Advances in Artificial Intelligence and Statistical Techniques with Applications to Health and Education

Advances in Artificial Intelligence and Statistical Techniques with Applications to Health and Education

Editors

Carmen Lacave
Ana Isabel Molina

MDPI • Basel • Beijing • Wuhan • Barcelona • Belgrade • Manchester • Tokyo • Cluj • Tianjin

Editors
Carmen Lacave
University of Castilla-La Mancha
Spain

Ana Isabel Molina
University of Castilla-La Mancha
Spain

Editorial Office
MDPI
St. Alban-Anlage 66
4052 Basel, Switzerland

This is a reprint of articles from the Special Issue published online in the open access journal *Mathematics* (ISSN 2227-7390) (available at: https://www.mdpi.com/si/mathematics/Artificial_Intelligence_Statistical_Techniques_Applications_Health_Education).

For citation purposes, cite each article independently as indicated on the article page online and as indicated below:

LastName, A.A.; LastName, B.B.; LastName, C.C. Article Title. *Journal Name* **Year**, *Volume Number*, Page Range.

ISBN 978-3-0365-7246-8 (Hbk)
ISBN 978-3-0365-7247-5 (PDF)

© 2023 by the authors. Articles in this book are Open Access and distributed under the Creative Commons Attribution (CC BY) license, which allows users to download, copy and build upon published articles, as long as the author and publisher are properly credited, which ensures maximum dissemination and a wider impact of our publications.

The book as a whole is distributed by MDPI under the terms and conditions of the Creative Commons license CC BY-NC-ND.

Contents

About the Editors . . . . **vii**

Carmen Lacave and Ana Isabel Molina
Advances in Artificial Intelligence and Statistical Techniques with Applications to Health and Education
Reprinted from: *Mathematics* **2023**, *11*, 1344, doi:10.3390/math11061344 . . . . **1**

Muhammad Arsalan, Adnan Haider, Ja Hyung Koo and Kang Ryoung Park
Segmenting Retinal Vessels Using a Shallow Segmentation Network to Aid Ophthalmic Analysis
Reprinted from: *Mathematics* **2022**, *10*, 1536, doi:10.3390/math10091536 . . . . **5**

Pedro Bonilla-Nadal, Andrés Cano, Manuel Gómez-Olmedo, Serafín Moral and Ofelia Paula Retamero
Using Value-Based Potentials for Making Approximate Inference on Probabilistic Graphical Models
Reprinted from: *Mathematics* **2022**, *10*, 2542, doi:10.3390/math10142542 . . . . **31**

Abdennour Boulesnane, Souham Meshoul and Khaoula Aouissi
Influenza-like Illness Detection from Arabic Facebook Posts Based on Sentiment Analysis and 1D Convolutional Neural Network
Reprinted from: *Mathematics* **2022**, *10*, 4089, doi:10.3390/math10214089 . . . . **59**

Eglė Butkevičiūtė, Aleksėjus Michalkovič and Liepa Bikulčienė
ECG Signal Features Classification for the Mental Fatigue Recognition
Reprinted from: *Mathematics* **2022**, *10*, 3395, doi:10.3390/math10183395 . . . . **81**

David Carneros-Prado, Cosmin C. Dobrescu, Iván González, Jesús Fontecha, Esperanza Johnson and Ramón Hervás
Analysis of Dual-Tasking Effect on Gait Variability While Interacting with Mobile Devices
Reprinted from: *Mathematics* **2023**, *11*, 202, doi:10.3390/math11010202 . . . . **99**

Cristian Gmez-Portes, José Jesús Castro-Schez, Javier Albusac, Dorothy N. Monekosso and David Vallejo
A Fuzzy Recommendation System for the Automatic Personalization of Physical Rehabilitation Exercises in Stroke Patients
Reprinted from: *Mathematics* **2021**, *9*, 1427, doi:10.3390/math9121427 . . . . **115**

Alicia Nieto-Reyes, Heather Battey and Giacomo Francisci
Functional Symmetry and Statistical Depth for the Analysis of Movement Patterns in Alzheimer's Patients
Reprinted from: *Mathematics* **2021**, *9*, 820, doi:10.3390/math9080820 . . . . **139**

Carmen Patino-Alonso, Marta Gómez-Sánchez, Leticia Gómez-Sánchez, Benigna Sánchez Salgado, Emiliano Rodríguez-Sánchez, Luis García-Ortiz and Manuel A. Gómez-Marcos
Predictive Ability of Machine-Learning Methods for Vitamin D Deficiency Prediction by Anthropometric Parameters
Reprinted from: *Mathematics* **2022**, *10*, 616, doi:10.3390/math10040616 . . . . **157**

Sergio Pozuelo-Campos, Víctor Casero-Alonso and Mariano Amo-Salas
Effect of Probability Distribution of the Response Variable in Optimal Experimental Design with Applications in Medicine
Reprinted from: *Mathematics* **2021**, *9*, 1010, doi:10.3390/math9091010 . . . . **173**

Àngela Sebastià Bargues, José-Luis Polo Sanz and Raúl Martín Martín
Optimal Experimental Design for Parametric Identification of the Electrical Behaviour of Bioelectrodes and Biological Tissues
Reprinted from: *Mathematics* **2022**, *10*, 837, doi:10.3390/math10050837 . . . . **189**

Bing Zhang and Jizhong Liu
Discriminative Convolutional Sparse Coding of ECG Signals for Automated Recognition of Cardiac Arrhythmias
Reprinted from: *Mathematics* **2022**, *10*, 2874, doi:10.3390/math10162874 . . . . **205**

Francisco Javier Díez, Manuel Arias, Jorge Pérez-Martín and Manuel Luque
Teaching Probabilistic Graphical Models with OpenMarkov
Reprinted from: *Mathematics* **2022**, *10*, 3577, doi:10.3390/math10193577 . . . . **225**

Daniel Alfredo Hernández-Carrasco, César Enrique Rose-Gómez, Samuel González-López, Aurelio López-López, Jesús Miguel García-Gorrostieta and Gilberto Borrego
A Framework to Assist in Didactic Planning at Undergraduate Level
Reprinted from: *Mathematics* **2022**, *10*, 1355, doi:10.3390/math10091355 . . . . **245**

Javier Alejandro Jiménez Toledo, César A. Collazos and Manuel Ortega
Discovery Model Based on Analogies for Teaching Computer Programming
Reprinted from: *Mathematics* **2021**, *9*, 1354, doi:10.3390/math9121354 . . . . **267**

Tieyuan Liu, Chang Wang, Liang Chang and Tianlong Gu
Predicting High-Risk Students Using Learning Behavior
Reprinted from: *Mathematics* **2022**, *10*, 2483, doi:10.3390/math10142483 . . . . **289**

María Morales, Antonio Salmerón, Ana D. Maldonado, Andrés R. Masegosa and Rafael Rumí
An Empirical Analysis of the Impact of Continuous Assessment on the Final Exam Mark
Reprinted from: *Mathematics* **2022**, *10*, 3994, doi:10.3390/math10213994 . . . . **305**

Alicia Nieto-Reyes, Rafael Duque and Giacomo Francisci
A Method to Automate the Prediction of Student Academic Performance from Early Stages of the Course
Reprinted from: *Mathematics* **2021**, *9*, 2677, doi:10.3390/math9212677 . . . . **327**

Oscar Revelo Sánchez, César A. Collazos and Miguel A. Redondo
Automatic Group Organization for Collaborative Learning Applying Genetic Algorithm Techniques and the Big Five Model
Reprinted from: *Mathematics* **13**, *9*, 1578, doi:10.3390/math9131578 . . . . **341**

Marina Segura, Jorge Mello and Adolfo Hernández
Machine Learning Prediction of University Student Dropout: Does Preference Play a Key Role?
Reprinted from: *Mathematics* **2022**, *10*, 3359, doi:10.3390/math10183359 . . . . **365**

Kyulee Shin and Sukkyung You
Quantile Regression Analysis between the After-School Exercise and the Academic Performance of Korean Middle School Students
Reprinted from: *Mathematics* **2022**, *10*, 58, doi:10.3390/math10010058 . . . . **385**

About the Editors

Carmen Lacave

Carmen Lacave, Ph.D., is currently a professor in the Department of Information Technologies and Systems at the University of Castilla–La Mancha (ULCM) in Spain. She received her M.Sc. degree in Mathematics from the Complutense University of Madrid, and her Ph.D. degree in Science from the National University of Distance Education. She has also been part of the Computer–Human Interaction and Collaboration (CHICO) research group of the Higher School of Informatics of Ciudad Real since 2014. Her research is based on three lines: the application of statistical techniques and artificial intelligence (Bayesian networks) to data analysis in the fields of medicine and education; the design of experiments for the evaluation of systems and notations; and the development and evaluation of tools for teaching programming.

Ana Isabel Molina

Ana Isabel Molina, Ph.D., is currently an associate professor in the area of Languages and Computer Systems at the University of Castilla–La Mancha (UCLM) in Spain. She received her M.Sc. degree in Computer Engineering from the University of Castilla–La Mancha in 2002, Ph.D. in Computer Engineering from the University of Castilla–La Mancha in 2007, and a degree in Psychology from the National University of Distance Education in 2019. She is an Expert Member of the Chair "Advanced Interaction Systems for Digital Education" of Telefónica Móviles Spain and the University of Castilla–La Mancha and has also been part of the Computer–Human Interaction and Collaboration (CHICO) research group of the Higher School of Informatics of Ciudad Real since 2002. Her main research lines are in the field of human–computer interaction, educational informatics and the evaluation of interactive systems combining objective and subjective techniques.

Editorial

Advances in Artificial Intelligence and Statistical Techniques with Applications to Health and Education

Carmen Lacave * and Ana Isabel Molina

Department of Information Technologies and Systems, Universidad de Castilla-La Mancha, Paseo de la Universidad, s/n, 13071 Ciudad Real, Spain; anaisabel.molina@uclm.es
* Correspondence: carmen.lacave@uclm.es

Citation: Lacave, C.; Molina, A.I. Advances in Artificial Intelligence and Statistical Techniques with Applications to Health and Education. *Mathematics* **2023**, *11*, 1344. https://doi.org/10.3390/math11061344

Received: 6 March 2023
Accepted: 8 March 2023
Published: 9 March 2023

Copyright: © 2023 by the authors. Licensee MDPI, Basel, Switzerland. This article is an open access article distributed under the terms and conditions of the Creative Commons Attribution (CC BY) license (https:// creativecommons.org/licenses/by/ 4.0/).

The COVID-19 pandemic highlighted the importance of health and education and also revealed the need for innovative solutions relative to the challenges confronting these disciplines. The pandemic led to a greater demand for remote healthcare services and online education, which has highlighted the potential for technology to transform these fields. With the increasing availability of big data and advancements in artificial intelligence, there is an opportunity to develop more efficient and effective approaches to healthcare and education. The integration of technology in healthcare and education has already shown promising results. In healthcare, machine learning algorithms have been used to predict the likelihood of disease progression, identify at-risk patients, and personalize treatment plans. In education, learning analytics has been used to track student progress and identify areas where they may need extra support. These technologies can provide valuable insights that can inform decision making and lead to better outcomes.

Therefore, the proposed Special Issue on the application of artificial intelligence to healthcare and education is timely and important. The challenges facing these disciplines require a multidisciplinary approach that combines technological advances with expertise in statistics, data analysis, and other related fields. By sharing new methods, applications, and case studies, this Special Issue can contribute to the development of innovative solutions that improve healthcare and education for all. Topics addressed in this Special Issue include data mining, machine learning, learning analytics, prediction methods, pattern recognition, decision analysis, probabilistic reasoning, fuzzy systems, student or patient modelling, adaptive systems, collaborative systems, recommendation systems, experimental design, and empirical study cases. Specifically, there are twenty rigorously reviewed papers included in this Special Issue, with eleven specializing in the field of medicine and health [1–11] and nine specializing in the field of education [12–20]. In total, fifteen papers (43% of the received) were rejected for publication.

In the area of **health**, most papers aim at improving the *diagnosis of a disease*, such as influenza [3], Alzheimer's disease [7], and cardiac arrhythmias [11], or of a specific symptom, such as changes in the retinal vasculature [1], mental fatigue [4], gait variability [5] or vitamin D deficiency [8]. There is one for the *personalization* of rehabilitation exercises for stroke patients [6], and there are three theoretical papers [2,9,10] aimed at *improving the representation of models*, which can be applied to different and actual medical problems.

Regarding the techniques used, those related to artificial intelligence prevail. Specifically, the majority make use of different machine learning algorithms [1–4,6,8,11], although with distinct objectives. For example, some works propose new specific classification models. In [1], a novel semantic segmentation network is developed to detect retinal vessels from original images, thus providing accurate support during ophthalmological analysis. In [4], a combination of electrocardiogram signal feature extraction, principal component analysis, and random forest classification was used to propose a novel approach to detect mental fatigue with a 94.5% of accuracy. In [11], a discriminative convolutional sparse coding framework and a classification strategy based on a linear support vector machine were combined to diagnose abnormal arrhythmias, exhibiting an accuracy of 99.32%. The study in [8] compares different supervised learning algorithms to predict the anthropometric parameter that is most strongly associated with vitamin D deficiency. They conclude that the Naïve Bayes model showed the best area under the curve in four of six parameters and the logistic regression model for the other two. In [3], the diagnosis of influenza-like illness was attained by using a new sentiment classification model based on one-dimensional convolutional neural networks from Facebook posts and based on the user's sentiments. The experimental results obtained an accuracy of 96.6%.

Another approach was proposed by [2] with respect to improving the efficiency of classification algorithms when there are memory limitations. Then, an improvement in value-based potentials to better represent approximate information and positive results was obtained after verifying it on several Bayesian networks representing medical problems.

A different proposal is that of [6] in which fuzzy logic was used to propose a system capable of recommending rehabilitation exercises for stroke patients depending on the variation in the patient's level of progress as the rehabilitation process evolves.

Statistical techniques have also been used, such as from the most basic ones, making use of descriptive statistics, discriminant analysis, and correlations [5], to more sophisticated ones such as functional data analysis [7] or an optimal experimental design [9,10]. Thus, basic statistical techniques in [5] were used to analyse the data obtained from an experiment performed with adults with the aim to characterize the gait parameters affected by mobile-based dual-tasking and the impact of normal cognitive decline due to aging. In [7], functional data analysis was used to provide insight into the nature of the difference in movement patterns of Alzheimer's patients according to their stage of the disease. The results indicate that the distribution of acceleration differs between each stage of the disease, mainly due to scale differences. In [9], an analysis of the effect of misspecification in the probability distribution of the response variable was performed by comparing a normal distribution with the Poisson or gamma distribution. The results show that assuming a homoscedastic normal distribution when obtaining optimal designs may led to a great loss in efficiency depending on the true distribution of the response variable and on the model function chosen. In [10], new algorithms were developed to calculate D-optimal designs by describing the electrical behaviour of bioelectrodes, cell membranes, or biological tissues; as a result, a substantial amount of observations obtained the same results as the classic design is saved.

It should be noted that the data used for the above studies have been obtained from public repositories in papers [1,2,11]. The other papers obtain their data from different types of experimental studies, most of them conducted with individuals [3–8].

In the field of **education**, work is mainly oriented towards improving teaching [12–14] or learning [18] and predicting educational performance [15–17,20] or drop-out rates [19].

Within the first group, there are different proposals to *improve teaching*. Thus, in [12] an open-source software tool, called *OpenMarkov*, was used as a pedagogical tool to teach the main concepts of Bayesian networks and influence diagrams using two models to represent and deal with uncertainty in artificial intelligence systems, which are difficult to convey. In [13], a framework based on natural language processing techniques to analyse college-level subjects' didactic planning was presented. Such a framework was supported by an ontology that considers the information from didactic plans approved by an evaluation committee. The statistical analysis of the framework's evaluation results indicated an agreement of 92% with the expert and a reduction in the workload of instructors. Natural language processing techniques are also used in [14], in which a knowledge discovery model based on machine learning and text mining was proposed for a structured development consisting of analogies to teach programming concepts. The input of the proposal is a didactic teaching strategy with analogies, and it obtained a series of patterns for possible scenarios that can be used with a greater degree of assertiveness when presenting an analogy on a CS1 course. The obtained structure was validated by the professors and the students.

A different approach is that of [18], in which genetic algorithms were used to automatically form groups in collaborative learning scenarios, considering the students' personality traits of the big five model as a criterion for grouping. As a result, a strategy was provided to assess, in each context, which type of approach (homogeneous, heterogeneous, or mixed) is the most appropriate for organising groups.

The papers that predict *educational performance* make use of different techniques, such as techniques from artificial intelligence and statistics. For example, in [15], the prediction of high-risk students was performed by a new hybrid deep learning model with respect to a student's learning behavior. The model is based on a combination of a gated unit neural network, a deep neural network, and a neural attention mechanism. The experimental results show better performances than other prediction models based on deep learning. In [17], a statistical depth-based supervised classification technique was used to develop a methodology to allow teachers to define the most appropriate variables in order to measure the academic performance of students. The proposal takes as input the data recorded in the first tasks of the academic year. The experimental results show an 80% success rate from the two first tasks (of six), increasing to 90% after the first four, in predicting the final grade. Moreover, the proposal of [16] compared different statistical and artificial intelligence techniques to determine if the performance of a student in the continuous assessment determines the score obtained in the final exam of the course. Those techniques are based on linear, quantile, and logistic regression; artificial neural networks; and Bayesian networks. The results obtained show that although continuous assessments influence the final exam score, it was not decisive in predicting it. However, in [20], only statistical techniques based on quantile regression were used to predict the relations between students' academic performance and their after-school exercise. Using empirical data collected from middle school students, they proved that there exists a positive relation among both variables.

This variety of techniques also appears in papers related to the prediction of *student dropout*. Thus, in [19], both machine learning models such as support vector machines, decision trees, and neural networks, together with logistic regression, were used to predict likely university dropout rates either at the beginning of the course of study or at the end of the first semester. The results show that dropout prediction cannot be made only with enrollment data, but that academic performance and the level of course preference must be considered. In general, machine learning techniques obtain similar predictions, although there are some areas in which those techniques offer worse results. Moreover, although logistic regression is never the best compared with other more sophisticated techniques, it can be used as a good approach in non-specialized audiences because of its ease of use.

In conclusion, the papers presented in this Special Issue provide a significant snapshot of the current research interests of the scientific community in the fields of medicine and education. In the medical field, there are clear efforts to develop and provide specialists with systems that can help make accurate diagnoses when problems are complex. This has led to the development of advanced technologies, such as machine learning algorithms, that can analyze vast amounts of medical data to help diagnose diseases more accurately and efficiently. Additionally, there is a crucial line of research focused on adapting treatments according to the needs and evolution of patients. This involves taking a personalized approach to medical care, where the individual needs of the patient are taken into account to create tailored treatment plans. This research is particularly important for conditions that have diverse symptoms and complex etiologies.

In the field of education, the focus is mainly on the early detection of school failure or dropout, with the aim of designing strategies that can address both problems in a timely manner and that can improve current failure rates. One significant area of research is the creation of tools or models that support students' learning based on their unique characteristics. This includes leveraging data-driven approaches to identify students' strengths and weaknesses, as well as creating personalized learning plans that are tailored to each student's learning style and abilities. Another important area of research in education is the creation of tools that support teachers in facilitating effective teaching. This includes the development of interactive learning tools and intelligent tutoring systems that can provide feedback to both teachers and students, as well as the use of data analytics to assess student progress and adjust teaching strategies accordingly.

Overall, the scientific community in both medicine and education is leveraging techniques from statistics and artificial intelligence to drive significant advances in their respective fields. These approaches hold great promise for improving patient outcomes and enhancing the quality of education for students around the world.

Conflicts of Interest: The authors declare no conflict of interest.

References

1. Arsalan, M.; Haider, A.; Koo, J.H.; Park, K.R. Segmenting Retinal Vessels Using a Shallow Segmentation Network to Aid Ophthalmic Analysis. *Mathematics* **2022**, *10*, 1536. [CrossRef]
2. Bonilla-Nadal, P.; Cano, A.; Gómez-Olmedo, M.; Moral, S.; Retamero, O.P. Using Value-Based Potentials for Making Approximate Inference on Probabilistic Graphical Models. *Mathematics* **2022**, *10*, 2542. [CrossRef]
3. Boulesnane, A.; Meshoul, S.; Aouissi, K. Influenza-like Illness Detection from Arabic Facebook Posts Based on Sentiment Analysis and 1D Convolutional Neural Network. *Mathematics* **2022**, *10*, 4089. [CrossRef]
4. Butkevičiūtė, E.; Michalkovič, A.; Bikulčienė, L. ECG Signal Features Classification for the Mental Fatigue Recognition. *Mathematics* **2022**, *10*, 3395. [CrossRef]
5. Carneros-Prado, D.; Dobrescu, C.C.; González, I.; Fontecha, J.; Johnson, E.; Hervás, R. Analysis of Dual-Tasking Effect on Gait Variability While Interacting with Mobile Devices. *Mathematics* **2023**, *11*, 202. [CrossRef]
6. Gmez-Portes, C.; Castro-Schez, J.J.; Albusac, J.; Monekosso, D.N.; Vallejo, D. A Fuzzy Recommendation System for the Automatic Personalization of Physical Rehabilitation Exercises in Stroke Patients. *Mathematics* **2021**, *9*, 1427. [CrossRef]
7. Nieto-Reyes, A.; Battey, H.; Francisci, G. Functional Symmetry and Statistical Depth for the Analysis of Movement Patterns in Alzheimer's Patients. *Mathematics* **2021**, *9*, 820. [CrossRef]
8. Patino-Alonso, C.; Gómez-Sánchez, M.; Gómez-Sánchez, L.; Sánchez Salgado, B.; Rodríguez-Sánchez, E.; García-Ortiz, L.; Gómez-Marcos, M.A. Predictive Ability of Machine-Learning Methods for Vitamin D Deficiency Prediction by Anthropometric Parameters. *Mathematics* **2022**, *10*, 616. [CrossRef]
9. Pozuelo-Campos, S.; Casero-Alonso, V.; Amo-Salas, M. Effect of Probability Distribution of the Response Variable in Optimal Experimental Design with Applications in Medicine. *Mathematics* **2021**, *9*, 1010. [CrossRef]
10. Sebastià Bargues, À.; Polo Sanz, J.-L.; Martín Martín, R. Optimal Experimental Design for Parametric Identification of the Electrical Behaviour of Bioelectrodes and Biological Tissues. *Mathematics* **2022**, *10*, 837. [CrossRef]
11. Zhang, B.; Liu, J. Discriminative Convolutional Sparse Coding of ECG Signals for Automated Recognition of Cardiac Arrhythmias. *Mathematics* **2022**, *10*, 2874. [CrossRef]
12. Díez, F.J.; Arias, M.; Pérez-Martín, J.; Luque, M. Teaching Probabilistic Graphical Models with OpenMarkov. *Mathematics* **2022**, *10*, 3577. [CrossRef]
13. Hernández-Carrasco, D.A.; Rose-Gómez, C.E.; González-López, S.; López-López, A.; García-Gorrostieta, J.M.; Borrego, G. A Framework to Assist in Didactic Planning at Undergraduate Level. *Mathematics* **2022**, *10*, 1355. [CrossRef]
14. Jiménez Toledo, J.A.; Collazos, C.A.; Ortega, M. Discovery Model Based on Analogies for Teaching Computer Programming. *Mathematics* **2021**, *9*, 1354. [CrossRef]
15. Liu, T.; Wang, C.; Chang, L.; Gu, T. Predicting High-Risk Students Using Learning Behavior. *Mathematics* **2022**, *10*, 2483. [CrossRef]
16. Morales, M.; Salmerón, A.; Maldonado, A.D.; Masegosa, A.R.; Rumí, R. An Empirical Analysis of the Impact of Continuous Assessment on the Final Exam Mark. *Mathematics* **2022**, *10*, 3994. [CrossRef]
17. Nieto-Reyes, A.; Duque, R.; Francisci, G. A Method to Automate the Prediction of Student Academic Performance from Early Stages of the Course. *Mathematics* **2021**, *9*, 2677. [CrossRef]
18. Revelo Sánchez, O.; Collazos, C.A.; Redondo, M.A. Automatic Group Organization for Collaborative Learning Applying Genetic Algorithm Techniques and the Big Five Model. *Mathematics* **2021**, *9*, 1578. [CrossRef]
19. Segura, M.; Mello, J.; Hernández, A. Machine Learning Prediction of University Student Dropout: Does Preference Play a Key Role? *Mathematics* **2022**, *10*, 3359. [CrossRef]
20. Shin, K.; You, S. Quantile Regression Analysis between the After-School Exercise and the Academic Performance of Korean Middle School Students. *Mathematics* **2022**, *10*, 58. [CrossRef]

Disclaimer/Publisher's Note: The statements, opinions and data contained in all publications are solely those of the individual author(s) and contributor(s) and not of MDPI and/or the editor(s). MDPI and/or the editor(s) disclaim responsibility for any injury to people or property resulting from any ideas, methods, instructions or products referred to in the content.

Article

Segmenting Retinal Vessels Using a Shallow Segmentation Network to Aid Ophthalmic Analysis

Muhammad Arsalan, Adnan Haider, Ja Hyung Koo and Kang Ryoung Park *

Division of Electronics and Electrical Engineering, Dongguk University, 30 Pildong-ro 1-gil, Seoul 04620, Korea; arsal@dongguk.edu (M.A.); adnanhaider@dgu.ac.kr (A.H.); koo6190@dongguk.edu (J.H.K.)
* Correspondence: parkgr@dongguk.edu

Abstract: Retinal blood vessels possess a complex structure in the retina and are considered an important biomarker for several retinal diseases. Ophthalmic diseases result in specific changes in the retinal vasculature; for example, diabetic retinopathy causes the retinal vessels to swell, and depending upon disease severity, fluid or blood can leak. Similarly, hypertensive retinopathy causes a change in the retinal vasculature due to the thinning of these vessels. Central retinal vein occlusion (CRVO) is a phenomenon in which the main vein causes drainage of the blood from the retina and this main vein can close completely or partially with symptoms of blurred vision and similar eye problems. Considering the importance of the retinal vasculature as an ophthalmic disease biomarker, ophthalmologists manually analyze retinal vascular changes. Manual analysis is a tedious task that requires constant observation to detect changes. The deep learning-based methods can ease the problem by learning from the annotations provided by an expert ophthalmologist. However, current deep learning-based methods are relatively inaccurate, computationally expensive, complex, and require image preprocessing for final detection. Moreover, existing methods are unable to provide a better true positive rate (sensitivity), which shows that the model can predict most of the vessel pixels. Therefore, this study presents the so-called vessel segmentation ultra-lite network (VSUL-Net) to accurately extract the retinal vasculature from the background. The proposed VSUL-Net comprises only 0.37 million trainable parameters and uses an original image as input without preprocessing. The VSUL-Net uses a retention block that specifically maintains the larger feature map size and low-level spatial information transfer. This retention block results in better sensitivity of the proposed VSUL-Net without using expensive preprocessing schemes. The proposed method was tested on three publicly available datasets: digital retinal images for vessel extraction (DRIVE), structured analysis of retina (STARE), and children's heart health study in England database (CHASE-DB1) for retinal vasculature segmentation. The experimental results demonstrated that VSUL-Net provides robust segmentation of retinal vasculature with sensitivity (Sen), specificity (Spe), accuracy (Acc), and area under the curve (AUC) values of 83.80%, 98.21%, 96.95%, and 98.54%, respectively, for DRIVE, 81.73%, 98.35%, 97.17%, and 98.69%, respectively, for CHASE-DB1, and 86.64%, 98.13%, 97.27%, and 99.01%, respectively, for STARE datasets. The proposed method provides an accurate segmentation mask for deep ophthalmic analysis.

Keywords: retina; fundus image; retinal vasculature; retinal disorders; semantic segmentation

MSC: 68T07; 68U10

Citation: Arsalan, M.; Haider, A.; Koo, J.H.; Park, K.R. Segmenting Retinal Vessels Using a Shallow Segmentation Network to Aid Ophthalmic Analysis. *Mathematics* **2022**, *10*, 1536. https://doi.org/10.3390/math10091536

Academic Editors: Carmen Lacave and Ana Isabel Molina

Received: 22 March 2022
Accepted: 29 April 2022
Published: 3 May 2022

Publisher's Note: MDPI stays neutral with regard to jurisdictional claims in published maps and institutional affiliations.

Copyright: © 2022 by the authors. Licensee MDPI, Basel, Switzerland. This article is an open access article distributed under the terms and conditions of the Creative Commons Attribution (CC BY) license (https://creativecommons.org/licenses/by/4.0/).

1. Introduction

Retinal vessel morphology is a clear biomarker for many retinal diseases and can be used to determine disease severity. The retinal disease causes changes in the retinal vasculature, which can be detected by tracking these changes. Such diseases include macular degeneration, macular edema, Alzheimer's disease (AD), diabetic retinopathy, hypertensive retinopathy, sickle cell retinopathy, and glaucoma, which involve retinal vascular changes and can lead to vision loss [1]. Diabetic retinopathy is a retinal disease that results in the swelling or leakage of retinal vessels due to high blood sugar [2]. Hypertensive retinopathy is a retinal disorder that results in narrowed retinal vessels due to high blood pressure, which can be particularly noticed in the microvasculature [3]. Central retinal vein occlusion (CRVO) and branch retinal vein occlusion (BRVO) is a common retinal disorder after diabetic retinopathy and a major cause of visual detachment. CRVO includes vascular changes [4]. Sickle cell retinopathy (SCR) is a vision loss-related disease that is characterized by vaso-occlusion caused by retinal ischemia. In SCR disease, the vasculature morphology changes with a reduction in vessel density. Retinal vessels are important biomarkers for early SCR detection [5]. Parkinson's disease (PD) is a neurodegenerative disorder that causes neuronal loss in the nervous system. Cell degeneration in PD causes symptoms that include impairment of the olfactory, visual, and nervous systems. The retinal vessel changes that occur during the progression of PD and subsequent vascular changes can be analyzed [6]. Retinal vascular changes, mainly observed in larger vessels, can be used to identify the area of retinal vascular occlusion. The morphologies of retinal vessels and other vascular pathologies are closely related to these retinal vascular diseases [7]. Table 1 enlists the abbreviations that are used in the paper.

Table 1. List of abbreviations.

Full Name	Abbreviations	Full Name	Abbreviations
Alzheimer's disease	AD	Sickle cell retinopathy	SCR
Parkinson's disease	PD	Retinopathy of prematurity	ROP
Contrast Limited Adaptive Histogram Equalization	CLAHE	U- shaped network	U-Net
Segmentation network	SegNet	generative adversarial network	GAN
Batch normalization and	BN	Rectified linear unit	ReLU
Generalized dice loss	GDL	Vertical flip and	VF
Horizontal flip	HF	Sensitivity	Sen
Specificity	Spe	Accuracy	Acc
Area under the curve	AUC	Gradient-weighted class activation map	Grad-cam
Convolutional neural network	CNN	Gaussian mixture model	GMM
iterative U-Net	IterNet	Cross-connected convolutional network	CcNet

Retinopathy of prematurity (ROP) proliferative retinal disorder affects premature infants, and most of these mild cases can be automatically resolved within a few months after birth. However, 5–10% of cases with severe ROP can lead to retinal detachment if not treated in time. Major ROP disease analyses were performed using manual morphological analysis of the retinal vessels of the patient. Ophthalmologists carefully analyze the arterial tortuosity and dilation of the posterior retinal vessels for disease diagnosis [8]. Glaucoma disease is a serious retinal disorder that has a huge impact on blindness globally [9]. Vascular factors play a vital role in the progression of glaucoma. Studies have shown that glaucoma is associated with blood pressure, perfusion pressure, and cardiovascular diseases. The retinal vasculature is the only visible biomarker that can be utilized for quantitative analysis of tortuosity, fractal dimensions, branching, etc., in glaucoma analysis [10]. AD is a common disease in the elderly that involves heterogeneous cognitive and functional impairments. Studies have shown that AD is coupled with retinal and neurovascular disorders, with which retinal morphological changes are also associated including changes in the retinal vasculature [11]. The retinal vessel-associated diseases are further discussed in [12].

Early ophthalmic diagnosis requires keen retinal image analysis. However, detecting minor changes is challenging. Many ophthalmic disorders are associated with retinal vessel morphology including position, thickness, tortuosity, creation, and elimination [13]. Ophthalmologists manually analyze the retinal vasculature and mark the changes. With the emergence of deep learning, automatic disease analysis is growing to help medical practitioners achieve faster and more reliable diagnoses [14–18].

Semantic segmentation is a method that can automatically detect retinal vessels for ophthalmic disease analysis in previous researches [19,20]. However, they are relatively inaccurate, expensive, and complex in architecture. They use more layers to accomplish the segmentation task, which increases the requirement of graphic processing unit memory. They also lack effective design, therefore, expensive preprocessing schemes are required to enhance the image before feeding it to a deep learning network. Moreover, most of the existing schemes cannot effectively provide a disease diagnosis solution. To address these issues, this study presents a deep-learning-based vessel segmentation ultra-lite-network (VSUL-Net) that can extract the retinal vasculature accurately from fundus images. VSUL-Net is a very shallow network that comprises only 0.37 million trainable parameters. It consists of very few layers and does not require conventional image-enhancement methods for preprocessing. This study showcases an ultra-lite semantic segmentation architecture specifically designed to detect retinal vessels to aid ophthalmic diagnosis and has the following advantageous novel contributions:

- This study presents a novel semantic segmentation architecture (VSUL-Net) that detects retinal vessels directly from original fundus images without preprocessing for image enhancement.
- VSUL-Net is a shallow architecture that comprises only 0.37 million trainable parameters with 10 convolutional layers with few filters.
- The feature retention block provides rich spatial features that help with better segmentation accuracy and true-positive rate.
- The proposed VSUL-Net trained models are made publicly available in [21].

The remainder of this paper is organized as follows. Section 2 presents a literature review on previous studies of retinal vessel segmentation. Section 3 describes the proposed method in detail. Section 4 presents the experimental results, evaluation of the proposed method, and discussion. Finally, conclusions are presented in Section 5.

2. Literature Review

Detection of retinal vessels can be useful for the early diagnosis of numerous retinal and non-retinal diseases, where automated methods are useful for reducing the diagnostic burden of medical specialists. Retinal vessel segmentation is performed using two main approaches: conventional image processing and machine/deep feature-based methods. Numerous research has been conducted based on conventional methods that use general image processing schemes. In Section 2.1, conventional image processing methods that have been researched recently are discussed. Learning-based methods have evolved with high stability and performance; recent deep-feature-based methods are discussed in detail in Section 2.2. Table 2 provides the pros and cons of the methods given in Sections 2.1 and 2.2.

2.1. Conventional Image Processing-Based Methods for Vessel Segmentation

2.1.1. Contrast Limited Adaptive Histogram Equalization (CLAHE) Based Methods

Conventional image processing-based schemes for vessel segmentation typically use various image-enhancement schemes before thresholding. Alhussein et al. presented a Wiener and morphological filtering-based method for segmentation and CLAHE to improve the contrast of fundus images [22]. Similarly, Ahamed et al. presented an automatic vessel segmentation method based on multiscale line detection. They used CLAHE on the green channel for contrast enhancement and integrated hysteresis and morphological thresholding for the final segmentation [23]. An unsupervised method was proposed by Naveed et al., who used an ensemble block-matching 3-D speckle filter for image enhancement after the CLAHE operation. In their model, a segmentation task was performed using a multiscale detector and a Frangi detector [24]. The above-listed methods are based on a conventional image processing scheme, which can suffer from minor image changes and lack segmentation performance.

2.1.2. Line Detection and Tube Based Methods

A line detector-based vessel detection method was proposed by Zhou et al., which was used to identify the major vessel area to which a Markov model was applied to detect retinal vessels after noise removal [25]. Shah et al. used a multiscale line-detection method for retinal vessel segmentation. Gabor wavelet superposition was used on the green channel, and a multiscale line detection method was used to enhance images for vessel extraction [26]. Another image-processing-based method used curvelet transform and line operation for vessel segmentation, where a combination of adaptive histogram equalization, anisotropic diffusion filtering, and color space transformation was employed for preprocessing [27]. Li et al. presented an unsupervised method in which image enhancement schemes were used for image preprocessing and a connected-tube marked point process was employed for the extraction of the vessel network. The final segmentation was performed using the detected tube width expansion [28]. Most of these listed methods include image processing schemes for image enhancement, which increase the overall cost of the system.

2.1.3. Thresholding, Morphology Based, and Other Methods

A three-stage method was proposed by Soto et al. using top-hat and homomorphic filtering. In the first stage, image smoothing was applied for image enhancement; then, the thin and thick vessels were segmented separately using two phases. In the final stage, morphological postprocessing was applied to improve segmentation results obtained in the second stage [29]. To detect retinal vessels, Aswini et al. presented an unsupervised method based on two-fold hysteresis thresholding. In their model, before thresholding, the fundus image was enhanced using morphological smoothing and background suppression [30]. A hybrid approach based on multiscale image enhancement combined with a bottom-hat transform was proposed by Sundaram et al., where the segmentation task was performed based on morphological operations [31]. Khawaja et al. proposed a probabilistic patch-based denoiser to alleviate the aggravated noise that obstructs vessel segmentation, in which a modified Frangi filter was used combined with a denoiser [32]. Similar to the methods listed in Section 2.1.2, most of these methods include image processing schemes for image enhancement and work on the specific threshold that suffers from changes in the image colors and contrasts.

2.2. Learned Feature-Based Methods for Vessel Segmentation

Learning-based methods are more widely recognized because they can mimic the knowledge of medical specialists through feature learning. In addition, image augmentation methods help accomplish the task with fewer training examples.

2.2.1. Encoder–Decoder Based Methods

The encoder–decoder-based methods are the methods in which the decoder is the same as the encoder. Jin et al. presented a deformable structure-based modified U-Net for improved performance, where they used an upsampling operator to enhance the resolution for better segmentation performance [33]. Khan et al. presented a fully convolutional network with a residual information transfer path. They used an encoder–decoder architecture, where the decoder structure was the same as that of the encoder. The final pixel-wise prediction was performed using a pixel classification layer [34]. Yan et al. suggested a deep learning-based scheme where they combined segmentation level loss with pixel-wise loss to associate these losses with a thin and thick vessel via a U-Net architecture in two branches at the segment and pixel levels [35]. A coarse-to-fine deep learning strategy was presented by Wang et al., who used two U-shaped SegNet architectures for coarse and fine segmentation. In their method, the coarse SegNet provided the probability maps of the patches, and the fine SegNet refined the patches [36]. Li et al. proposed an iterative

U-Net (IterNet) to segment the cloaked information of retinal vessels. They iterated the mini-U-Net with weight sharing using skip paths for improved segmentation [37]. Zhao et al. presented an end-to-end matting algorithm to retrieve vessels existing in unknown areas, where an encoder–decoder deep-learning method was used to create the matte. Then, the final segmentation was performed by incorporating both local matting loss and global pixel loss [38]. Zhang et al. proposed a pyramid U-Net approach for retinal vessel segmentation. They used pyramid-scale aggregation, which is based on the residual block to create different scales [39]. Similarly, another U-Net-based approach was presented by Gengundez-Arias et al. In detail, they modified the U-Net architecture to allow for a reduced structure and the use of a low number of parameters [40]. Most of these listed methods are based on an encoder–decoder, and decoders are the same as an encoder, which increases the overall depth of the network with a substantial increase in the number of trainable parameters. Moreover, these methods lack segmentation performance.

2.2.2. Generative Adversarial Networks-Based Methods

He et al. presented an end-to-end generative adversarial network (GAN) to distinguish the vessel area from the background. They used patches to feed the model along with the patches predicted by the network. Then, they merged all of these patches again to obtain the final result [41]. Guo et al. presented a combined GAN and dense U-Net-based approach to distinguish retinal vessels from the background. Specifically, they used a dense U-Net with an inception module implementation, where the short skip connections of the U-Net were replaced by dense blocks to benefit from the fusing of spatial information obtained from the initial layers. Dense inception was used as a generator, and a multilayered CNN was used as a discriminator with a loss function tuned for segmentation and GAN losses [42]. Lal et al. discussed the adversarial attacks for diabetic retinopathy recognition and used adversarial training in the defense of adversarial speckle-noise attacks [43]. Chudzik et al. presented a two-stage framework. In the first phase, a codebook was generated by a CNN with correlated features extracted from expert annotation. In the second phase, the generative features of the codebook were utilized for retinal vessel prediction and detection [44]. The generative adversarial approaches are relatively complex and require more computational power.

2.2.3. Machine Learning-Based Methods

Palanivel et al. proposed a novel Gaussian mixture model (GMM) for retinal vessel detection. They used multi-fractional characterization for noise removal and vessel enhancement and a holder component based on Gabor wavelet responses to approximate the regularity of the retinal vessels. In the final stage, a GMM classifier was applied to classify the pixels between the vessel and background classes [45]. A coarse-to-fine strategy for vessel segmentation was presented by Tchinda et al., who used conventional edge detection methods to extract the feature vector. These feature vectors were then sent to the artificial neural network to find pixel-wise labels in the image-to-vessel and non-vessel classes [46]. These methods are complex and have a lower true positive rate.

2.2.4. Multiscale/Multi Networks-Based Methods

A fully convolutional deep learning scheme for supervised vessel segmentation was proposed by Oliveira et al. They utilized a multiscale fully convolutional neural network analyzed by a stationary wavelet transform in a patch-based scenario [47]. Guo et al. presented a deeply supervised short-connection-based fully convolutional method for retinal vessel segmentation. They utilized two widely known networks, VGG-Net and ResNet-101, with short connections to transfer low-level detail information with short connections [48]. Feng et al. used a green channel-based 1-D image to feed the cross-connected deep learning architecture in a multiscale scenario, where the final segmentation was performed with fusion [49]. An accurate three-stage deep-learning-based vessel segmentation method was presented by Yang et al., where separate deep-learning models were used to segment the thick and narrow vessels separately. Finally, another deep-learning model was used to fuse both results for the final segmentation [50]. These methods perform segmentation with deep networks and keep the size of the final feature maps small, which results in lower sensitivity.

2.2.5. Other CNN-Based Methods

Hu et al. presented a CNN method to detect retinal vessels. They utilized a cross-entropy loss function for vessel segmentation, in which a conditional random field-based scheme was employed to boost the segmentation mask using a neural network [51]. A CNN-based scheme was proposed by Kromm et al. to detect vessels and their centerlines. They used Capsule-Net integrated with an inception network to tackle the segmentation task [52]. Considering the most recent learning-based methods, Samuel et al. proposed a supervised VGG-16 network with two-vessel extraction layers. These extraction layers were responsible for localizing the blood vessels; they used skip chain convolutional layers for rich feature flow between the network layers for superior segmentation [53]. Wu et al. presented a novel deep learning scheme in which a front network was used to generate a retinal vessel probabilistic map and a subsequent network to refine the map. They also employed an inner-network skip connection to unite identical features, where probabilistic maps were averaged for the final segmentation [54]. Similar to the methods listed in Section 2.2.5, these methods provide lower accuracy and sensitivity.

Table 2. Pros and cons of the literature.

Type	Method	Pros	Cons
Local feature-based methods	CLAHE [22–24]	Relatively simpler hardware is required	Suffer from the changes in contrast and quality of images
	Line detection [25–27]	Simple image processing-based approach	Multiple preprocessing is required
	Tubular approach [28]	Tube Marked Point Process model approximation for vessel	Low sensitivity
	Morphology and Thresholding [29–31]	Thresholding is the simplest segmentation approach	The threshold may change with each image
	Patch-based denoiser [32]	Frangi filter is good for a vessel like structure	Low sensitivity
Learned feature-based methods	Encoder-decoder [33–40]	U-Net and SegNet are famous for pixel-wise segmentation	The decoder is the same as the encoder increase the number of trainable parameters
	GAN [41–43]	Adversarial approaches are good for a small amount of data	Complex structure with a large number of trainable parameters
	Machine Learning [45,46]	Relatively simpler compared to deep learning approaches	Pre and postprocessing are required
	Multiscale CNN [47]	Multiscale CNN is famous to deal with multiple resolutions	Patch-based scheme
	VGG and ResNet [48]	Skip connection overcomes the vanishing gradient problem	Two networks are combined for the task
	Cross-connected CNN [49]	Cross connected multiscale CNN share the spatial information of different scales	Only the Green channel is used
	Three-stage CNN [50]	Multiple network benefits are achieved	Three networks make the overall system complex
	Cross Entropy-based CNN [51]	Multiscale CNN performs better	A conditional random field is required to boost segmentation performance

Table 2. Cont.

Type	Method	Pros	Cons
	Capsule-Net [52]	CapsuleNet in combination with Inception is used for better performance	Overall complex
	VGG-16 [53]	Skip connection improves segmentation performance	Preprocessing is required
	NFN+ [54]	The network is followed by another network for better performance	Patch-based approach with preprocessing

3. Proposed Method

3.1. Summary of Retinal Vessels Detection Using Deep Learning

The deep networks that deal with pixel-wise segmentation are called semantic segmentation networks. Unlike classification networks, which predict the image level label, semantic segmentation networks provide pixel-level predicted labels. A semantic segmentation network takes an image as input and applies many trained filters according to the learning from the training examples in an encoder–decoder manner, and at the end of the network, the pixel classification layers provide a binary output mask for each class in one go. Similarly, the morphological properties of retinal vessels are important for various ophthalmic disease assessments and semantic segmentation can help to find each vessel pixel in the image for analysis. The VSUL-Net is a deep learning-based segmentation network that learns from the example training images and utilizes that learned knowledge for pixel-wise retinal vessel prediction. The overview of the proposed network is provided in Section 3.2.

3.2. Overview of the Proposed Method

This study proposes a vessel segmentation ultra-lite network that can be used to aid ophthalmic analysis applications. Figure 1 presents the overall working procedure of the proposed method, which is based on the concatenation of features obtained from the backbone and retention blocks. This feature aggregation allows the network to learn powerful features to segment the retinal vasculature without a preprocessing stage. The proposed VSUL-Net takes the original image and applies a convolutional operation to extract meaningful features to detect retinal vessels. The final pixel classification block provides a binary segmentation mask that represents vessel and background pixels, and can be used for ophthalmic analysis.

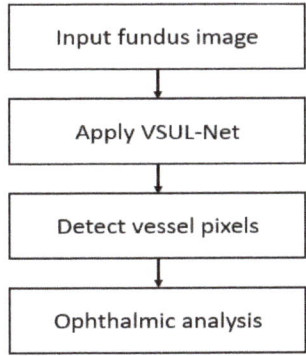

Figure 1. The working overall procedure of the proposed method for vessel segmentation for ophthalmic analysis. Abbreviation: VSUL-Net, vessel segmentation ultra-lite-network.

3.3. Structure of Proposed VSUL-Net

Generally, segmentation tasks are based on deep learning using a fully convolutional network in which the fully connected layers are removed and an upsampling procedure is adopted. Conventional semantic segmentation networks [55,56] are designed for other applications, and they use the same number of convolutions for the encoder and decoder while maintaining the same architectural design. This principle increases the overall depth of the network and the number of trainable parameters. Moreover, the conventional networks [56] use multiple pooling layers to reduce the size of the feature map, and the final feature map size becomes too small, which cannot represent the minor objects in the image. That small final feature map vanishes the small object in the image, which results in lower performance for the smaller classes. Hypothetically considering the vessel segmentation applications, the retinal vessel has a very complex structure. In addition, the smaller size of vessels makes segmentation tasks challenging. The accurate detection of these vessels is very important for ophthalmic disease analysis, and keeping the final feature map larger can save the important spatial information. VSUL-Net is a custom-designed vessel segmentation network that is specifically designed to detect retinal vessels with better sensitivity. Figure 2 illustrates the structure of the proposed VSUL-Net. Observe (Figure 2) that VSUL-Net is composed of three main blocks, namely, the backbone block (shown on the left of Figure 2), feature retention block (shown in the middle of Figure 2), and upsampling block (shown on the right side of Figure 2). Considering the importance of the true positive rate (sensitivity), which represents how effectively our model detects the true vessel pixels, the retention block keeps the feature map size larger and provides the low-level spatial information to the later layers.

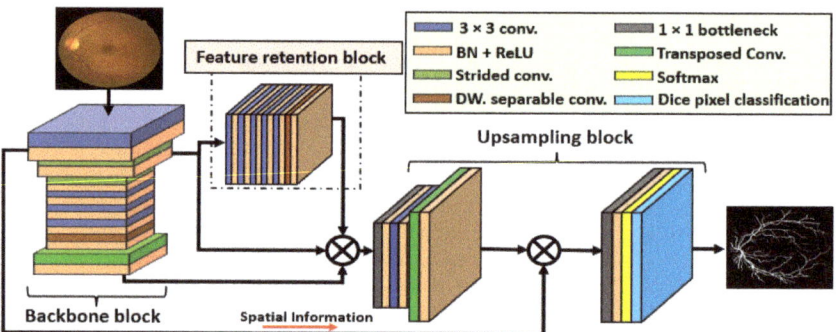

Figure 2. The structure of the proposed VSUL-Net. In this figure, 3×3 kernel convolution (3×3 conv.), 1×1 convolution (1×1 bottleneck), batch normalization and rectified linear unit (BN + ReLU), 2×2 transposed convolution with stride = 2 (Transposed Conv.), 3×3 convolution with stride = 2 (Strided conv.), and 3×3 depth-wise separable convolution (DW. separable conv.) are represented.

The backbone block consists of four 3×3 general convolutions and two strided convolutions with stride = 2. The strided convolution is used to reduce the feature map size by half, replacing the max-pooling layers used in conventional architectures. Overall, the feature map is reduced twice in the backbone block. Convolutional layers with many channels require more trainable parameters; therefore, the convolution on the deeper side of the backbone block is replaced by depth-wise separable convolutions to reduce the complexity of the network. Keeping in mind that these vessels are small compared to the background, these vessels can be eliminated if the feature map size is reduced significantly inside the network. Observe from Table 3 that the smallest feature map size in the backbone block was 163×163, which is sufficient to represent most of the vessels available in the image. Moreover, with this 163×163 feature map, minor vessels can be eliminated;

therefore, the feature retention block is used to apply continuous convolutions without resizing the feature map size. The retention block retains the future map size for a flat feature map size of 325 × 325 (as shown in Table 3), which can contain most of the valuable features that can represent most of the vessels. The upsampling block is mainly based on two transposed convolutions that are used along with a few general convolutions and batch normalizations. Two transposed convolutions are used to resize the feature map to its original size. Softmax and pixel classification layers are used at the end of the upsampling block. A further description of the pixel classification layer is provided in Section 3.3.

Table 3. Feature map size details of the VSUL-Net layers.

Block	Layer Name	Layer Size K × K × C, (Stride)	Filters/Groups	Output
Input Block	Input Conv	1 × 1 × 3 (S = 1)	8	650 × 650 × 8
Backbone	Conv-BB-A	3 × 3 × 8 (S = 2)	8	325 × 325 × 8
	Conv-BB-B	3 × 3 × 8 (S = 2)	8	163 × 163 × 8
	Conv-BB-C	3 × 3 × 8 (S = 1)	8	163 × 163 × 8
	Conv-BB-D	3 × 3 × 8 (S = 1)	16	163 × 163 × 16
	Conv-BB-E	3 × 3 × 16 (S = 1)	24	163 × 163 × 24
	DW-Sep-Conv-BB-A	3 × 3 × 24 (S = 1)	24	163 × 163 × 24
	T-Conv-BB-A	2 × 2 × 24 (S = 2)	32	325 × 325 × 32
Retention	Conv-RT-A	3 × 3 × 8 (S = 1)	8	325 × 325 × 8
	Conv-RT-B	3 × 3 × 8 (S = 1)	8	325 × 325 × 8
	Conv-RT-C	3 × 3 × 8 (S = 1)	16	325 × 325 × 16
	Conv-RT-D	3 × 3 × 16 (S = 1)	24	325 × 325 × 24
	Conv-RT-E	3 × 3 × 24 (S = 1)	32	325 × 325 × 32
	DW-Sep-Conv-RT-A	3 × 3 × 32 (S = 1)	32	325 × 325 × 32
Concatenation-A	T-Conv-BB-A © DW-Sep-Conv-RT-A © Conv-BB-A			325 × 325 × 72
Upsampling	B-Neck-Conv	1 × 1 × 72 (S = 1)	32	325 × 325 × 32
	Conv-US-A	3 × 3 × 32 (S = 1)	32	325 × 325 × 32
	T-Conv-US-A	2 × 2 × 32 (S = 2)	16	650 × 650 × 16
Concatenation-B	Input Conv © T-Conv-US-A			650 × 650 × 24
Final	Class-Mask-Conv	1 × 1 × 24 (S = 1)	2	650 × 650 × 2

Figure 3 illustrates the VSUL-Net connectivity and dense feature aggregation principle. The backbone block takes the input feature F_i, passes it through several convolutional layers to extract meaningful features for the retinal vessel analysis and provides the F_B feature. This F_B is densely aggregated with the rich feature F_{Ret} coming from the retention block. The retention block features are without extensive pooling operations; therefore, they contain features that represent most of the vessels in the image. Both F_B and F_{Ret} are aggregated by depth-wise concatenation to create the S_1 feature that is expressed by Equation (1).

$$S_1 = F_B © F_{Ret}. \tag{1}$$

Here, S_1 is the densely aggregated feature created by the depth-wise concatenation of F_B (feature coming from the backbone block) and F_{Ret} (coming from the retention block), where © represents the depth-wise concatenation.

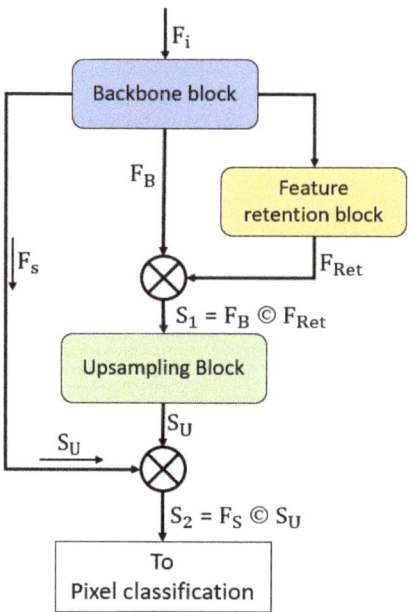

Figure 3. Understanding of VSUL-Net connectivity and dense feature aggregation principle.

The upsampling block uses the S_1 feature and upsamples it so that it is equal to the input size of the network. The upsampling block outputs an S_U feature that can be used for the final pixel-wise classification. However, to compensate for the spatial loss created by the continuous convolution operation, another dense concatenation is required. The low-level spatial information F_s is imported from the initial layers of the network to be aggregated with the S_U feature to build the rich compensated feature S_2, which is expressed by Equation (2).

$$S_2 = F_S \copyright S_U \qquad (2)$$

Here, the S_2 feature is the combined aggregated powerful feature created by the depth-wise concatenation of F_S (coming from the initial layers of the network) and S_U (coming from the upsampling block), where $\copyright$ represents the depth-wise concatenation.

3.4. Dealing with Class Imbalance Using Dice Loss

The pixel classification layer is responsible for providing pixel-wise markings according to the predicted class. Feature S_2, taken from the upsampling block, is sent to a Softmax block. The number of vessel pixels in the image is less than that of the background pixels; therefore, the class imbalance deteriorates the final segmentation performance. The generalized dice loss (GDL) is an effective method for addressing class imbalances [57]. In VSUL-Net, the pixel classification layer is used with the GDL. The GDL is expressed by Equation (3)

$$L_{GDL} = 1 - \left(\frac{2 \times \sum_i^K P_{Pred-i} G_{True-i}}{\sum_i^K P_{Pred-i}^2 + \sum_i^K G_{True-i}^2} \right), \qquad (3)$$

where K belongs to all pixels available in the image; i is the pixel under consideration; and P and G are the predicted labels and actual ground truth labels, respectively. P_{Pred-i} is the predicted probability of pixel i belonging to a specific class and G_{True-i} is the actual ground truth label.

4. Experimental Results

4.1. Datasets

In our experiments, we used three publicly available datasets, namely, DRIVE [58], CHASE-DB1 [59], and STARE [60]. The DRIVE [58] dataset consists of 40 RGB images with pixel-wise expert annotations of retinal vessels. The images were captured using a Canon CR5 fundus camera (45° field of view (FOV)). The DRIVE dataset was provided with a predefined official data split of 20 training and 20 testing images. The CHASE-DB1 [59] dataset consists of 28 RGB images with pixel-wise expert annotations of retinal vessels. The images were captured using a Nidek NM-200D fundus camera (30° FOV). The CHASE-DB1 dataset was provided with a predefined official data split of the first 20 images for training and the remaining eight images for testing. The STARE [60] dataset consists of 20 RGB images with pixel-wise expert annotations of retinal vessels. The images were captured using a TopCon TRV-50 fundus camera (35° FOV). For the STARE dataset, we performed leave-one-out cross-validation, in which 19 images were used for training and one image for testing, and 20 experiments were performed independently for each testing image. The final result was obtained by averaging the 20 experimental results. Figure 4a–c shows example images and expert annotations taken from the DRIVE, CHASE-DB1, and STARE datasets, respectively. Table 4 summarizes the experimental details for each dataset used in our experiments. Further details can be found in [58–60] for DRIVE, CHASE-DB-1, and STARE, respectively.

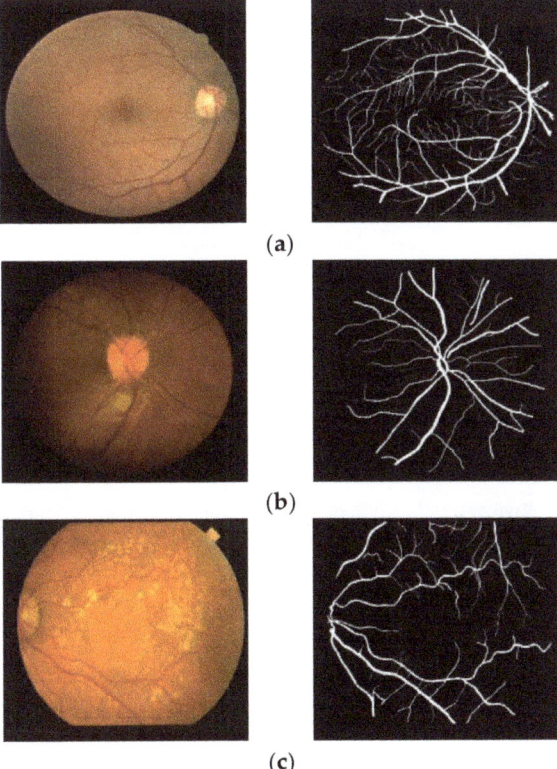

(a)

(b)

(c)

Figure 4. Example fundus images used in our experiments. (**a–c**) are examples taken from the DRIVE, CHASE-DB1, and STARE datasets, respectively.

Table 4. Description of the DRIVE, STARE, and CHASE-DB1 datasets and experimentation details.

Dataset Name	Total Images	Experiment Details
DRIVE [58]	40	Pre-defined Training = 20, Testing = 20 (one experiment)
CHASE-DB1 [59]	28	Pre-defined Training = 20, Testing = 8 (one experiment)
STARE [60]	20	Training = 19, Testing = 1 (20 experiments)

4.2. Data Augmentation

The segmentation performance of deep learning is directly related to the amount of labeled training data; successful training requires a significant quantity of labeled training data. Therefore, we utilized image flipping and translation to increase the amount of data. Figure 5 presents the adopted augmentation procedure, where 20 original images were flipped vertically and horizontally to create 60 images. Then, these 60 images were iteratively translated into both X and Y values combined with flipping to create 3200 images from the DRIVE dataset. The same augmentation approach was adopted for the CHASE-DB1 and STARE datasets to create 1280 and 1520 images, respectively.

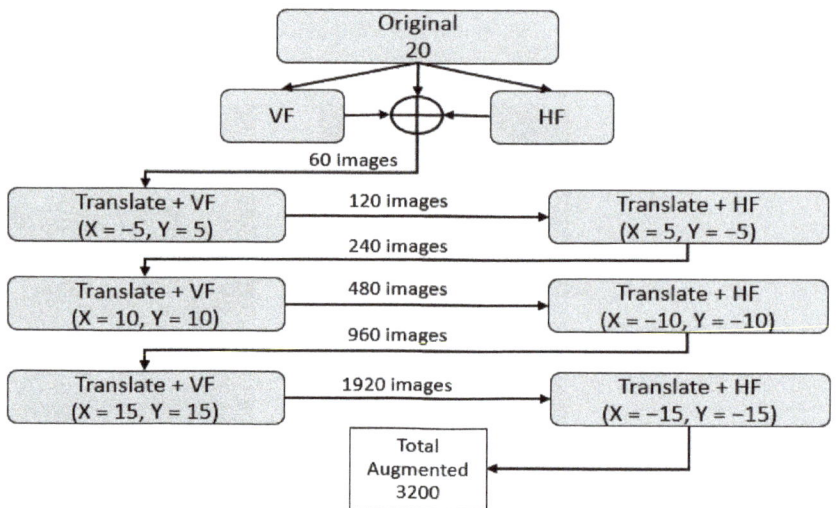

Figure 5. Data augmentation scheme used to synthetically increase training data, where VF and HF represent vertical flip and horizontal flip, respectively.

4.3. Experimental Environment and Training of Proposed Method

The proposed VSUL-Net architecture was implemented, trained, and tested using MATLAB 2021b on a desktop computer with an Intel® Core i7-3770K CPU, NVIDIA RTX 3080 GPU, and 28 GB of RAM. The proposed method was trained from scratch without using weight initialization, migration, or transfer learning. Adam optimizer [61] was adopted to train 35 epochs of training using an initial learning rate of 0.0001 and an epsilon of 0.000001 with global L2-normalization. We picked the optimal models with parameters that were with the lowest training loss and highest training accuracy. In our experiments, we shuffled the images for each epoch. Figure 6 depicts the training accuracy and loss curves of the VSUL-Net experiment using the DRIVE dataset. The curves demonstrate that our proposed network achieved high training accuracy and low training loss.

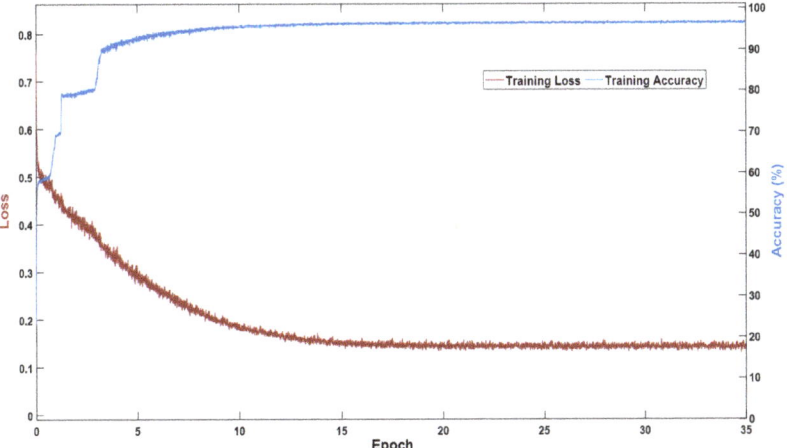

Figure 6. VSUL-Net training accuracy and loss curves for the DRIVE dataset.

4.4. Evaluation of Proposed Method

VSUL-Net provides a mask for the network output. This mask represents all the vessel and background pixels as "1" and "0", respectively. To measure the segmentation performance, the output mask of the proposed network was compared with expert annotations to compute the segmentation performance using sensitivity (Sen), specificity (Spe), accuracy (Acc), and area under the curve (AUC), which are commonly used to evaluate the segmentation performance of retinal images [19]. Sen is the true positive rate that shows how good the model is to detect vessel pixels. Spe is the true negative rate that shows the ability to detect the non-vessel pixels. Acc represents the overall number of correct predictions by the method. Sen, Spe, and Acc are expressed by Equations (4)–(6), respectively. TP denotes a pixel that is predicted as a vessel pixel and is categorized as a vessel pixel in the expert annotation. FN denotes a pixel that is predicted as a background pixel and is categorized as a vessel pixel in the expert annotation. TN denotes a pixel that is predicted as a background pixel and is categorized as a background pixel in the expert annotation. FP denotes a pixel that is predicted as a vessel pixel and is categorized as a background pixel in the expert annotation.

$$\text{Sen} = \frac{\text{TP}}{(\text{TP} + \text{FN})} \quad (4)$$

$$\text{Spe} = \frac{\text{TN}}{(\text{TN} + \text{FP})} \quad (5)$$

$$\text{Acc} = \frac{(\text{TP} + \text{TN})}{(\text{TP} + \text{FN} + \text{FP} + \text{TN})} \quad (6)$$

4.5. Ablation Study for Proposed VSUL-Net

The initial layers of the network contain low-level valuation features that contain edge information. Importing this information through skip connections aids the convergence of the network by reducing the vanishing gradient problem [62]. Dense connectivity [63] reduces feature latency and performs better than residual networks [62]. An ablation study was conducted to compare the performance of residual and dense connectivity for the proposed network. In the ablation experiments, the VSUL-Net structure was trained using element-wise addition (VSUL-Net-R) and depth-wise concatenation (VSUL-Net-D). Table 5 reports that VSUL-Net with dense connectivity performed better, with a higher true positive rate (Sen) compared to the residual one keeping the same number of parameters.

Table 5. Ablation study results for proposed VSUL-Net. The processing time is measured in milliseconds (ms) for an image with size 650 × 650 pixels.

Method	Sen	Spe	Acc	AUC	Parameters	Process Time (ms)
VSUL-Net (Residual)	83.19	98.15	96.84	98.45	0.37 M	35
VSUL-Net (Dense)	83.80	98.21	96.95	98.54	0.37 M	34

4.6. Comparison of Proposed Method with Existing Schemes

This section compares the proposed method with existing vessel segmentation schemes. Tables 6–8 list numerical comparison results with the DRIVE, CHASE-DB1, and STARE datasets, respectively. The comparisons were performed based on the Sen, Spe, Acc, and AUC metrics described in Section 4.4. Most of the methods that are provided in Tables 6–8 only provided the numerical results by describing the number of trainable parameters. A few methods have provided details of trainable parameters, which is an important parameter to judge the network's cost and its resource utilization along with the performance measures provided in Section 4.4. Considering this fact, the proposed method provided high sensitivity in combination with other metrics for all three datasets presented in Tables 6–8. The method presented by Soomro et al. [64] was based on SegNet, which is a famous semantic segmentation network, but the performances for the Sen, Spe, Acc, and AUC were 74.60%, 91.70%, 94.80%, and 94.60%, which were lower than the proposed VSUL-Net while using 29.4 million trainable parameters. Lv et al. [65] presented two methods of U-Net, and AA-UNet, where it can be seen from Tables 6 and 8, that for the DRIVE dataset, both U-Net and AA-UNet provided lower Sen, Spe, Acc, and AUC of 78.49%, 98.02%, 95.54%, 97.19%, and 79.41%, 97.98%, 95.58%, and 98.24%, respectively, which were lower compared to the proposed VSUL-Net. In the case of CHASE-DB1, the Sen of U-Net and AA-UNet was slightly higher, but considering other metrics, the Spe, and AUC were lower than the proposed VSUL-Net with only 0.37 million trainable parameters where U-Net and AA-UNet consumed 31.03 million and 28.28 million trainable parameters, respectively. Considering Vess-Net [14], a relative with a lower number of parameters achieved Sen, Spe, and AUC of 80.22%, 98.21%, and 96.27% respectively, where the Sen was lower than that proposed, which consumed much fewer trainable parameters. Very few researchers have focused on utilizing shallower architectures because as the network depth decreases, the performance of the network also deteriorates. Li et al. proposed LACNN [66], which only consumes 0.4 million trainable parameters with few layers. It can be noticed from Tables 6–8, that LACNN provided better segmentation performance compared to many famous studies described in the same tables, but with an effective architecture, the proposed VSUL-Net provided a much better Sen, Spe, Acc, and AUC for all three datasets. The DSF-Net and DSA-Net are effective shallow architectures that performed better than LACNN and other famous methods listed in Tables 6 and 8 with a better true positive rate, but the proposed VSUL-Net provided further enhanced Sen. The Spe with DSF-Net and DSA-Net was slightly high but the number of trainable parameters was much higher than the proposed VSUL-Net.

To prove the effectiveness of a model, a 2-tailed *t*-test [67] can be performed that can compare two methods. According to Table 4, the training and testing images were pre-defined for just one experiment for the DRIVE and CHASE-DB1 datasets according to the database providers, and we followed this experimental protocol for fair comparisons with the previous research available in Tables 6 and 7. The results available in Tables 6 and 7 were taken from the corresponding papers, therefore, statistical testing such as the ANOVA test or *t*-tests with DRIVE and CHASE-DB1 cannot be performed due to the unavailability of variance.

However, the training and testing images are not pre-defined in the STARE dataset, according to the database providers. Therefore, as shown in Table 4, the STARE dataset includes 20 experiments with leave-one-out cross-validation (following the same experimental protocol for fair comparisons with the previous research available in Table 8), and consequently, there exists variances to perform statistical testing. Nevertheless, the accuracies of all the previous research, except for the second-best one [20] in Table 8, were also referred to in corresponding papers, and we used the same STARE dataset and experimental protocols as those used by the previous researchers presented in Table 8. Consequently, there was no reported variance in the accuracies by their methods except for the second-best one [20]. However, we performed the experiments with the algorithm of the method [20] implemented by us, so we could obtain the variance from all 20 experiments.

The ANOVA test is usually used to statistically compare the differences of more than two methods (observations) [68,69]. Because no variance was available for the methods except for the second-best one [20] in Table 8, it was not possible to perform the ANOVA test. As the *t*-test offers the statistical comparison of two methods (observations), we only performed the *t*-test between the proposed VSUL-Net and the second-best one of DSA-Net [20].

Table 9 presents a 2-tailed *t*-test [67] comparison between the proposed method and the second-best method [20] for the STARE dataset in Table 8. The *t*-test is generally performed to enlighten the performance difference of two models quantitatively using a null hypothesis (H), which assumes that the two models have a similar performance (i.e., H = 0). A hypothesis rejection score (*p*-value) was calculated with a confidence score for the rejection of the null hypothesis. The proposed method rejected the null hypothesis with a confidence score of 93.6%, 98.8%, and 99.9% for Sen, Spe, and Acc, respectively, which confirmed that our method outperformed the second best one [20] in a statistical manner.

Table 6. Numerical comparison of the proposed VSUL-Net with existing methods for the DRIVE dataset.

Method	Sen	Spe	Acc	AUC	#Pram
Soomro et al. SegNet [64]	74.60	91.70	94.80	94.60	29.4
Lv et al. U-Net [65]	78.49	98.02	95.54	97.19	31.03
Lv et al. AA-UNet [65]	79.41	97.98	95.58	98.24	28.25
Arsalan et al. Vess-Net [14]	80.22	98.10	96.55	98.20	9.7
Samuel et al. VSSCNet [53]	78.27	98.21	96.27	-	8.0
Zhang et al. BIWT [70]	78.95	97.01	94.63	-	-
Zhang et al. BIWT (postprocessing) [70]	78.61	97.12	94.66	-	-
Tan et al. Single CNN [71]	75.37	96.94	-	-	-
Zhu et al. EML [72]	71.40	98.68	96.07	-	-
Girard et al. [73]	78.40	98.10	95.7	97.20	-
Hu et al. MCNN [51]	77.72	97.93	95.33	97.59	-
Fu et al. DeepVessel [74]	76.03	-	95.23	-	-
Wang et al. C-CNN [75]	76.48	98.17	95.41	-	-
Soomro et al. BS-CNN [64]	74.60	91.70	94.60	83.10	-
Chudzik et al. DISCERN [44]	78.81	97.41	-	96.46	-
Yan et al. 3-stage DL [50]	76.31	98.20	95.38	97.50	-
Soomro et al. FCNN [76]	73.90	95.60	94.8	84.40	-

Table 6. *Cont.*

Method	Sen	Spe	Acc	AUC	#Pram
Jin et al. DUNet [33]	79.63	98.00	95.66	98.02	-
Leopold et al. [77]	69.63	95.73	91.06	82.68	-
Wang et al. PixelBNN [78]	79.86	97.36	95.11	97.40	-
Feng et al. CCCN [49]	76.25	98.09	95.28	96.78	-
Oliveira et al. FCNN [47]	80.39	98.04	95.76	98.21	-
Guo et al. Image BTS-DSN [48]	78.00	98.06	95.51	97.96	-
Guo et al. Patch BTS-DSN [48]	78.91	98.04	95.61	98.06	-
Khan et al. VessSeg [79]	82.55	97.60	96.20	97.30	-
Kromm et al. ICN [52]	76.51	98.18	95.47	97.50	-
Li et al. LACNN [66]	79.21	98.10	95.68	98.06	0.4
Arsalan et al. DSF-Net [20]	81.94	98.38	96.93	98.30	1.5
Arsalan et al. DSA-Net [20]	82.68	98.30	96.93	98.42	1.5
Width-wise bifurcation [80]	81.25	97.63	96.10	-	-
Zhang et al. RU-Net [81]	78.31	98.02	95.47	98.05	-
Zhang et al. Bridge-Net [81]	78.53	98.18	95.65	98.34	-
Zhang et al. [39]	82.13	98.07	96.15	98.15	-
VSUL-Net (Proposed)	83.80	98.21	96.95	98.54	0.37

Table 7. Numerical comparison of the proposed VSUL-Net with existing methods for the CHASE-DB1 dataset.

Methods	Sen	Spe	Acc	AUC	#Pram
Zhang et al. BIWT [70]	77.86	96.94	94.97	-	-
Zhang et al. BIWT (Postprocessing) [70]	76.44	97.16	95.02	-	-
Fu et al. DeepVessel [74]	71.30	-	94.89	-	-
Wang et al. C-CNN [75]	77.30	97.92	96.03	-	-
Yan et al. 3-stage DL [50]	76.41	98.06	96.07	97.76	-
Jin et al. DUNet [33]	81.55	97.52	96.10	98.04	-
Leopold et al. [77]	86.18	89.61	89.36	87.90	-
Lv et al. U-Net [65]	83.99	96.98	95.77	97.80	31.03
Lv et al. AA-UNet [65]	81.76	97.04	96.08	98.65	28.25
Oliveira et al. FCNN [47]	77.79	98.64	96.53	98.55	-
Image BTS-DSN [48]	78.88	98.01	96.27	98.40	-
Khan et al. VessSeg [79]	82.91	97.30	96.20	97.65	-
Li et al. LACNN [66]	78.18	98.19	96.35	98.10	-
Width-wise bifurcation [80]	80.12	97.30	95.78	-	-
RU-Net [81]	81.03	98.40	96.65	98.86	-
Bridge-Net [81]	81.32	98.40	96.67	98.93	-
VSUL-Net (Proposed)	81.73	98.35	97.19	98.69	0.37

Table 8. Numerical comparison of the proposed VSUL-Net with existing methods for the STARE dataset.

Method	Sen	Spe	Acc	AUC	#Pram
Zhang et al. BIWT [70]	77.24	97.04	95.13	-	-
Zhang et al. BIWT (Postprocessing) [70]	78.82	97.29	95.47	-	-
Hu et al. MCNN [51]	75.43	98.14	96.32	97.51	-
Fu et al. DeepVessel [74]	74.12	-	95.85	-	-
Wang et al. C-CNN [75]	75.23	98.85	96.40	-	-
Soomro et al. FCNN [64]	74.8	92.2	94.8	83.5	-
Chudzik et al. DISCERN [44]	82.69	98.04	-	98.37	-
Hajabdollahi et al. CNN [82]	78.23	97.70	96.17	-	-
Hajabdollahi et al. Q-CNN [82]	77.92	97.40	95.87	-	-
Hajabdollahi et al. PQ-CNN [82]	75.99	97.57	95.81	-	-
Yan et al. 3-stage DL [50]	77.35	98.57	96.38	98.33	-
Soomro et al. FCNN [76]	74.8	96.2	94.7	85.5	-
Jin et al. DUNet [33]	75.95	98.78	96.41	98.32	-
Leopold et al. [77]	64.33	94.72	90.45	79.52	-
Wang et al. PixelBNN [78]	79.14	97.22	95.38	97.04	-
Feng et al. CCCN [49]	77.09	98.48	96.33	97.0	-
Oliveira et al. FCNN [47]	83.15	98.58	96.94	99.05	-
Arsalan et al. Vess-Net [14]	85.26	97.91	96.97	98.83	9.7
Guo et al. Image BTS-DSN [48]	82.01	98.28	96.60	98.72	-
Guo et al. Patch BTS-DSN [48]	82.12	98.43	96.74	98.59	-
Khan et al. VessSeg [79]	83.18	97.58	96.23	97.58	-
Li et al. LACNN [66]	83.52	98.23	96.78	98.75	-
Width-wise bifurcation [80]	80.78	97.21	95.86	-	-
Arsalan et al. DSA-Net [20]	86.07	98.00	97.00	98.65	1.5
Zhang et al. RU-Net [81]	79.81	98.56	96.58	98.62	-
Zhang et al. Bridge-Net [81]	80.02	98.64	96.68	99.01	-
VSUL-Net (Proposed)	86.64	98.13	97.27	99.01	0.37

Table 9. The *t*-test performance difference analysis (*p*-value and confidence score) for the STARE dataset.

Proposed VSUL-Net vs. DSA-Net [20]	Sen	Spe	Acc
p-Value	0.064	0.012	0.001
Confidence score (%)	93.6	98.8	99.9

4.7. Visual Results of Proposed Method for Vessel Segmentation

The visual results provided by the proposed method on three publicly available fundus image datasets, DRIVE, CHASE-DB1, and STARE, for retinal vasculature detection, are presented in this section. Figures 7–9 depict the vessel segmentation visual results obtained by the proposed VSUL-Net compared with expert annotation. Figures 7–9 display the (a) input fundus image, (b) expert annotation, and (c) VSUL-Net predicted mask.

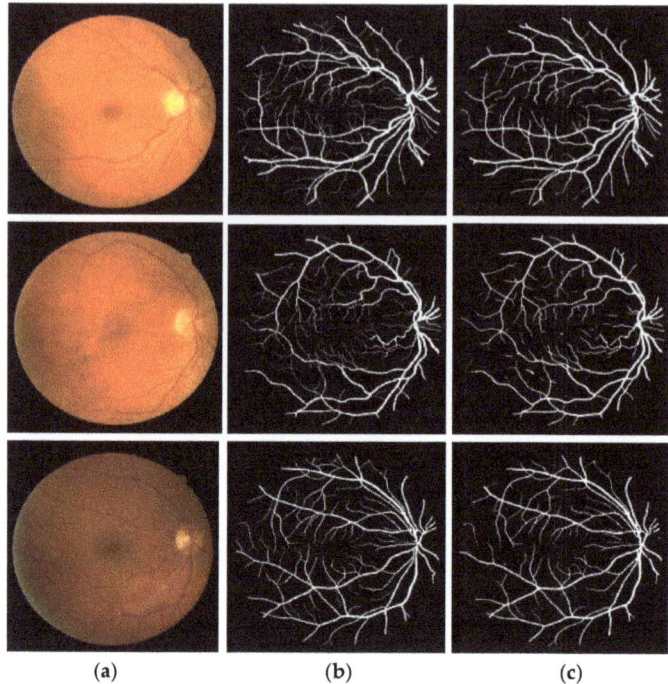

Figure 7. VSUL-Net visual results for the DRIVE dataset: (**a**) original fundus image, (**b**) expert annotation, and (**c**) VSUL-Net predicted mask.

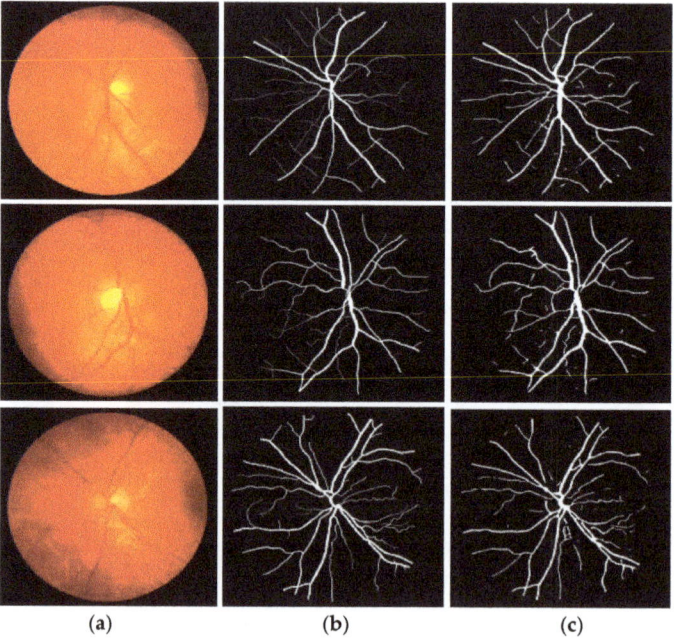

Figure 8. VSUL-Net visual results for the CHASE-DB1 dataset: (**a**) original fundus image, (**b**) expert annotation, and (**c**) VSUL-Net predicted mask.

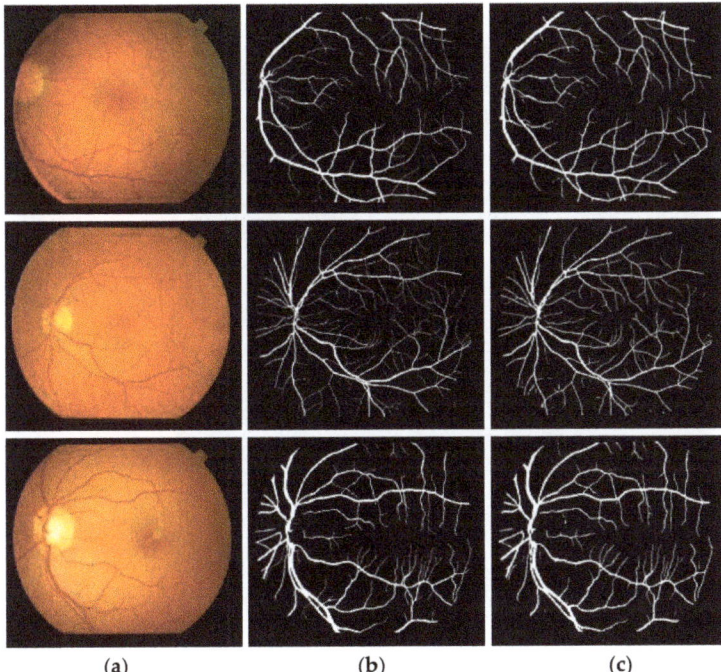

Figure 9. VSUL-Net visual results for the STARE dataset: (**a**) original fundus image, (**b**) expert annotation, and (**c**) VSUL-Net predicted mask.

4.8. Discussion

The proposed VSUL-Net depends on the quality of the input data. Similar to other methods, the VSUL-Net is a learning-based method that learns the valuable features from the training data, and the quality and amount of data can affect the segmentation performance. As mentioned at the end of the Introduction section (Section 1), unlike other famous methods, the proposed VSUL-Net does not use any preprocessing schemes for image enhancement, which increases the overall cost of the system. The VSUL-Net uses the original image and provides pixel-wise segmentation of the retinal vessels. As the VSUL-Net is a learning-based system, there can be misses, discontinuities, and over-segmentation. Figure 10 presents example images of these misses, discontinuities, and over-segmentation based on TP, FP, and FN (defined in Section 4.4) for the DRIVE, CHASE-DB1, and STARE datasets (top to down) in comparison with expert annotation. According to Figure 10, the blue color represents the TP, the red color presents the FN (misses or discontinuities), and the green color presents the FP (over-segmentation). It can be noted from Figure 10d that most of the pixels (blue) belonged to TP and there existed errors (FN, FP) in the smaller vessels that were not clearly visible in the original image (Figure 10a). These misses and discontinuities were smaller compared to the existing approaches as shown by the better segmentation performance in Tables 6–8. These discontinuities can cause problems with the diagnosis. Therefore, the predicted mask by the proposed method cannot be used directly for disease diagnosis. This can be an alternative for aiding in ophthalmic analysis and can provide an opportunity for the ophthalmologist to detect the retinal morphology in a faster way to reduce the manual detection burden. The retinal diseases that are related to the central retinal vein or optic nerve head can be helped. Moreover, suspicious cases can be keenly verified by the medical specialist.

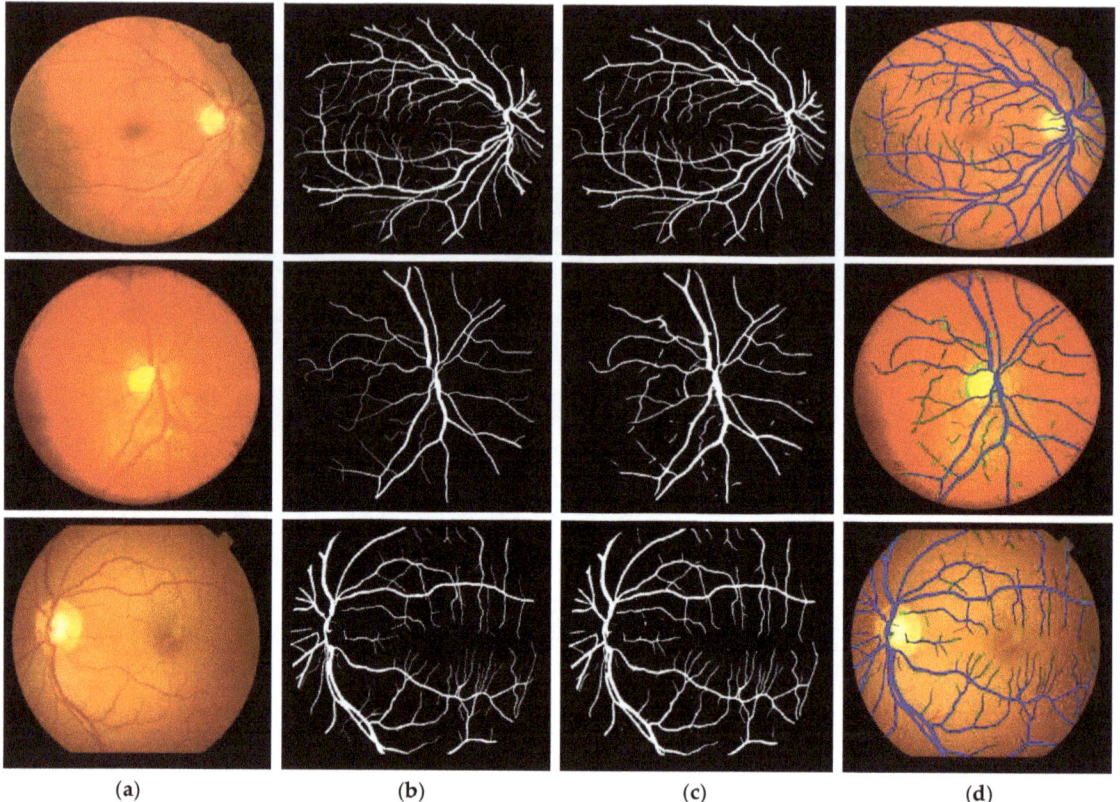

Figure 10. VSUL-Net output mask analysis for misses, discontinuities, and over-segmentation: (**a**) original fundus image, (**b**) expert annotation, (**c**) VSUL-Net predicted mask, and (**d**) mask-annotation overlapping image (TP is presented in blue, FN in red, and FP in green).

The prediction obtained from the network is based on specific features, which are important for the development of a robust segmentation network. The deep learning network behaves like a black box, without explaining the discriminative features that contribute to predicting a specific pixel label. Gradient-weighted class activation map (Grad-cam) [83] is a method for visualizing discriminative features that contribute to detecting vessel pixels from an image. In Grad-cam, a color close to red represents high-class confidence, whereas blue represents evidence of class presentation. Figure 11 shows examples of Grad-cam images taken from the DRIVE, CHASE-DB1, and STARE datasets. These Grad-cam images were extracted via the ReLU function of T-Conv-BB-A present in the backbone block (shown in Figure 11c), DW-Sep-Conv-RT-A present in the retention block (shown in Figure 11d), T-Conv-US-A present in the upsampling block (shown in Figure 11e), and Class-Mask-Conv located at the end of the network (shown in Figure 11f). The Grad-cam results show that our network gradually learns without bias.

4.9. Alternative for Aiding the Ophthalmic Analysis by Proposed Method

Retinal vessels are biomarkers of various ophthalmic and other diseases. Accurate pixel-wise detection of these retinal vessels can be an alternative in aiding with the ophthalmic analysis [5–7]. Accurate detection of the retinal vasculature helps ophthalmologists detect these diseases and identify changes, which are crucial for early diagnoses. The proposed VSUL-Net can be an alternative for aiding in ophthalmic analysis and can provide an opportunity for the ophthalmologist to detect the retinal morphology in a faster way. Suspicious cases can be keenly verified by the medical specialist for better diagnosis.

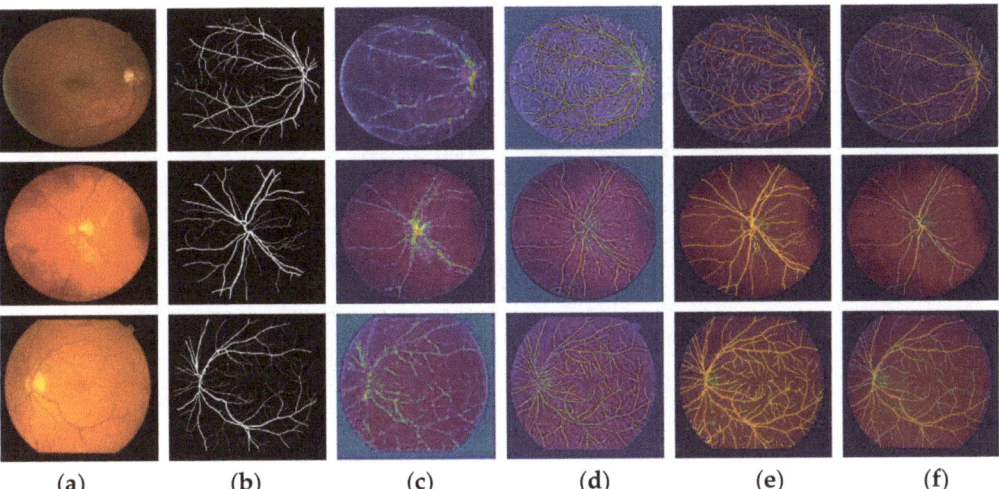

Figure 11. VSUL-Net Grad-cam visualization for the DRIVE (row-1), CHASE-DB1 (row-2), and STARE datasets (row-3): (**a**) original fundus image, (**b**) expert annotation, and Grad-cam extracted from the ReLU of (**c**) T-Conv-BB-A, (**d**) DW-Sep-Conv-RT-A, (**e**) T-Conv-US-A, (**f**) Class-Mask-Conv of Table 3.

4.10. Limitations of the Proposed Method

Although the proposed VSUL-Net detects retinal vessels with superior segmentation performance, there are still certain limitations of the proposed method. The proposed VSUL-Net is a learning-based segmentation method that mainly relies on the input training data. The medical data for disease analysis are very difficult to arrange in quantity. Therefore, data augmentation is required to artificially increase the amount of training data. Moreover, the learning-based methods provide the output masks based on the learned knowledge, and there can exist misses (false negative) and false positive pixels in the final prediction of the network.

5. Conclusions

The main objective of this study was to develop an effective low-cost vessel segmentation network specifically designed to address vessel segmentation with a better true positive rate to aid ophthalmic diagnosis with a simpler design. Conventional architectures continuously downsample the feature map, which causes the loss of important minor features available in the image. This continuous downsampling causes the loss of important low-level features, and many minor morphologies from the image disappear, which finally results in low sensitivity. The thin vessel can completely vanish during this process. The effective design of VSUL-Net with a retention block allows the network to perform better, even with a few layers and only 0.37 million trainable parameters. The proposed VSUL-Net provides an accurate pixel-wise classification of fundus images without preprocessing. Unlike conventional semantic segmentation networks, VSUL-Net uses a few transposed convolutions to upsample the image back to its original size. The proposed VSUL-Net outputs a binary segmentation mask that represents the vessel and background pixels. The subsequently obtained predicted mask can be utilized to monitor changes in the retinal vasculature during ophthalmic disease analyses.

In the future, we plan to use different image enhancement schemes to increase the quality of the training data for better performance with the same network. This preprocessing will help reduce the misses and discontinuities of the network. In addition, we plan to collect the related disease sample with pixel number annotation for accurate ophthalmic diagnosis with a better true positive rate.

Author Contributions: Methodology, M.A.; conceptualization, A.H.; validation, J.H.K.; supervision, K.R.P.; writing—original draft, M.A.; writing—review and editing, K.R.P. All authors have read and agreed to the published version of the manuscript.

Funding: This research was supported in part by the National Research Foundation of Korea (NRF) funded by the Ministry of Science and ICT (MSIT) through the Basic Science Research Program (NRF-2021R1F1A1045587), in part by the NRF funded by the MSIT through the Basic Science Research Program (NRF-2020R1A2C1006179), and in part by the MSIT, Korea, under the ITRC (Information Technology Research Center) support program (IITP-2022-2020-0-01789) supervised by the IITP (Institute for Information & Communications Technology Planning & Evaluation).

Institutional Review Board Statement: Not applicable.

Informed Consent Statement: Not applicable.

Data Availability Statement: Not applicable

Conflicts of Interest: The authors declare no conflict of interest.

References

1. Abràmoff, M.D.; Garvin, M.K.; Sonka, M. Retinal Imaging and Image Analysis. *IEEE Rev. Biomed. Eng.* **2010**, *3*, 169–208. [CrossRef] [PubMed]
2. Alyoubi, W.L.; Shalash, W.M.; Abulkhair, M.F. Diabetic Retinopathy Detection through Deep Learning Techniques: A Review. *Inform. Med. Unlocked* **2020**, *20*, 100377. [CrossRef]
3. Dai, G.; He, W.; Xu, L.; Pazo, E.E.; Lin, T.; Liu, S.; Zhang, C. Exploring the Effect of Hypertension on Retinal Microvasculature Using Deep Learning on East Asian Population. *PLoS ONE* **2020**, *15*, e0230111. [CrossRef]
4. Cho, B.-J.; Bae, S.H.; Park, S.M.; Shin, M.C.; Park, I.W.; Kim, H.K.; Kwon, S. Comparison of Systemic Conditions at Diagnosis between Central Retinal Vein Occlusion and Branch Retinal Vein Occlusion. *PLoS ONE* **2019**, *14*, e0220880. [CrossRef]
5. Cano, J.; Farzad, S.; Khansari, M.M.; Tan, O.; Huang, D.; Lim, J.I.; Shahidi, M. Relating Retinal Blood Flow and Vessel Morphology in Sickle Cell Retinopathy. *Eye* **2020**, *34*, 886–891. [CrossRef] [PubMed]
6. Kromer, R.; Buhmann, C.; Hidding, U.; Keserü, M.; Keserü, D.; Hassenstein, A.; Stemplewitz, B. Evaluation of Retinal Vessel Morphology in Patients with Parkinson's Disease Using Optical Coherence Tomography. *PLoS ONE* **2016**, *11*, e0161136. [CrossRef] [PubMed]
7. Bek, T. Regional Morphology and Pathophysiology of Retinal Vascular Disease. *Prog. Retin. Eye Res.* **2013**, *36*, 247–259. [CrossRef]
8. Brown, J.M.; Campbell, J.P.; Beers, A.; Chang, K.; Ostmo, S.; Chan, R.V.P.; Dy, J.; Erdogmus, D.; Ioannidis, S.; Kalpathy-Cramer, J.; et al. Automated Diagnosis of Plus Disease in Retinopathy of Prematurity Using Deep Convolutional Neural Networks. *JAMA Ophthalmol.* **2018**, *136*, 803–810. [CrossRef]
9. Mahum, R.; Rehman, S.U.; Okon, O.D.; Alabrah, A.; Meraj, T.; Rauf, H.T. A Novel Hybrid Approach Based on Deep CNN to Detect Glaucoma Using Fundus Imaging. *Electronics* **2022**, *11*, 26. [CrossRef]
10. Chan, K.K.W.; Tang, F.; Tham, C.C.Y.; Young, A.L.; Cheung, C.Y. Retinal Vasculature in Glaucoma: A Review. *BMJ Open Ophthalmol.* **2017**, *1*, e000032. [CrossRef]
11. Querques, G.; Borrelli, E.; Sacconi, R.; De Vitis, L.; Leocani, L.; Santangelo, R.; Magnani, G.; Comi, G.; Bandello, F. Functional and Morphological Changes of the Retinal Vessels in Alzheimer's Disease and Mild Cognitive Impairment. *Sci. Rep.* **2019**, *9*, 63. [CrossRef] [PubMed]
12. Heier, J.S.; Singh, R.P.; Wykoff, C.C.; Csaky, K.G.; Lai, T.Y.Y.; Loewenstein, A.; Schlottmann, P.G.; Paris, L.P.; Westenskow, P.D.; Quezada-Ruiz, C. The Angiopoietin/Tie Pathway in Retinal Vascular Diseases: A Review. *RETINA* **2021**, *41*, 1–19. [CrossRef] [PubMed]
13. Miri, M.; Amini, Z.; Rabbani, H.; Kafieh, R. A Comprehensive Study of Retinal Vessel Classification Methods in Fundus Images. *J. Med. Signals Sens.* **2017**, *7*, 59–70.
14. Arsalan, M.; Owais, M.; Mahmood, T.; Cho, S.W.; Park, K.R. Aiding the Diagnosis of Diabetic and Hypertensive Retinopathy Using Artificial Intelligence-Based Semantic Segmentation. *J. Clin. Med.* **2019**, *8*, 1446. [CrossRef] [PubMed]
15. Arsalan, M.; Baek, N.R.; Owais, M.; Mahmood, T.; Park, K.R. Deep Learning-Based Detection of Pigment Signs for Analysis and Diagnosis of Retinitis Pigmentosa. *Sensors* **2020**, *20*, 3454. [CrossRef] [PubMed]
16. Owais, M.; Arsalan, M.; Mahmood, T.; Kang, J.K.; Park, K.R. Automated Diagnosis of Various Gastrointestinal Lesions Using a Deep Learning–Based Classification and Retrieval Framework With a Large Endoscopic Database: Model Development and Validation. *J. Med. Internet Res.* **2020**, *22*, e18563. [CrossRef] [PubMed]

17. Arsalan, M.; Haider, A.; Choi, J.; Park, K.R. Detecting Blastocyst Components by Artificial Intelligence for Human Embryological Analysis to Improve Success Rate of In Vitro Fertilization. *J. Pers. Med.* **2022**, *12*, 124. [CrossRef]
18. Wang, L.; Wang, H.; Huang, Y.; Yan, B.; Chang, Z.; Liu, Z.; Zhao, M.; Cui, L.; Song, J.; Li, F. Trends in the Application of Deep Learning Networks in Medical Image Analysis: Evolution between 2012 and 2020. *Eur. J. Radiol.* **2022**, *146*, 110069. [CrossRef]
19. Islam, M.M.; Yang, H.-C.; Poly, T.N.; Jian, W.-S.; Li, Y.-C. Deep Learning Algorithms for Detection of Diabetic Retinopathy in Retinal Fundus Photographs: A Systematic Review and Meta-Analysis. *Comput. Methods Programs Biomed.* **2020**, *191*, 105320. [CrossRef]
20. Arsalan, M.; Haider, A.; Choi, J.; Park, K.R. Diabetic and Hypertensive Retinopathy Screening in Fundus Images Using Artificially Intelligent Shallow Architectures. *J. Pers. Med.* **2022**, *12*, 7. [CrossRef]
21. VSUL-Net Models. Available online: http://dm.dgu.edu/link.html (accessed on 12 March 2022).
22. Alhussein, M.; Aurangzeb, K.; Haider, S.I. An Unsupervised Retinal Vessel Segmentation Using Hessian and Intensity Based Approach. *IEEE Access* **2020**, *8*, 165056–165070. [CrossRef]
23. Ahamed, A.T.U.; Jothish, A.; Johnson, G.; Krishna, S.B.V. Automated System for Retinal Vessel Segmentation. In Proceedings of the Second International Conference on Inventive Communication and Computational Technologies, Coimbatore, India, 20–21 April 2018; pp. 717–722.
24. Naveed, K.; Abdullah, F.; Madni, H.A.; Khan, M.A.U.; Khan, T.M.; Naqvi, S.S. Towards Automated Eye Diagnosis: An Improved Retinal Vessel Segmentation Framework Using Ensemble Block Matching 3D Filter. *Diagnostics* **2021**, *11*, 114. [CrossRef] [PubMed]
25. Zhou, C.; Zhang, X.; Chen, H. A New Robust Method for Blood Vessel Segmentation in Retinal Fundus Images Based on Weighted Line Detector and Hidden Markov Model. *Comput. Methods Programs Biomed.* **2020**, *187*, 105231. [CrossRef] [PubMed]
26. Shah, S.A.A.; Shahzad, A.; Khan, M.A.; Lu, C.; Tang, T.B. Unsupervised Method for Retinal Vessel Segmentation Based on Gabor Wavelet and Multiscale Line Detector. *IEEE Access* **2019**, *7*, 167221–167228. [CrossRef]
27. Chalakkal, R.J.; Abdulla, W.H. Improved Vessel Segmentation Using Curvelet Transform and Line Operators. In Proceedings of the Asia-Pacific Signal and Information Processing Association Annual Summit and Conference, Honolulu, HI, USA, 12–15 November 2018; pp. 2041–2046.
28. Li, T.; Comer, M.; Zerubia, J. An Unsupervised Retinal Vessel Extraction and Segmentation Method Based On a Tube Marked Point Process Model. In Proceedings of the IEEE International Conference on Acoustics, Speech and Signal Processing, Barcelona, Spain, 4–8 May 2020; pp. 1394–1398.
29. Ramos-Soto, O.; Rodríguez-Esparza, E.; Balderas-Mata, S.E.; Oliva, D.; Hassanien, A.E.; Meleppat, R.K.; Zawadzki, R.J. An Efficient Retinal Blood Vessel Segmentation in Eye Fundus Images by Using Optimized Top-Hat and Homomorphic Filtering. *Comput. Methods Programs Biomed.* **2021**, *201*, 105949. [CrossRef]
30. Aswini, S.; Suresh, A.; Priya, S.; Krishna, B.V.S. Retinal Vessel Segmentation Using Morphological Top Hat Approach On Diabetic Retinopathy Images. In Proceedings of the Fourth International Conference on Advances in Electrical, Electronics, Information, Communication and Bio-Informatics, Chennai, India, 27–28 February 2018; pp. 1–5.
31. Sundaram, R.; Ks, R.; Jayaraman, P.; B, V. Extraction of Blood Vessels in Fundus Images of Retina through Hybrid Segmentation Approach. *Mathematics* **2019**, *7*, 169. [CrossRef]
32. Khawaja, A.; Khan, T.M.; Naveed, K.; Naqvi, S.S.; Rehman, N.U.; Nawaz, S.J. An Improved Retinal Vessel Segmentation Framework Using Frangi Filter Coupled With the Probabilistic Patch Based Denoiser. *IEEE Access* **2019**, *7*, 164344–164361. [CrossRef]
33. Jin, Q.; Meng, Z.; Pham, T.D.; Chen, Q.; Wei, L.; Su, R. DUNet: A Deformable Network for Retinal Vessel Segmentation. *Knowl. Based Syst.* **2019**, *178*, 149–162. [CrossRef]
34. Khan, T.M.; Alhussein, M.; Aurangzeb, K.; Arsalan, M.; Naqvi, S.S.; Nawaz, S.J. Residual Connection-Based Encoder Decoder Network (RCED-Net) for Retinal Vessel Segmentation. *IEEE Access* **2020**, *8*, 131257–131272. [CrossRef]
35. Yan, Z.; Yang, X.; Cheng, K.-T. Joint Segment-Level and Pixel-Wise Losses for Deep Learning Based Retinal Vessel Segmentation. *IEEE Trans. Biomed. Eng.* **2018**, *65*, 1912–1923. [CrossRef]
36. Wang, K.; Zhang, X.; Huang, S.; Wang, Q.; Chen, F. CTF-Net: Retinal Vessel Segmentation via Deep Coarse-To-Fine Supervision Network. In Proceedings of the IEEE 17th International Symposium on Biomedical Imaging, Iowa City, IA, USA, 3–7 April 2020; pp. 1237–1241.
37. Li, L.; Verma, M.; Nakashima, Y.; Nagahara, H.; Kawasaki, R. IterNet: Retinal Image Segmentation Utilizing Structural Redundancy in Vessel Networks. In Proceedings of the IEEE Winter Conference on Applications of Computer Vision, Snowmass, CO, USA, 1–5 March 2020; pp. 3645–3654.
38. Zhao, H.; Li, H.; Cheng, L. Improving Retinal Vessel Segmentation with Joint Local Loss by Matting. *Pattern Recognit.* **2020**, *98*, 107068. [CrossRef]
39. Zhang, J.; Zhang, Y.; Xu, X. Pyramid U-Net for Retinal Vessel Segmentation. In Proceedings of the IEEE International Conference on Acoustics, Speech and Signal Processing, Toronto, ON, Canada, 6–11 June 2021; pp. 1125–1129.
40. Gegundez-Arias, M.E.; Marin-Santos, D.; Perez-Borrero, I.; Vasallo-Vazquez, M.J. A New Deep Learning Method for Blood Vessel Segmentation in Retinal Images Based on Convolutional Kernels and Modified U-Net Model. *Comput. Methods Programs Biomed.* **2021**, *205*, 106081. [CrossRef] [PubMed]

41. He, J.; Jiang, D. Fundus Image Segmentation Based on Improved Generative Adversarial Network for Retinal Vessel Analysis. In Proceedings of the 3rd International Conference on Artificial Intelligence and Big Data, Chengdu, China, 28–31 May 2020; pp. 231–236.
42. Guo, X.; Chen, C.; Lu, Y.; Meng, K.; Chen, H.; Zhou, K.; Wang, Z.; Xiao, R. Retinal Vessel Segmentation Combined With Generative Adversarial Networks and Dense U-Net. *IEEE Access* **2020**, *8*, 194551–194560. [CrossRef]
43. Lal, S.; Rehman, S.U.; Shah, J.H.; Meraj, T.; Rauf, H.T.; Damaševičius, R.; Mohammed, M.A.; Abdulkareem, K.H. Adversarial Attack and Defence through Adversarial Training and Feature Fusion for Diabetic Retinopathy Recognition. *Sensors* **2021**, *21*, 3922. [CrossRef]
44. Chudzik, P.; Al-Diri, B.; Calivá, F.; Hunter, A. DISCERN: Generative Framework for Vessel Segmentation Using Convolutional Neural Network and Visual Codebook. In Proceedings of the 40th Annual International Conference of the IEEE Engineering in Medicine and Biology Society, Honolulu, HI, USA, 18–21 July 2018; pp. 5934–5937.
45. Palanivel, D.A.; Natarajan, S.; Gopalakrishnan, S. Retinal Vessel Segmentation Using Multifractal Characterization. *Appl. Soft Comput.* **2020**, *94*, 106439. [CrossRef]
46. Saha Tchinda, B.; Tchiotsop, D.; Noubom, M.; Louis-Dorr, V.; Wolf, D. Retinal Blood Vessels Segmentation Using Classical Edge Detection Filters and the Neural Network. *Inform. Med. Unlocked* **2021**, *23*, 100521. [CrossRef]
47. Oliveira, A.; Pereira, S.; Silva, C.A. Retinal Vessel Segmentation Based on Fully Convolutional Neural Networks. *Expert Syst. Appl.* **2018**, *112*, 229–242. [CrossRef]
48. Guo, S.; Wang, K.; Kang, H.; Zhang, Y.; Gao, Y.; Li, T. BTS-DSN: Deeply Supervised Neural Network with Short Connections for Retinal Vessel Segmentation. *Int. J. Med. Inform.* **2019**, *126*, 105–113. [CrossRef]
49. Feng, S.; Zhuo, Z.; Pan, D.; Tian, Q. CcNet: A Cross-Connected Convolutional Network for Segmenting Retinal Vessels Using Multi-Scale Features. *Neurocomputing* **2019**, *392*, 268–276. [CrossRef]
50. Yan, Z.; Yang, X.; Cheng, K.T. A Three-Stage Deep Learning Model for Accurate Retinal Vessel Segmentation. *IEEE J. Biomed. Health Inform.* **2018**, *23*, 1427–1436. [CrossRef]
51. Hu, K.; Zhang, Z.; Niu, X.; Zhang, Y.; Cao, C.; Xiao, F.; Gao, X. Retinal Vessel Segmentation of Color Fundus Images Using Multiscale Convolutional Neural Network with an Improved Cross-Entropy Loss Function. *Neurocomputing* **2018**, *309*, 179–191. [CrossRef]
52. Kromm, C.; Rohr, K. Inception Capsule Network for Retinal Blood Vessel Segmentation and Centerline Extraction. In Proceedings of the IEEE 17th International Symposium on Biomedical Imaging, Iowa City, IA, USA, 3–7 April 2020; pp. 1223–1226.
53. Samuel, P.M.; Veeramalai, T. VSSC Net: Vessel Specific Skip Chain Convolutional Network for Blood Vessel Segmentation. *Comput. Methods Programs Biomed.* **2021**, *198*, 105769. [CrossRef] [PubMed]
54. Wu, Y.; Xia, Y.; Song, Y.; Zhang, Y.; Cai, W. NFN+: A Novel Network Followed Network for Retinal Vessel Segmentation. *Neural Netw.* **2020**, *126*, 153–162. [CrossRef] [PubMed]
55. Ronneberger, O.; Fischer, P.; Brox, T. U-Net: Convolutional Networks for Biomedical Image Segmentation. In Proceedings of the Medical Image Computing and Computer-Assisted Intervention, Munich, Germany, 5–9 October 2015; pp. 234–241.
56. Badrinarayanan, V.; Kendall, A.; Cipolla, R. SegNet: A Deep Convolutional Encoder-Decoder Architecture for Image Segmentation. *IEEE Trans. Pattern Anal. Mach. Intell.* **2017**, *39*, 2481–2495. [CrossRef]
57. Sudre, C.H.; Li, W.; Vercauteren, T.; Ourselin, S.; Jorge Cardoso, M. Generalised Dice Overlap as a Deep Learning Loss Function for Highly Unbalanced Segmentations. In Proceedings of the Deep Learning in Medical Image Analysis and Multimodal Learning for Clinical Decision Support, Québec City, QC, Canada, 14 September 2017; pp. 240–248.
58. Staal, J.; Abramoff, M.D.; Niemeijer, M.; Viergever, M.A.; Ginneken, B. van Ridge-Based Vessel Segmentation in Color Images of the Retina. *IEEE Trans. Med. Imaging* **2004**, *23*, 501–509. [CrossRef]
59. Fraz, M.M.; Remagnino, P.; Hoppe, A.; Uyyanonvara, B.; Rudnicka, A.R.; Owen, C.G.; Barman, S.A. Blood Vessel Segmentation Methodologies in Retinal Images—A Survey. *Comput. Methods Programs Biomed.* **2012**, *108*, 407–433. [CrossRef]
60. Hoover, A.; Kouznetsova, V.; Goldbaum, M. Locating Blood Vessels in Retinal Images by Piecewise Threshold Probing of a Matched Filter Response. *IEEE Trans. Med. Imaging* **2000**, *19*, 203–210. [CrossRef]
61. Kingma, D.P.; Ba, J. Adam: A Method for Stochastic Optimization. In Proceedings of the International Conference for Learning Representations, San Diego, CA, USA, 7–9 May 2015; pp. 1–15.
62. He, K.; Zhang, X.; Ren, S.; Sun, J. Deep Residual Learning for Image Recognition. In Proceedings of the IEEE Conference on Computer Vision and Pattern Recognition, Las Vegas, NV, USA, 27–30 June 2016; pp. 770–778.
63. Huang, G.; Liu, Z.; van der Maaten, L.; Weinberger, K.Q. Densely Connected Convolutional Networks. In Proceedings of the IEEE Conference on Computer Vision and Pattern Recognition, Honolulu, HI, USA, 21–26 July 2017.
64. Soomro, T.A.; Afifi, A.J.; Gao, J.; Hellwich, O.; Khan, M.A.U.; Paul, M.; Zheng, L. Boosting Sensitivity of a Retinal Vessel Segmentation Algorithm with Convolutional Neural Network. In Proceedings of the International Conference on Digital Image Computing: Techniques and Applications, Sydney, NSW, Australia, 29 November–1 December 2017; pp. 1–8.
65. Lv, Y.; Ma, H.; Li, J.; Liu, S. Attention Guided U-Net With Atrous Convolution for Accurate Retinal Vessels Segmentation. *IEEE Access* **2020**, *8*, 32826–32839. [CrossRef]
66. Li, X.; Jiang, Y.; Li, M.; Yin, S. Lightweight Attention Convolutional Neural Network for Retinal Vessel Segmentation. *IEEE Trans. Ind. Inform.* **2020**, *17*, 1958–1967. [CrossRef]
67. Livingston, E.H. Who Was Student and Why Do We Care so Much about His *t*-Test?1. *J. Surg. Res.* **2004**, *118*, 58–65. [CrossRef]

68. *t*-Test and ANOVA. Available online: https://www.iuj.ac.jp/faculty/kucc625/method/anova.html (accessed on 1 March 2022).
69. Kao, L.S.; Green, C.E. Analysis of Variance: Is There a Difference in Means and What Does It Mean? *J. Surg. Res.* **2008**, *144*, 158–170. [CrossRef] [PubMed]
70. Zhang, J.; Chen, Y.; Bekkers, E.; Wang, M.; Dashtbozorg, B.; Romeny, B.M. ter H. Retinal Vessel Delineation Using a Brain-Inspired Wavelet Transform and Random Forest. *Pattern Recognit.* **2017**, *69*, 107–123. [CrossRef]
71. Tan, J.H.; Acharya, U.R.; Bhandary, S.V.; Chua, K.C.; Sivaprasad, S. Segmentation of Optic Disc, Fovea and Retinal Vasculature Using a Single Convolutional Neural Network. *J. Comput. Sci.* **2017**, *20*, 70–79. [CrossRef]
72. Zhu, C.; Zou, B.; Zhao, R.; Cui, J.; Duan, X.; Chen, Z.; Liang, Y. Retinal Vessel Segmentation in Colour Fundus Images Using Extreme Learning Machine. *Comput. Med. Imaging Graph.* **2017**, *55*, 68–77. [CrossRef]
73. Girard, F.; Kavalec, C.; Cheriet, F. Joint Segmentation and Classification of Retinal Arteries/Veins from Fundus Images. *Artif. Intell. Med.* **2019**, *94*, 96–109. [CrossRef]
74. Fu, H.; Xu, Y.; Lin, S.; Kee Wong, D.W.; Liu, J. DeepVessel: Retinal Vessel Segmentation via Deep Learning and Conditional Random Field. In Proceedings of the International Conference on Medical Image Computing and Computer-Assisted Intervention, Athens, Greece, 17–21 October 2016; pp. 132–139.
75. Wang, X.; Jiang, X.; Ren, J. Blood Vessel Segmentation from Fundus Image by a Cascade Classification Framework. *Pattern Recognit.* **2019**, *88*, 331–341. [CrossRef]
76. Soomro, T.A.; Hellwich, O.; Afifi, A.J.; Paul, M.; Gao, J.; Zheng, L. Strided U-Net Model: Retinal Vessels Segmentation Using Dice Loss. In Proceedings of the Digital Image Computing: Techniques and Applications, Canberra, Australia, 10–13 December 2018; pp. 1–8.
77. Leopold, H.A.; Orchard, J.; Zelek, J.S.; Lakshminarayanan, V. PixelBNN: Augmenting the PixelCNN with Batch Normalization and the Presentation of a Fast Architecture for Retinal Vessel Segmentation. *J. Imaging* **2019**, *5*, 26. [CrossRef]
78. Wang, C.; Zhao, Z.; Ren, Q.; Xu, Y.; Yu, Y. Dense U-Net Based on Patch-Based Learning for Retinal Vessel Segmentation. *Entropy* **2019**, *21*, 168. [CrossRef]
79. Khan, T.M.; Naqvi, S.S.; Arsalan, M.; Khan, M.A.; Khan, H.A.; Haider, A. Exploiting Residual Edge Information in Deep Fully Convolutional Neural Networks For Retinal Vessel Segmentation. In Proceedings of the International Joint Conference on Neural Networks, Glasgow, UK, 19–24 July 2020; pp. 1–8.
80. Khan, T.M.; Khan, M.A.U.; Rehman, N.U.; Naveed, K.; Afridi, I.U.; Naqvi, S.S.; Raazak, I. Width-Wise Vessel Bifurcation for Improved Retinal Vessel Segmentation. *Biomed. Signal Processing Control* **2022**, *71*, 103169. [CrossRef]
81. Zhang, Y.; He, M.; Chen, Z.; Hu, K.; Li, X.; Gao, X. Bridge-Net: Context-Involved U-Net with Patch-Based Loss Weight Mapping for Retinal Blood Vessel Segmentation. *Expert Syst. Appl.* **2022**, *195*, 116526. [CrossRef]
82. Hajabdollahi, M.; Esfandiarpoor, R.; Najarian, K.; Karimi, N.; Samavi, S.; Reza-Soroushmeh, S.M. Low Complexity Convolutional Neural Network for Vessel Segmentation in Portable Retinal Diagnostic Devices. In Proceedings of the 25th IEEE International Conference on Image Processing, Athens, Greece, 7–10 October 2018; pp. 2785–2789.
83. Selvaraju, R.R.; Cogswell, M.; Das, A.; Vedantam, R.; Parikh, D.; Batra, D. Grad-CAM: Visual Explanations From Deep Networks via Gradient-Based Localization. In Proceedings of the IEEE International Conference on Computer Vision, Venice, Italy, 22–29 October 2017; pp. 618–626.

Article

Using Value-Based Potentials for Making Approximate Inference on Probabilistic Graphical Models

Pedro Bonilla-Nadal [†], Andrés Cano [†], Manuel Gómez-Olmedo *,[†], Serafín Moral [†] and Ofelia Paula Retamero [†]

Computer Science and Artificial Intelligent Department, University of Granada, 18071 Granada, Spain; pedrobn@ugr.es (P.B-N.); acu@decsai.ugr.es (A.C.); smc@decsai.ugr.es (S.M.); oretamero@decsai.ugr.es (O.P.R.)
* Correspondence: mgomez@decsai.ugr.es; Tel.: +34-958248487
† These authors contributed equally to this work.

Abstract: The computerization of many everyday tasks generates vast amounts of data, and this has lead to the development of machine-learning methods which are capable of extracting useful information from the data so that the data can be used in future decision-making processes. For a long time now, a number of fields, such as medicine (and all healthcare-related areas) and education, have been particularly interested in obtaining relevant information from this stored data. This interest has resulted in the need to deal with increasingly complex problems which involve many different variables with a high degree of interdependency. This produces models (and in our case probabilistic graphical models) that are difficult to handle and that require very efficient techniques to store and use the information that quantifies the relationships between the problem variables. It has therefore been necessary to develop efficient structures, such as probability trees or value-based potentials, to represent the information. Even so, there are problems that must be treated using approximation since this is the only way that results can be obtained, despite the corresponding loss of information. The aim of this article is to show how the approximation can be performed with value-based potentials. Our experimental work is based on checking the behavior of this approximation technique on several *Bayesian networks* related to medical problems, and our experiments show that in some cases there are notable savings in memory space with limited information loss.

Keywords: probabilistic graphical models; bayesian networks; value-based potentials; approximate inference; medical applications

MSC: 68T37; 62C10; 62F15

Citation: Bonilla-Nadal, P.; Cano, A.; Gómez-Olmedo, M.; Moral, S.; Retamero, O.P. Using Value-Based Potentials for Making Approximate Inference on Probabilistic Graphical Models. *Mathematics* **2022**, *10*, 2542. https://doi.org/10.3390/math10142542

Academic Editors: Carmen Lacave and Ana Isabel Molina

Received: 13 June 2022
Accepted: 14 July 2022
Published: 21 July 2022

Publisher's Note: MDPI stays neutral with regard to jurisdictional claims in published maps and institutional affiliations.

Copyright: © 2022 by the authors. Licensee MDPI, Basel, Switzerland. This article is an open access article distributed under the terms and conditions of the Creative Commons Attribution (CC BY) license (https://creativecommons.org/licenses/by/4.0/).

1. Introduction

Probabilistic Graphical Models (*PGMs*) [1–3] are a powerful framework to encode problems under uncertainty. *PGMs* are able to combine graphs and probability theory to compactly represent the probabilistic dependency between random variables. Any *PGM* can be defined by its two components:

- Qualitative component, given by a directed, acyclic graph (*DAG*), where each node represents a random variable, and the presence of an edge connecting two of these implies mutual dependency.
- Quantitative component, given by a set of parameters that quantify the degree of dependence between the variables.

One of the most interesting properties of *PGMs* over discrete domains such as *Bayesian networks* (*BNs*) [4,5] and *influence diagrams* (*IDs*) [6,7] is the efficient representation of joint probability distributions, and traditionally marginal or conditional probability distributions and utility functions are represented with *tables* or *unidimensional arrays* (*1DA* in general). However, as the size of *1DAs* grows exponentially with the number of variables, an exact representation might be arduous or even impossible (due to memory space restrictions).

Even in cases where problem representation using *1DA* is possible, it may be difficult to perform subsequent inference tasks as new potentials may appear larger than the initial ones.

This difficulty originates some works focused on improving the way of performing operations with probability distribution and utility functions as a way to alleviate the computational cost in complex models [8]. And another approaches have been explored over the years in the search for efficient alternative representations to *1DAs*, which are able to work with complex models. Successful examples are standard and binary probability trees (*PTs* and *BPTs*) [9–13]. Despite the advantages that these offer compared to the use of *1DA*, they also present certain limitations, and not all context-specific independencies can result in smaller representations and therefore in memory space savings.

Another very well-studied strategy for saving memory space is to approximate the structures, such as in *PTs*, by accepting a loss of information [14,15]. This operation is called pruning and the *PTs* which have been pruned are called *pruned probability trees* (*PPTs*). This operation consists of replacing certain contiguous values with their average value, always remembering to select those values that produce the smallest information loss.

Value-based potentials (*VBPs*) [16] were recently introduced. These structures take advantage of the repetition of values, regardless of the order in which they appear. *VBPs* were tested with several *BNs* included in the bnlearn repository [17,18] and the *UAI* inference competitions [19,20]. The paper compares the memory spaces required for representing potentials with *1DAs*, *PTs*, *PPTs*, and *VBPs*. The comparison demonstrates that there is an overall reduction in memory space when *VBPs* are used. Their use is justified by observing that, in a large number of *BNs* representing real-world problems (in the medical field, for example), many repeated values appear in the potentials which quantify the probabilistic relationships. For example, all those impossible events will have been assigned a probability value equal to 0. Another source of repetition can occur in situations in which the models include subjectively assigned probabilities through interviews with experts. Normally, the assigned probabilities are reduced to a very limited set of values (for example, 0.25, 0.4, etc., and it is difficult for an expert to indicate that the probability of an event occurring is 0.23678).

Taking into account all of the previously mentioned work, the aim of our study will be to make *VBPs* even more compact and to define an algorithm to approximate them. Such an algorithm will be an iterative process, and each step will keep the approximated *VBP* with the minimum Kullback–Leibler divergence in relation to the original one, thereby minimizing loss of information.

This paper is organized as follows: Section 2 defines some necessary basic concepts and notation; Section 3 contains the theory about classical structures and alternative *VBPs*; Section 4 introduces the prerequisites for the approximation of *VBPs* and the approximation algorithm itself; Section 5 studies the empirical evaluation of the algorithm by applying it to real *BNs*; and finally Section 6 outlines our conclusions and presents our future lines of research.

2. Basic Definitions and Notation

Let $\mathbf{X} = \{X_1, X_2, \ldots, X_N\}$ be a finite set of discrete random variables. For the sake of simplicity, the states of each variable X_i (its *domain*) are assumed to be integers and represented as Ω_{X_i}. The values for X_i are noted in lowercase $\Omega_{X_i} = \{x_{i,j} \ : \ j = 1, 2, \ldots, k_i\}$. $|\Omega_{X_i}|$ denotes the *cardinality* of the variable, i.e., the number of elements in its domain ($|\Omega_{X_i}| = k_i$).

The Cartesian product $\prod_{X_i \in \mathbf{X}} \Omega_{X_i}$ will be denoted as $\Omega_\mathbf{X}$ and its elements, called *configurations* of $\mathbf{X}$, are defined by $\mathbf{x} := \{X_1 = x_1, X_2 = x_2, \ldots, X_N = x_n\}$, or $\mathbf{x} := \{x_1, x_2, \ldots, x_n\}$ (if the variables are obvious from the context). A function defined over a subset of variables $\mathbf{Y} \subseteq \mathbf{X}$ and taking values in $\mathbb{R}_0^+$ will be termed as a *potential* $\phi(\mathbf{Y})$.

Example 1. *Let us consider the variables X_1, X_2, and X_3, with 2, 3, and 2 possible states, respectively. Then $\phi(X_1, X_2, X_3)$ is a potential defined on such variables with the values assigned to each configuration shown in Figure 1. This potential expresses the conditional distribution $P(X_3 | X_1, X_2)$.*

index	x_1	x_2	x_3	$\phi(x_1, x_2, x_3)$
0	0	0	0	0.1
1	0	0	1	0.9
2	0	1	0	0.5
3	0	1	1	0.5
4	0	2	0	0.0
5	0	2	1	1
6	1	0	0	0.8
7	1	0	1	0.2
8	1	1	0	0.2
9	1	1	1	0.8
10	1	2	0	0.9
11	1	2	1	0.1

Figure 1. Representation of the potential $\phi(X_1, X_2, X_3)$ as a mapping that assigns a numeric value to each configuration.

In order for some of the structures considered in our work to be better understood, we need to clarify the concept of the *index of configuration*. This is a unique, numeric identifier which represents each configuration on a given domain Ω_X. Let us consider that the indices start at 0 and end on $|\Omega_X| - 1$. In the given Example 1, index 0 is associated with the configuration $\{0, 0, 0\}$, index 1 to $\{0, 0, 1\}$, and so on until the last one, 11, which is associated with $\{1, 2, 1\}$ (these indices are shown in the left-most column in Figure 1).

There is a relation between indices and configurations based on the concept of *weight* (otherwise known as *stride* or *step size*). Assuming an order between variables $\mathbf{X} = \{X_1 \ldots X_N\}$, each variable $X_i \in \mathbf{X}$ has an associated weight w_i that may be computed as follows (variable with index N has the lowest weight):

$$w_i = \begin{cases} 1 & \text{if } i = N \\ |\Omega_{X_{i+1}}| \cdot w_{i+1} & \text{otherwise.} \end{cases} \quad (1)$$

The index corresponding to a certain configuration $\mathbf{x} = \{x_1, x_2, \ldots, x_N\}$ can be computed as:

$$index(\mathbf{x}) = \prod_{i=1}^{N} x_i \cdot w_i. \quad (2)$$

Example 2. *Considering the potential described in Example 1, the weights are $w_3 = 1, w_2 = 2, w_1 = 6$, and the indices assigned to configurations are presented below:*

$$index(\{0,0,0\}) = 0 \cdot 6 + 0 \cdot 2 + 0 \cdot 1 = 0$$
$$index(\{0,0,1\}) = 0 \cdot 6 + 0 \cdot 2 + 1 \cdot 1 = 1$$
$$index(\{0,1,0\}) = 0 \cdot 6 + 1 \cdot 2 + 0 \cdot 1 = 2$$
$$\ldots\ldots\ldots\ldots\ldots\ldots\ldots\ldots\ldots\ldots\ldots\ldots$$
$$index(\{1,2,1\}) = 1 \cdot 6 + 2 \cdot 2 + 1 \cdot 1 = 11$$

More specifically, the value of a particular variable X_i in a configuration linked to an index k, denoted by $\mathbf{x}^{(k)}$ and satisfying $index(\mathbf{x}^{(k)}) = k$, can be computed as:

$$x_i = (k // w_i) \% |\Omega_{X_i}|, \quad (3)$$

where $//$ denotes integer division and $\%$ the modulus of the division.

As we mentioned previously, the association between indices and configurations requires that the variable order in the domain be known. Any order is valid, but by default, we will consider the order in which variables are written (e.g., for potential $\phi(X, Y, Z)$, the first variable would be X). Additionally, we consider that the first variable has the highest weight. However, the opposite approach could also be considered.

The links in the network define a set of conditional dependences and independences that are expressed as $X \perp_Z Y$. This expression indicates that X is independent of Y once the values of the variables in Z are known. The *Markov blanket* of X, $mb(X)$, contains its parents $pa(X)$, its children $ch(X)$, and the parents of the children $pa(ch(X))$; it is the set of variables that makes X be independent of the other variables Z, $Z = X \setminus \{X \cup mb(X)\}$, once the value of variables in $mb(X)$ is known, i.e., $X \perp_{mb(X)} Z$. The *in-degree* of X is the number of parents $|pa(X)|$, and the *out-degree* is the number of children $|ch(X)|$. The *average degree* considers the values of *in-degree* and *out-degree*. These values are used to characterize the *BNs* used for experiments (see details in Table 5).

3. Representation of Potentials

3.1. Classic Structures

3.1.1. 1D-Arrays

A *one-dimensional* or *single-dimensional array (1DA)* is a storage structure for elements of the same nature, which enables every element to be accessed individually by specifying the index corresponding to the position where it is located.

Let ϕ be a potential defined over a set of N variables, ϕ can be represented by an *array* $\mathcal{A}_\phi$ as:

$$\mathcal{A}_\phi := \left[\phi(0,\ldots 0), \phi(0,\ldots 1), \ldots, \phi(|\Omega_{X_1}|-1, \ldots, |\Omega_{X_N}|-1)\right]. \tag{4}$$

The size of a *1DA*, denoted by $size(\mathcal{A}_\phi)$, is the number of entries, or the number of configurations of the potential.

Example 3. *The potential $\phi(X_1, X_2, X_3)$ given in Example 1 can be represented as the following 1DA with 12 entries (see Figure 2).*

0	1	2	3	4	5	6	7	8	9	10	11
0.1	0.9	0.5	0.5	0.0	1.0	0.8	0.2	0.2	0.8	0.9	0.1

Figure 2. $\phi(X_1, X_2, X_3)$ as *1DA*.

3.1.2. Probability Trees

A *probability tree (PT)* represents a given potential $\phi : \Omega_X \to \mathbb{R}_0^+$, and allows exact or approximate operations over it [11–13]. A *probability tree* $\mathcal{T}$ is a directed and labeled tree, where each internal node represents one variable and each leaf node a non-negative real number. Each internal node will have as many exiting arcs as the number of states that the variable labeling the node has. The size of a *PT*, $size(\mathcal{T})$, is defined as the number of nodes it contains.

Example 4. *The same potential given in the previous example is presented in Figure 3 as a PT. This PT has 21 nodes (12 leaves and 9 internal nodes).*

PTs can take advantage of context-specific independences [9] by combing equal values into a single one. This operation is called pruning, and once *PTs* have been pruned, they are known as *pruned probability trees (PPTs)*.

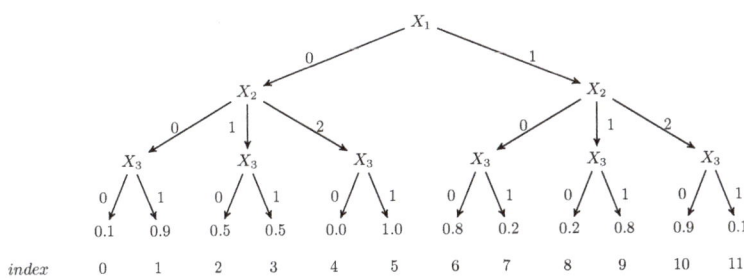

Figure 3. $\phi(X_1, X_2, X_3)$ as PT.

Example 5. *The potential in the previous examples presents a context-specific independence that enables its size to be reduced: the value for $X_1 = 0, X_2 = 1$ is 0.5, regardless of the value of X_3. Once the pruning is complete, the result is a PPT consisting of 19 nodes (11 leaves and 8 internal nodes) and this is shown in Figure 4.*

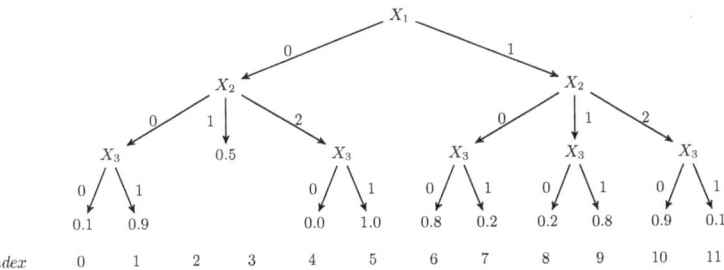

Figure 4. $\phi(X_1, X_2, X_3)$ as PPT.

A variant to a *PT* is the *binary probability tree* or *BPT* ([10,14,15]). In *BPTs*, two arcs exit from each internal node, so one variable can label several nodes in a path from root to leaf node. An example of *BPT* is presented in Figure 5 and described in the following example.

Example 6. *On the left, a given PT is represented, and two equal values (0.4) can be observed for c configuration (left sub-tree) but related to two different values of X_k. Both values can therefore be combined to produce the BPT on the right-hand side of Figure 5. It is now apparent that the leftmost branch of X_k simultaneously represents values for $X_k = 0$ and $X_k = 2$.*

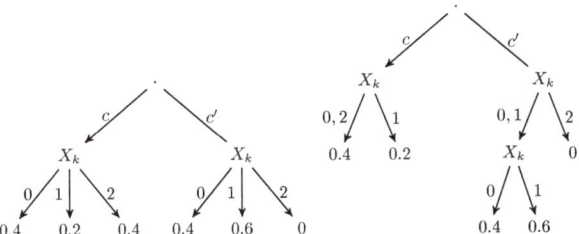

Figure 5. Binary tree representation.

With this property, although *BPTs* can avoid more repetitions of values than *PPTs*, there are still situations in which repetitions cannot be avoided. This is the case for the values 0.4 of the configurations given by c', $x_k = 2$ and c, $x_k = 0$. Therefore, as we mentioned previously, both *PPTs* and *BPTs* introduce the possibility of saving memory space by combining values under pretty specific circumstances, but are not able to make the structure more efficient otherwise. This fact opens various possible avenues of research into how to exploit different patterns. In many cases, some combinations of values are not allowed and are represented by 0's or some values are repeated several times; a proper efficient structure should be able to somehow compact the information using such patterns.

3.2. Alternative Structures: Value-Based Potentials

Valued-based potentials were recently introduced [16] as an alternative representation based exclusively on the values. Once such new structure was applied on several *BNs* from two different sources (*bnlearn* repository [17,18] and *UAI* competitions [19,20]) and compared with *1DAs*, *PTs*, and *PPTs*. It has been proven that the use of *VBP* structures saves memory space. In *VBPs*, values must be stored paired with the indices (or configurations) that define the events in which they appear. How these pairs value-indices are stored determines two different *VBP* categories:

- Structures driven by values, using dictionaries in which the keys will be values: *value-driven with grains* (*VDG*) and *value-driven with indices* (*VDI*).
- Structures driven by indices, where keys are indices: *index-driven with pair of arrays* (*IDP*) and *index-driven with map* (*IDM*).

In all of these alternatives, a default value is set (in our case, 0.0) and any related index will not be stored (in order to reduce memory space). Such a default value can be defined in advance or may be conveniently selected as the most repeated one. As *VBPs* represent potentials, it will be easy to adapt inference algorithms to use *VBPs*. A more complete definition of *VBPs* can be found in [16].

A simple visual idea of how *VBPs* work can be presented as a set of conveniently arranged probability values (i.e., each value is stored near its corresponding indices). Our studied example will appear as in Figure 6. It should be observed that the index 4, relating to value 0.0 (the default value), is not stored at all. This would be similar to storing the values using a *1DA* structure. However, the goal is to avoid storing duplicated values. The example shows how each of the values, 0.1, 0.2, 0.5, 0.8, and 0.9, appear to be associated with two different indices (or configurations).

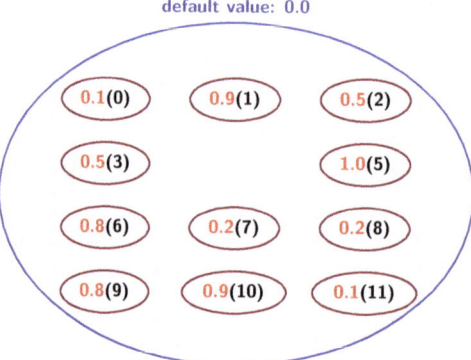

Figure 6. $\phi(X_1, X_2, X_3)$ as the relation between values and indices.

By using *VBPs*, therefore, each value is represented only once and all the indices in which it appears are linked to it. Figure 7 shows the groupings made and this highlights the fact that only 6 probability values are stored. The purpose of *VBPs* is therefore to make as many groups as different probability values exist to avoid repetitions and associate the related indices of configurations.

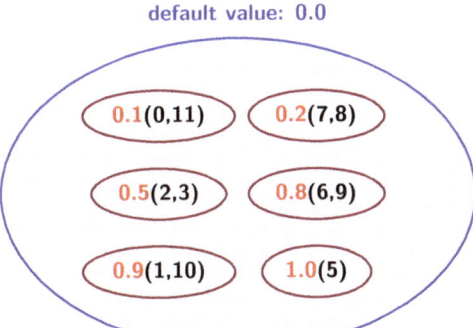

Figure 7. Visual idea of $\phi(X_1, X_2, X_3)$ as grouping equal probability values.

From the alternatives presented in [16], in this paper we will focus on *value-driven with indices* (VDI) and *index-driven with pairs* (IDP), since both of these performed extremely well on most of the studied *BNs*.

3.2.1. VDI: Value-Driven with Indices

Let us consider a certain potential ϕ defined over **X**. A VDI for ϕ, VDI_ϕ, is a dictionary D in which each entry $< v, L_v >$ contains a value (as the key) and a list of indices L_v, such that $\phi(l) = v$, for each $l \in L_v$.

Example 7. *The potential $\phi(X_1, X_2, X_3)$ used before and described in Figure 1 will be represented as VDI as shown in Figure 8. The outermost rectangle represents the dictionary and the entry keys (values) are drawn as circles. Keys give access to the index lists (inner rectangles with rounded corners). It can be seen that this dictionary faithfully represents the grouping of values shown in Figure 7 as an intuitive explanation of the purpose of VBP structures.*

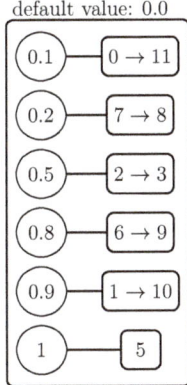

Figure 8. $\phi(X_1, X_2, X_3)$ as *VDI*.

3.2.2. IDP: Index-Driven with Pair of Arrays

Let ϕ be a potential defined over **X**. A structure *IDP* representing ϕ, IPD_ϕ, is a pair of arrays V and L. Non-repeated values in ϕ (excluding the default value) are stored in $V = \{v_0 \ldots v_{d-1}\}$. Let nd_ϕ represent the number of indices storing non-default values. The array L is then defined as follows:

$$L := \{(i,j) : \phi(\mathbf{x}_i) = v_j, i \in nd_\phi\}. \tag{5}$$

This means that *IDP* is based on two components: firstly, an array storing the values (without repetitions and excluding 0.0 as the default value), and secondly, an array of pairs (index in potential, index in array of values). The second index of the pair saves the relationship between the indices and values.

Example 8. *The representation of potential $\phi(X_1, X_2, X_3)$ as IDP is presented in Figure 9. The upper array (V) stores non-default values. The lower one includes pairs of indices. The fourth one $(3,2)$ represents the fact that $\phi(\mathbf{x}_3) = V(2) = 0.5$.*

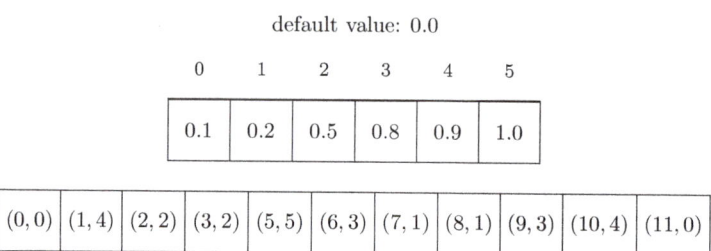

Figure 9. $\phi(X_1, X_2, X_3)$ as *IDP*.

4. Approximating Value-Based Potentials

As we previously mentioned in Section 3, *tables* or *1DA* were widely used in the bibliography to represent quantitative information in *BNs* or *IDs*. There is, however, a limitation of representing potentials with the 1DA structure and that is that they increase exponentially in size as the number of variables increases. Inferring or even dealing with these may therefore be (in the case of complex models) computationally unfeasible. For this purpose, it is convenient not only to define new structures which are able to compactly represent such potentials, but also methods to approximate them so that the memory space may be reduced without any significant loss of information. *PTs* can take advantage of context-specific independences, thereby reducing the number of stored values, but can also be approximated and so produce *PPTs* (this feature was presented as an additional advantage of *PTs* from their definition). However, the guiding procedure for the approach is computationally very expensive as it is necessary to determine the degree of information of each variable in order to ensure that the most informative ones appear as close as possible to the root. This ensures that the values stored in the tree leaves are most similar and, therefore, the loss of information is less when various values are replaced with their average value.

VBP structures [16] may produce a relevant decrease in the memory space when repeated values are present. Moreover, the approximation operation can be applied in a very simple way. This work presents an algorithm for this operation and also provides a theoretical justification for it. Our experimental work will show the performance of the algorithm using two different alternatives for *VBPs*: *value-driven with indices* (*VDI*) and *index-driven with pairs* (*IDP*).

4.1. Algorithm

The method to approximate a given potential $\phi : \Omega_\mathbf{X} \to \mathbb{R}_0^+$ is explained by considering potentials represented as *VDI* because this structure is simpler, but the practical application follows the same idea as for any other alternative (such as *IDP*, for example). Let the *VBP* potential to approximate be denoted as V. Let us assume that it stores n different values, denoted as $v_1 \ldots v_n$ in increasing order of size. As we mentioned in our description of *VBPs*, although each different value v_i is only stored once, the information about the set of corresponding indices (or configurations) is saved, where $\mathbf{S}_i$ is $n_i = |\mathbf{S}_i|$ (which means that n_i is the number of configurations in $\mathbf{S}_i$).

Definition 1. *The basic approximation step consists of reducing the number of values by applying a reduction operation. This operation replaces two consecutive values, v_i and v_{i+1}, with their weighted average. Reduction can generally be described using the following notation:*

- v_a and v_b will be the values to reduce with $\mathbf{S}_a$ and $\mathbf{S}_b$ as their sets of indices, with $n_a = |\mathbf{S}_a|$ and $n_b = |\mathbf{S}_b|$.
- v_r is the new value that replaces v_a and v_b, with $\mathbf{S}_r = \mathbf{S}_a \cup \mathbf{S}_b$ and $n_r = |\mathbf{S}_r|$. This value is computed as:

$$v_r = \frac{n_a \cdot v_a + n_b \cdot v_b}{n_a + n_b}.$$

- It is important to observe that this operation does not modify the total sum of the potential values. Therefore, if ϕ is the original potential and V the result of successive reductions, then $sum(\phi) = sum(V)$.

Consequently, at the end of this operation, the number of values is reduced. The complete algorithm employed for approximating V_ϕ can now be intuitively described as follows:

1. There are a number of different approximation alternatives resulting in candidate structures which will become the one chosen for the final approximation. As there are n different values, there will be $n-1$ candidate structures produced by reducing every pair of consecutive values. Iterate from $i=1$ to $i=n-1$:
    1.1 Let us consider two successive values: v_i and v_{i+1}. The candidate structure is then obtained by reducing both values as previously explained in Definition 1. The result of this operation will be V_i.
    1.2 Calculate the Kullback–Leibler divergence between the original potential V and V_i. This value is denoted by $D(V, V_i)$.
2. Select the candidate structure $V_m = \underset{j=1\ldots n-1}{\arg\min} D(V, V_j)$.
3. Repeat the previous steps until the selected stopping condition has been satisfied.

Before presenting a detailed description of the algorithm, we wish to include a number of considerations:

- It is evident that it is not necessary to build the candidate structures but only to evaluate the loss of information of the corresponding *reduction* operations.
- The Kullback–Leibler divergence between a candidate structure V_i and the original one can be computed by taking into account only those values and indices involved in the *reduction*, and the measure to compute is in fact the loss of information produced by this operation. The way to compute this measure will be explained below.
- A possible stopping criteria (this is the one used in the experimental work although others could be considered) consists of setting a global information loss threshold, t_l. Therefore, the procedure of reducing consecutive values will continue as long as the addition of information losses does not reach the threshold t_l.

4.2. Theoretical Background

Let us consider a potential $\phi(\mathbf{X})$ where $V(\mathbf{X})$ is its representation as *VBP*. The degree of approximation between them will be measured with the Kullback–Leibler divergence [21] between the corresponding normalized potentials ($\overline{\phi}$ and $\overline{V}$):

$$D(\phi, V) = \sum_{\mathbf{x} \in \Omega_{\mathbf{X}}} \overline{\phi}(\mathbf{x}) \log \frac{\overline{\phi}(\mathbf{x})}{\overline{V}(\mathbf{x})}. \qquad (6)$$

The divergence is a non-negative real number which would only be equal to zero if V provides an exact representation of ϕ. As we explained previously, the key operation for approximating ϕ represented as V is *reduction*, as described in Definition 1 and Algorithm 1.

Algorithm 1 Approximation of a potential ϕ represented as V (VBP).

```
 1: function APPROXIMATE(V, t_l)                              ▷ t_l: global loss threshold
 2:     loss ← 0
 3:     while loss < t_l do                                   ▷ loss threshold is not reached
 4:         n ← number of values in φ
 5:         for i ∈ {1, ..., n − 1} do
 6:             consider the reduction of v_i and v_{i+1}
 7:             // compute information loss in V due to reduction
 8:             compute I(V, S_i, S_{i+1})
 9:         end for
10:         choose V_m which minimizes I(V, S_i, S_{i+1}), i = 1 ... n − 1)
11:         loss ← loss + I(V, S_m, S_{m+1})
12:         V ← V_m                                           ▷ keeps reducing V if possible
13:     end while
14:     return V                                              ▷ return V after reaching the loss threshold
15: end function
```

Definition 2. *Let us use V_j to denote the approximated VBP structure obtained in the j-th iteration of the algorithm under consideration in the $j + 1$-th iteration. The new reduction to consider will be described in the previously presented terms. The **information loss** produced by this **reduction** is defined as:*

$$I(V_j, S_a, S_b) = D(\phi, V_j) - D(\phi, V_{j+1}). \tag{7}$$

The selection of the pair of values minimizing the information loss will consequently lead to the minimum value of the Kullback–Leibler divergence between the original potential and the approximate one.

Proposition 1. *The information loss obtained by reducing v_a and v_b in V can be computed as follows:*

$$I(V, S_a, S_b) = \frac{1}{sum(V)} \left[log(v_r)sum(V^{\downarrow S_r}) - log(v_a)sum(V^{\downarrow S_a}) - log(v_b)sum(V^{\downarrow S_b}) \right]. \tag{8}$$

where $sum(V)$ denotes the addition of every value of V and $V^{\downarrow S}$ represents the potential V restricted to the configurations included in S and all remaining values are discarded. If we consider ϕ to be the original potential and V its representation as VBP (perhaps after applying several reduction operations), then $sum(\phi) = sum(V)$ and the previous equation can be expressed as:

$$I(V, S_a, S_b) = \frac{1}{sum(\phi)} \left[log(v_r)sum(\phi^{\downarrow S_r}) - log(v_a)sum(\phi^{\downarrow S_a}) - log(v_b)sum(\phi^{\downarrow S_b}) \right]. \tag{9}$$

Proof. Let ϕ be a potential represented by V (a VBP). V_j denotes the potential obtained from V as a result of the j-th iteration of the approximation algorithm. According to Definition 2:

$$I(V_j, S_a, S_b) = D(\phi, V_j) - D(\phi, V_{j+1}). \tag{10}$$

This difference can be calculated by separating the configurations defined in **X** into three different subsets: $\Omega_X = \{\Omega_X \setminus S_r\} \cup S_a \cup S_b$:

$$I(V_j, \mathbf{S}_a, \mathbf{S}_b) = D(\phi, V_j) - D(\phi, V_{j+1}) =$$

$$\sum_{\mathbf{x} \in \{\Omega_\mathbf{X} \setminus \mathbf{S}_r\}} \left[\overline{\phi}(\mathbf{x}) \log(\frac{\overline{\phi}(\mathbf{x})}{\overline{V}_j(\mathbf{x})}) - \overline{\phi}(\mathbf{x}) \log(\frac{\overline{\phi}(\mathbf{x})}{\overline{V}_{j+1}(\mathbf{x})}) \right] +$$

$$\sum_{\mathbf{x} \in \mathbf{S}_a} \left[\overline{\phi}(\mathbf{x}) \log(\frac{\overline{\phi}(\mathbf{x})}{v_a/sum(\phi)}) - \overline{\phi}(\mathbf{x}) \log(\frac{\overline{\phi}(\mathbf{x})}{v_r/sum(\phi)}) \right] + \quad (11)$$

$$\sum_{\mathbf{x} \in \mathbf{S}_b} \left[\overline{\phi}(\mathbf{x}) \log(\frac{\overline{\phi}(\mathbf{x})}{v_b/sum(\phi)}) - \overline{\phi}(\mathbf{x}) \log(\frac{\overline{\phi}(\mathbf{x})}{v_r/sum(\phi)}) \right].$$

It should be noted that the first part of the summation is equal to 0 since the values of the configurations that are not involved in the reduction ($\mathbf{x} \in \Omega_{\mathbf{X} \setminus \mathbf{S}_r}$) are identical in V_j and V_{j+1}. Additionally, when the properties of the logarithm are considered, the previous equation can be expressed as follows:

$$\sum_{\mathbf{x} \in \mathbf{S}_a} \overline{\phi}(\mathbf{x}) \left[\log(\overline{\phi}(\mathbf{x})) - \log(\frac{v_a}{sum(\phi)}) - \log(\overline{\phi}(\mathbf{x})) + \log(\frac{v_r}{sum(\phi)}) \right] +$$

$$\sum_{\mathbf{x} \in \mathbf{S}_b} \overline{\phi}(\mathbf{x}) \left[\log(\overline{\phi}(\mathbf{x})) - \log(\frac{v_b}{sum(\phi)}) - \log(\overline{\phi}(\mathbf{x})) + \log(\frac{v_r}{sum(\phi)}) \right] = \quad (12)$$

$$\sum_{\mathbf{x} \in \mathbf{S}_a} \overline{\phi}(\mathbf{x}) \log(\frac{v_r}{v_a}) + \sum_{\mathbf{x} \in \mathbf{S}_b} \overline{\phi}(\mathbf{x}) \log(\frac{v_r}{v_b}).$$

Since $\overline{\phi}(\mathbf{x}) = \frac{\phi(\mathbf{x})}{sum(\phi)}$ and if we remove the logarithm from the sum as it does not depend on the configurations, the previous equation can then be written as follows:

$$\log(\frac{v_r}{v_a}) \sum_{\mathbf{x} \in \mathbf{S}_a} \frac{\phi(\mathbf{x})}{sum(\phi)} + \log(\frac{v_r}{v_b}) \sum_{\mathbf{x} \in \mathbf{S}_b} \frac{\phi(\mathbf{x})}{sum(\phi)} =$$

$$\frac{1}{sum(\phi)} \left[\log(v_r) sum(\phi^{\downarrow \mathbf{S}_a}) - \log(v_a) sum(\phi^{\downarrow \mathbf{S}_a}) + \log(v_r) sum(\phi^{\downarrow \mathbf{S}_b}) - \log(v_b) sum(\phi^{\downarrow \mathbf{S}_b}) \right] = \quad (13)$$

$$\frac{1}{sum(\phi)} \left[\log(v_r) sum(\phi^{\downarrow \mathbf{S}_r}) - \log(v_a) sum(\phi^{\downarrow \mathbf{S}_a}) - \log(v_b) sum(\phi^{\downarrow \mathbf{S}_b}) \right].$$

□

4.3. Example

The application of the approximation algorithm will be exemplified using the potential presented in Example 1 and stored as a *VDI*, as shown in Figure 10. The practical implementation of the algorithm attempts to simplify computations as much as possible. Therefore, the global sum of the potential values in Equation (8) can be avoided, as it is not needed for determining the candidate structure with lower loss of information.

As the potential stores 6 different probability values, the initial iteration must therefore consider 5 candidate structures, i.e., 5 different *reduction* operations, and then calculate their respective information losses. This information is presented in Table 1. Each row considers the values to be reduced (v_a and v_r) and the new value (v_r) in addition to their corresponding sets of indices ($\mathbf{S}_a$, $\mathbf{S}_b$ and $\mathbf{S}_r$). The alternative with the lowest information loss is presented in bold.

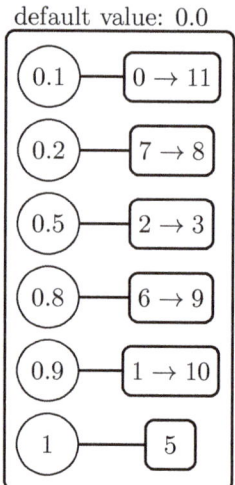

Figure 10. Potential to approximate.

Table 1. Candidate structures for the first iteration. Bold typeface is used for the preferred candidate structure.

$v_a - S_a$	$v_b - S_b$	$v_r - S_r$	$I(V, S_a, S_b)$
$0.1 - \{0, 11\}$	$0.2 - \{7, 8\}$	$0.15 - \{0, 7, 8, 11\}$	0.014757
$0.2 - \{7, 8\}$	$0.5 - \{2, 3\}$	$0.35 - \{2, 3, 7, 8\}$	0.057686
$0.5 - \{2, 3\}$	$0.8 - \{6, 9\}$	$0.65 - \{2, 3, 6, 9\}$	0.030339
$0.8 - \{6, 9\}$	$0.9 - \{1, 10\}$	$0.85 - \{1, 6, 9, 10\}$	0.002556
$\mathbf{0.9 - \{1, 10\}}$	$\mathbf{1 - \{5\}}$	$\mathbf{0.93333 - \{1, 5, 10\}}$	**0.001533**

Therefore, the preferred candidate structure is the final one and the resulting approximate structure is the one presented in Figure 11. The total loss is 0.001533.

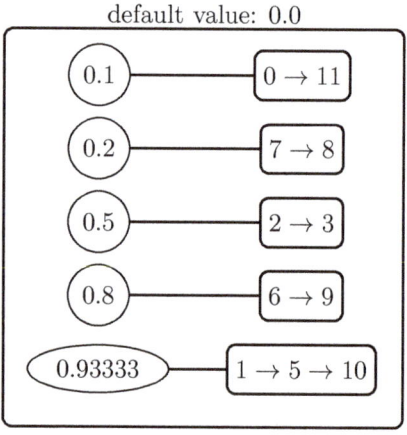

Figure 11. Approximation of ϕ obtained in the first iteration.

In the second iteration, there are only 4 candidate structures to consider, as shown in Table 2.

Table 2. Candidate structures for the second iteration. The best reduction is presented with bold typeface.

$v_a - S_a$	$v_b - S_b$	$v_r - S_r$	$I(V, S_a, S_b)$
$0.1 - \{0, 11\}$	$0.2 - \{7, 8\}$	$0.15 - \{0, 7, 8, 11\}$	0.014757
$0.2 - \{7, 8\}$	$0.5 - \{2, 3\}$	$0.35 - \{2, 3, 7, 8\}$	0.057686
$0.5 - \{2, 3\}$	$0.8 - \{6, 9\}$	$0.65 - \{2, 3, 6, 9\}$	0.030339
$0.8 - \{6, 9\}$	$\mathbf{0.93333 - \{1, 5, 10\}}$	$\mathbf{0.88 - \{1, 5, 6, 9, 10\}}$	**0.005323**

The *reduction* of the values 0.8 and 0.93333 therefore performs the best. The approximate structure after this iteration is presented in Figure 12. The global loss is now 0.006856.

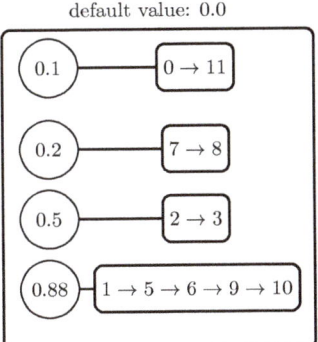

Figure 12. Approximation of ϕ obtained in the second iteration.

In the next step, we will consider a third iteration by selecting from among the candidate *reductions* presented in Table 3.

Table 3. Candidate structures for the third iteration. The best reduction is presented with bold typeface.

$v_a - S_a$	$v_b - S_b$	$v_r - S_r$	$I(V, S_a, S_b)$
$\mathbf{0.1 - \{0, 11\}}$	$\mathbf{0.2 - \{7, 8\}}$	$\mathbf{0.15 - \{0, 7, 8, 11\}}$	**0.014757**
$0.2 - \{7, 8\}$	$0.5 - \{2, 3\}$	$0.35 - \{2, 3, 7, 8\}$	0.057686
$0.5 - \{2, 3\}$	$0.88 - \{1, 5, 6, 9, 10\}$	$0.65 - \{2, 3, 6, 9\}$	0.063298

If we combine the values 0.1 and 0.2, we obtain the new approximated potential shown in Figure 13.

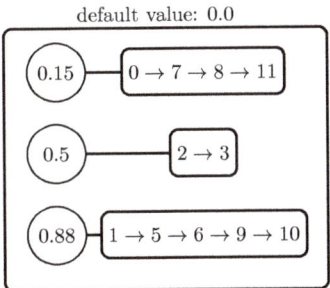

Figure 13. Final approximation of ϕ obtained in the third iteration.

The loss of information in relation to the original potential is now 0.021613. The next iteration must select between only two *reductions*, as shown in Table 4.

Table 4. Candidate structures for the fourth iteration.

$v_a - S_a$	$v_b - S_b$	$v_r - S_r$	$I(V, S_a, S_b)$
0.15 – {0, 7, 8, 11}	0.5 – {2, 3}	0.5333 – {0, 2, 3, 7, 8, 11}	0.123074
0.5 – {2, 3}	0.88 – {1, 5, 6, 9, 10}	0.65 – {2, 3, 6, 9}	0.063298

If the global loss threshold is 0.05, then there are no more *reductions* to apply and the process ends with the approximate potential shown in Figure 13. We need to make one last comment about the operation of the algorithm. If we look at the tables, it is apparent that information loss values for each *reduction* remain constant, regardless of the other values. This facilitates the consideration of alternative structures by storing the already calculated loss values, thereby avoiding repeated computations.

5. Empirical Evaluation

The application of the approximation algorithm will be evaluated by considering various *BNs* developed for modeling medical problems. All of these are included in the *bnlearn* repository (see [17,18]) and are either categorized as large (*HEPAR II*) or very large (*diabetes*, *munin*, and *pathfinder*) networks. The main features of these are described below.

- The *hepar2* network was defined by A. Onisko in her Ph.D. dissertation [22] as part of the *HEPAR II* project. The project was inspired by the *HEPAR* system [23], the aim of which is to support the diagnosis of liver and biliary tract disorders.
- *pathfinder* ([24]) is a system which, when combined with expert knowledge from surgical pathologists, can assist in the diagnosis of lymphnode diseases. As a result of this study, the discrete *pathfinder* network was defined.
- The *munin* network was defined while creating the expert system identified by the same acronym *MUNIN* (MUscle and Nerve Inference Network) [25]. The aim of this system was to help electromyographics (EMCs), which are designed to localize and characterize lesions of the neuro-muscular system, from a patho-physiological approach combined with expert knowledge.
- The *diabetes* [26] BN represents a differential equation model which attempts to adjust the insulin therapy for diabetic people. The model considers the patient's state by measuring blood glucose, biologically active insulin, and the amount of undigested carbohydrate within an hour gap in addition to other known variables involved in the glucose metabolism process. The *diabetes* network enabled predictions to be extended to 24-hour blood glucose profiles and the insulin treatment to be adjusted.

Table 5 presents a summary of the information for each network: number of nodes, number of arcs, number of parameters (*np*), average *Markov blanket* (M.B.) size, *average degree*, and *maximum in-degree*. The networks are ordered according to the number of parameters because this is the most relevant feature in terms of the experimental work.

Table 5. *Bayesian network* features.

Network	Nodes	arcs	np	avg. M.B. Size	avg. deg	Max. in-deg
hepar2	70	123	2139	4.51	3.51	6
pathfinder	223	338	97,851	5.61	3.03	6
munin	1041	1397	98,423	3.54	2.68	3
diabetes	413	606	461,069	3.97	2.92	2

The experimental section is organized in the following way:

1. Analysis of the memory space necessary to store the complete networks using the different representation alternatives in order to compare it with the representation using 1DA, since this is considered to be the base representation (see Section 5.1).

2. Analysis of the main characteristics of the specific potentials of some variables that will later be used to perform inference, as well as the memory space necessary for their representation with the different structures considered (see Section 5.2).
3. Examination of the effect of the approximation on the memory space necessary for the storage of each network (see Section 5.3). The relationship with the memory space required by the base representation is determined, as well as the reduction produced in relation to the alternative representations but without any approximation. In this case, the results are presented by means of a specific table for each network in order to collect the information on the threshold values considered.
4. Propagation errors produced by the approximation, both local (only the potential of the target variable is approximated) and global (all potentials are approximated) (see Section 5.4). A table is presented for each network and this collects the results for the selected variables and for the set of thresholds used.
5. In order to obtain further information about the effect of the approximation, some charts are also included to show the effect of the approximation on the order of the probabilities of the marginal distributions obtained as a result of the propagation. If these distributions are used to make decisions, it is important that the alternatives are kept in the same order (according to their probability value) in which they appear in the exact result, without approximation (see Section 5.5).

5.1. Global Memory Size Analysis

This section analyzes the networks in order to determine the necessary memory size for each form of representation being considered: *1DA*, *PT*, *PPT*, *VDI*, and *IPD*. This part serves to check the convenience of using alternative *VBP*-type representations in networks modeling real-world medical problems. In this way, a base memory size is available and it will enable the effect of the approximation on memory spaces required for the *VBP*-type representations to be subsequently checked. Table 6 includes the following information:

- *network*: name of the network;
- *1DA*: memory size indispensable for *1DA* storing the complete set of potentials;
- *PT*: memory size required for *PT* representation and the saving or increase in space in terms of *1DA*. This last value is included in the second line and is computed as

$$\frac{as * 100}{bs} - 100, \tag{14}$$

where *as* refers to the memory size of the alternative representation, and *bs* to the memory size of the *1DA* representation;
- *PPT*, *VDI*, and *IDP*: the same as the previous line for the remaining representations: pruned probability trees, *VDI* and *IDP*.

In Table 6, the best savings values are shown in bold. The results show that *VBP* structures behave better than *PT* and *PPT* in every network, although in some of these there are no savings in terms of the space required for the simplest representation of all: *1DA*. Some more specific comments are included below:

- In *hepar2*, we can see that *PPT* offers little improvement in relation to *PT*, which indicates that in reality there are few repeated values that can be used by the *PPT* pruning operation. The *VDI* structure provides a saving of approximately 44% compared to *PT*, while *IPD* represents a saving of 62%.
- In the case of *pathfinder*, there are notable savings in relation to *1DA* and very important ones with respect to *PT* and *PPT*. The biggest savings come from the *VDI* structure.
- With respect to the *munin* network, *VDI* representation needs almost the same memory space as *1DA* and there is a saving of about 23% in *IDP* (moreover, significant reductions can also be seen with respect to *PT* and *PPT*).
- Finally, for *diabetes*, both *VBP* structures represent a substantial reduction in memory space and this is slightly greater in the case of *VDI*.

Table 6. Global memory size analysis. Bold typeface denotes the structure with the best saving percentage (or with the smallest increase percentage).

Network	1DA	PT	PPT	VDI	IDP
hepar2	32,530	132,026 305.8592	131,756 305.0292	74,070 127.6975	49,602 **52.4808**
pathfinder	806,982	4,249,768 426.6249	3,779,470 368.3463	301,602 **−62.6259**	482,438 −40.2170
munin	994,672	3,393,878 241.2057	3,353,900 237.1865	997,864 0.3209	766,072 **−22.9825**
diabetes	3,773,200	10,044,948 166.2183	10,044,810 166.2146	964,380 **−74.4413**	1,105,728 −70.6952

In short, these data show the capacity of these structures to offer efficient mechanisms for representing quantitative information, and, as will be seen below, they allow the use of the approximation operation with the possibility of achieving additional memory savings.

5.2. Local Memory Size Analysis

This experiment gathers information about the selected variables of each network in order to determine their features and verify the relationship between representation and memory size. These variables will later be used as target variables using the *VE* algorithm ([27–29]) to compute their marginal distributions. The columns included in Table 7 are:

- *network*: name of the network;
- *variable*: name of the variable being examined;
- *np*: global number of parameters of the target variable potential;
- *nd*: number of different values in the potential (these are the values actually stored in the *VBP* representation);
- *1DA*: memory size for the *1DA* representation;
- *PT*: memory size required for *PT* representation and saving or increase regarding *1DA*. This last value is included in the second line and computed as before;
- *PPT*, *VDI*, and *IDP*: the same as the previous line for *PPT*, *VDI*, and *IDP*.

In this experiment, we have selected the variables with the largest number of parameters: *hepar2* (*ggtp*, *ast*, *alt*, and *bilirubin*); *pathfinder* (*F39*, *F74*, and *F40*); *munin* (*v1* (L_LNLPC5_DELT_MUSIZE), *v2* (L_LNLE_ADM_MUSIZE), and *v3* (L_MED_ALLCV_EW)); and *diabetes* (*cho_0*, *cho_1*, and *cho_2*). The best savings values are shown in bold. We wish to make the following comments about the results in Table 7:

- In *hepar2* variables, the number of different probability values is slightly lower than the number of parameters. This justifies the fact that memory space requirements do not reduce those required by *1DA*, although they do offer significant savings with respect to *PT* and *PPT*.
- Selected *pathfinder* variables present a high degree of repetition, so the number of different values is significantly lower than the number of parameters. This produces very significant memory savings in relation to *1DA* which are larger in the case of *VDI*.
- For the first two *munin* variables, there are only 12 different values but 600 parameters. This accounts for the notable memory space savings for *VBP* structures. In the case of the third variable, there are more different values (133), although this does suppose a high degree of repetition compared to the 600 necessary parameters.
- *Diabetes* variables have similar characteristics: only 45 different values (and 7056 possible values). Consequently, the memory space savings are very noticeable and appreciably better in the case of *VDI*.

Table 7. Local memory size analysis. Numbers in bold typeface denotes the best saving percentages (or with the smallest increase percentage).

Network	Variable	np	nd	1DA	PT	PPT	VDI	IDP
hepar2	ggtp	384	334	3454	19,452 463.1731	19,452 463.1731	9990 189.2299	6150 **78.0544**
	ast	288	231	2636	13,648 417.7542	13,648 417.7542	7084 168.7405	4508 **71.0167**
	alt	288	249	2636	13,648 417.7542	13,648 417.7542	7516 185.1290	4652 **76.4795**
	bilirubin	288	244	2636	13,426 409.3323	13,426 409.3323	7396 180.5766	4612 **74.9621**
pathfinder	F39	8064	30	64,794	376,442 480.9828	359,850 455.3755	15,114 **−76.6738**	28,698 −55.7089
	F74	7560	111	60,712	293,736 383.8187	152,072 150.4810	28,676 **−52.7672**	52,632 −13.3087
	F40	4032	43	32,488	116,076 257.2888	114,588 252.7087	5640 **−82.6397**	9280 −71.4356
munin	v1	600	12	5032	19,132 280.2067	19,132 280.2067	1112 **−77.9014**	1464 −70.9062
	v2	600	12	5032	19,132 280.2067	19,132 280.2067	1112 **−77.9014**	1464 −70.9062
	v3	600	133	4982	15,012 201.3248	15,012 201.3248	4066 −18.3862	2582 **−48.1734**
diabetes	cho_0	7056	45	56,630	139,546 146.4171	139,546 146.4171	9454 **−83.3057**	16,878 −70.1960
	cho_1	7056	45	56,630	139,546 146.4171	139,546 146.4171	9454 **−83.3057**	16,878 −70.1960
	cho_2	7056	45	56,630	139,546 146.4171	139,546 146.4171	9454 **−83.3057**	16,878 −70.1960

5.3. Global Memory Size with Approximation

This experiment considers the effect of the approximation on every potential in the network in terms of the necessary memory space after approximating with different thresholds. This determines the degree to which the approximation enables a reduction in the memory size for storing the networks. The results for this section are divided into various tables, one for each network (Tables 8–11), and all have a similar structure.

- The first column shows the threshold.
- The second presents data relating to the *VDI* structure: memory size after approximation, savings over *1DA* and savings with respect to the exact *VDI* representation.
- The third column is identical to the second but with data for the *IDP* structure.

5.3.1. *hepar2* Network

The number of parameters is 2139, and the memory sizes of *1DA*, *PT*, and *PPT* structures are 32,530, 132,026, and 131,756, respectively. Table 8 includes savings when approximation is applied.

Table 8. *hepar2*—Global approximation memory size analysis.

Threshold	VDI	IDP
0.00001	63,846 (96.2681/−13.8032)	46,194 (42.0043/−6.8707)
0.00005	58,062 (78.4875/−21.6120)	44,266 (36.0775/−10.7576)
0.00010	55,302 (70.0031/−25.3382)	43,346 (33.2493/−12.6124)
0.00050	48,558 (49.2714/−34.4431)	41,098 (26.3388/−17.1445)
0.00100	45,678 (40.4181/−38.3313)	40,138 (23.3876/−19.0799)
0.00500	39,798 (22.3425/−46.2697)	38,178 (17.3624/−23.0313)
0.01000	37,518 (15.3335/−49.3479)	37,418 (15.0261/−24.5635)
0.05000	33,798 (3.8979/−54.3702)	36,178 (11.2143/−27.0634)
0.10000	32,550 (0.0615/−56.0551)	35,762 (9.9354/−27.9021)

Table 9. *pathfinder*—Global approximation memory size analysis.

Threshold	VDI	IDP
0.00001	293,178 (−63.6698/−2.7931)	479,630 (−40.5650/−0.5820)
0.00005	290,682 (−63.9791/−3.6207)	478,798 (−40.6681/−0.7545)
0.00010	289,266 (−64.1546/−4.0902)	478,326 (−40.7266/−0.8523)
0.00050	285,450 (−64.6275/−5.3554)	477,054 (−40.8842/−1.1160)
0.00100	283,170 (−64.9100/−6.1114)	476,294 (−40.9784/−1.2735)
0.00500	277,002 (−65.6743/−8.1564)	474,238 (−41.2331/−1.6997)
0.01000	274,050 (−66.0401/−9.1352)	473,254 (−41.3551/−1.9037)
0.05000	267,090 (−66.9026/−11.4429)	470,934 (−41.6426/−2.3846)
0.10000	264,450 (−67.2298/−12.3182)	470,054 (−41.7516/−2.5670)

Table 10. *munin*—Global approximation memory size analysis.

Threshold	VDI	IDP
0.00001	880,744 (−11.4538/−11.7371)	727,032 (−26.9074/−5.0961)
0.00005	829,096 (−16.6463/−16.9129)	709,816 (−28.6382/−7.3434)
0.00010	800,584 (−19.5128/−19.7702)	700,312 (−29.5937/−8.5840)
0.00050	725,440 (−27.0674/−27.3007)	675,264 (−32.1119/−11.8537)
0.00100	692,296 (−30.3996/−30.6222)	664,216 (−33.2226/−13.2959)
0.00500	615,976 (−38.0725/−38.2705)	638,776 (−35.7802/−16.6167)
0.01000	587,848 (−40.9003/−41.0894)	629,400 (−36.7229/−17.8406)
0.05000	533,728 (−46.3413/−46.5130)	611,360 (−38.5365/−20.1955)
0.10000	518,272 (−47.8952/−48.0619)	606,208 (−39.0545/−20.8680)

Here are some comments about Table 8:

- For *VDI*, it is apparent that there is a very noticeable increase in memory space savings as the threshold used for the approximation becomes greater, reaching very similar sizes to those of *1DA* for the threshold 0.1. For every threshold, there is a reduction in relation to the exact *VDI* structure (without the use of approximation).
- With the *IDP* structure, the behavior is similar, although the reductions are not as notable as with *VDI*.

Table 11. *diabetes*—Global approximation memory size analysis.

Threshold	VDI	IDP
0.00001	843,180 (−77.6535/−12.5677)	1,065,328 (−71.7659/−3.6537)
0.00005	799,932 (−78.7996/−17.0522)	1,050,912 (−72.1480/−4.9575)
0.00010	776,868 (−79.4109/−19.4438)	1,043,224 (−72.3517/−5.6527)
0.00050	719,148 (−80.9406/−25.4290)	1,023,984 (−72.8617/−7.3928)
0.00100	694,908 (−81.5831/−27.9425)	1,015,904 (−73.0758/−8.1235)
0.00500	644,076 (−82.9302/−33.2135)	998,960 (−73.5249/−9.6559)
0.01000	626,172 (−83.4047/−35.0700)	992,992 (−73.6830/−10.1956)
0.05000	594,324 (−84.2488/−38.3724)	982,376 (−73.9644/−11.1557)
0.10000	585,636 (−84.4791/−39.2733)	979,480 (−74.0411/−11.4176)

5.3.2. *pathfinder* Network

This contains $97,851$ parameters, and the memory sizes for *1DA*, *PT*, and *PPT* are $806,982$, $4,249,768$, and $3,779,470$. The memory sizes for several degrees of approximation are presented in Table 9.

It is worth remembering that in this network, the *VDI* structure without approximation already represented a saving of approximately 62.7% in relation to *1DA*, which increases as the threshold value grows. For the highest threshold value, the saving is 12.3% with respect to the *VDI* structure without approximation. Similar results can be observed for *IDP*.

5.3.3. *munin* Network

This network requires $994,672$ parameters to store the quantitative information and the memory sizes required for alternative representation structures with approximation operation are $994,672$, $3,393,878$, and $3,353,900$ for *1DA*, *PT*, and *PPT*. The effect of approximation can be observed in Table 10.

In this network, the reduction of space is extremely notable both with respect to *1DA* and also to the exact representations through *VDI* and *IDP*, although the reduction is more important in the case of *VDI*.

5.3.4. *diabetes* Network

In the *diabetes* network, the number of parameters is $461,069$, and the memory sizes for representations as *1DA*, *PT*, and *PPT* are $3,773,200$, $10,044,948$, and $10,044,810$. The effect of approximation in memory sizes is presented in Table 11.

As in the case of the *munin* network, memory size reductions are important and especially relevant for *VDI*.

5.4. Propagation Errors with Approximation

The objective of this part is to check the effect of approximation on propagation errors using the *VE* algorithm on the set of selected variables. For each target variable, two different values are presented: the error when approximation is limited to the potential of the target variable and when approximation is applied to the entire set of potentials. As *VDI* and *IDP* approximations will produce the same potentials, this experiment will be performed exclusively on the *VDI* representation. The steps followed to produce the results are:

1. Perform a *VE* propagation on each target variable for storing the marginal obtained as the ground result V_g.
2. Modify the network by approximating the potential of the target variable, saving the remaining ones as defined in the network specification.
3. Perform a second *VE* propagation on the modified network setting the selected target variable. The result is termed as V_{la}.
4. Apply the approximation on the entire set of potentials.

5. Compute a third VE propagation for the selected variable, producing V_{ga}.
6. Compute the divergences between the ground result and the approximate ones: $D(V_g, V_{la})$ and $D(V_g, V_{ga})$.

In order to introduce the results obtained, Tables 12–15 are organized as follows. Threshold values are presented in the first column; for each variable the *local* columns contain the errors of propagation with approximation on target variable, that is $D(V_g, V_{la})$; and *global* columns show the errors of propagation when approximation is applied on all the potentials ($D(V_g, V_{ga})$). It should be noted that the values presented in the following tables are rounded to include only three decimal places. Therefore, the value of divergence $d_l = 0.001$ will be referred to as the limit value.

5.4.1. hepar2 Network

It is apparent that if the threshold value is below 0.005, then the errors remain below d_l. Errors above this threshold value only appear for the last three threshold values, and even for these values there are variables in which both the global and local approximations remain below d_l. The largest error value is 0.005 (quite small) for the *ggtp* variable in the case of global approximation with a threshold value of 0.1.

Table 12. *hepar2*—local and global approximation propagation error analysis.

Threshold	ggtp		ast		alt		bilirubin	
	Local	Global	Local	Global	Local	Global	Local	Global
0.00001	0.000	0.000	0.000	0.000	0.000	0.000	0.000	0.000
0.00005	0.000	0.000	0.000	0.000	0.000	0.000	0.000	0.000
0.00010	0.000	0.000	0.000	0.000	0.000	0.000	0.000	0.000
0.00050	0.000	0.000	0.000	0.000	0.000	0.000	0.000	0.000
0.00100	0.000	0.000	0.000	0.000	0.000	0.000	0.000	0.000
0.00500	0.000	0.000	0.000	0.000	0.000	0.000	0.000	0.000
0.01000	0.000	0.001	0.000	0.000	0.000	0.000	0.000	0.001
0.05000	0.002	0.004	0.001	0.001	0.000	0.000	0.000	0.001
0.10000	0.002	0.005	0.003	0.004	0.001	0.002	0.001	0.001

Table 13. *pathfinder*—local and global approximation propagation error analysis.

Threshold	F39		F74		F40	
	Local	Global	Local	Global	Local	Global
0.00001	−0.000	0.000	0.000	0.000	0.000	0.000
0.00005	0.000	0.000	0.000	0.000	0.000	0.000
0.00010	0.000	0.000	0.000	0.000	0.000	0.000
0.00050	0.000	0.000	0.000	0.000	0.000	0.000
0.00100	0.000	0.000	0.000	0.000	0.000	0.000
0.00500	0.000	0.000	0.000	0.000	0.000	0.000
0.01000	0.000	0.000	0.000	0.000	0.000	0.000
0.05000	0.000	0.004	0.000	0.000	0.000	0.005
0.10000	0.000	0.005	0.000	0.001	0.000	0.006

Table 14. munin—local and global approximation propagation error analysis.

Threshold	v1		v2		v3	
	Local	Global	Local	Global	Local	Global
0.00001	0.000	0.000	0.000	0.000	0.000	0.000
0.00005	0.000	0.000	0.000	0.000	0.000	0.000
0.00010	0.000	0.000	0.000	0.000	0.000	0.000
0.00050	0.000	0.000	0.000	0.000	0.000	0.001
0.00100	0.000	0.000	0.000	0.000	0.000	0.001
0.00500	0.000	0.001	0.000	0.001	0.000	0.005
0.01000	0.000	0.001	0.000	0.001	0.000	0.006
0.05000	0.000	0.002	0.000	0.003	0.000	0.096
0.10000	0.000	0.002	0.000	0.003	0.000	0.093

Table 15. diabetes—local and global approximation propagation error analysis.

Threshold	cho_0		cho_1		cho_2	
	Local	Global	Local	Global	Local	Global
0.00001	0.000	0.000	0.000	0.000	0.000	0.000
0.00005	0.000	0.000	0.000	0.000	0.000	0.000
0.00010	0.000	0.000	0.000	0.000	0.000	0.000
0.00050	0.001	0.001	0.000	0.001	0.000	0.000
0.00100	0.001	0.001	0.000	0.001	0.000	0.000
0.00500	0.001	0.001	0.000	0.000	0.000	0.000
0.01000	0.001	0.001	0.000	0.000	0.000	0.000
0.05000	0.000	0.000	0.000	0.001	0.000	0.000
0.10000	0.001	0.001	0.001	0.002	0.000	0.002

5.4.2. *pathfinder* Network

The results for this network are similar to those obtained for the *hepar2* network. All errors are below d_l for threshold values between 0.00001 and 0.01. Even above these values, the local approximation produces errors that are below d_l in every variable. The largest error occurs for the threshold 0.1 and global approximation for the variable *F40*.

5.4.3. *munin* Network

In the case of the *munin* network, there are only significant errors for the case of global approximation and with high thresholds (0.0096 for threshold 0.05 and 0.093 for threshold 0.1 and variable $v3$). The local approximation always produces error values lower than the limit value d_l.

5.4.4. *diabetes* Network

For the *diabetes* network, the variable *cho_0* is the one that offers the worst results, with errors equal to the limit value d_l in the case of local approximation and with threshold values over 0.0005. In any case, all the error values are very small, even for global approximation and large threshold values.

5.5. Order of Preferences

As stated earlier, the results of propagation can be used to aid in a decision-making process. It is therefore important that the errors are kept low (as demonstrated by the previous experiments) but that the order between the probability values of the states of the variables on which the propagation is performed is also maintained. In the charts included in this experimentation (see Tables 16–20), the possible states of the variables are denoted as si. Let us imagine a variable with the three states: $s1, s2, s3$. Let us also suppose that exact propagation indicates that the order of the states according to their probability, from highest to lowest, is $s2, s11, s3$. This will therefore be the order of preferences that should be maintained so that the decision does not change as a result of errors produced by the approximation. In this way, the ideal situation will be one in which the order of preferences is not altered despite the approximation made, whether global or local. The colors in the tables also represent the differences between the probability values obtained for each alternative (with respect to the probability values obtained in the exact propagation), with colors ranging from green for the lowest differences to red for the highest values and those in between in varying shades of yellow.

Table 16. Preferences for *hepar2* variables.

Table 17. Preferences for *pathfinder* variables.

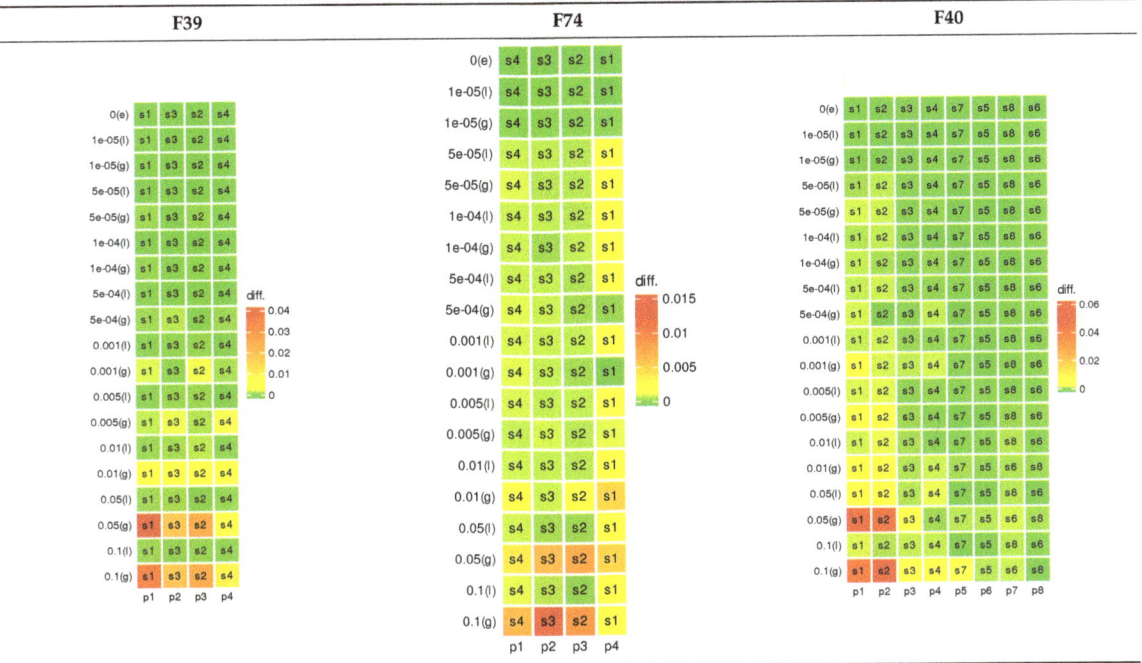

Table 18. Preferences for *munin* variables.

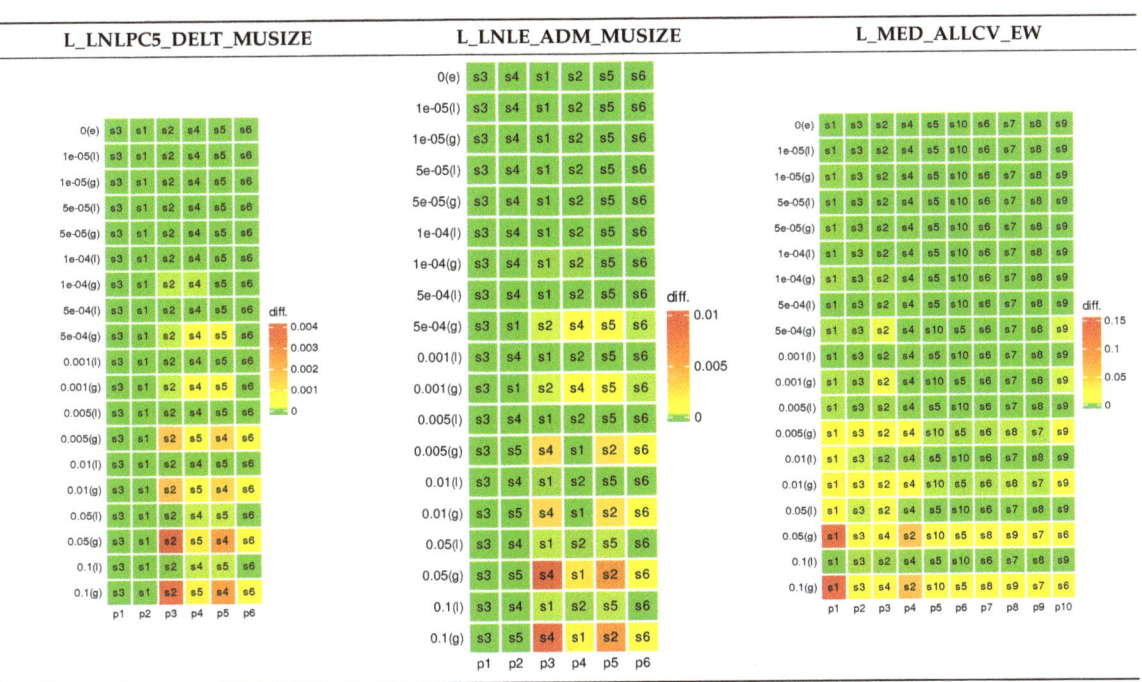

Table 19. Preferences for *cho_0* and *cho_1*.

Table 20. Preferences for *cho_2*.

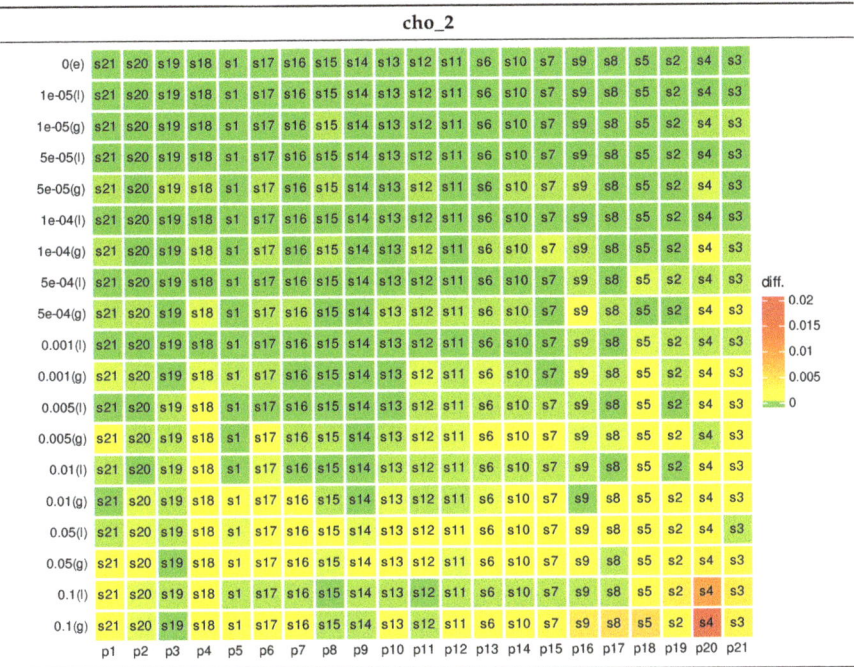

5.5.1. hepar2 Network

For this network, the order of preferences (*s*3, *s*3, *s*2, *s*1 for *ggtp* and *bilirubin*, and *s*3, *s*4, *s*2, *s*1 for *ast* and *alt*) are always maintained, both for global and local approximation as well as for every threshold value. Similarly, it can be seen that the probability differences are always small, with maximum values of 0.04 for the case of the *ggtp* and *ast* variables.

5.5.2. pathfinder Network

For the three variables in this network, the same behavior is observed as in the case of the previous network: the preference orders are maintained for every threshold and for both forms of approximation. The largest probability difference value is 0.06 for the variable *F40*, and this appears in the global approximation case with the highest threshold values.

5.5.3. munin Network

For this network, there are changes in the order of preferences, although these do not affect the most probable alternatives. For the three variables, the changes appear with threshold values starting at 0.0005 and always for the case of global approximation. The highest values of probability difference occur for the third variable, reaching 0.15 with high thresholds and global approximation.

5.5.4. diabetes Network

The results for this network have been divided into two tables due to the number of states of the variables considered (21 in total).

For these two variables, there are changes in the orders of preferences for threshold values from 0.005 with both types of approximation. It should be noted that the differences between probability values are very low (the maximum is 0.02) and that the changes do not affect the first preferences (3 first in the case of *cho_0* and 6 first in the case of *cho_1*).

For the last variable, there are no changes in the preference orders and the difference between probability values is very small, even in the case of large thresholds and global approximation (the maximum value is 0.02).

6. Discussion

In this work, we have analyzed the characteristics of some *BNs* that model real medical problems. This analysis has allowed us to observe that the probability distributions that quantify the uncertainty of the problem have various common characteristics, and these include the fact that there are many impossible events and that some probability values tend to appear several times. For example, when analyzing the *pathfinder* network (see Table 7), it can be seen that although the probability distribution for the variable *F39* has 8064 parameters, there are only 30 different values for these. However, these repetitions do not always appear in a way that can be used by tree-like structures such as *PPT* or *BPT*. This justifies the use of the considered *VBP* structures, which in some cases enable a considerable saving of memory space in relation to other possible representation structures.

The need to deal with increasingly complex problems may subsequently lead to situations where models cannot be evaluated by exact inference algorithms, such as the *VE* algorithm. In such cases, our work considers the possibility of approximating the *VBP* structures, forcing an additional saving of space at the cost of losing information. Our work presents the way in which this operation should be carried out and experimentally demonstrates that the errors it induces in the results of the inference algorithms are small and that in many cases they do not alter the preference orders between variable alternatives. In this way, the decision-making process based on the approximate results would match the one performed if the exact propagation could be computed.

Author Contributions: Writing–review & editing, P.B.-N., A.C., M.G.-O., S.M. and O.P.R. All authors have read and agreed to the published version of the manuscript.

Funding: This paper is supported by the Spanish Ministry of Education and Science under project PID2019-106758GB-C31 and the European Regional Development Fund (FEDER). Funding for open access publication has been provided by the *Universidad de Granada/CBUA*.

Data Availability Statement: The software used in this paper was implemented in **Scala**. The code is available at https://github.com/mgomez-olmedo/VBPots (accessed on 15 June 2022).. This repository also stores the information required for reproducing the experiments.

Conflicts of Interest: The authors declare no conflict of interest.

Abbreviations

The following abbreviations are used in this manuscript:

BN	Bayesian network
BPT	Binary probability tree
DAG	Decision acyclic graph
ID	Influence diagram
IDM	Index-driven with map
IDP	Index-driven with pair of arrays
PGM	Probabilistic graphical model
PPT	Pruned probability tree
PT	Probability tree
VBP	Value-based potential
VDG	Value-driven with grains
VDI	Value-driven with indices
1DA	Unidimensional array

References

1. Koller, D.; Friedman, N. *Probabilistic Graphical Models: Principles and Techniques*; MIT Press: Cambridge, MA, USA, 2009.
2. Lauritzen, S.L. *Graphical Models*; Oxford University Press: Oxford, UK, 1996.
3. Pearl, J. *Probabilistic Reasoning in Intelligent Systems: Networks of Plausible Inference*; Morgan Kaufmann: Burlington, MA, USA, 1988.
4. Pearl, J. *Bayesian Networks: A Model of Self-Activated Memory for Evidential Reasoning*; Computer Science Department, University of California, California, LA, USA, 1985.
5. Pearl, J.; Russell, S. Bayesian Networks. Computer Science Department, University of California. 1998. Available online: https://people.eecs.berkeley.edu/~russell/papers/hbtnn-bn.pdf (accessed on 15 June 2022).
6. Howard, R.A.; Matheson, J.E. Influence diagram retrospective. *Decis. Anal.* **2005**, *2*, 144–147. [CrossRef]
7. Olmsted, S.M. On Representing and Solving Decision Problems. Ph.D. Thesis, Department of Engineering-Economic Systems, Stanford University, Stanford, CA, USA, 1983.
8. Arias, M.; Díez, F. Operating with potentials of discrete variables. *Int. J. Approx. Reason.* **2007**, *46*, 166–187. [CrossRef]
9. Boutilier, C.; Friedman, N.; Goldszmidt, M.; Koller, D. Context-specific independence in Bayesian networks. In Proceedings of the 12th Annual Conference on Uncertainty in Artificial Intelligence (UAI-96), Portland, OR, USA, 1–3 August 1996; pp. 115–123.
10. Cabañas, R.; Gómez, M.; Cano, A. Using binary trees for the evaluation of influence diagrams. *Int. J. Uncertain. Fuzziness Knowl. Based Syst.* **2016**, *24*, 59–89. [CrossRef]
11. Cano, A.; Moral, S.; Salmerón, A. Penniless propagation in join trees. *Int. J. Approx. Reason* **2000**, *15*, 1027–1059. [CrossRef]
12. Gómez-Olmedo, M.; Cano, A. Applying numerical trees to evaluate asymmetric decision problems. In *Symbolic and Quantitative Approaches to Reasoning with Uncertainty of Lecture Notes in Computer Science*; Nielsen, T., Zhang, N., Eds.; Springer: Berlin/Heidelberg, Germany, 2003; Volume 2711.
13. Salmerón, A.; Cano, A.; Moral, S. Importance sampling in Bayesian networks using probability trees. *Comput. Stat. Data Anal.* **2000**, *34*, 387–413. [CrossRef]
14. Cabañas, R.; Gómez-Olmedo, M.; Cano, A. Approximate inference in influence diagrams using binary trees. In Proceedings of the Sixth European Workshop on Probabilistic Graphical Models (PGM-12), Granada, Spain, 19–21 September 2012.
15. Cano, A.; Gómez-Olmedo, M.; Moral, S. Approximate inference in Bayesian networks using binary probability trees. *Int. J. Approx. Reason.* **2011**, *52*, 49–62. [CrossRef]
16. Gómez-Olmedo, M.; Cabañas, R.; Cano, A.; Moral, S.; Retamero, O.P. Value-Based Potentials: Exploiting Quantitative Information Regularity Patterns in Probabilistic Graphical Models. *Int. J. Intell. Syst.* **2021**, *36*, 6913–6943. [CrossRef]
17. Scutari, M. Learning Bayesian networks with the bnlearn R package. *J. Stat. Softw.* **2010**, *35*, 1–22. [CrossRef]
18. Scutari, M. Bayesian network constraint-based structure learning algorithms: Parallel and optimized implementations in the bnlearn R package. *J. Stat. Softw.* **2017**, *77*, 1–20. [CrossRef]
19. UAI 2014 Inference Competition. 2014. Available online: https://personal.utdallas.edu/~vibhav.gogate/uai14-competition/index.html (accessed on 15 June 2022).
20. UAI 2016 Inference Competition. 2016. Available online: https://personal.utdallas.edu/~vibhav.gogate/uai16-evaluation/index.html (accessed on 15 June 2022).
21. Kullback, S.; Leibler, R.A. On information and sufficiency. *Ann. Math. Stat.* **1951**, *22*, 76–86. [CrossRef]
22. Onisko, A. Probabilistic Causal Models in Medicine: Application to Diagnosis of Liver Disorders. Ph.D. Dissertation, Institute of Biocybernetics and Biomedical Engineering, Polish Academy of Science, Warsaw, March 2003.
23. Bobrowski, L. HEPAR: Computer system for diagnosis support and data analysis. In *Prace IBIB 31*; Institute of Biocybernetics and Biomedical Engineering, Polish Academy of Science: Warsaw, Poland, 1992.
24. Heckerman, D.; Horwitz, E.; Nathwani, B. Towards Normative Expert Systems: Part I. The Pathfinder Project. *Methods Inf. Med.* **1992**, *31*, 90–105. [CrossRef] [PubMed]
25. Andreassen, S.; Jensen, F.V.; Andersen, S.K.; Falck, B.; Kjærulff, U.; Woldbye, M.; Sørensen, A.R.; Rosenfalck, A.; Jensen, F. MUNIN—An Expert EMG Assistant. In *Computer-Aided Electromyography and Expert Systems*; Elsevier: Amsterdam, The Netherlands, 1989; Chapter 21.
26. Andreassen, S.; Hovorka, R.; Benn, J.; Olesen, K.G.; Carson, E.R. A Model-based Approach to Insulin Adjustment. In Proceedings of the 3rd Conference on Artificial Intelligence in Medicine, Vienna, Austria, 21–24 June 1991; pp. 239–248.
27. Dechter, R. Bucket elimination: A unifying algorithm for Bayesian inference. *Artif. Intell.* **1997**, *93*, 1–27.
28. Shenoy, P.P.; Shafer, G.R. Axioms for probability and belief-function propagation. In *Uncertainty in Artificial Intelligence of Machine Intelligence and Pattern Recognition*; Shachter, R.D., Levitt, T.S., Kanal, L.N., Lemmer, J.F., Eds.; North-Holland: Amsterdam, The Netherlands, 1990; Volume 9.
29. Zhang, N.L.; Poole, D. Exploiting causal independences in Bayesian networks inference. *J. Artif. Intell. Res.* **1996**, *5*, 301–328. [CrossRef]

Article

Influenza-like Illness Detection from Arabic Facebook Posts Based on Sentiment Analysis and 1D Convolutional Neural Network

Abdennour Boulesnane [1],*, Souham Meshoul [2],* and Khaoula Aouissi [3]

[1] BIOSTIM Laboratory, Medicine Faculty, Salah Boubnider University Constantine 03, Constantine 25001, Algeria
[2] Department of Information Technology, College of Computer and Information Sciences, Princess Nourah bint Abdulrahman University, P.O. Box 84428, Riyadh 11671, Saudi Arabia
[3] Department of Pharmacy, Medicine Faculty, Salah Boubnider University Constantine 03, Constantine 25001, Algeria
* Correspondence: aboulesnane@univ-constantine3.dz (A.B.); sbmeshoul@pnu.edu.sa (S.M.)

Abstract: The recent large outbreak of infectious diseases, such as influenza-like illnesses and COVID-19, has resulted in a flood of health-related posts on the Internet in general and on social media in particular, in a wide range of languages and dialects around the world. The obvious relationship between the number of infectious disease cases and the number of social media posts prompted us to consider how we can leverage such health-related content to detect the emergence of diseases, particularly influenza-like illnesses, and foster disease surveillance systems. We used Algerian Arabic posts as a case study in our research. From data collection to content classification, a complete workflow was implemented. The main contributions of this work are the creation of a large corpus of Arabic Facebook posts based on Algerian dialect and the proposal of a new classification model based on sentiment analysis and one-dimensional convolutional neural networks. The proposed model categorizes Facebook posts based on the users' feelings. To counteract data imbalance, two techniques have been considered, namely, SMOTE and random oversampling (ROS). Using a 5-fold cross-validation, the proposed model outperformed other baseline and state-of-the-art models such as SVM, LSTM, GRU, and BiLTSM in terms of several performance metrics.

Keywords: influenza-like illness; COVID-19; Arabic sentiment analysis; disease classification; Facebook; Algerian dialect

MSC: 68T07

1. Introduction

The huge increase in the use of social media platforms has made them an important source of massive amounts of data. Users of social media are now sharing every aspect of their lives, including their political beliefs, emotional feelings, health status, anxiety, anger, and even their wishes. Based on Social Media Analysis (SMA) [1], such data have been used for a variety of purposes, including product marketing [2], political elections [3], tourism [4], healthcare [5], and renewable energy [6,7], among others.

With over 2.9 billion users [8], Facebook is one of the world's largest social networking platforms, allowing the sharing of diverse data in a variety of daily life domains. Algeria has an estimated 27 million Internet users, accounting for 60% of the total population. About 22.4 million of these people use Facebook. As a result, Facebook is the most popular social media platform in this country [9].

As is the case in the rest of the world, Algerian Facebook users have recently and extensively shared a great deal of health-related information, including requests for medical advice and fears of certain diseases, especially in light of the rising incidence of rapidly spreading infectious diseases such as Influenza-Like Illnesses (ILI) and COVID-19. The Centers for Disease Control and Prevention [10] define ILI as "a fever, cough, and/or sore throat with no other known cause than influenza". While COVID-19 can have severe consequences and cause organ damage, its clinical manifestations are comparable to those of the common cold, such as fever, cough, and sore throat [11,12].

On the other hand, health systems still rely significantly on health center data to detect diseases and follow their spread, which is a time-consuming and labor-intensive process prior to issuing public warnings. Therefore, it has become imperative to strengthen existing health systems by leveraging health-related data on social media and developing intelligent systems that help in monitoring the spread of infectious diseases such as ILI, anticipating and controlling outbreaks, providing early warnings, and identifying the emergence of new symptoms.

Several studies have been undertaken to improve public health systems by leveraging social media health-related data, machine or deep learning models, and Natural Language Processing (NLP) techniques, such as text mining and sentiment analysis. These studies include the detection of various diseases through social networks, such as COVID-19 [13–15], latent infectious diseases [16], infectious diseases [17], depression [18–20], mental illness [21,22], mosquito-borne diseases [23], Asperger syndrome [24], dengue disease [25], avian influenza [26], and influenza [27–31], among others.

However, as these works rely on an in-depth comprehension of the natural language used to analyze emotions and detect diseases from published texts, their use is mostly limited to this language, and they cannot be used for other natural languages. Moreover, to the best of our knowledge, no previous research has used sentiment analysis on social media data written in the Algerian Arabic dialect to detect diseases.

In this paper, we present a new sentiment classification model based on one-dimensional convolutional neural networks (1D-CNN) and sentiment analysis to detect and monitor ILI in Facebook postings from Algeria. The suggested approach is able to interpret the emotions of Algerian-speaking patients and identify ILI-positive instances. This work's contributions can be summarized as follows: (1) A corpus of 21,885 Facebook posts written in Arabic Algerian dialect was compiled. This data set comprises health-related information that can be utilized by a variety of medical applications for the benefit of the public health. (2) All acquired data were manually annotated by professionals, enabling the development of a model capable of comprehending how a patient with ILI is feeling. (3) We examined, balanced, and preprocessed the data as part of the data preparation phase by implementing novel NLP approaches, such as recommending new stop words appropriate to the Algerian Arabic dialect. (4) Multiple Feature Extraction (FE) approaches were employed, and a methodology called "Feature concatenation" was introduced to improve the extraction process by merging these methods. (5) We propose a new 1D-CNN-based model architecture with many layers trained to identify and classify ILI from Facebook postings. Finally, an extensive evaluation process was undertaken to show the effectiveness of the proposed approach.

The remainder of the paper is organized as follows: Section 2 discusses the most recent works on Arabic sentiment analysis related to public health. Section 3 describes the proposed approach in detail. The results of the experiments are discussed and analyzed in Section 4. Section 5 includes a conclusion and presents future work plans.

2. Background and Related Work

Compared to other languages such as English, Spanish, and Chinese, Arabic remains considerably less prevalent on the Internet. Moreover, for the purposes of NLP, Arabic content requires significantly more effort to extract the sentiment and core idea behind the text, as nearly every Arabic-speaking nation utilizes a different dialect. Furthermore, regarding Arabic health-related content on social media, it is not being used effectively to benefit public health on the one hand, and on the other hand, users lack the awareness required to safeguard their sensitive data [32].

In this section, we will present an overview of recent works in the literature that apply sentiment analysis techniques [33] based on deep or machine learning and use social media health-related data written in the Arabic language and/or its dialects.

In [34,35], sentiment analysis using Machine Learning (ML) was adopted to understand and analyze the social behavior of Saudi individuals towards certain health services (such as mHealth apps) and to assess the extent of their awareness of the quarantine during the COVID-19 pandemic. Each study collects, labels, processes, and sentimentally classifies Arabic tweets into three categories, namely, "positive", "negative", and "neutral".

An Arabic language dialect identification system is proposed in [36], aiming to analyze and classify COVID-19-related tweets into four Arabic dialects: Modern Standard Arabic (MSA), Egyptian, Gulf, and Levantine. In this study, BERT-based models were adopted to locate the source region of COVID-19 Arabic tweets, thus helping to monitor the epidemic outbreaks in the Arab world. Furthermore, the data from [37,38] were used, and the features were extracted based on Term Frequency-Inverse Document Frequency (TF-IDF) and word embedding. As a result, the proposed system achieved a very strong performance in determining the tweets' sources with an accuracy of 97.36%.

In [39], COVID-19 vaccine-related tweets were collected and analyzed for six Gulf countries to study people's feelings about different types of vaccines to support the vaccination process. The collected data were cleaned, tokenized, and then scored using three sentiment analysis methods, TextBlob, Ratio, and VADER, producing positive and negative instances. After that, the LSTM was used to extract deep features and provide them to ML classifiers, including SVM, Fine-KNN, and Ensemble Boost. The best sentiment classification results were achieved for fine-KNN and Ensemble boost classifiers with accuracy of 94.01%.

In [40], more than 4.5 million Arabic tweets were collected related to the topic of COVID-19. The main objective of this study was to detect rumors and misinformation about COVID-19 in Arabic content. For this purpose, 8786 tweets were annotated into two categories—"misinformation" and "not", based on a list of misinformation collected from reliable sources. Furthermore, using TF-IDF and other word embedding methods such as word2veca and FASTTEXT, the features were extracted and then fed to several ML and deep learning models.

In another similar study [41], an AraBERT-based model was proposed that can determine whether Arabic health-related tweets are accurate or not. This work focuses on training and evaluating the performance of various deep learning models that use transformer models and pretrained word embeddings. The results demonstrated the efficacy of the AraBERT-based model over the other deep learning models in identifying the medical accuracy of Arabic tweets.

In [42], Arab tweets were used to build a monitoring system to track and analyze people's emotions during the spread of COVID-19, as well as to monitor the symptoms that appear as a result this disease. Using rule-based (if-then) techniques, 5.5 million tweets were collected and annotated for their study. Additionally, two types of classification were adopted, namely, emotion-based multi-class classification and symptom-based binary classification. Initially, the LSTM deep learning model is used to classify Arabic tweets into six emotions, including "anger", "disgust", "fear", "joy", "sadness", and "surprise". Then, a second LSTM classifier is introduced to classify tweets into either "symptom" or "non-symptom" categories.

Another similar study [43] intends to build a health monitoring system in order to discover concerns associated with the COVID-19 epidemic and to assess the sentiments of Moroccan users on Facebook, Twitter, YouTube, and other popular websites. In addition to the Arabic language, the researchers focused on the Moroccan dialect and developed MD-ULM, the first Universal Language Model for the Moroccan dialect. This proposed model is mainly based on LSTM to classify text comments by topic and emotion.

Two BERT-based models for analyzing Arabic tweets and evaluating the influence of COVID-19 on users' mental health were proposed in [44]. In this paper, the authors propose a new method called dynamically weighted loss function to address the issue of unbalanced data. Word and contextual embeddings were used to extract features from tweets, and emojis were substituted with more expressive ones in terms of sentiment and emotion. On the basis of these methodologies, BERT-based transformers were utilized to detect sentiment in Arabic COVID-19 tweets, thereby protecting individuals from mental diseases such as depression, anxiety, and so on.

In [45], several ML models, including Random Forest (RF), AdaBoostM1, Naïve Bayes (NB), and Liblinear, were used to determine whether Twitter users in the Arab Gulf region were suffering from depression. Based on sentiment analysis and NLP, each tweet was categorized as either "Depressed" or "non-depressed". In addition to tweets written in MSA, the authors of this work also considered Arabian Gulf languages to train ML classifiers and produce more accurate models.

A similar study was conducted to aid in the diagnosis of depression in [46]. After collecting and thoroughly analyzing 4542 tweets based on nine depression symptoms, the tweets were classified into three broad sentiment categories: "non-depressed", "depressed", and "neutral". In their research, the authors extract data features from processed Arabic tweets using N-grams and TF-IDF techniques. These features were then fed into several classifiers based on ML.

On the other hand, the authors of [47] used sentiment analysis to cluster and categorize depression levels and causes accordingly. Facebook groups were used as the data source to detect and evaluate depression among Egyptian women. In addition, a cluster LSTM model was presented to determine the sex and depression levels of Facebook users based on their text comments. Furthermore, Word2vec and LSTM were employed to classify each comment into a variety of causes of depression, such as family issues, education, employment problems, sicknesses, newborns, etc.

Another interesting study [48] used YouTube comments to protect people with diabetes from misinformation by analyzing sentiments in the comments for herbal treatment videos. For this purpose, a newly compiled dataset of 4111 comments called ADHTD was developed. This dataset was split into positive and negative classes based on the annotators' analysis. Furthermore, the Synthetic Minority Oversampling Technique (SMOTE) was employed to address the uneven distribution of the ADHTD dataset. Upon this basis, the suggested ML classifiers, particularly Support Vector Machine (SVM) and Logistic Regression (LR) models, achieved great performance with up to 92% accuracy.

In [49], sentiment analysis was used to monitor influenza epidemics in tweets from Arab countries. In their work, several ML models were proposed to classify Arabic tweets into two different classes: A valid class representing influenza-related tweets and an invalid class for tweets unrelated to influenza. Although the proposed models in this study demonstrated promising results for interpreting Arabic tweets, they did not account for the diverse Arabic dialects spoken in other Arab countries. Moreover, Twitter is less popular in the Maghreb than in the Middle East.

In [50], a significant study was discussed that concerns detecting rumors and misinformation about cancer treatment spread in Arabic content on social media. In this regard, a corpus of Arabic tweets was collected and annotated into two classes: "Rumor" and "non-Rumor". As in many studies, data were processed, and features were extracted using TF-IDF. After that, several models were proposed using several feature extraction methods, with and without oversampling techniques.

Table 1 provides a brief summary of the above-discussed works related to Arabic sentiment analysis in public health. As can be seen, various text data representations and ML models were employed. The proposed models are closely related to the used language/dialect. There has been no research into the Algerian spoken dialect related to health-based content to the best of our knowledge.

Table 1. A summary of related work for recent Arabic sentiment analysis related to public health.

Articles	Model	Disease	Social Network	#Instances	#Classes	Result
[34]	SVM with AraVec Embeddings	COVID-19	Twitter	4719	3	85.00% F1
[35]	SVM with Bigram in TF-IDF	COVID-19	Twitter	242,525	3	85.00% F1
[43]	LSTM	COVID-19	Twitter, Facebook, Youtube	747,018	6	70.00% Acc
[42]	LSTM	COVID-19	Twitter	5.5 M	6	83.00% F1
[39]	ML Classifiers based on LSTM deep features	COVID-19	Twitter	685	2	94.01% Acc
[36]	BERT-based Models	COVID-19	Twitter	1.8 M	4	97.36% Acc
[40]	ML Classifiers	COVID-19	Twitter	8786	2	87.80% Acc
[41]	AraBERT-based Model	General	Twitter	779	2	87.70% Acc
[44]	BERT-based Models	COVID-19, Mental Health	Twitter	10,000	11	72.50% F1
[46]	ML Classifiers	Depression	Twitter	4542	3	82.39% Acc
[45]	ML Classifiers	Depression	Twitter	2722	2	87.50% Acc
[47]	LSTM	Depression	Facebook	10,000	>3	85.00% Acc
[48]	ML Classifiers with SMOTE	Diabetes	YouTube	4111	2	95.00% Acc
[50]	ML Classifiers	Cancer	Twitter	208	2	83.50% Acc
[49]	ML Classifiers	Influenza	Twitter	6300	2	89.06% Acc

3. Methodology and Proposed Approach

As previously stated, the aim of this study is to propose a framework that can be integrated as part of a disease surveillance system to help in detecting, tracking, and monitoring ILIs. This section describes our proposed system architecture for detecting ILI in people based on their Facebook postings using deep learning and NLP. The model's overall architecture is depicted in Figure 1. It consists of five modules designed to process and analyze Facebook post data. The initial module consists of data collection and annotation. The second module includes all preprocessing techniques used to work with the Arabic Algerian dialect. The third module encompasses FE techniques that turn text posts into meaningful representations. The fourth module utilizes oversampling and undersampling approaches to balance the dataset. Finally, the last module is related to the suggested deep learning model for sentiment classification. The subsequent subsections provide a full description of each module.

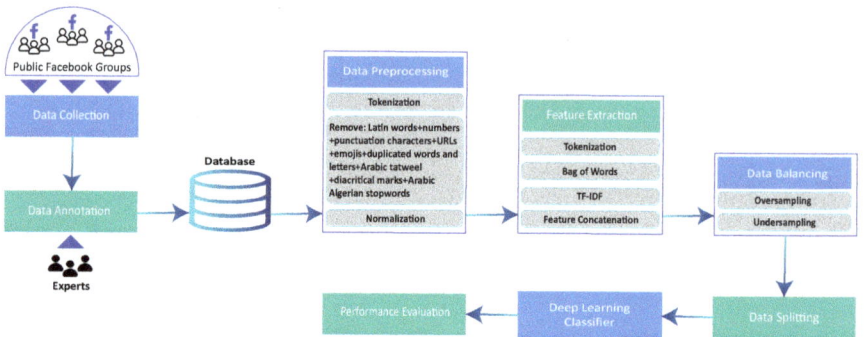

Figure 1. Adopted Methodology.

3.1. Data Collection

The data were collected from the most popular public Facebook groups in Algeria concerned with diseases and health issues. In each group, individuals express their health concerns (through wall posts) in order to receive medical advice or treatment from medical professionals or even non-medical group members. One of the benefits of using Facebook groups as a data source is that they provide data for a specific region in a specific language and area of interest, which facilitates data collection.

During the collection process, only textual content was retained; postings including photos or videos, as well as posts from group administrators, were discarded. Using multiple Facebook profiles, we collected data from March 2021 to 31 July 2021, until we obtained 21,885 postings.

The collected data consist of posts dating back to the inception of these Facebook groups on 24 April 2016. Since our analysis focuses on the detection of ILI, we have only included the data associated with the spread of COVID-19 in Algeria, i.e., from 01/01/2020 [51]. (see Figure 2).

On the other hand, it should be noted that the collected data respect the privacy and anonymity of each Facebook group's members and do not reveal the names of the posts' authors.

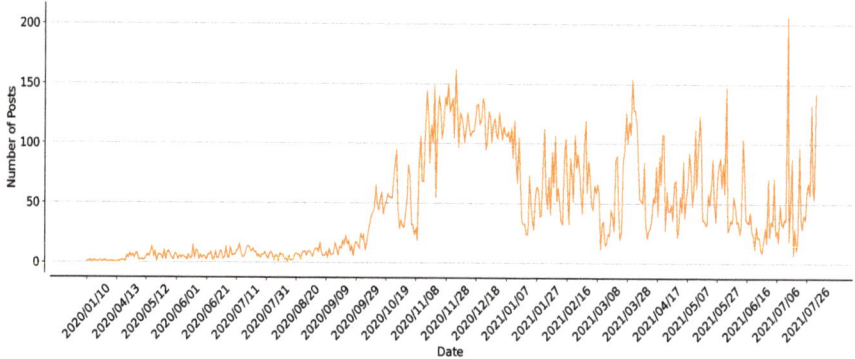

Figure 2. The volume of data collected from 01/01/2020 to 31/07/2021.

3.2. Data Annotation

After collecting data, the labeling process is performed based on the sentiment expressed in each Facebook post. This annotation stage is essential for preparing the data for the classification phase [52].

In our study, we manually annotated Facebook postings depending on the symptoms of ILI contained inside each post. They were categorized, with the aid of two annotators who are conversant with Algerian dialect, into the following three emotional categories:

- Positive: This category contains the postings whose authors claim they are experiencing ILI symptoms (such as fever, cough, sore throat, runny or stuffy nose, headaches, muscle aches, etc.) or new symptoms connected with COVID-19 (e.g., loss of taste or smell, difficulty breathing, chest pain).
- Negative-related: This category covers posts that do not indicate that the person is ill, but do provide medical advice or information regarding ILI symptoms.
- Unrelated: This category contains posts that are not related to ILI.

Table 2 illustrates examples of each of the above categories.

Table 2. Examples of posts in each sentiment class.

Class	Post in Arabic (Algerian Dialect)	Translated Post to English
Unrelated	نحتاج طبيب جلد مليح لنزع الشعر بالليزر تكون نتيجة مليحة شكون يعرف ولا تعرف	I need a good dermatologist for laser hair removal, with a good result, who knows a good doctor.
Negative-related	الكحة هي واحدة من الأعراض المُصاحبة لمرضٍ ما كالإنفلونَزا والرشح وغيرها من الأمراض المُنتشرة بالأخص في فصل الشتاء وقد تكون علامةً وإشارة للشخص لينتبه لوجود أمرٍ خطير في جسده	Cough is one of the symptoms that accompanies a disease such as influenza, cold and other diseases that are prevalent, especially in the winter season, and it may be a sign and signal for a person to be aware of the presence of something dangerous in his body.
Positive	السلام عليكم عندى السعال بزاف عندها يومين كاش دوا تع السعلة الله يجازيكم	Peace be upon you. I have a cough and I have been coughing a lot for two days. Is there a medicine for the cough, thank you.

The annotation procedure lasted around two months and yielded the following distribution of classes: Unrelated classes = 20,711 (94.63%), Positive classes = 936 (4.28%), and Negative-related classes = 238 (1.09%).

3.3. Data Analysis and Motivation

The collected data contain a wealth of information that can be used to benefit public health. Many diseases that are prevalent in Algerian society are mentioned in this information. According to N-gram analysis, the most common diseases and symptoms are: blood pressure (ضغط الدم), thyroid (الغدة الدرقية), nervous colon (قولون عصبى), shortness of breath (ضيق تنفس), blood sugar (سكر دم), and others.

In the context of our study, we compared the positive ILI cases in our database (Positive instances) with the COVID-19 cases recorded in Algeria by Johns Hopkins University's Center for Systems Science and Engineering (CSSE) [53]. We previously mentioned that COVID-19 has symptoms that are very similar to ILI, and some studies have even classified COVID-19 as an ILI [54,55]. Figure 3 shows the data from both databases normalized to the 0–1 scale.

The comparison of the graphs reveals that these two curves share certain similarities. Due to the paucity of data obtained from June to October 2020, the normalized curves exhibit a gap between instances from June to October 2020. However, there is a strong correlation between the two curves for the majority of the remaining months. Thus, we may conclude that the positive ILI patients in our dataset were related to the two waves of COVID-19 in Algeria. The first wave of COVID-19 began in October 2020 and ended in March 2021, while the second wave began in May 2021 and peaked in late July of the same year. The aforementioned investigations inspire us to present a sentiment classification system that detects ILI cases and contributes to the field of public health through intelligent systems for disease surveillance.

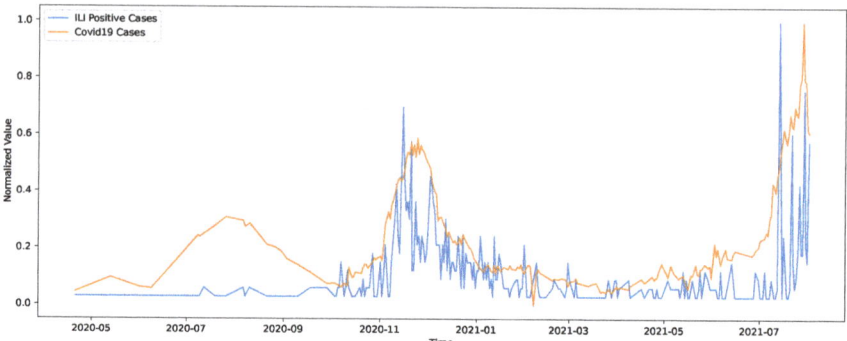

Figure 3. The positive ILI cases observed in our data compared to the COVID-19 cases from 20/04/2020 to 01/08/2021.

3.4. Data Preprocessing

Preprocessing is an important step in sentiment analysis [56]. At this stage, we eliminate all irrelevant and noisy data from the raw Facebook posts used in the sentiment classification process.

Each post was tokenized using N-grams (unigram) in order to facilitate the preparation of the raw data. Both character and word tokenization were considered. We will refer to them as Character-Tokenization and Word-Tokenization, respectively. In NLP, N-grams are sequences of N consecutive words (or characters) retrieved from textual data [57], where N = 1 corresponds to the use of uni-grams, N = 2 to bi-grams, N = 3 to tri-grams, etc.

Since Arabic is most commonly used to express opinions on Facebook in Algeria, all Latin letters and words were removed. In addition, we removed any numerals, punctuation, URLs, emojis, and repetitive words and letters from the same Facebook post. Additionally, any text posts with fewer than three words were deleted.

In addition, we eliminated Arabic stopwords (1574 words [58,59]) that do not contribute significantly to the meaning of the post. Furthermore, we suggest a new list of Arabic stopwords (400 words) based on the Algerian Arabic dialect that should likewise be eliminated.

We also converted some Arabic letters to another form (normalization). For example, "أ","إ","آ" were converted to "ا", "ى" was converted to "ي", and "ه" was converted to "ة". Moreover, for each word in the post, we removed Arabic tatweel (lengthening) and all Arabic diacritical marks (fatHah, kasrah, dhammah, shaddah, sukoon).

Before this phase, there were 21,885 raw data postings; after preprocessing, 1519 were eliminated, resulting in 20,366 posts.

The preceding preprocessing steps were applied to each Facebook post. Table 3 illustrates a data preprocessing application.

Table 3. Data preprocessing outcome on one Facebook post.

Before Data Preprocessing Phase
انا، عندي، فقدان، حساسة، الشم، والذوق، مع، انو، معنديش، حرارة، مرتفعة، هل، انا، مصاب؟ (I, have, loss, sense, smell, and taste, with, that, I don't have, high, temperature, is, I, injured?)
After Data Preprocessing Phase
فقدان، حساسة، شم، ذوق، حرارة، مرتفعة، مصاب (Loss, sensitivity, smell, taste, temperature, high, injured)

3.5. Feature Engineering

Typically, before using text data in deep learning-based NLP models, feature representations for each text instance in the dataset should be generated or extracted. All Facebook posts are integer-encoded at two levels in this regard: word-level and character-level. We used several techniques, including Tokenization, Bag of Words (BoW), Term Frequency-Inverse Document Frequency (TF-IDF), and Feature Concatenation, to convert raw texts into numerical values, as follows:

Tokenization: Each word and character is represented by a distinct integer. Following that, the integer vector representations at the word and character levels were padded with zeros to have the same lengths of $Nw = 447$ and $Nc = 2973$, which correspond to the number of words and characters in the longest text post, respectively.

BoW: This is a straightforward FE technique that counts the occurrences of each word/character in textual data to generate a numerical feature vector. BoW is widely used for topic modeling, NLP, text classification, and information retrieval due to its simplicity and effectiveness [60–62]. The size of the resulting feature vector is determined by the number of words or characters in the data.

TF-IDF: The weight of each term (word, letter) in the document is calculated using TF-IDF to determine its importance and rarity [63]. This weight is given based on its term frequency (TF) and inverse document frequency (IDF), as described in the formula below:

$$\text{TF-IDF}(t,d) = \text{TF}_{t,d} \times \text{IDF}_{t,d,N} = frq_{t,d} \times \log\left(\frac{N}{Nd_t}\right) \quad (1)$$

where $frq_{t,d}$ is the frequency of term t in document d. N is the total number of documents in the corpus. Nd_t is the number of documents containing the term t.

Feature concatenation: In addition to the previously mentioned FE approaches, we suggest feature concatenation using three different combination schemes: (1) word tokenization and character tokenization; (2) tokenization and BoW features; (3) tokenization and TF-IDF features. All of these concatenation schemes operate on word representations and/or character representations under various N-grams, including uni-grams, bi-grams, and tri-grams.

The encoding representation does not capture syntactic and semantic word relationships within text sequences [64,65]. In order to learn a mapping between words/characters during training, a word and/or character embedding layer is employed to receive the feature vector. Based on a vocabulary size of 22,752 words (135 characters), the embedding layer will generate a dense vector with dimensions $S \times E$, where S denotes the size of the feature vector and E represents the output embedding dimension. Thus, words and/or characters with similar meanings and common contexts will be mapped closely together in the vector space.

3.6. Data Balancing

Significant patient information and medical history are stored in healthcare databases. The statistics reveal that the number of diagnosed disease cases (positive) has always been less than the number of healthy instances (negative) [66]. Interestingly, this also holds true for our obtained data, where the number of people suspected of having influenza is significantly smaller than the number of healthy people (see Figure 4a). This indicates that the data set collected is imbalanced in terms of class distribution. Using imbalanced data to train sentiment classification models, according to numerous studies [67,68], may result in erroneous precision and biased predictions.

Re-sampling methods, including undersampling and oversampling techniques, are among the most effective strategies that have been widely used in the literature to address the problem of imbalanced data [69–71]. Simply put, undersampling methods remove samples from the majority class, whereas oversampling methods increase the number of samples in the minority class [70].

In our case, SMOTE [72,73] and Random Over Sampling (ROS) are used to oversample the "Positive" and "Negative-related" classes. On the other hand, from the Unrelated class that represents the majority class, we randomly selected 3000 instances to make the size of the three classes equal, as can be seen in Table 4.

The primary distinction between the two oversampling methods is that ROS is the most basic oversampling technique, in which minority class samples are randomly replicated. SMOTE, on the other hand, generates synthetic instances of the minority class along the line connecting this minority class to its nearest neighbor [72].

Figure 4 depicts the ratio of sentiment classes before and after applying balancing methods.

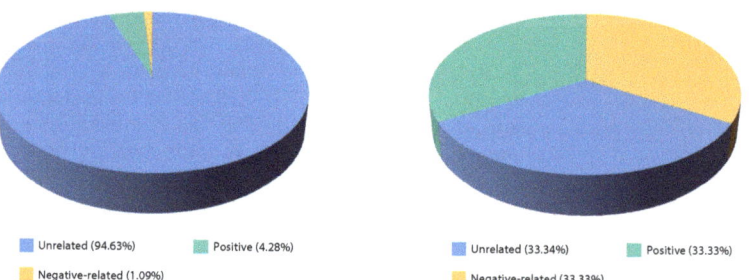

(a) Sentiment classes without balancing   (b) Sentiment classes with balancing

Figure 4. Ratio of sentiment classes with and without balancing.

Table 4. The number of instances for each class after SMOTE, ROS oversampling.

	Positive	Negative-Related	Unrelated	Total
Imbalanced	927	238	3000	4165
SMOTE	3000	3000	3000	9000
ROS	3000	3000	3000	9000

3.7. Sentiment Classification Using Deep Learning Model

In this study, we propose a deep learning model based on a convolutional neural network (CNN) [74] for ILI detection in Algerian Facebook posts.

Although CNNs have primarily been used in computer vision, they have also been used in NLP and produced impressive results [75–77]. CNNs can capture advanced features and handle input data in multiple dimensions. 2D-CNN and 3D-CNN are the most commonly used computer vision algorithms for images and video. Concurrently, 1D-CNN is used for 1D-signal processing, including biomedical data classification, speech recognition, structural health monitoring, and so on [78], as well as NLP [75,79].

Figure 5 depicts a graphical representation of the proposed 1D-CNN-based deep learning model. The proposed model's 13 layers include an input layer, an embedding layer, three 1D-convolutional layers, two max-pooling layers, four dropout layers, a global max-pooling layer, and a fully connected layer.

The input layer of our CNN model accepts each post as an integer-encoded vector. The embedding layer obtains the integer vector representation of S dimensions in order to map each word/character of a text post to an E-dimensional feature vector, producing a $S \times E$ matrix, where E represents the embedding dimension.

The output embedding matrix $S \times E$, followed by a dropout layer of 0.2, is then fed to the first 1D-convolutional layer with a filter size of 128 and a kernel size of 3. Faster than 2D-CNN [78], the kernel function in the 1D-CNN layer convolves the $S \times E$ matrix to extract hidden features and to detect local associations between adjacent characters. To capture the most relevant features and thus reduce the dimension of the preceding layer, the features from the first 1D-CNN layer are transmitted to the 1D max pooling layer, which is then followed by a dropout layer with a dropout rate of 0.2 to prevent overfitting.

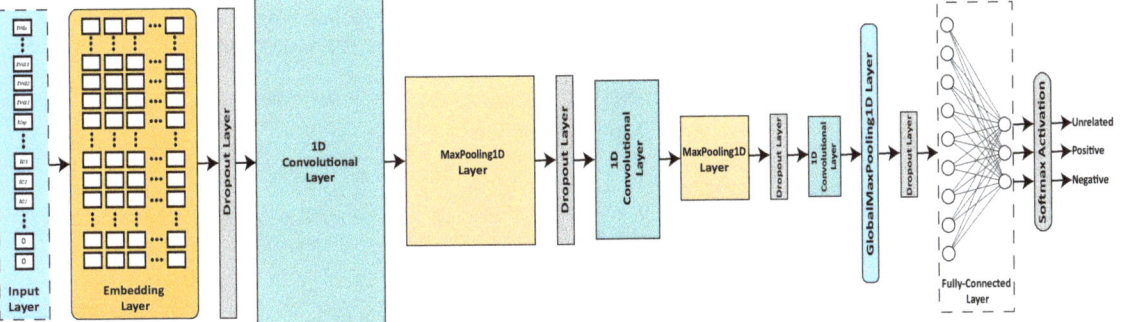

Figure 5. Architecture of the proposed 1D-CNN-based deep learning model.

To extract deeper features, an additional sequence of layers consisting of a 1D-convolutional layer with 64 filters, a 1D max pooling layer, and a dropout layer is added to the proposed model. The output of these layers is then transferred to the third 1D-CNN layer, which has a filter size of 16 and is followed by a global max pooling and dropout layer in order to reduce the network's complexity.

The final layer is the dense layer, a fully connected layer with the softmax activation function. As there are three classes, Positive, Negative-related, and Unrelated, the softmax function evaluates the probability value to return the class with the largest value.

It is important to note that several empirical attempts were made before settling on the 1D-CNN-based model, as evidenced by the results and explained in Section 4.

4. Experiments and Analysis

The aim of the conducted experiments is to evaluate the performance of the proposed 1D CNN-based model with various FE approaches and data balancing strategies. Moreover, the proposed model is compared to other baseline and state-of-the-art methods to evaluate its efficacy for sentiment classification.

A 5-fold cross-validation technique was used in our experimental study where each fold used for testing represents 20% of the data set, and the remaining 80% are used as training samples. Performance measures, including accuracy, precision, recall, F1-score, Receiver Operating Characteristics (ROC) curve, and Area Under the ROC Curve (AUC), were used to compare and evaluate the performances of the proposed model.

Furthermore, we took into account the embedding dimension (E), batch size, dropout rate, optimizer, and early stopping patience when tuning hyperparameters. Table 5 depicts the optimal parameter settings of our model.

We conducted all the experiments in Google Colab Pro (https://colab.research.google.com, accessed on 1 March 2021) Python 3 (CPU: Intel(R) Xeon(R) CPU @ 2.20 GHz; RAM: 25.46 GBs; Disk space: 166.83 GBs; GPU: Tesla P100-PCIE-16GB).

Table 5. Hyperparameter Setting.

Hyperparameter	Values Range	Optimal Value
Embedding dimension (E)	10, 20, 32, 64, 128	20
Batch size	32, 50, 64,128	128
Dropout rate	0.1, 0.2, 0.3, 0.4, 0.5	0.2
Optimizer	'SGD', 'RMSprop', 'adam', 'Nadam'	'adam'
Early stopping patience	1, 5, 10, 15, 20, 30	20

4.1. Evaluation Metrics

In this work, we adopt four evaluation metrics, including accuracy, precision, recall, and F1-score to evaluate the model's performance [80]. Each of these metrics is reported as an average of five folds. The value of each metric ranges between 0.0 (i.e., worst performance) and 1.0 (i.e., best performance), where the greater the value, the more efficient the model.

Accuracy is the proportion of correct predictions to total predictions. It is defined as:

$$\text{Accuracy} = \frac{TP + TN}{TP + TN + FP + FN} \quad (2)$$

Precision refers to the proportion of positive predictions that actually belong to the positive class, which is defined as:

$$\text{Precision} = \frac{TP}{TP + FP} \quad (3)$$

Recall denotes the proportion of real positives that are predicted correctly, calculated as follows:

$$\text{Recall} = \frac{TP}{TP + FN} \quad (4)$$

F1-score is defined as the harmonic mean of the precision and recall. It is considered as an essential performance evaluation measure for imbalanced data. F1-score is defined as follows:

$$\text{F1-score} = 2 \times \frac{\text{Precision} \times \text{Recall}}{\text{Precision} + \text{Recall}} \quad (5)$$

where, TP, FP, TN, and FN, in the above equations, refer to the number of True Positive, False Positive, True Negative, and False Negative cases, respectively.

4.2. Performance Results and Analysis

To account for the specificities of the Algerian Arabic dialect, we need to identify the best method extracting features and making sentiment classification more accurate. To identify an appropriate FE method for our dataset, we performed several feature concatenation schemes through various combinations between several feature engineering techniques, as illustrated in Table 6. Additionally, this experiment was conducted on imbalanced and oversampled data using SMOTE and ROS techniques to investigate their impact on sentiment classification.

Table 6 reveals a significant performance boost for the model using the oversampled data with ROS at all levels. Regardless of the FE approach, the proposed model achieved excellent results, with an average accuracy of 96.60%, as well as 96.60% precision, 96.50% recall, and 96.60% in F1-score while using feature concatenation between character-tokenization and word-level BoW with N-grams = 2.

Table 6. Performance of the proposed model with different FE techniques on imbalanced and oversampled data.

	#FE	FE Technique	Level	N-Grams	Performance Metrics			
					Accuracy	Precision	Recall	F1-Score
Imbalanced Dataset	1	Tokenization	Character	1	0.878	0.881	0.875	0.882
	2	Tokenization	Word	1	0.811	0.811	0.810	0.817
	3	Tokenization	Character + Word	1	0.807	0.808	0.807	0.815
	4	Tokenization + BoW	Character	1	0.883	0.886	0.881	0.885
	5	Tokenization + BoW	Character	1-2	0.892	0.895	0.888	0.895
	6	Tokenization + BoW	Character	1-3	0.891	0.894	0.888	0.894
	7	Tokenization + TF-IDF	Character	1	0.889	0.892	0.887	0.893
	8	Tokenization + TF-IDF	Character	1-2	0.896	0.898	0.893	0.898

Table 6. *Cont.*

	#FE	FE Technique	Level	N-Grams	Performance Metrics			
					Accuracy	Precision	Recall	F1-Score
	9	Tokenization + TF-IDF	Character	1-3	0.894	0.897	0.891	0.898
	10	Tokenization + BoW	Word	1	0.807	0.808	0.807	0.812
	11	Tokenization + BoW	Word	1-2	0.815	0.815	0.815	0.822
	12	Tokenization + BoW	Word	1-3	0.829	0.829	0.828	0.836
	13	Tokenization + TF-IDF	Word	1	0.822	0.825	0.821	0.828
	14	Tokenization + TF-IDF	Word	1-2	0.827	0.827	0.827	0.833
	15	Tokenization + TF-IDF	Word	1-3	0.821	0.822	0.820	0.828
	16	Tokenization + BoW	Character + Word	1	0.899	0.902	0.895	0.901
	17	Tokenization + BoW	Character + Word	1-2	0.894	0.896	0.891	0.897
	18	Tokenization + BoW	Character + Word	1-3	0.888	0.894	0.886	0.892
	19	Tokenization + TF-IDF	Character + Word	1	0.883	0.887	0.879	0.886
	20	Tokenization + TF-IDF	Character + Word	1-2	0.887	0.892	0.884	0.890
	21	Tokenization + TF-IDF	Character + Word	1-3	0.897	0.900	0.891	0.899
SMOTE	1	Tokenization	Character	1	0.884	0.886	0.883	0.882
	2	Tokenization	Word	1	0.706	0.710	0.702	0.698
	3	Tokenization	Character + Word	1	0.746	0.749	0.742	0.739
	4	Tokenization + BoW	Character	1	0.888	0.890	0.886	0.890
	5	Tokenization + BoW	Character	1-2	0.893	0.895	0.891	0.891
	6	Tokenization + BoW	Character	1-3	0.891	0.893	0.889	0.893
	7	Tokenization + TF-IDF	Character	1	0.888	0.890	0.885	0.893
	8	Tokenization + TF-IDF	Character	1-2	0.894	0.896	0.892	0.899
	9	Tokenization + TF-IDF	Character	1-3	0.895	0.897	0.892	0.895
	10	Tokenization + BoW	Word	1	0.719	0.722	0.714	0.706
	11	Tokenization + BoW	Word	1-2	0.721	0.723	0.718	0.713
	12	Tokenization + BoW	Word	1-3	0.738	0.745	0.735	0.740
	13	Tokenization + TF-IDF	Word	1	0.709	0.712	0.705	0.703
	14	Tokenization + TF-IDF	Word	1-2	0.727	0.733	0.721	0.712
	15	Tokenization + TF-IDF	Word	1-3	0.727	0.731	0.720	0.721
	16	Tokenization + BoW	Character + Word	1	0.893	0.894	0.890	0.893
	17	Tokenization + BoW	Character + Word	1-2	0.893	0.895	0.891	0.889
	18	Tokenization + BoW	Character + Word	1-3	0.891	0.893	0.888	0.892
	19	Tokenization + TF-IDF	Character + Word	1	0.898	0.900	0.896	0.899
	20	Tokenization + TF-IDF	Character + Word	1-2	0.894	0.897	0.893	0.890
	21	Tokenization + TF-IDF	Character + Word	1-3	0.893	0.894	0.890	0.891
ROS	1	Tokenization	Character	1	0.950	0.951	0.950	0.949
	2	Tokenization	Word	1	0.958	0.958	0.958	0.959
	3	Tokenization	Character + Word	1	0.950	0.951	0.950	0.952
	4	Tokenization + BoW	Character	1	0.960	0.960	0.960	0.959
	5	Tokenization + BoW	Character	1-2	0.963	0.963	0.963	0.965
	6	Tokenization + BoW	Character	1-3	0.958	0.959	0.958	0.961
	7	Tokenization + TF-IDF	Character	1	0.963	0.964	0.963	0.964
	8	Tokenization + TF-IDF	Character	1-2	0.964	0.964	0.964	0.966
	9	Tokenization + TF-IDF	Character	1-3	0.963	0.964	0.963	0.966
	10	Tokenization + BoW	Word	1	0.958	0.958	0.958	0.961
	11	Tokenization + BoW	Word	1-2	0.963	0.963	0.963	0.965
	12	Tokenization + BoW	Word	1-3	0.961	0.961	0.961	0.963
	13	Tokenization + TF-IDF	Word	1	0.961	0.962	0.961	0.962
	14	Tokenization + TF-IDF	Word	1-2	0.956	0.957	0.956	0.959
	15	Tokenization + TF-IDF	Word	1-3	0.964	0.964	0.963	0.966
	16	Tokenization + BoW	Character + Word	1	0.960	0.961	0.960	0.962
	17	Tokenization + BoW	Character + Word	1-2	**0.966**	**0.966**	**0.965**	**0.966**
	18	Tokenization + BoW	Character + Word	1-3	0.963	0.963	0.963	0.965
	19	Tokenization + TF-IDF	Character + Word	1	0.963	0.963	0.962	0.965
	20	Tokenization + TF-IDF	Character + Word	1-2	0.955	0.956	0.955	0.957
	21	Tokenization + TF-IDF	Character + Word	1-3	0.962	0.963	0.962	0.965

The values in bold are the best results for each metric.

Figure 6 displays the learning curves for the accuracy and loss of the proposed 1D-CNN-Based model during the training and validation phases while considering feature concatenation and data balance. These curves demonstrate that the proposed model was trained appropriately and that no overfitting was observed. For instance, the achieved training and validation accuracies were 98.50% and 96.70%, respectively, at epoch 155.

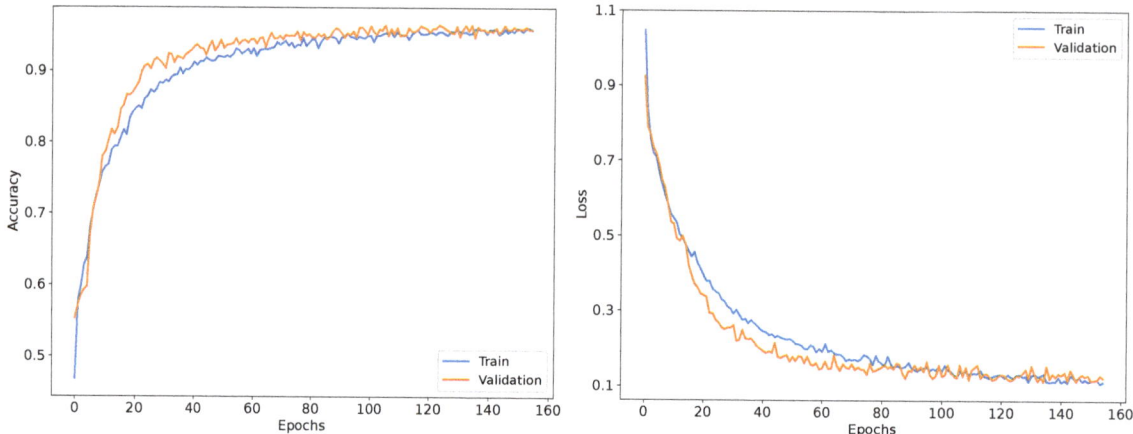

Figure 6. Accuracy and loss curves of our proposed 1D-CNN-based model.

On the other hand, a comparison of imbalanced and oversampled data using SMOTE reveals that neither has a significant advantage over the other. As we can see, the model trained on imbalanced data achieved an accuracy of 89.90%, precision of 90.20%, recall of 89.50%, and F1-score of 90.10%, while the model trained on SMOTE oversampled data achieved an accuracy of 89.80%, precision of 90.00%, recall of 89.60%, and 89.90% F1-score. In particular, the proposed model performed best with a feature concatenation that combines character-tokenization and word-level BoW using N-grams = 1 and imbalanced data. However, using SMOTE oversampled data, the proposed 1D-CNN-based model performs best with a feature concatenation combining character-tokenization and word-level TF-IDF using N-grams = 1.

Moreover, based on the results in Table 6, we graphically represented the proposed model's F1-score (suitable for imbalanced data), as illustrated in Figure 7. As such, it becomes clear that the performance of the proposed model on unbalanced and SMOTE oversampled data is negatively impacted when the FE process is based solely on words (see FE techniques: 2, 3, 10, 11, 12, 13, 14, 15). On ROS oversampled data, however, model results are unaffected when words and characters are utilized independently in the FE process. However, the performance improves when feature concatenation is employed.

As another way to evaluate these results, we present the confusion matrices depicted in Figure 8 corresponding to the proposed 1D-CNN-based model on the different datasets. A confusion matrix compares the true classes and the classes predicted by the proposed model. As shown in Figure 8a, the model using imbalanced data underperforms in identifying Positive and Negative-related sentiments, while it can achieve 92% correct predictions for the Unrelated class due to the availability of data in this category. Therefore, overfitting is most likely to occur in this case. The confusion matrix depicted in Figure 8b shows the results of the model with balanced data using SMOTE. As can be seen, 15% of positive instances were classified as Unrelated cases, which shows a misclassification issue which can be explained by the over-generalization problem related to SMOTE-based techniques.

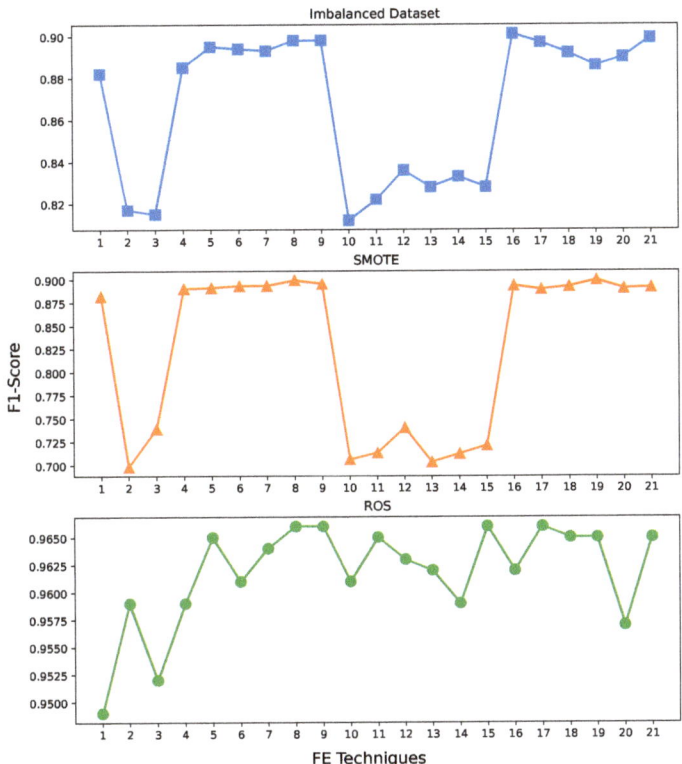

Figure 7. F1-score comparison with different FE techniques on imbalanced and oversampled data.

Finally, the confusion matrix for the model on ROS oversampled data (see Figure 8c) displays better and more accurate results in identifying all classes, resulting in high true positive rates ([94, 100%]) for Negative-related, Positive, and Unrelated sentiments.

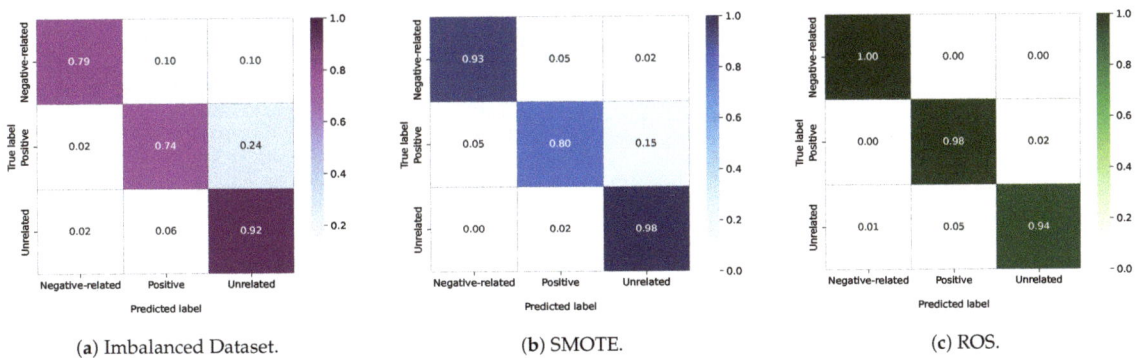

(**a**) Imbalanced Dataset.   (**b**) SMOTE.   (**c**) ROS.

Figure 8. Confusion matrix of the proposed 1D-CNN-based model on imbalanced and oversampled data.

4.3. Comparison with Baselines

To show the validity and the effectiveness of the proposed 1D-CNN-based model, the performance of our algorithm was compared with the following sentiment classification baselines:

- LSTM is a type of recurrent neural network that uses different gates to learn long-term dependencies. It has been widely used for several sentiment classification tasks [81]. In this study, this model uses one LSTM layer with 128 neurons;
- GRU is a simpler and faster version of LSTM used widely in sequence problems. It consists of two gated functions: an update gate and a reset gate. The architecture of this model consists of one GRU layer with 64 neurons;
- BiLSTM is a sequence processing model with two LSTMs, one of which processes sequence data forward and the other backward. For this model, we use one bidirectional LSTM layer with 64 neurons;
- 1D-CNN is a feed-forward artificial neural network [82] that has been successfully used in various tasks related to NLP due to its remarkable ability to extract syntactic and semantic features. The architecture of this baseline consists of one 1D-CNN layer with 64 neurons, MaxPooling1D layer, and Flatten layer;
- 1D-CNN + LSTM is a hybrid deep learning model constructed by CNN and LSTM networks and thus combines the advantages of these two networks. In this model, we use the same layers in a 1D-CNN baseline with 128 neurons, followed by an LSTM layer with 64 neurons.

In order to obtain unbiased outcomes, in each baseline model, the data are oversampled using ROS, and the same feature concatenation is adopted, combining character tokenization and word-level BoW using N-grams = 2. Furthermore, all the above models incorporate an embedding layer and one dropout layer before the fully-connected dense layer with a softmax activation function, as described before in Figure 5. Additionally, we train each baseline using the same hyperparameters setting (see Table 5).

Table 7 compares the performance results of the proposed 1D-CNN-based model to those of the five baseline models. As can be seen, the proposed 1D-CNN-based model outperforms all the previously mentioned baseline models across all evaluation metrics. Particularly, according to accuracy, our model outperforms LSTM by 16.50%, GRU by 18.80%, BiLSTM by 34.90%, 1D-CNN by 1.30%, and 1D-CNN+LSTM by 17.70%. Furthermore, the results show the effectiveness of all CNN-based models, including the 1D-CNN baseline model, compared to other methods and confirm the superior ability of CNN models in extracting the most discriminative features.

Table 7. Performance comparison of the proposed model with different baselines.

Model	Performance Metrics			
	Accuracy	Precision	Recall	F1-Score
LSTM	0.801	0.858	0.741	0.761
GRU	0.778	0.870	0.666	0.685
BiLSTM	0.617	0.840	0.464	0.490
1D-CNN	0.953	0.953	0.953	0.955
1D-CNN+LSTM	0.789	0.866	0.685	0.713
Proposed 1D-CNN-based model	**0.966**	**0.966**	**0.965**	**0.966**

The values in bold are the best results for each metric.

With an accuracy of 61.70%, the BiLSTM baseline demonstrates the futility of using backward features. LSTM and GRU outperformed BiLSTM, with LSTM achieving the best results with an accuracy of 80.10%. The above results motivated us to combine LSTM and 1D-CNN (1D-CNN + LSTM) to improve sentiment classification performance. However, the obtained results did not show the expected improvement. Therefore, we focused our research on the 1D-CNN model by introducing more 1D-convolution layers, which resulted in the proposed 1D-CNN-based architecture in Figure 5.

To further evaluate the models, we generated the corresponding ROC curves to graphically represent and compare their performance (see Figure 9). The mean AUC was calculated as 0.81, 0.84, 0.80, 0.98, 0.81, and 0.99 for the LSTM, GRU, BiLSTM, 1D-CNN,

1D-CNN+LSTM, and the proposed model, respectively. This clearly demonstrates that the proposed 1D-CNN-based model outperforms the other baseline methods.

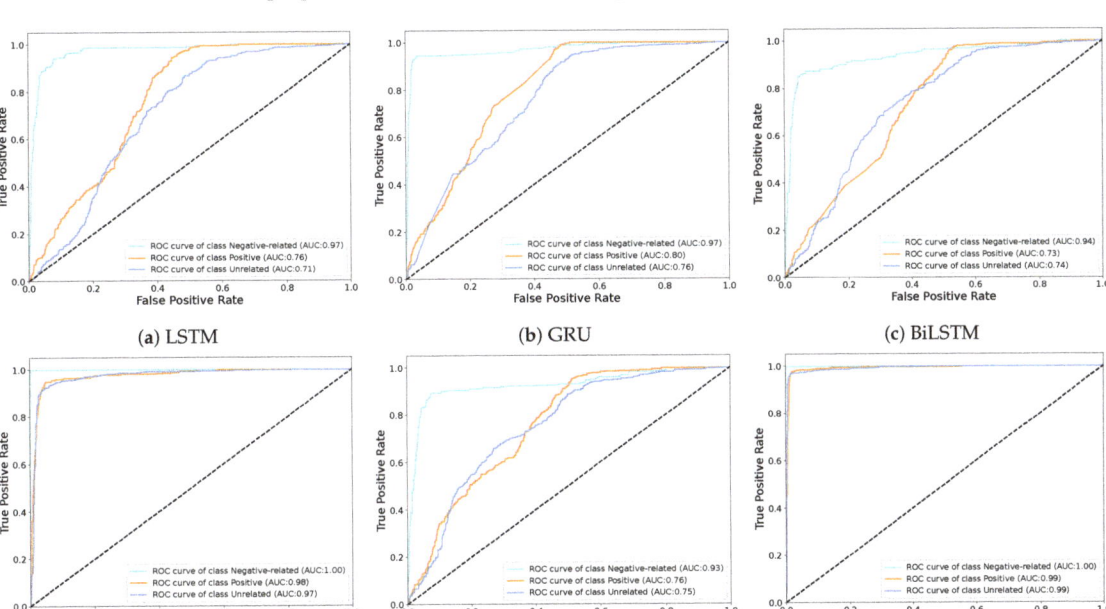

Figure 9. ROC curve comparison for (**a**) LSTM, (**b**) GRU, (**c**) BiLSTM, (**d**) 1D-CNN, (**e**) 1D-CNN+LSTM, and (**f**) the proposed 1D-CNN-based model.

4.4. Comparison with the State-of-the-Art Models

As shown in Table 8, we compared our proposed model with other state-of-the-art methods, including LSTM [42], SVM Bigram-TF-IDF [35], SVM Trigram-TF-IDF [48], Naive Bayes (NB) [49], and Random Forest (RF) [50]. The comparison was conducted using both unbalanced and balanced data based on ROS. As can be observed, the majority of comparison methods are based on traditional ML. This can be explained by the good performance of these algorithms in several sentiment classification studies, as shown in the section describing related work (see Table 1). These works are predominately based on simple feature extraction techniques, such as TF-IDF and tokenization, using various N-grams.

When balanced data are used, the results in Table 8 show that SVM-based methods perform very well, demonstrating their effectiveness in approaching sentiment classification problems [83,84], particularly in SVM Bigram-TF-IDF [35]. With an accuracy of 96.70%, the latter performed very similarly to our proposed 1D-CNN-based model, which had an accuracy of 96.60%. Other models, such as LSTM [42], SVM Trigram-TF-IDF [48], and RF [50], also performed well and were very close to each other. In contrast, the NB model has significant shortcomings when it comes to resolving the classification problem. Figure 10 depicts the confusion matrix of each model on oversampled data, which shows more details on the classification abilities of each method.

On the other hand, model comparison on imbalanced data revealed a clear difference between our proposed model and the other state-of-the-art methods, with our proposed model outperforming LSTM [42] by 7.10%, SVM Bigram-TF-IDF [35] by 9.20%, SVM Trigram-TF-IDF [48] by 14.10%, NB [49] by 62.40%, and RF [50] by 15.60%. Therefore, these results show the superiority of our proposed 1D-CNN model over the other models.

Table 8. Performance comparison of the proposed model with state-of-the-art methods.

	Model	Performance Metrics			
		Accuracy	Precision	Recall	F1-Score
ROS	LSTM [42]	0.948	0.949	0.948	0.951
	SVM Bigram-TF-IDF [35]	**0.967**	**0.968**	**0.967**	**0.967**
	SVM Trigram-TF-IDF [48]	0.955	0.960	0.955	0.955
	NB [49]	0.582	0.516	0.582	0.498
	RF [50]	0.937	0.947	0.937	0.937
	Proposed 1D-CNN-based model	0.966	0.966	0.965	0.966
Imbalanced Dataset	LSTM [42]	0.823	0.825	0.821	0.828
	SVM Bigram-TF-IDF [35]	0.802	0.819	0.802	0.766
	SVM Trigram-TF-IDF [48]	0.753	0.797	0.753	0.673
	NB [49]	0.270	0.526	0.270	0.143
	RF [50]	0.738	0.799	0.738	0.639
	Proposed 1D-CNN-based model	**0.894**	**0.896**	**0.891**	**0.897**

The values in bold are the best results for each metric.

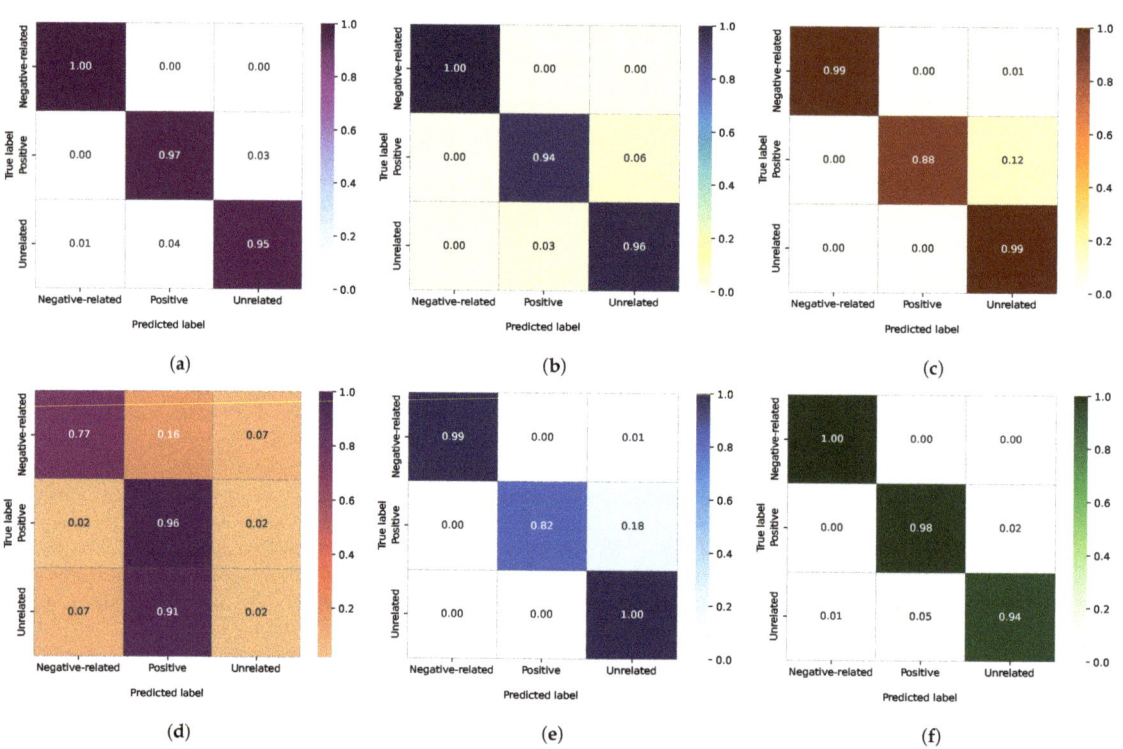

Figure 10. Confusion matrix of the proposed model compared to other state-of-the-art methods on oversampled data. (**a**) LSTM [42]. (**b**) SVM Bigram-TF-IDF [35]. (**c**) SVM Trigram-TF-IDF [48]. (**d**) NB[49]. (**e**) RF [50]. (**f**) Proposed 1D-CNN-based model.

5. Conclusions and Future Work

A framework for developing intelligent tools for disease surveillance based on social media posts is described in this paper. Core components of the proposed framework are the generation of a large dataset or corpus from Facebook posts written in the Algerian Arabic dialect and a multi-classification model based on 1D-CNN and sentiment analysis. Advanced NLP techniques were used to accurately analyze sentiments during an intensive data collection, labelling, and preparation task that led to the creation of the dataset.

Furthermore, to extract features from text data, we suggested using feature concatenation schemes that combine widely-used feature engineering techniques. In addition, ROS and SMOTE oversampling techniques were used to address the data imbalance problem. After data preprocessing, the proposed 1D-CNN classification model is a 13-layer deep learning model that has been trained and tested on the generated corpus. The experimental results demonstrate the effectiveness of the methods used for feature extraction and data balancing, and the proposed model achieved high performance with an average accuracy of 96.60% compared with the most popular models used in similar contexts such as SVM, BiLSTM, LSTM, and GRU. We intend to expand the current study to include the detection of even more diseases, which will benefit public health systems, as part of our future work. In addition, we plan to include other Arabic dialects in the proposed classification system. Combining our proposed model with a real-time data collection system to produce an online monitoring system would also be an interesting attempt.

Author Contributions: Conceptualization, A.B.; methodology, A.B. and S.M.; software, A.B.; validation, S.M. and K.A.; investigation, A.B. and K.A.; data curation, A.B. and K.A.; writing—original draft preparation, A.B.; writing—review and editing, S.M.; visualization, A.B.; supervision, A.B. and S.M. All authors have read and agreed to the published version of the manuscript.

Funding: This work is supported by Princess Nourah Bint Abdulrahman University Researchers Supporting Project number (PNURSP2022R196), Princess Nourah Bint Abdulrahman University, Riyadh, Saudi Arabia.

Institutional Review Board Statement: Not applicable.

Informed Consent Statement: Not applicable.

Data Availability Statement: All of the data and program code used in this study are available at the public repository: https://github.com/boulesnane/ILI-Detection (accessed on 1 November 2022).

Acknowledgments: The authors would like to acknowledge the Princess Nourah Bint Abdulrahman University Researchers Supporting Project number (PNURSP2022R196), Princess Nourah Bint Abdulrahman University, Riyadh, Saudi Arabia.

Conflicts of Interest: The authors declare no conflict of interest.

References

1. Rathore, A.K.; Kar, A.K.; Ilavarasan, P.V. Social Media Analytics: Literature Review and Directions for Future Research. *Decis. Anal.* **2017**, *14*, 229–249. [CrossRef]
2. Alalwan, A.A.; Rana, N.P.; Dwivedi, Y.K.; Algharabat, R. Social media in marketing: A review and analysis of the existing literature. *Telemat. Inform.* **2017**, *34*, 1177–1190. [CrossRef]
3. Anstead, N.; O'Loughlin, B. Social Media Analysis and Public Opinion: The 2010 UK General Election. *J. Comput.-Mediat. Commun.* **2014**, *20*, 204–220. [CrossRef]
4. Zeng, B.; Gerritsen, R. What do we know about social media in tourism? A review. *Tour. Manag. Perspect.* **2014**, *10*, 27–36. [CrossRef]
5. Yang, F.C.; Lee, A.J.; Kuo, S.C. Mining Health Social Media with Sentiment Analysis. *J. Med. Syst.* **2016**, *40*, 236. [CrossRef]
6. Haber, I.E.; Toth, M.; Hajdu, R.; Haber, K.; Pinter, G. Exploring Public Opinions on Renewable Energy by Using Conventional Methods and Social Media Analysis. *Energies* **2021**, *14*, 3089. [CrossRef]
7. Corbett, J.; Savarimuthu, B.T.R. From tweets to insights: A social media analysis of the emotion discourse of sustainable energy in the United States. *Energy Res. Soc. Sci.* **2022**, *89*, 102515. [CrossRef]
8. DataReportal. Digital 2022: Global Overview Report. 2022. Available online: https://datareportal.com/reports/digital-2022-global-overview-report (accessed on 1 September 2022).
9. DataReportal. Digital 2022: Algeria. 2022. Available online: https://datareportal.com/reports/digital-2022-algeria (accessed on 1 September 2022).
10. CDC. Overview of Influenza Surveillance in United States. USA: Department of Health and Human Services, Center for Disease Control. 2020. Available online: https://www.cdc.gov/flu/weekly/overview.htm (accessed on 8 February 2021).
11. Guan, W.-J.; Ni, Z.-Y.; Hu, Y.; Liang, W.-H.; Ou, C.-Q.; He, J.-X.; Liu, L.; Shan, H.; Lei, C.-L.; Hui, D.S.; et al. Clinical Characteristics of Coronavirus Disease 2019 in China. *N. Engl. J. Med.* **2020**, *382*, 1708–1720. [CrossRef]
12. Murtas, R.; Decarli, A.; Russo, A.G. Trend of pneumonia diagnosis in emergency departments as a COVID-19 surveillance system: A time series study. *BMJ Open* **2021**, *11*, e044388. [CrossRef]

13. Rustam, F.; Khalid, M.; Aslam, W.; Rupapara, V.; Mehmood, A.; Choi, G.S. A performance comparison of supervised machine learning models for Covid-19 tweets sentiment analysis. *PLOS ONE* **2021**, *16*, e0245909. [CrossRef]
14. Chakraborty, K.; Bhatia, S.; Bhattacharyya, S.; Platos, J.; Bag, R.; Hassanien, A.E. Sentiment Analysis of COVID-19 tweets by Deep Learning Classifiers—A study to show how popularity is affecting accuracy in social media. *Appl. Soft Comput.* **2020**, *97*, 106754. [CrossRef] [PubMed]
15. Naseem, U.; Razzak, I.; Khushi, M.; Eklund, P.W.; Kim, J. COVIDSenti: A Large-Scale Benchmark Twitter Data Set for COVID-19 Sentiment Analysis. *IEEE Trans. Comput. Soc. Syst.* **2021**, *8*, 1003–1015. [CrossRef] [PubMed]
16. Lim, S.; Tucker, C.S.; Kumara, S. An unsupervised machine learning model for discovering latent infectious diseases using social media data. *J. Biomed. Inform.* **2017**, *66*, 82–94. [CrossRef] [PubMed]
17. García-Díaz, J.A.; Apolinario-Arzube, Ó.; Medina-Moreira, J.; Luna-Aveiga, H.; Lagos-Ortiz, K.; Valencia-García, R. Sentiment Analysis on Tweets related to infectious diseases in South America. In Proceedings of the Euro American Conference on Telematics and Information Systems, Fortaleza, Brazil, 12–15 November 2018. [CrossRef]
18. Babu, N.V.; Kanaga, E.G.M. Sentiment Analysis in Social Media Data for Depression Detection Using Artificial Intelligence: A Review. *SN Comput. Sci.* **2021**, *3*, 74. [CrossRef]
19. Hassan, A.U.; Hussain, J.; Hussain, M.; Sadiq, M.; Lee, S. Sentiment analysis of social networking sites (SNS) data using machine learning approach for the measurement of depression. In Proceedings of the 2017 International Conference on Information and Communication Technology Convergence (ICTC), Jeju, Korea, 18–20 October 2017. [CrossRef]
20. Joshi, M.L.; Kanoongo, N. Depression detection using emotional artificial intelligence and machine learning: A closer review. *Mater. Today Proc.* **2022**, *58*, 217–226. [CrossRef]
21. Hinduja, S.; Afrin, M.; Mistry, S.; Krishna, A. Machine learning-based proactive social-sensor service for mental health monitoring using twitter data. *Int. J. Inf. Manag. Data Insights* **2022**, *2*, 100113. [CrossRef]
22. Sumathy, B.; Kumar, A.; Sungeetha, D.; Hashmi, A.; Saxena, A.; Shukla, P.K.; Nuagah, S.J. Machine Learning Technique to Detect and Classify Mental Illness on Social Media Using Lexicon-Based Recommender System. *Comput. Intell. Neurosci.* **2022**, *2022*, 5906797. [CrossRef]
23. Jain, V.K.; Kumar, S. Effective surveillance and predictive mapping of mosquito-borne diseases using social media. *J. Comput. Sci.* **2018**, *25*, 406–415. [CrossRef]
24. Gabarron, E.; Dechsling, A.; Skafle, I.; Nordahl-Hansen, A. Discussions of Asperger Syndrome on Social Media: Content and Sentiment Analysis on Twitter. *JMIR Form. Res.* **2022**, *6*, e32752. [CrossRef]
25. Amin, S.; Uddin, M.I.; Hassan, S.; Khan, A.; Nasser, N.; Alharbi, A.; Alyami, H. Recurrent Neural Networks With TF-IDF Embedding Technique for Detection and Classification in Tweets of Dengue Disease. *IEEE Access* **2020**, *8*, 131522–131533. [CrossRef]
26. Yousefinaghani, S.; Dara, R.; Poljak, Z.; Bernardo, T.M.; Sharif, S. The Assessment of Twitter's Potential for Outbreak Detection: Avian Influenza Case Study. *Sci. Rep.* **2019**, *9*, 18147. [CrossRef] [PubMed]
27. Zhang, F.; Luo, J.; Li, C.; Wang, X.; Zhao, Z. Detecting and Analyzing Influenza Epidemics with Social Media in China. In *Advances in Knowledge Discovery and Data Mining*; Springer International Publishing: Berlin/Heidelberg, Germany, 2014; pp. 90–101. [CrossRef]
28. Alessa, A.; Faezipour, M. A review of influenza detection and prediction through social networking sites. *Theor. Biol. Med. Model.* **2018**, *15*. [CrossRef] [PubMed]
29. Jain, V.K.; Kumar, S. An Effective Approach to Track Levels of Influenza-A (H1N1) Pandemic in India Using Twitter. *Procedia Comput. Sci.* **2015**, *70*, 801–807. [CrossRef]
30. Zuccon, G.; Khanna, S.; Nguyen, A.; Boyle, J.; Hamlet, M.; Cameron, M. Automatic detection of tweets reporting cases of influenza like illnesses in Australia. *Health Inf. Sci. Syst.* **2015**, *3*, S4. [CrossRef] [PubMed]
31. Alkouz, B.; Aghbari, Z.A.; Al-Garadi, M.A.; Sarker, A. Deepluenza: Deep learning for influenza detection from Twitter. *Expert Syst. Appl.* **2022**, *198*, 116845. [CrossRef]
32. Asiri, E.; Khalifa, M.; Shabir, S.A.; Hossain, M.N.; Iqbal, U.; Househ, M. Sharing sensitive health information through social media in the Arab world. *Int. J. Qual. Health Care* **2016**, *29*, 68–74. [CrossRef]
33. Birjali, M.; Kasri, M.; Beni-Hssane, A. A comprehensive survey on sentiment analysis: Approaches, challenges and trends. *Knowl.-Based Syst.* **2021**, *226*, 107134. [CrossRef]
34. Binkheder, S.; Aldekhyyel, R.N.; AlMogbel, A.; Al-Twairesh, N.; Alhumaid, N.; Aldekhyyel, S.N.; Jamal, A.A. Public Perceptions around mHealth Applications during COVID-19 Pandemic: A Network and Sentiment Analysis of Tweets in Saudi Arabia. *Int. J. Environ. Res. Public Health* **2021**, *18*, 13388. [CrossRef]
35. Aljameel, S.S.; Alabbad, D.A.; Alzahrani, N.A.; Alqarni, S.M.; Alamoudi, F.A.; Babili, L.M.; Aljaafary, S.K.; Alshamrani, F.M. A Sentiment Analysis Approach to Predict an Individual's Awareness of the Precautionary Procedures to Prevent COVID-19 Outbreaks in Saudi Arabia. *Int. J. Environ. Res. Public Health* **2020**, *18*, 218. [CrossRef]
36. Essam, N.; Moussa, A.M.; Elsayed, K.M.; Abdou, S.; Rashwan, M.; Khatoon, S.; Hasan, M.M.; Asif, A.; Alshamari, M.A. Location Analysis for Arabic COVID-19 Twitter Data Using Enhanced Dialect Identification Models. *Appl. Sci.* **2021**, *11*, 11328. [CrossRef]
37. Addawood, A. Coronavirus: Public Arabic Twitter Data Set. 2020. Available online: https://openreview.net/forum?id=ZxjFAfD0pSy (accessed on 22 October 2022).

38. Zaidan, O.; Callison-Burch, C. The arabic online commentary dataset: An annotated dataset of informal arabic with high dialectal content. In Proceedings of the 49th Annual Meeting of the Association for Computational Linguistics: Human Language Technologies, Portland, OR, USA, 19–24 June 2011; pp. 37–41.
39. Alabrah, A.; Alawadh, H.M.; Okon, O.D.; Meraj, T.; Rauf, H.T. Gulf Countries' Citizens' Acceptance of COVID-19 Vaccines—A Machine Learning Approach. *Mathematics* **2022**, *10*, 467. [CrossRef]
40. Alqurashi, S.; Hamoui, B.; Alashaikh, A.; Alhindi, A.; Alanazi, E. Eating Garlic Prevents COVID-19 Infection: Detecting Misinformation on the Arabic Content of Twitter. *arXiv* **2021**, arXiv:2101.05626.
41. Albalawi, Y.; Nikolov, N.S.; Buckley, J. Pretrained Transformer Language Models Versus Pretrained Word Embeddings for the Detection of Accurate Health Information on Arabic Social Media: Comparative Study. *JMIR Form. Res.* **2022**, *6*, e34834. [CrossRef] [PubMed]
42. Al-Laith, A.; Alenezi, M. Monitoring People's Emotions and Symptoms from Arabic Tweets during the COVID-19 Pandemic. *Information* **2021**, *12*, 86. [CrossRef]
43. Ghanem, A.; Asaad, C.; Hafidi, H.; Moukafih, Y.; Guermah, B.; Sbihi, N.; Zakroum, M.; Ghogho, M.; Dairi, M.; Cherqaoui, M.; et al. Real-Time Infoveillance of Moroccan Social Media Users' Sentiments towards the COVID-19 Pandemic and Its Management. *Int. J. Environ. Res. Public Health* **2021**, *18*, 12172. [CrossRef]
44. Alturayeif, N.; Luqman, H. Fine-Grained Sentiment Analysis of Arabic COVID-19 Tweets Using BERT-Based Transformers and Dynamically Weighted Loss Function. *Appl. Sci.* **2021**, *11*, 10694. [CrossRef]
45. Almouzini, S.; khemakhem, M.; Alageel, A. Detecting Arabic Depressed Users from Twitter Data. *Procedia Comput. Sci.* **2019**, *163*, 257–265. [CrossRef]
46. Musleh, D.A.; Alkhales, T.A.; Almakki, R.A.; Alnajim, S.E.; Almarshad, S.K.; Alhasaniah, R.S.; Aljameel, S.S.; Almuqhim, A.A. Twitter Arabic Sentiment Analysis to Detect Depression Using Machine Learning. *Comput. Mater. Contin.* **2022**, *71*, 3463–3477. [CrossRef]
47. ElDin, D.M.; Hamed, M.; Eldeen, N. SentiNeural: A Depression Clustering Technique for Egyptian Women Sentiments. *Int. J. Adv. Comput. Sci. Appl.* **2019**, *10*. [CrossRef]
48. Yafooz, W.M.; Alsaeedi, A. Sentimental Analysis on Health-Related Information with Improving Model Performance using Machine Learning. *J. Comput. Sci.* **2021**, *17*, 112–122. [CrossRef]
49. Baker, Q.; Shatnawi, F.; Rawashdeh, S.; Al-Smadi, M.; Jararweh, Y. Detecting Epidemic Diseases Using Sentiment Analysis of Arabic Tweets. *JUCS J. Univers. Comput. Sci.* **2020**, *26*, 50–70. [CrossRef]
50. Saeed, F.; Yafooz, W.M.S.; Al-Sarem, M.; Abdullah, E. Detecting Health-Related Rumors on Twitter using Machine Learning Methods. *Int. J. Adv. Comput. Sci. Appl.* **2020**, *11*. [CrossRef]
51. Lounis, M. Epdemiology of coronavirus disease 2020 (COVID-19) in Algeria. *New Microbes New Infect.* **2021**, *39*, 100822. [CrossRef] [PubMed]
52. Al-Twairesh, N.; Al-Khalifa, H.; Al-Salman, A.; Al-Ohali, Y. AraSenTi-Tweet: A Corpus for Arabic Sentiment Analysis of Saudi Tweets. *Procedia Comput. Sci.* **2017**, *117*, 63–72. [CrossRef]
53. Dong, E.; Du, H.; Gardner, L. An interactive web-based dashboard to track COVID-19 in real time. *Lancet Infect. Dis.* **2020**, *20*, 533–534. [CrossRef]
54. Amin, M.T.; Fatema, K.; Arefin, S.; Hussain, F.; Bhowmik, D.R.; Hossain, M.S. Obesity, a major risk factor for immunity and severe outcomes of COVID-19. *Biosci. Rep.* **2021**, *41*, BSR20210979. [CrossRef]
55. Kumar, R.; Arora, R.; Bansal, V.; Sahayasheela, V.J.; Buckchash, H.; Imran, J.; Narayanan, N.; Pandian, G.N.; Raman, B. Accurate Prediction of COVID-19 using Chest X-Ray Images through Deep Feature Learning model with SMOTE and Machine Learning Classifiers. *medRxiv* **2020**. [CrossRef]
56. Symeonidis, S.; Effrosynidis, D.; Arampatzis, A. A comparative evaluation of pre-processing techniques and their interactions for twitter sentiment analysis. *Expert Syst. Appl.* **2018**, *110*, 298–310. [CrossRef]
57. Sidorov, G.; Velasquez, F.; Stamatatos, E.; Gelbukh, A.; Chanona-Hernández, L. Syntactic N-grams as machine learning features for natural language processing. *Expert Syst. Appl.* **2014**, *41*, 853–860. [CrossRef]
58. El-Khair, I.A. Effects of stop words elimination for Arabic information retrieval: A comparative study. *Int. J. Comput. Inf. Sci.* **2006**, *4*, 119–133.
59. PyArabic. PyPI. Available online: https://pypi.org/project/PyArabic/ (accessed on 1 September 2021).
60. Qin, Z.; Cong, Y.; Wan, T. Topic modeling of Chinese language beyond a bag-of-words. *Comput. Speech Lang.* **2016**, *40*, 60–78. [CrossRef]
61. HaCohen-Kerner, Y.; Miller, D.; Yigal, Y. The influence of preprocessing on text classification using a bag-of-words representation. *PLoS ONE* **2020**, *15*, e0232525. [CrossRef] [PubMed]
62. Passalis, N.; Tefas, A. Learning bag-of-embedded-words representations for textual information retrieval. *Pattern Recognit.* **2018**, *81*, 254–267. [CrossRef]
63. Zhang, W.; Yoshida, T.; Tang, X. A comparative study of TF* IDF, LSI and multi-words for text classification. *Expert Syst. Appl.* **2011**, *38*, 2758–2765. [CrossRef]
64. Lauriola, I.; Lavelli, A.; Aiolli, F. An introduction to Deep Learning in Natural Language Processing: Models, techniques, and tools. *Neurocomputing* **2022**, *470*, 443–456. [CrossRef]

65. Kumar, V.; Recupero, D.R.; Riboni, D.; Helaoui, R. Ensembling Classical Machine Learning and Deep Learning Approaches for Morbidity Identification From Clinical Notes. *IEEE Access* **2021**, *9*, 7107–7126. [CrossRef]
66. Kaur, H.; Pannu, H.S.; Malhi, A.K. A Systematic Review on Imbalanced Data Challenges in Machine Learning. *ACM Comput. Surv.* **2019**, *52*, 1–36. [CrossRef]
67. Singla, Z.; Randhawa, S.; Jain, S. Sentiment analysis of customer product reviews using machine learning. In Proceedings of the 2017 International Conference on Intelligent Computing and Control (I2C2), Coimbatore, India, 23–24 June 2017; pp. 1–5. [CrossRef]
68. Tolba, M.; Ouadfel, S.; Meshoul, S. Hybrid ensemble approaches to online harassment detection in highly imbalanced data. *Expert Syst. Appl.* **2021**, *175*, 114751. [CrossRef]
69. Ramos-Pérez, I.; Arnaiz-González, Á.; Rodríguez, J.J.; García-Osorio, C. When is resampling beneficial for feature selection with imbalanced wide data? *Expert Syst. Appl.* **2022**, *188*, 116015. [CrossRef]
70. Liang, D.; Yi, B.; Cao, W.; Zheng, Q. Exploring ensemble oversampling method for imbalanced keyword extraction learning in policy text based on three-way decisions and SMOTE. *Expert Syst. Appl.* **2022**, *188*, 116051. [CrossRef]
71. Houssein, E.H.; Hassaballah, M.; Ibrahim, I.E.; AbdElminaam, D.S.; Wazery, Y.M. An automatic arrhythmia classification model based on improved Marine Predators Algorithm and Convolutions Neural Networks. *Expert Syst. Appl.* **2022**, *187*, 115936. [CrossRef]
72. Chawla, N.V.; Bowyer, K.W.; Hall, L.O.; Kegelmeyer, W.P. SMOTE: Synthetic minority over-sampling technique. *J. Artif. Intell. Res.* **2002**, *16*, 321–357. [CrossRef]
73. Elreedy, D.; Atiya, A.F. A Comprehensive Analysis of Synthetic Minority Oversampling Technique (SMOTE) for handling class imbalance. *Inf. Sci.* **2019**, *505*, 32–64. [CrossRef]
74. Li, Z.; Liu, F.; Yang, W.; Peng, S.; Zhou, J. A Survey of Convolutional Neural Networks: Analysis, Applications, and Prospects. *IEEE Trans. Neural Netw. Learn. Syst.* **2021**, 1–21. [CrossRef] [PubMed]
75. Kim, Y. Convolutional Neural Networks for Sentence Classification. *arXiv* **2014**, arXiv:1408.5882.
76. Giménez, M.; Palanca, J.; Botti, V. Semantic-based padding in convolutional neural networks for improving the performance in natural language processing. A case of study in sentiment analysis. *Neurocomputing* **2020**, *378*, 315–323. [CrossRef]
77. Conneau, A.; Schwenk, H.; Barrault, L.; Lecun, Y. Very Deep Convolutional Networks for Text Classification. *arXiv* **2016**, arXiv:1606.01781.
78. Kiranyaz, S.; Avci, O.; Abdeljaber, O.; Ince, T.; Gabbouj, M.; Inman, D.J. 1D convolutional neural networks and applications: A survey. *Mech. Syst. Signal Process.* **2021**, *151*, 107398. [CrossRef]
79. Sharma, A.K.; Chaurasia, S.; Srivastava, D.K. Sentimental Short Sentences Classification by Using CNN Deep Learning Model with Fine Tuned Word2Vec. *Procedia Comput. Sci.* **2020**, *167*, 1139–1147. [CrossRef]
80. Grandini, M.; Bagli, E.; Visani, G. Metrics for Multi-Class Classification: An Overview. *arXiv* **2020**, arXiv:2008.05756.
81. Joseph, J.; Vineetha, S.; Sobhana, N. A survey on deep learning based sentiment analysis. *Mater. Today Proc.* **2022**, *58*, 456–460. [CrossRef]
82. Gu, J.; Wang, Z.; Kuen, J.; Ma, L.; Shahroudy, A.; Shuai, B.; Liu, T.; Wang, X.; Wang, G.; Cai, J.; et al. Recent advances in convolutional neural networks. *Pattern Recognit.* **2018**, *77*, 354–377. [CrossRef]
83. Li, X.; Li, J.; Wu, Y. A Global Optimization Approach to Multi-Polarity Sentiment Analysis. *PLoS ONE* **2015**, *10*, e0124672. [CrossRef] [PubMed]
84. AlBadani, B.; Shi, R.; Dong, J. A Novel Machine Learning Approach for Sentiment Analysis on Twitter Incorporating the Universal Language Model Fine-Tuning and SVM. *Appl. Syst. Innov.* **2022**, *5*, 13. [CrossRef]

Article

ECG Signal Features Classification for the Mental Fatigue Recognition

Eglė Butkevičiūtė [1,*], Aleksėjus Michalkovič [2] and Liepa Bikulčienė [2]

[1] Department of Software Engineering, Kaunas University of Technology, Studentu Str. 50, 51368 Kaunas, Lithuania
[2] Department of Applied Mathematics, Kaunas University of Technology, Studentu Str. 50, 51368 Kaunas, Lithuania
* Correspondence: egle.butkevicute@ktu.lt

Abstract: Mental fatigue is a major public health issue worldwide that is common among both healthy and sick people. In the literature, various modern technologies, together with artificial intelligence techniques, have been proposed. Most techniques consider complex biosignals, such as electroencephalogram, electro-oculogram or classification of basic heart rate variability parameters. Additionally, most studies focus on a particular area, such as driving, surgery, etc. In this paper, a novel approach is presented that combines electrocardiogram (ECG) signal feature extraction, principal component analysis (PCA), and classification using machine learning algorithms. With the aim of daily mental fatigue recognition, an experiment was designed wherein ECG signals were recorded twice a day: in the morning, i.e., a state without fatigue, and in the evening, i.e., a fatigued state. PCA analysis results show that ECG signal parameters, such as Q and R wave amplitude values, as well as QT and T intervals, presented with the largest differences between states compared to other ECG signal parameters. Furthermore, the random forest classifier achieved more than 94.5% accuracy. This work demonstrates the feasibility of ECG signal feature extraction for automatic mental fatigue detection.

Keywords: machine learning; ECG; mental fatigue; signal analysis; classification

MSC: 62P10; 68T09

Citation: Butkevičiūtė, E.; Michalkovič, A.; Bikulčienė, L. ECG Signal Features Classification for the Mental Fatigue Recognition. *Mathematics* **2022**, *10*, 3395. https://doi.org/10.3390/math10183395

Academic Editor: Manuel Franco

Received: 29 July 2022
Accepted: 15 September 2022
Published: 19 September 2022

Publisher's Note: MDPI stays neutral with regard to jurisdictional claims in published maps and institutional affiliations.

Copyright: © 2022 by the authors. Licensee MDPI, Basel, Switzerland. This article is an open access article distributed under the terms and conditions of the Creative Commons Attribution (CC BY) license (https://creativecommons.org/licenses/by/4.0/).

1. Introduction

Fatigue is a phenomenon that has not been conventionally defined and relates, in particular, to reactions to various loads and conditions, including experiences and states of mind. Fatigue is also defined as a subjective lack of physical and/or mental energy perceived by an individual to interfere with their usual or desired activities [1].

Usually, fatigue is a state associated with a weakening or depletion of an individual's physical and/or mental resources, ranging from a general state of lethargy to a specific burning sensation in a particular muscle. Physical fatigue leads to an inability to continue functioning at a normal level of activity. Mental fatigue is a state of tiredness that sets in when brain energy levels are depleted. In the literature, fatigue is differentiated into six types: social, emotional, physical, pain, mental, and chronic illnesses; furthermore, these types are often distinguished in terms of physical and mental fatigue [2].

Many people experience mental fatigue (MF) in daily life or work activities that require sustained mental efficiency [3]. MF can be defined as a psychobiological state caused by prolonged episodes of cognitive exertion [4]. Overwork-related disorders, such as cerebrovascular/cardiovascular diseases, diabetes, and cancer, are major health issues worldwide [5,6]. However, fatigue is a common symptom in both sick and healthy people [7]. Fatigue is one of the most crucial factors contributing to decreased performance among aircraft pilots; car drivers [8]; individual athletes [9]; and team sport athletes, such as soccer players [10]; among other professions. Furthermore, mental fatigue may reduce cognitive resources and impair balance performance [11]. In some literature reports, cognitive fatigue (CF) is considered the main component of mental fatigue. CF is known to cause attention deficits, leading to poor situational awareness and impaired vigilance [12]. Various cognitive tests are used to detect mental fatigue, such as the psychomotor vigilance task, the Stroop task, the AX-continuous performance test, and the TloadDback test; however, such tasks takes time and require additional performance [13].

In the literature, electroencephalographic (EEG) signal features are studied and analyzed as a relevant tool for the detection of mental fatigue [14,15]. However, it is not always possible to record EEG signals and conduct measurements in real-life environments due to electric line noise or noise from electronic equipment [16]. In other research, electromyography (EMG) and electro-oculography (EOG) signals, as well as inertial measurement unit (IMU) sensors, 3D optical tracking techniques, infrared cameras, and accelerometer signals, have been analyzed [17,18]. Scientists have proposed artificial intelligence and expert system-based solutions that combine several sensors and devices [19]. EEG, together with ECG signal recordings, are very common in fatigue detection tasks for drivers, for whom exhaustion and distraction may lead to serious accidents [20]. In the literature, real-time monitoring systems are used to detect heart anomalies [21]. In such cases, ECG signals are classified for in an alert configuration to notify designated healthcare providers. However, most systems are designed to detect various heart anomalies and might not be applicable to fatigue recognition.

When the sympathetic nervous system is active to a heightened degree, the heart regularly beats at a faster pace, whereas the opposite occurs when the parasympathetic nervous system is active to a heightened degree. Therefore, during mental fatigue or stress, heart rate variability (HRV) is lower than normal. This parameter is a convenient tool to monitor personal health using simple smart devices, such as watches; however, the results are consistently inaccurate and depend on individual human characteristics. Furthermore, to acquire accurate results, the non-linear characteristics of heart rate (HR) must be investigated [22].

Usually, a classification algorithm consists of two main parts: primary signal transformation and classification. The primary transformation process is based on feature analysis to extract the raw signal and reduce its dimensions [23]. Classifying ECG signals into pathologies or health stages is a complicated task that requires recognition of the signal structure. Generally, a combination of several classification algorithms is used to solve this problem [24]. A similar classification problem is considered in the fatigue identification process. In this article, the research object is not a continuous ECG signal or its segments but separate signals that were recorded at different times of the day (in the morning and the evening). Usually, fatigue occurs after intensive physical or mental activity, mostly at the end of the working day. Instant physical fatigue detection after an intensive training session is a simple task because the heart is loaded and works faster. However, mental fatigue detection is a more complicated task because there is no clear difference in terms of ECG signal parameters.

Another technique used in medicine is principal component analysis (PCA). This method of analysis is used to detect early stages of diseases and to diagnose the cardiac health of patients [25–30]. This technique was used in the present study to evaluate the differences between ECG features in different states and to detect mental fatigue symptoms.

This research focuses on mental fatigue recognition in healthy individuals based on their health condition at different times of the day. All data are split into two datasets. Data gathered in the first subset corresponds to a normal state without fatigue, whereas the second subset consists of data recorded in the evening, representing a fatigued state. The main purpose of this paper is to determine whether ECG signal features reveal differences in mental states. However, the proposed framework is not designed for diagnostic purposes and should be tested on clinical patients for use as a specific criterion for mental fatigue diagnosis.

The structure of this article is as follows: Section 2 highlights the recent literature on mental fatigue detection using various biosignal classification methods and other techniques. The experimental design, data description, and applied methods are presented in Section 3. Section 4 consists of data analysis using the PCA method, and analysis of the performance of ML algorithms. Finally, a discussion and conclusions are presented in Section 5.

2. Related Work

Modern wearable devices, such as eye-tracking technologies, are becoming increasingly popular. Li et al. [31] demonstrated the feasibility of applying wearable eye-tracking technology to identify and classify mental fatigue in construction equipment operators. The Toeplitz inverse covariance-based clustering (TICC) method was used to determine multiple levels of mental fatigue, and the classification task was performed using support vector machine (SVM) methods. However, this study consisted of a narrow target group and might not be applicable in other fields.

In [32], EEG and HRV signals were observed and analyzed to detect the impacts of prolonged cognitive activity on the central nervous system and the autonomic nervous system. EEG signal wavelet packet parameters and HRV spectral indices were combined to measure changes in mental fatigue. Although 91% classification accuracy was achieved, two separate devices for EEG and HRV recordings are not efficient and barely usable in daily life activities. Furthermore, EEG signals are most likely contaminated by muscle artifacts, which may lead to incorrect interpretation. For this reason, various filtering and feature extraction methods have been proposed [33,34]. Preprocessed EEG signals can be used in multilevel fatigue recognition tasks. In [35], EEG signals were classified using a K-nearest neighbor (KNN) classifier, achieving 100% accuracy. These results demonstrate the feasibility of using EEG signals and extracted features to successfully detect mental fatigue. However, in this case, the data were collected using a driving simulator and a brain cap with 32 electrodes placed on the skin surface, which may not be applicable in real-world environments.

Portable single-channel electrocardiogram equipment ("LaPatch") was used in [5] to record and analyze ECG signals. Eight heart rate variability (HRV) indicators were considered and classified using SVM, KNN, naïve Bayes (NB), and logistic regression (LR) models. Although the technique is promising, due to the small sample size, only 75.5% accuracy was achieved. In another study, researchers developed an automatic mental stress detection system based on ECG signals recorded from T-shirts and analyzed using machine learning (ML) classifiers: decision tree (DT), random forest (RF), NB, and LR [6]. The best-performing model achieved an accuracy of 94.1%. However, in this research only mental stress detection was considered, and the same technique may not be applicable to mental fatigue recognition.

Wearable devices for HRV recordings are usually user-friendly and convenient. Furthermore, they do not require electrodes to be attached directly to the skin surface. Many studies have focused on heart rate (HR) and time- or spectral-domain HRV analysis. For example, in [36], mental and physical fatigue detection methods were applied based on HR, HRV, skin temperature, and pulse. Causal convolutional neural networks (cCNN) and RF models were used to detect and distinguish between mental and physical fatigue. However, only 66.2% accuracy was achieved in the mental fatigue recognition task. Other similar research used a polar H10 chest strap and photoplethysmography (PPG) technology for HRV detection [37]. Results were compared with those obtained with a Bittium FarosTM 360 device, which records a single ECG lead. Furthermore, the study included several watches, such as the Actigraph wGT3X-BT, Garmin, and Polar Vantage V. Various time- and spectral-domain HRV parameters were estimated and compared. However, no decision-making or fatigue recognition techniques were applied.

Modern wearable electronics have been developed in recent years, such as epidermal electronics systems (EES) and electronic tattoos (E-tattoos), with which ECG signals, respiration rate, and galvanic skin responses (GSR) can be recorded [38]. Comparing three

ML models (SVM, KNN, and DT) the obtained signals were classified with 89% accuracy. Although these technologies are promising, the equipment has not been fully tested and prepared for production. A transparent eye detection system can also be considered a modern wearable device [39]. Such a system can acquire movement in the pupil and detect blinking based on the light that is reflected from the eye. A summary of these and similar wearable devices and corresponding research in recent literature is presented in Table 1.

Table 1. Wearable devices used to detect mental fatigue in recent literature.

Wearable Device	Target Group	Sensor	Method
Neuroscan system Synamps Scan 4.3 [3]	Drivers	EEG, ECG, HRV	Spectral and statistical analysis, entropy
"LaPatch" [5]	Healthy adults	ECG, HRV	SVM, KNN, NB, LR
Wearable eye-tracking technology [31]	Construction equipment operators	TICC	SVM
T-shirt [6]	Healthy adults	ECG	DT, RF, NB, LR
32-electrode ActiCapTM and BrainAmpTM systems [17]	-	EEG, EOG, ECG	SVM, ANOVA
Medtronic PL-Winsor 2.35 EEG system [16]	-	EEG	SVM
IMU sensors [18]	Young healthy adults	IMU, HRV	RF, SVM, LR
Neuroscan 32-channel system [32]	Healthy adults	EEG, ECG, HRV	Spectral analysis, SVM
Everion device [36]	Healthy adults	HRV, skin temperature	Statistical analysis, CNN, RF
Polar H10 chest strap [37]	Military members	HRV, ECG	Statistical analysis
Neuroscan Scan 4.3 [15]	Drivers (men)	EEG	SVM, DT, RF, KNN, and others
[20]	Train drivers	EOG, EEG, ECG	Correlation analysis, ANOVA, SVM, PCA
Driving simulator and brain cap [35]	Drivers	EEG	KNN
E-tattoos [38]	Healthy adults	ECG, respiration, GSR	SVM, KNN, DT
Transparent eye detection system [39]	National Aeronautics	Eye blinks	Statistical analysis

Because HRV analysis cannot achieve high accuracy in mental fatigue recognition and EEG signals are not reliable in daily life activities, in this paper, a novel framework is proposed for mental fatigue detection that involves analysis and classification of ECG signal features. Furthermore, principal component analysis (PCA) is applied to distinguish between ECG signal parameters in two different states (in the morning, i.e., a non-fatigued state, and in the evening, i.e., fatigue condition). The classification task is performed using several models: KNN, LDA, DT, and RF.

3. Materials and Methods

In this section, we describe the proposed data analysis and classification processes that are essential for mental fatigue recognition. The whole process flow consists of five main parts: ECG signal recording, ECG signal preprocessing, feature extraction, PCA analysis, and ML performance (see Figure 1). The experiment was designed with ECG signal registration twice a day (in the morning and in the evening). HRV analysis or whole ECG signal classification techniques failed on the mental fatigue recognition task, so we proposed the extraction of ECG signal features only when applying classification algorithms, such as KNN, DT, RF, etc. Before implementation of a machine learning technique, PCA analysis was applied to make sure that there were significant differences between ECG signal features in separate states. This research was conducted with the approval of the Kaunas Regional Research Ethics Committee of our institution under the project name, "Various directionalities on physical exercise effects that are based on differential learning methodology, and impact on heart and cardiovascular system" (biomedical ethics permission number BE-2–38, Lithuania).

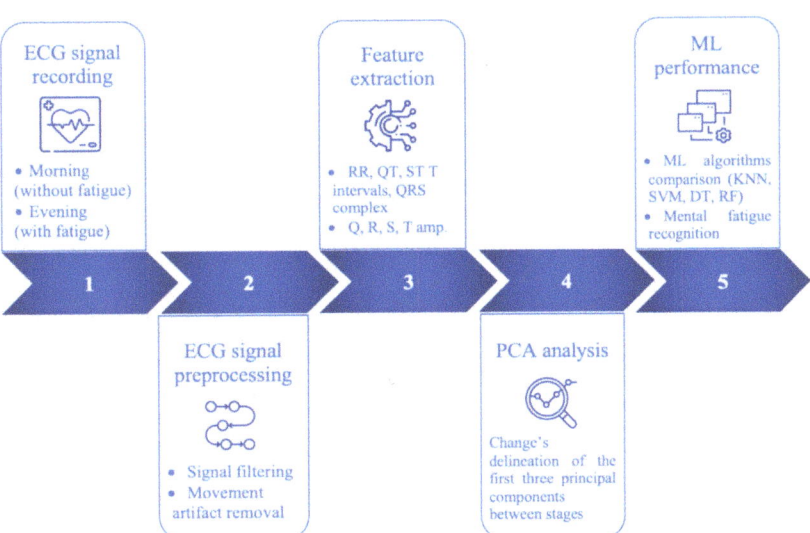

Figure 1. Proposed framework for mental fatigue detection.

3.1. ECG Signal Characteristics and Data Analysis

In this study, various ECG signal features were analyzed and classified. The protocol consisted of two 60 sec recordings of each participant. These recordings enabled the detection of differences in ECG signal parameters, which were estimated at the beginning of the day and in the evening. V5 lead was selected in this research (see an example in Figure 2), with each parameter representing a separate component of heart activity (see Table 2).

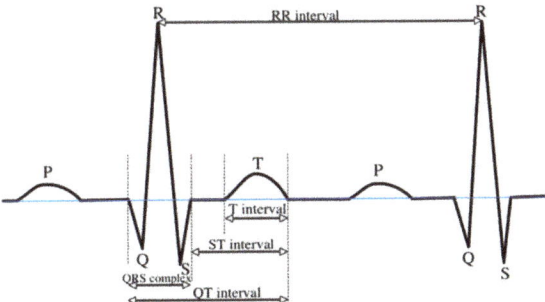

Figure 2. ECG signal features in the V5 lead.

All ECG signal features are visible in the properly filtered data. Numerous methods can be applied to ECG signal preprocessing, such as moving average (MA), exponential smoothing, or linear Fourier transformation. Usually, biological signals are contaminated with various environmental disturbances. The main purpose of signal filtering algorithms is to divide separate components into informative parts and undesirable noise. Furthermore, biological signals that are recorded during movement are highly contaminated by various disturbances, and sometimes, noise overlaps the signal itself. The main problem associated with movement-contaminated signals is non-stationary, low-frequency noise (a trend resulting from movement artifacts). In such cases, ordinary filtering methods for signal processing are insufficient or unreliable. In this research, ECG signals were recorded while each participant was standing so that only small movement artifacts might affect the signal. Therefore, a Butterworth filter was used for noise reduction [40].

Table 2. ECG signal features and causes of electrical impulses in the heart (based on [41]).

Wave Type and Parameter	Heart Activity
Q wave	The anteroseptal part of the myocardial ventricle is activated
R wave	Depolarization of myocardial ventricles
S wave	The posterior diaphragmatic part of the ventricles is activated
T wave	Rapid ventricular repolarization
QT interval	Time required for the electrical system to fire an impulse through the ventricles and then recharge
ST interval	The initial, slow phase of ventricular repolarization
RR interval	Time elapsed between two successive R waves of the QRS signal on an electrocardiogram (and its reciprocal, the HR); a function of intrinsic properties of the sinus node, as well as autonomic influence
QRS complex	A combination of the Q wave, R wave, and S wave; the "QRS complex" represents ventricular depolarization

ECG signal preprocessing continues with feature extraction (ECG parameter estimation). ECG feature extraction starts with R peak detection and QRS complex identification. All other parameters, such as Q and S peaks, RR interval, and T wave, are based on R peaks or QRS complex positions. In this research, 9 ECG parameters were estimated: Q, R, S, and T amplitudes; QT, ST, RR, and QRS intervals; and T-wave intervals. All ECG features were estimated using the NeuroKit2 toolbox in Python programming language [42].

3.2. Research Design and Data Acquisition

In this research, a CardioScout Multi-device was used to record ECG signals and transmit them to mobile devices or tablets. The signal recording frequency was 500 Hz, and each segment was 60 s long. In this article, the analyzed experiments comprise data recorded twice a day (in the morning and in the evening) for signal parameter classification and fatigue recognition. In Table 3, two different states are defined: A1 in the morning and A2 in the evening.

Table 3. ECG signal recordings in different states.

State	Description	Recording Duration
A1	In the morning, i.e., a state without fatigue	60 s
A2	In the evening, i.e., fatigued condition	60 s

In total, 60 healthy adults were recruited (aged between 24 and 34 years) without a diagnosis of health pathologies or overwork-related problems. In this research, 8271 measurements were estimated from 60 participants via ECG signal recordings: 4195 corresponding to state A1 and 4076 corresponding to state A2.

3.3. Data Description and Visualization

As mentioned in the previous section, two states were analyzed in this study (A1 in the morning and A2 in the evening). All parameter data were normalized by subtracting means and dividing by the standard deviation. This type of data normalization is needed to eliminate differences in individual heart rate characteristics of each person. For example, some participants may have higher (or lower) ECG signal amplitude values compared to others in both states (in the morning and in the evening), which may affect classification results, indicating fatigued state in both datasets. Furthermore, normalization increases data integrity without distorting differences in the ranges of values. The distribution and scatter plots are shown in Figure 3. Pearson correlation coefficients are presented in Figure 4 (Y represents the state: a value of 1 corresponds to the fatigued condition or state (A2), and a value of 0 corresponds to the fatigue-free condition of state (A1)). Comparing data from different states, clear differences could be noticed. For example, histograms of the Sa parameter look similar, but A2 data are shifted, with higher values compared to state A1 values (see Figure 3). Furthermore, some ECG signal parameter values overlap. For example, there is no significant difference between states A1 and A2 in terms of RR interval values. Therefore, typical HRV analysis fails in mental fatigue detection, with low classification accuracies.

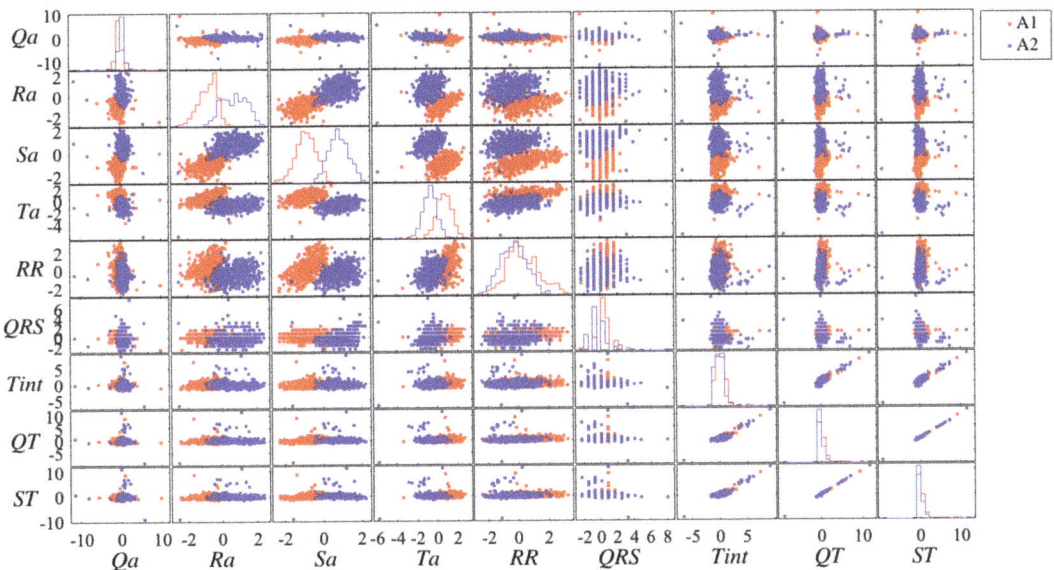

Figure 3. Histograms and scatter plots of ECG signal parameters in different states.

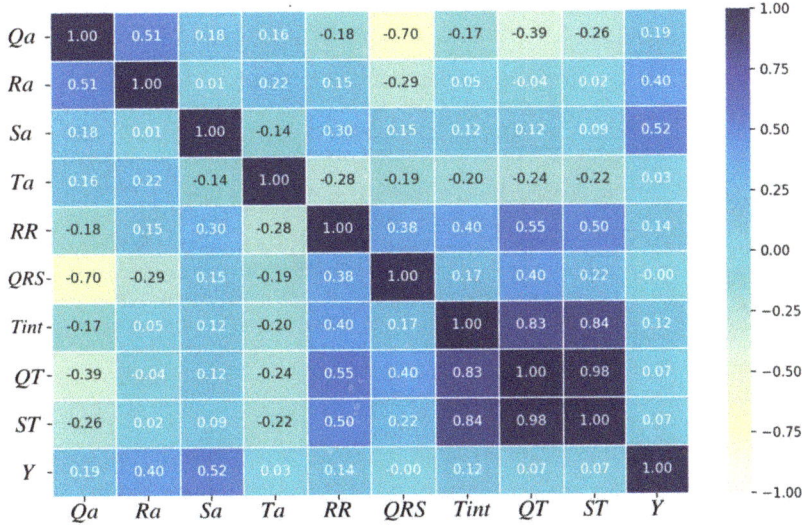

Figure 4. Pearson correlation coefficients between ECG signal parameters.

Figure 3 shows linear dependences between several parameters (for example, between parameters QT and ST). Similar results are shown in Figure 4 (for example, the Pearson correlation coefficient for ST and QT reaches 0.98). Additionally, a strong dependence (Pearson correlation coefficient > 0.8) is evident between Tint and QT or ST. Although some parameters may be eliminated in the classification step, it is not clear which parameters have a greater impact on classification accuracy. In the initial stage of the classification process, all ECG signal features were included (all 9 ECG parameters).

3.4. Principal Component Analysis

Principal component analysis (PCA) was applied to distinguish between ECG features in the morning and in the evening. The general idea behind this technique is to obtain new latent variables based on the original data. The newly defined principal components reflect directions of maximal variance of the projected data and form a new orthonormal basis of the original vector space.

PCA is commonly used to reduce the dimensions of the collected data matrix by choosing k principal components (PC1, PC2, ..., PCk) and evaluating the amount of information explained by the chosen components as follows:

$$\sum_{i=1}^{k} \frac{\lambda_i}{Tr(C)}, \qquad (1)$$

where λ_i is the i-th eigenvalue of the covariance matrix (C), and $Tr(C)$ is its trace, i.e., the sum of all entries on the main diagonal. Furthermore, the original data are projected to the low-dimension hyperplane spanned by components PC1, PC2, ..., PCk, thus extracting the essential information from the initial data cloud. In this study, three principal components were considered, and the obtained results were visualized via 3D plots to emphasize the desired differences in mental states.

3.5. Machine Learning Technique

The use of social media, smartphones, smartwatches, computers, and even portable devices provides big data about various mental and physical health disorders. Effective algorithms for big data processing are usually based on machine learning (ML) techniques.

Various ML algorithms have been created for data classification and prognosis. There are three main categories: Supervised learning: examples of such methods include support vector machine (SVM), k-nearest neighbors (KNN), decision tree (DT), and random forest (RF); Unsupervised learning: these methods include neural networks (NN) and clustering; Semi-supervised learning: this category includes methods such as semi-supervised SVM, mixed models, etc. [43].

Supervised learning is used to analyze the labeled data and make predictions or classify data into different categories, whereas unsupervised learning methods can learn from unlabeled data and extract similar patterns. The third group is semi-supervised learning, which involves the analysis of data with and without labels; such methods are used when there is not enough labeled data for classification or prognosis.

One way to evaluate the potential accuracy of predictions is to use a confusion matrix [44]. The entries in this matrix indicate the correctness of the prediction or classification of distinct fault categories compared to actual observed values. To evaluate the quality of the selected predictions or data classifications, additional measurements can be considered. Two widely used standard statistics are accuracy (*acc*) and *F*1 score. These are estimated using Equation (2).

$$acc = \frac{TP + TN}{TP + TN + FP + FN}, \quad F1 = \frac{2 \cdot TP}{2 \cdot TP + FP + FN}; \qquad (2)$$

where *TN* corresponds to true-negative elements after prediction (correctly predicted as not correct), *TP* represents true-positive elements (correctly predicted as correct), *FP* represents false-positive elements, and *FN* represents false-negative elements. Although popular in ML analysis, both *acc* and *F*1 ignore the size of each category in the confusion matrix. Therefore, the additional statistic called Matthew's correlation coefficient (*MCC*) was measured [45]. This coefficient is calculated as follows:

$$MCC = \frac{TP \cdot TN - FP \cdot FN}{\sqrt{(TP+FP) \cdot (TP+FN) \cdot (TN+FP) \cdot (TN+FN)}}, \quad (3)$$

The value of this coefficient is in the range $[-1; 1]$, where -1 is interpreted as the worst-case scenario, whereas 1 is the best possible value.

Additionally, in 1960 J. Cohen revealed that there is a level of algorithm precision when the algorithm is no longer capable of predicting correctly, i.e., the prediction becomes as accurate as a simple guess. This level is called Cohen's Kappa (κ) statistic and can be expressed as follows:

$$\kappa = \frac{accuracy - d}{1-d}, \text{ where } d = \frac{TP+FN}{TP+TN+FP+FN}. \quad (4)$$

Three main intervals are considered: if $\kappa > 0.75$, then the value is viewed as perfect; if κ is in the range of $[0.4, 0.75]$ the value is sufficient; and if $\kappa < 0.4$, it is considered weak [46].

In this research, we compared multiple ML methods, revealing that the RF algorithm classifies signal parameters with the highest accuracy. For RF algorithms in the feature extraction process, the Gini coefficient needs to be estimated. If n is defined as the number of samples in node t and each node has c classes, then the number of samples belonging to class i is n_i. The ratio ($p(i|t)$) is expressed as:

$$p(i|t) = \frac{n_i}{n}. \quad (5)$$

In this case, the Gini coefficient G for each node is defined as [47]:

$$G_c(t) = 1 - \sum_{i=1}^{c} p(i|t)^2. \quad (6)$$

Generally, the RF classifier is based on DT and consists of three main steps: input all data into root nodes for every DT; minimize the Gini coefficient by dividing data into separate nodes; recursively repeat all steps at each node that needs to be split until the root mean square error (RMSE) value for the node falls below a threshold value or the tree reaches a defined depth.

RF may consist of many separate decision trees that train each model concurrently using random data samples. This type of RF is also called a bagged tree algorithm. Consistent DT models that are trained consecutively are called boosted trees. In this case, every DT model learns from previous model errors. Usually, this type of RF has more nodes [48]. Like any other classifier, the random forest algorithm requires two datasets: one for training and one for testing. In ML techniques, the more data provided, the higher the classification accuracy. Additionally, in every ML technique, overfitting of training data should be considered, which may negatively affect algorithm performance, thereby reducing prediction accuracy. Cross validation can be applied to avoid overfitting. This method involves splitting data into different groups and estimating the classification accuracy for each group. In this case, the training dataset is divided into two groups: a training set and a validation set. If cross validation is performed several times, in each iteration, different data samples are assigned to the testing data subset [49].

4. Experimental Results

4.1. PCA Implementation

In this research, PCA was applied in two ways. First, all collected data were considered at once. Then, the data were factored into morning and evening subsets, and PCA was performed on each subset separately.

Considering all collected data, the main parameters of Tint, QT, and ST, which reflect the first principal component, have an interval, whereas the second principal component mainly covers amplitude parameters, i.e., Qa and Ra. These results are consequential, as during casual daytime activity, the amplitude of the heart rate changes less than the intervals between two waves. A summary of the PCA results for the whole dataset is presented in Table 4. A 3D plot of the obtained results was drawn using RStudio tools (see Figure 5). A significant difference was observed between the two groups: yellow dots represent the morning state, and e blue pyramids represent the evening state. The change in parameters is more noticeable in the evening subset. Moreover, the evening data can be further grouped into several clusters, whereas the morning data are mainly concentrated in the center.

Table 4. Summary of principal components using factored data.

Data	PC1	PC2	PC3	PC4	PC5	PC6	PC7	PC8
Qa	0.241	−0.581	0.033	−0.219	0.138	−0.107	0.443	−0.573
Ra	0.026	−0.568	0.026	0.552	0.280	0.459	−0.203	0.202
Sa	−0.131	−0.232	−0.608	−0.625	0.164	0.212	−0.238	0.200
Ta	−0.311	−0.230	−0.367	0.243	−0.787	0.035	0.024	−0.189
RR	−0.365	−0.150	−0.295	0.280	0.341	−0.722	0.104	0.173
QRS	−0.279	0.421	−0.355	0.217	0.333	0.414	0.387	−0.345
Tint	−0.417	−0.153	0.326	−0.211	−0.099	0.185	0.606	0.489
QT	−0.483	−0.012	0.246	−0.089	0.123	0.060	−0.244	−0.314
ST	−0.456	−0.102	0.337	−0.141	0.061	−0.023	−0.342	−0.261

To explore the visible difference between the two investigated states, the data were split into two separate subsets. The obtained PCA results for each of the individual states show that the interval parameters are considerably represented in the first component. This influence remains consistent, regardless of the considered state. On the other hand, the influence of the amplitude parameters changed significantly. This difference is even more obvious in the second principal component, where these parameters outshine most other parameters in the case of the morning data subset. The explicit expressions of the first three principal components are presented for each of the states, along with the percentage of data explained by these components in parentheses (see Table 5).

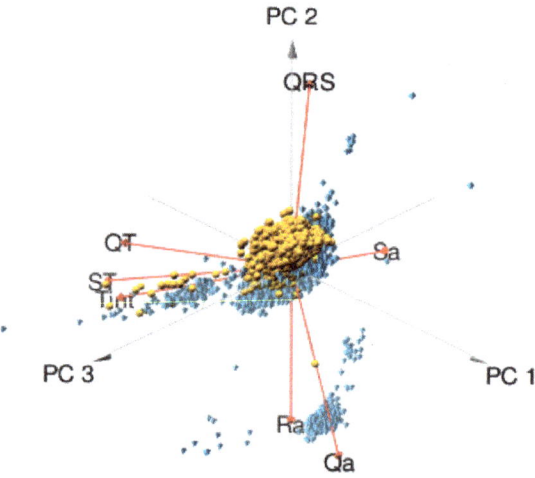

Figure 5. 3D plot of PCA results for both data subsets: yellow dots represent the morning state; blue pyramids—evening state.

Table 5. Summary of the first three principal components using factored data (morning data (M): 73.6%; evening data (E): 79.5%).

Data	PC1M	PC2M	PC3M	PC1E	PC2E	PC3E
Qa	0.083	0.651	0.181	0.313	−0.482	−0.187
Ra	0.102	−0.614	0.251	0.060	−0.585	−0.303
Sa	−0.341	0.217	−0.443	0.118	0.241	−0.518
Ta	−0.279	−0.384	−0.266	−0.328	−0.050	−0.426
RR	−0.371	0.019	−0.121	−0.341	−0.069	−0.537
QRS	−0.245	−0.034	−0.529	−0.287	0.480	−0.185
Tint	−0.402	−0.024	0.388	−0.402	−0.253	0.194
QT	−0.469	0.036	0.269	−0.472	−0.108	0.148
ST	−0.458	0.041	0.346	−0.440	−0.232	0.204

Based on the PCA results for the two considered states, we assume that the fatigue factor is represented by the significant changes in the influence of the amplitude parameters on the first and second principal components. Moreover, substantial changes occurred in the distribution of points in 3D plots obtained for the first three principal components for each of the states (see Figure 6).

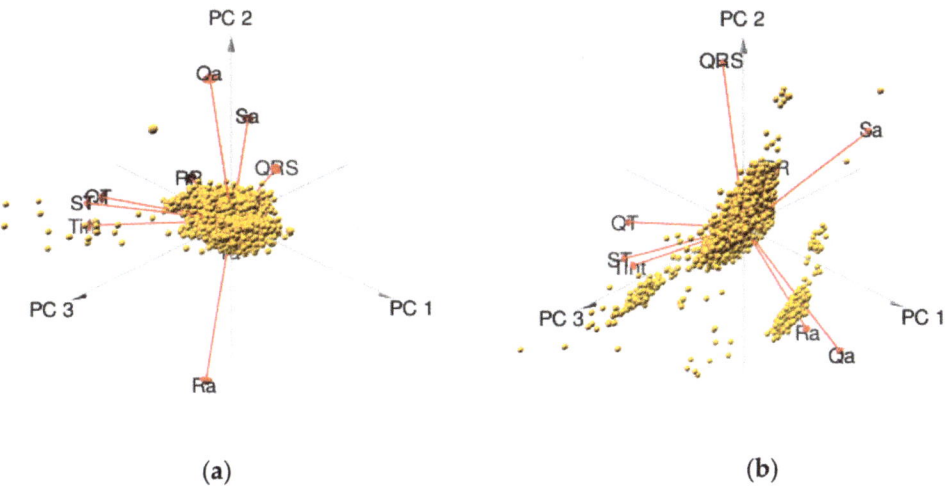

Figure 6. 3D plots of the PCA performed on factorial data: (**a**) morning; (**b**) evening.

4.2. Machine Learning Performance

At the beginning of this research, multiple ML algorithms were compared (see Table 6 and Figure 7) using all 9 ECG parameters. In this case, the input dataset was split into training with validation (70%) and testing (30%) subsets. Analysis of data shows that a lower allocation of data to the testing subset slightly reduces the overall accuracy of the KNN, DT, and RF algorithms. For example, reducing the testing dataset to 20% of the total data for the RF model resulted in a reduction in accuracy of 2%. This may also result in lower quality and feasibility of selected classifiers. To ensure that the model did not overfit the training data, 10-fold cross validation was applied for all ML methods. In Figure 7 shows the validation accuracy results following 100 calculations. Table 6 shows averaged, F1, and MCC values for a better comparison of the analyzed ML algorithms.

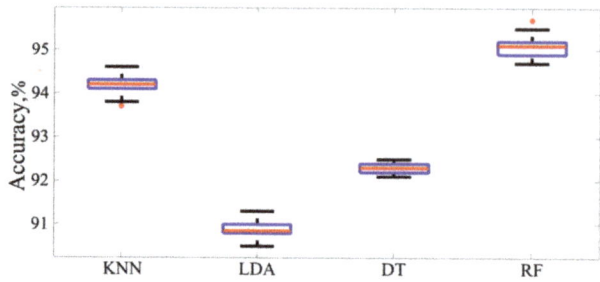

Figure 7. Boxplots of ML algorithm accuracies.

According to the results presented in Table 6 and Figure 7, the best algorithm for physiological fatigue recognition is the random forest model, which classified states A1 and A2 with a validation accuracy of more than 95%. Multiple hyperparameter values were analyzed for all compared ML techniques. The best results were obtained when DT had 100 maximum splits and 9 maximum surrogates in each node. In this case, the selected RF algorithm consisted of 30 DTs, with a maximum of 20 splits for every tree. Based on these results (see Table 6), a random forest algorithm was selected for further analysis.

Table 6. Average accuracy of ML algorithms.

Method	Accuracy	F1	MCC
KNN	94.19%	0.94	0.87
LDA	76.82%	0.75	0.46
SVM	90.89%	0.91	0.82
DT	92.31%	0.92	0.83
RF	95.08%	0.95	0.90

RF algorithms include multiple DTs, in which every node is a condition of a single feature and is designed to split the dataset into two subsets. Basically, similar response values end up in the same dataset. As previously mentioned, different ECG signal features may have varying impacts on the final classification result. Usually, the importance of a feature is estimated based on the degree to which it decreases the entropy in each tree.

Only four ECG signal characteristics (Sa, Ra, Ta, and QT) are important for A1 and A2 state classification (mental fatigue recognition) if the selected threshold is equal to 0.8 (see Figure 8). Based on these results, the final RF model was designed using only those four ECG parameters.

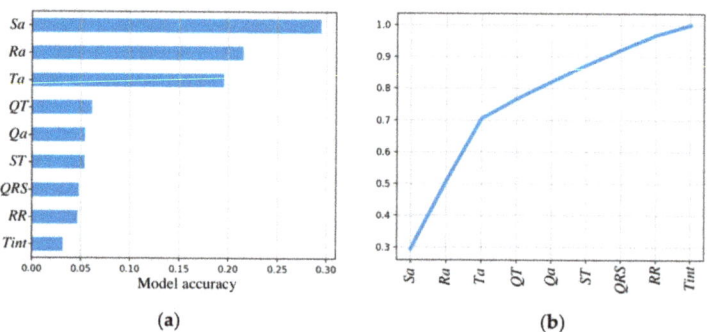

Figure 8. The importance of ECG parameters for classification of states A1 and A2: (**a**) ECG parameters and FR accuracy; (**b**) cumulative accuracy curve for the RF model.

A random forest is a complex algorithm with multiple hyperparameters, all of which should be optimized. In this research, a random search algorithm was selected based on a grid search technique; this algorithm attempts every possible combination. However, the number of iterations is limited, and possible randomly selected hyperparameter values are declared in advance. Only the best hyperparameter values are saved to maximize the FR validation accuracy. The optimal RF model identified in this research consists of 40 DTs with a maximum tree height of 7 and a minimum of 40 samples in a node for a split.

K-times cross validation was used in the RF model training process. The training dataset was split into two subsets: the training set and the testing set. In this case, the same steps were repeated 10 times, and averaged results were estimated. Receiver operating characteristic curves (ROCs) are commonly used to visually represent of k-fold cross validation. These curves help to plot and illustrate the true-positive (TP, correctly classified values of state A2 presented on the y-axis) and false-positive (FP, misclassified A1 state values presented on the x-axis) rates. The 10-fold cross validation and averaged curve for states A1 and A2 are illustrated in Figure 9. In this figure, the area under the ROC curve (AUC) provides an accumulated measure of performance across all possible classification thresholds. In this research, the AUC indicated the probability that the model ranks a random value from state A2 more highly than a random value from state A1. Analysis of multiple scenarios with various k values shows that in most cases, a lower number of k-folds may negatively affect recall or precision values. However, the AUC value remains similar, and further investigation is needed to determine the number of k-folds in the cross-validation process. Due to small changes in the results, we decided not to present all possible combinations and instead use only 10-fold cross validation as an example.

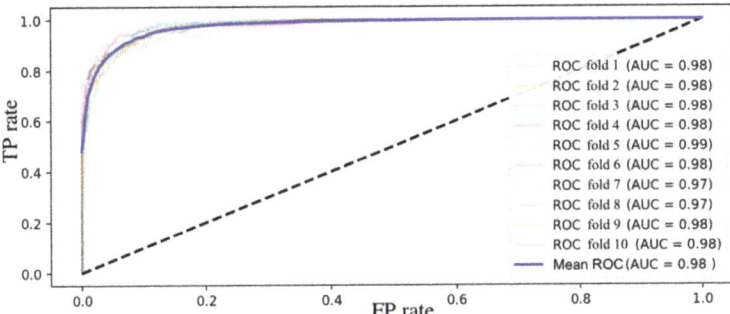

Figure 9. 10-fold cross validation of the RF model.

Based on cross-validation results (see Figure 9), and accuracy of 98% can be expected for A1 and A2 state classification. The next step is to test the final RF model using a separate dataset (30% of all input data). The testing accuracy of the constructed RF model is equal to 94.5%, which is lower than expected (validation accuracy, 98%). However, this model can sufficiently classify and correctly assign values to states A1 and A2. True-positive (state A2) and false-positive (state A1) values are predicted with similar accuracy (95% and 94%, respectively) (Figure 10).

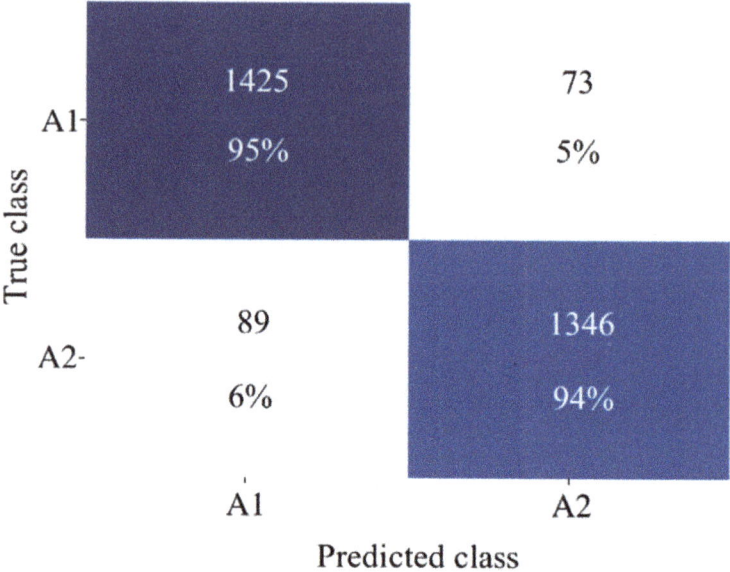

Figure 10. Confusion matrix of classification results for states A1 and A2.

Finally, Cohen's Kappa coefficient was estimated as an essential measurement to evaluate a model's suitability and reliance on random samples. This value was calculated as $\kappa = 0.886$, indicating "perfect" model reliability. Therefore, the constructed RF classifier sufficiently classifies data into states A1 and A2, meaning that the model can identify fatigued conditions using ECG signal parameter values.

5. Discussion and Conclusions

5.1. Discussion and Future Work

In this paper, we proposed a framework for mental fatigue detection combining ECG signal recording twice a day corresponding to different mental states: fatigued and without mental fatigue. Extracted ECG signal features, such as R, S, and T wave amplitude values, as well as QT intervals, increased the classification accuracy compared to similar methods reported in the literature. For example, in [5], heart rate variability (HRV) indicators achieved an accuracy of 75.5%. Additionally, in [6], the proposed methods achieved an accuracy of 93.3%. However, this research considered mentally stressed participants (after 12 h of intense work), which may have resulted in an increased impact on HRV parameter values. This research enables the detection of smaller changes in mental health conditions compared to previously mentioned literature reports. Furthermore, statistical analysis of several ECG signal features showed that RR interval values (used in HRV analysis) overlap in between states, which is why HRV analysis and parameter estimation are not efficient and may reduce classification accuracies. PCA analysis showed that other ECG features present with larger differences between states. Due to the use of several ECG signal features, an accuracy of 94.5% was achieved.

Although the proposed technique shows promising results, it is also subject to some weaknesses. ECG signals should be recorded using professional devices, such as CardioScout Multi, which is expensive and inconvenient. User-friendly devices, such as a Polar v10 belt or Garmin watch, do not record full ECG signals, and data from such devices are not sufficiently reliable. Furthermore, in this research, the gathered data were not suitable for diagnostic purposes because we did not include patients with diagnosed mental illness. Future research should focus on gathering more data and improving classification accuracies. We suggest that 60 sec ECG signal recordings could be expanded and compared with HRV analysis results.

5.2. Conclusions

Considering gaps identified in recent literature, we presented a novel framework that combines ECG signal feature extraction, PCA analysis, and ML classification algorithms. The obtained results show that the proposed framework is feasible for automatic mental fatigue detection.

To ensure daily fatigue recognition, we designed an experiment involving separate recordings registered twice a day. Each recording represents a mental state, i.e., a state without fatigue recorded in the morning and a fatigued state recorded in the evening. A total of 60 healthy adults (ages 24 to 34) without a diagnosis of health pathologies or overwork-related problems were recruited for this experiment. All ECG signals were filtered using a Butterworth filter, and features were extracted using Python toolbox NeuroKit2. Using these methods, the following high-quality ECG parameters were obtained: Q, R, S, and T wave amplitude values; QRS complexes; and RR, ST, QT, and T intervals.

Data visualization processes and statistical analysis show that RR interval values overlap between states, which is why only RR interval analysis alone, such as HRV parameter estimation, is not an efficient way to detect mentally fatigued states. To overcome this issue, other ECG signal parameters were considered in this paper.

PCA analysis showed a significant difference between states (with and without fatigue). As the most representative ECG signal features Q and R wave amplitude values and QT and T intervals were observed. Changes in the first three principal components were evident, indicating the importance of ECG signal feature extraction for mental fatigue recognition.

Finally, machine learning algorithms were applied for automatic classification of ECG signal features into separate states. Four ECG signal parameters (Sa, Ra, Ta, and QT) were identified as the most important for the mental fatigue classification process. The final RF model was able to detect daily mental fatigue with an accuracy of more than 94.5%.

Although the proposed technique shows promising results, it is also subject to some weaknesses. Future work should focus on user-friendly devices for the ECG signal gathering process to ensure that a wide range of participants can be included in experiments.

Author Contributions: Conceptualization, E.B. and L.B.; methodology, E.B. and A.M.; software, E.B. and A.M.; validation, E.B., L.B. and A.M.; formal analysis, L.B.; investigation, E.B. and A.M.; resources and data curation, E.B.; writing—original draft preparation, E.B. and A.M.; writing—review and editing, L.B.; visualization, E.B. and A.M.; supervision, L.B. and A.M. All authors have read and agreed to the published version of the manuscript.

Funding: This research received no external funding.

Institutional Review Board Statement: The study was conducted in accordance with the Declaration of Helsinki, and approved by the Kaunas Regional Research Ethics Committee board (protocol code BE-2-38, 2016-09-07).

Informed Consent Statement: Informed consent was obtained from all subjects involved in the study.

Data Availability Statement: Not applicable.

Conflicts of Interest: The authors declare no conflict of interest.

Abbreviations

ANOVA	Analysis of variance
AUC	Area under the ROC curve
cCNN	Causal convolutional neural network
CF	Cognitive fatigue
DT	Decision tree
ECG	Electrocardiogram
EEG	Electroencephalogram
EES	Epidermal electronic system
EMG	Electromyogram
EOG	Electrooculogram
E-tattoos	Electronic tattoos
G	Gini coefficient
GSR	Galvanic skin response
HR	Heart rate
HRV	Heart rate variability
IMU	Inertial measurement unit
KNN	K-nearest neighbor
LDA	Linear discriminant analysis
LR	Logistic regression
MA	Moving average
MCC	Matthew's correlation coefficient
MF	Mental fatigue
ML	Machine learning
NB	Naïve Bayes
NN	Neural network
PCA	Principal component analysis
PPG	Photoplethysmography
RF	Random forest
ROC	Receiver operating characteristic curve
RPCA	Robust principal component analysis
SVM	Support vector machine
TICC	Toeplitz inverse covariance-based clustering

References

1. Eldadah, B.A. Fatigue and Fatigability in Older Adults. *PMRJ* **2010**, *2*, 406–413. [CrossRef] [PubMed]
2. Ruvalcaba, N.M.M.; Humboldt, S.; Villavicencio, M.E.F.; García, I.F.D. Psychological Fatigue. In *Encyclopedia of Gerontology and Population Aging*; Springer: Cham, Switzerland, 2019; pp. 1–5. [CrossRef]
3. Zhao, C.; Zhao, M.; Liu, J.; Zheng, C. Electroencephalogram and Electrocardiograph Assessment of Mental Fatigue in a Driving Simulator. *Accid. Anal. Prev.* **2012**, *45*, 83–90. [CrossRef] [PubMed]
4. Proost, M.; Habay, J.; De Wachter, J.; De Pauw, K.; Rattray, B.; Meeusen, R.; Roelands, B.; Van Cutsem, J. How to Tackle Mental Fatigue: A Systematic Review of Potential Countermeasures and Their Underlying Mechanisms. *Sport. Med.* **2022**, *52*, 2129–2158. [CrossRef]
5. Huang, S.; Li, J.; Zhang, P.; Zhang, W. International Journal of Medical Informatics Detection of Mental Fatigue State with Wearable ECG Devices. *Int. J. Med. Inform.* **2018**, *119*, 39–46. [CrossRef]
6. Bin Heyat, M.B.; Akhtar, F.; Abbas, S.J.; Al-Sarem, M.; Alqarafi, A.; Stalin, A.; Abbasi, R.; Muaad, A.Y.; Lai, D.; Wu, K. Wearable Flexible Electronics Based Cardiac Electrode for Researcher Mental Stress Detection System Using Machine Learning Models on Single Lead Electrocardiogram Signal. *Biosensors* **2022**, *12*, 427. [CrossRef]
7. Tanaka, M.; Mizuno, K.; Yamaguti, K.; Kuratsune, H.; Fujii, A.; Baba, H.; Matsuda, K.; Nishimae, A.; Takesaka, T.; Watanabe, Y. Autonomic Nervous Alterations Associated with Daily Level of Fatigue. *Behav. Brain Funct.* **2011**, *7*, 46. [CrossRef] [PubMed]
8. Hu, X.; Lodewijks, G. Detecting Fatigue in Car Drivers and Aircraft Pilots by Using Non-Invasive Measures: The Value of Differentiation of Sleepiness and Mental Fatigue. *J. Saf. Res.* **2020**, *72*, 173–187. [CrossRef]
9. Habay, J.; Van Cutsem, J.; Verschueren, J.; De Bock, S.; Proost, M.; De Wachter, J.; Tassignon, B.; Meeusen, R.; Roelands, B. Mental Fatigue and Sport-Specific Psychomotor Performance: A Systematic Review. *Sport. Med.* **2021**, *51*, 1527–1548. [CrossRef]
10. Kunrath, C.A.; Cardoso, F.D.S.L.; Calvo, T.G.; Costa, I.T.D. Mental fatigue in soccer: A systematic review. *Rev. Bras. Med. Esporte* **2020**, *26*, 172–178. [CrossRef]

11. Brahms, M.; Heinzel, S.; Rapp, M.; Mückstein, M.; Hortob, T.; Stelzel, C.; Granacher, U. The Acute Effects of Mental Fatigue on Balance Performance in Healthy Young and Older Adults—A Systematic Review and Meta-Analysis. *Acta Psychol.* **2022**, *225*, 103540. [CrossRef]
12. Kodithuwakku, A.S.N.; Burch, R.F.V.; Chander, H.; Turner, A.J.; Knight, A.C. Theoretical Issues in Ergonomics Science The Use of Wearable Devices in Cognitive Fatigue: Current Trends and Future Intentions. *Theor. Issues Ergon. Sci.* **2022**, *23*, 374–386. [CrossRef]
13. Keeffe, K.O.; Hodder, S.; Lloyd, A. A Comparison of Methods Used for Inducing Mental Fatigue in Performance Research: Individualised, Dual-Task and Short Duration Cognitive Tests Are Most Effective. *Ergonomics* **2020**, *63*, 1–12. [CrossRef]
14. Tran, Y.; Craig, A.; Craig, R.; Chai, R.; Nguyen, H. The Influence of Mental Fatigue on Brain Activity: Evidence from a Systematic Review with Meta-Analyses. *Psychophysiology* **2020**, *57*, e13554. [CrossRef] [PubMed]
15. Hu, J. Comparison of Different Features and Classifiers for Driver Fatigue Detection Based on a Single EEG Channel. *Comput. Math. Methods Med.* **2017**, *2017*, 5109530. [CrossRef]
16. Shen, K.; Li, X.; Ong, C.; Shao, S.; Wilder-smith, E.P. V EEG-Based Mental Fatigue Measurement Using Multi-Class Support Vector Machines with Confidence Estimate. *Clin. Neurophysiol.* **2008**, *119*, 1524–1533. [CrossRef]
17. Laurent, F.; Valderrama, M.; Besserve, M.; Guillard, M.; Lachaux, J.P.; Martinerie, J.; Florence, G. Biomedical Signal Processing and Control Multimodal Information Improves the Rapid Detection of Mental Fatigue. *Biomed. Signal Process. Control* **2013**, *8*, 400–408. [CrossRef]
18. Maman, S.Z.; Chen, Y.; Baghdadi, A.; Lombardo, S.; Cavuoto, L.A.; Megahed, F.M. A Data Analytic Framework for Physical Fatigue Management Using Wearable Sensors. *Expert Syst. Appl.* **2020**, *155*, 113405. [CrossRef]
19. Butkevičiūtė, E.; Eriņš, M.; Bikulčienė, L. An Adaptable Human Fatigue Evaluation System. *Procedia Comput. Sci.* **2021**, *192*, 1274–1284. [CrossRef]
20. Fan, C.; Huang, S.; Lin, S.; Xu, D.; Peng, Y.; Yi, S. Types, Risk Factors, Consequences, and Detection Methods of Train Driver Fatigue and Distraction. *Comput. Intell. Neurosci.* **2022**, *2022*, 8328077. [CrossRef]
21. Badr, A.; Badawi, A.; Rashwan, A.; Elgazzar, K. XBeats: A Real-Time Electrocardiogram Monitoring and Analysis System. *Signals* **2022**, *3*, 189–208. [CrossRef]
22. Delliaux, S.; Delaforge, A.; Deharo, J.; Chaumet, G. Mental Workload Alters Heart Rate Variability, Lowering Non-Linear Dynamics. *Front. Physiol.* **2019**, *10*, 565. [CrossRef] [PubMed]
23. Wei, J.X.; Wang, J.; Zhu, Y.X.; Sun, J.; Xu, H.M.; Li, M. Traditional Chinese Medicine Pharmacovigilance in Signal Detection: Decision Tree-Based Data Classification. *BMC Med. Inform. Decis. Mak.* **2018**, *18*, 19. [CrossRef] [PubMed]
24. Shao, M.; Bin, G.; Wu, S.; Bin, G.; Huang, J.; Zhou, Z. Detection of Atrial Fibrillation from ECG Recordings Using Decision Tree Ensemble with Multi-Level Features. *Physiol. Meas.* **2018**, *39*, 094008. [CrossRef]
25. Balagué, N.; González, J.; Javierre, C.; Hristovski, R.; Aragonés, D.; Álamo, J.; Niño, O.; Ventura, J.L. Cardiorespiratory Coordination after Training and Detraining. A Principal Component Analysis Approach. *Front. Physiol.* **2016**, *7*, 35. [CrossRef] [PubMed]
26. Ye, W.; Lu, W.; Tang, Y.; Chen, G.; Li, X.; Ji, C.; Hou, M.; Zeng, G.; Lan, X.; Wang, Y.; et al. Identification of COVID-19 Clinical Phenotypes by Principal Component Analysis-Based Cluster Analysis. *Front. Med.* **2020**, *7*, 570614. [CrossRef]
27. Wang, J.; Liao, X.; Zheng, P.; Xue, S.; Peng, R. Classification of Chinese Herbal Medicine by Laser-Induced Breakdown Spectroscopy with Principal Component Analysis and Artificial Neural Network. *Anal. Lett.* **2018**, *51*, 575–586. [CrossRef]
28. Kara, S.; Dirgenali, F. A System to Diagnose Atherosclerosis via Wavelet Transforms, Principal Component Analysis and Artificial Neural Networks. *Expert. Syst. Appl.* **2007**, *32*, 632–640. [CrossRef]
29. Papi, M.; Caracciolo, G. Principal Component Analysis of Personalized Biomolecular Corona Data for Early Disease Detection. *Nano Today* **2018**, *21*, 14–17. [CrossRef]
30. Martis, J.R.; Acharya, U.R.; Mandana, K.M.; Ray, A.K.; Chakraborty, C. Application of Principal Component Analysis to ECG Signals for Automated Diagnosis of Cardiac Health. *Expert. Syst. Appl.* **2012**, *39*, 11792–11800. [CrossRef]
31. Li, J.; Li, H.; Umer, W.; Wang, H.; Xing, X.; Zhao, S.; Hou, J. Identification and Classification of Construction Equipment Operators' Mental Fatigue Using Wearable Eye-Tracking Technology. *Autom. Constr.* **2020**, *109*, 103000. [CrossRef]
32. Zhang, C.; Yu, X. Estimating Mental Fatigue Based on Electroencephalogram and Heart Rate Variability. *Pol. J. Med. Phys. Eng.* **2010**, *16*, 67–84. [CrossRef]
33. Phadikar, S.; Sinha, N.; Ghosh, R.; Ghaderpour, E. Automatic Muscle Artifacts Identification and Removal from Single-Channel EEG Using Wavelet Transform with Meta-Heuristically Optimized Non-Local Means Filter. *Sensors* **2022**, *22*, 2948. [CrossRef] [PubMed]
34. Ahmed, M.Z.I.; Sinha, N.; Phadikar, S.; Ghaderpour, E. Automated Feature Extraction on AsMap for Emotion Classification Using EEG. *Sensors* **2022**, *22*, 2346. [CrossRef] [PubMed]
35. Tuncer, T.; Dogan, S.; Subasi, A. EEG-Based Driving Fatigue Detection Using Multilevel Feature Extraction and Iterative Hybrid Feature Selection. *Biomed. Signal Process. Control* **2021**, *68*, 102591. [CrossRef]
36. Luo, H.; Lee, P.-A.; Clay, I.; Jaggi, M.; De Luca, V. Assessment of Fatigue Using Wearable Sensors: A Pilot Study. *Emerg. Appl.* **2020**, *4*, 59–72. [CrossRef]
37. Hinde, K.; White, G.; Armstrong, N. Wearable Devices Suitable for Monitoring Twenty Four Hour Heart Rate Variability in Military Populations. *Sensors* **2021**, *21*, 1061. [CrossRef]

38. Zeng, Z.; Huang, Z.; Leng, K.; Han, W.; Niu, H.; Yu, Y.; Ling, Q.; Liu, J.; Wu, Z.; Zang, J. Nonintrusive Monitoring of Mental Fatigue Status Using Epidermal Electronic Systems and Machine-Learning Algorithms. *ACS Sensors* **2020**, *5*, 1305–1313. [CrossRef]
39. Sampei, K.; Ogawa, M.; Cesar, C.; Torres, C.; Sato, M.; Miki, N. Mental Fatigue Monitoring Using a Wearable Transparent Eye Detection System. *Micromachines* **2016**, *7*, 20. [CrossRef]
40. Liu, M.; Hao, H.Q.; Xiong, P.; Lin, F.; Hou, Z.G.; Liu, X. Constructing a Guided Filter by Exploiting the Butterworth Filter for ECG Signal Enhancement. *J. Med. Biol. Eng.* **2018**, *38*, 980–992. [CrossRef]
41. Prasad, S.T.; Varadarajan, S. ECG Signal Analysis: Different Approaches. *Int. J. Eng. Trends Technol.* **2014**, *7*, 212–216. [CrossRef]
42. Makowski, D.; Pham, T.; Lau, Z.J.; Brammer, J.C.; Lespinasse, F.; Pham, H.; Schölzel, C.; Chen, S.H.A. NeuroKit2: A Python Toolbox for Neurophysiological Signal Processing. *Behav. Res. Methods* **2021**, *53*, 1689–1696. [CrossRef] [PubMed]
43. Bi, Q.; Goodman, K.E.; Kaminsky, J.; Lessler, J. What Is Machine Learning? A Primer for the Epidemiologist. *Pract. Epidemiol.* **2019**, *188*, 2222–2239. [CrossRef] [PubMed]
44. Bowes, D.; Hall, T.; Gray, D. DConfusion: A Technique to Allow Cross Study Performance Evaluation of Fault Prediction Studies. *Autom. Softw. Eng.* **2014**, *21*, 287–313. [CrossRef]
45. Halimu, C.; Kasem, A.; Newaz, S.H.S. Empirical Comparison of Area under ROC Curve (AUC) and Mathew Correlation Coefficient (MCC) for Evaluating Machine Learning Algorithms on Imbalanced Datasets for Binary Classification. In Proceedings of the 3rd International Conference on Machine Learning and Soft Computing (ICMLS 2019), Marakesh, Morocco, 28–30 October 2019; pp. 10–15. [CrossRef]
46. McHugh, M.L. Lessons in Biostatistics Interrater Reliability: The Kappa Statistic. *Biochem. Medica* **2012**, *22*, 276–282. [CrossRef]
47. Oeda, S.; Chieda, M. Visualization of Programming Skill Structure by Log-Data Analysis with Decision Tree. *Procedia Comput. Sci.* **2019**, *159*, 582–589. [CrossRef]
48. Spanakis, G.; Weiss, G.; Roefs, A. Bagged Boosted Trees for Classification of Ecological Momentary Assessment Data. In *Ebook: ECAI 2016*; IOS Press: Amsterdam, The Netherlands, 2016; pp. 1612–1613. [CrossRef]
49. Chicco, D. Ten Quick Tips for Machine Learning in Computational Biology. *BioData Min.* **2017**, *10*, 35. [CrossRef]

Article

Analysis of Dual-Tasking Effect on Gait Variability While Interacting with Mobile Devices

David Carneros-Prado, Cosmin C. Dobrescu, Iván González, Jesús Fontecha, Esperanza Johnson and Ramón Hervás *

Department of Information Technologies and Systems, University of Castilla-La Mancha, Paseo de la Universidad 4, 13071 Ciudad Real, Spain
* Correspondence: ramon.hlucas@uclm.es

Citation: Carneros-Prado, D.; Dobrescu, C.C.; González, I.; Fontecha, J.; Johnson, E.; Hervás, R. Analysis of Dual-Tasking Effect on Gait Variability While Interacting with Mobile Devices. *Mathematics* 2023, 11, 202. https://doi.org/10.3390/math11010202

Academic Editor: Francesco Calimeri

Received: 10 October 2022
Revised: 8 December 2022
Accepted: 26 December 2022
Published: 30 December 2022

Copyright: © 2022 by the authors. Licensee MDPI, Basel, Switzerland. This article is an open access article distributed under the terms and conditions of the Creative Commons Attribution (CC BY) license (https://creativecommons.org/licenses/by/4.0/).

Abstract: Cognitive deficits are very difficult to diagnose during the initial stages; tests typically consist of a patient performing punctual dual-task activities, which are subjectively analyzed to determine the cognitive decline impact on gait. This work supports novel and objective diagnosis methods by stating a baseline on how neurotypical aging affects dual tasks while using a smartphone on the move. With this aim, we propose a twofold research question: Which mobile device tasks performed on the move (dual tasking) have characteristic changes in gait parameters, and which are especially characteristic at older ages? An experiment was conducted with 30 healthy participants where they performed 15 activities (1 single task, 2 traditional dual-tasks and 12 mobile-based dual-tasks) while walking about 50 m. Participants wore a wireless motion tracker (15 sensors) that made the concise analysis of gait possible. The results obtained characterized the gait parameters affected by mobile-based dual-tasking and the impact of normal cognitive decline due to aging. The statistical analysis shows that using smartphone-based dual-tasking produces more significant results than traditional dual-tasking. In the study, 3 out of 10 gait parameters were very significantly affected ($p < 0.001$) when using the traditional dual tasks, while 5 out of 10 parameters were very significantly affected ($p < 0.001$) in mobile-based dual-tasking. Moreover, the most characteristic tasks and gait parameters were identified through the obtained results. Future work will focus on applying this knowledge to improve the early diagnosis of MCI.

Keywords: mobile computing; dual tasking; cognitive decline; human motion tracking; gait analysis

MSC: 68W99

1. Introduction

One of the most common stages that precede dementia is known as Mild Cognitive Impairment [1] (MCI). It is defined as "cognitive impairment that is greater than expected for an individual's age and educational level but does not markedly interfere with activities of daily living" [2]. An increasing prevalence of MCI has been reported, estimated in up to 19% of adults over 65 years of age, with a risk of progression to dementia in up to 33% of cases within 2 years and up to 50% of cases progressing to dementia within 5 years [3]. These statistics show that dementia is one of the most common disorders among older adults, and the number of people affected is expected to triple by 2050 [4].

Gait performance is affected by neurodegeneration in aging and has traditionally been used as a clinical marker for progression from MCI to dementia [5,6]. Usually, a dual-tasking gait test evaluating the cognitive-motor interface is performed to diagnose MCI [7] and to monitor its progression to dementia [8–11]. In this type of test, the geriatrician first observes the patient's gait pace while performing a single motor task without interference from any other high cognitive load tasks. Then gait is evaluated while the patient performs some tasks with a high cognitive load (e.g., counting backwards or remembering items) in a dual-tasking model [12]. Different spatiotemporal parameters of the gait (e.g., gait speed or stride time) have been quantitively analyzed in the related literature about dual-tasking. The most relevant ones, as well as frequently used cognitive tasks, are listed in Section 2.3.

In general, the association between aging and gait changes has been demonstrated [13–15], increasing its impact on human gait when older adults are affected by MCI. In this sense, there is growing evidence that supports the use of dual-tasking gait tests instead of single-task (only gait) as a more powerful tool to discriminate the progression between different levels of cognitive impairment [10,16]. For instance, it has been reported that gait speed monitoring, as part of dual-tasking gait trials, could be more valuable than acquiring gait speed in a single-task trial to discriminate between older adults with and without MCI [17]. In particular, the impact of dual-tasking as a cognitive-motor interface has been widely researched in both cross-sectional and longitudinal prospective studies as a potential clinical marker of cognitive impairment progression in older adults [18–21].

This work contributes a basis for the development of a novel method for early diagnosis of cognitive impairment while monitoring gait in a dual-tasking model. An innovative approach for the selection and performance of cognitive tasks is proposed for evaluation, instead of using only the classic ones (such as listing collections of related items or subtracting/counting numbers) [9]. We aim to study the impact on different gait cycle characteristics/parameters (spatiotemporal measures) while dual cognitive tasks are simultaneously performed, specifically, common tasks with the smartphone. The use of mobile devices has proven to be a powerful tool for obtaining data for medical purposes [22,23] and, particularly, for diagnosis [24–26] and behavioral analysis [27].

The current contribution is part of the first phase of a longer study. In this phase, we have carried out the analysis with a sample of adults within a wide age range and without cognitive impairment. In a future phase of this project, we will include adults with mild cognitive impairment in the study to perform tasks under the same terms and to determine if there is still correspondence with the findings of the current work. This characterization could provide a ground truth to support early diagnosis of cognitive impairment in the future by performing tasks with a mobile device while analyzing gait parameters.

Through this study, we aim to identify the types of cognitive tasks that have a greater impact on gait performance and determine whether this impact can be seen across all age ranges. Alongside this, we also aim to observe whether older age causes gait to be more affected in the presence of specific cognitive tasks. Thus, considering all this background, the twofold research question guiding this work is: *Which mobile device tasks performed on the move (dual-tasking) have characteristic changes in gait parameters, and which are especially characteristic at older ages?*

2. Materials and Methods

2.1. Participants

The study had a population of $n = 30$ (33.33% female and 66.67% male), without any gait pathology and with a mean age of 44.27 ± 19.55. The study did not focus on gender, so gender parity was not considered. To observe the variability of gait in different age groups, three groups were created with equal populations in each. Group 1 was aged between 18 and 34 years; group 2 from 35 to 55 years; and the last group with ages over 55 years. This grouping follows the stages of adulthood according to Carl Jung's theory [28]. The subjects had the following anthropometric measurements taken prior to testing: height, foot length, shoulder height, elbow span, wrist extension, knee height and ankle height. Table 1 summarizes the population characteristics divided by age group.

The inclusion criteria to participate in the experiment were (a) daily use of the smartphone; (b) weekly use of applications for communication, internet searches and multimedia (categories in which all the tasks carried out in the experiment are included); (c) not having been diagnosed with any cognitive impairment; and (d) not having any motor pathology or injury affecting gait.

Table 1. Anthropometric measurements of participants divided by groups and total. Values are mean ± standard deviations.

Group	Age	Height (cm)	Foot Length (cm)	Shoulder Height (cm)	Elbow Span (cm)	Wrist Span (cm)	Knee Height (cm)	Ankle Height (cm)
$18 \leq x \leq 34$	23.30 ± 4.32	178.95 ± 8.01	27.45 ± 2.02	153.05 ± 6.93	90.60 ± 7.29	140.52 ± 9.57	52.10 ± 3.52	10.35 ± 1.06
$35 \leq x \leq 55$	41.50 ± 4.99	175.15 ± 8.66	27.15 ± 1.83	150.15 ± 8.02	88.35 ± 4.65	138.70 ± 8.49	51.88 ± 3.92	10.50 ± 1.39
$x > 56$	68.00 ± 8.08	169.3 ± 10.44	26.45 ± 2.06	146.95 ± 10.47	87.05 ± 8.77	136 ± 11.97	51.15 ± 3.35	10.19 ± 1.26
	44.27 ± 19.55	174.46 ± 9.66	27.02 ± 1.95	150.05 ± 8.68	88.67 ± 7.02	138.5 ± 9.92	51.71 ± 3.50	10.35 ± 1.21

As we included people in our evaluation, we ensured the experiment was conducted according to the guidelines of the authors' institution research ethics commission and in accordance with the principles of the WMA declaration of Helsinki. The authors oversaw the research conducted, while respecting all ethical and privacy implications, ensuring human rights, autonomy and dignity. The personal data and monitoring dataset were handled confidentially and anonymously. Only encoded data was used for analysis and dissemination purposes. Before participation in the experiment each participant was given a document explaining the objective of the study, the description of the experiment, the researchers responsible for data collection, their rights regarding confidentiality of the data and the voluntary nature of the experiment.

2.2. Technological Requirements

The experiment was carried out in a 24 m long and 3 m wide corridor with a wireless human motion tracker at the School of Computer Science of the University of Castilla-La Mancha, Ciudad Real. The system, named MTw Awinda [29] and developed by Xsens, consists of 15 devices called MTw (Motion Tracker Wireless), which can synchronize with a transmitter/receiver base (Awinda Station). The Awinda protocol uses 2.4 GHz and is based on the IEEE 802.15.4, with an accuracy of 10 us at a frequency of 60 Hz using 15 devices. By using a technology in the same band as the 2.4 GHz WIFI, these devices have a specific definition of channels that overlap with the WIFI channels; however, unlike the WIFI channels, they do not overlap with each other. An analysis of the occupation of these channels must be made when carrying out the different tests, choosing the one that is the freest. The set offers a wireless transmission autonomy of 20–50 m, depending on environmental interferences and the load on the WIFI channels. To obtain good accuracy the station was placed on one side of the corridor within the path of the participant, 4 m from the starting point.

The data were processed and analyzed in real time by the MVN Analyze v2021.2.0 software on a computer with an i7 10700F processor and a GTX3060Ti graphics card for smooth processing. MTw devices contain an inertial measurement unit (IMU) and a barometer, with the IMU having nine degrees of freedom (DOF) and three degrees for each magnitude: (i) acceleration, (ii) velocity and (iii) magnetometer. By using multiple MTws distributed along the human body and based on the units of measurement that they bring, the system can model movement in a three-dimensional space [30], obtaining spatiotemporal and kinematic parameters. The set comes with a series of Velcro bands, t-shirts and accessories for proper placement of the devices. One of the more useful accessories that allow increased precision of the anthropometric measurements of the participant is the segmometer. This tool is normally used in medical fields to take different body measurements, and in this experiment, it was used to obtain the dimensions specified.

2.3. Dual-Tasking

Some of the most common spatiotemporal gait parameters gathered in dual-tasking studies are cadence, gait speed, stride length, step length, step width, swing phase percentage or swing duration, stance phase percentage or stance duration, double support percentage or double support duration, step duration, stride duration and step symmetry, among others. The mean and standard deviation dispersion measures are calculated to characterize the participant's gait. For this purpose, these measures of the spatiotemporal parameters of the stride for each gait are calculated so that the gait can be quantitatively characterized. We can also determine how gait is affected while performing another highly cognitive dual task compared to the gait-only recording (single-task).

Regarding highly cognitive tasks in the dual-tasking model, related works consider the following capabilities: (i) working memory (e.g., listing the alphabet by alternating letters or reciting months of the year backward); (ii) verbal and arithmetic fluency (e.g., reciting related words that are part of a specific collection, such as animals, professions, home appliances . . . , and subtracting N by N or counting backwards for the arithmetic type); and (iii) attention and visuomotor abilities (e.g., a trail-making test over a paper sheet) [18].

In order to have a point of reference with respect to the dual-tasking research literature, two frequently used or classic dual-tasks were added. The tasks chosen as a baseline were counting backwards from 100 by 3 s, and naming animals or professions.

In this research, tasks like those proposed by Cabañero et al. have been chosen and adapted to the particularities of the experiment; these follow the taxonomy "Human-Smartphone Basic Interactions Taxonomy" HuSBIT [23]. This taxonomy classifies interactions into four groups directly related to human senses: touch, sight, speech and hearing. Additionally, each of these interactions can be classified as active or passive, depending on the user's interaction with a smartphone. Based on this taxonomy, a series of dual-tasks are defined and classified under AMPEC terminology. This acronym corresponds to the grouping of tasks into 5 different groups: Automated, Psychomotor, Production, Exploration and Consumption. The adapted tasks, together with the assigned identifiers and their description, can be found in Table 2.

Table 2. List of tasks classification based on AMPEC and according to HuSBIT approach.

Task Category	Id	Description
Base	B1	Counting backwards from 100 by 3 s.
	B2	Naming animals or professions aloud.
Psychomotor	M2	Moving the icons of mobile applications between the different screens.
	M3	Opening as many applications as possible on the participant's mobile device and close them one at a time at the start of the walk. If the participant closes them all, they must reopen others and close them again.
	M5	Reading a text in which the participant must select the words that start with "a" or "e".
Production	P1	Writing a text message talking about an activity they did in the past.
	P2	Recording a voice message talking about an activity the participant is going to do in the future.
	P3	Recording a video while keeping the black dot placed at the end of the corridor as centered as possible, starting with max zoom and decreasing it as the participant goes along. Perform the same procedure when returning.
Exploration	E2	Counting the people with hats in an image from the classic "Where's Waldo?" game.
	E3	The participant is told about two actions they must perform, found in the mobile device settings. These tasks are chosen according to the capabilities of the participant.
	E4	The participant is provided with an interactive map on which they can move, zoom, and see the direction of the streets. They must trace a route between 4 locations indicated on the map.
Consumption	C1	Reading a text provided to the participant as they walk along the corridor.
	C2	Listening to an audio recording with a shopping list and memorizing the items.
	C3	Watching a cooking video and memorizing the ingredients used to determine what recipe is being prepared.

2.4. Instrumentation Procedure and Trials Specification

The procedure to follow consists of (i) taking anthropometric dimensions, (ii) placing instrumentation, (iii) calibrating the system and (iv) performing single and dual-tasks (shown in Figure 1). The time of the first, second and third phases depends on the persons in charge of the experiment, and the last phase depends directly on the participants, with a time frame between 30 and 80 min. The time difference is due to several factors, such as age of the participants, as older people took longer to perform the tasks. In addition, some sensors occasionally were misadjusted during the tests, which meant that the system had to be recalibrated (approximately 10 min).

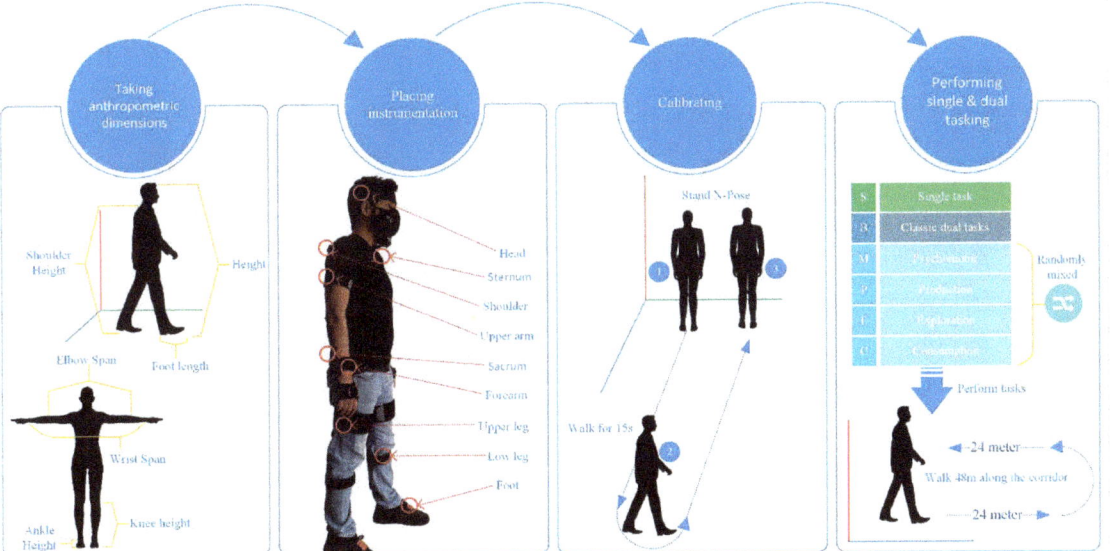

Figure 1. Procedure to complete the experiment with one participant.

The MVN Analysis software requires only two anthropometric dimensions: body height and foot length. The accuracy of the gait analysis varies depending on the number of additional measurements and their accuracy. Given the complexity of accurately measuring shoulder width, hip height and hip width, it has been decided to leave the self-generated values based on an anthropometric model.

A "full body no hands" suit configuration was used in this research. Each foot was instrumented with three MTws: one between the second and third metatarsal, one at the level of the soleus muscle and another at the level of the biceps femoris. The trunk was instrumented with four MTws: one located on the L5 vertebra above the sacral region, two on each shoulder and one on the sternum. Finally, each arm had two MTws: one on the biceps and another on the forearm.

The system used for this project requires a three-phase calibration procedure based on inertial measurement units. The duration depends on the number of devices and the capacity of the computer used, reaching two minutes in the worst case. First, the participant must start in a position called N-pose. This consists on the person standing upright with hands close to the body, feet together and as straight as possible. Then they must start walking for approximately 15 s so the system can make the necessary adjustments and detect interferences from the environment. After this time, the participant must remain in N-pose but not necessarily in the same location in which they started the calibration process. Finally, a visual check is made to ensure that the movements made by the participant and the virtual model match. At this point, it is possible to see if a mistake was made in the placement of a MTw device.

While participants were carrying out the tests, the researchers in charge of the experiment noted any incident regarding the participant's performance of the test. Once the participant had completed the assigned task, a series of questions were asked to confirm that the experiment had been carried out correctly. Based on these criteria, the test was considered valid or not.

The tasks of the experiment can be started once the participant is instrumented and the system calibrated with the anthropometric data. At all times the normal task is the first to be performed, followed by the classic/basic dual-tasks. Tasks are performed in a random order so that fatigue does not influence the participant in the performance of the different dual-tasks with a mobile device. Figure 2 depicts the instrumentation and experiment environment.

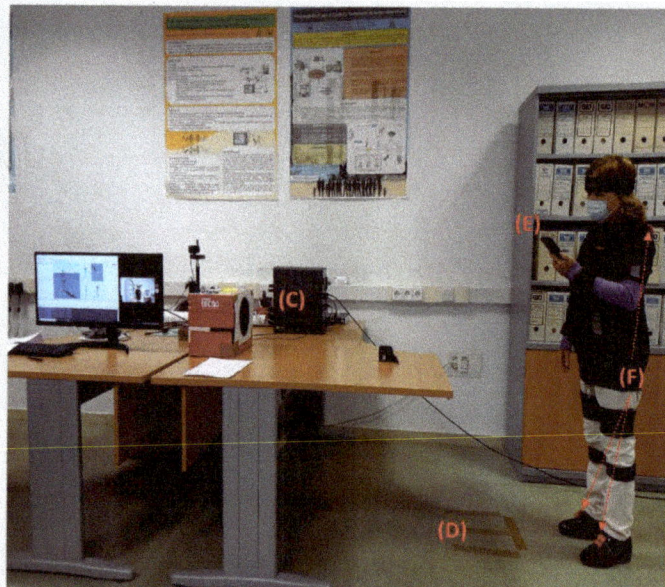

Figure 2. Instrumentation and experiment environment. (A) 24-m-long corridor the participants must walk. (B) Monitor where the movement of the person is visualized in real time. (C) Computer with motion capture software. (D) Start position marks. (E) Personal mobile device. (F) Some of the MTw IMUs.

2.5. Data Analysis

The raw inertial data obtained from the MTw IMUs, together with complementary information from the recordings provided by the Xsens MVN Analyze software, were processed and analyzed using the following specialized Python libraries: Pandas, NumPy and SciPy. With the motion capture system, the acceleration/velocity/position information is obtained from each of the sensors in addition to the information calculated by the software of the acceleration/velocity/position of the joints and body segments. This software also provides the contact information of the heels and toes with the ground for each frame of the recording.

Using the heel and toe contact data calculated by the motion capture system software, the Heel Strike and Toe Off events were calculated using a state machine, obtaining the time and frame at which the events occurred for both feet.

With the inertial data and gait events, the following spatiotemporal data of the human gait were calculated: stride length (mm), stride duration (s), maximum heel height (mm), maximum foot height (mm), stance phase duration (s), swing phase duration (s), double stance duration (s), velocity (m/s), cadence (steps/min) and the acceleration of the center of gravity in the mediolateral axis (m/s^2). Table 3 shows the spatiotemporal parameters of single task (ST) and dual-tasking (DT) gait divided by age group.

Table 3. Spatiotemporal parameters obtained by volunteers separated into age groups for single task (only gait) and dual tasks. Values are mean ± standard deviations.

Gait Parameter	Group $18 \leq x < 35$		Group $35 \leq x \leq 55$		Group $x > 55$	
	Single Task	DT	Single Task	DT	Single Task	DT
Cadence (steps/min)	106.81 ± 7.79	101.08 ± 7.04	105.46 ± 7.43	102.35 ± 8.36	108.05 ± 7.60	93.63 ± 12.09
Speed (m/s)	1.23 ± 0.11	1.06 ± 0.12	1.21 ± 0.16	1.12 ± 0.14	1.09 ± 0.17	0.83 ± 0.20
Stride length (cm)	138.52 ± 6.25	125.74 ± 10.52	137.14 ± 12.65	130.98 ± 9.72	122.01 ± 16.71	105.29 ± 17.75
Max. Heel height (mm)	160.73 ± 12.97	156.67 ± 13.63	166.66 ± 19.28	162.68 ± 18.57	145.73 ± 17.57	134.39 ± 18.59
Max. Toe height (mm)	120.21 ± 10.69	109.20 ± 13.02	130.10 ± 19.28	122.57 ± 16.86	103.96 ± 17.45	92.81 ± 18.15
Stance phase (s)	0.64 ± 0.05	0.69 ± 0.05	0.65 ± 0.07	0.68 ± 0.08	0.65 ± 0.06	0.77 ± 0.15
Swing phase (s)	0.49 ± 0.03	0.50 ± 0.04	0.49 ± 0.02	0.5 ± 0.03	0.47 ± 0.04	0.53 ± 0.09
Double support (s)	0.16 ± 0.03	0.19 ± 0.03	0.16 ± 0.05	0.18 ± 0.05	0.19 ± 0.04	0.33 ± 0.18
Acc. Mediolateral (m/s^2)	1.74 ± 0.42	1.59 ± 0.37	1.59 ± 0.45	1.53 ± 0.37	1.71 ± 0.47	1.38 ± 0.46

A normalization of the spatiotemporal parameters was performed to reduce the bias caused by the anthropometric characteristics of the subjects. These were presented in a dimensionless form so they were less susceptible to the variability of the anthropometric factors [31]. The variables for double stance duration, swing phase duration and support phase duration were divided by the stride time (t_0), obtaining the percentage that corresponds to the duration of this phase of the total stride duration [32–34]. Stride length was normalized by the height of the person [35] as were speed and cadence (in which gravity was also included) [31,36]. Alternatively, for the normalization of the maximum heel and foot height parameters, the Pearson correlation coefficient was calculated after assuming normality using the Saphiro-Wilk test with a confidence level of 95% ($\alpha = 0.05$). With this it was observed that the anthropometric variable that most affected maximum heel height and maximum foot height was height, with $r = 0.61$ ($p = 0.0003$) and $r = 0.53$ ($p = 0.002$), respectively. Therefore, these two parameters were also normalized by the height of the subject. In addition, these values remained very small because of the normalization of the maximum heel and foot height parameters. Thus, a Min-Max normalization was also applied to these values to make them range [0, 1]. The maximum acceleration in the mediolateral axis was normalized by gravity [31]. See Table 4 for the dimensionless normalization of the spatiotemporal parameters.

Table 4. Dimensionless normalization of gait parameters [31], where l_0 is the subject's height, t_0 is the stride length and g is gravity (9.81 m/s^2).

Gait Parameter	Dimension	Dimensionless Magnitude
Stride length	L	$\hat{l} = l/l_0$
Max. Heel height	L	$\hat{l} = l/l_0$
Max. Foot height	L	$\hat{l} = l/l_0$
Speed	LT^{-1}	$\hat{v} = v/\sqrt{gl_0}$
Cadence	T^{-1}	$\hat{c} = c/\sqrt{g/l_0}$
Duration of stance phase	T	$\hat{t} = t/t_0$
Duration of swing phase	T	$\hat{t} = t/t_0$
Double support time	T	$\hat{t} = t/t_0$
Acc mediolateral axis	LT^{-2}	$\hat{a} = a/g$

The initial and final strides were eliminated to avoid the effects of acceleration/decelerations produced when starting the gait, when finishing it or when approaching the turning point. For this purpose, the velocity information of the subject's center of gravity in the anteroposterior axis, smoothed with the Savizky-Golay filter [37], was used to detect strides that were far away from the walking speed. In addition, outliers that deviated by 30% or more from the average, which may be caused by interferences between the sensors, were also eliminated. A total of 55 ± 8 strides was analyzed from each recording.

Descriptive statistics are presented as mean $\pm$ SD. A general outline of the analyses carried out is presented in Figure 3, with more details to follow in the next section. The t-student test was used for each gait parameter for the comparison between the normal gait and the dual-tasking group. For further exploration, and in order to test the initial hypothesis, a paired t-student test was performed between normal gait and all the dual-tasking activities (the baseline and the proposed). In all cases the significance level was set at 95% ($\alpha = 0.05$), so it could be said to be significant when its p-value was $<\alpha$ and very significant (or higher significance) when its p-value was much lower than α; this will be emphasized by setting "<0.001" instead of its p-value. Finally, Pearson's correlation coefficient was calculated to look for relationships between age and gait variability when performing the dual-tasks.

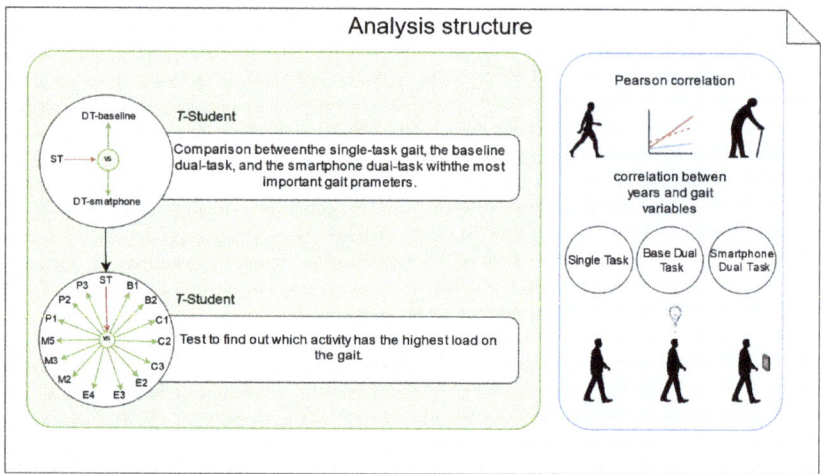

Figure 3. Structure of the analysis carried out in this paper (the included graphs are just for illustration, results are explained in Section 3).

3. Results

The results section is divided into two parts: the first one shows the statistical analyses to answer the research question "Which mobile device tasks performed on the move (dual-tasking) have characteristic changes in gait parameters?"; the second part focuses on answering the question "Which are especially characteristic at older ages?" through a study of the correlation of gait variables with age for the different activities.

3.1. Inferential Analysis

In the first analysis, a Student's t-test is performed between single-task gait versus dual-task baseline gait (used in traditional tests) and single task versus smartphone dual-task gait. The results of applying the t-test can be seen in Appendix A, Table A1. Figure 4 shows the boxplots of the gait variables with the highest level of significance. First, we performed a comparison between the single-task gait with the baseline dual-task gait. This shows that the variables stride length, velocity and cadence are the most significant variables ($p < 0.001$). The parameters of acceleration of the axis of gravity in the mediolateral axis, stride length, swing and stance phase ($p = 0.013$, $p = 0.020$, $p = 0.041$ and $p = 0.041$ respectively) are also significant. The variables maximum foot height ($p = 0.211$) and maximum heel height ($p = 0.504$) are not significant.

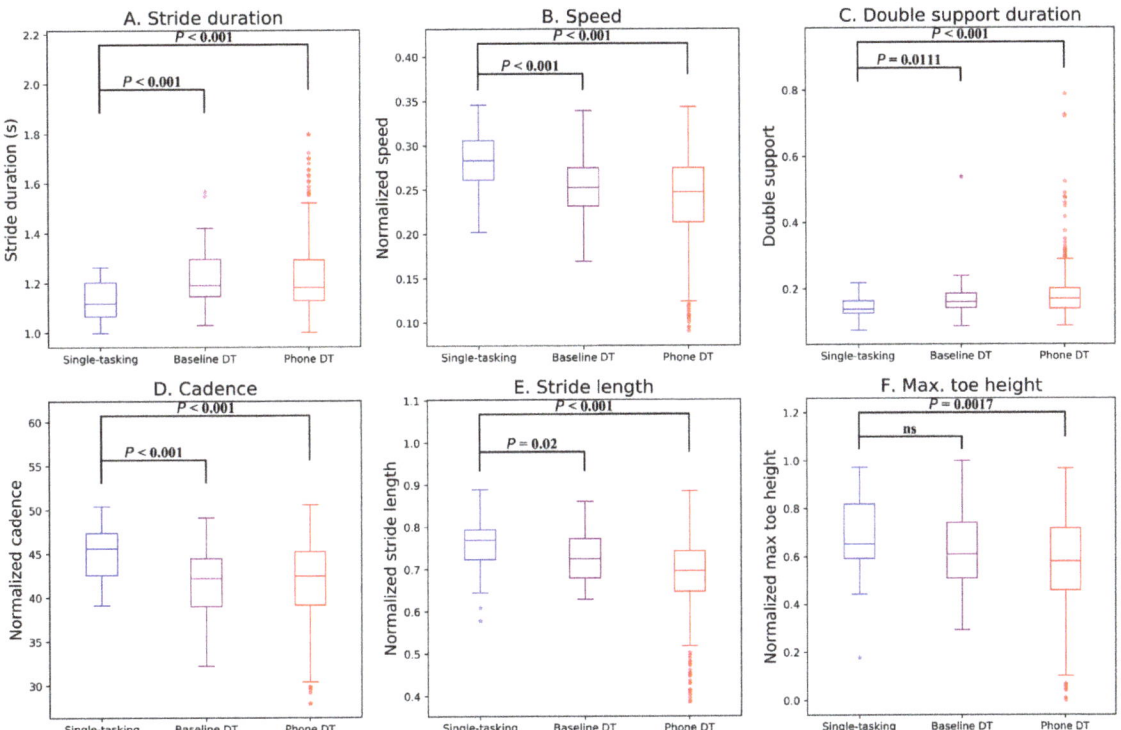

Figure 4. Boxplots with the effects of the baseline dual task and mobile phone dual task on single gait of the 6 gait variables with the highest significance (lowest *p*-value). The five-pointed stars represent outliers, which are data points that fall outside the upper and lower quartiles of the data set. See Appendix A, Table A1.

On the other hand, the gait variables are more affected when performing the double task with the smartphone. The variables stride duration, speed, double support phase, cadence and stride length have a higher level of significance ($p < 0.0001$). The other variables max heel height, acc. mediolateral, support phase, swing phase and max toe height ($p = 0.031$, $p = 0.039$, $p = 0.005$, $p = 0.005$ and $p = 0.002$, respectively) are also significant.

To evaluate which dual-task activities affect gait parameters the most, a separate Student's *t*-test was performed between each dual activity and single-task gait. Table 5 shows which dual tasks with the smartphone present more significant variations with single-task gait and compare them with the reference dual tasks (B1 and B2). Figure 5 shows the boxplots of the dual tasks with the mobile device with the largest effect on gait. We can see how tasks E4 and P3 have the greatest influence on gait with $p < 0.05$ for all gait parameters. Tasks E2 and M5 have $p < 0.05$ in 7/10 and 8/10 parameters, respectively. It can be highlighted how the performance of the dual tasks with the smartphone causes variations in a greater number of gait parameters than the base dual tasks, such as the percentage in double support or the maximum foot height.

Table 5. Results of applying the *t*-test of each dual-tasking task vs. single-task gait for each normalized gait parameter.

Feature	ST-B1	ST-B2	ST-C1	ST-C2	ST-C3	ST-E2	ST-E3	ST-E4	ST-M2	ST-M3	ST-M5	ST-P1	ST-P2	ST-P3
Stride duration	<0.001	0.001	0.004	0.021	0.011	<0.001	0.003	<0.001	0.006	0.010	<0.001	<0.001	ns	<0.001
Speed	<0.001	0.002	<0.001	0.008	<0.001	<0.001	<0.001	<0.001	<0.001	0.001	<0.001	<0.001	ns	<0.001
Double support	ns	ns	0.021	ns	0.035	0.004	0.016	0.010	0.009	0.017	0.020	0.026	ns	<0.001
Cadence	<0.001	<0.001	0.004	0.020	0.010	<0.001	0.003	<0.001	0.005	0.008	<0.001	<0.001	ns	<0.001
Stride length	0.045	ns	0.002	0.029	0.003	<0.001	<0.001	<0.001	<0.001	0.004	<0.001	<0.001	ns	<0.001
Max toe height	ns	ns	ns	Ns	0.048	0.005	0.023	<0.001	0.009	ns	0.004	0.008	ns	0.002
Swing phase	ns	ns	ns	ns	ns	ns	ns	0.041	ns	ns	ns	ns	ns	0.024
Stance phase	ns	ns	ns	ns	ns	ns	ns	0.041	ns	ns	ns	ns	ns	0.023
Max heel height	ns	ns	ns	ns	ns	0.047	ns	0.022	ns	ns	0.040	ns	ns	0.008
Acc. Mediolateral	0.026	ns	ns	ns	ns	ns	ns	0.026	ns	ns	0.031	ns	ns	<0.001

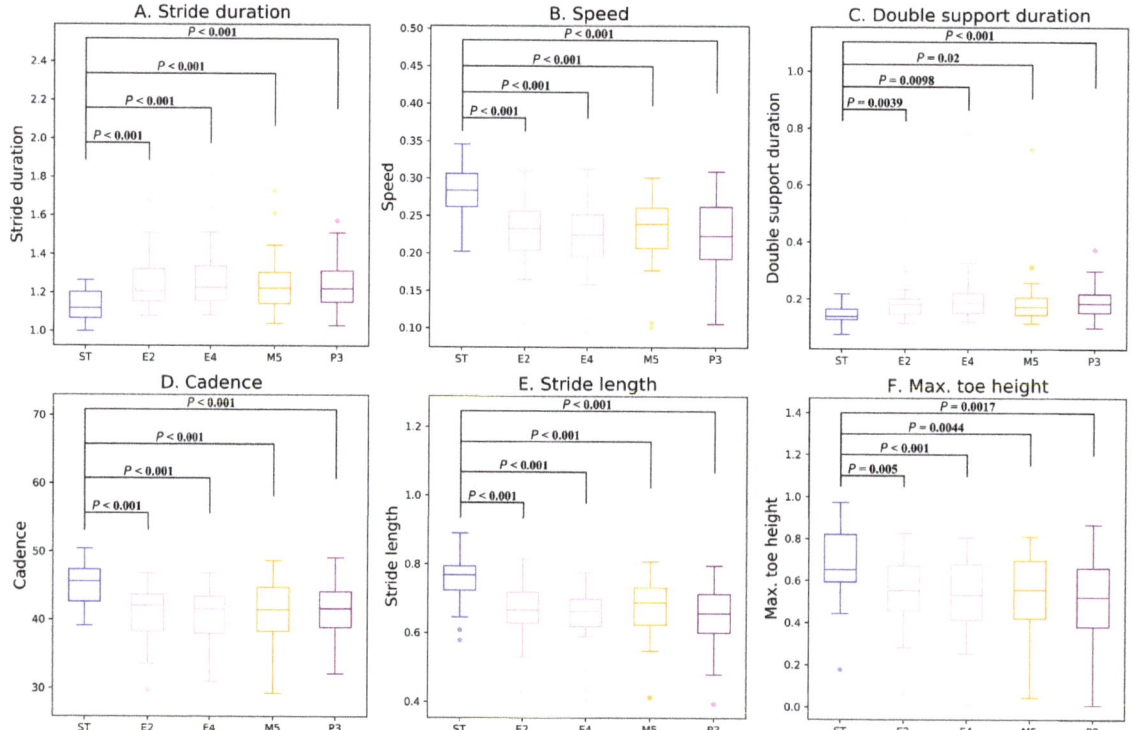

Figure 5. Boxplots showing the dual-tasking activities with the highest load on the gait for the most significant parameters (see Table 5).

If we look at Table 5 by rows rather than by columns, we can see how the significant gait parameters for the baseline dual tasks are stride duration, speed, cadence and stride length. On the other hand, when performing the dual tasks with the smartphone, it can be observed how more gait parameters are affected compared to the baseline tasks, such as double support, swing phase, stance phase and maximum foot height.

3.2. Correlation Analysis

Finally, Pearson's correlation coefficient was calculated to examine the relationships between age and the variability of gait parameters in the performance of the dual-task baseline activities, the dual-task activities with the mobile phone and with the gait without an additional task. Appendix A, Table A2 shows a moderate/strong relationship in the parameters of speed ($r = -0.58$), cadence ($r = -0.57$), stride length ($r = 0.5$), double stance phase ($r = 0.5$) and stride length ($r = 0.49$), with age in the dual-task performance using the mobile device, all with $p < 0.001$. A relationship also exists (though not as strong) between age and the previously mentioned gait parameters with the baseline dual tasks, and likewise with the single-task gait. Figure 6 shows the regression lines with the effects of age on the gait parameters on the performance of the different tasks.

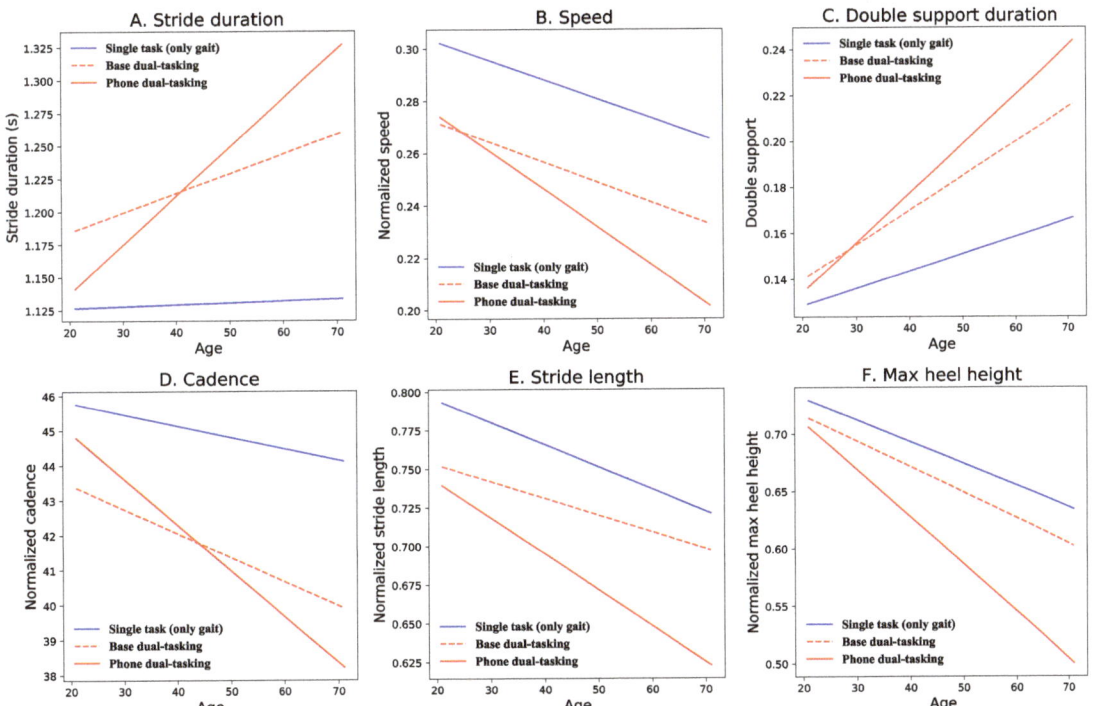

Figure 6. Associations of age (in years) with the normalized gait parameters that showed the best correlation results (see Appendix A, Table A2).

4. Discussion

This work provides knowledge on how various gait parameters are affected when performing typical tasks with a smartphone and compares them with single and baseline dual-tasking tests typically used to diagnose cognitive impairment.

The present work aims to obtain a ground truth in terms of dual-tasking effect on gait variability while interacting with mobile devices. The most relevant parameters and the most representative mobile device tasks were identified, both based on their statistical significance. The data obtained also served as a model to characterize normal age-related cognitive decline—key information for this model as an early diagnostic tool.

In general terms, after analyzing the impact on gait performance for the entire sample during single and dual-tasking, the results obtained are in line with the existing research literature on dual-tasking [18] when considering baseline dual-tasking and when using a mobile device. Particularly, Figure 4 shows that stride duration tends to increase (as indicated by the median of boxplot A), as does stride length variability, which is observable by a slightly higher interquartile range (IQR) and more separated extreme values (wider whiskers in the boxplot) when compared to ambulation without dual-tasking.

Regarding gait speed and cadence (boxplots B and D in Figure 4), both parameters tend to decrease for the entire sample, while their variability increases in the presence of dual-tasking for both DT-baseline and DT-smartphone, having much higher outliners in the dual-tasks with smartphone. Alternatively, for both groups, the double support time (gait phase in which both feet coincide on the ground) increases in a slightly observable manner (boxplot C), also showing higher dispersion values than those from single-task trials (only gait). From this general perspective, spatial gait parameters, such as stride length and max toe height (boxplots E and F in the same figure), decrease in value during dual-tasking performance, possibly due to the consequent reduction in walking pace and the inertia of the movement itself. At the same time, higher variability is also observed, both in the interquartile range and in the distance between their extreme ranges. This can be seen in most of the cognitive tasks in Figure 5 and reinforces what was previously said. Considering Figure 4 and Table A1, Appendix A most of the parameters (except Mediolateral Acc.Mediolateral) have a higher variability in the dual tasks with smartphone. This indicates that smartphone use may be a significant factor to consider when studying gait variability, and it appears to be at least as good (or better) as the "classic" dual tasks in this regard.

However, it is difficult to indicate which of these spatiotemporal gait parameters is the most affected in terms of variability compared to single-task trials (only gait). If we observe the interquartile range closely, perhaps it is cadence or speed; if we look at the length of the boxplots with their whiskers (and without outliers), maybe it is the stride duration.

Table 5 shows that dual tasks that use a smartphone have a greater impact on gait parameters than the baseline tasks when reading by columns. Reading by rows, the results for the baseline dual tasks match what is found in the literature, impacting stride duration, speed and cadence. However, dual tasks involving a smartphone have a greater effect on gait, altering more parameters.

Nevertheless, some interesting conclusions can be drawn by studying the evolution of the gait parameters most affected by dual-tasking in relation to age. The regression lines of dual-tasking with a smartphone show a greater slope than the lines of the base dual-tasking and the lines of single-tasking, as shown in Figure 6. Specifically, moderate direct correlation between stride duration and age, and moderate inverse correlations between speed and age and cadence and age can be observed. Furthermore, it should be highlighted that the biggest difference between single-task and smartphone dual-task correlation coefficients is found in the stride duration parameter, which is reflected by a larger angle formed at the point of intersection of the two lines in the figure.

This work also opens up the possibility of future work that takes diagnosis from punctual tests in controlled environments to long-term testing in everyday life. The next steps will focus on the use of low-cost sensorized insoles, based on previous work by the authors [38], to obtain information on the performance of dual-tasking activities while people carry out their daily life in a more complete and objective way.

In addition to the contributions highlighted above, this work has served to identify some limitations. First, the sample of 30 people, although statistically conclusive, should be expanded to make the results for each age range more consistent. Similarly, future work should consist of replicating the tests with people diagnosed with MCI to create expert systems that can identify the initial stages of MCI, which can help in early diagnosis before symptomatology is evident.

In this initial experiment with the XSENS system, we aimed to identify which activities cause the most variability in gait parameters. Based on these results, future studies should be designed to examine the relationship between these variables (gait parameters) and to apply a factorial ANOVA analysis. Additionally, Tukey's method can be used to further investigate the interaction of different activities with the smartphone to determine their significance in gait analysis.

5. Conclusions

The results show how the performance of dual-tasking (either base or with the use of a smartphone) significantly affects a person's gait. The results show that different dual tasks affect gait parameters differently. Specifically, dual-tasks involving a smartphone were found to have a greater impact on gait, resulting in more significant parameters. In the baseline task, 8 out of 10 gait parameters were significant, with only 3 having a p-value less than 0.001. In contrast, all 10 parameters were affected in the dual task using a smartphone, with 5 having a p-value less than 0.001. These findings indicate that smartphone use should be considered when studying gait variability and may be a useful tool for early diagnosis of cognitive impairment.

Returning to one of the research questions: Which mobile device tasks performed on the move (dual-tasking) have characteristic changes in gait parameters? Overall, it can be concluded that all smartphone tasks affect gait more than baseline tasks, except for task P2 (recording a voice message while walking). These findings indicate the importance of considering smartphone use when studying gait variability and for early diagnosis of cognitive impairment.

Based on the results presented in Figure 6, there is a moderate to strong relationship between age and certain gait parameters (speed, cadence, stride length, double support phase) in the dual-task performance using a smartphone. This relationship is also present, though not as strong, in the performance of the dual-task baseline activities and the single-task gait. So, regarding the question: Which are especially characteristic at older ages? we can also conclude that the effect of dual-tasking with a smartphone increases with age; this is well-observed in stride duration, speed and cadence.

Author Contributions: Conceptualization, R.H. and I.G.; methodology, R.H. and I.G.; software, D.C.-P. and C.C.D.; validation, D.C.-P., C.C.D., R.H. and I.G.; formal analysis, D.C.-P. and C.C.D.; investigation, R.H., J.F. and I.G.; resources, E.J., D.C.-P. and C.C.D.; data curation, D.C.-P. and C.C.D.; writing—original draft preparation, D.C.-P. and C.C.D.; writing—review and editing, R.H., I.G., E.J. and J.F.; visualization, D.C.-P. and C.C.D.; supervision, I.G. and R.H.; project administration, R..H.; funding acquisition, R.H. and J.F. All authors have read and agreed to the published version of the manuscript.

Funding: This research was funded by the MINISTERIO DE CIENCIA, INNOVACIÓN Y UNIVERSIDADES, grant number projects: RTI2018-098780-B-I00 and PDC2022-133457-I00 (M^{4}S national research project and derived proof of concept project) and EQC2019-006053-P (WeCareLab); the PTA2020-018436-I technical support personnel contract; and the 2022-PRED-20651 predoctoral contract by UNIVERSITY OF CASTILLA-LA MANCHA.

Institutional Review Board Statement: The study was conducted in accordance with the Declaration of Helsinki, and following the Ethics Committee guidelines of University of Castilla-La Mancha (https://www.uclm.es/misiones/investigacion/serviciosinvestigacion/portaleticacientifica).

Informed Consent Statement: Informed consent was obtained from all subjects involved in the study.

Data Availability Statement: The dataset generated and analyzed for this study can be found in https://mamilab.eu/datasets/.

Acknowledgments: We would like to thank all the people who collaborated as participants in this experiment. We would also like to thank Victor Casero-Alonso for clearing up our questions regarding statistical analysis.

Conflicts of Interest: The authors declare no conflict of interest.

Appendix A

Table A1. Results of applying the student's *t*-test for each gait parameter normalized between single task (only gait) and gait during dual-tasking (baseline and mobile device tasks). Variables are sorted in ascending order of *p*-values. The mean ± SD of the parameters are reported.

Gait Parameter	Single Task	Baseline DT	Phone DT	*p*-Value	*p*-Value
Stride duration (s)	1.13 ± 0.08	1.22 ± 0.11	1.23 ± 0.14	<0.001	<0.001
Speed	0.29 ± 0.04	0.25 ± 0.04	0.24 ± 0.05	0.001	<0.001
Double support phase	0.15 ± 0.03	0.18 ± 0.08	0.19 ± 0.08	0.011	<0.001
Cadence	44.99 ± 3.04	41.76 ± 3.59	41.73 ± 4.47	<0.001	<0.001
Stride length	0.76 ± 0.07	0.73 ± 0.06	0.69 ± 0.00	0.020	<0.001
Max toe height	0.68 ± 0.17	0.63 ± 0.17	0.57 ± 0.18	0.211	0.002
Swing phase	0.43 ± 0.02	0.42 ± 0.02	0.42 ± 0.03	0.041	0.005
Stance phase	0.57 ± 0.02	0.58 ± 0.02	0.58 ± 0.03	0.041	0.005
Max heel height	0.69 ± 0.16	0.66 ± 0.15	0.61 ± 0.18	0.504	0.031
Acc. Mediolateral	0.17 ± 0.04	0.15 ± 0.04	0.15 ± 0.04	0.0132	0.039

Table A2. Results of applying Pearson to search for correlations between normalized gait variables and age when performing normal gait and dual-tasking.

	Single-Task		Base Dual-Tasking		Phone Dual-Tasking	
Gait Parameter	*r*	*p*-Value	*r*	*p*-Value	*r*	*p*-Value
Stride duration (s)	0.03	ns	0.26	0.046	0.49	<0.001
Speed	−0.40	0.031	−0.42	<0.001	−0.58	<0.001
Double Support	0.46	0.011	0.38	0.003	0.50	<0.001
Cadence	−0.21	ns	−0.37	0.003	−0.57	<0.001
Stride length	−0.40	0.026	−0.36	0.005	−0.50	<0.001
Max toe height	−0.34	ns	−0.19	ns	−0.34	<0.001
Swing phase	−0.33	ns	−0.25	ns	−0.25	<0.001
Stance phase	0.33	ns	0.25	0.049	0.25	<0.001
Max heel height	−0.24	ns	−0.28	0.031	−0.43	<0.001
Acc. Mediolateral	−0.07	ns	0.02	ns	−0.29	<0.001

References

1. Grundman, M.; Petersen, R.C.; Ferris, S.H.; Thomas, R.G.; Aisen, P.S.; Bennett, D.A.; Foster, N.L.; Jack, C.R.; Galasko, D.R.; Doody, R.; et al. Mild Cognitive Impairment Can Be Distinguished from Alzheimer Disease and Normal Aging for Clinical Trials. *Arch. Neurol.* **2004**, *61*, 59–66. [CrossRef]
2. Gauthier, S.; Reisberg, B.; Zaudig, M.; Petersen, R.C.; Ritchie, K.; Broich, K.; Belleville, S.; Brodaty, H.; Bennett, D.; Chertkow, H.; et al. Mild Cognitive Impairment. *Lancet* **2006**, *367*, 1262–1270. [CrossRef] [PubMed]
3. Ritchie, K. Mild Cognitive Impairment: An Epidemiological Perspective. *Dialogues Clin. Neurosci.* **2004**, *6*, 401–408. [CrossRef] [PubMed]
4. Jeong, J. EEG Dynamics in Patients with Alzheimer's Disease. *Clin. Neurophysiol.* **2004**, *115*, 1490–1505. [CrossRef]
5. Montero-Odasso, M.M.; Sarquis-Adamson, Y.; Speechley, M.; Borrie, M.J.; Hachinski, V.C.; Wells, J.; Riccio, P.M.; Schapira, M.; Sejdic, E.; Camicioli, R.M.; et al. Association of Dual-Task Gait with Incident Dementia in Mild Cognitive Impairment. *JAMA Neurol.* **2017**, *74*, 857. [CrossRef] [PubMed]
6. Bovonsunthonchai, S.; Vachalathiti, R.; Hiengkaew, V.; Bryant, M.S.; Richards, J.; Senanarong, V. Quantitative Gait Analysis in Mild Cognitive Impairment, Dementia, and Cognitively Intact Individuals: A Cross-Sectional Case–Control Study. *BMC Geriatr.* **2022**, *22*, 767. [CrossRef]
7. Zheng, Y.; Lang, S.; Liang, J.; Jiang, Y.; Zhao, B.; Chen, H.; Huang, D.; Li, Q.; Liu, H.; Chen, S.; et al. Effects of Motor-Cognitive Interaction Based on Dual-Task Gait Analysis Recognition in Middle Age to Aging People with Normal Cognition and Mild Cognitive Impairment. *Front. Aging Neurosci.* **2022**, *14*, 969822. [CrossRef]
8. Lamoth, C.J.; van Deudekom, F.J.; van Campen, J.P.; Appels, B.A.; de Vries, O.J.; Pijnappels, M. Gait Stability and Variability Measures Show Effects of Impaired Cognition and Dual Tasking in Frail People. *J. Neuroeng. Rehabil.* **2011**, *8*, 1–9. [CrossRef]
9. Ansai, J.H.; Andrade, L.P.D.; Rossi, P.G.; Almeida, M.L.; Carvalho Vale, F.A.; Rebelatto, J.R. Association Between Gait and Dual Task with Cognitive Domains in Older People with Cognitive Impairment. *J. Mot. Behav.* **2018**, *50*, 409–415. [CrossRef]

10. Åhman, H.B.; Cedervall, Y.; Kilander, L.; Giedraitis, V.; Berglund, L.; McKee, K.J.; Rosendahl, E.; Ingelsson, M.; Åberg, A.C. Dual-Task Tests Discriminate between Dementia, Mild Cognitive Impairment, Subjective Cognitive Impairment, and Healthy Controls—A Cross-Sectional Cohort Study. *BMC Geriatr.* **2020**, *20*, 258. [CrossRef]
11. Bragatto, V.S.R.; Andrade, L.P.D.; Rossi, P.G.; Ansai, J.H. Dual-Task during Gait between Elderly with Mild Cognitive Impairment and Alzheimer: Systematic Review. *Fisioterapia em Movimento* **2017**, *30*, 849–857. [CrossRef]
12. Leone, C.; Moumdjian, L.; Patti, F.; Vanzeir, E.; Baert, I.; Veldkamp, R.; van Wijmeersch, B.; Feys, P. Comparing 16 Different Dual-Tasking Paradigms in Individuals with Multiple Sclerosis and Healthy Controls: Working Memory Tasks Indicate Cognitive–Motor Interference. *Front. Neurol.* **2020**, *11*, 918. [CrossRef] [PubMed]
13. González, I.; Fontecha, J.; Hervás, R.; Bravo, J. Estimation of Temporal Gait Events from a Single Accelerometer Through the Scale-Space Filtering Idea. *J. Med. Syst.* **2016**, *40*, 1–10. [CrossRef] [PubMed]
14. González, I.; Fontecha, J.; Bravo, J. Relationship between Stride Interval Variability and Aging: Use of Linear and Non-Linear Estimators for Gait Variability Assessment in Assisted Living Environments. *J. Ambient Intell. Humaniz. Comput.* **2019**, *10*, 2095–2109. [CrossRef]
15. Droby, A.; Varangis, E.; Habeck, C.; Hausdorff, J.M.; Stern, Y.; Mirelman, A.; Maidan, I. Effects of Aging on Cognitive and Brain Inter-Network Integration Patterns Underlying Usual and Dual-Task Gait Performance. *Front. Aging Neurosci.* **2022**, *14*, 1157. [CrossRef]
16. Muir, S.W.; Speechley, M.; Wells, J.; Borrie, M.; Gopaul, K.; Montero-Odasso, M. Gait Assessment in Mild Cognitive Impairment and Alzheimer's Disease: The Effect of Dual-Task Challenges across the Cognitive Spectrum. *Gait Posture* **2012**, *35*, 96–100. [CrossRef]
17. MacAulay, R.K.; Wagner, M.T.; Szeles, D.; Milano, N.J. Improving Sensitivity to Detect Mild Cognitive Impairment: Cognitive Load Dual-Task Gait Speed Assessment. *J. Int. Neuropsychol. Soc.* **2017**, *23*, 493–501. [CrossRef]
18. Ramírez, F.; Gutiérrez, M. Dual-Task Gait as a Predictive Tool for Cognitive Impairment in Older Adults: A Systematic Review. *Front. Aging Neurosci.* **2021**, *13*, 769462. [CrossRef]
19. Veldkamp, R.; Goetschalckx, M.; Hulst, H.E.; Nieuwboer, A.; Grieten, K.; Baert, I.; Leone, C.; Moumdjian, L.; Feys, P. Cognitive–Motor Interference in Individuals with a Neurologic Disorder: A Systematic Review of Neural Correlates. *Cogn. Behav. Neurol.* **2021**, *34*, 79–95. [CrossRef]
20. Tsang, C.S.-L.; Wang, S.; Miller, T.; Pang, M.Y.-C. Degree and Pattern of Dual-Task Interference during Walking Vary with Component Tasks in People after Stroke: A Systematic Review. *J. Physiother.* **2022**, *68*, 26–36. [CrossRef]
21. Rooney, S.; Ozkul, C.; Paul, L. Correlates of Dual-Task Performance in People with Multiple Sclerosis: A Systematic Review. *Gait Posture* **2020**, *81*, 172–182. [CrossRef] [PubMed]
22. Bravo, J.; Villarreal, V.; Hervás, R.; Urzaiz, G. Using a Communication Model to Collect Measurement Data through Mobile Devices. *Sensors* **2012**, *12*, 9253–9272. [CrossRef]
23. Cabañero, L.; Hervás, R.; González, I.; Fontecha, J.; Mondéjar, T.; Bravo, J. Characterisation of Mobile-Device Tasks by Their Associated Cognitive Load through EEG Data Processing. *Future Gener. Comput. Syst.* **2020**, *113*, 380–390. [CrossRef]
24. Lupton, D.; Jutel, A. "It's like Having a Physician in Your Pocket!" A Critical Analysis of Self-Diagnosis Smartphone Apps. *Soc. Sci. Med.* **2015**, *133*, 128–135. [CrossRef] [PubMed]
25. Klimova, B. Mobile Phone Apps in the Management and Assessment of Mild Cognitive Impairment and/or Mild-to-Moderate Dementia: An Opinion Article on Recent Findings. *Front. Hum. Neurosci.* **2017**, *11*, 461. [CrossRef]
26. Bravo, J.; Hervás, R.; Fontecha, J.; González, I. M-Health: Lessons Learned by m-Experiences. *Sensors* **2018**, *18*, 1569. [CrossRef]
27. Harari, G.M.; Lane, N.D.; Wang, R.; Crosier, B.S.; Campbell, A.T.; Gosling, S.D. Using Smartphones to Collect Behavioral Data in Psychological Science: Opportunities, Practical Considerations, and Challenges. *Perspect. Psychol. Sci.* **2016**, *11*, 838–854. [CrossRef]
28. Jung, C.G.H. *Collected Works of C.G. Jung, Volume 8: Structure & Dynamics of the Psyche*; Princeton University Press: Princeton, NJ, USA, 2014.
29. Paulich, M.; Schepers, M.; Rudigkeit, N.; Bellusci, G. Xsens MTw Awinda: Miniature Wireless Inertial-Magnetic Motion Tracker for Highly Accurate 3D Kinematic Applications. *Xsens Enschede Neth.* **2018**, *MW0404P*, 1–9. [CrossRef]
30. Song, Z.; Cao, Z.; Li, Z.; Wang, J.; Liu, Y. Inertial Motion Tracking on Mobile and Wearable Devices: Recent Advancements and Challenges. *Tsinghua Sci. Technol.* **2021**, *26*, 692–705. [CrossRef]
31. Hof, A.L. Scaling Gait Data to Body Size. *Gait Posture* **1996**, *4*, 222–223. [CrossRef]
32. Chao, E.Y.; Laughman, R.K.; Schneider, E.; Stauffer, R.N. Normative Data of Knee Joint Motion and Ground Reaction Forces in Adult Level Walking. *J. Biomech.* **1983**, *16*, 219–233. [CrossRef]
33. Macellari, V.; Giacomozzi, C.; Saggini, R. Spatial-Temporal Parameters of Gait: Reference Data and a Statistical Method for Normality Assessment. *Gait Posture* **1999**, *10*, 171–181. [CrossRef] [PubMed]
34. Gill, H.S.; O'Connor, J.J. Heelstrike and the Pathomechanics of Osteoarthrosis: A Pilot Gait Study. *J. Biomech.* **2003**, *36*, 1625–1631. [CrossRef]
35. Owings, T.M.; Grabiner, M.D. Variability of Step Kinematics in Young and Older Adults. *Gait Posture* **2004**, *20*, 26–29. [CrossRef] [PubMed]
36. Titianova, E.B.; Pitkänen, K.; Pääkkönen, A.; Sivenius, J.; Tarkka, I.M. Gait Characteristics and Functional Ambulation Profile in Patients with Chronic Unilateral Stroke. *Am. J. Phys. Med. Rehabil.* **2003**, *82*, 778–786. [CrossRef] [PubMed]

37. Savitzky, A.; Golay, M.J.E. Smoothing and Differentiation of Data by Simplified Least Squares Procedures. *Anal. Chem.* **1964**, *36*, 1627–1639. [CrossRef]
38. González, I.; Fontecha, J.; Hervás, R.; Bravo, J. An Ambulatory System for Gait Monitoring Based on Wireless Sensorized Insoles. *Sensors* **2015**, *15*, 16589–16613. [CrossRef]

Disclaimer/Publisher's Note: The statements, opinions and data contained in all publications are solely those of the individual author(s) and contributor(s) and not of MDPI and/or the editor(s). MDPI and/or the editor(s) disclaim responsibility for any injury to people or property resulting from any ideas, methods, instructions or products referred to in the content.

Article

A Fuzzy Recommendation System for the Automatic Personalization of Physical Rehabilitation Exercises in Stroke Patients

Cristian Gmez-Portes [1,†], José Jesús Castro-Schez [1,†], Javier Albusac [1,†], Dorothy N. Monekosso [2,†] and David Vallejo [1,*,†]

1 Department of Information Technologies and Systems, University of Castilla-La Mancha Paseo de la Universidad 4, 13071 Ciudad Real, Spain; Cristian.Gomez2@alu.uclm.es (C.G.-P.); JoseJesus.Castro@uclm.es (J.J.C.-S.); JavierAlonso.Albusac@uclm.es (J.A.)
2 School of Built Environment, Engineering and Computing, Leeds-Beckett University, Leeds LS6 3QT, UK; D.N.Monekosso@leedsbeckett.ac.uk
* Correspondence: David.Vallejo@uclm.es
† These authors contributed equally to this work.

Citation: Gmez-Portes, C.; Castro-Schez, J.J; Albusac, J.; Monekosso, D.N.; Vallejo, D. A Fuzzy Recommendation System for the Automatic Personalization of Physical Rehabilitation Exercises in Stroke Patients. *Mathematics* 2021, 9, 1427. https://doi.org/10.3390/math9121427

Academic Editor: Daniel Gómez Gonzalez

Received: 17 May 2021
Accepted: 17 June 2021
Published: 19 June 2021

Publisher's Note: MDPI stays neutral with regard to jurisdictional claims in published maps and institutional affiliations.

Copyright: © 2021 by the authors. Licensee MDPI, Basel, Switzerland. This article is an open access article distributed under the terms and conditions of the Creative Commons Attribution (CC BY) license (https://creativecommons.org/licenses/by/4.0/).

Abstract: Stroke is among the top 10 leading causes of death and disability around the world. Patients who suffer from this disease usually perform physical exercises at home to improve their condition. These exercises are recommended by therapists based on the patient's progress level, and may be remotely supervised by them if technology is an option for both. At this point, two major challenges must be faced. The first one is the lack of specialized medical staff to remotely handle the growing number of stroke patients. The second one is the difficulty of dynamically adapt the patient's therapy plan in real time whilst they rehabilitate at home, since their evolution varies as the rehabilitation process progresses. In this context, we present a fuzzy system that is able to automatically adapt the rehabilitation plan of stroke patients. The use of fuzzy logic greatly facilitates the monitoring and guidance of stroke patients. Moreover, the system is capable of automatically generating modifications of existent exercises whilst considering their particularities at any given time. A preliminary experiment was conducted to show the advantages of the proposal, and the results suggest that the application of fuzzy logic may help make correct decisions based on the patient's progress level.

Keywords: remote rehabilitation; recommender system; stroke; fuzzy logic; telemedicine

1. Introduction

One in six people will suffer a stroke during their lifetime. Globally, stroke causes more than 6 million deaths each year, according to statistics provided by the World Health Organization [1]. Approximately two-thirds of stroke survivors leave hospital with some form of disability. Current predictions for the coming years are, unfortunately, negative, due to factors such as the incidence of stroke in middle-income countries [2]. In fact, 70% of strokes globally occur in low- and middle-income countries. This figure has doubled in recent decades, while in high-income countries, it has fallen by 42% [1]. The impact of this unresolved clinical challenge on health systems is enormous, due to issues such as the continuous need for physical rehabilitation and face-to-face supervision by qualified medical staff. In addition, stroke often affects people who are at the productive peak of their working careers, which can also have an impact on a country's socioeconomic development [3].

Much of the post-stroke rehabilitation process focuses on the physical rehabilitation of patients. In this process, both physiotherapists and occupational therapists guide the patient to regain day-to-day autonomy by addressing the movement and mobility difficulties resulting from stroke. In this sense, rehabilitation plans are usually designed around the concept of *self-care*, i.e., based on activities and exercises that the patient can progressively perform at home and in an independent way, whenever possible. The intensity of rehabilitation will depend on the condition of each patient, although it is quite common to carry out daily sessions of 45 min for periods of between 2 and 6 weeks. In more severe cases of stroke, rehabilitation may last several months.

In recent years, a significant number of applied research studies have appeared in which technology has been used to deploy virtual home rehabilitation systems [4,5]. These pursue the dual goal of facilitating patient monitoring and motivating patients to carry out rehabilitation exercises at home. These systems generally provide natural interaction mechanisms in a 3D virtual environment, guiding and helping patients to perform rehabilitation exercises in a playful and enjoyable way. Typically, a system offering such features will consist of (i) a device that can detect the patient's movements by means of a tracking system that calculates the positions and orientations of the joints in 3D space; (ii) a laptop running the system's software; and (iii) a monitor that provides visual feedback. It should be noted that technological solutions based on the low-cost Microsoft Kinect™ device have underpinned much of the research work conducted in recent years [6], with numerous studies giving credit to the clinical validity of the generated tools [7,8]. However, this device has already been replaced by more modern and scalable alternatives.

In order for a remote rehabilitation system to be used effectively from home, different aspects need to be considered. Firstly, usability is essential. If the underlying technology involves an entry barrier for the patient, then the system will be discontinued. Such a system can be considered usable when technology becomes transparent and natural for the patient. In this sense, natural interfaces based on gesture and movement detection are particularly relevant. At the same time, the system must be able to offer continuous assistance to the patient, making it as easy as possible to use the system, especially when approaching the system for the first time. Secondly, the ability to motivate the patient is another fundamental element to guarantee the continuous use of the system, since rehabilitation routines are usually based on the systematic repetition of a limited set of exercises. The integration of gamification techniques has been used in recent years to increase patient motivation [9]. Thirdly, the system must be able to recognize, with a certain precision and in an automatic way, the movements or exercises performed by the patient, which are usually previously assigned by the therapist. Home rehabilitation systems are often designed to encourage the patient to complete the entire routine, even if the execution is not perfect. In this regard, it is often desirable to strike a balance between the economic cost of the tracking system and the accuracy of the system.

A system that integrates these three fundamental characteristics will maximize the chances of successful use, guiding the patient through the rehabilitation process at home, facilitating the therapist's work, and ultimately, improving the quality and effectiveness of remote rehabilitation. However, the therapist would still be responsible for the individualized supervision of each patient according to their inherent condition (considering aspects such as their age, physical condition, or severity of the stroke) and their level of progress according to the assigned rehabilitation routine. Ideally, a remote rehabilitation system may incorporate an intelligent module that would automatically and dynamically adapt this routine for each patient, thus incorporating the notion of personalization. This adaptation would serve, among other things, to recommend more difficult exercises or to suggest variations of exercises based on the patient's performance.

In the previously introduced research context, our work has been essentially focused on the creation of a comprehensive remote rehabilitation system capable of automatically evaluating and classifying rehabilitation exercises [10]. On these foundations, we also designed a language whose sentences are processed by a software that can automatically generate personalized exergames that motivate the patient to perform rehabilitation exercises. In this article, we focus on the automated and intelligent personalization of the rehabilitation process adapted to each patient [11]. Thus, this paper proposes a fuzzy system for the recommendation of rehabilitation exercises for stroke patients. This system integrates an expert knowledge base defined by means of fuzzy rules and variables that reflects aspects such as the performance of a patient when performing rehabilitation exercises. The system is capable of adapting the rehabilitation plan initially assigned by the therapist. This adaptation takes the form of recommendations for new exercises, or exercises already performed by the patient, depending on the variation in the patient's level of progress as the rehabilitation process progresses.

The remainder of this article is structured as follows. Section 2 positions our work in the context of recommender systems, and particularly, those that operate automatically in remote rehabilitation systems. Subsequently, Section 3 presents our contribution, discussing the fundamental aspects and addressing the integration in a remote rehabilitation system. Section 4 presents the results obtained after conducting an experiment that illustrates with examples of how the fuzzy recommender system adapts a patient's rehabilitation routine. These results are discussed in Section 5, and the article ends with a series of conclusions in Section 6.

2. Related Work

When designing remote rehabilitation systems, it is essential to take into account the personalization of the patient's rehabilitation process. A symbiosis must be sought between the patient, the system, and the clinician, which seeks to adapt to the patient's progress according to the state of their injury. Achieving this involves the design of recommendation systems that are adaptive to the patient.

The design of a recommender system depends to a large extent on the used information and the available knowledge. Recommender systems can be classified into different groups [12]: (i) user profile recommendation systems; (ii) content recommendation systems; (iii) hybrid recommendation systems; (iv) filter-based recommendation systems; and (v) feature-based recommendation systems.

In the field of remote rehabilitation, recommendation systems based on the user's profile are commonly used. These systems analyze the patient's profile, considering their condition and evolution, and based on this, recommend a rehabilitation routine from the established plan for the recovery of their injury.

One of the main problems to be faced when studying a patient's profile is the uncertainty and vagueness with which the patient's condition is usually assessed. Furthermore, determining how well they are performing a certain exercise or even establishing how they are progressing represent similar challenges. In this sense, fuzzy logic and linguistic variables [13,14] are well-validated tools to be taken into account when dealing with uncertainty and vagueness.

In the context of remote rehabilitation systems, González-González et al. [15] presented a proposal in which the general objective is the design of an intelligent rehabilitation system based on exergames, consisting of an exercise player and a tool for designing them. The system includes a recommendation module that analyses the user's interactions, physical history, and preferences to assign the exergames to be performed. In turn, this module handles the concepts of difficulty levels and user skills. The recommendation algorithm revolves around three simple assumptions based on the patient's most recent performance (last exergame performed): (i) if the performance was low, the algorithm chooses an easier exergame; (ii) if the performance was good, the algorithm assigns a more difficult exercise; (iii) otherwise, the algorithm chooses an exercise of medium difficulty. The system was evaluated with domain experts, users and therapists, with positive results in terms of gesture-based interaction and medical applications.

Esfahlani et al. [16] discussed a serious game designed for the user to perform a series of tasks based on a dynamic of reaching virtual goals with a therapeutic objective. The difficulty levels of these tasks are adjusted based on a fuzzy controller, which has the user's skeleton tracking data (position and orientation of joints in 3D space) as input and the difficulty level of the game that the patient will perform later as output. In this sense, the proposed system allows to guide, in an automatic way, the patient's rehabilitation routine through continuous and personalized learning. The fuzzy rules are derived from consultancy and collaboration with physiotherapists, along with the various tests carried out. On the other hand, the authors of [17] describe related work in which a grammar is used to enable therapists to specify rehabilitation exercises. The system includes a fuzzy logic-based component that evaluates, in real time, whether the patient performs the exercises according to the exercise definition. In a related context, the prototype of the patient rehabilitation station that integrates video games for rehabilitation based on computational intelligence techniques is presented in [18], both for the online monitoring of the execution of movements during the games and for the adaptation of the game to the patient's condition. The prototype integrates a fuzzy system to monitor the execution of the exercises, in real time, according to the clinical constraints defined by the therapist at the time of configuration, and to provide direct feedback to the patients. At the same time, the system adapts to modify the game according to the patient's current performance and progress and to the exercise plan specified by the therapist. This latter work represents one of the pillars of the methodology for the design of safe, therapeutic exergames introduced by these same authors [19].

In a line of research more linked to the management of expert knowledge, a tele-rehabilitation system for the remote selection, evaluation and management of physical therapies is proposed in [20]. The main contribution of this work is the creation of an integral system for tele-rehabilitation, although the authors place special emphasis on the extraction and use of knowledge through the definition of an ontology composed of 2300 classes and 100 properties, to appropriately select the exercises assigned to each patient. To do this, a knowledge base is used that contains information about the patient's medical history and the previously assigned treatment.

On the other hand, Karime et al. [21] proposed a web-based framework for wrist rehabilitation that makes use of fuzzy logic to offer adaptive tasks to the patient, in parallel with the supervision performed by the therapist. In this work, an evaluation of the effectiveness of the framework is carried out, considering the adjustment of various parameters used in the rehabilitation process in a framework that combines the level of personalization of the rehabilitation based on the patient's performance and the feedback offered by the therapist. The use of fuzzy logic is also present in articles focusing on patient rehabilitation using robots or exoskeletons, such as the work discussed in [22], where a system based on deterministic adaptive robust control is introduced whose control parameters are optimized thanks to a novel approach based upon cooperative game theory. External disturbances (possibly time-varying) are managed through fuzzy logic and its ability to work with uncertainty.

Our proposal, which is described in detail in Section 3, which falls within the scope of several lines of research that are currently considered popular research topics. Particularly noteworthy is the line that contemplates the definition of artificial intelligence models and the use of expert knowledge to guide or orientate the patient's evolution, based on their clinical data and the context of their illness. This line is closely related to the impact that precision medicine has had on the medical domain, and whose ideas can be borrowed with the ultimate aim of adapting or personalizing the rehabilitation process to each patient. Furthermore, this work is also framed in the field of telemedicine tools in the context of physical rehabilitation, thus trying to respond to an unresolved clinical challenge as a consequence of the lack of specialized clinical staff to supervise patients affected by stroke or, from a more general point of view, by neurological diseases requiring physical rehabilitation.

Thus, the main contributions of this research article are as follows:

- Firstly, a recommendation module which can automatically modify rehabilitation plans previously devised by physicians is proposed. Conditional knowledge is defined to select the most suitable exercise for the patients, depending on their current condition and how they progress in terms of rehabilitation;

- Secondly, the gap between the rehabilitation system in which the recommendation module is integrated and the patients/physicians is reduced, thanks to the use of fuzzy logic to both represent and infer knowledge. This approach facilitates the understanding of the artificial system, and particularly, how the recommendation module operates. We think that this contribution is especially relevant when it comes to explain how artificial systems make decisions. Furthermore, the feedback provided to the patients can be used to guide the rehabilitation process in a dynamic way;
- Thirdly, the proposal sets the foundations for providing physicians with a tool that reduces the time spent supervising stroke patients. Currently, there is a lack of specialized personnel to supervise, face-to-face and on a regular basis, patients affected by neurological diseases that require physical rehabilitation. Our work may eventually help improve the quality and effectiveness of remote rehabilitation by addressing the automatic adaptation of rehabilitation routines.

3. Material and Methods

3.1. Remote Rehabilitation System Overview

In this section, a fuzzy system for automatically recommending rehabilitation exercises for stroke patients is proposed. Particularly, the exercises recommended by this system are therapeutic exergames, which involve physical effort guided by gamification techniques. Fundamentally, this system was mainly designed to enable patients to perform home rehabilitation exercises, according to their condition and situation at a given moment of their therapy. The proposed approach employs the therapist's knowledge to evaluate the patient mobility and recommend, in consequence, a rehabilitation exercise according to such information. However, it should be pointed out that the recommendation of an exercise when patients perform rehabilitation at home is exacerbated, since the adjustment of the therapy turns into a more complex process by having a fuzzy idea of their current situation. This system bears this in mind, and is able to automatically generate personalized modifications of existent exercises by considering the particularities of the patients. Despite this, it should be noted that the system does not pretend to remove the therapist's role. On the contrary, it aims to complement it in order to reduce their workload by delegating tasks to the proposed intelligent system.

The system introduced herein consists of several components that interact between them. Figure 1 depicts the overall architecture, whose interrelated components are the domain knowledge module (i); the interface module (ii); the tracking module (iii); the evaluation module (iv); and the recommender module (v). Each component is briefly described below.

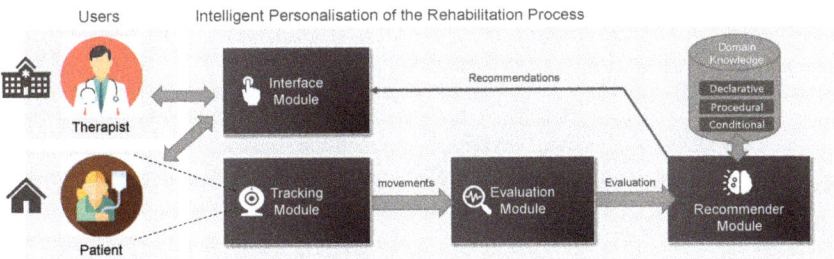

Figure 1. Architectural overview of the proposed system.

The **domain knowledge module** integrates the knowledge necessary for the system to correctly work. This module considers the following aspects: knowledge about the physical rehabilitation of stroke patients, knowledge about the performance of rehabilitation exercises, knowledge about managing their rehabilitation plan, knowledge about the patient's body, their injury, their condition, and the evolution in their rehabilitation. This module is referred to as the knowledge of domain experts from a higher perspective. Specifically, this is structured and organized in three specific classes of knowledge, which are clearly differentiated: declarative knowledge, procedural knowledge, and conditional knowledge:

- *Declarative knowledge.* It refers to the facts or static knowledge. In this regard, it defines the set of existent body joints that can be exercised during the rehabilitation, which will be recognized by the system (i.e., $J = \{j_1, j_2, \ldots, j_{31}\}$ https://docs.microsoft.com/bs-latn-ba/azure/kinect-dk/body-joints, accessed on 11 June 2021), the constraints associated with them (i.e., $C(J) = \{C(j_1), C(j_2), \ldots, C(j_{31})\}$), the associated variables to monitor the rehabilitation exercise of patients (i.e., $V = \{v_1, v_2, \ldots, v_k\}$);
- *Procedural knowledge.* This knowledge defines the rehabilitation exercises and the game dynamics associated with them (i.e., $E = \{e_1, e_2, \ldots, e_n\}$. In each $e_i \in E$, the patient works out a concrete joint (i.e., $j_x \in J$) with a different degree of complexity, trying to rehabilitate a body member with low mobility. The procedural knowledge also includes the knowledge required to check how well the patient performs an exercise and to determine how the patient is progressing in the rehabilitation process;
- *Conditional knowledge.* This knowledge will be used to recommend the next exercise to be performed in the patients' rehabilitation plan (i.e., $e_i \in E$), based on their degree of injury and their progress towards recovery. Fundamentally, it makes use of a set of fuzzy (if–then) rules (i.e., $R = \{r_1, r_2, \ldots, r_m\}$) to achieve the aforementioned goal. This will be deepened in the following section.

The **interface module** enables the communication between the patient/therapist and the system. On the one hand, it includes the adequate interaction mechanisms so that patients perform rehabilitation exercises as if they played games. On the other hand, it provides the software components to the therapists in order to define rehabilitation exercises and game dynamics associated with them.

The **tracking module** is responsible for recognizing in real time the users' movements to perform rehabilitation exercises. In essence, it captures the body tracking results from a sensor device, in this case Microsoft Azure Kinect DK https://azure.microsoft.com/es-es/services/kinect-dk/, accessed on 11 June 2021. These results represent the 3D spatial coordinates of the human body joints, i.e., positions $(x, y$ and $z) \in \mathbb{R}^3$, and rotations $(w, a, b$ and $c) \in \mathbb{R}^4$. The latter is expressed as a normalized quaternion.

The **evaluation module** assesses the performance of a rehabilitation exercise according to the level of complexity that it entails for the patient. This information is necessary to know the patient's status within the context of the rehabilitation plan and to recommend new rehabilitation exercises.

The **recommendation module** is responsible for modifying the patient's rehabilitation plan according to the patient's current condition. This module will make use of conditional knowledge to determine the most appropriate exercise for the patient based on their injury and their current level of progress within their rehabilitation plan. This module, which is the core of the paper, is fully detailed in the next section.

As described above, procedural knowledge contains the exercises used in this system. These are physical activities to be executed by patients within the rehabilitation plan with a motivational approach that is based on play, i.e., exergames. The exergame constitutes the core of the system and it is defined as a 8-tuple, consisting of the following elements:

$$e_i = <D_i, JI_i, SET_i, VE_i, T_i, RG_i, C_i(JI_i), KPI_i> \tag{1}$$

where each element represents the following:

- D_i is a description of the exercise e_i;
- JI_i is the set associated with the joints involved in the rehabilitation exercise e_i, i.e., $JI_i \subseteq J$;
- SET_i is the setup of the exercise which is defined as a 4-tuple (sc, rp, t, c). sc indicates the degree of success by achieving a step in the rehabilitation exercise e_i ($sc \in \mathbb{N}$); rp are the repetitions required to perform the exercise e_i ($rp \in \mathbb{N}$); t is the time needed to finish the exercise e_i ($t \in \mathbb{R}$); and c is the degree of complexity of the exercise ($c \in \mathbb{N}$);

- VE_i represents the virtual objects positioned in a playable scene in the 3D space. Examples of this objects may be rings, spheres and hoops, among others;
- T_i refers to the trajectories associated with the movements that a patient will make when performing the exergame e_i. T_i is defined as a set of virtual points that establish the movements the patient must perform;
- RG_i is a set of rules that contains the game mechanics of the exercise e_i, which are based on the interaction between JI_i and T_i in the 3D space to achieve an objective. Formally, $RG_i = (rg_{i1}, rg_{i2}, \ldots, rg_{in})$, where each particular rule of the game rg_{ij} is used to define the function $JI_i \times VE_i \times O \longrightarrow GM$ where:
    - JI_i establishes the joints that interact with the game rule;
    - VE_i establishes the virtual nodes that interact with the game rule;
    - O is a set of objectives defined to satisfy the game rules ($O = \{o_1, o_2, \ldots, o_m\}$);
    - GM is a set of game mechanics to be triggered when a joint involved JI_i interacts with a virtual node VE_i meeting a certain objective o_j. Example of game mechanics may be visual feedback provided to the patient to correct a bad movement.
- $C_i(JI_i)$ is a set of constraints that are associated with joints that the patient should not ideally move to compensate for the lack of mobility or strength in the exercise e_i (i.e., $(C_i(JI_i) \subseteq C(J))$;
- KPI_i is a set of key performance indicators that are used to monitor the patient's evolution according to the performance of the exercise e_i.

3.2. Proposed Recommendation Module

This module aims to help therapists recommend new exercises to patients who perform home rehabilitation. Generally, therapists ask patients to carry out a series of exercises at home, when the therapy has not yet been completed in the rehabilitation center. Once the patients return to the clinic, therapists interview them about how they have performed the exercises and evaluate their progress in order to be able to recommend new exercises. Without the use of technology, the therapists' knowledge may be inaccurate regarding the patients' progress as they do not know their commitment at home.

The developed system will collect data on how the patients have performed exercises at home within their rehabilitation plan. In addition, the system, using an intelligent recommender, is able to adapt the rehabilitation plan to the patients' needs. This section presents the architecture devised for the intelligent rehabilitation module which will be used by the general system to autonomously modify the patients' rehabilitation plan according to their evolution.

However, entering before fully into detail of the formal model, the next subsection shows the fundamental ideas of the proposed system.

3.2.1. Fundamental Ideas

This system allows therapists to define a rehabilitation therapy based on the patients' injury and the their initial assessment regarding the patients' condition (their injury state, their physical condition, and their age).

Particularly, the overall rehabilitation system makes use of the gym metaphor to define a rehabilitation therapy. This means that our approach is based on the global concept of patient's rehabilitation plan, which can be considered as a succession of exercises taken from E and ordered by their complexity, which must be carried out by the patient in a sequential way. However, the plan should be able to be altered according to the patient's progress. Thus, provided that the system detects that the patient is finding difficulties to perform an exercise in the plan, the system should be capable of recommending an exercise with lower complexity. It even may modify an existent exercise, reducing the number of repetitions or increasing the time to be spent on it. On the other hand, the system should behave in a similar way when in a situation in which complex exercises are easily performed.

Thus, a rehabilitation plan for a patient p_i, denoted as $P(p_i)$, is defined as follows: $P(p_i) = \{e_x, e_y, \ldots, e_k\}$ where each $e_j \in P(p_i)$ is also an element of E (i.e., $e_j \in E$) and it is satisfied that $Complexity(e_x) \leq Complexity(e_y) \leq \ldots \leq Complexity(e_k)$ with $Complexity(e_j)$ being a function that returns the complexity of the exergame e_j (taken from $c \in SET\_j$).

As mentioned above, the exercises that form part of a patient's plan are initially selected and organized by the therapists according to the patient's injury and condition. The recommendation module will automatically adjust the plan according to the patient's performance, acting on the set of exercises included, their order or even their configuration (values of parameters rp (number of repetitions) and t (time needed to finish the exercise) taken from SET_x).

3.2.2. Recommender Module Definition

The recommendation system presented herein has been proposed as a function that will determine an action on the patient's rehabilitation plan to be adjusted, as much as possible, to the patient's state of recovery. Therefore, this function models the existing relationship between the domain, i.e., the patient's condition in the recovery of the injured limb, and the codomain, i.e., an action to be performed in the rehabilitation plan.

The challenge to be faced is the domain of definition of such a function. This should provide information on how the patients are progressing in their recovery. It will be determined by how they have performed the last exercise of the plan as well as the state in which they are found regarding their recovery.

The variables, which can be recorded by the system, and can provide information on how the patient performed the last exercise of the plan, are defined below:

- *difference_number_steps* (V_1) is the difference between the number of steps that the patients and the therapists performed to carry out the last rehabilitation exercise *last_exg* (i.e., the patient fails to pass through all the virtual points that establish the exercise trajectory);
- *accumulated_deviation* (V_2) is the cumulative spatial deviation between the patient's exercise and that gold standard or the therapist's exercise (i.e., this calculation is based on the distance accumulated when traversing the trajectory associated to the last exercise *last_exg*);
- *difference_time* (V_3) is the temporal difference regarding the execution of the last exercise *last_exg* between the patient and the therapist.

These variables collect information about the patients' status, i.e., how they have performed the last exercise of the allocated plan. However, they do not take into account their evolution, that is, how they have progressed. Significantly, it becomes essential to add this information to the domain to know the actual state of the patient in detail. Thus, the variable *progress_level* (*PPL*) was included in order to track the state in which a patient is found before performing the last exercise. Its value belongs to the range $[0, 10]$, and the initial one is determined by the therapists when they assess the patient for the first time. It should be noted that the value of the previous variable is considered to choose the exercises for the patient's rehabilitation plan. Furthermore, this variable is modified depending on the patient's evolution towards the last recovery session.

On the other hand, the codomain should reflect the next exercise to be performed by the patients according to their condition. In this research work, the initial rehabilitation plan established by the therapist is modified by proposing a new exercise based on a desirable difficulty recommended to the patient. Thus, the output will consist of a new exercise, which will be established depending on the difficulty given by one of the following functions:

- *propose_exercise*. It chooses an exercise from E whose lesion and joint JI_i are similar to the last exercise *last_exg*. This function takes into account an exercise that has not yet been performed, since the system internally stores information about the patients

and the exercises they performed, i.e., their level of success regarding the exercise, their points, as well as the time spent by the patient to complete it. To do this, this function takes two parameters: (1) a label indicating the complexity of the exercise to be searched for (*MC*, more complexity; *SC*, same complexity; *LC*, less complexity) based on the (2) last performed exercise (*last_exg*);
- *repeat_last_exg*. It recommends the repetition of the last exercise performed by the patient *last_exg* based on modifying its configuration. This function takes as parameters *rp* (number of repetitions) and *t* (time needed to finish the exercise) from SET_{last_exg}.

It is important to highlight that the execution of the last exercise influences the patient's progress level, i.e., the results from the execution of the *last_exg* affects the value of the variable *progress_level* (*PPL*). This is why any action on this variable will also be included as an output of the recommender system. This variable, denoted as *EPPL*, is named *Effect_on_PPL*.

When modeling the function that relates the domain or inputs to the codomain or outputs, a mechanism is used to understand why the recommendation was made. At the same time, this mechanism also deals with the imprecision and uncertainty that exists when evaluating the performance of the last exercise performed by the patient. Even when evaluating the level of progress of the patient within the context of their rehabilitation plan. For this reason, a set of IF-THEN fuzzy rules (*R*), which model the function $V_1 \times V_2 \times V_3 \times PPL \longrightarrow E \times EPPL$, are defined.

The linguistic variable *V* (i.e., $V = \{V_1, V_2, V_3\}$) considers the following domain of definition: $DDV_x = \{$ very low (*VL*), low (*L*), medium (*M*), high (*H*), very high (*VH*)$\}$ being *x* defined from 1 to 3. Each linguistic value in DDV_x is defined by means of a trapezoidal function (Π), enclosed by a lower limit *a*, an upper limit *d*, a lower support limit *b*, and an upper support limit *c*, where $a < b < c < d$ (see Equation (2)). If the values of *b* and *c* are equal, a triangular function is obtained:

$$\Pi(x;a,b,c,d) = \begin{cases} 0 & iff \quad x < a \\ (x-a)/(b-a) & iff \quad a \leq x < b \\ 1 & iff \quad b \leq x \leq c \\ (d-x)/(d-c) & iff \quad c < x \leq d \\ 0 & iff \quad x > d \end{cases} \quad (2)$$

The choice of the trapezoidal function to construct the membership function, for each of the values that the variables used in the system can take, is justified because it is the only one that gives us the necessary freedom to represent any type of value (i.e., ordered-discrete or ordinal, unordered-discrete or nominal, boolean, numerical, ranking or the most frequent continuous) [23].

The domain of the definition of each variable $V_x \in V$, i.e., DDV_x, is matched to the normalized measurements $\{0, 0.25, 0.5, 0.75, 1.0\}$. The membership value was confined to the closed range $[0, 1]$. The corresponding fuzzy membership set is depicted in Figure 2.

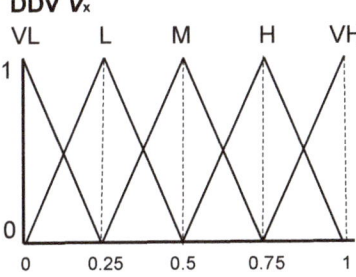

Figure 2. Domain of definition of the variable V_x, i.e., *V*1, *V*2, *V*3.

On the other hand, the linguistic input variable PPL may take the following values: "excellent achievement" (EA, equivalent to 9 or 10); "outstanding achievement" (OA, equivalent to 7 or 8); "satisfactory achievement" (SA, equivalent to 5 or 6); and "not achieved" (NA, smaller than 5). Each linguistic value that this variable can take is defined by means of a trapezoidal function—as can be seen Figure 3.

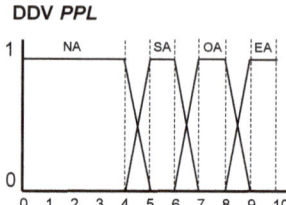

Figure 3. Domain of definition of the variable PPL.

The linguistic output variable $EPPL$ takes the following values: "substantial decrease" (SD, equivalent to decrease 1 point); "moderate decrease" (MD, equivalent to decrease 0.5 point); "no change" (NC); "moderate increase" (MI, equivalent to increase 0.5 point); and "substantial increase" (SI, equivalent to increase 1 point). Each one of these linguistic values will also be defined by means of a trapezoidal function—as can be seen in Figure 4. It is purely used to modify the patient's level of progress as the patient recovery level potentially suffers a change after a physical activity. The operations to be considered are three: increasing the patient's progress, decreasing it or maintaining it.

Knowledge engineering techniques have been used during the design of the system, mainly based on interviews with physicians, using designs and executions which have been fine-tuned in different stages as a basis. Thanks to this process, the rules and the variables and values they take have been determined, seeking a compromise between understandability and efficiency.

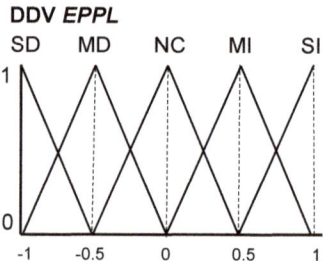

Figure 4. Domain of definition of the variable $EPPL$.

As for the other output of the system, it will be a recommended exercise for the patient by invoking the function *propose_exercise*, as mentioned above. This function will recommend an exercise from the set $P(p_i)$ with higher, lower or same complexity as the last exercise performed by the patient. Otherwise, if the exercise to be recommended is not found, E will be used. The function is shown in Algorithm 1. It should be pointed out that we assume an exercise will certainly be taken from E.

Invoking the function *repeat_last_exg*(rp, t) involves recommending to the patient the repetition of the last performed exercise e_y, however, altering some of its configuration parameters from SET_y, namely rp by setting a different number of repetitions, or t by giving a different time to finish the exercise e_y. The modification of the values may be an increase (+) or reduction (-) in the parameters rp and t.

Algorithm 1: Behavior of proposed exergame function.

Input: degree of complexity DC, i.e., HC (higher complexity), SC (same complexity), LC (lower complexity); and the last exergame $last\_exg$ performed
Output: recommended exergame, e_{out}

1 **if** $last\_exg \notin P(p_i)$ **then**
2   **switch** DC **do**
3   **case** HC **do**
4   Select e_i from $P(p_i)$ such that $SET_i(c) > SET_{last\_exg}(c)$
5   **end**
6   **case** SC **do**
7   Select e_i from $P(p_i)$ such that $SET_i(c) = SET_{last\_exg}(c)$
8   **end**
9   **case** LC **do**
10   Select e_i from E such that $SET_i(c) = SET_{last\_exg}(c)$
11   **end**
12   **end**
13 **else**
14   **switch** DC **do**
15   **case** HC **do**
16   Select e_i from $P(p_i)$ such that $SET_i(c) > SET_{last\_exg}(c)$
17   **end**
18   **case** SC **do**
19   Select e_i from E such that $SET_i(c) = SET_{last\_exg}(c)$
20   **end**
21   **case** LC **do**
22   Select e_i from E such that $SET_i(c) = SET_{last\_exg}(c)$
23   **end**
24   **end**
25 **end**
26 **return** e_i

Each rule $r_i \in R$ has the following form: IF V_1 is $DDV_1(i)$ AND V_2 is $DDV_2(i)$ AND V_3 is $DDV_3(i)$ AND PPL is $DDV_{PPL}(i)$ THEN e_y and $EPPL$ is $DDV_{EPPL}(i)$. On the one hand, e_y represents the exercise to be recommended. On the other hand, $DDV_x(i)$ represents the values that the variable V_x takes in the rule i, that is, $DDV_x(i) \subseteq DDV_x$. Similarly, $DDV_{PPL}(i)$ and $DDV_{EPPL}(i)$ represent the values that the variables PPL and $EPPL$ take in the rule i, respectively, where $DDV_{PPL}(i) \subseteq DDV_{PPL}$ and $DDV_{EPPL}(i) \subseteq DDV_{EPPL}$. The set DDV_x is a global set that represents the values that must take the variable V. Furthermore, the set DDV_{PPL} and DDV_{EPPL} are the global sets that represent the values that must take the variables PPL and $EPPL$.

Lastly, some of the rules defined in this system to model the behavior of the recommender system, which will constitute the conditional knowledge of the remote rehabilitation system, are shown below:

r_1:   IF $difference\_number\_steps$ is $\{VL\}$
       AND $accumulated\_deviation$ is $\{VL\}$
       AND PPL is $\{EA, OA\}$
       THEN $propose\_exercise(HC, last\_exg)$ AND $EPPL$ is $\{SI\}$

r_5:   IF $difference\_number\_steps$ is $\{M\}$
       AND $difference\_time$ is $\{M\}$
       AND PPL is $\{SA\}$
       THEN $propose\_exercise(SC, last\_exg)$ AND $EPPL$ is $\{NC\}$

r_9:   IF $accumulated\_deviation$ is $\{VH\}$
       AND $difference\_time$ is $\{VH, H\}$
       AND PPL is $\{SA\}$
       THEN $propose\_exercise(LC, last\_exg)$ AND $EPPL$ is $\{SD\}$

r_{11}:   IF $difference\_number\_steps$ is $\{M\}$
       AND $accumulated\_deviation$ is $\{M\}$
       AND $difference\_time$ is $\{M\}$
       AND PPL is $\{NA\}$
       THEN $repeat\_last\_exg(-rp, +t)$ AND $EPPL$ is $\{NC\}$

At this point, we must clarify that a variable not appearing in a rule means that all the values of its definition domain may be taken. For example, in the rule r_1, the variable $difference\_time$ (V_3) takes the following values: $\{VL, L, M, H, VH\}$. As can be seen, the rules are highly explainable, which will help understand why the system makes a new recommendation.

3.2.3. Functions Of The Proposed Recommender System

In this section, we present how the proposed system uses the fuzzy rules presented above to recommend a new rehabilitation exercise and to alter a patient's progress level.

Given that the output of the rules consists of two elements, that is, the recommended exercise and an alteration in the value of the patient's progress level, two outputs need to be obtained for each occurrence of the inputs ($V_1 \times V_2 \times V_3 \times PPL$). Therefore, the system infers two situations for each input, which are enumerated below:

1. The next rehabilitation exercise that the patient should perform;
2. How to alter the value of the patient's progress level.

For this purpose, we will consider that the rules inform of the following two relations, since the consequent is related to a logical AND: $V_1 \times V_2 \times V_3 \times PPL \longrightarrow E$ and $V_1 \times V_2 \times V_3 \times PPL \longrightarrow EPPL$.

To infer within the first relationship, we will check the activation degree of each rule. This will be done by evaluating the antecedent of each one. This evaluation is performed as discussed subsequently.

A function φ_{ji} will be associated with each variable V_i in the rule j, whose definition depends on the values taken by the variable V_i in it. Therefore, if the variable takes a single linguistic label L_x (i.e., $L_x \in DDV_i$), the definition of the function φ_{ji} will be the same as the one defining the linguistic value (i.e., $\varphi_{ji} = \Pi_{L_x}$). However, when the variable takes more than one linguistic value, this function will be built based on whether or not the values are close to the domain of definition of the variable V_i, i.e., DDV_i. For consecutive linguistic values, we will refer to this set as C. The function φ_{ji} will be defined as a trapezoidal one with the following parameters:

$$a = \min_{a}\{\Pi_{L_x}(x; a, b, c, d) | L_x \in C\} \tag{3}$$

$$b = \min_{b}\{\Pi_{L_x}(x; a, b, c, d) | L_x \in C\} \tag{4}$$

$$c = \max_{c}\{\Pi_{L_x}(x; a, b, c, d) | L_x \in C\} \tag{5}$$

$$d = \max_{d}\{\Pi_{L_x}(x; a, b, c, d) | L_x \in C\} \tag{6}$$

If the variable V_i in a rule takes non-consecutive values, or there are two non-consecutive groups of values, the function φ_{ji} will be defined with as many trapezoidal functions as there are non-consecutive values or non-consecutive groups (Figure 5).

Example 1. *For the rule r_1 shown above, which is: IF V_1 is {VL} AND V_2 is {VL} AND V_3 is {VL,L,M,H,VH} AND PPL(V_4) is {OA,EA} THEN propose_exercise(MC, last_exg) AND EPPL is {SI}, the φ_{1i} functions will be defined as follows:*

$$\varphi_{11}(x) = \Pi_{VL}(x; 0, 0, 0, 0.25)$$
$$\varphi_{12}(x) = \Pi_{VL}(x; 0, 0, 0, 0.25)$$
$$\varphi_{13}(x) = \Pi_{\{VL,L,M,H,VH\}}(x; 0, 0, 1, 1)$$
$$\varphi_{14}(x) = \Pi_{\{OA,EA\}}(x; 6, 7, 10, 10)$$

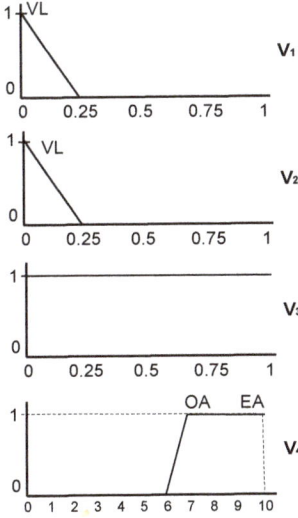

Figure 5. φ_{1i} functions for each variable V_i in the rule r_1.

The *activation degree* of a rule r_j for an input (x_1, x_2, x_3, x_4), where x_i is the input value (crisp value) taken by the variable V_i, will be calculated by determining the membership value of each input x_i to the function that defines the input variable V_i, i.e., $\varphi_{ji}(x_i)$. Given that the antecedent of our rules has more than one part related with a logical AND operator, the t-norm [24] of the minimum has been applied to obtain a single membership value. The definition of this calculus is as follows:

$$\text{activation degree}(r_j) = \min_{i=1,\ldots,4} \{\varphi_{ji}(x_i)\} \tag{7}$$

To obtain the output of this first inference process, the t-conorm [24] of the maximum will be used (i.e., the t-conorm corresponding to the minimum t-norm). As a result, the system will recommend the exercise that proposes the rule with the highest activation degree:

$$\text{output\_exercise}(r_j) = \max_{j=1,\ldots,n} \{\text{activation degree}(r_j)\} \tag{8}$$

On the other hand, the inference of the second relationship has been carried out by using the Mamdani's fuzzy inference method [25], whose output is a fuzzy set. This fuzzy inference process is composed of the following steps:

1. Evaluate the antecedent for each rule $r_j \in R$ to obtain a single membership value, i.e., *activation degree* (r_j). We will do this as in the previous case;
2. Obtain the conclusion of each rule in $EPPL$. To do this, we truncate the fuzzy value taken by the consequent of the rule in the variable $EEPL$ using the minimum with the *activation degree*(r_j) on its membership function. The output will be a new fuzzy set defined by means of a membership function μ_j where:

$$\mu_j : [-1, 1] \longrightarrow [0, \text{activation degree}(r_j)]$$

and it is defined as

$$\mu_j(x) = min\{\Pi_{L_x}(x), \text{activation degree}(r_j)\} \quad (9)$$

with L_x being the value that the variable $EPPL$ takes in the rule r_j ($L_x \in DDV_{EPPL}$).

3. Aggregate rule's conclusions into a single fuzzy set defined by means of the function μ, using a fuzzy aggregation operator. The t-conorm of the maximum has been used to aggregate the truncated output functions returned by the previous step:

$$\mu(x) = \max_{j=1,\ldots,|R|} \{\mu_j(x)\} \quad (10)$$

4. Defuzzification. Since we want to obtain a crisp value that affects to the PPL value, which we recall is confined to the range $[0, 10]$, so we need to transform the fuzzy set obtained in step 3 into a single numerical value. To do this, we used the defuzzification method of the centroid, which returns the center of the area under the fuzzy set obtained in step 3. It should be pointed out that the total area of the membership function distribution used to represent the combined control action is divided into a number of sub-areas. We denote the centroid as $EPPL_{co}$ and it is calculated as

$$EPPL_{co} = \frac{\sum_{i=1}^{N} x_i \mu(x_i)}{\sum_{i=1}^{N} \mu(x_i)} \quad (11)$$

where N indicates the number of sub-areas, $\mu(x_i)$ and x_i represent the area and the centroid of the area, respectively, of the ith sub-area.

The value $EPPL_{co}$ ($EPPL_{co} \in [-1, 1]$) is used to modify the patient's progress level (PPL) with the aim of updating their progress:

$$PPL = \begin{cases} 0 & iff \quad PPL + EPPL_{co} \leq 0 \\ PPL + EPPL_{co} & iff \quad 0 < PPL + EPPL_{co} < 10 \\ 10 & iff \quad PPL + EPPL_{co} \geq 10 \end{cases} \quad (12)$$

We would like to conclude by stressing that Zadeh's conventional t-operators of Min and Max, which have been used in this system, perform significantly well within the context of our problem [26].

4. Proposed System In Operation

This section describes an experimental case study conducted to show the benefits of the proposal discussed in this research work. Then, an example that describes how the fuzzy system that underpins our proposal would work in a real-world situation is presented.

However, before fully entering the description of the experimental case study, let us take a look at the holistic view of the whole recommender system presented in Figure 6 in order to understand how it works with all the modules involved.

1. The system proposes an exercises ($e_x \in E$) to the patient through the **interface module**;
2. The patient performs an exercise whose movements are captured by the **tracking module**;
3. The system evaluates, through the **evaluation module**, the performance of the patient. Particularly, it obtains the value of the variables (V_1, V_2, V_3);
4. The system, based upon the values of the variables (V_1, V_2, V_3, and PPL), triggers the rules following the next criteria:
   (a) It computes the activation degree of the rules belonging to the knowledge base (i.e., *conditional knowledge*);
   (b) It selects, employing the first inference system, the rule whose activation degree is greater among the set of rules. Its consequent contains the exercise to be recommended, which may be a new one or a modification of the last exercise performed;
   (c) It modifies, employing the second inference system, the patient's progress level ($EEPL$). It should be noted that this modification takes into account the last exercise performed.

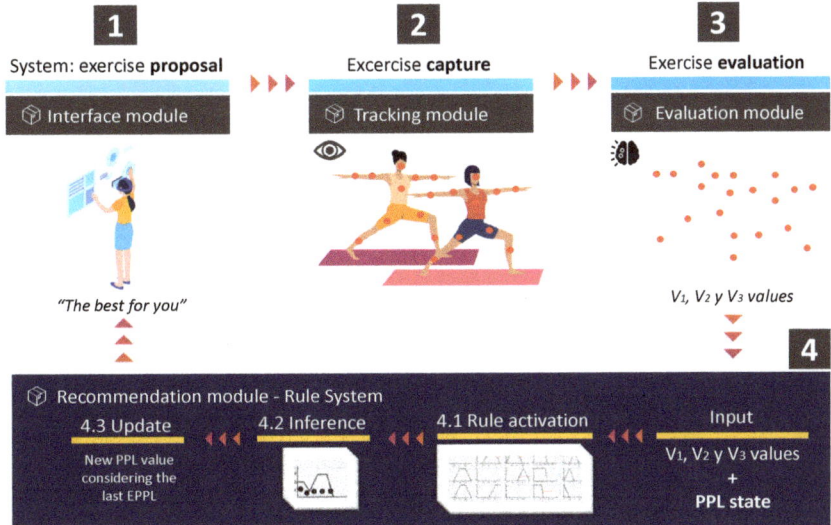

Figure 6. Holistic view of the recommender system.

Consider a stroke patient whose mobility on the left side of the body has been substantially reduced. Fortunately, the patient's progress has relatively improved over the past few sessions. Imagine that the last exercises performed consisted in, from an upright bipedal posture, raising the left arm from the hip to the shoulder, passing the hand in red color through the spheres placed in the 3D world that draw a trajectory. Fundamentally, the hand must pass first through the sphere close to the hip and with the largest size, ending the repetition when the colored joint reaches the sphere close to the shoulder and with the smallest size. This exercise comprises three repetitions and it must be completed under two minutes. Figure 7 graphically shows the left shoulder abduction by means of a virtual system in which the patient simulates the movement, so that their left hand touches the colored spheres.

Figure 7. Left elbow flexion representation.

Example 2. *Assume that the value of the variable PPL is assigned to 4.5 based on the last session. After performing the last exercise, the values of the variables V_1, V_2 and V_3 were obtained. They are 0.75, 0.80 and 0.55, respectively. The process to obtain the EPPL value is described below.*

The previous description means that the patient took more steps than the therapist. The trajectory between them differed considerable. However, the patient did not spend much more time on completing the exercise than the therapist. It should be reminded that the values of these variables are the result of the mean after the patient performing all repetitions.

It should be highlighted that the previous values of the input scores are computed taking into account the configuration SET_i and the performance of the therapist. However, the underlying details of this process are not provided as it is beyond the scope of this paper.

Considering this situation as an starting point, the inference process that this system carries out is discussed subsequently. At this point, it is important to point out that the system infers two situations for each input, i.e., $V_1 \times V_2 \times V_3 \times PPL \longrightarrow E$ and $V_1 \times V_2 \times V_3 \times PPL \longrightarrow EPPL$.

The first inference process consists of proposing a physical rehabilitation exercise that is best suited according to the patient's situation. Initially, the values associated with each input v_i are applied to each rule r_j to obtain its activation degree. We show below only the rules from R whose activation degree is greater than 0 (i.e., $\{r_i \mid r_i \in R \land \text{activation degree}(r_i) > 0\}$):

r_3:   IF *accumulated_deviation* is $\{M, H\}$
      AND *difference_time* is $\{L, M\}$
      AND *PPL* is $\{NA, SA\}$
      THEN *repeat_last_exg*$(-rp, +t)$ AND *EPPL* is $\{NC\}$

r_8:   IF *difference_number_steps* is $\{M, H\}$
      AND *difference_time* is $\{H\}$
      AND *PPL* is $\{NA, SA\}$
      THEN *propose_exercise*$(LC, last\_exg)$ AND *EPPL* is $\{MD\}$

r_{12}:   IF *difference_number_steps* is $\{M, H\}$
      AND *accumulated_deviation* is $\{H, VH\}$
      AND *PPL* is $\{NA\}$
      THEN *propose_exercise*$(LC, last\_exg)$ AND *EPPL* is $\{SD\}$

Their activation degrees are as follows:

$$\text{activation degree}(r_3) = 0.80$$
$$\text{activation degree}(r_8) = 0.20$$
$$\text{activation degree}(r_{12}) = 0.50$$

Therefore, the best compelling exercise to be recommended is obtained from the rule whose activation degree is greater among the set from the previous step. In other words:

$$max\{\text{activation degree}(r_3), \text{activation degree}(r_8), \text{activation degree}(r_{12})\}$$

As a result, the recommended exercise is the one related to the rule r_3 which proposes the repetition of the last performed exercise, but reducing the repetitions and increasing the time. Given that the system infers that the exercise was not well performed because of time, the algorithm responsible for this update proposes two repetitions in 3 min. That is, the system subtracts one repetition and adds one minute. The underlying details of this algorithm are not provided as it is beyond the scope of this paper. This new configuration for the proposed exercise will be used later so as to see the reliability level of the system in terms of decisions making.

On the other hand, the inference of the second relationship was also performed in order to update the patient's progress level. Clearly, the completion of the last rehabilitation exercise must have had some effect on their progress. Let us see how that effect is computed.

As from the activation degrees previously obtained, the output fuzzy set is truncated with the aforementioned values by using the minimum method. That is, the output fuzzy set is reshaped for each rule r_j, whose output is represented by the following new sets defined as membership functions:

$$\mu_3(x) = min\{\Pi_{NC}(x), 0.80\}$$
$$\mu_8(x) = min\{\Pi_{MD}(x), 0.20\}$$
$$\mu_{12}(x) = min\{\Pi_{SD}(x), 0.50\}$$

From the outputs calculated in the previous step, an aggregation process is employed to unify these values in a single fuzzy set. The outputs of each rule (i.e., activation degree) are combined into a single fuzzy set as follows:

$$\mu(x) = max\{\mu_3(x), \mu_8(x), \mu_{12}(x)\}$$

In Figure 8, all three rules, which are activated, are displayed to show how their outputs are aggregated into a single fuzzy set ($\mu(x)$). The membership function of this fuzzy set assigns a weight for every output $EPPL$ value.

Finally, a representative value is obtained after performing the defuzzification step that uses the $EPPL_{co}$ defined in Equation (11). In the aggregated fuzzy set, as shown in Figure 8, the total area is divided into five sub-areas. This value and with the centroid of each sub-area are calculated in Table 1.

Table 1. Result of each sub-area and centroid related to example 2.

Sub-Area Number	Area ($\mu(x_i)$)	Centroid of Area (x_i)	Area * x_i
1	0.375	−0.625	−0.234375
2	0.0875	−0.7084	−0.061985
3	0.2	−0.534	−0.1068
4	0.16	0	0
5	0.16	0.234	0.03744
	$\sum$ Area = 0.9825		$\sum$ Area * x_i = −0.36572

The defuzzified value $EPPL_{co}$ is: $\sum Area * x_i / \sum Area$; $-0.36572/0.9825 \simeq -0.38$. Therefore, the new PPL value is updated through Equation (12), that is, $4.5 - 0.38 = 4.12$. This result indicates that the patient's progress level should be reduced.

The system now proposes performing the last exercise with reduced repetitions but increased time (output of the rule r_3). The repetitions to be taken are 2 and the time is 3 min.

Example 3. *After performing the last proposed exercise, the values of the variables V_1, V_2 and V_3 are 0.2, 0.45 and 0.15, respectively. The PPL value is 4.12, whose result was obtained in the previous example. The process to obtain the new EPPL value is described below, omitting unnecessary steps.*

It is remarkable that the patient correctly performed the exercise. They took almost the same number of steps as the therapist. The trajectory was relatively low. Furthermore, the time spent completing the exercise was also similar to that of the therapist.

As in the previous example, we show below only the rules from R whose activation degrees are greater than 0:

r_2: IF *difference_number_steps* is $\{L\}$
AND *accumulated_deviation* is $\{L\}$
AND *PPL* is $\{NA, SA\}$
THEN *propose_exercise(HC, last_exg)* AND *EPPL* is $\{MI\}$

r_7: IF *accumulated_deviation* is $\{L, M\}$
AND *difference_time* is $\{L, M\}$
AND *PPL* is $\{NA, SA\}$
THEN *propose_exercise(SC, last_exg)* AND *EPPL* is $\{NC\}$

r_{13}: IF *difference_number_steps* is $\{L\}$
AND *accumulated_deviation* is $\{M\}$
AND *PPL* is $\{NA, SA\}$
THEN *propose_exercise(SC, last_exg)* AND *EPPL* is $\{MI\}$

Furthermore, their activation degrees are as follows:

$$\text{activation degree}(r_2) = 0.20$$
$$\text{activation degree}(r_7) = 0.60$$
$$\text{activation degree}(r_{13}) = 0.80$$

As a result of applying the output exercise function 8, the rule r_{13} is triggered as its activation degrees is greater among the others. Therefore, the best compelling exercise to be proposed by the system is one whose complexity is the same as the last exercise performed. This exercise consists of a left arm abduction, that is, a movement which implies raising the left arm around the shoulder, moving it laterally away from the body. This exercise comprises two repetitions and it must be completed under three minutes. Figure 9 graphically shows the left shoulder abduction by means of a virtual system in which the patient simulates the movement, so that their left hand touches the colored spheres.

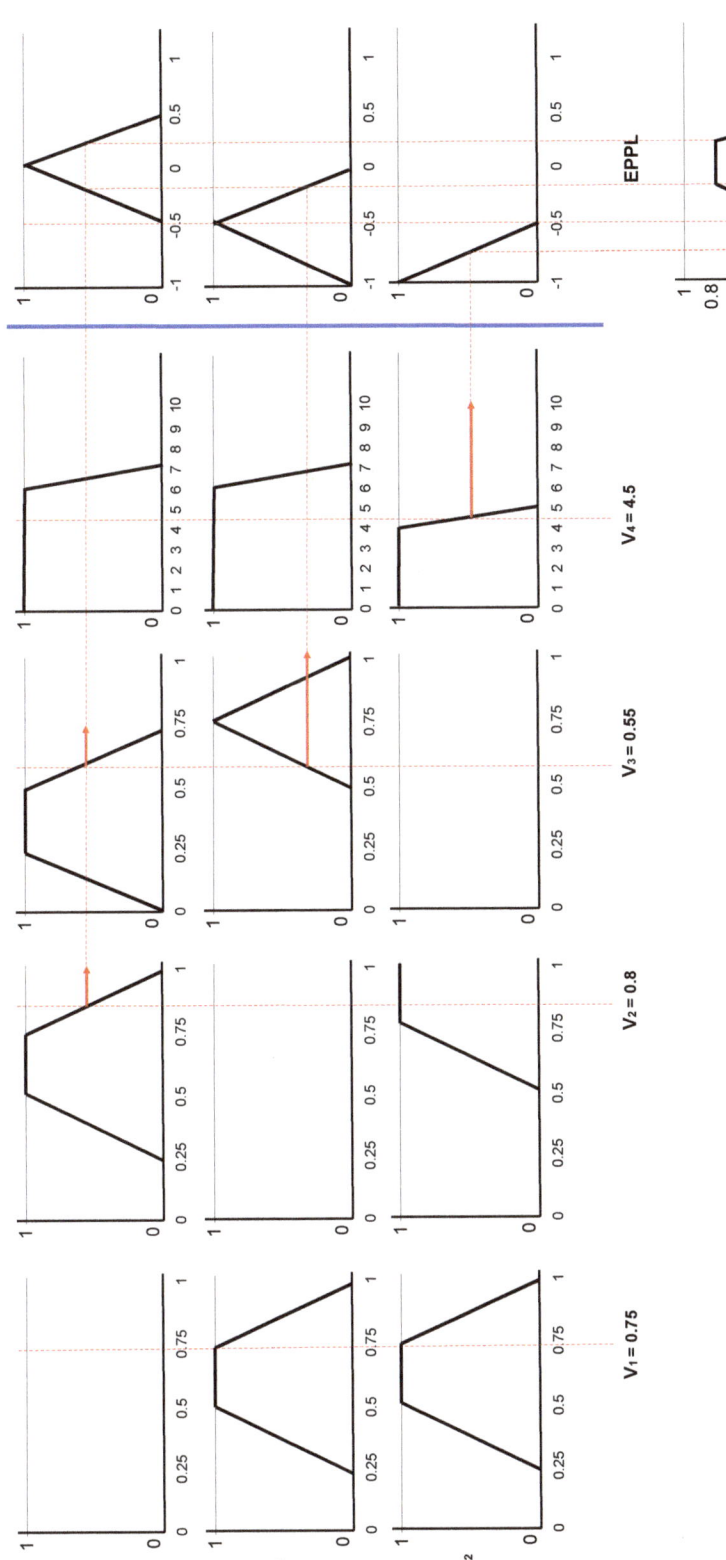

Figure 8. Visual representation and results when applying the aggregation method (max) related to example 2.

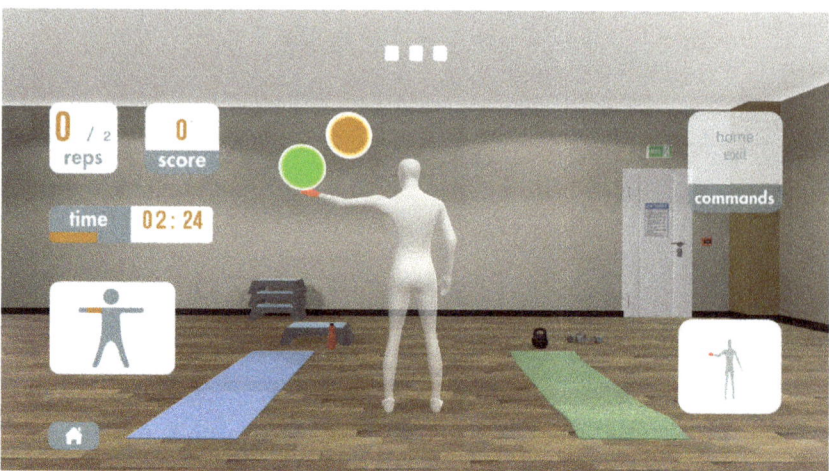

Figure 9. Left shoulder abduction representation.

Then, the new membership functions are computed as a consequence of truncating the output fuzzy sets with the values previously obtained. In other words:

$$\mu_2(x) = min\{\Pi_{MI}(x), 0.20\}$$
$$\mu_7(x) = min\{\Pi_{NC}(x), 0.60\}$$
$$\mu_{13}(x) = min\{\Pi_{SD}(x), 0.80\}$$

After that, a single fuzzy set is obtained by combining the previous outputs using the function 10. The result is as follows:

$$\mu(x) = max\{\mu_2(x), \mu_7(x), \mu_{13}(x)\}$$

Finally, the output, i.e., $EPPL_{co}$, is computed using the centroid function defined in (11). Similar to the previous example, the total area is divided into six sub-areas. Table 2 shows the area and centroid of each sub-area. Furthermore, Figure 10 depicts the new aggregated fuzzy set.

Table 2. Result of each sub-area and centroid related to example 3.

Sub-Area Number	Area ($\mu(x_i)$)	Centroid of Area (x_i)	Area * x_i
1	0.09	−0.3	−0.234375
2	0.24	0	0
3	0.0275	0.2167	0.005995925
4	0.0975	0.35	0.034125
5	0.16	0.5	0.08
6	0.16	0.74	0.1184
	$\sum$ Area = 0.775		$\sum$ Area * x_i = 0.21148425

The defuzzified value $EPPL_{co}$ is: $\sum Area * x_i / \sum Area$; $0.21148425/0.775 \simeq 0.27$. Therefore, the new PPL value is updated through Equation (12), that is, $4.12 + 0.27 = 4.39$. This result indicates that the patient's progress level has relatively improved.

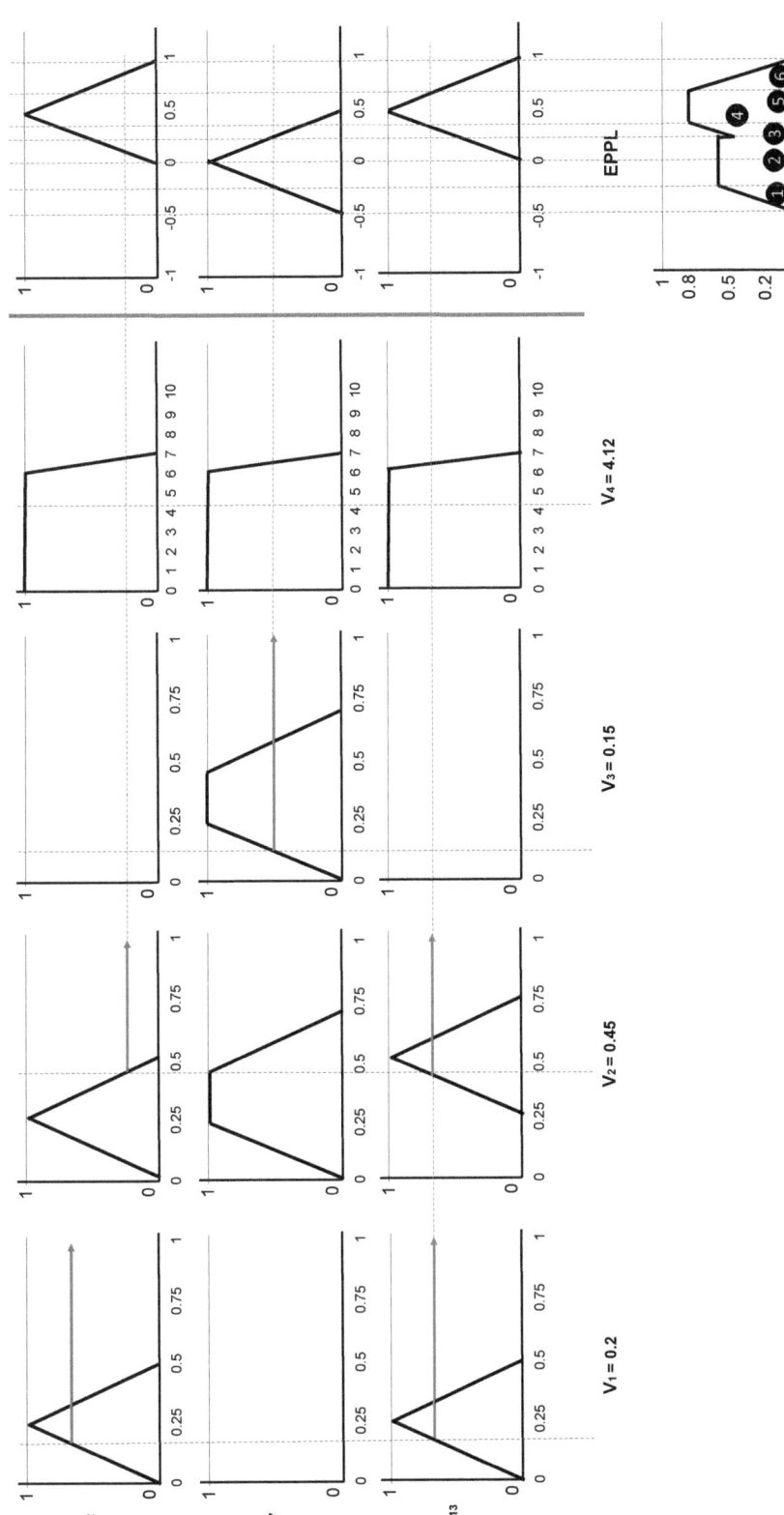

Figure 10. Visual representation and results when applying the aggregation method (max) related to example 3.

5. Discussion

A preliminary evaluation was carried out and the results obtained appear to be quite interesting. The discussed case study showed that the system proposed in this research work is capable of inferring the next rehabilitation exercise and appropriately updating the patient's progress level. Both tasks are based on the performance of the last exercise made by the patient.

The main goal of the experiment conducted was oriented towards demonstrating the utility of the proposed system. This is the first step before using the system for a clinical trial with patients, who have a suffered moderate or severe stroke, according to the levels measured by the National Institutes of Health Stroke Scale (NIHSS) scoring system. These clinical trials will test the efficacy of the system in the recovery of stroke patients.

Interestingly, the results of the evaluation are in accordance with the values of the input variables v_i. The patient's progress level was relatively low ($PPL = 4.5$). The time invested was not too bad with respect to the time spent by the therapist ($V_1 = 0.55$), but the number of steps between the patient and the therapist was significantly different ($V_2 = 0.75$). In addition, the trajectory greatly differed from the one charted by therapist ($V_3 = 0.8$). In other words, the exercise was not accurately performed by the patient. This means that the patient preferred to sacrifice accuracy over time. In this regard, the system automatically concluded that the patient needs to keep working out to positively upgrade their progress. Additionally, the system suggested that the patient repeats the last performed exergame, considering that the number of repetitions should be reduced but the time spent in performing the exercise should be increased. Remarkably, the result of this system's suggestion is coherent taking into account the progress level of the patient ($PPL = 4.12$) and also the performance of the last exercise proposed ($V_1 = 0.2$, $V_2 = 0.45$, $V_3 = 015$). As a result, the patient's progress level was moderately upgraded, highlighting that this increase is reasonable based on two previous performances. In view of these facts, the reliability of the system is noteworthy. The system adequately performs recommendations and updates the progress of the patient accordingly.

However, one limitation of our research work is the difficulty to test the proposed system with a representative sample of stroke patients due to the current COVID-19 pandemic. To date, we focused our work on evaluating the system from an internal point of view, that is, according to case studies such as the one described in Section 4. Therefore, the results presented in this paper need to be interpreted with caution.

Despite the limitations of this evaluation, our findings suggest that the use of Fuzzy Logic for physical rehabilitation seems to make sense as it enables making decisions in an automatic and understandable way. What this approach offers is to dynamically monitor and guide the home rehabilitation process, whose supervision is difficult to be made by a therapist because of their lack of time and the need for a face-to-face supervision. However, the developed system does not aim at replacing the therapist. On the contrary, it is intended to relieve the therapists' workload and help them interpret, through an inference process similar to the human one, how the patient progresses as the rehabilitation plan is being completed.

This research aims to be complemented, in a second phase, with a clinical trial to evaluate the impact of using our system on the recovery process of real stroke patients. In a third phase, another clinical trial will be conducted to analyze the efficacy of the system for its intended use, which is to improve physical rehabilitation at home.

6. Conclusions

In order for a remote rehabilitation system to be used continuously and effectively by stroke patients, three essential characteristics must be provided: (i) usability, to remove the barrier that the use of technology may represent, and adequately guide the user in the process of autonomous rehabilitation; (ii) motivation, to encourage the continued use of the system and reduce the possibility of abandonment by the patient; and (iii) autonomy, to be able to automatically recognize and evaluate the rehabilitation exercises performed by the patient without the need for continuous supervision and presence of the therapist. A significant part of the existing research work focuses on one or more of these features, with the therapist being responsible for adjusting the rehabilitation routine according to the level of progress of their patients. Ideally, a remote rehabilitation system that offers an integral solution should be able to offer suggestions or recommendations that enable the ability to customize the rehabilitation routine automatically or semi-automatically.

In this paper, we proposed a new recommender system to determine the next action that should be performed by the patient in their rehabilitation plan. The system is based on a set of fuzzy rules and a double inference process on them. The use of fuzzy logic is justified because it provides patients and physicians with guidance that they can understand. In this sense, the use of linguistic variables makes it easier for them to interpret this information. On the other hand, the recommender system provides the patients with detailed feedback on the work they have done, with an explanation about the areas in which they have performed well, and others which may still need improvement. In addition, on a broader level, patients will be informed whether they have truly performed the rehabilitation routine well.

The approach presented herein shows the potential of automating the work of monitoring and guiding the steps in a patient's rehabilitation. The idea of this method is not to replace the role of the physician, but to support them with tools that enable them to conduct an efficient rehabilitation process, dedicating their time to higher level tasks. The proposed system is intended to speed up the assignment of exercises to patients and to obtain data that can be provided to physicians. All these data allow them to evaluate and determine the patient's state of evolution in their injury.

The discussed case study shows the potential of our approach in terms of adapting the rehabilitation process to the patient's progress level. Particularly, the adoption of fuzzy logic to guide the processes of knowledge representation and inference of recommendations greatly facilitates the automatic customization of rehabilitation routines, since the way such processes are described is inherently close to the way therapists adjust rehabilitation routines. Thus, this research work contributes to increase the level of autonomy for remote rehabilitation systems thanks to the capacity of dynamically adjusting the rehabilitation process.

As future lines of research, we can stress the need to work on a main objective: evaluating the degree of improvement on stroke patients using the proposed system in a real treatment. For doing so, once the system has been validated by the research community, two clinical trials will be conducted. The first will study the impact of using the recommender system on real stroke patients over a significant period of time. The second will study the efficacy of the system on patient recovery. The data collected in these clinical trials will be used for improving the system and exploring other solutions that may be of interest to be included in it.

Author Contributions: Conceptualization, J.J.C.-S., D.V., C.G.-P., J.A. and D.N.M.; methodology, J.J.C.-S., D.V. and D.N.M.; software, C.G.-P.; validation, J.A., J.J.C.-S.; investigation, J.J.C.-S., J.A.; visualization, J.A., C.G.-P.; writing—original draft preparation, C.G.-P., D.V.; writing—review and editing, J.A., J.J.C.-S., D.V. and D.N.M.; supervision, D.V.; project administration, D.V.; funding acquisition, J.A., J.J.C.-S., D.V. and D.N.M. All authors have read and agreed to the published version of the manuscript.

Funding: This research was funded by Instituto de Salud Carlos III grant number DTS18/00122, co-funded by the European Regional Development Fund, European Social Fund "Investing in your future".

Informed Consent Statement: Informed consent was obtained from all subjects involved in the study.

Conflicts of Interest: The authors declare no conflict of interest.

References

1. Johnson, W.; Onuma, O.; Owolabi, M.; Sachdev, S. Stroke: A global response is needed. *Bull. World Health Organ.* **2016**, *94*, 634–644. [CrossRef]
2. Semrau, M.; Evans-Lacko, S.; Alem, A.; Ayuso-Mateos, J.L.; Chisholm, D.; Gureje, O.; Hanlon, C.; Jordans, M.; Kigozi, F.; Lempp, H.; et al. Strengthening mental health systems in low-and middle-income countries: The Emerald programme. *BMC Med.* **2015**, *13*, 1–9. [CrossRef] [PubMed]
3. Mensah, G.A.; Norrving, B.; Feigin, V.L. The global burden of stroke. *Neuroepidemiology* **2015**, *45*, 143–145. [CrossRef] [PubMed]
4. Sarfo, F.S.; Ulasavets, U.; Opare-Sem, O.K.; Ovbiagele, B. Tele-rehabilitation after stroke: An updated systematic review of the literature. *J. Stroke Cerebrovasc. Dis.* **2018**, *27*, 2306–2318. [CrossRef] [PubMed]
5. Moral-Munoz, J.A.; Zhang, W.; Cobo, M.J.; Herrera-Viedma, E.; Kaber, D.B. Smartphone-based systems for physical rehabilitation applications: A systematic review. *Assist. Technol.* **2019**. [CrossRef] [PubMed]
6. Webster, D.; Celik, O. Systematic review of Kinect applications in elderly care and stroke rehabilitation. *J. Neuroeng. Rehabil.* **2014**, *11*, 108. [CrossRef] [PubMed]
7. Clark, R.A.; Pua, Y.; Fortin, K.; Ritchie, C.; Webster, K.E.; Denehy, L.; Bryant, A.L. Validity of the Microsoft Kinect for assessment of postural control. *Gait Posture* **2012**, *36*, 372–377. [CrossRef]
8. Mobini, A.; Behzadipour, S.; Saadat, F.M. Accuracy of Kinect's skeleton tracking for upper body rehabilitation applications. *Disabil. Rehabil. Assist. Technol.* **2014**, *9*, 344–352. [CrossRef]
9. Sardi, L.; Idri, A.; Fernández-Alemán, J.L. A systematic review of gamification in e-Health. *J. Biomed. Inform.* **2017**, *71*, 31–48. [CrossRef]
10. Schez-Sobrino, S.; Vallejo, D.; Monekosso, D.N.; Glez-Morcillo, C.; Remagnino, P. A distributed gamified system based on automatic assessment of physical exercises to promote remote physical rehabilitation. *IEEE Access* **2020**, *8*, 91424–91434. [CrossRef]
11. Vallejo, D.; Gmez-Portes, C.; Albusac, J.; Glez-Morcillo, C.; Castro-Schez, J.J. Personalized Exergames Language: A Novel Approach to the Automatic Generation of Personalized Exergames for Stroke Patients. *Appl. Sci.* **2020**, *10*, 7378. [CrossRef]
12. Bhaskaran, S.; Marappan, R.; Santhi, B. Design and Analysis of a Cluster-Based Intelligent Hybrid Recommendation System for E-Learning Applications. *Mathematics* **2021**, *9*, 197. [CrossRef]
13. Zadeh, L.A. Fuzzy sets. *Inf. Control* **1965**, *8*, 338–353. [CrossRef]
14. Zadeh, L.A. The concept of a linguistic variable and its application to approximate reasoning-I. *Inf. Control* **1975**, *8*, 199–249. [CrossRef]
15. González-González, C.S.; Toledo-Delgado, P.A.; Muñoz-Cruz, V.; Torres-Carrion, P.V. Serious games for rehabilitation: Gestural interaction in personalized gamified exercises through a recommender system. *J. Biomed. Inform.* **2019**, *97*, 103266–103285. [CrossRef] [PubMed]
16. Esfahlani, S.S.; Cirstea, S.; Sanaei, A.; Wilson, G. An adaptive self-organizing fuzzy logic controller in a serious game for motor impairment rehabilitation. In Proceedings of the 2017 IEEE 26th International Symposium on Industrial Electronics (ISIE), Edinburgh, UK, 19–21 June 2017; pp. 1311–1318.
17. Fernandez-Cervantes, V.; Stroulia, E.; Oliva, L.E.; Gonzalez, F.; Castillo, C. Serious games: Rehabilitation fuzzy grammar for exercise and therapy compliance. In Proceedings of the 2015 IEEE Games Entertainment Media Conference (IEEE), Toronto, ON, Canada, 14–16 October 2015; pp. 1–8.
18. Pirovano, M.; Mainetti, R.; Baud-Bovy, G.; Lanzi, P.L.; Borghese, N.A. Self-adaptive games for rehabilitation at home. In Proceedings of the 2012 IEEE Conference on Computational Intelligence and Games (IEEE), Granada, Spain, 11–14 September 2012; pp. 179–186.
19. Pirovano, M.; Surer, E.; Mainetti, R.; Lanzi, P.L.; Borghese, N.A. Exergaming and rehabilitation: A methodology for the design of effective and safe therapeutic exergames. *Entertain. Comput.* **2016**, *14*, 55–65. [CrossRef]
20. Anton, D.; Berges, I.; Bermúdez, J.; Goñi, A.; Illarramendi, A. A telerehabilitation system for the selection, evaluation and remote management of therapies. *Sensors* **2018**, *18*, 1459. [CrossRef]
21. Karime, A.; Mohamad, E.; Alja'Am, J.M.; El Saddik, A.; Gueaieb, W. A fuzzy-based adaptive rehabilitation framework for home-based wrist training. *IEEE Trans. Instrum. Meas.* **2013**, *63*, 135–144. [CrossRef]
22. Han, J.; Yang, S.; Xia, L.; Chen, Y. Deterministic adaptive robust control with a novel optimal gain design approach for a fuzzy 2DOF lower limb exoskeleton robot system. *IEEE Trans. Fuzzy Syst.* **2021**. [CrossRef]
23. Castro-Schez, J.J.; Castro, J.L.; Zurita, J.M Fuzzy Repertory Table: A Method for Acquiring Knowledge About Input Variables to Machine Learning Algorithm. *IEEE Trans. Fuzzy Syst.* **2004**, *12*, 123–139. [CrossRef]
24. Klement, E.P.; Mesiar, R.; Pap, E. Fuzzy set theory, Cap. In *Triangular Norms*; Springer: Berlin/Heidelberg, Germany, 2000; pp. 249–264.
25. Mandami, E.H; Assilian, S. An experiment in linguistic synthesis with a fuzzy logic controller. *Int. J. Man Mach. Stud.* **1975**, *7*. [CrossRef]
26. Gupta, M.M.; Qi, J. Theory of T-norms and fuzzy inference methods. *Fuzzy Sets Syst.* **1991**, *40*, 431–450. [CrossRef]

Article

Functional Symmetry and Statistical Depth for the Analysis of Movement Patterns in Alzheimer's Patients

Alicia Nieto-Reyes [1,*,†], Heather Battey [2] and Giacomo Francisci [1,3]

1. Department of Mathematics, Statistics and Computer Science, University of Cantabria, 39005 Santander, Spain
2. Department of Mathematics, Imperial College London, London SW7 2BZ, UK; h.battey@imperial.ac.uk
3. Department of Mathematics, University of Trento, 38122 Trento, Italy; giacomo.francisci@unitn.it
* Correspondence: alicia.nieto@unican.es
† Current address: Faculty of Science, Avd. Los Castros s/n, 39005 Santander, Spain.

Abstract: Black-box techniques have been applied with outstanding results to classify, in a supervised manner, the movement patterns of Alzheimer's patients according to their stage of the disease. However, these techniques do not provide information on the difference of the patterns among the stages. We make use of functional data analysis to provide insight on the nature of these differences. In particular, we calculate the center of symmetry of the underlying distribution at each stage and use it to compute the functional depth of the movements of each patient. This results in an ordering of the data to which we apply nonparametric permutation tests to check on the differences in the distribution, median and deviance from the median. We consistently obtain that the movement pattern at each stage is significantly different to that of the prior and posterior stage in terms of the deviance from the median applied to the depth. The approach is validated by simulation.

Keywords: Alzheimer's disease; dementia; functional data analysis; functional depth; statistical data depth; symmetry

1. Introduction

Alzheimer's disease is a neurodegenerative condition that affects 15 million people worldwide [1]. The evolution of the patient passes through different stages of the disease, which, according to the Global Deterioration Scale (GDS) [2], are:

(GDS 1) no cognitive impairment,
(GDS 2) early cognitive impairment,
(GDS 3) mild cognitive impairment,
(GDS 4) mild dementia,
(GDS 5) moderate dementia,
(GDS 6) moderately severe dementia and
(GDS 7) severe dementia.

An important aspect is diagnosing when a patient evolves from his or her current stage into the next one, which usually entails a complex physical examination carried by the patient's medical doctor. As an additional tool for the doctor to consider in taking that decision, [3,4] analyzed the movement patterns of Alzheimer's sufferers when moving freely in a daycare facility. The objective of those papers was supervised classification, so that given the movement patterns of a set of patients and their disease stage, the stage of other patients could be predicted based on their movement patterns. The analysis used neural networks applied to multivariate time series data. This is a black-box technique that results in high success rates, 83% in [4] and 91% in [3], but does not reveal which characteristics of the data helped with the classification. In [4], also an attempt to analyze the data as functional data was made. However, no significant findings were obtained that way.

The analyzed real data are recordings made by the accelerometer device of an Android smartphone with a sampling rate of 8 Hz. These acceleration forces are measured in the three spatial dimensions over time while the patients carry the smartphone in their pocket. The data comprise repeated trivariate measurements on 35 patients in different stages of Alzheimer's disease:

- 7 patients in a mild stage of the disease (GDS 2 and 3),
- 18 patients in a moderate stage of the disease (GDS 4 and 5) and
- 10 patients in a severe stage of the disease (GDS 6 and 7).

The data are unusually complex in that the number of repeated measurements is different for each patient, between 2 and 8, with a total of 187 measurements (187 three-dimensional curves). Moreover, the length of the domain over which the trivariate functional data are observed is different for each measurement and the grid of discretization points is also different for each measurement.

This type of data is functional in nature, in fact, it can be viewed as longitudinal functional data [5]. The modern research theme of functional data analysis (FDA) [6,7], in which collections of measurements are viewed as partially observed realizations of random functions (a natural viewpoint for e.g., growth trajectory data, brain imaging data and handwriting data), belongs primarily to the area of non-parametric statistics and will allow us to further develop the analysis of these data from an exploratory perspective. This will provide information for a more interpretable model, in contrast to the widespread black-box approaches to classification. For this, we will use the concepts of statistical symmetry [8] and data depth [9].

Statistical depth functions provide an order for the elements of a given space $\mathcal{X}$ by making use of a probability distribution P on that space. The deepest element(s) are generally referred to as the median, coinciding with the center of symmetry of P when a unique center of symmetry exists for some notion of symmetry. Although providing an order in spaces of dimension higher than one is a non-trivial task, it is important because statistics of order are the basis of many established nonparametric procedures, for instance, inference based on ranks and the detection of outliers. Outlier detection is a necessary preliminary stage in many statistical investigations and inference based on ranks can be used, for example, in supervised classification and clustering.

Just as in the case of $\mathcal{X} = \mathbb{R}^p$, there is no unique definition of symmetry when $\mathcal{X}$ is a function space $\mathcal{F}$. Thus, in Section 2, we discuss difficulties associated with some potential notions of symmetry for distributions on $\mathcal{X} = \mathcal{F}$ and show there are situations whereby a distribution on a functional space would be deemed symmetric with respect to several of these notions, despite possessing important topological asymmetries. After highlighting such difficulties, we describe the notion of functional symmetry used to explore the Alzheimer's dataset. Simultaneously, we will explain the complexity involved in defining a statistical functional depth and give details of the one relevant for our application, which allows for multivariate functional data. It will require specification of an appropriate metric space and the aforementioned notion of functional symmetry. In Section 3, we perform a simulation to illustrate that the notion of functional symmetry employed is preserved through the use of derivatives. This is important as the acceleration is the second derivative of the position with respect to the time. Section 4 provides the data analysis and a suitable metric space for it. We finalize with a discussion in Section 5.

2. Methodology

2.1. Symmetry

Symmetry is a fundamental concept, and has been the focus of much contemplation throughout history due to its manifestation in natural and scientific phenomena, as well as in man-made structures. Its usage is common in modern language as a means to express a particular type of structure or regularity, often geometric, that of exact correspondence between parts of an object with reference to a point or axis of symmetry. Typically though, the mathematical formalization of symmetry entails invariance under a family of measurable transformations [10]. In simple geometric contexts, this might be invariance under sign changes or under rotation.

We focus on symmetry in statistics, in this case, it is not the random objects themselves to which a notion of symmetry applies, but rather their distributions. In Figure 1, essential features of a symmetric probability distribution P are depicted, for: a space of dimension one, $\mathcal{X} = \mathbb{R}$; a multivariate space, $\mathcal{X} = \mathbb{R}^p$; and space of functions, $\mathcal{X} = \mathcal{F}$. We explain in detail the concept of depth later in the manuscript; however, it is worth saying that, in the figure, symmetries in the distribution with respect to an element ζ of $\mathcal{X}$ are discernible in the color, with ζ the *center of symmetry*. In fact, the changes in the colors show that the datasets are ordered from the center outward.

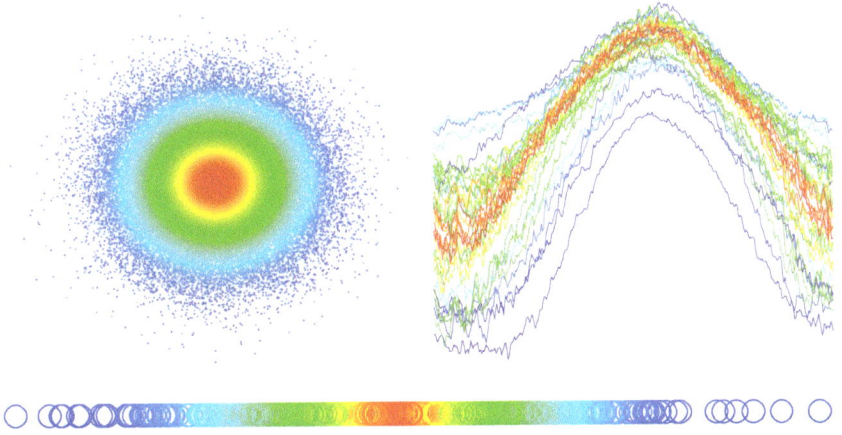

Figure 1. Top panels: 10^5 sample draws from a standard bivariate normal distribution (**left**) and a dataset of raw univariate functional data (**right**). Bottom panel: 10^3 sample draws from a standard normal distribution in dimension one. The color of the elements in each of the three plots represent the depth based on the distance to the center of symmetry of the sample.

2.1.1. Difficulties with Notions of Functional Symmetry

The intangibility of distributions on function space leads to great difficulties in formulating a well conceived notion of symmetry in this domain, as naïve point-wise extensions of familiar notions in $\mathbb{R}$ or $\mathbb{R}^p$ ignore topological features such as continuity, contiguity and smoothness. We illustrate the difficulties in formulating a notion of functional symmetry through a prototypical example of a distribution on function space, asymmetric by construction, but symmetric with respect to many topologically apathetic notions of functional symmetry.

For that, we make use of ([11], Example 2) where X denotes a mixture of three processes on $[0,1]$, with probabilities $p_1 = 0.2$, $p_2 = 0.3$ and $p_3 = 0.5$, each following a mean zero Gaussian distribution. They differ according to the correlation length parameter m in their covariance structure:

$$\text{Cov}(s,t) = e^{-\frac{(s-t)^2}{2m^2}},$$

where $m \in \{1, 0.25, 0.1\}$.

Figure 2 depicts $n = 11$ typical realizations of this process, with the different panels emphasizing the elements of the sample corresponding to the different correlation lengths. A symmetry notion exclusive for spaces of functions should naturally consider topological characteristics, for instance, shape and roughness. Note the difference among the three processes in the mixture by observing the differences in the curves of the three panels of Figure 2, from those with less curvature on the left to those with more curvature on the right. Thus, by making use of an appropriate metric on the functional space, the notion of symmetry we will apply here correctly recognizes that mixtures of Gaussian distributions like X are asymmetric.

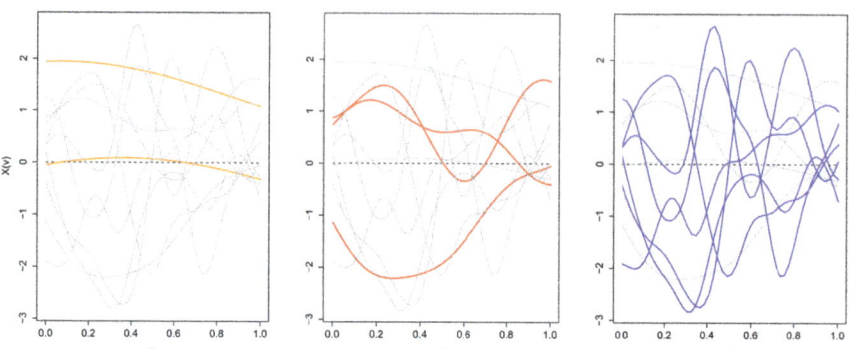

Figure 2. Observations from a mixture of Gaussian processes on [0,1]. Mixture components are mean zero and have covariance structure $\text{Cov}(s,t) = \exp\{-(s-t)^2/(2m^2)\}$ where $m = 1$ with probability 0.2, $m = 0.25$ with probability 0.3 and $m = 0.1$ with probability 0.5. Realizations corresponding to each mixture component are highlighted in the respective panels from left ($m = 1$) to right ($m = 0.1$).

However, X is clearly symmetric around the zero function for several extensions of multivariate symmetry; for example:

(i) X and $-X$ are equal in law,
(ii) for any $v \in [0,1]$, the distribution of $X(v)$, or of its derivative at v, is symmetric on $\mathbb{R}$ around zero and
(iii) for any reasonable notion of symmetry in multivariate spaces, any finite linear combination of the random coefficients in the Karhunen-Loève expansion [12] of the process X, or of its derivative process, is symmetric around the zero element.

There is no inconsistency between X not being functional symmetric and being symmetric with respect to plausible extensions of multivariate notions. The notions are complementary. If the mixture of Gaussian distributions is asymmetric in terms of shape or roughness, there should be a type of symmetry that is sensitive to this, as described below.

2.1.2. Metric δ-Symmetry

The notion of symmetry employed in this paper was recently defined in [11] and is suitable for any function space, $\mathcal{F}$, endowed with a metric, or pseudo-metric, which we denote by d. For any fixed $\delta \in [0, \infty)$, a distribution P on $\mathcal{F}$ with support $\mathfrak{S}$ is (d, δ)-symmetric about a center

$$\zeta(\delta) := \zeta(\delta, P) \in \mathfrak{S}$$

if

$$P(\mathfrak{H}_x^{\zeta(\delta)}) \geq 0.5 - \delta$$

for all $x \in \mathfrak{S}$, with

$$\mathfrak{H}_x^{\zeta(\delta)} := \mathfrak{H}_x^{\zeta(\delta)}(P) = \{z \in \mathfrak{S} : d(z,x) \geq \max[d\{x,\zeta(\delta)\}, d\{z,\zeta(\delta)\}]\}.$$

Denoting,

$$\mathcal{Z}(\delta) := \mathcal{Z}(\delta, P) = \{z \in \mathfrak{S} : P(\mathfrak{H}_x^z) \geq \frac{1}{2} - \delta \text{ for all } x \in \mathfrak{S}\}, \tag{1}$$

we have that any

$$\zeta(\delta) \in \mathcal{Z}(\delta)$$

is a *center of* (d,δ)-*symmetry* of the space $\mathcal{F}$ with respect to the distribution P.

The (d,δ)-symmetry induces a functional median of the space $\mathcal{F}$ with respect to the distribution P, the *metric median*, which is

$$\mathcal{M}(P) := \arg\min_{z \in \mathfrak{S}}\{\delta \in [0,\infty) : P(\mathfrak{H}_x^z) \geq \tfrac{1}{2} - \delta \text{ for all } x \in \mathfrak{S}\}.$$

A distribution on a metric function space is generally understood as symmetric if it is $(d,0)$-symmetric. The δ for which $M(P)$ is obtained when being larger than 0 is the degree of departure from $(d,0)$-symmetry. As it occurs with the median in $\mathbb{R}$, a center of (d,δ)-symmetry is not necessarily unique (as observable from Equation (1)). Additionally, it is functional affine invariant and has a consistent and qualitatively robust sample version [11].

This definition of symmetry shares some common ground with the notion of multivariate half-space symmetry in that both notions are generalizations of Equation (2) below. Half-space symmetry is introduced in [8] for distributions on $\mathbb{R}^p$, as a means to generalize the previously existing notions of multidimensional symmetry such as central symmetry and angular symmetry. In the particular case of $p = 1$, according to [8] a distribution P on $\mathbb{R}$ is half-space symmetric about a center ζ if

$$P(H_x^\zeta) \geq \frac{1}{2}$$

for all $x \in \mathbb{R} \backslash \zeta$, with

$$H_x^\zeta := \{z \in \mathbb{R} : |z - x| \geq \max\{|x - \zeta|, |z - \zeta|\}\}. \tag{2}$$

An important point illustrating the generality of (d,δ)-symmetry, and equivalently of half-space symmetry, is that, in this special case of $p = 1$, all distributions are $(d,0)$-symmetric with center of symmetry at the median, despite not necessarily being so with respect to more geometrically intuitive notions of symmetry.

The concept of (d,δ)-symmetry is the first one designed specifically for functional data. Apparently, it could be applied to any metric space, however, it is indeed exclusive to functional data in the sense that it has no useful analogue in a multivariate context. This can be deduced from the reasoning in Section 2.1.1.

2.2. Statistical Depth

Just as in other disciplines, symmetry is a recurrent theme in statistics. For instance, symmetric laws frequently arise as limit laws of empirical processes [13,14], and, as we have just seen, the notion of symmetry helps to generalize the concept of median beyond the one dimensional case, for which it has a simple and unambiguous definition. In addition to being of independent interest, a notion of symmetry is required for constructing statistical depth functions, as is clear from the property based definition of depth appearing in [9,15]. According to this definition, the deepest element in a space $\mathcal{X}$ computed with respect to a distribution P on $\mathcal{X}$ coincides with the center of symmetry of P when a unique center of symmetry exists for some notion of symmetry. The other properties in this definition are: distance invariance, strictly decreasing with respect to the deepest element, upper semi-continuity, receptivity to convex hull width across the domain and continuity in distribution.

Loosely speaking, statistical depth orders the elements of a space with respect to a distribution, or a dataset (an empirical distribution). Thus, it lays the foundation for many nonparametric and exploratory data analysis tools such as rank-based inference and outlier detection, whose potential applications are wide ranging. We will employ statistical functional depth here as an exploratory tool to gain insight into the movement patterns of Alzheimer's patients.

2.2.1. Difficulties with Functional Depth Constructions

Refs. [16,17] report a problematic feature of certain depth constructions, both multivariate depths (half-space [18], simplicial [19], projection [9]) and functional depths (band [20], half region [21]). This feature is their degenerate behavior when applied in some common functional spaces. Therefore, in formulating a functional depth, it does not suffice to simply extend the finite dimension to infinity. The literature contains several instances of functional depth (h-depth [22], random Tukey depth [23,24], modified band depth [20], modified half region depth [21], spatial depth [25], for instance) and an axiomatic definition of functional depth put forward in [15]. However, the above cited commonly used proposals violate at least one of these axioms.

Recently, Ref. [11] has given a functional depth construction designed for functional metric spaces, and not multivariate. This construction was proved to satisfy the axiomatic definition of statistical functional depth under a mild condition on the metric. That condition is met by most metrics, including the Lebesgue and Sovolev metrics, but not the supremum metric. The construction, which we describe below, makes use of the set of centers of (d,δ)-symmetry. As a result of the relation of this set with the multivariate half-space depth median, a depth that suffers from the problem reported in [17], one might expect it to inherit this degeneracy. However the non-vanishing of the half-space depth median ([17], Theorem 3) guarantees that this is not the case.

2.2.2. Metric Depth

Given a (d,δ)-symmetric distribution P on a functional metric space $(\mathcal{F},d)$, with $\mathcal{Z}$ the set of centers, the *metric depth* of an element x of $\mathcal{F}$ with respect to a distribution P is defined in [11] as

$$D_m(x,P) := \frac{1}{I_m(x,P)+1} \qquad (3)$$

with

$$I_m(x,P) := \frac{d(x,\mathcal{Z})}{d(\xi,\xi')} := \inf_{\zeta \in \mathcal{Z}} \frac{d(x,\zeta)}{d(\xi,\xi')} \qquad (4)$$

and

$$\xi := \xi(P) \text{ and } \xi' := \xi'(P) \in \mathcal{F}$$

satisfying $d(\xi,\xi') > 0$ and independent of x.

This depth function computes the distance of the element of the space to the set of centers of functional symmetry and then standardizes so that the axiomatic properties in [15] are satisfied, under a mild condition on the metric. This is a general framework to be specified through the distance, for instance:

(i) A distance that makes use of the distribution with respect to which the depth is computed. In the space of continuous functions, the distance between two elements of the space can be defined through the probability of the band determined by them.

(ii) A Sobolev distance that takes into account how rough the datum is with respect to the functional center of symmetry.

In the context of the Alzheimer's data, it suffices to make use of

$$I_M(x,P) := d(x,\mathcal{Z}) := \inf_{\zeta \in \mathcal{Z}} d(x,\zeta) \qquad (5)$$

in (3) instead of (4) because, given P, $d(\xi,\xi')$ is constant for every x in the space, (see [11]).

3. Illustration

The dataset of Alzheimer's patients, analyzed later, consists of the accelerations recorded by the accelerometer of an Android smartphone while the patients move freely in a daycare facility. On exploring this dataset, we aim to study whether the underlying distribution generating the data is symmetric. The acceleration is the derivative of the velocity with respect to time, which, as well, is the derivative of the position with respect to time. Accelerometers provide directly the acceleration, without the need for differentiating the data. However, in studying the distribution underlying the movement of Alzheimer's patients, it is relevant that symmetries are perpetuated through derivatives, particularly, the first and the second.

We provide an example to illustrate that the notion of symmetry we use has the distinctive feature of inducing symmetry in other domains. Let X denote a Gaussian process with mean zero, covariance structure

$$\text{Cov}(s,t) = e^{-\frac{(s-t)^2}{m^2}}$$

and correlation length $m = 1$ and $X_1, \ldots, X_n$, $n = 1000$ independent realizations drawn from X.

For $i = 1, \ldots, n$, we plot

$$\int (X_i - \zeta)(v) dv$$

versus

$$\int (X_i^{(1)} - \zeta^{(1)})(v) dv$$

in the left plot of Figure 3 and

$$\int (X_i^{(1)} - \zeta^{(1)})(v) dv$$

versus

$$\int (X_i^{(2)} - \zeta^{(2)})(v) dv$$

in the right plot of Figure 3. There, $X_i^{(j)}$ denotes the jth derivative of X_i, for $j = 1, 2$ and $i = 1, \ldots, 1000$.

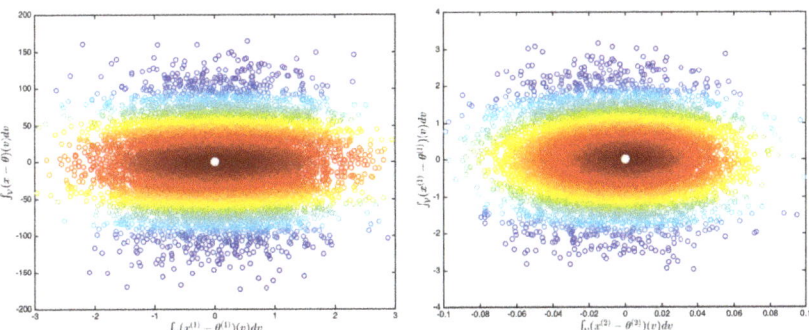

Figure 3. Symmetries induced in the domain of the integration of a Gaussian process with correlation length 1 minus its center of symmetry versus the integral of its first derivative (**left**) and of the first derivative versus the second (**right**). The color represents the metric depth in Sobolev-(2,2) distance (**left**) and in the Sobolev-(2,2) distance minus the $\mathbb{L}_2$ distance (**right**), with the center depicted by a white dot.

To illustrate that our notion of symmetry has the distinctive feature of inducing symmetry in these two domains, we compute the set of sample centers of $(d, 0)$-symmetry based on the empirical distribution of $X_1, \ldots, X_{1000}$, P_n, and the corresponding metric depth of X_i with respect to P_n for each $i = 1, \ldots, n$. We depict in Figure 3 the center of symmetry as a white dot and the metric depth of each point by the color (from dark red for high depth to dark blue for low depth).

Let us denote by $\mathbb{L}_2$ the standard Lebesgue 2-integrable norm and by Sobolev-(2,k) the standard Sobolev inner product norm for k derivatives. To illustrate the importance of taking into account the topology of the elements in the support of the distribution, we use the Sobolev-(2,2) distance for the left panel of the figure and the Sobolev-(2,2) distance minus the $\mathbb{L}_2$ distance for the right panel. Thus, the colors in the right panel, given by the center and depth, only make use of a distance based on the first and second derivatives.

4. Application

As mentioned in the introduction, the dataset consists of the acceleration values, in the three spatial dimensions over time, of patients that move freely in a daycare facility. Although non-standard, these data are easily accommodated by the (d,δ)-symmetry and the metric depth as shown below in Section 4.1. We make use of nonparametric tests on the depth results as described in Section 4.2 and evaluate this methodology through Monte Carlo simulations in Section 4.3. Section 4.4 summarizes and explains the real data we analyze. The results of such analysis are in Section 4.5.

4.1. Functional Metric Space Construction

We denote by n the total number of studied patients and by x_i the acceleration values recorded for patient i, $i = 1, \ldots, n$. As the accelerations of each patient were recorded in separate days, we have repeated measurements for each patient, we denote by k_i the number of repeated measurements for patient i and by $x_{i1}, \ldots, x_{ik_i}$ the repeated measurements, $i = 1, \ldots, n$. We later refer to these repeated measurements as repetitions. Thus,

$$x_i = (x_{i1}, \ldots, x_{ik_i}) \text{ for } i = 1, \ldots, n. \tag{6}$$

As each measurement is a three dimensional functional datum, we have that

$$x_{ik} : [l_{ik}, u_{ik}] \to \mathbb{R}^3$$

is the kth measurement on patient i and

$$L(x_{ik}) := u_{ik} - l_{ik}$$

is the length of the domain. A particularity of this dataset is that the domain, $[l_{ik}, u_{ik}]$, and its length, $L(x_{ik})$, differ for each $k = 1, \ldots, k_i$ and $i = 1, \ldots, n$. This requires non-standard FDA methodologies like the ones we apply here.

A characteristic of real functional data is that they are observed on a grid, not being recorded in every point of the domain. That is, $x_{ik}(t)$ is not recorded at each $t \in [l_{ik}, u_{ik}]$, but at each t in the finite set

$$\mathcal{T}_{i,k} := \{t_{1,i,k}, \ldots, t_{T_{i,k},i,k}\}$$

with

$$l_{ik} \le t_{1,i,k} < t_{2,i,k} < \cdots < t_{T_{i,k},i,k} \le u_{ik},$$

not necessarily equally spaced. Part of the complexity of this dataset is that $\mathcal{T}_{i,k}$ differs for each $k = 1, \ldots, k_i$ and $i = 1, \ldots, n$.

The (d,δ)-symmetry and the metric depth require of a metric functional space for their application. Then, given any pair $(x_{ik}, x_{j\ell})$ with $k \in \{1, \ldots, k_i\}$, $\ell \in \{1, \ldots, k_j\}$ and $i, j \in \{1, \ldots n\}$, we define our distance between x_{ik} and $x_{j\ell}$ as

$$d_S(x_{ik}, x_{j\ell}) := \max\{d(x_m, x_M(\mathcal{V}_h)) \ : \ h \in [0, L(x_M) - L(x_m)]\} \tag{7}$$

where the notation $x_i(\mathfrak{S})$ means $\{x(t) : t \in \mathfrak{S}\}$ and, additionally,

$$x_m := \arg\min\{L(x_{ik}), L(x_{j\ell})\},$$

$$x_M := \arg\max\{L(x_{ik}), L(x_{j\ell})\}$$

and $\mathcal{V}_h$ is such that

$$x_M(\mathcal{V}_h) = \{x_M(t) : 0 \le t - l_M - h \le L(x_m)\}.$$

It is easy to see that $d_S(\cdot, \cdot)$ satisfies the definition of a distance, for any distance d. In the data analysis, for two three dimensional functional data objects

$$f = \{f_1, f_2, f_3\}$$

and

$$g = \{g_1, g_2, g_3\},$$

which are defined over the same domain, we take

$$d(f,g) = 1/3 \sum_{i=1}^{3} \|f_i - g_i\|, \tag{8}$$

where $\|\cdot\|$ is a norm, for instance the $\mathbb{L}_2$ norm. We then aggregate the information from the repeated measurements as

$$\frac{1}{k_i k_j} \sum_{k=1}^{k_i} \sum_{\ell=1}^{k_j} d_S(x_{ik}, x_{j\ell}),$$

and use this to construct the set of centers of (d, δ)-symmetry and the metric depth as described previously.

4.2. Tests on the Statistical Depth Values

The dataset consists of patients at three different stages of the disease and the analysis will provide a depth value for each. Let

$$D_m := \{D_{m,1}, \ldots D_{m,l_m}\}$$

be the depth values for the patients in a mild stage of the disease,

$$D_o := \{D_{o,1}, \ldots D_{o,l_o}\}$$

the depth values for those in a moderate stage and

$$D_s := \{D_{s,1}, \ldots D_{s,l_s}\}$$

the depth values for those in a severe stage. Abusing of the notation, D_m, D_o and D_s will stand also for the corresponding depth random variables. Note that $l_m + l_o + l_s = n$. We will illustrate the methodology using D_m and D_o. Analogous ideas apply to all combinations of depths for mild, moderate and severe disease stages.

Depth values have an inherent rank structure. To test for differences between the distributions of the trivariate acceleration functions, we apply two sided nonparametric tests to the associated depth values. One of them is an omnibus test, a test that can potentially pick any difference between two distributions with independence of the nature of the difference. It is also important to know where the differences lie. Thus, we propose to perform two further tests, one on the median differences and another on the scale differences. The scale test is a test on the deviance from the median [26]. We do them on the median, as opposed to the mean, in order to perform non-parametric robust tests. These last two tests have hypotheses of the form

$$H_0: \mathfrak{p}_m \leq \mathfrak{p}_o$$
$$H_a: \mathfrak{p}_m > \mathfrak{p}_o,$$

where $\mathfrak{p}_m$ refers respectively to the population median and the deviance from the population median in the mild group and $\mathfrak{p}_o$ is the same parameter in the moderate group.

Given D_m and D_o and a statistic G, all of these tests are permutation tests [27] of the following form:

1. Compute the value of the statistic on the observed depth values

$$g_{obs} := G(D_m, D_o).$$

2. Compute the permutations of the $l_m + l_o$ depth values between two groups, one with l_m elements and the other with l_o. There is a total of

$$N := (l_m + l_o)!/(l_m! l_o!)$$

permutations.

3. Compute the value of the statistic on each of the permutations, $g_1, \ldots, g_N$.
4. The resulting p-value for the test is

$$p := \#\{i = 1, \ldots, N : g_i \geq g_{obs}\}/N.$$

For the omnibus test, we apply the Kolmogorov–Smirnov test [28,29] to the depths. The associated test statistic is

$$G_{KS}(D_m, D_o) := \max_{t \in \mathbb{R}} |F_{D_m}(t) - F_{D_o}(t)|,$$

where $F_D(t)$ is the cumulative distribution of D at time t. As G_{KS} involves an absolute value, performing the above steps for the permutation test will result in this case on a test for the null hypothesis of equality of distributions against the distributions being different. For the test on the median differences, the test statistic is

$$G_M(D_m, D_o) := \text{Med}(D_m) - \text{Med}(D_o),$$

where $\text{Med}(D)$ denotes the median of D. For the deviance from the median test, the statistic is

$$G_S(D_m, D_o) := \frac{\sum_{i=1,\ldots,l_m} |D_{m,i} - \text{Med}(D_m)|}{\sum_{i=1,\ldots,l_o} |D_{o,i} - \text{Med}(D_o)|}.$$

4.3. Simulation

We perform a Monte Carlo study to evaluate the performance of the methodology described above. The following simple example was used for illustration in ([11], Example 1). Functional random variables X are generated as

$$X(t) = Y \cos(\pi t)$$

with Y a real random variable and $t \in [0, 1]$. As studied in [11], the distribution of X is $(d, 0)$-symmetric independently of d and the choice of distribution for Y. To emulate the different populations of patients in the Alzheimer's data, we generate observations $X_{m,1}, \ldots, X_{m,l_m}$ from one population, Population m say, by taking Y to be standard normally distributed. We generate, independently, observations $X_{o,1}, \ldots, X_{o,l_o}$ from Population o by drawing Y from a distribution Q, taken in turn as standard normal, standard uniform and beta of parameters 2 and 1. We use of a grid of 50 equi-spaced points on $[0,1]$ and, to emulate the Alzheimer's data, we take $l_m = l_o = 10$.

For the analysis, we use the metric depth, based on the set of (d,0)-centers of symmetry, with respect to the pooled sample with d taken as the Sobolev-(2,2) distance; obtaining the depth values $\{D_{m,1}, \ldots D_{m,l_m}\}$ and $\{D_{o,1}, \ldots D_{o,l_o}\}$. We then apply the methodology described in Section 4.2 to these depth values. When Q is the standard normal distribution, the distributions of $X_{m,j}$ and $X_{o,i}$ are the same for any i and j and we expect the tests to reject infrequently. Specifically, we expect the proportion of rejections over the Monte Carlo replications to be roughly equal to the nominal level of the test. When Q is one of the other distributions, the proportion of rejections will ideally be large, as this indicates strong ability to distinguish between distributions of the functional random variables on the basis of their functional depth values.

The median and deviance from the median tests used are exact permutation tests. As the distribution test has more computational cost, we have performed an approximated permutation test based on 1000 permutations. The proportion of Monte Carlo replications in which the test rejects the null hypothesis of equal distributions is reported in Table 1 for each of the three scenarios. It is observable from the table that the power of rejection is higher when the $X_{0,i}$s are drawn using the beta distribution with parameters (2,1) than when using the uniform distribution. Additionally, under the alternative, the deviance from the median test is more powerful than the median test, which is also more powerful than the distribution test. The low rejection rate of the distribution test under the null hypothesis can be due to an approximated permutation test is performed.

Table 1. Rate of rejection based on 1000 repetitions for three permutation tests: distribution, median and deviance from the median. The permutation tests for the median and deviation from the median are exact. The permutation test for the distribution is approximated, based on 1000 permutations. The first sample is based on the standard normal distribution, N(0,1), and the second on the N(0,1) (first column), the uniform in the (0,1) interval, U(0,1), (second column) and the beta with parameters (2,1), $\beta(2,1)$, (third column).

	N(0,1)	U(0,1)	$\beta(2,1)$
Distribution	0.034	0.591	0.749
Median	0.053	0.795	0.891
Deviance	0.042	0.801	0.913

4.4. The Data

The real data were measured in the patients' natural environment rather than a controlled environment as in [30]. Patients' movements were recorded while they perform their usual activities throughout the day under the supervision of a neuropsychologist, in a room of a day care facility. The smartphone is oriented and placed in a pocket of the patient by the neuropsychologist. Thus, the orientation and placement of the smartphone is never exactly the same, neither among patients nor among the different days in which the accelerations of a particular patient are recorded.

From a purely statistical point of view, it is always advantageous to use data from a controlled experiment. However, for the statistical classifier to be a valuable and widely applicable diagnostic tool, it is necessary to use observational data of the type studied here. Ref. [31] asserts that the everyday behavior of Alzheimer's patients is detectable by using only an accelerometer, without the need for an additional gyroscope for standardization. For a more detailed discussion, see [4], where these data were first analyzed.

The study comprises data on $n = 35$ patients for whom repeated measurements are available corresponding to different days. The repetitions k_i in (6), vary between 2 and 8 depending on the patient labeled as $i = 1, \ldots, n$. The value of k_i, for each i, is displayed in Table 2, column two, under the heading repetitions. There, the disease stage of each patient is also shown in column three. The information obtained from these two columns is summarized in Table 3, from which we observe that:

- 7 patients are in the mild stage of the disease with a total of 41 repetitions.
- 18 patients are in the moderate stage of the disease with a total of 100 repetitions.
- 10 patients are in the severe stage of the disease with a total of 46 repetitions.

Table 2. Synopsis of the studied dataset. For each of the 35 patients (column i), labeled from 1 to 35, it is displayed the number of repeated measurements (column ii), the disease stage of the patient (column iii), the range, among the repetitions for each patient, of the time domain upper-bounds, in seconds, (column iv) and the range, among the repetitions for each patient, of the number of grid points (column v).

Patient	Repetitions	Disease Stage	Maximum Range	Grid Range
1	5	moderate	3273.8–4149.3	457,352–574,918
2	3	severe	2721.6–3573.2	380,756–493,117
3	3	mild	3077.8–3679.8	426,027–508,825
4	6	mild	3168.5–3847.7	447,858–542,706
5	5	severe	2786.6–4109.3	396,699–583,914
6	3	severe	3356.4–3587.0	469,298–498,984
7	7	severe	2993.3–3878.0	426,625–545,839
8	8	mild	2610.7–3778.1	366,541–531,256
9	3	severe	3419.6–3633.7	474,456–500,270
10	6	moderate	3090.3–3952.5	427,229–547,061
11	8	mild	2718.5–3870.4	267,288–385,509
12	5	moderate	3069.8–4112.8	257,796–388,149
13	8	moderate	2802.8–5003.5	245,309–520,520
14	7	severe	3365.1–5942.7	327,976–560,693
15	7	mild	3590.9–4127.8	295,551–344,340
16	7	severe	3472.2–5452.3	327,583–496,692
17	4	mild	3405.0–4008.7	182,260–295,130
18	6	moderate	3168.1–4068.7	211,480–389,936
19	5	mild	3189.9–3667.0	298,743–339,375
20	7	moderate	2765.9–4469.5	259,898–354,498
21	5	moderate	3309.3–5427.6	322,132–521,646
22	4	severe	3465.3–5303.9	301,622–527,696
23	6	moderate	3040.7–6346.4	246,077–491,322
24	2	severe	4666.8–4666.8	399,909–399,909
25	7	moderate	3305.3–5076.6	322,957–484,066
26	4	moderate	3203.1–6108.5	281,369–590,537
27	7	moderate	3535.9–5345.0	305,482–481,180
28	3	moderate	3147.6–4033.7	307,455–376,297
29	7	moderate	3502.5–5807.5	342,543–558,649
30	4	moderate	3605.4–5908.8	266,367–537,241
31	5	moderate	3043.7–5991.5	295,878–469,712
32	6	moderate	3326.8–4494.0	320,243–419,402
33	3	moderate	3078.7–4753.0	263,053–462,177
34	6	moderate	2329.4–5002.6	215,536–529,828
35	5	severe	3143.6–4576.0	302,221–469,318

Table 3. Summary of Table 2 encapsulating the number of patients and total number of repetitions per stage of the disease: mild, moderate and severe.

	Mild	Moderate	Severe
Number of patients	7	18	10
Number of repetitions	41	100	46

Furthermore, in Table 2 column four, under the heading maximum range, we have displayed, for each patient $i = 1, \ldots, n$,

$$\min\{u_{ik} : k = 1, \ldots k_i\} - \max\{u_{ik} : k = 1, \ldots k_i\}. \tag{9}$$

Additionally, to report the size of each $\mathcal{T}_{i,k}$, in Table 2 column five, under the heading grid range, we have displayed

$$\min\{T_{i,k} : k = 1, \ldots k_i\} - \max\{T_{i,k} : k = 1, \ldots k_i\}, \tag{10}$$

for each patient $i = 1, \ldots, n$. This is then a report on the range of the amount of recorded elements of each time series, per patient.

In Figure 4, we exemplify the nature of the dataset by plotting, for three of the patients, the recorded accelerations, in meters per second squared (m/s^2), with respect to the time in seconds (s).

- In the left column panels: the five repetitions of patient 19, who is in a mild stage of the disease.
- In the central column panels: the six repetitions of patient 34, who is in a moderate stage of the disease.
- In the right column panels: the five repetitions of patient 35, who is in a severe stage of the disease.

The top row in Figure 4 corresponds to the accelerations with respect to time in the OX coordinate axis, the middle row to the OY coordinate axis and the bottom row to the OZ axis. It is observable from these plots that each repetition is recorded for a different length of time, $L(x_{ik})$. Additionally, note that the plots show no apparent difference among the three stages of the disease.

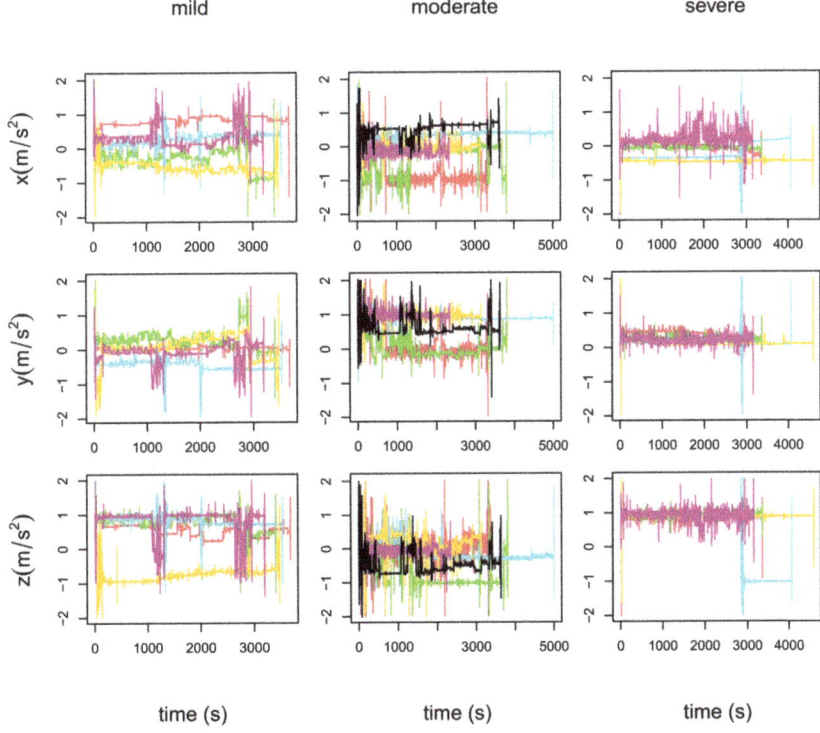

Figure 4. Display of the accelerations (m/s^2), in the three coordinate axis (OX: top row, OY: central row and OZ: bottom row) over the time domain (s), of the repetitions of three patients. Each patient is in a different stage of the disease. Left column: mild stage (patient 19). Central column: moderate stage (patient 34). Right column: severe stage (patient 35).

4.5. Results

We find functional $(d,0)$-symmetry when the Sobolev-(2,2) distance is used, in Equation (7) through the use of Equation (8), in the complete sample as well as in the three subsamples corresponding to different severity of dementia (mild, moderate and severe). This is an important finding to get insight into this type of movement data as it tells us information on the symmetry of the underlying distributions. The same results are obtained using the $\mathbb{L}_2$ distance due to the functional data points exhibiting little variability over the domain, which is observable from the elements of the dataset displayed in Figure 4.

The corresponding set of centers of $(d,0)$-symmetry can be used to compute the metric depth as outlined in Section 2. Unlike most other functional depth constructions appearing in the literature, the metric depth is known to satisfy the fifth property of the axiomatic definition of statistical functional depth [15]. That property establishes the depth function has to be receptive to the convex hull width across the domain. This is especially relevant here as the elements of functional spaces show a small amount of variation over large parts of the domain. This depth construction automatically accounts for this, giving greater importance to the regions of the domain in which the functional data points exhibit the most variability.

To illustrate the findings, in Figure 5 we display the I_M value of the metric depth, Equation (5), of the elements in each of the three subsets computed with respect to the center of $(d,0)$-symmetry of the complete sample (left plot) and of the three subsamples separately (right plot). As observable from the figure, the center of $(d,0)$-symmetry of the complete sample, which takes I_M value 0, belongs to the subgroup with mild dementia and coincides with the center of symmetry of this subgroup when the center of $(d,0)$-symmetry is computed separately for each of the three subsamples. In fact, the patient corresponding to the center of $(d,0)$-symmetry when computed with respect to the complete sample is the patient labeled as 3 in Table 2. When computing the center of $(d,0)$-symmetry of the patients in the moderate stage of the disease, we obtain that the center of $(d,0)$-symmetry corresponds to the patient labeled as 10. For the severe stage, we obtain the patient labeled as 9.

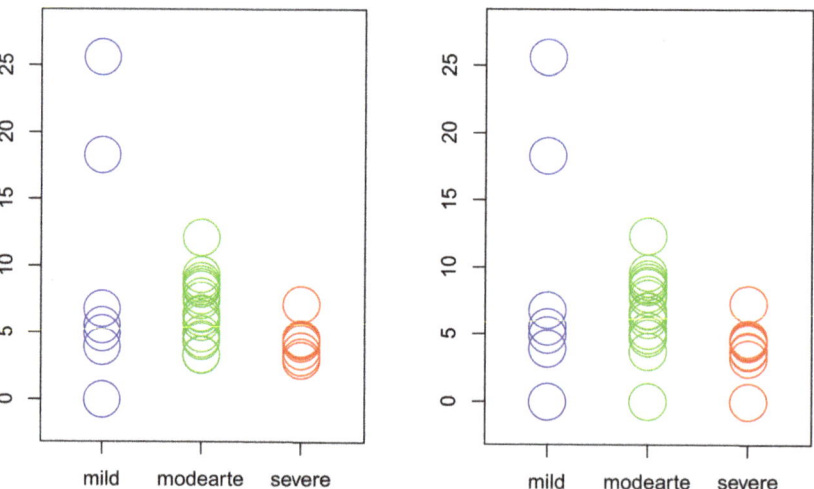

Figure 5. Representation of the I_M depth value for the 35 Alzheimer's patients computed with respect to the center of symmetry of the complete sample (**left plot**) and of the three subsamples separately (**right plot**).

From the two plots in Figure 5, it can be easily deduced that the variability of the depth values for the mild patients is higher than that for moderate, which likewise is higher than for the severe patients. To check whether this is indeed the case, we perform the permutation tests on the depth commented above in Section 4.2. All the tests are exact permutation tests in this subsection. The *p*-values resulting from these tests are displayed in Table 4. We have arranged them in two cases:

- The metric depth is computed with respect to the center of $(d, 0)$-symmetry of the complete sample. This corresponds to the left plot in Figure 5.
- The metric depth is computed with respect to the center of $(d, 0)$-symmetry of each of the three subsamples separately. This corresponds to the right plot in Figure 5.

For each of the two cases, we have included in the table the *p*-values resulting of testing whether each two groups of distributions are equal against the alternative in which they differ. The heading of the table is for the greater than alternative instead of not equal so the resulting *p*-value will coincide, as explained in Section 4.2. Additionally, the table includes a test on which the median on a stage of the disease is less or equal than in the next stage against the alternative in which it is greater and an equivalent test but on the deviation from the median.

Table 4. *p*-values resulting from performing the permutation test on the depth to find distribution, median and deviance from the median differences. The top three rows refer to the tests performed on depth values computed with respect to the complete sample while the bottom three to tests performed on depth values computed for each of the three stages separately. Thus, *Complete sample* is for using the depth values of the pooled sample and *Subsamples* for using the depth values computed with respect to each sample separately. The alternative hypothesis for each test is greater than, but for the distribution case that coincides with the not equal alternative. *p*-values resulting in a rejection at 0.05 significance level are emphasized in bold.

H_a :	$\mathbb{P}_{mild} > \mathbb{P}_{moderate}$	$\mathbb{P}_{moderate} > \mathbb{P}_{severe}$
	Complete Sample	
Distribution	0.0202	0.0027
Median	0.8090	0.0158
Deviance	0.0339	0.0030
	Subsamples	
Distribution	0.6672	0.0001
Median	0.8242	0.0140
Deviance	0.0320	0.0332

The results in Table 4 show a significant difference on the distribution for three out of the four run tests. However, we can say that there is a significant difference in the distribution in the four cases, as the deviance from the median test is able to detect the difference every time. The median test also detects a difference when studying the pair moderate and severe. However, no such difference is detected with the pair mild and moderate. For this case of the median test with the pair mild and moderate, it is worth saying that neither a rejection is obtained for the less than alternative nor for the not equal alternative, although the *p*-values decrease.

5. Discussion

Many modern datasets consist of functional observations, i.e., data most naturally viewed as realizations of random functions. Typical examples of such data include gene expression levels over time, blood oxygen levels throughout the volume of the brain and, as used for illustration in the present work, accelerations of Alzheimer's patients when moving freely in a daycare facility. The ease of recording such data make it practically useful, although they present difficulties for its analysis due to their unusual features. Notably:

- There are a different number of recordings for each patient.
- Each recording is over a different time domain.

- Each recording is observed over a different grid.

Our functional data analysis based on new notions of functional symmetry and depth introduced in [11] applies without complications in this setting. This notion of functional symmetry has the advantage of being truly conceived for functional data and it adapts to the characteristics of the data, through the metric. Thus, it is not an extension of a multivariate notion like the others existing in the literature. The instance of depth used, the metric depth, does have two advantages over the others in the literature:

- The involved center of symmetry is a truly functional center of symmetry.
- It is the only existing instance of depth that satisfies the notion of statistical functional depth.

Most existing data of this type are recorded in a controlled environment such as a laboratory and not just by the use of a smartphone in a quite free environment. This dataset, however, has been previously used in [3,4] with the aim of performing supervised classification. There, black-box techniques were applied and so the objective in this paper has been to understand the characteristic(s) that differentiate among the distributions of the stages of Alzheimer's disease. The proposed methodology is able to distinguish between patients at different stages of the disease based on the accelerometer data. In particular, we found that the distribution of acceleration differs between each stage of the disease. We observe that those differences are mainly due to scale differences. As for ensuring the validity of the methodology used, in addition to the broad results covered in [11], we have provided a simulation study to emulate the analysis performed on the real data when the ground truth is known. Analogous to the performed analysis based on the recorded accelerations, future research could include an analysis on the velocities.

Author Contributions: Conceptualization, A.N.-R.; Formal analysis, A.N.-R., H.B. and G.F.; Supervision, A.N.-R.; Writing—original draft, A.N.-R. and H.B. All authors have read and agreed to the published version of the manuscript.

Funding: For A.N.-R., this research was funded by grant number MTM2017-86061-C2-2-P of the Spanish Ministry of Science, Innovation and Universities. H.B was supported by the EPSRC under grant number EP/P002757/1.

Institutional Review Board Statement: Not applicable.

Informed Consent Statement: Not applicable.

Acknowledgments: We are thankful to the Association of Relatives of Alzheimer's patients in Cantabria, Spain, for the Alzheimer's dataset.

Conflicts of Interest: The authors declare no conflict of interest.

Abbreviations

This paper contains the below abbreviations:

FDA Functional Data Analysis
GDS Global Deterioration Scale

References

1. Mayeux, R.; Sano, M. Treatment of Alzheimer's disease. *N. Engl. J. Med.* **1999**, *341*, 1670–1679. [CrossRef]
2. Reisberg, B.; Ferris, S.H.; de Leon, M.J.; Crook, T. The Global Deterioration Scale for assessment of primary degenerative dementia. *Am. J. Psychiatry* **1982**, *139*, 1136–1139. [PubMed]
3. Bringas, S.; Salomón, S.; Duque, R.; Lage, C.; Montaña, J.L. Alzheimer's Disease stage identification using deep learning models. *J. Biomed. Inform.* **2020**, *109*, 103514. [CrossRef] [PubMed]
4. Nieto-Reyes, A.; Duque, R.; Montaña, J.L.; Lage C. Classification of Alzheimer's patients through ubiquitous computing. *Sensors* **2017**, *17*, 1679. [CrossRef] [PubMed]
5. Park, S.Y.; Staicu, A.M. Longitudinal functional data analysis. *STAT Int. Stat. Inst.* **2015**, *4*, 212–226. [CrossRef]
6. Ferraty, F.; Vieu, P. *Nonparametric Functional Data Analysis*; Springer Series in Statistics; Springer: New York, NY, USA, 2006.
7. Ramsay, J.O.; Silverman, B.W. *Functional Data Analysis*; Springer Series in Statistics; Springer: New York, NY, USA, 2005.

8. Zuo, Y.; Serfling, R. On the performance of some robust nonparametric location measures relative to a general notion of multivariate symmetry. *J. Statist. Plann. Inference* **2000**, *84*, 55–79. [CrossRef]
9. Zuo, Y.; Serfling, R. General notions of statistical depth function. *Ann. Statist.* **2000**, *28*, 461–482. [CrossRef]
10. Kallenberg, O. *Probabilistic Symmetries and Invariance Principles*; Probability and Its Applications; Springer: New York, NY, USA, 2005.
11. Nieto-Reyes, A.; Battey, H. A topologically valid construction of depth for functional data. *J. Multivar. Anal.* **2021**, *184*, 104738.
12. Fukunaga, K.; Koontz, W.L.G. Application of the Karhunen-Loève Expansion to Feature Selection and Ordering. *IEEE Trans. Comput.* **1970**, *19*, 311–318. [CrossRef]
13. Dudley, R.M. *Uniform Central Limit Theorems*; Cambridge Studies in Advanced Mathematics, Series Number 63; Cambridge University Press: Cambridge, UK, 1999.
14. Hall, P. Two-sided bounds on the rate of convergence to a stable law. *Zeitschrift für Wahrscheinlichkeitstheorie und Verwandte Gebiete* **1981**, *57*, 349–364. [CrossRef]
15. Nieto-Reyes, A.; Battey, H. A topologically valid definition of depth for functional data. *Stat. Sci.* **2016**, *31*, 61–79. [CrossRef]
16. Chakraborty, A.; Chaudhuri, P. On data depth in infinite dimensional spaces. *Ann. Inst. Stat.* **2014**, *66*, 303–324. [CrossRef]
17. Dutta, S.; Ghosh, A-K.; Chaudhuri, P. Some intriguing properties of Tukey's halfspace depth. *Bernoulli* **2011**, *17*, 1420–1434. [CrossRef]
18. Tukey, J. Mathematics and the picturing of data. In Proceedings of the International Congress of Mathematicians, Vancouver, BC, Canada, 21–29 August 1974; Canadian Mathematical Congress: Montreal, QC, Canada, 1975; pp. 523–531.
19. Liu, R.Y. On a notion of data depth based on random simplices. *Ann. Statist.* **1990**, *18*, 405–414. [CrossRef]
20. López-Pintado, S.; Romo, J. On the concept of depth for functional data. *J. Amer. Statist. Assoc.* **2009**, *104*, 718–734. [CrossRef]
21. López-Pintado, S.; Romo, J. A half-region depth for functional data. *Comput. Statist. Data Anal.* **2011**, *55*, 1679–1695. [CrossRef]
22. Cuevas, A.; Febrero, M.; Fraiman, R. Robust estimation and classification for functional data via projection-based depth notions. *Comput. Statist.* **2007**, *22*, 481–496. [CrossRef]
23. Cuesta-Albertos, J.A.; Nieto-Reyes, A. The random Tukey depth. *Comput. Statist. Data Anal.* **2008**, *52*, 4979–4988. [CrossRef]
24. Cuesta-Albertos, J.A.; Nieto-Reyes, A. Functional Classification and the Random Tukey Depth: Practical Issues. In *Combining Soft Computing and Statistical Methods in Data Analysis*; Borgelt, C., González-Rodríguez, G., Trutschnig, W., Lubiano, M.A., Gil, M.Á., Grzegorzewski, P., Hryniewicz, O., Eds.; Springer: Berlin/Heidelberg, Germany, 2010; pp. 123–130.
25. Chakraborty, A.; Chaudhuri, P. The spatial distribution in infinite dimensional spaces and related quantiles and depths. *Ann. Statist.* **2014**, *42*, 1203–1231. [CrossRef]
26. Richter, S.J.; McCann, M.H. Permutation tests of scale using deviances. *Commun. Stat. Simul. Comput.* **2017**, *46*, 5553–5565. [CrossRef]
27. Higgins, J.J. *An Introduction to Modern Nonparametric Statistics*; Brooks/Cole: Pacific Grove, CA, USA, 2003.
28. Kolmogorov, A. Sulla determinazione empirica di una legge di distribuzione. *Giorn. Ist. Ital. Attuar.* **1933**, *4*, 83–91.
29. Smirnov, N. Table for estimating the goodness of fit of empirical distributions. *Ann. Math. Stat.* **1948**, *19*, 279–281. [CrossRef]
30. Ijmker T.; Lamoth, C.J.C. Gait and cognition: The relationship between gait stability and variability with executive function in persons with and without dementia. *Gait Posture* **2012**, *35*, 126–130. [CrossRef]
31. Kirste, T.; Hoffmeyer, A.; Koldrack, P.; Bauer,A; Schubert, S.; Schroeder, S; Teipel, S. Detecting the effect of Alzheimer's disease on everyday motion behavior. *J. Alzheimer's Dis.* **2014**, *38*, 121–132. [CrossRef] [PubMed]

Article

Predictive Ability of Machine-Learning Methods for Vitamin D Deficiency Prediction by Anthropometric Parameters

Carmen Patino-Alonso [1,2,*], Marta Gómez-Sánchez [2], Leticia Gómez-Sánchez [2], Benigna Sánchez Salgado [2,3], Emiliano Rodríguez-Sánchez [2,3,4], Luis García-Ortiz [2,3,5,†] and Manuel A. Gómez-Marcos [2,3,4,†]

[1] Department of Statistics, University of Salamanca, 37007 Salamanca, Spain
[2] Primary Care Research Unit of Salamanca (APISAL), Biomedical Research Institute of Salamanca (IBSAL), 37005 Salamanca, Spain; martas_111@hotmail.com (M.G.-S.); leticiagmzsnchz@gmail.com (L.G.-S.); benissanchez@gmail.com (B.S.S.); emiliano@usal.es (E.R.-S.); lgarcia@usal.es (L.G.-O.); magomez@usal.es (M.A.G.-M.)
[3] Health Service of Castilla and Leon (SACyL), 37005 Salamanca, Spain
[4] Department of Medicine, University of Salamanca, 37007 Salamanca, Spain
[5] Department of Biomedical and Diagnostic Sciences, University of Salamanca, 37007 Salamanca, Spain
* Correspondence: carpatino@usal.es
† These authors contributed equally to this work.

Abstract: Background: Vitamin D deficiency affects the general population and is very common among elderly Europeans. This study compared different supervised learning algorithms in a cohort of Spanish individuals aged 35–75 years to predict which anthropometric parameter was most strongly associated with vitamin D deficiency. Methods: A total of 501 participants were recruited by simple random sampling with replacement (reference population: 43,946). The analyzed anthropometric parameters were waist circumference (WC), body mass index (BMI), waist-to-height ratio (WHtR), body roundness index (BRI), visceral adiposity index (VAI), and the Clinical University of Navarra body adiposity estimator (CUN-BAE) for body fat percentage. Results: All the anthropometric indices were associated, in males, with vitamin D deficiency ($p < 0.01$ for the entire sample) after controlling for possible confounding factors, except for CUN-BAE, which was the only parameter that showed a correlation in females. Conclusions: The capacity of anthropometric parameters to predict vitamin D deficiency differed according to sex; thus, WC, BMI, WHtR, VAI, and BRI were most useful for prediction in males, while CUN-BAE was more useful in females. The naïve Bayes approach for machine learning showed the best area under the curve with WC, BMI, WHtR, and BRI, while the logistic regression model did so in VAI and CUN-BAE.

Keywords: vitamin D; machine learning; decision making; anthropometric parameters

Citation: Patino-Alonso, C.; Gómez-Sánchez, M.; Gómez-Sánchez, L.; Sánchez Salgado, B.; Rodríguez-Sánchez, E.; García-Ortiz, L.; Gómez-Marcos, M.A. Predictive Ability of Machine-Learning Methods for Vitamin D Deficiency Prediction by Anthropometric Parameters. *Mathematics* 2022, 10, 616. https://doi.org/10.3390/math10040616

Academic Editors: Carmen Lacave, Ana Isabel Molina and Florin Leon

Received: 30 November 2021
Accepted: 14 February 2022
Published: 17 February 2022

Publisher's Note: MDPI stays neutral with regard to jurisdictional claims in published maps and institutional affiliations.

Copyright: © 2022 by the authors. Licensee MDPI, Basel, Switzerland. This article is an open access article distributed under the terms and conditions of the Creative Commons Attribution (CC BY) license (https://creativecommons.org/licenses/by/4.0/).

1. Introduction

Published work, at different latitudes and on both sexes, has indicated that serum 25-hydroxyvitamin D concentrations are lower in obese subjects as compared to normal-weight subjects [1–5]. Moreover, intervention studies and clinical trials have shown an inverse association between the duration and dosage of 25-hydroxyvitamin D supplementation according to BMI and body fat [2,6,7]. Excess adiposity is associated with risk factors for cardiovascular diseases (CVD), such as hypertension, diabetes mellitus, and dyslipidemia. Body mass index (BMI) is the most widely used measure to evaluate the presence of obesity in adults, and it is associated with an increase in morbimortality by cardiovascular diseases and cancer [8]. Waist circumference (WC) has been used to evaluate central obesity and predict the risk of mortality more accurately than BMI [9]. However, it has some limitations, as it considers neither the height nor the weight of the individual [9]. To solve these limitations, alternatives have been developed that include height (e.g., the waist-to-height ratio (WHtR)) [10], the lipid profile (e.g., the visceral adiposity index (VAI)) [11], body fat percentage (e.g., the body adiposity estimator (CUN-BAE)) [12], and body roundness index (BRI) [13]. The epidemic of vitamin D deficiency has been correlated with a wide variety of diseases [14]. The study of vitamin D deficiency and its relation to different diseases has gained increasing interest in recent decades. Vitamin D deficiency affects the general population and is very common in European populations, especially among the elderly [15,16]. This deficit has also been associated with several diseases, such as cancer and cardiovascular diseases [17,18], obesity [19], and even mortality rates for COVID-19 [20]. Aleksova et al. [21] found a U-shaped, nonlinear relationship between vitamin D levels and myocardial infarction. Although evidence has been found [22] for the association of anthropometric parameters regarding vitamin D, such association is not yet fully understood. It would be helpful to better identify individuals with a greater likelihood of vitamin D deficiency, which could improve the efficiency of the determination.

Machine learning (ML) is a technology that was originally intended to mimic human intelligence [23]. Currently, it has been transformed into a tool that can use algorithms to identify patterns and formulate predictions. ML methods have acquired great importance in the health sector for disease prediction. Their versatility means they can derive a model from available data without prior knowledge of the relationships between variables [24]. These methods make fewer assumptions about the data, which allows them to use variables with a non-normal distribution. In the medical field, ML has been used to predict different traits, such as cardiovascular disease [25], diabetes [26,27], and hypertension [28]. These methods, in theory, can provide more accurate predictions as compared to traditional linear methods [29]. However, one of the reasons why conventional methods such as regression are still used is that despite the theoretical potential of ML, its practical application has not always proven superior to traditional linear modeling. Furthermore, it has been difficult to forecast which method will result in the higher accuracy when predicting a particular disease [30]. In practice, there are many different ML techniques that may be suitable for predicting a variable of interest. This challenge has resulted in a trial-and-error approach to find the best method for each circumstance [31]. In summary, ML is an interdisciplinary field closely related to artificial intelligence, pattern recognition, and probability theory, through which computer algorithms can automatically extract patterns from the available data. ML has mainly been divided into three categories: supervised, unsupervised and semisupervised learning approaches, depending on the availability of types and categories of training data. Supervised ML involves predetermined output attributes in addition to the use of input attributes, and all the data are labeled. Unsupervised learning approaches are in contrast to supervised learning approaches, in that they do not require any training process, and all the data are unlabeled. The difference between both is the existence of labels in the training data subset [32]. Semisupervised ML is an approach that incorporates both unsupervised and supervised machine learning; that is, in the presence of both labeled and unlabeled data [33]. In this paper, supervised learning approaches, which are widely used in the data classification process, were applied. The naïve Bayes (NB) probabilistic classifier and the linear logistic regression (LR) and random forest (RF) were used.

Recently, prediction models for 25-hydroxyvitamin D have been developed using conventional regression analysis [34,35]. However, ML is a data analysis technique that creates algorithms to predict outcomes by "learning" from the data. It increasingly stands out as a competitive alternative to regression analysis. However, although ML can outperform conventional regression, it develops fewer assumptions about the data, possibly due to its ability to capture nonlinearities between predictor variables [36]. Despite this, only two studies [37,38] have used machine-learning algorithms to predict 25-hydroxyvitamin D, neither of which studied the relationship of 25-hydroxyvitamin D deficit using anthropometric parameters.

Although ML predication models have already been tested in other pathologies, such as coronary artery disease [39], this was the first study to use them in the analysis of the association of different anthropometric parameters with vitamin D. Therefore, the aims of this study were, firstly, to explore the association of the different anthropometric parameters (i.e., BMI, WC, WHtR, BRI, VAI, and CUN-BAE) with vitamin D, and secondly, to analyze which anthropometric parameters were the most efficient in predicting vitamin D levels while comparing the results to those of other methods, including LR, NB, and RF.

2. Methods

2.1. Design

This was a cross-sectional, descriptive study of individuals recruited for a study entitled "Association between Different Risk Factors and Early Vascular Ageing (EVA study)" (NCT02623894) [40].

2.2. Study Population

The sample was recruited from an urban population of 43,946 people from 5 healthcare centers. Through random sampling with replacement and stratifying by age groups (35, 45, 55, 65, and 75 years) and sex, 501 individuals were selected, with 100 in each group (i.e., 50 males and 50 females) aged between 35 and 75 years old. The recruitment was conducted from June 2016 to November 2017. Inclusion criteria included those aged 35–75 years old and willing to sign the informed consent to participate. The exclusion criteria included individuals with terminal illnesses, as well as those who could not move into the healthcare centers, had a history of CVD, had a glomerular filtration rate below 30%, had chronic inflammatory disease or acute inflammatory processes in the last three months, or were under treatment with estrogen, testosterone, or growth hormone.

2.3. Variables and Measurement Instruments

A detailed description of the variables gathered and tests performed was included in the protocol of the EVA study [40]. The nurses who collected the tests and questionnaires of the EVA study were previously trained following a standardized protocol.

2.3.1. Measurement of the Anthropometric Parameters

The anthropometric variables were gathered through physical examination.

Weight: mean of 2 measures recorded using an approved and calibrated Seca-770 scale (precision ± 0.1 kg), with the participant barefoot and wearing light clothing.

Height: mean of 2 measures using a Seca-222 wall-mounted height rod, with the participant standing barefoot and aligning their midsagittal line with the middle line of the height rod.

BMI: this was calculated as weight in kg/height in m^2. We considered obesity for participants with BMI $\geq$ 30 [41].

WC: this was measured in the superior border of the iliac crest parallel to the floor, at the end of a normal exhalation. Obesity was considered for WC values $\geq$88 cm in females and $\geq$102 cm in males [41]. Hip circumference (HC) was measured at the level of the trochanters.

WHtR: this was calculated using the following equation [42,43]: WHtR = waist circumference (cm)/height (cm).

CUN-BAE: the body fat percentage was calculated according to the Clinical University of Navarra, following the recommendations of Gómez-Ambrosi et al. [12]: CUN-BAE = $-44988 + (0.503 \times$ age$) + (10689 \times$ sex$) + (3172 \times$ BMI$) - (0.026 \times$ BMI2$)$ $+ (0.181 \times$ BMI sex$) - ($BMI $0.02 \times$ age$) - (0.005 \times$ BMI2 sex$) + (0.00021 \times$ BMI2 age$)$, considering males = 0 and females = 1.

BRI: this was based on height (m) and waist perimeter (m), and it was calculated using the following equation [13]:

$$(BRI) = 364.2 - (365.5 \times SQR(1 - ((WC/(2 \times 3.141516))^2)/(0.5 \times Height)^2))$$

VAI: this was calculated using the following equations [11]:

$$\text{Males}: \text{VAI} = \left(\frac{\text{WC}}{39.68 + (1.88 \times \text{BMI})}\right) \times \left(\frac{\text{TG}}{1.03}\right) \times \left(\frac{1.31}{\text{HDL}}\right)$$

$$\text{Females}: \text{VAI} = \left(\frac{\text{WC}}{36.58 + (1.89 \times \text{BMI})}\right) \times \left(\frac{\text{TG}}{0.81}\right) \times \left(\frac{1.51}{\text{HDL}}\right)$$

2.3.2. Vitamin Intake

The level of 25-hidroxyvitamin D was calculated using an immunoassay technique in a venous blood sample taken at 8–9 a.m. The participants fasted and were instructed not to consume any alcohol or caffeine for 12 h prior to the collection of the blood samples. Fasting plasma glucose, creatinine, total serum cholesterol, high-density lipoprotein (HDL) cholesterol, and triglycerides were measured by standard automatized enzymatic methods.

Vitamin D deficiency was determined as levels below 20 ng/mL [44].

2.4. Statistical Analysis

The continuous variables were expressed as means ± standard deviations, whereas the categorical variables were expressed as numbers and percentages. The comparison of the means between two independent groups was carried out using Student's *t*-test, applying χ^2 for the categorical variables.

The missing values were imputed according to the rate of missing values. If the rate was <1%, the missing values were replaced with the mean in the continuous variables. The missing values of the variables with a proportion of missing values between >1% and <5% were replaced with the hot-deck imputation.

Three logistic regression models were performed, using each of the anthropometric parameters (i.e., BMI, WC, WHtR, VAI, BRI, and CUN-BAE) as independent variables and vitamin D as the dependent variable in two categories (model 0 for ≥20 ng/mL; model 1 for <20 ng/mL). Model 1 was carried out without controlling for any variables, model 2 was controlled for age and sex, and model 3 was controlled for age, sex, cardiovascular risk score, and consumption of hypotensive, hypoglycemic, and hypolipidemic drugs (0 = no consumption; 1 = consumption).

In this study, three classifiers were used: LR, NB, and RF. The data were divided into a training set and a test set (70% and 30%, respectively). The training set was used to build the classifier; however, to calculate the precision measurements of the models in order to validate them, the data from the test set were applied. The parameters used to evaluate the efficacy of the individual classifiers and compare them included sensitivity, specificity, precision, and error.

All the ML methods used in this study could provide a confidence score on the classification of vitamin D deficiency vs. no vitamin D deficiency. By varying the threshold of this confidence score, it was possible to compensate for the rate of true positive outcomes (sensitivity) with the rate of false positive outcomes (1-specificity) and, therefore, generate a curve of the receiver operating characteristic (ROC). The standard measure of the area under the ROC curve (AUC) was used to report and compare the efficiency of the models.

2.4.1. Machine Learning Techniques: LR, NB, RF

ML is a form of artificial intelligence that enables machines to learn and respond under specific conditions. It employs techniques and algorithms that can predict future events or classify data by identifying and learning the patterns in the existing data.

2.4.2. Logistic Regression

Logistic regression (LR) is a statistical-inferential machine-learning technique employed by researchers to analyze and classify binary and proportional response datasets that dates back to the 1960s [45,46]. LR analysis extends multiple regression analysis techniques to research situations in which the outcome variable is categorical. The model for logistic regression analysis assumes that the outcome variable, Y, is categorical, but LR does not model this outcome variable directly. It is based on probabilities associated with the values of Y. It is a type of regression that predicts the probability of an occurrence by fitting data to a logistic function; that is, it is about finding a sigmoid function that maximizes the probability of the observed values in the dataset [47]. The logit of the LR model is transformed by the following equation:

$$\text{logit}(y) = b_0 + b_1 x_1 + b_2 x_2 + \ldots + b_n x_n$$

where b_0 is the intercept of the equation, and $b_1, b_2, \ldots, b_n$ are the coefficients of independent variables $x_1, x_2, \ldots, x_n$. The logistic (logit) transformation is the logarithm of the odds of the positive response, and it is defined as:

$$\ln\left(\frac{p}{1-p}\right) = x\beta$$

The probability $P(Y = 1/X)$ is calculated in the LR model as follows:

$$P(Y = 1/x_1, x_2 \ldots x_n) = p(x)$$

The general equation is:

$$p(x) = \frac{1}{1 + e^{-\beta x_i}} = \frac{1}{1 + e^{-(b_0 + b_1 x_1 + b_2 x_2 + \ldots + b_n x_n)}} = \frac{1}{1 + e^{-(b_0 + \sum \beta_i X_i)}}$$

The regression coefficients are usually estimated using maximum likelihood (ML) estimation [48]. The ML method is based on the joint probability density of the observed data, and acts as a function of the unknown parameters in the model. Now, with the assumption that the observations are independent, the likelihood function is:

$$L(\beta) = \prod_{i=1}^{n}(p_i)^{y_i}(1-p_i)^{1-y_i} = \prod_{i=1}^{n}\left(\frac{e^{x_i\beta}}{1+e^{x_i\beta}}\right)^{y_i}\left(\frac{1}{1+e^{x_i\beta}}\right)^{1-y_i}$$

The log-likelihood is:

$$\ln L(\beta) = \sum_{i=1}^{n}\left(y_i \ln\left(\frac{e^{x_i\beta}}{1+e^{x_i\beta}}\right) + (1-y_i)\ln\left(\frac{1}{1+e^{x_i\beta}}\right)\right)$$

Some of the main advantages of LR are that it can naturally provide probabilities and extend to multiclass classification problems [49].

2.4.3. Naïve Bayes

Naïve Bayes (NB) is a supervised classifier based on Bayes' theorem. An NB classifier assumes that the existence or absence of a specific feature of a class is independent of and unrelated to the presence (or absence) of any other feature [50]. The method is based on the class-conditional independence assumption. Despite the naïve design, some studies have exhibiting the effectiveness of the NB [51]. NB presents several advantages: the structure is predefined, it is very efficient when the features are not strongly correlated, and it requires a small amount of training data to estimate the necessary parameters [52]. One limitation is that the attribute independence assumption is often violated in the real world.

It is defined as:

- $X < X_1, \ldots, X_k >$ as an instance (vector of random variables denoting observed attribute values);
- $x < x < x_1, \ldots, x_k >$ as a particular instance;
- C as a random variable denoting the class of an instance;
- c represents the value that C takes.

Each instance is assumed to belong to one class $C \in \{c_1, c_2, \ldots, c_m\}$. In NB, all attributes are assumed to be independent given the value of the class variable (conditional independence assumption): $P(C = c_s / X = x_i)$. Applying Bayes' theorem, it is obtained by:

$$P(c_s/x_i) = \frac{P(x_i/c_s)P(c_s)}{P(x_i)}$$

$P(x_i/c_s)P(c_s)$ is the joint probability of x_i and c_s. Let us assume that the individual x_i are independent from each other. Thus, the joint probability of x and c_s is:

$$P(x/c_s)P(c_s) = P(x_1/c_s) \ldots P(x_k/c_s)P(c_s) = \prod_{n=1}^{k} P(x_k/c_s)P(c_s)$$

Thus, it is obtained by:

$$P(c_s/X) = \frac{\prod_{n=1}^{k} P(x_k/c_s)P(c_s)}{P(x)}$$

$P(x)$ does not depend on the class; it is the same for all classes. NB aims to determine the class using the maximum a posteriori (MAP) decision rule, and it is calculated as $\hat{y}$ for the instance x as follows:

$$\hat{y} = \mathrm{argmax}_{c_s} \prod_{n=1}^{k} P(x_n/c_s)P(c_s)$$

2.4.4. Random Forest

The Random Forest (RF) algorithms form a family of classification methods that rely on several decision trees for building a predictor ensemble with a set of decision trees that grow in randomly selected subspaces of data. The RF algorithm was introduced by Breiman [53], and it is defined as the group of decision trees whose nodes are defined at the preprocessing step. RF handles a huge number of input variables without the deletion of variables. It uses two randomizations: bagging and random feature selection, which introduces randomization in the choice of the splitting test designed for each node of the tree. The choice is usually based on an impurity measure that is used as a criterion to determine the best feature for the partition of the current node into several child nodes [54]. Each tree in the collection is formed by first selecting at random, at each node, a small group of input coordinates on which to split, and secondly, by calculating the best split based on these features in the training set. The tree is grown using the CART methodology of Breiman et al. [55] to maximum size without pruning.

A random forest is a classifier consisting of a of a collection of randomized base regressions $\{k(x, \Theta n), n = 1, \ldots, J\}$ in which $\{\Theta k\}$ are independent and identically distributed random vectors, and each tree $h(x, \Theta n)$ casts a unit vote for the most popular class at input x [53].

The general growing and voting process of RF was as follows. A bootstrap sample was chosen from the training set to grow each tree of RF. In the RF, the number of trees and the number of predictor variables chosen at each node were the tuning parameters determining the RF overall fit. Because the RF was composed of many individual decision trees (DTs), an RF algorithm was required to determine the suitable number. The error of the RF was approximated by the out-of-bag (OOB) score. This method allowed us to find the proper size of the RF. Each tree was built on a different bootstrap sample.

Machine learning has been used in different fields of health and medicine. Various other machine-learning techniques have attracted attention in recent years. A low vitamin D status is common in the general population. This finding is of concern because it has been associated with several chronic diseases, including cardiovascular diseases (CVD) [17,18], the leading causes of death. Therefore, different artificial intelligence methods, such as classification algorithms, should be used to significantly improve the efficiency of vitamin D deficiency detection. This study compared multiple LR, a linear method, with NB and RF, two nonlinear machine-learning methods. All the analyses were performed using the statistical software SPSS for Windows, version 23.0 (IBM Corp, Armonk, NY, USA), and R, version 3.4.1. In the hypothesis test, an α risk of 0.05 was established as the limit of statistical significance.

Figure 1 presents a summary flow diagram of the approach proposed in this study.

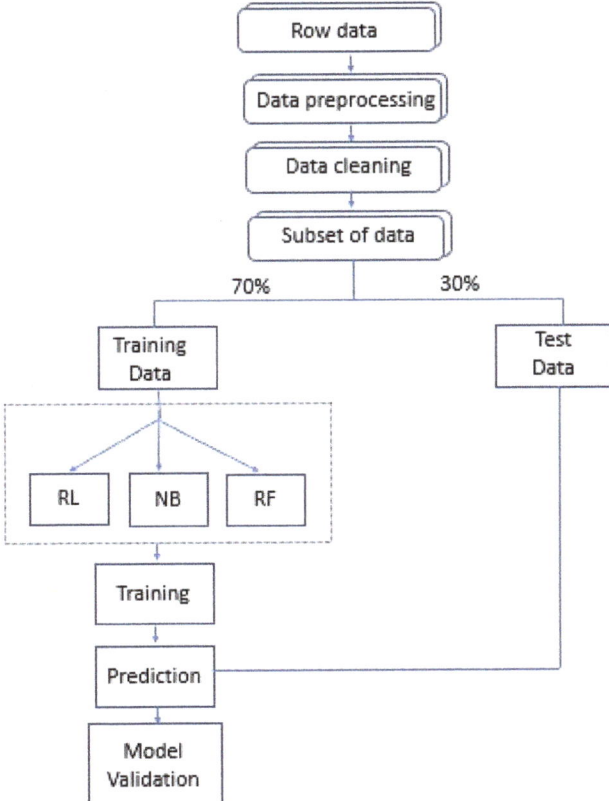

Figure 1. Flow diagram.

3. Results

3.1. Characteristics of the Population

The general characteristics of the individuals included in this study are shown in Table 1, including their sex and their levels of vitamin D. The mean age was 55.90 ± 14.24 years. The males showed higher values of arterial pressure, blood glucose, triglycerides, LDL cholesterol, and RCV, and lower values of HDL cholesterol, as compared to the females. The prevalence of smokers, hypertensives, and diabetics was greater in males. The mean values of BMI, WC, WhtR, and BRI were higher in males, whereas hip circumference and CUN-BAE were greater in females. A total of 174 individuals (%) presented values of vitamin D of <20 ng/mL. The patients with <20 ng/mL vitamin D presented greater values in all the analyzed anthropometric parameters.

Table 1. Baseline demographic and clinical characteristics of participants in the overall sample by sex and with and without vitamin D deficiency.

Variables	Overall (n = 501)	Females (n = 252)	Males (n = 249)	p1	Normal Levels of Vitamin D (n = 327)	Vitamin D Deficit (n = 174)	p2
Cardiovascular risk factors							
Age, years	55.90 ± 14.24	55.85 ± 14.19	55.95 ± 14.30	0.934	55.77 ± 14.43	56.14 ± 13.90	0.782
Smoker, n (%)	90 (18.00)	41 (16.30)	49 (19.70)	0.320	47 (14.4)	43 (24.7)	0.004
SBP, mmHg	120.69 ± 23.13	114.95 ± 24.96	126.47 ± 19.52	<0.001	120.62 ± 25.78	120.83 ± 17.14	0.921
DBP, mmHg	75.53 ± 10.10	73.67 ± 10.46	77.40 ± 9.37	<0.001	75.30 ± 10.39	75.95 ± 9.54	0.496
Hypertension, n (%)	147 (25.80)	65 (29.30)	82 (32.90)	0.079	96 (29.4)	51 (29.3)	0.991
Total cholesterol, (mg/dL)	194.76 ± 32.50	196.88 ± 32.64	192.61 ± 32.26	0.142	193.96 ± 32.21	196.27 ± 33.07	0.450
LDL-C, mg/dL	115.51 ± 29.37	113.61 ± 28.54	117.43 ± 14.12	0.148	114.37 ± 28.68	117.65 ± 30.59	0.236
HDL-C, mg/dL	58.88 ± 16.15	64.27 ± 16.14	53.43 ± 14.23	<0.001	60.27 ± 16.33	56.27 ± 15.51	0.008
Triglycerides, mg/dL	103.12 ± 53.11	94.07 ± 50.48	112.27 ± 54.23	<0.001	97.90 ± 46.63	112.93 ± 62.51	0.002
Dyslipidemia, n (%)	191 (38.1)	96 (38.2)	95 (38.1)	0.905	208 (64.0)	118 (67.8)	0.393
Glycemia, mg/dL	88.21 ± 17.37	86.30 ± 15.73	90.14 ± 18.71	0.013	87.05 ± 15.20	90.39 ± 20.72	0.040
HbA1c, (%)	5.49 ± 0.56	5.44 ± 0.47	5.54 ± 0.63	0.043	5.48 ± 0.50	5.51 ± 0.65	0.466
Diabetes mellitus, n (%)	38 (7.60)	12 (4.8)	26 (10.50)	0.016	23 (7.0)	15 (8.6)	0.523
CVR score (%)	11.80 ± 13.00	6.48 ± 6.67	17.22 ± 15.43	<0.001	10.99 ± 12.38	13.33 ± 14.02	0.056
Vitamin D	25.56 ± 19.30	26.55 ± 25.60	24.61 ± 10.11	0.276	—	—	—
Drugs							
Antihypertensive drugs, n (%)	96 (19.20)	46 (18.30)	50 (20.10)	0.604	58 (17.7)	38 (21.8)	0.267
Lipid-lowering drugs, n (%)	102 (20.40)	53 (21.00)	49 (19.70)	0.707	72 (22.0)	30 (17.2)	0.206
Antidiabetic drugs, n (%)	35 (7.00)	12 (4.8)	23 (9.20)	0.049	22 (6.7)	13 (7.5)	0.756
Anthropometric parameters							
Height, cm	165.11 ± 9.68	158.70 ± 6.98	171.60 ± 7.46	<0.001	165.59 ± 9.67	164.21 ± 9.67	0.128
Weight, kg	72.41 ± 13.61	65.67 ± 11.87	79.22 ± 11.75	<0.001	71.68 ± 12.99	73.76 ± 4.65	0.104
WC, (cm)	93.33 ± 11.99	87.95 ± 11.68	98.76 ± 9.65	<0.001	92.32 ± 11.78	95.21 ± 12.20	0.010
Hip circumference, (cm)	103.13 ± 9.24	103.55 ± 9.34	102.71 ± 9.13	0.313	102.29 ± 9.38	104.72 ± 8.78	0.005
BMI ≥ 30, n (%)	94 (18.80)	52 (20.6)	42 (16.90)	0.280	52 (15.9)	42 (24.1)	0.025
BMI, (kg/m²)	26.52 ± 4.23	26.14 ± 4.79	26.90 ± 3.54	0.044	26.11 ± 4.08	27.28 ± 4.40	0.003
WHtR	0.57 ± 0.07	0.56 ± 0.08	0.58 ± 0.06	0.001	0.56 ± 0.07	0.58 ± 0.07	0.001
BRI	4.79 ± 1.57	4.59 ± 1.73	4.98 ± 1.36	0.005	4.62 ± 1.55	5.09 ± 1.56	0.002
VAI	3.26 ± 2.42	3.22 ± 2.59	3.30 ± 2.25	0.728	3.02 ± 2.26	3.71 ± 2.65	0.002
CUN-BAE	33.20 ± 7.86	38.50 ± 6.37	27.82 ± 5.07	<0.001	32.73 ± 7.74	34.07 ± 8.02	0.068

BMI, body mass index; SBP, systolic blood pressure; DBP, diastolic blood pressure; HDL-C, high-density lipoprotein cholesterol; HbA1c, glycohemoglobin; WC, waist circumference; WHtR, waist-to-height ratio; VAI, visceral adiposity index; LDL-C, low-density lipoprotein cholesterol; BRI, body roundness index; CUN-BAE, Clinical University of Navarra body adiposity estimator. Normal value if vitamin D ≥ 20 ng/mL, and a deficiency if vitamin D < 20 ng/mL. The continuous variables are presented as average ± standard deviation; the categorical variables are presented as numbers and percentages. Column p1 shows differences between males and females, and column p2 shows differences between participants in the sample with and without vitamin D deficiency.

3.2. Association of the Anthropometric Parameters with Vitamin D

The logistic regression analysis, both globally and stratified by sex, is presented in Table 2. In the global analysis, higher values of all the parameters analyzed in the three models were associated with lower 25-hydroxyvitamin D values. In model 3, the OR ranged from 1.249 with BRI to 1.005 with WHTr*1000. No statistically significant association was found with CUN-BAE in any of the three models. In the analysis by sex, the association was maintained in males for all parameters except CUN-BAE, with an OR ranging between 1.467 for BRI and 1.008 for WHtR*1000. Therefore, we concluded that the results for males were similar to the overall sample. In contrast, in females, the only anthropometric parameter associated with 25-hydroxyvitamin D deficiency was CUN-BAE, with an OR ranging from 1.044 to 1.060.

Table 2. Anthropometric parameters associated with low values of vitamin D levels determined using logistic regression analysis.

Variable	Overall			Females			Males		
	OR	IC 95%	p	OR	IC 95%	p	OR	IC 95%	p
WC									
Model 1	1.021	1.005–1.037	0.011	1.016	0.993–1.038	0.177	1.038	1.009–1.067	0.009
Model 2	1.021	1.005–1.038	0.010	1.017	0.994–1.041	0.149	1.039	1.009–1.070	0.010
Model 3	1.022	1.005–1.039	0.011	1.014	0.990–1.040	0.252	1.040	1.010–1.071	0.010
BMI									
Model 1	1.068	1.022–1.116	0.003	1.061	1.005–1.121	0.034	1.080	1.003–1.163	0.042
Model 2	1.069	1.022–1.118	0.004	1.065	1.007–1.127	0.027	1.078	1.001–1.162	0.048
Model 3	1.068	1.021–1.118	0.004	1.059	0.999–1.123	0.056	1.078	1.000–1.163	0.050
WHtR*1000									
Model 1	1.004	1.002–1.007	0.001	1.003	1.000–1.006	0.089	1.007	1.002–1.011	0.003
Model 2	1.005	1.002–1.008	0.001	1.003	1.000–1.007	0.055	1.008	1.003–1.013	0.002
Model 3	1.005	1.002–1.008	0.001	1.003	0.999–1.007	0.118	1.008	1.003–1.014	0.001
VAI									
Model 1	1.119	1.038–1.207	0.003	1.073	0.973–1.183	0.157	1.188	1.054–1.339	0.005
Model 2	1.120	1.038–1.208	0.003	1.080	0.976–1.194	0.135	1.189	1.055–1.340	0.005
Model 3	1.122	1.039–1.212	0.003	1.064	0.959–1.181	0.242	1.203	1.064–1.360	0.003
BRI									
Model 1	1.209	1.073–1.361	0.002	1.126	0.969–1.308	0.122	1.362	1.118–1.660	0.002
Model 2	1.250	1.095–1.426	0.001	1.157	0.982–1.363	0.080	1.447	1.152–1.818	0.002
Model 3	1.249	1.092–1.430	0.001	1.126	0.945–1.340	0.184	1.467	1.163–1.851	0.001
CUN-BAE									
Model 1	1.022	0.998–1.046	0.068	1.044	1.001–1.089	0.044	1.052	0.998–1.108	0.061
Model 2	1.024	0.999–1.050	0.065	1.060	1.011–1.113	0.016	1.057	0.996–1.122	0.067
Model 3	1.025	0.999–1.052	0.062	1.056	1.005–1.110	0.030	0.070	0.995–1.122	0.070

%CI, 95% confidence interval; WC, waist circumference; BMI, body mass index; WHtR, waist-to-height ratio; VAI, visceral adiposity index; BRI, body roundness index; CUN-BAE, Clinical University of Navarra body adiposity estimator; OR, odds ratio. Dependent variable in the logistic regression analysis was vitamin D (0 = ≥20 ng/mL; 1 = levels less than 20 ng/mL). Independent variables were WC, BMI, WHtR, and VAI, and adjustment variables were age, cardiovascular risk score, hypotensive, hypoglycemic, and hypolipidemic drugs. For risk factors: 1 = presence and 0 = absence. Model 1: unadjusted; Model 2: adjusted by age; Model 3: adjusted by age, cardiovascular risk score, hypotensive, hypoglycemic, and hypolipidemic drugs (1 = yes, 0 = no).

3.3. Comparing the Performance of Data-Mining Algorithms in the Prediction of Vitamin D Deficiency

Table 3 presents the percentages of success, error, sensitivity, specificity, and AUC-ROC obtained for each classifier. It can be observed that the logistic regression built models with the greatest precision in WC and CUN-BAE (92.4%), BMI (91.9%), WHtR (91%), and BRI (91%). In the case of CUN-BAE, the RL was closely followed by the NB classifier (92.3%). However, for the anthropometric parameter VAI, it was the NB classifier that presented the highest value, 94.2%. NB exceeded the logistic regression in the area under the curve for WC (AUC = 0.528; CI: 0.494–0.563), BMI (AUC = 0.538; CI: 0.502–0.574), WHtR (AUC = 0.538; CI: 0.499–0.575), and BRI (AUC = 0.533; CI: 0.497–0.570). However, for VAI and CUN-BAE, the logistic regression presented higher values in the area under the curve (AUC = 0.531, CI: 0.494–0.568; and AUC= 0.536, CI: 0.501–0.572, respectively).

Table 3. Comparison of area under receiver-operating characteristic curve among the different models for prediction.

Variable	Accuracy	Error	Precision	Specificity	Sensitivity	AUC-ROC (95% CI)
Algorithms						
Logistic Regression						
WC	0.635	0.365	0.924	0.500	0.650	0.528 (0.494–0.563)
BMI	0.641	0.359	0.919	0.526	0.655	0.538 (0.502–0.574)
WHtR	0.638	0.362	0.910	0.512	0.654	0.538 (0.499–0.575)
BRI	0.635	0.365	0.910	0.500	0.653	0.533 (0.497–0.570)
VAI	0.633	0.367	0.906	0.488	0.652	0.531 (0.494–0.568)
CUN-BAE	0.641	0.359	0.924	0.528	0.654	0.536 (0.501–0.572)
Naïve Bayes						
WC	0.607	0.393	0.856	0.118	0.669	0.546 (0.487–0.604)
BMI	0.653	0.347	0.885	0.333	0.697	0.555 (0.495–0.616)
WHtR	0.620	0.380	0.875	0.133	0.674	0.556 (0.499–0.613)
BRI	0.620	0.380	0.875	0.133	0.674	0.556 (0.499–0.613)
VAI	0.687	0.313	0.942	0.455	0.705	0.503 (0.458–0.547)
CUN-BAE	0.640	0.360	0.923	0.000	0.676	0.503 (0.465–0.542)
Random Forest						
WC	0.580	0.420	0.786	0.185	0.667	0.449 (0.388–0.509)
BMI	0.607	0.393	0.817	0.240	0.680	0.474 (0.412–0.536)
WHtR	0.640	0.360	0.885	0.250	0.687	0.486 (0.434–0.537)
BRI	0.653	0.347	0.894	0.313	0.694	0.501 (0.447–0.556)
VAI	0.633	0.367	0.846	0.304	0.693	0.499 (0.436–0.562)
CUN-BAE	0.613	0.387	0.827	0.250	0.683	0.479 (0.417–0.540)

CI, confidence interval; AUC-ROC, area under the receiver-operating characteristic curve; BMI, body mass index; WC, waist circumference; WHtR, waist-to-height ratio; VAI, visceral adiposity index; BRI, body roundness index; CUN-BAE, Clinical University of Navarra body adiposity estimator.

The highest values in terms of sensitivity were obtained by NB in WC, BMI, and VAI (66.9%, 69.7%, and 70.5%, respectively), and by RF in WHtR, BRI, and CUN-BAE (68.7%, 69.4%, and 68.3%, respectively). Regarding specificity in all the anthropometric parameters, the highest values were obtained by LR. Sensitivity for all three algorithms and for all anthropometric parameters showed similar results, with values ranging from 0.650 to 0.705. The highest values in terms of sensitivity for the anthropometric parameters VAI, BMI, and WC (70.5%, 69.7%, and 66.9%, respectively) were obtained with NB. The highest values in terms of sensitivity for BRI, WHtR, and CUN-BAE (69.4%, 68.7%, and 68.3%, respectively) were achieved with RF. Regarding specificity in all the anthropometric parameters, the highest values were obtained by LR, ranging from 0.488 to 0.528. RF and NB presented very low values in specificity in all anthropometric parameters, with the exception of the NB algorithm for the anthropometric parameter VAI.

4. Discussion and Conclusions

Through a logistic regression model, we explored the capacity of anthropometric parameters to predict vitamin D deficiency, and we concluded that the behavior of these parameters differed according to sex; thus, in males, WC, WHtR, VAI, and BRI were associated with low levels of vitamin D, whereas in females, CUN-BAE was associated with low vitamin D.

To the best of our knowledge, this was the first study to use ML algorithms for the detection of vitamin D and investigate its predictability using anthropometric parameters.

Vitamin D deficiency (<20 ng/mL) in our study affected 34.7% of the participants. These results were in line with the systematic review conducted by Manios et al. [56], who reported that in Southern European countries, over one-third of the population had vitamin D levels <20 ng/mL, and 10% of the population had values <10 ng/mL. A cross-sectional, retrospective study with 21,490 patients (74.3% females) aged between 14 and 105 years who had used primary healthcare in La Rioja (Spain) showed that the mean levels of 25(OH)D were 18.3 (SD, 11.6) ng/mL in the entire sample [57], with males presenting lower values than females (17.6 vs. 18.5 ng/mL, $p < 0.001$). However, our study did not obtain significant differences according to sex, and the mean levels were above 25.56 (SD, 19.30), likely due to the differences in age, sex, and associated diseases between the study populations.

The relationship between low concentrations of 25(OH)D and obesity has been previously reported [58,59]. Jääskeläine et al. [60] used data from the 2000–2011 Health Survey and suggested that vitamin D deficiency may be a risk factor for abdominal obesity among males, but not among females. These results were in line with those of our study; in males, in the logistic regression analysis, WC and BMI were associated with vitamin D deficiency. Nevertheless, these results disagreed with those of Cătoi et al. [61], who explored the complex relationship between the levels of 25(OH)D and overweight/obesity, insulin resistance, systemic inflammation, and oxidative stress, revealing that overweight and an increasing degree of obesity were not significantly associated with a decrease in the levels of 25(OH)D.

A Danish study with 4909 children and adolescents in the Danish Childhood Obesity Biobank (2860 females) found that vitamin D deficiency was common among Danish children and adolescents with obesity. Our results were in line with those of that study, as the individuals with vitamin D deficiency showed greater BMI, WHtR, and frequency in males, which indicated that the degree of obesity was independently associated with lower serum concentrations of 25(OH)D [62]. Moreover, it is known that obese people need higher vitamin D loading doses to reach the same amount of serum 25-hydroxyvitamin D as people with normal body weight [5]. However, not all studies have found this association. The results of Pereira Santos et al. [4] indicated that overweight and obese individuals in different age groups have a similar probability of presenting with vitamin D deficiency. These discrepancies could be due to the origins of the different study populations.

In a study conducted with young Italian females, Adami et al. [15] found that the main determinants of vitamin D deficiency were an increase in BMI and exposure to sunlight. In a more recent study performed to identify the best combination of predictors for the serum concentration of vitamin D in adults aged between 18 and 70 years old, the multivariate linear regression model included age, sex, BMI, sunlight exposure in the previous week and during the month of blood sample collection, skin phototype, job position, smoking status, physical activity, latitude, and administration of vitamin D supplements in the previous year [63]. However, these results differed from some of our results, in that BMI was not found to be significant in females; we considered that these differences could be due to differences in age ranges and ethnicities.

The relationship we found between vitamin D deficiency and VAI was in disagreement with the study by Izadi et al. [64], who analyzed a sample of 57 males and 26 females with nonalcoholic fatty liver disease (NAFLD) and despite controlling for age and sex, they found a reverse association between VAI and vitamin D levels. Nevertheless, a study by Zubiaga et al. [65] reported that body fat percentage (BFP), when calculated with CUN-BAE as a predictive marker of cardiovascular risk in patients with morbid obesity before and after being subjected to vertical gastrectomy (VG), was significantly correlated with three biochemical factors associated with greater cardiovascular risk (i.e., cortisol, vitamin D, and TG/HDL-C ratio), which was in line with our results, as we only found an association between CUN-BAE and vitamin D in females.

Several studies have analyzed the association (i.e., predictive ability) of 25-hydroxyvitamin D concentrations with various health problems, using different ML techniques. Luo et al. [66]

analyzed whether 25-hydroxyvitamin D deficiency was associated with an increased incidence of COVID-19 and disease severity using multivariable logistic regression techniques in order to propose a predictive model. These authors observed that subjects with COVID-19 had lower 25-hydroxyvitamin D concentrations as compared to the controls without COVID-19, and that 25-hydroxyvitamin D deficiency influenced both hospitalization rates and the severity of COVID-19 in the Chinese subjects. Deschasaux et al. [67] used logistic regression in 1557 middle-aged adults without prior 25-hydroxyvitamin D treatment to develop a scale to predict 25-hydroxyvitamin D deficiency and identify adults at risk of deficiency. This scale indicated that in subjects with scores of ≥ 7 points, 70% were deficient in 25-hydroxyvitamin D, and when the score was >9, 80% were deficient in 25-hydroxyvitamin D, with a sensitivity of 0.67 and a specificity of 0.63. Therefore, the application of this scale could avoid unjustified 25-hydroxyvitamin D supplementation and unnecessary blood tests. Garcia-Carretero et al. [37] analyzed 1002 hypertensive patients to establish predictive models to identify patients unlikely to have 25-hydroxyvitamin D deficiency or to undergo plasma 25-hydroxyvitamin D concentration measurements. To do so, they used the classifiers logistic regression, support vector machine (SVM), RF, NB, and extreme gradient boosting to calculate classification accuracy, sensitivity, specificity, and predictive values to assess the performance of each method. These authors found that the radial kernel, SVM-based method performed better than the other algorithms in terms of sensitivity (98%), negative predictive value (71%), and classification accuracy (73%). Therefore, they concluded that the combination of a feature-selection method such as elastic regularization, as well as a classification approach, produced well-fitted models. This combined approach allowed them to develop a prediction model with high sensitivity but low specificity, which was consistent with the results of our study, to identify the population that could benefit from a laboratory determination of serum 25-hydroxyvitamin D levels. Guo et al. [38] analyzed MLR and RBF-SVR techniques in 594 Caucasian adults to develop a score for predicting serum 25-hydroxyvitamin D concentration. The best results were found using the RBF-SVR model, which provided a better prediction of serum 25-hydroxyvitamin D concentrations and vitamin D deficiency, as compared to an MLR model. Lopes et al. [68] analyzed 908 community-dwelling older people using logistic regression to propose a model for detecting 25-hydroxyvitamin D deficiency. The model was able to identify older people at risk of 25-hydroxyvitamin D deficiency with a sensitivity of 55.9%, a specificity of 72.3%, and an ROC area of 0.685. These authors suggested that a clinical use of these parameters could help to identify and design appropriate public health interventions. Finally, Sohl et al. [69], in a longitudinal aging study in Amsterdam with 1509 subjects, developed a risk profile based on backward logistic regression to identify older people at high risk of 25-hydroxyvitamin D deficiency. In this study, two total risk scores were developed that included either 10 or 13 variables that were capable of predicting serum 25(OH)D concentrations of less than 0.50 and 0.30 nmol/L, respectively. This scale may be useful in clinical practice to identify individuals at risk of 25-hydroxyvitamin D deficiency.

Given the association between 25-hydroxyvitamin D deficiency and obesity, and that healthcare professionals deal with many variables that can influence health problems, ML algorithms have potential clinical application.

Recent research has further explored linking these techniques to provide hybrid ML algorithms. Therefore, the approach of this paper, which indicated that the predictive ability of different anthropometric parameters differed according to sex, could be useful in future research. However, additional studies are needed to confirm our results.

4.1. Limitations of the Study

This study had several limitations. Firstly, this was a cross-sectional study, which hindered the establishment of causal relationships between vitamin D levels and anthropometric parameters. Secondly, there may have been confounding variables that were not considered in this study. Lastly, the number of patients with vitamin D deficiency in our study was unbalanced as compared to the number of people with normal levels.

4.2. Conclusions

The capacity of anthropometric parameters to predict vitamin D deficiency differed according to sex; thus, WC, BMI, WHtR, VAI, and BRI were useful predictors in males, while CUN-BAE was more useful in females. In all the anthropometric parameters, the LR model presented the highest values in terms of specificity to predict vitamin D deficiency. The NB approach of ML showed the best area under the curve in WC, BMI, WHtR, and BRI, whereas the LR model did so for VAI and CUN-BAE.

Author Contributions: Conceptualization, C.P.-A., M.A.G.-M., L.G.-O. and E.R.-S.; methodology, M.G.-S., L.G.-S., M.A.G.-M., E.R.-S. and B.S.S.; data analysis, C.P.-A., M.A.G.-M. and L.G.-O.; writing—review and editing, all authors; supervision, C.P.-A.; funding acquisition, M.A.G.-M. All authors have read and agreed to the published version of the manuscript.

Funding: The project was funded by the Institute of Health Carlos III of the Spanish Ministry of Science, Innovation, and Universities through Red de investigación en cronicidad, atención primaria y promoción de la salud (RD21/0016/0010), and cofinanced by the European Union Health Institute/European Regional Development Fund (ERDF), the Autonomous Government of Castilla and León (GRS 1193/B/15, GRS 1821/B/18), and intensification of a research program (INT/M/08/19, INT/M/9/19/INT/M/14/19).

Institutional Review Board Statement: The study was approved by the Drug Research Ethics Committee of the Health Area of Salamanca on 4 May 2015 under registry number PI15/01039. All procedures conducted with human participants complied with the ethical rules of the institutional and/or national research committee and with the 2013 Declaration of Helsinki [70]. All participants signed an informed consent form before participating in this study.

Informed Consent Statement: Informed consent was obtained from all subjects involved in the study.

Data Availability Statement: Not applicable.

Conflicts of Interest: The authors declare that they have no known competing financial interest or personal relationships that could have influenced the work reported in this paper.

References

1. Bassatne, A.; Chakhtoura, M.; Saad, R.; Fuleihan, G. Vitamin D supplementation in obesity and during weight loss: A review of randomized controlled trials. *Metabolism* **2019**, *92*, 193–205. [CrossRef] [PubMed]
2. Cordeiro, A.; Santos, A.; Bernardes, M.; Ramalho, A.; Martins, M. Vitamin D metabolism in human adipose tissue: Could it explain low vitamin D status in obesity? *Horm. Mol. Biol. Clin. Investig.* **2017**, *33*. [CrossRef] [PubMed]
3. Lagunova, Z.; Porojnicu, A.; Lindberg, F.; Hexeberg, S.; Moan, J. The dependency of vitamin D status on body mass index, gender, age and season. *Anticancer Res.* **2009**, *29*, 3713–3720. [CrossRef] [PubMed]
4. Pereira-Santos, M.; Costa, P.R.F.; Assis, A.M.O.; Santos, C.A.S.T.; Santos, D.B. Obesity and vitamin D deficiency: A systematic review and meta-analysis. *Obes. Rev.* **2015**, *16*, 341–349. [CrossRef]
5. Walsh, J.S.; Bowles, S.; Evans, A.L. Vitamin D in obesity. *Curr. Opin. Endocrinol. Diabetes Obes.* **2017**, *24*, 389–394. [CrossRef]
6. Orces, C. The Association between Body Mass Index and Vitamin D Supplement Use among Adults in the United States. *Cureus* **2019**, *11*, e5721. [CrossRef]
7. Camozzi, V.; Frigo, A.C.; Zaninotto, M.; Sanguin, F.; Plebani, M.; Boscaro, M.; Schiavon, L.; Luisetto, G. 25-hydroxycholecalciferol response to single oral cholecalciferol loading in the normal weight, overweight, and obese. *Osteoporos. Int.* **2016**, *27*, 2593–2602. [CrossRef]
8. Forouzanfar, M.H.; Alexander, L.; Bachman, V.F.; Biryukov, S.; Brauer, M.; Casey, D.; Coates, M.M.; Delwiche, K.; Estep, K.; Frostad, J.J.; et al. Global, regional, and national comparative risk assessment of 79 behavioural, environmental and occupational, and metabolic risks or clusters of risks in 188 countries, 1990–2013: A systematic analysis for the Global Burden of Disease Study 2013. *Lancet* **2015**, *386*, 2287–2323. [CrossRef]
9. Nishida, C.; Ko, G.T.; Kumanyika, S. Body fat distribution and noncommunicable diseases in populations: Overview of the 2008 WHO Expert Consultation on Waist Circumference and Waist-Hip Ratio. *Eur. J. Clin. Nutr.* **2010**, *64*, 2–5. [CrossRef]
10. Ashwell, M.; Cole, T.J.; Dixon, A.K. Ratio of waist circumference to height is strong predictor of intraabdominal fat. *BMJ* **1996**, *313*, 559–560. [CrossRef]
11. Amato, M.C.; Giordano, C.; Galia, M.; Criscimanna, A.; Vitabile, S.; Midiri, M.; Galluzzo, A. Visceral adiposity index: A reliable indicator of visceral fat function associated with cardiometabolic risk. *Diabetes Care* **2010**, *33*, 920–922. [CrossRef] [PubMed]

12. Gómez-Ambrosi, J.; Silva, C.; Catalán, V.; Rodríguez, A.; Galofré, J.C.; Escalada, J.; Valentí, V.; Rotellar, F.; Romero, S.; Ramírez, B.; et al. Clinical usefulness of a new equation for estimating body fat. *Diabetes Care* **2012**, *35*, 383–388. [CrossRef] [PubMed]
13. Thomas, D.M.; Bredlau, C.; Bosy-Westphal, A.; Mueller, M.; Shen, W.; Gallagher, D.; Maeda, Y.; McDougall, A.; Peterson, C.M.; Ravussin, E.; et al. Relationships between body roundness with body fat and visceral adipose tissue emerging from a new geometrical model. *Obesity* **2013**, *21*, 2264–2271. [CrossRef] [PubMed]
14. Rosas-Peralta, M.; Holick, M.F.; Borrayo-Sánchez, G.; Madrid-Miller, A.; Ramírez-Árias, E.; Arizmendi-Uribe, E. Efectos inmunometabólicos disfuncionales de la deficiencia de vitamina D y aumento de riesgo cardiometabólico. Potencial alerta epidemiológica en América? *Endocrinol. Diabetes y Nutr.* **2017**, *64*, 162–173. [CrossRef] [PubMed]
15. Adami, S.; Bertoldo, F.; Braga, V.; Fracassi, E.; Gatti, D.; Gandolini, G.; Minisola, S.; Battista Rini, G. 25-hydroxy vitamin D levels in healthy premenopausal women: Association with bone turnover markers and bone mineral density. *Bone* **2009**, *45*, 423–426. [CrossRef]
16. Cashman, K.D.; Dowling, K.G.; Škrabáková, Z.; Gonzalez-Gross, M.; Valtueña, J.; De Henauw, S.; Moreno, L.; Damsgaard, C.T.; Michaelsen, K.F.; Mølgaard, C.; et al. Vitamin D deficiency in Europe: Pandemic? *Am. J. Clin. Nutr.* **2016**, *103*, 1033–1044. [CrossRef]
17. Danik, J.S.; Manson, J.A.E. Vitamin D and cardiovascular disease. *Curr. Treat. Options Cardiovasc. Med.* **2012**, *14*, 414–424. [CrossRef]
18. Gandini, S.; Boniol, M.; Haukka, J.; Byrnes, G.; Cox, B.; Sneyd, M.J.; Mullie, P.; Autier, P. Meta-analysis of observational studies of serum 25-hydroxyvitamin D levels and colorectal, breast and prostate cancer and colorectal adenoma. *Int. J. Cancer* **2011**, *128*, 1414–1424. [CrossRef]
19. Foss, Y.J. Vitamin D deficiency is the cause of common obesity. *Med. Hypotheses* **2009**, *72*, 314–321. [CrossRef]
20. Ilie, P.C.; Stefanescu, S.; Smith, L. The role of vitamin D in the prevention of coronavirus disease 2019 infection and mortality. *Aging Clin. Exp. Res.* **2020**, *32*, 1195–1198. [CrossRef]
21. Aleksova, A.; Beltrami, A.P.; Belfiore, R.; Barbati, G.; Di Nucci, M.; Scapol, S.; De Paris, V.; Carriere, C.; Sinagra, G. U-shaped relationship between vitamin D levels and long-term outcome in large cohort of survivors of acute myocardial infarction. *Int. J. Cardiol.* **2016**, *223*, 962–966. [CrossRef] [PubMed]
22. Elizondo-Montemayor, L.; Castillo, E.; Rodríguez-López, C.; Villarreal-Calderón, J.; Gómez-Carmona, M.; Tenorio-Martínez, S.; Nieblas, B.; García-Rivas, G. Seasonal Variation in Vitamin D in Association with Age, Inflammatory Cytokines, Anthropometric Parameters, and Lifestyle Factors in Older Adults. *Mediators Inflamm.* **2017**, *2017*, 5719461. [CrossRef] [PubMed]
23. Michalski, R.; Carbonell, J.; Mitchell, T. *Machine Learning: An Artificial Intelligence Approach*; Springer Science & Business Media: Berlin, Germany, 2013.
24. Kotsiantis, S.; Zaharakis, I.; Pintelas, P. Supervised machine learning: A review of classification techniques. *Emerg. Artif. Intell. Appl. Comput. Eng.* **2007**, *160*, 3–24.
25. Dey, D.; Diaz Zamudio, M.; Schuhbaeck, A.; Juarez Orozco, L.E.; Otaki, Y.; Gransar, H.; Li, D.; Germano, G.; Achenbach, S.; Berman, D.S.; et al. Relationship between Quantitative Adverse Plaque Features from Coronary Computed Tomography Angiography and Downstream Impaired Myocardial Flow Reserve by 13N-Ammonia Positron Emission Tomography: A Pilot Study. *Circ. Cardiovasc. Imaging* **2015**, *8*, e003255. [CrossRef]
26. Kavakiotis, I.; Tsave, O.; Salifoglou, A.; Maglaveras, N.; Vlahavas, I.; Chouvarda, I. Machine Learning and Data Mining Methods in Diabetes Research. *Comput. Struct. Biotechnol. J.* **2017**, *15*, 104–116. [CrossRef]
27. Zou, Q.; Qu, K.; Luo, Y.; Yin, D.; Ju, Y.; Tang, H. Predicting Diabetes Mellitus With Machine Learning Techniques. *Front. Genet.* **2018**, *9*, 515. [CrossRef]
28. Krittanawong, C.; Bomback, A.S.; Baber, U.; Bangalore, S.; Messerli, F.H.; Wilson Tang, W.H. Future Direction for Using Artificial Intelligence to Predict and Manage Hypertension. *Curr. Hypertens. Rep.* **2018**, *20*, 75. [CrossRef]
29. Qawqzeh, Y.K.; Bajahzar, A.S.; Jemmali, M.; Otoom, M.M.; Thaljaoui, A. Classification of Diabetes Using Photoplethysmogram (PPG) Waveform Analysis: Logistic Regression Modeling. *Biomed Res. Int.* **2020**, *2020*, 3764653. [CrossRef]
30. Tiwari, P.; Colborn, K.; Smith, D.; Xing, F.; Ghosh, D.; Rosenberg, M. Assessment of a machine learning model applied to harmonized electronic health record data for the prediction of incident atrial fibrillation. *JAMA Netw. Open* **2020**, *3*, e1919396. [CrossRef]
31. Uddin, S.; Khan, A.; Hossain, M.E.; Moni, M.A. Comparing different supervised machine learning algorithms for disease prediction. *BMC Med. Inform. Decis. Mak.* **2019**, *19*, 281. [CrossRef]
32. Saravanan, R.; Sujatha, P. A State of Art Techniques on Machine learning algorithms: A perspective of supervised learning approaches in data classification. In Proceedings of the 2018 Second International Conference on Intelligent Computing and Control Systems (ICICCS), Madurai, India, 14–15 June 2018; pp. 945–949.
33. Zhu, X.; Goldberg, A. Introduction to semi-supervised learning. *Synth. Lect. Artif. Intell. Mach. Learn.* **2009**, *31*, 1–130. [CrossRef]
34. Narang, R.K.; Gamble, G.G.; Khaw, K.T.; Camargo, C.A.; Sluyter, J.D.; Scragg, R.K.R.; Reid, I.R. A prediction tool for vitamin D deficiency in New Zealand adults. *Arch. Osteoporos.* **2020**, *15*, 172. [CrossRef] [PubMed]
35. Heo, J.-C.; Kim, D.; An, H.; Son, C.-S.; Cho, S.; Lee, J.-H. A Novel Biosensor and Algorithm to Predict Vitamin D Status by Measuring Skin Impedance. *Sensors* **2021**, *21*, 8118. [CrossRef] [PubMed]

36. Miller, D.D.; Brown, E.W. Artificial Intelligence in Medical Practice: The Question to the Answer? *Am. J. Med.* **2018**, *131*, 129–133. [CrossRef]
37. Garcia Carretero, R.; Vigil-Medina, L.; Barquero-Perez, O.; Mora-Jimenez, I.; Soguero-Ruiz, C.; Ramos-Lopez, J. Machine learning approaches to constructing predictive models of vitamin D deficiency in a hypertensive population: A comparative study. *Informatics Heal. Soc. Care* **2021**, *46*, 355–369. [CrossRef]
38. Guo, S.; Lucas, R.M.; Ponsonby, A.L.; Chapman, C.; Coulthard, A.; Dear, K.; Dwyer, T.; Kilpatrick, T.; McMichael, T.; Pender, M.P.; et al. A novel approach for prediction of vitamin D status using support vector regression. *PLoS ONE* **2013**, *8*, e79970. [CrossRef]
39. Ricciardi, C.; Cantoni, V.; Improta, G.; Iuppariello, L.; Latessa, I.; Cesarelli, M.; Triassi, M.; Cuocolo, A. Application of data mining in a cohort of Italian subjects undergoing myocardial perfusion imaging at an academic medical center. *Comput. Methods Programs Biomed.* **2020**, *189*, 105343. [CrossRef]
40. Gomez-Marcos, M.A.; Martinez-Salgado, C.; Gonzalez-Sarmiento, R.; Hernandez-Rivas, J.M.; Sanchez-Fernandez, P.L.; Recio-Rodriguez, J.I.; Rodriguez-Sanchez, E.; Garca-Ortiz, L. Association between different risk factors and vascular accelerated ageing (EVA study): Study protocol for a cross-sectional, descriptive observational study. *BMJ Open* **2016**, *6*, e011031. [CrossRef]
41. Salas-Salvadó, J.; Rubio Hererra, M.A.; Barbany, M.; Moreno, B. Consensus for the evaluation of overweight and obesity and the establishment of therapeutic intervention criteria. *Med. Clin. (Barc).* **2007**, *128*, 184–196. [CrossRef]
42. Oliveros, E.; Somers, V.K.; Sochor, O.; Goel, K.; Lopez-Jimenez, F. The concept of normal weight obesity. *Prog. Cardiovasc. Dis.* **2014**, *56*, 426–433. [CrossRef]
43. Browning, L.M.; Hsieh, S.D.; Ashwell, M. A systematic review of waist-to-height ratio as a screening tool for the prediction of cardiovascular disease and diabetes: 05 could be a suitable global boundary value. *Nutr. Res. Rev.* **2010**, *23*, 247–269. [CrossRef] [PubMed]
44. Bouillon, R.; Carmeliet, G. Vitamin D insufficiency: Definition, diagnosis and management. *Best Pract. Res. Clin. Endocrinol. Metab.* **2018**, *32*, 669–684. [CrossRef] [PubMed]
45. Kleinbaum, D.; Kupper, L.; Nizam, A.; Muller, K. *Applied Regression Analysis and Multivariable Methods*, 4th ed.; Duxbury Press: Pacific Grove, CA, USA, 2007.
46. Hilbe, J. *Logistic Regression Models*; Chapman & Hall/CRC: Boca Raton, FL, USA, 2009.
47. Kleinbaum, D. *Logistic Regression: A Self-Learning Text*; Springer: New York, NY, USA, 1994.
48. Maalouf, M. Logistic regression in data analysis: An overview. *Int. J. Data Anal. Tech. Strateg.* **2011**, *3*, 281–299. [CrossRef]
49. Hastie, T.; Tibshirani, R.; Friedman, J. *The Elements of Statistical Learning: Data Mining, Inference, and Prediction*; Springer: New York, NY, USA, 2009.
50. Berrar, D. Bayes' Theorem and Naive Bayes Classifier. *Encycl. Bioinform. Comput. Biol.* **2018**, *1*, 403–412. [CrossRef]
51. Hand, D.; Chan, Y. Idiot's Bayes—Not so stupid after all? *Int. Stat. Rev.* **2001**, *69*, 385–398.
52. Jahan, R. Applying Naive Bayes Classification Technique for Classification of Improved Agricultural Land soils. *Int. J. Res. Appl. Sci. Eng. Technol.* **2018**, *6*, 189–193. [CrossRef]
53. Breiman, L. Random forests. *Mach. Learn.* **2001**, *45*, 5–32. [CrossRef]
54. Bernard, S.; Adam, S.; Heutte, L. Dynamic Random Forests. *Pattern Recognit. Lett.* **2012**, *33*, 1580–1586. [CrossRef]
55. Breiman, L.; Friedman, J.; Olshen, R.; Stone, C. *Classification and Regression Trees*; Chapman & Hall: New York, NY, USA, 1984.
56. Manios, Y.; Moschonis, G.; Lambrinou, C.P.; Tsoutsoulopoulou, K.; Binou, P.; Karachaliou, A.; Breidenassel, C.; Gonzalez-Gross, M.; Kiely, M.; Cashman, K.D. *A Systematic Review of Vitamin D Status in Southern European Countries*; Springer: Berlin/Heidelberg, Germany, 2018; Volume 57, ISBN 0039401715.
57. Díaz-López, A.; Paz-Graniel, I.; Alonso-Sanz, R.; Marqués-Baldero, C.; Mateos-Gil, C.; Arija-Val, V. Vitamin D deficiency in primary health care users at risk in Spain. *Nutr. Hosp.* **2021**, *38*, 1058–1067.
58. Mansouri, M.; Miri, A.; Varmaghani, M.; Abbasi, R.; Taha, P.; Ramezani, S.; Rahmani, E.; Armaghan, R.; Sadeghi, O. Vitamin D deficiency in relation to general and abdominal obesity among high educated adults. *Eat. Weight Disord.* **2019**, *24*, 83–90. [CrossRef]
59. Vanlint, S. Vitamin D and obesity. *Nutrients* **2013**, *5*, 949–956. [CrossRef] [PubMed]
60. Jääskeläinen, T.; Männistö, S.; Härkänen, T.; Sääksjärvi, K.; Koskinen, S.; Lundqvist, A. Does Vitamin D status predict weight gain or increase in waist circumference? Results from the longitudinal Health 2000/2011 Survey. *Public Health Nutr.* **2020**, *23*, 1266–1272. [CrossRef] [PubMed]
61. Cătoi, A.F.; Iancu, M.; Pârvu, A.E.; Cecan, A.D.; Bidian, C.; Chera, E.I.; Pop, I.D.; Macri, A.M. Relationship between 25 hydroxyvitamin d, overweight/obesity status, pro-inflammatory and oxidative stress markers in patients with type 2 diabetes: A simplified empirical path model. *Nutrients* **2021**, *13*, 2889. [CrossRef] [PubMed]
62. Plesner, J.L.; Dahl, M.; Fonvig, C.E.; Nielsen, T.R.H.; Kloppenborg, J.T.; Pedersen, O.; Hansen, T.; Holm, J.C. Obesity is associated with Vitamin D deficiency in Danish children and adolescents. *J. Pediatr. Endocrinol. Metab.* **2018**, *31*, 53–61. [CrossRef]
63. Viprey, M.; Merle, B.; Riche, B.; Freyssenge, J.; Rippert, P.; Chakir, M.A.; Thomas, T.; Malochet-guinamand, S.; Cortet, B.; Breuil, V.; et al. Development and validation of a predictive model of hypovitaminosis d in general adult population: SCOPYD study. *Nutrients* **2021**, *13*, 2526. [CrossRef]
64. Izadi, A.; Aliasghari, F.; Gargari, B.P.; Ebrahimi, S. Strong association between serum vitamin D and vaspin levels, AIP, VAI and liver enzymes in NAFLD patients. *Int. J. Vitam. Nutr. Res.* **2020**, *90*, 59–66. [CrossRef]

65. Toro, L.Z.; Polo, J.R.T.; Díez-Tabernilla, M.; Bernal, L.G.; Sebastián, A.A.; Rico, R.C. Fórmula CUN-BAE y factores bioquímicos como marcadores predictivos de obesidad y enfermedad cardiovascular en pacientes pre y post gastrectomía vertical. *Nutr. Hosp.* **2014**, *30*, 281–286.
66. Luo, X.; Liao, Q.; Shen, Y.; Li, H.; Cheng, L. Vitamin D deficiency is associated with COVID-19 incidence and disease severity in Chinese people. *J. Nutr.* **2021**, *151*, 98–103. [CrossRef]
67. Deschasaux, M.; Souberbielle, J.C.; Andreeva, V.A.; Sutton, A.; Charnaux, N.; Kesse-Guyot, E.; Latino-Martel, P.; Druesne-Pecollo, N.; De Edelenyi, F.S.; Galan, P.; et al. Quick and easy screening for Vitamin D insufficiency in adults a scoring system to be implemented in daily clinical practice. *Medicine* **2016**, *95*, e2783. [CrossRef]
68. Lopes, J.B.; Fernandes, G.H.; Takayama, L.; Figueiredo, C.P.; Pereira, R.M.R. A predictive model of vitamin D insufficiency in older community people: From the São Paulo Aging & Health Study (SPAH). *Maturitas* **2014**, *78*, 335–340.
69. Sohl, E.; Heymans, M.W.; De Jongh, R.T.; Den Heijer, M.; Visser, M.; Merlijn, T.; Lips, P.; Van Schoor, N.M. Prediction of vitamin D deficiency by simple patient characteristics. *Am. J. Clin. Nutr.* **2014**, *99*, 1089–1095. [CrossRef] [PubMed]
70. World Medical Association. World Medical Association Declaration of Helsinki: Ethical principles for medical research involving human subjects. *JAMA* **2013**, *310*, 2191–2194. [CrossRef] [PubMed]

Article

Effect of Probability Distribution of the Response Variable in Optimal Experimental Design with Applications in Medicine [†]

Sergio Pozuelo-Campos *,[‡], Víctor Casero-Alonso [‡] and Mariano Amo-Salas [‡]

Department of Mathematics, University of Castilla-La Mancha, 13071 Ciudad Real, Spain; victormanuel.casero@uclm.es (V.C.-A.); Mariano.Amo@uclm.es (M.A.-S.)
* Correspondence: Sergio.Pozuelo@uclm.es
† This paper is an extended version of a published conference paper as a part of the proceedings of the 35th International Workshop on Statistical Modeling (IWSM), Bilbao, Spain, 19–24 July 2020.
‡ These authors contributed equally to this work.

Abstract: In optimal experimental design theory it is usually assumed that the response variable follows a normal distribution with constant variance. However, some works assume other probability distributions based on additional information or practitioner's prior experience. The main goal of this paper is to study the effect, in terms of efficiency, when misspecification in the probability distribution of the response variable occurs. The elemental information matrix, which includes information on the probability distribution of the response variable, provides a generalized Fisher information matrix. This study is performed from a practical perspective, comparing a normal distribution with the Poisson or gamma distribution. First, analytical results are obtained, including results for the linear quadratic model, and these are applied to some real illustrative examples. The nonlinear 4-parameter Hill model is next considered to study the influence of misspecification in a dose-response model. This analysis shows the behavior of the efficiency of the designs obtained in the presence of misspecification, by assuming heteroscedastic normal distributions with respect to the D-optimal designs for the gamma, or Poisson, distribution, as the true one.

Keywords: elemental information matrix; gamma distribution; poisson distribution; D-optimization; misspecification

Citation: Pozuelo-Campos, S.; Casero-Alonso, V.; Amo-Salas, M. Effect of Probability Distribution of the Response Variable in Optimal Experimental Design with Applications in Medicine. *Mathematics* **2021**, *9*, 1010. https://doi.org/10.3390/math9091010

Academic Editor: Lev Klebanov

Received: 18 March 2021
Accepted: 27 April 2021
Published: 29 April 2021

Publisher's Note: MDPI stays neutral with regard to jurisdictional claims in published maps and institutional affiliations.

Copyright: © 2021 by the authors. Licensee MDPI, Basel, Switzerland. This article is an open access article distributed under the terms and conditions of the Creative Commons Attribution (CC BY) license (https://creativecommons.org/licenses/by/4.0/).

1. Introduction

To obtain optimal designs, it is common to assume a homoscedastic normal distribution of the response variable and under this assumption there is vast literature focused mainly on nonlinear models. However, there are also papers that use probability distributions different from a normal distribution [1–7]. At this point, it is important to remember that the probability distribution of the response variable is assumed, on many occasions, from the nature of the experiment to be performed. However, there are usually no prior observations to allow this assumption to be checked.

There are very few available references that set out a general framework for optimal experimental design for any probability distribution of the response variable. Ref. [8] present a method to compute the D-optimal designs for Generalized Linear Models with a binary response allowing uncertainty in the link function, ref. [9] study the Generalized Linear Model from the perspective of optimal experimental design, ref. [10] present the "elemental information matrix" for different probability distributions, and [11] compute optimal designs based on the maximum quasi-likelihood estimator to avoid the misspecification in the probability distribution of the response. The aim of this paper is to analyze the effect of misspecification in the probability distribution in optimal design. In other words, it allows those cases to be identified in which it is important to pay special attention to the assumed probability distribution. In this study, apart from theoretical results, real applications involving the linear quadratic model and a dose-response model are considered. For the latter, we focus on the well-known Hill model, widely used to describe dependence between the concentration of a substance and a variety of responses in biochemistry, physiology or pharmacology. From the point of view of optimal experimental design, this model is studied in many papers [12–15]. Specifically, ref. [13] study the effect of some drugs which inhibit the growth of tumor cells providing D-optimal designs under the assumption of the response variable follows a heteroscedastic normal distribution with a given structure for the variance.

The article is organized as follows. Section 2 introduces the model used and the theory of optimal experimental design. Section 3 presents the structure of the variance of the heteroscedastic normal distribution and proves a general theoretical result. Section 4 focuses on the linear quadratic model and provides some theoretical results for gamma or Poisson distributions. This section also shows applications of these results to real examples found in the literature. Finally, the 4-parameter Hill model is studied in Section 5. Assuming the heteroscedastic normal distribution, as in [13], an efficiency analysis is performed, considering the Poisson, or gamma, as the true probability distribution. A sensitivity analysis with respect to a parameter of the variance structure is also performed. The paper concludes with a summary and conclusions section.

2. Model and Optimal Experimental Design

The model of interest to the practitioner is expressed in a general way as

$$E[y] = g^{-1}(\eta(x;\theta)), \tag{1}$$

where y is the response variable, following a probability distribution with pdf $d(y;\rho)$, where ρ is the vector of parameters of the assumed distribution, $\eta(x;\theta)$ is the regression function (linear or nonlinear in the parameters), x is the vector of controllable variables and θ the vector of unknown parameters that must be estimated. Lastly, g is the link function relating the regression function to the mathematical expectation of the response. Ref. [16] carry out an in-depth study of the link function and Generalized Linear Models. In line with these authors, this paper considers the canonical link function for the probability distributions involved in the study, as it guarantees that the maximum likelihood estimators of the model parameters, $\hat{\theta}$, are sufficient.

An exact design of size n is defined as a set of values of the explanatory variables, $x_1, \ldots, x_n$, in which some may be repeated. These values belong to a compact set called design space $\mathcal{X}$, which is usually a subset of $\mathbb{R}^N$. However, the real applications, examples and results in this study consider the one-dimensional case. Assuming that only q of these values are distinct, we may consider the set $x_1, \ldots, x_q$ and associate with it a probability measure defined by $w_1, \ldots, w_q$, where each w_i represents the proportion of experiments carried out under the condition x_i. This suggests a more general definition of approximate design as a probability measure ξ over the design space $\mathcal{X}$:

$$\xi = \begin{Bmatrix} x_1 & \ldots & x_q \\ w_1 & \ldots & w_q \end{Bmatrix} \in \Xi, \quad \sum_{i=1}^{q} w_i = 1,$$

where $\xi(x_i) = w_i$ and Ξ represents the set of all approximate designs.

The scenario studied in this work is the estimation of a single parameter of the probability distribution of the response, with the rest being fixed. Thus, the elemental information matrix (EIM), introduced by [10], is scalar and is defined as

$$\nu(\eta(x;\theta)) = -E\left[\frac{\partial^2 \log d(y;\eta(x;\theta))}{\partial \eta(x;\theta)^2}\right], \tag{2}$$

which contains information about the probability distribution of the response variable y, given by the pdf $d(y;\rho)$. The relationship between the parameters to estimate, ρ, of the probability distribution and the regression function $\eta(x;\boldsymbol{\theta})$ is established by the link function, g, shown in (1). Table 1 sets out the canonical link function, the mathematical expectation of the response variable as a function of $\eta(x;\boldsymbol{\theta})$ and the EIM for the probability distributions used in this paper, some of which are derived in Section 3.

Table 1. Density function, link function, expectation of the response variable as a function of $\eta = \eta(x;\boldsymbol{\theta})$ and the EIM for the probability distributions used in this paper.

Distribution	pdf, $d(y;\rho)$	$g(E[y])$	$E[y]$	EIM
$\mathcal{N}(\mu,\sigma^2)$ constant σ^2	$\frac{1}{\sqrt{2\pi\sigma^2}}\exp\left(-\frac{(y-\mu)^2}{2\sigma^2}\right)$	Identity	$\mu = \eta$	$\frac{1}{\sigma^2}$
$\mathcal{N}(\mu,k\mu^{2r})$	$\frac{1}{\sqrt{2k\pi\mu^{2r}}}\exp\left(-\frac{(y-\mu)^2}{2k\mu^{2r}}\right)$	Identity	$\mu = \eta$	$\frac{2r^2}{\eta^2}+\frac{1}{k\eta^{2r}}$
$\mathcal{P}(\lambda)$	$\frac{\lambda^y e^{-\lambda}}{y!}$	Log	$\lambda = e^\eta$	e^η
$\Gamma(\alpha,\beta)$ constant α	$\frac{\beta^\alpha}{\Gamma(\alpha)}y^{\alpha-1}e^{-y\beta}$	Reciprocal	$\frac{\alpha}{\beta}=\frac{1}{\eta}$	$\frac{\alpha}{\eta^2}$

The single-point information matrix in $x \in \mathcal{X}$ is given by

$$I(x;\boldsymbol{\theta}) = -E\left[\frac{\partial^2 \log d(y;\eta(x;\boldsymbol{\theta}))}{\partial \theta_i \partial \theta_j}\right] = \nu(\eta(x;\boldsymbol{\theta}))f^T(x;\boldsymbol{\theta})f(x;\boldsymbol{\theta}), \quad \forall i,j = 1,\ldots,m,$$

where $\nu(\eta(x;\boldsymbol{\theta}))$ is the EIM defined in (2) and

$$f^T(x;\boldsymbol{\theta}) = \frac{\partial \eta(x;\boldsymbol{\theta})}{\partial \boldsymbol{\theta}}.$$

Finally, the Fisher information matrix (FIM) is defined for the approximate design with probability measure ξ as

$$M(\xi;\boldsymbol{\theta}) = \int_{\mathcal{X}} I(x;\boldsymbol{\theta})\xi(x)dx.$$

The FIM establishes a connection between optimal experimental design and the Generalized Regression Model. The standard form of FIM under the normality hypothesis can be generalized to any probability distribution by including the EIM. By definition, the inverse of the FIM is asymptotically proportional to the variance and covariance matrix of estimators of $\boldsymbol{\theta}$, the parameters of the model. This matrix may depend on these parameters, so nominal values for them are necessary and therefore locally optimal designs can be obtained. By Carathéodory's theorem, it is known that for any design there is always another with the same information matrix of at most $m(m+1)/2+1$ different points, where m is the number of unknown parameters to be estimated for the model $\eta(x;\boldsymbol{\theta})$ [17]. Therefore, it is sufficient to seek designs with finite support.

Optimization criteria express functions of the FIM that allow this matrix to be optimized in different ways. Consider the criterion function Φ as a real convex bounded function defined over the space of the information matrix $\mathcal{M} = \{M(\xi) : \xi \in \Xi\}$. A design ξ^* will then be Φ-optimal if $\xi^* = \arg\min_{\xi \in \Xi} \Phi(M(\xi;\boldsymbol{\theta}))$. A number of studies, for example Chapter 10 of [18], give the criteria most commonly used in the literature. This paper uses the D-optimality criterion, whose goal is to minimize the volume of the confidence ellipsoid of $\hat{\boldsymbol{\theta}}$, the estimators of $\boldsymbol{\theta}$. This criterion may be expressed by

$$\Phi_D(M(\xi;\boldsymbol{\theta})) = \log|M^{-1}(\xi;\boldsymbol{\theta})|.$$

In practice this criterion is equivalent to maximizing the determinant of the information matrix. The General Equivalence Theorem (see [19]) is a tool that allows optimality of a given design under a specific criterion to be checked. The sensitivity function $\varphi(x;\xi,\theta)$ is defined as a directional derivative

$$\varphi(x;\xi;\theta) = \lim_{\alpha\to 0^+} \frac{\partial}{\partial \alpha}\Phi[M((1-\alpha)\xi + \alpha\bar{\xi}_x;\theta)],$$

where $\bar{\xi}_x$ is an arbitrary design centered on a point x. Given an optimal design, ξ^*, we find that $\varphi(x;\xi^*,\theta) \geq 0$, and the equality is found in the support points of the optimal design. The sensitivity function for the D-optimization criterion is given by

$$\varphi(x;\xi,\theta) = m - \nu(\eta(x;\theta))f^T(x;\theta)M^{-1}(\xi;\theta)f(x;\theta). \tag{3}$$

The efficiency allows any design ξ to be compared to the Φ-optimal design ξ^*,

$$\text{eff}_\Phi(\xi|\xi^*) = \frac{\Phi(M(\xi^*;\theta))}{\Phi(M(\xi;\theta))}.$$

Also, if Φ is positively homogeneous, the value of the efficiency can be interpreted practically. If the efficiency value is 0.7, this means that the Φ-optimal design can be used to obtain the same information, or equivalently, the same statistical inference of the estimators of the model parameters, with a saving of 30% of the observations. For D-optimization criterion, which is positively homogeneous, D-efficiency is calculated as follows:

$$\text{eff}_D(\xi|\xi^*) = \left(\frac{|M(\xi;\theta)|}{|M(\xi^*;\theta)|}\right)^{1/m}. \tag{4}$$

This expression will be termed "efficiency" from here on, as there is no possible confusion.

3. Variance Structure and EIM for a Heteroscedastic Normal Distribution

In most applications in the context of optimal experimental design, the homoscedastic normal distribution is used. However, when the response follows the gamma or the Poisson distribution the variance depends on the explanatory variable. To compare in a fair way with these distributions it is considered the heteroscedastic normal distribution with a variance structure given by

$$\text{Var}[y] = k\text{E}[y]^{2r}, \tag{5}$$

where $k \in \mathbb{R}^+$ and $r \in \mathbb{R}$ are constants and $\text{E}[y] = \eta(x;\theta)$. Thus, taking $k=1$, for a value of $r=0.5$ the variance structure for the heteroscedastic normal distribution is similar to that of the Poisson distribution ($\text{Var}[y] = \text{E}[y]$). On the other hand, with $k=1/\alpha$ and $r=1$, the structure of the variance for the heteroscedastic normal distribution is $\text{Var}[y] = \text{E}[y]^2/\alpha$, similar to the variance of the gamma distribution, $\Gamma(\alpha,\beta)$, when parameter α is constant. Finally, the case $r=0$ corresponds to the homoscedastic normal distribution.

Then, using (2), the EIM for the heteroscedastic normal distribution with variance given by (5) is

$$\nu_\mathcal{N}(\eta(x;\theta);r,k) = \frac{2r^2}{\eta(x;\theta)^2} + \frac{1}{k\eta(x;\theta)^{2r}}.$$

Theorem 1. *Let $\eta(x;\theta) > 0$ be the function of some regression model, for any optimization criterion Φ based on the FIM, then the Φ-optimal designs for the heteroscedastic normal distribution with $r=1$ in the variance defined in (5) and for the gamma distribution with constant α coincide. Also, the Φ-optimal design obtained is independent of α and k.*

Proof. Taking $r = 1$ in the variance given by (5), the EIM for the heteroscedastic normal distribution is $v_\mathcal{N}(\eta(x;\boldsymbol{\theta})) = (2k+1)/(k\eta(x;\boldsymbol{\theta})^2)$, while the EIM for the gamma distribution is $v_\Gamma(\eta(x;\boldsymbol{\theta})) = \alpha/\eta(x;\boldsymbol{\theta})^2$, and so

$$M_\mathcal{N}(\xi;\boldsymbol{\theta}) = \frac{2k+1}{k}\frac{1}{\eta(x;\boldsymbol{\theta})^2}f^T(x;\boldsymbol{\theta})f(x;\boldsymbol{\theta}) \propto \frac{\alpha}{\eta(x;\boldsymbol{\theta})^2}f^T(x;\boldsymbol{\theta})f(x;\boldsymbol{\theta}) = M_\Gamma(\xi;\boldsymbol{\theta}).$$

Therefore the Φ-optimal design calculated with any of the matrices will agree. Also, the parameters k and α are constants, multiplied in each expression of the FIM, and so do not affect Φ-optimal design. □

The form of the EIMs of heteroscedastic normal ($r = 0.5$) and Poisson distribution are hardly proportional. Therefore, in this case, there is no possible similar result to Theorem 1.

4. Linear Quadratic Model

The linear quadratic model is considered in many studies which assume different probability distributions, such as gamma or Poisson distributions (for instance, refs. [1,4]). The regression function of the model is given by

$$\eta(x;\boldsymbol{\theta}) = \theta_0 + \theta_1 x + \theta_2 x^2, \quad x \in \mathcal{X}$$

The aim of this section is to provide D-optimal designs for this model when the response variable follows first a gamma and then a Poisson distribution. It also discusses the influence of misspecification for an assumed heteroscedastic normal distribution.

4.1. Gamma Distribution

Gamma models are suitable when the response is non-negative, continuous, skewed and heteroscedastic [7]. The introduction of the cited reference mentions several papers with real applications. From the point of view of optimal experimental design some papers could be cited, for example [6,20] for the case of multivariate gamma models, and [4] for the univariate case. In the present study, this last reference is revisited as an example of the applicability of the following results.

Theorem 2. *Let $\eta(x;\boldsymbol{\theta}) = \theta_0 + \theta_1 x + \theta_2 x^2 + \ldots \theta_p x^p > 0$ be the function of a linear regression model of order $p \geq 1$, where x is defined on a design space $\mathcal{X} = [x_l, x_u]$. If the response variable follows a gamma distribution with constant parameter α, the D-optimal design is supported in $p + 1$ equally weighted points with $x_1 = x_l$ and $x_{p+1} = x_u$. It can be expressed by*

$$\xi_\Gamma^* = \begin{Bmatrix} x_1 & x_2 & \ldots & x_p & x_{p+1} \\ 1/(p+1) & 1/(p+1) & \ldots & 1/(p+1) & 1/(p+1) \end{Bmatrix}.$$

For the linear quadratic model ($p = 2$), the D-optimal design is

$$\xi_\Gamma^* = \begin{Bmatrix} x_l & x_2 & x_u \\ 1/3 & 1/3 & 1/3 \end{Bmatrix},$$

where $x_2 \in (x_l, x_u)$ is a root of the linear quadratic equation

$$(\theta_1 + \theta_2(x_l + x_u))x_2^2 - (2\theta_2 x_l x_u - 2\theta_0)x_2 - (\theta_0(x_l + x_u) + \theta_1 x_l x_u) = 0. \quad (6)$$

Thus, it will be one of the solutions of

$$x_2 = \frac{2\theta_2 x_l x_u - 2\theta_0 \pm \sqrt{(2\theta_2 x_l x_u - 2\theta_0)^2 + 4(\theta_1 + \theta_2(x_l + x_u))(\theta_0(x_l + x_u) + \theta_1 x_l x_u)}}{2(\theta_1 + \theta_2(x_l + x_u))}.$$

Proof. Particularizing the sensitivity function given in (3) using the EIM for the gamma distribution (Table 1) gives

$$\varphi(x;\xi,\theta) = (p+1) - \frac{\alpha}{\eta(x;\theta)^2} f(x)^T M^{-1}(\xi;\theta) f(x).$$

By the General Equivalence Theorem, if ξ_Γ^* is the D-optimal design, $\varphi(x;\xi_\Gamma^*,\theta) \geq 0$ must be satisfied for all $x \in [x_l, x_u]$, and there must be equality in the support points of the design. It is, therefore, necessary to study the zeros of the function

$$g(x) = (p+1)\eta(x;\theta)^2 - \alpha f(x)^T M^{-1}(\xi_\Gamma^*;\theta) f(x),$$

which is a $2p$-order polynomial and its zeros coincide with the zeros of $\varphi(x;\xi_\Gamma^*;\theta)$. First, the number of support points of the D-optimal design must be greater or equal to the number of unknown parameters in the model, $m = p+1$, in order for the FIM to be regular. Suppose, then, that the D-optimal design ξ_Γ^* has $p+2$ support points. In this case, there will be at least p internal points with multiplicity two for the sensitivity function and its derivative to vanish, and the polynomial $g(x)$ will have at least $2p+2$ roots, contradicting its order, which is $2p$. Therefore, the D-optimal design cannot have more than nor fewer than $p+1$ points, and so must have exactly $p+1$ points. Now suppose that one extreme of $\mathcal{X}$ is not a support point of the design. Then it is assumed, without loss of generality, that the support points of the optimal design $x_1, \ldots, x_{p+1}$ satisfies $x_l < x_1 < \ldots < x_{p+1} = x_u$. The points $x_1, x_2, \ldots, x_p$ are roots of multiplicity 2 of $g(x)$, and by Rolle's Theorem, there exist $c_1 \in (x_1, x_2)$, $c_2 \in (x_2, x_3), \ldots c_p \in (x_p, x_{p+1})$ such that $g'(c_i) = 0, i = 1, \ldots p$. Therefore, $g'(x)$ vanishes at $2p$ points, once again contradicting the order of the polynomial $g'(x)$, of order $2p - 1$. By analogous reasoning, for the case $x_l = x_1 < \ldots < x_{p+1} < x_u$, the conclusion is that the D-optimal design should have the two extremes in its support, and by the above, $p - 1$ internal points.

Finally, D-optimal design is equally weighted because the weights can be separated out in the optimization of the determinant in the way

$$|M(\xi;\theta)| = \left(\prod_{i=1}^{p+1} \nu(\eta(x_i;\theta))\right) F(x_1, \ldots x_{p+1}) w_1 \ldots w_{p+1}$$

where

$$F(x_1, \ldots, x_{p+1}) = \prod_{\substack{i=1, j=2 \\ i<j}}^{p+1} (x_i - x_j)^2$$

only depends on the support points. Thus, the maximum product of the $p+1$ weights, which are restricted to being positive and summing to 1, is reached for $w_i = 1/(p+1)$.

For $p = 2$, the internal point of the design is found by solving, with $x_1 = x_l$ and $x_3 = x_u$, the equation

$$\frac{\partial |M(\xi;\theta)|}{\partial x_2} = \frac{2(x_2 - x_l)(x_2 - x_u)(x_l - x_u)^2 a(x_2;\theta) w_1 w_2 w_3}{\eta(x_2;\theta)^3 \eta(x_l;\theta)^2 \eta(x_u;\theta)^2} = 0 \qquad (7)$$

where $a(x_2;\theta) = (\theta_1 + \theta_2(x_l + x_u))x_2^2 - (2\theta_2 x_l x_u - 2\theta_0)x_2 - (\theta_0(x_l + x_u) + \theta_1 x_l x_u)$. To solve Equation (7) is equivalent to solve $a(x_2) = 0$, which is a linear quadratic equation with roots

$$x_2 = \frac{2\theta_2 x_l x_u - 2\theta_0 \pm \sqrt{(2\theta_2 x_l x_u - 2\theta_0)^2 + 4(\theta_1 + \theta_2(x_l + x_u))(\theta_0(x_l + x_u) + \theta_1 x_l x_u)}}{2(\theta_1 + \theta_2(x_l + x_u))}.$$

By the previous results, only one of the two roots can be on the interval (x_l, x_u). □

Corollary 1. Let $\eta(x;\boldsymbol{\theta}) = \theta_0 + \theta_1 x + \theta_2 x^2 + \ldots \theta_p x^p > 0$ be the function of a linear regression model of order $p \geq 1$, where x is defined on a design space $\mathcal{X} = [x_l, x_u]$. If the response variable follows a heteroscedastic normal distribution, with $r = 1$ in the variance defined by Equation (5), then $\zeta_{\mathcal{N}}^* = \zeta_{\Gamma}^*$.

Proof. This is a direct consequence of Theorems 1 and 2. □

Corollary 2. By the hypothesis of Theorem 2, the following specific cases exist where the internal point of the design, x_2, does not depend on the values of the parameters $\boldsymbol{\theta}$ of the model:

- If $\theta_1 = -\theta_2(x_l + x_u)$ and $\theta_0 \neq \theta_2 x_l x_u$, Equation (6) is linear and gives $x_2 = (x_l + x_u)/2$. In this case, the designs for the gamma distribution with constant α and the homoscedastic normal ($r = 0$ in (5)) agree.
- If $\theta_0 = \theta_2 x_l x_u$ and $x_l x_u > 0$, then $x_2^2 = x_l x_u$. Therefore $x_2 = \pm\sqrt{x_l x_u}$, where x_2 is the point found on the interval (x_l, x_u).
- If $\theta_1 = -\theta_0(x_l + x_u)/(x_l x_u)$ with $x_l, x_u \neq 0$ and $x_l + x_u \neq 0$, then $x_2 = 0$ or $x_2 = 2 x_l x_u/(x_l + x_u)$.

Proof. The cases can be computed by algebraic manipulation from Equation (6). □

In [4], Bayesian, A- and D-optimal designs are computed for linear models assuming gamma distribution. In the case of linear quadratic model D-optimal designs are computed for different nominal values. Some of them are not equally weighted or even they are supported in two points (singular designs). This might seem in contradiction to Theorem 2 above. However, it happens only for the nominal values $\boldsymbol{\theta}^{(0)}$ for which the linear predictor $\eta(x;\boldsymbol{\theta}) \leq 0$ for, at least, one $x \in \mathcal{X}$. If $\eta(x;\boldsymbol{\theta}) = 0$, a problem occurs in the definition of EIM ($v(\eta(x;\boldsymbol{\theta})) = 1/\eta(x;\boldsymbol{\theta})^2$). On the other hand, the case $\eta(x;\boldsymbol{\theta}) < 0$ does not make mathematical sense since $\eta(x;\boldsymbol{\theta})^{-1} = E[y] = \alpha/\beta$, where $\alpha, \beta > 0$ are the parameters of the gamma distribution (see Table 1).

For all nominal values $\boldsymbol{\theta}^{(0)}$ for which $\eta(x;\boldsymbol{\theta}^{(0)}) > 0$, Theorem 2 can be applied to obtain D-optimal designs. Thus, both extremes of the design space are included in D-optimal designs, all of which are equally weighted, and the inner points, x_2, are obtained by solving (6) (Table 2). The D-optimality condition is verified by the General Equivalence Theorem, through the sensitivity function (3). In addition, for the nominal values $\boldsymbol{\theta}^{(0)} = (0.3, -0.3, 0.3)$, the first condition of Corollary 2 is satisfied. Thus, it can be shown that the D-optimal design is supported in the midpoint of $\mathcal{X}$, which agrees with the D-optimal design for a homoscedastic normal distribution.

Table 2. Locally D-optimal designs $\{x_1 = 0, x_2, x_3 = 1\}$ equally weighted obtained for the linear quadratic regression model when the probability distribution of the response is gamma. The nominal values of the parameters of the model are those considered in [4].

θ_0	0.3	0.3	0.3	0.3	0.3	1
θ_1	0.3	2	5	10	-0.3	1
θ_2	0.3	0.3	0.3	0.3	0.3	-0.3
x_2	0.366	0.254	0.188	0.144	0.5	0.434

4.2. Poisson Distribution

Generalized Linear Models for Poisson distribution are widely used in the literature. Special attention is paid to linear quadratic models in oncology [21–24]. A reference involving optimal designs and Poisson distribution is [1], where different linear regression models are considered.

Theorem 3. Let $\eta(x;\theta) = \theta_0 + \theta_1 x + \theta_2 x^2$ be the function of the linear quadratic regression model, with x defined on the design space $\mathcal{X} = [x_l, x_u]$, and the response variable following a Poisson distribution. Then, for the 3-point D-optimal design, we have the following sufficient conditions:

- If $\theta_2 < 0$ and $\theta_1 + 2x_l\theta_2 < 4/(x_u - x_l)$, the lower extreme of $\mathcal{X}$, x_l, is included in the D-optimal design.
- If $\theta_2 < 0$ and $\theta_1 + 2x_u\theta_2 > 0$, the upper extreme of $\mathcal{X}$, x_u, is included in the D-optimal design.

Also, if both extremes of $\mathcal{X}$ are included in the design, the internal point x_2 will be the solution, included in $\mathcal{X}$, of the cubic equation

$$-2\theta_2 x_2^3 + [2\theta_2(x_u + x_l) - \theta_1]x_2^2 + [\theta_1(x_u + x_l) - 2x_l x_u \theta_2 - 4]x_2$$
$$+ [2x_u + x_l(2 - x_u\theta_1)] = 0. \tag{8}$$

Proof. Consider the 3-point D-optimal design

$$\xi_\mathcal{P}^* = \begin{Bmatrix} x_1 & x_2 & x_3 \\ 1/3 & 1/3 & 1/3 \end{Bmatrix}$$

with $x_l \leq x_1 < x_2 < x_3 \leq x_u$. The design is equally weighted because the weights can be separated out in the optimization of the determinant (see Proof of Theorem 2).

The explicit expression of the derivative with respect to x_1 is

$$\frac{\partial |M(\xi;\theta)|}{\partial x_1} = \frac{1}{27} \exp\left\{\sum_{i=1}^{3} \eta(x_i;\theta)\right\}(x_2 - x_1)(x_3 - x_1)(x_3 - x_2)^2$$
$$\times ((4x_1 - 2x_2 - 2x_3) + (x_2 - x_1)(x_3 - x_1)(\theta_1 + 2x_1\theta_2)),$$

If $\partial |M(\xi;\theta)|/\partial x_1 < 0$ on $[x_l, x_2)$, then the maximum of the determinant will be reached at $x_1 = x_l$. Thus

$$\frac{\partial |M(\xi;\theta)|}{\partial x_1} < 0 \iff \theta_1 + 2x_1\theta_2 < \frac{2x_2 + 2x_3 - 4x_1}{(x_2 - x_1)(x_3 - x_1)}. \tag{9}$$

If we consider $\theta_2 < 0$, we have $\theta_1 + 2x_1\theta_2 \leq \theta_1 + 2x_l\theta_2$ and the inequalities

$$\frac{2x_2 + 2x_3 - 4x_1}{(x_2 - x_1)(x_3 - x_1)} > \frac{4(x_2 - x_1)}{(x_2 - x_1)(x_3 - x_1)} = \frac{4}{(x_3 - x_1)} > \frac{4}{(x_u - x_l)}.$$

are satisfied.

Therefore, the inequality (9) is true if the following is satisfied

$$\theta_1 + 2x_l\theta_2 < \frac{4}{(x_u - x_l)}.$$

Also,

$$\frac{\partial |M(\xi;\theta)|}{\partial x_3} = \frac{1}{27}\exp\left\{\sum_{i=1}^{3}\eta(x_i;\theta)\right\}(x_3 - x_1)(x_3 - x_2)(x_2 - x_1)^2$$
$$\times ((4x_3 - 2x_1 - 2x_2) + (x_3 - x_1)(x_3 - x_2)(\theta_1 + 2x_3\theta_2)),$$

and if $\partial |M(\xi;\theta)|/\partial x_3 > 0$ on $(x_2, x_u]$ the maximum will be found at $x_3 = x_u$. This gives

$$\frac{\partial |M(\xi;\theta)|}{\partial x_3} > 0 \iff \frac{2x_1 + 2x_2 - 4x_3}{(x_3 - x_1)(x_3 - x_2)} < \theta_1 + 2x_3\theta_2. \tag{10}$$

If $\theta_2 < 0$, we have $\theta_1 + 2x_u\theta_2 \leq \theta_1 + 2x_3\theta_2$. Thus,

$$\frac{2x_1 + 2x_2 - 4x_3}{(x_3 - x_1)(x_3 - x_2)} < 0,$$

and so if $0 < \theta_1 + 2x_u\theta_2$, the inequality in (10) is satisfied.

Finally, if x_l and x_u are in the support of the design, like in Theorem 2, the internal point will be a solution of the equation $\partial |M(\xi;\theta)|/\partial x_2 = 0$, which is equivalent to the cubic equation given by (8). □

As mentioned above, the linear quadratic model plays an important role in oncology, and optimal experimental design has an important practical role in determining the best doses for carrying out the experiment and fitting the model. To illustrate the previous result, we consider the example in [1] where the response variable y explains the number of living cells in a system and the explanatory variable x is the dose of an injected oncology drug. Hence, the expected number of living cells for any dose x_i is given by

$$\lambda_i = E[y_i] = e^{\theta_0 + \theta_1 x_i + \theta_2 x_i^2}, \quad x_i \geq 0.$$

From the context of the problem, the relationship between x and y must be inverse: the higher the dose inoculated the lower the number of living cells and vice versa. For the examples, $\theta_1 \leq 0$ and $\theta_2 < 0$ are considered to satisfy this relationship for all $x \in \mathcal{X}$. Furthermore, to consider a high dose would not be realistic, as the number of living cells could be very low and might compromise the survival of the system. Let $\lambda_c = e^{\theta_0}$ be the mean of the number of surviving cells for a control dose ($x = 0$). Then, the expected survival proportion for any dose x_i is $\lambda_i/\lambda_c \geq c$, where $c \in (0,1]$ is the minimal survival proportion. The value of c is a characteristic for each system and for the context of the problem. For this study we consider $c = 0.4$. When $\theta_1^2/\theta_2 \geq -4\log c$, the survival proportion is not less than the minimal survival proportion in the design space $\mathcal{X} = [0, x_u]$, where x_u is expressed as a function of the parameters of the model (see details in [1]).

Based on the above, the first condition of the Theorem 3 is satisfied and therefore a control dose $x = 0$ is always included on the D-optimal design. Table 3 shows D-optimal designs when the response variable follows heteroscedastic normal (with $r = 0.5$ in (5)) or Poisson distributions. The nominal values considered fulfill the relationship in [1]. Moreover, all D-optimal designs are supported on the upper extreme, so only the inner points x_2 of D-optimal designs are shown. For a Poisson distribution the point x_2 may be computed by solving Equation (8) of Theorem 3. Finally, an efficiency study is carried out. The efficiencies of the designs are calculated by adapting (4) as

$$\text{eff}_D(\xi_A|\xi_T) = \left(\frac{|M_T(\xi_A;\theta)|}{|M_T(\xi_T;\theta)|}\right)^{1/m}, \tag{11}$$

where ξ_A is the D-optimal design for the probability distribution assumed by the researcher (for this example, heteroscedastic normal with $r = 0.5$), while ξ_T is the D-optimal design and M_T is the FIM, both for the true probability distribution (in this example, a Poisson distribution). The last column of Table 3 shows that efficiencies. Unlike the results obtained for the gamma distribution, where the D-optimal designs coincide with the heteroscedastic normal distribution when the relationship between mean and variance agrees (Corollary 1), there is a non-negligible loss efficiency, around 20% or more, in this case. It is noteworthy that the inner point of the Poisson distribution is lower than that for a heteroscedastic normal distribution for the designs computed.

Table 3. Locally D-optimal designs $\{x_1 = 0, x_2, x_3 = x_u\}$ equally weighted obtained for the linear quadratic model when the probability distribution of the response is heteroscedastic normal or Poisson. The nominal values are $\theta^{(0)} = (0.95, -1, \theta_2)$ and the minimal survival fraction is $c = 0.4$. The last column shows the efficiency when comparing the design for the heteroscedastic normal distribution with $r = 0.5$ to the Poisson distribution.

		$\xi_\mathcal{N}$ ($r = 0.5$)	$\xi_\mathcal{P}$	
θ_2	x_u	x_2	x_2	$\text{eff}_D(\xi_\mathcal{N}|\xi_\mathcal{P})$
$-1/50$	0.9001	0.7017	0.3993	0.7724
$-1/20$	0.8778	0.6826	0.3895	0.7748
$-1/10$	0.8449	0.6546	0.3751	0.7785
$-1/5$	0.7911	0.6091	0.3515	0.7845
-1	0.5799	0.4354	0.2585	0.8073

5. Extended Hill Model

The Hill model is a dose-response model commonly used in practice to describe the relationship between the concentration of a drug and its effect. Several papers [12,14,15] have addressed this issue from the point of view of optimal experimental design. This model may explain both discrete and continuous responses, such as counting cells [25] or the effect of a drug on cell growth [13], among many others. Here we focus on the 4-parameter Hill model.

If we consider x to be the dose of an administered drug, the function of the regression model which explains the effect can be expressed as

$$\eta(x; \theta) = \frac{(E_{con} - b)\left(\frac{x}{IC_{50}}\right)^s}{1 + \left(\frac{x}{IC_{50}}\right)^s} + b, \tag{12}$$

where $\theta = (E_{con}, b, IC_{50}, s)$ are the parameters to be estimated. The parameter E_{con} is the effect on the control, i.e., where there is no dose. The parameter b corresponds to the asymptotic value of the response when the concentration of the drug tends to infinity and IC_{50} corresponds to the dose at which a response would be found equal to the middle of the effect range, $E_{con} - b$. Finally, the parameter s is a form parameter: if $s > 0$, $\eta(x; \theta)$ will be strictly increasing, and if $s < 0$, strictly decreasing. Thus, when the parameter $b > 0$ and $s < 0$ the drug has an inhibitory effect where b implies that the whole cell population is not destroyed, as shown in Figure 1. This is the case considered in this paper. Here it is studied from two perspectives simultaneously, where the gamma, or Poisson, is the true distribution of the response variable and the practitioner assumes a heteroscedastic normal distribution with the variance structure given by (5).

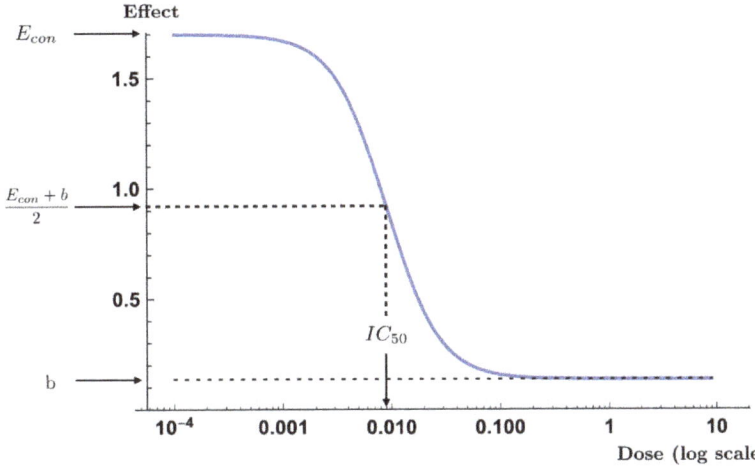

Figure 1. Graph of the regression function $\eta(x;\theta)$ of the 4-parameter Hill model with nominal values corresponding to the drug TMTX, shown in Table 4.

Ref. [13] bring together different maximum likelihood estimations of the parameters of (12) for different types of drugs. Table 4 shows these nominal values and the 4-point D-optimal designs obtained for different probability distributions of the response variable: ξ_Γ (gamma distribution with constant α), $\xi_\mathcal{N}$ (heteroscedastic normal distribution with variance structure given by (5)) and $\xi_\mathcal{P}$ (Poisson distribution). By Theorem 1, when $r=1$ in (5) ξ_Γ and $\xi_\mathcal{N}$ coincide. However, the designs $\xi_\mathcal{P}$ and $\xi_\mathcal{N}$ with $r=0.5$ are distinct, even though both comparisons show a similar relationship between the mean and the variance. Table 4 shows only the inner points (intermediate doses) of the D-optimal designs, as the extremes of the design space $\mathcal{X}=[0,D_{max}]$ are included in all the cases studied. The maximum dosage D_{max} was given by the value $1000 \cdot IC_{50}$, except for the drug AG2009, since the authors considered this dosage to be impractical. It can be seen that the D-optimal design leads to experimenting with three very low doses, and at the maximum dose (D_{max}), except for drug AG2009, where the doses are more spread out.

Table 4. Locally D-optimal designs $\{x_1=0, x_2, x_3, x_4=D_{max}\}$ equally weighted for the 4-parameter Hill model for different drugs and probability distributions. The nominal values $E_{con}^{(0)}=1.70$ and $b^{(0)}=0.137$ were considered for all the drugs. Columns 2–4 show the nominal values of the parameters and columns 5–10 show the internal points of the D-optimal designs $\xi_\mathcal{N}$, ξ_Γ and $\xi_\mathcal{P}$. The last column shows the efficiency when comparing the design for the heteroscedastic normal distribution with $r=0.5$ to the Poisson distribution.

	Nominal Values			$\xi_\Gamma = \xi_\mathcal{N}\ (r=1)$		$\xi_\mathcal{N}\ (r=0.5)$		$\xi_\mathcal{P}$		
Drug	$IC_{50}^{(0)}$	$s^{(0)}$	D_{max}	x_2	x_3	x_2	x_3	x_2	x_3	$\mathrm{eff}_D(\xi_\mathcal{N}|\xi_\mathcal{P})$
TMTX	0.00895	−1.79	8.95	0.00918	0.03568	0.00748	0.03010	0.00407	0.01283	0.729
MTX	0.0223	−2.74	22.3	0.02265	0.05502	0.01982	0.04922	0.01330	0.02817	0.728
AG2032	0.453	−0.825	453	0.07837	0.15728	0.07057	0.14411	0.05159	0.09299	0.728
AG2034	0.0774	−3.49	77.4	0.43634	7.70106	0.28694	5.46295	0.08152	0.96714	0.743
AG2009	111	−1.03	1500	63.1061	432.616	49.5552	361.701	23.4549	156.114	0.836

The last column of Table 4 shows that the efficiency computed by (11) of the D-optimal designs when a heteroscedastic normal distribution with $r=0.5$ is assumed with respect to the Poisson distribution, is around 73%, except for the drug AG2009, whose efficiency is higher. Again, in this practical case there is a considerable loss of efficiency in estimating the model parameters, with regard to misspecification in the probability distribution. All D-optimal designs in this section have been computed using the Wynn-Fedorov's algorithm [26].

Sensitivity Analysis

The main aim of this section is to study the effect of the relationship between $E[y]$ and $Var[y]$, characterized by the parameter r in (5), on the efficiency. So, a sensitivity analysis of this parameter is done. Ref. [11] studies the influence of misspecification in the structure of the variance in an analysis carried out for the gamma distribution and the heteroscedastic normal distribution separately. Here, a similar study was carried out with a point of view in which a practitioner considers a heteroscedastic normal response, but the true distribution of the response is gamma, or Poisson. For both distributions, efficiencies, using (11), are computed by comparing D-optimal designs for heteroscedastic normal distribution with the D-optimal design for the true probability distribution, as a function of the values of r.

The efficiencies achieved for different drugs are shown in Figure 2. It can be seen how, when the true distribution is gamma (Figure 2a), the efficiency is 1 for $r = 1$ (dot), since in this case the designs coincide as proven in Theorem 1. However, when the true distribution is the Poisson (Figure 2b), maximum efficiency is not obtained for $r = 0.5$ (dots), as might be expected. It is achieved in this case for negative values of r, close to $r = 0$, and so it would have been better, in terms of efficiency, for the practitioner to have assumed the homoscedastic normal distribution rather than heteroscedastic normal with $r = 0.5$. Furthermore, it does not reach the value 1 for any value of r. Finally, for this model in the neighborhood of $r = 0$ (homoscedastic normal distribution) opposite effects are produced on the efficiency for each of the distributions: greater efficiencies when the true distribution is the Poisson, and lower in the case of the gamma. It is important to highlight that there is no analytic explanation for this effect, and it is motivated by the model and nominal values.

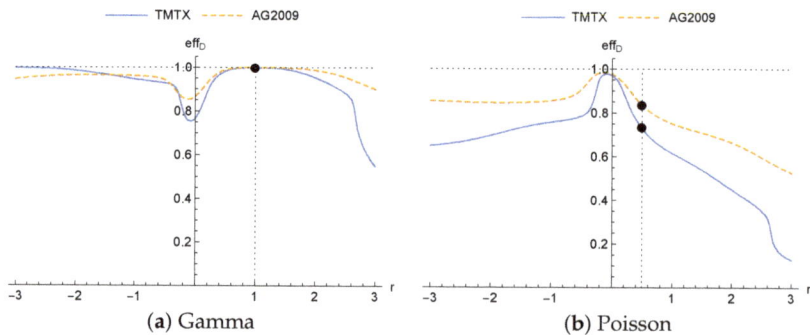

(a) Gamma (b) Poisson

Figure 2. Efficiencies when comparing the designs obtained for the heteroscedastic normal distribution with variance given by (5) and different values of r when the true distributions are the gamma (a) and Poisson (b), for the 4-parameter Hill model using the nominal values of Table 4. The graphs for the drugs MTX, AG2032 and AG2034 are similar to the graph for the drug TMTX.

For that, the effect of r on the trend of the efficiency is studied depending on the values taken by $\eta(x; \theta)$. Again, in this analysis, it is assumed that y follows a heteroscedastic normal distribution with variance structure given by (5) when the distribution of y is the Poisson or the gamma and a misspecification takes place.

First, for sufficiently large values of r and $\eta(x;\boldsymbol{\theta}) > 1$, $\forall x \in \mathcal{X}$, given that $\eta(x;\boldsymbol{\theta})^{-2r}/k \approx 0$, we have

$$v_\mathcal{N}(\eta(x;\boldsymbol{\theta}),r,k) = 2r^2/\eta(x;\boldsymbol{\theta})^2 + \eta(x;\boldsymbol{\theta})^{-2r}/k \approx 2r^2/\eta(x;\boldsymbol{\theta})^2$$
$$\propto \alpha/\eta(x;\boldsymbol{\theta})^2 = v_\Gamma(\eta(x;\boldsymbol{\theta})).$$

Thus, when the true probability distribution is a gamma distribution, Figure 3a (solid line) shows how, on increasing the value of r the efficiency tends to 1. On the other hand, the lower the value of r, the greater the difference between $v_\mathcal{N}(\eta(x;\boldsymbol{\theta});r,k)$ and $v_\Gamma(\eta(x;\boldsymbol{\theta}))$, therefore the efficiency tends to 0 as can be seen in Figure 3a. However, if $0 < \eta(x;\boldsymbol{\theta}) \leq 1$ (dashed line), $\forall x \in \mathcal{X}$, the effect of r on the trend of the efficiencies of the designs obtained for the heteroscedastic normal distribution when the true distribution is a gamma distribution is the opposite. As it is shown in Figure 3a, if r increases, the efficiency tends to 0, and if r decreases, the efficiency tends to 1.

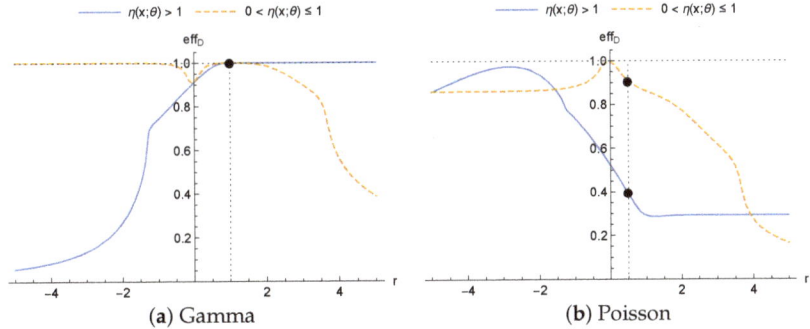

Figure 3. Study of efficiency trend when comparing the designs obtained for the heteroscedastic normal distribution as a function of the parameter r of (5) considering the gamma (**a**) or Poisson (**b**) distributions as the true distributions, for the 4-parameter Hill model in $\mathcal{X} = [0, 1500]$. Solid lines assume $E_{con} = 10$ and $b = 1$ (therefore $\eta(x;\boldsymbol{\theta}) > 1$), while for dashed lines $E_{con} = 1$ and $b = 0.1$ ($0 < \eta(x;\boldsymbol{\theta}) \leq 1$). Both cases use the nominal values $IC_{50} = 550$ and $s = -2$.

When the true distribution is a Poisson distribution there is no direct comparison between its EIM and the EIM of a heteroscedastic normal distribution. However, it can be seen in Figure 3b how the efficiency reaches a maximum for a particular value of r and loses efficiency for values away from that value. This is because the study looks at values of $s < 0$, and so $\eta(x;\boldsymbol{\theta})$ and $v_\mathcal{P}(\eta(x;\boldsymbol{\theta}))$ are monotonic. Therefore, the maximum efficiency is at the value of r where the distance between $v_\mathcal{N}(\eta(x;\boldsymbol{\theta}))$ and $v_\mathcal{P}(\eta(x;\boldsymbol{\theta}))$ is minimal (independently of whether $\eta(x;\boldsymbol{\theta}) > 1$ or $0 < \eta(x;\boldsymbol{\theta}) \leq 1$). Although the 4-parameter Hill model is taken as an example and the graphs in Figure 3 are obtained based on that model, the whole study on the trend of r on the efficiency is general for any regression function satisfying the inequalities.

Finally, it is interesting to point out differences between the graphs in Figures 2 and 3. First, the trends in the efficiencies as a function of r do not coincide. This is because, for the drugs in the study for the 4-parameter Hill model, the inequalities $\eta(x;\boldsymbol{\theta}) > 1$ or $0 < \eta(x;\boldsymbol{\theta}) \leq 1$ are not satisfied on the design spaces considered in the examples. Secondly, when the true distribution is the Poisson distribution, maximum efficiency in Figure 3b is obtained for a value close to $r = 0$ when $0 < \eta(x;\boldsymbol{\theta}) \leq 1$, as also it takes place in Figure 2b, while for the case with $\eta(x;\boldsymbol{\theta}) > 1$ maximum efficiency is obtained close to $r = -3$, i.e., for the same model, the nominal values defined by the context of the problem affect the loss of efficiency.

6. Summary and Conclusions

This study has been carried out to analyze the effect of misspecification in the probability distribution of the response variable. We measure that effect by calculating the efficiency of the optimal design obtained with an assumed or working distribution compared to that obtained with the true probability distribution. The typical case is when a researcher assumes a normal distribution, even a heteroscedastic one, for the response variable of his or her problem, but at a greater depth, another distribution is more appropriate, for example a gamma (or Poisson) distribution. When there is misspecification in the probability distribution, there is a loss of efficiency which depends both on the assumed probability distribution and on the regression function $\eta(x; \boldsymbol{\theta})$.

We provide some theoretical results, as well as practical ones. The first is quite general, valid for any regression function and any criterion based on FIM which guarantees that there is no loss of efficiency when the response variable follows a gamma distribution, and there is assumed to be a heteroscedastic normal distribution with $r = 1$ in the variance structure given by (5). For the linear quadratic model, analytical results are obtained on computing the optimal design for Poisson and gamma distributions. These theoretical results have been used in real applications from the literature, providing designs useful for practitioners.

Finally, the 4-parameter Hill model was used to illustrate and quantify the loss of efficiency. Assuming a heteroscedastic normal distribution, taking values close to $r = 0$ in (5), between about 18% and 25% efficiency is lost for all the drugs looked at in the study when the true distribution is a gamma distribution. Thus, in this case, the usual assumption of normality and homoscedasticity ($r = 0$) of the response variable is not a good option. However, when the true distribution is the Poisson, the loss of efficiency is less severe, reaching maximum values of efficiency for values close to $r = 0$ for all the drugs. This is a striking case, as one might expect maximum efficiency to be achieved at the value $r = 0.5$, which leads to the same relationship between the mean and the variance for the heteroscedastic normal and the Poisson distributions.

It is worth finishing this paper by mentioning that the EIM is an essential tool, as it collects information both about the regression function and the probability distribution of the response variable. As already mentioned, to assume the homoscedastic normal distribution when obtaining optimal designs may lead to a great loss of efficiency. Nonetheless, the examples given show that this will depend on the true distribution of the response variable and on the model function chosen. The existence of uncertainty about the probability distribution of the response variable will therefore lead to the future goal of obtaining robust designs to reduce this uncertainty.

Author Contributions: Conceptualization, M.A.-S., V.C.-A. and S.P.-C.; methodology, M.A.-S., V.C.-A. and S.P.-C.; software, M.A.-S., V.C.-A. and S.P.-C.; formal analysis, M.A.-S., V.C.-A. and S.P.-C.; investigation, M.A.-S., V.C.-A. and S.P.-C.; writing—original draft preparation, M.A.-S., V.C.-A. and S.P.-C.; writing—review and editing, M.A.-S., V.C.-A. and S.P.-C. All authors have read and agreed to the published version of the manuscript.

Funding: All authors were sponsored by Ministerio de Economía y Competitividad and fondos FEDER MTM2016-80539-C2-1-R and by Junta de Comunidades de Castilla-La Mancha SBPLY/17/180501/000380.

Institutional Review Board Statement: Not applicable.

Informed Consent Statement: Not applicable.

Data Availability Statement: Not applicable.

Conflicts of Interest: The authors declare no conflict of interest.

References

1. Wang, Y.; Myers, R.H.; Smith, E.P.; Ye, K. D-optimal designs for Poisson regression models. *J. Stat. Plan. Inference* **2006**, *136*, 2831–2845. [CrossRef]
2. García-Camacha, I.; Martín-Martín, R. The Construction of Locally D-Optimal Designs by Canonical Forms to an Extension for the Logistic Model. *Appl. Math.* **2014**, *5*, 824–831.
3. Amo-Salas, M.; Delgado-Márquez, E.; Filová, L.; López-Fidalgo, J. Optimal designs for model discrimination and fitting for the flow particles. *Stat Pap.* **2016**, *57*, 875–891. [CrossRef]
4. Aminenjad, M.; Jafari, H. Bayesian A- and D-optimal designs for gamma regression model with inverse link function. *Commun. Stat. Simul. Comput.* **2017**, *46*, 8166–8189. [CrossRef]
5. Casero-Alonso, V.; López-Fidalgo, J.; Torsney, B. A computer tool for a minimax criterion in binary response and heteroscedastic simple linear regression models. *Comput. Methods Programs Biomed.* **2017**, *138*, 105–115. [CrossRef]
6. Idais, O. Locally optimal designs for multivariate generalized linear models. *J. Multivar. Anal.* **2020**, *180*, 104663. [CrossRef]
7. Idais, O.; Schwabe, R. Analytic solutions for locally optimal designs for gamma models having linear predictors without intercept. *Metrika* **2020**, *86*, 1–16. [CrossRef]
8. Woods, D.C.; Lewis, S.M.; Eccleston, J.A.; Russell, K.G. Designs for Generalized Linear Models With Several Variables and Model Uncertainty. *Technometrics* **2006**, *48*, 284–292. [CrossRef]
9. Stufken, J.; Yang, M. Optimal designs for generalized linear models. In *Design and Analysis of Experiments, Special Design and Applications*; Hinkelmann, K., Ed.; Wiley: New York, NY, USA, 2012; Chapter 4, pp. 137–164.
10. Atkinson, A.C.; Fedorov, V.V.; Herzberg, A.M.; Zang, R. Elemental information matrices and optimal experimental design for generalized regression models. *J. Stat. Plan. Inference* **2014**, *144*, 81–91. [CrossRef]
11. Shen, G.; Hyun, S.W.; Wong, W.K. Optimal designs based on the maximum quasi-likelihood estimator. *J. Stat. Plan. Inference* **2016**, *178*, 128–139. [CrossRef]
12. Bezeau, M.; Endrenyi, L. Design of Experiments for the Precise Estimation of Dose-Response Parameters: The Hill Equation. *J. Theor. Biol.* **1986**, *123*, 415–430. [CrossRef]
13. Khinkis, L.A.; Levasseur, L.; Faessel, H.; Greco, W.R. Optimal Design for Estimating Parameters of the 4-Parameter Hill Model. *Nonlinearity Biol. Toxicol. Med.* **2003**, *1*, 363–377. [CrossRef] [PubMed]
14. Fang, H.B.; Ross, D.D.; Sausville, E.; Tan, M. Experimental design and interaction analysis of combination studies of drugs with log-linear dose responses. *Stat. Med.* **2008**, *27*, 3071–3083. [CrossRef]
15. Sperrin, M.; Thygesen, H.; Su, T.; Harbron, C.; Whitehead, A. Experimental designs for detecting synergy and antagonism between two drugs in a pre-clinical study. *Pharm. Stat.* **2015**, *14*, 216–225. [CrossRef] [PubMed]
16. McCullagh, P.; Nelder, J.A. *Generalized Linear Models*; Chapman & Hall/CRC: Boca Raton, FL, USA, 1989.
17. Karlin, S.; Studden, W.J. Optimal Experimental Designs. *Ann. Math. Stat.* **1966**, *37*, 783–815. [CrossRef]
18. Atkinson, A.; Donev, A.N.; Tobias, R.D. *Optimum Experimental Designs, with SAS*; Oxford University Press: New York, NY, USA, 2007; Volume 34.
19. Kiefer, J.; Wolfowitz, J. The equivalence of two extremum problems. *Can. J. Math.* **1960**, *12*, 363–365. [CrossRef]
20. Gaffke, N.; Idais, O.; Schwabe, R. Locally optimal designs for gamma models. *J. Stat. Plan. Inference* **2019**, *203*, 199–214. [CrossRef]
21. Tucker, S.L. Tests for the fit of the linear-quadratic model to radiation isoeffect data. *Int. J. Radiat. Oncol.* **1984**, *10*, 1933–1939. [CrossRef]
22. Roch-Lefèvre, S.; Martin-Bodiot, C.; Grègoire, E.; Desbrée, A.; Roy, L.; Barquinero, J.F. A mouse model of cytogenetic analysis to evaluate caesium137 radiation dose exposure and contamination level in lymphocytes. *Radiat. Environ. Biophys.* **2016**, *55*, 61–70. [CrossRef]
23. McMahon, S.J. The linear quadratic model: Usage, interpretation and challenges. *Phys. Med. Biol.* **2019**, *64*, 01TR01. [CrossRef]
24. Shuryak, I.; Cornforth, M.N. Accounting for overdispersion of lethal lesions in the linear quadratic model improves performance at both high and low radiation doses. *Int. J. Radiat. Biol.* **2021**, *97*, 50–59. [CrossRef] [PubMed]
25. Minkin, S. Experimental Design for Clonogenic Assays in Chemotherapy. *J. Am. Stat. Assoc.* **1993**, *88*, 410–420. [CrossRef]
26. Wynn, H.P. The sequential generation of D-optimum experimental designs. *Ann. Math. Stat.* **1970**, *41*, 1655–1664. [CrossRef]

Article

Optimal Experimental Design for Parametric Identification of the Electrical Behaviour of Bioelectrodes and Biological Tissues

Àngela Sebastià Bargues [1], José-Luis Polo Sanz [2] and Raúl Martín Martín [1,*]

[1] Department of Mathematics, University of Castilla-La Mancha, Avda. Carlos III s/n, 45071 Toledo, Spain; angela.sbargues@uclm.es

[2] Escuela de Ingeniería Industrial y Aeroespacial de Toledo, University of Castilla-La Mancha, Avda. Carlos III s/n, 45071 Toledo, Spain; joseluis.polo@uclm.es

* Correspondence: raul.mmartin@uclm.es

Citation: Sebastià Bargues, À.; Polo Sanz, J.-L.; Martín Martín, R. Optimal Experimental Design for Parametric Identification of the Electrical Behaviour of Bioelectrodes and Biological Tissues. *Mathematics* 2022, 10, 837. https://doi.org/10.3390/math10050837

Academic Editor: Christophe Guyeux

Received: 30 January 2022
Accepted: 2 March 2022
Published: 6 March 2022

Publisher's Note: MDPI stays neutral with regard to jurisdictional claims in published maps and institutional affiliations.

Copyright: © 2022 by the authors. Licensee MDPI, Basel, Switzerland. This article is an open access article distributed under the terms and conditions of the Creative Commons Attribution (CC BY) license (https://creativecommons.org/licenses/by/4.0/).

Abstract: The electrical behaviour of a system, such as an electrode–tissue interface (ETI) or a biological tissue, can be used for its characterization. One way of accomplishing this goal consists of measuring the electrical impedance, that is, the opposition that a system exhibits to an alternating current flow as a function of frequency. Subsequently, experimental impedance data are fitted to an electrical equivalent circuit (EEC model) whose parameters can be correlated with the electrode processes occurring in the ETI or with the physiological state of a tissue. The EEC used in this paper is a reasonable approach for simple bio-electrodes or cell membranes, assuming ideal capacitances. We use the theory of optimal experimental design to identify the frequencies in which the impedance is measured, as well as the number of measurement repetitions, in such a way that the EEC parameters can be optimally estimated. Specifically, we calculate approximate and exact D-optimal designs by optimizing the determinant of the information matrix by adapting two of the most algorithms that are routinely used nowadays (REX random exchange algorithm and KL exchange algorithm). The D-efficiency of the optimal designs provided by the algorithms was compared with the design commonly used by experimenters and it is shown that the precision of the parameter estimates can be increased.

Keywords: optimal experimental design; bioimpedance; impedance spectroscopy; algorithm

1. Introduction

The electrical behaviour of cells, biological tissues, or electrode-tissue interfaces can be used for their characterization [1–4]. One way to do this is by measuring the electrical impedance, that is, the opposition that the system under study exhibits to an alternating current flow as a function of frequency. Subsequently, experimental impedance data are fitted to an electrical equivalent circuit (EEC), which is a mathematical model that approximates the electrical behaviour of the system under study. Thus, the EEC parameters give information about the physiological state of a tissue or about the electrode processes occurring in the electrode-tissue interface (ETI). For instance, it is useful to know the electrical/electrochemical behaviour of the ETI plays a significant role in the biopotential measurements or also in the propagation of an applied stimuli. It should be mentioned that the experimental impedance data are analysed by using an impedance function. This impedance function can be proposed from a plausible physical theory (that predicts the impedance) or from an EEC, that aids in the visualization of the physical processes occurring in the system under study [1].

In this paper, we work with linear time-invariant (LTI) circuits, that is, LTI systems that fulfil the properties of linearity and invariance in time, meaning that the superposition and proportionality principles are hold. From the study of the circuit theory, a LTI circuit in which the input $i(t)$ is an electrical current (amperes), the output $v(t)$ is a voltage (volts), and t is the time (seconds) can be described by an ordinary, linear differential equation (ODE) with constant coefficients $a_i, b_j \in \mathbb{R}$ and order n for $n, m \in \mathbb{N}$ as [5]:

$$\frac{d^n v(t)}{dt^n} + a_{n-1}\frac{d^{n-1} v(t)}{dt^{n-1}} + \cdots + a_0 v(t) = b_m \frac{d^m i(t)}{dt^m} + b_{m-1}\frac{d^{m-1} i(t)}{dt^{m-1}} + \cdots + b_0 i(t) \quad (1)$$

Without loss of generality, we have assumed that $a_n = 1$.

Let us now consider the input $i(t) = e^{st}$, where s is a time-independent parameter. It can be shown that the output (refer to Equation (1)) can be written as $v(t) = Z(s)e^{st}$, where $Z(s)$ is an impedance function (in units of ohms, Ω), which relates the voltage to the current:

$$Z(s) = \frac{b_m s^m + b_{m-1} s^{m-1} + \cdots + b_0}{s^n + a_{n-1} s^{n-1} + \cdots + a_0} \quad (2)$$

The input given by e^{st} is extremely versatile. It allows us to obtain the forced response to a constant input ($s = 0$) or to a sinusoidal input ($s = j\omega$, where j is the imaginary unit and ω is the angular frequency in rad/s with $\omega = 2\pi f$, where f is frequency in Hz). This latter response is known as frequency response of systems, that is, the response of a system to input sinusoids of different frequencies. Moreover, e^{st} constitutes a basis function involving the Fourier series and the Fourier and Laplace transforms [5].

Note in particular that the parameter s in (2) can be interpreted as the variable that appears in the Laplace transform or as the differential operator ($\frac{d}{dt}$, typically denoted by p) [6]. When $s = j\omega$, the circuit is operating at sinusoidal steady-state. Specifically, by considering the Laplace transform of Equation (1), assuming zero initial conditions, we can write $V(s) = Z(s)I(s)$, where $I(s)$ and $V(s)$ are the Laplace transforms of the input $i(t)$ and the output $v(t)$, respectively. Interestingly, the unit-impulse ($i(t) = \delta(t)$, $I(s) = 1$, where $\delta(t)$ is Dirac delta function) response is $V(s) = Z(s)$, that is, the Laplace transfom of the voltage output equal the impedance $Z(s)$.

Electrical impedance has been usually defined in the context of a single sinusoidal signal and phasor analysis [6]. The impedance $Z(j\omega)$ at the frequency ω, is a complex number whose magnitude and phase are $|Z(j\omega)|$ and $\arg[Z(j\omega)]$, respectively. Equivalently, $Z(j\omega)$ can also be expressed in terms of its real and imaginary components, that is, the resistance $R(\omega)$ and the reactance $X(\omega)$, respectively.

$$Z(j\omega) = |Z(j\omega)|_{\arg[Z(j\omega)]} = R(\omega) + jX(\omega) \quad (3)$$

Note that for physical frequencies ($s = j\omega$), the impedance in Equation (2) can be written according to Equation (3). Hereinafter, the impedance $Z(j\omega)$ is also denoted by $Z(\omega)$.

Regarding the sinusoidal signal, it should be mentioned that the square of the rms (root mean square) value of a sinusoidal signal is the average power associated with it, that is, the average power is concentrated at frequency ω. Importantly, the average power associated with a periodic signal is the sum of the squared rms values (sum of the average powers) of all its components (Parseval's theorem for periodic signals). Therefore, the power spectral density (which, when integrated over the whole spectrum frequency, gives the total average power) for a periodic signal (power signal) consists of a series of impulses [7].

In this paper, we focus on finding the input frequencies to the circuit which maximises the amount of information obtained from an experiment, given that the true system is a priori known. Optimal input designs concern finding the input signal, which assures that the estimates become as good as possible. The use of optimal input signals will increase the precision of the parameter estimators [8]. This problem, called optimal input design, arises from the works of Mehra [9,10]. The theory of optimal design of experiments for the construction of optimal input signals in control theory, involving the frequency domain, can be found in [11–18]. However, its use for electrical impedance models has been scarcely reported in the scientific literature. Considerations of optimal multisine input signals are analysed in [19–21]. Specifically, a D-optimal multisine excitation for broadband impedance spectroscopy measurements is proposed in [20]. These optimal designs are based on simple first-order LTI circuits, that is, they are described by an ODE of order 1. The objective of this work is to design the D-optimal frequencies in which to carry out the electrical impedance measurements to achieve the best statistical estimates. Specifically, we calculate approximate and exact optimal designs by optimizing the determinant of the information matrix by adapting the REX random exchange algorithm and KL exchange algorithm. To the best of the authors' knowledge, there is no previous report of modifying those algorithms to calculate D-optimal designs in the frequency domain. In Section 2, we provide an introduction to the D-optimal input design applied to the study of a simple impedance model, which approaches the electrical behaviour of basic bio-electrodes or cell membranes. The definition of the Fisher Information Matrix (FIM) and the spectral density function are presented. Section 3 is devoted to the D-optimization criterion, the directional derivative, the equivalence theorem and the two algorithms adapted. Finally, in Section 4, we include a real application. The results obtained from an experimental test carried out with the two algorithms adapted to compare the efficiency of the design commonly used by experimenters with the D-optimal designs obtained from the algorithms are also discussed in this section.

2. Optimal Experimental Design for the Identification of LTI Systems

In general, the procedure for the identification of a system can be divided into three steps. The first one will be the experimental design, that is, planning and selecting the input signals to be introduced into the model. The set where to take the observations is known as the design space and is denoted by χ. From now on we will assume that it is a compact set. Once the input signals have been selected within the design space, the second step will be to collect data. The third step will be to estimate the parameters of the model.

2.1. Design of Experiments Background

Let χ be the compact design space and $y(t)$ the response variable, assumed as a random variable of a parametric distribution with a vector of parameters θ. We assume that the observations $y(t)$ verify the following model:

$$y(t) = \eta(t, \theta) + \varepsilon(t) \tag{4}$$

The model exhibits a random error ε and the function η is called the response surface and it is a partially known function, that is, it is within a parametric set of functions where the parameters $\theta^T = (\theta_1, \ldots, \theta_k) \in \mathbb{R}^k$ are unknown and their specification determines η totally. The response variable depends on the variable t, which we will call the independent or design variable, which can be freely chosen by the experimenter.

We will say that an exact design, ξ_N is a collection of N different support points, $t_1, t_2, \ldots, t_N$, where there could be repetitions. An approximate design, ξ, is a collection of M different support points, $t_1, t_2, \ldots, t_M$, and weights, $\xi(t_1), \xi(t_2), \ldots, \xi(t_M)$, that defines a discrete probability at χ. If the design ξ has weight $\xi(t_i)$ at t_i, $i = 1, \ldots, M$ and the total number of observations made is N, approximately $N\xi(t_i)$ observations will be taken at t_i, $i = 1, \ldots, M$. By choosing a sufficiently large N, it is possible to approximate a design with these characteristics to an exact design. The approximations will be better the larger the N [22].

One of the most important tools in the optimal experimental design is the FIM induced by ξ. The variance-covariance matrix $Var[\hat{\theta}]$ of the maximum likelihood estimator $\hat{\theta}$ can be asymptotically approximated by the inverse of the FIM, $M^{-1}(\xi)$, and under certain regularity conditions it reaches the lower limit of Cramer-Rao [23]. Once the estimator has been specified, we can consider the optimal design problem, as the selection of predictors that somehow lead to the minimization of the variance-covariance matrix $Var[\hat{\theta}] \approx M^{-1}(\xi)$, or equivalently to the maximization of $M(\xi)$. Therefore, the objective of the optimal design of experiments will be to find the best of the designs that maximizes $M(\xi)$ or minimizes $M^{-1}(\xi)$ in some sense.

Optimal design theory was initially developed for linear models. However, in practice it is common to find experiments where the response is explained from non-linear models in the parameters to be estimated, as this case study. The most common method for analysing data from a non-linear model is based on the use of the linear Taylor series approximation of the response surface.

$$\eta(t,\theta) \approx \eta(t,\theta^{(0)}) + [\nabla_\theta \eta(x,\theta)|_{\theta^{(0)}}]^T (\theta - \theta^{(0)}) \tag{5}$$

where ∇_θ denotes the gradient with respect θ and being $\theta^{(0)}$ a prior value of θ, for example an estimate calculated on the basis of an initial experiment or suitable values found in the literature. Thus, the FIM will depend on the values of the unknown parameters and, consequently, the optimal designs will also depend on these values,

$$M(\xi,\theta) = \int_\xi \nabla_\theta \eta(t,\theta) \nabla_\theta^T \eta(t,\theta) \xi(dt) \tag{6}$$

2.2. Electrical Circuit Model

Let us consider the EEC of Figure 1A. It comprises a resistance R_1 in series with the parallel combination of a capacitor C and a resistance R_2. Currents and voltages have been labelled in each element. $i(t)$ and $v(t)$ are the current input and the voltage output, respectively. $i_C(t)$ and $i_{R_2}(t)$ are the currents flowing through the capacitor C and the resistance R_2, respectively. $v_C(t)$ is the voltage across C (the same than that of R_2).

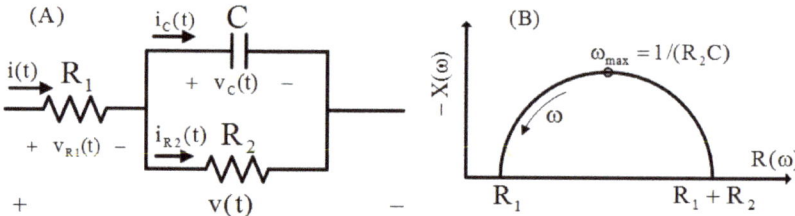

Figure 1. Electrical circuit model (**A**) and Nyquist plot (**B**).

The ODE of the EEC shown in Figure 1A is written as (refer to Appendix A)

$$\frac{dv(t)}{dt} + a_0 v(t) = b_1 \frac{di(t)}{dt} + b_0 i(t), \quad t \in [0,T] \tag{7}$$

Let us define $\theta^T = (b_1, b_0, a_0)$ for $b_1, b_0, a_0 \in \mathbb{R}$ and $k = 3$ the unknown vector parameters with

$$\begin{cases} b_1 = R_1 \\ b_0 = \dfrac{R_1 + R_2}{R_2 C} \\ a_0 = \dfrac{1}{R_2 C} \end{cases} \tag{8}$$

As we saw in Section 1, the impedance from Equation (7) is obtained as

$$Z(s) = \frac{b_1 s + b_0}{s + a_0} \tag{9}$$

For physical frequencies $s = j\omega$, Equation (9) is written as

$$Z(\omega) = \frac{b_1 j\omega + b_0}{j\omega + a_0} \tag{10}$$

where $\omega \in (0, \infty)$.

Figure 1B shows the Nyquist plot ($-X(\omega)$ vs. $R(\omega)$ in the complex plane). Equation (10) sketches a semicircle, which intersects the real axis at R_1 and $R_1 + R_2$, at the frequencies $\omega = \infty$ and $\omega = 0$, respectively (ω is positive and increases counterclockwise). The maximum of $-X(\omega)$ vs. $R(\omega)$ is reached at $\omega_{\max} = \frac{1}{R_2 C}$.

Now, let the parameter s (refer to Equation (9)) be considered the differential operator, that is, $p = d/dt$ (see above). The unknown parameters θ must be estimated from measures of the form:

$$v(t) = Z(p)i(t) + \varepsilon(t) \tag{11}$$

where $Z(p)$ is a new differential operator [6] and $\varepsilon(t)$ is a random error $N(0, \sigma^2)$ that includes both the errors of the tests and the specification of the model. The Fourier transform of Equation (11) is given by

$$V(\omega) = Z(\omega)I(\omega) + E(\omega) \tag{12}$$

where $V(\omega) = \mathcal{F}[v](\omega) \in \mathbb{C}$, $I(\omega) = \mathcal{F}[i](\omega) \in \mathbb{C}$ and $E(\omega) = \mathcal{F}[\varepsilon](\omega) \in \mathbb{C}$, with $\mathcal{F}$ the Fourier transform.

It should be mentioned that the impedance of (9) can also be obtained by considering the impedance of each of R_1, R_2 and C, that is, R_1, R_2 and $\frac{1}{sC}$, respectively, resulting in $Z(s) = R_1 + (R_2 \parallel \frac{1}{sC})$, $\parallel$ denotes parallel, which gives Equation (9).

2.3. The FIM for the Electrical Circuit Model

In this section, we will consider that the input signal $i(t)$ is a time stationary process and we will go from the time domain to the frequency domain in order to apply the optimal design theory for this type of LTI SISO (single-input, single-output) systems. In this domain, the properties for the approximation of the information matrices used in the theory of the optimal design of experiments, given by Kiefer-Wolfowitz [24], Karlin-Studden [25] and Fedorov [26], are preserved. According to Mehra [9], if a SISO system is LTI, the number of data points N is large and $i(t)$ is a stationary process, the optimal inputs can be calculated much more efficiently using frequency domain techniques.

Let Equation (10) be the impedance model to be estimated, where θ is the vector of parameters of the impedance model defined in (8). Then,

$$\nabla_\theta Z(\omega) = \begin{pmatrix} \frac{j\omega}{j\omega + a_0} \\ \frac{1}{j\omega + a_0} \\ -\frac{j(b_1\omega - b_0 j)}{(j\omega + a_0)^2} \end{pmatrix} \tag{13}$$

By Parseval's Theorem, we find that, for a continuous time model (10), the FIM in the frequency domain is given by (refer to Appendix B)

$$M(\Phi) = \frac{1}{2\pi} \int_{-\infty}^{+\infty} \tilde{M}(\omega, \theta) \Phi(\omega) d\omega \tag{14}$$

where Φ is the power spectral density of $i(t)$ and $\tilde{M}(\omega, \theta)$ is the single-frequency FIM, which defines the information associated with the model (10) with respect to θ, defined as

$$\tilde{M}(\omega, \theta) = \Re\left\{ \nabla_\theta Z(\omega) \cdot \nabla_\theta Z(\omega)^H \right\} \tag{15}$$

where the superscript H denotes the conjugate transpose operator and $\Re\{z\}$ is the real part of the number $z \in \mathbb{C}$. From the model (10), the single-frequency FIM as defined in (15) is

$$\tilde{M}(\omega, \theta) = \begin{pmatrix} \frac{\omega^2}{a_0^2+\omega^2} & 0 & \frac{\omega^2(b_0-b_1 a_0)}{(a_0^2+\omega^2)^2} \\ 0 & \frac{1}{a_0^2+\omega^2} & -\frac{b_1\omega^2+b_0 a_0}{(a_0^2+\omega^2)^2} \\ \frac{\omega^2(b_0-b_1 a_0)}{(a_0^2+\omega^2)^2} & -\frac{b_1\omega^2+b_0 a_0}{(a_0^2+\omega^2)^2} & \frac{b_1^2\omega^2+b_0^2}{(a_0^2+\omega^2)^2} \end{pmatrix} \tag{16}$$

Note that in the frequency domain, the role of the probability measure is played by the power spectral density function Φ. Therefore, Φ is the design measure (or design), ζ, that we call in the context of design of experiments.

We define by Ξ the set of non-decreasing, continuous design measures of bounded variation, corresponding to input power spectral density functions, that is,

$$\Xi = \left\{ \Phi \ : \ \int_{\omega_I}^{\omega_E} \Phi(\omega) d\omega = 1 \right\} \tag{17}$$

The design can be limited to a finite range $[\omega_I, \omega_E]$, where ω_I and ω_E are the lowest and highest angular frequencies, respectively, at which impedance has been measured. This frequency range will be the design space χ.

3. Construction of D-Optimal Input Signals

Among a set of designs, it is not easy to decide which is "the best" of them. Therefore, we need to choose a criterion, a scalar measure of the FIM, $\Psi : \mathcal{M}(\Xi) \longrightarrow \mathbb{R} \cup \{\infty\}$, called optimality criterion, that helps us to find the best design. The choice will depend on the interests sought by conducting the experiment. A design that minimizes Ψ over all the designs on χ is called an optimum design, that is

$$\Phi^* = \arg\min_{\Phi \in \Xi} \Psi[M(\Phi)] \tag{18}$$

The most popular criterion is D-optimality. This criterion consists of minimizing the volume of the confidence ellipsoid of estimators of the parameters of the model, i.e., it maximizes the determinant of the FIM. For a given $\theta^{(0)}$, D-optimality is defined by the criterion function:

$$\Psi_D[M(\Phi)] = [\det M(\Phi)]^{-\frac{1}{k}} \tag{19}$$

When an optimal design is sought among all approximate designs on the design space and the design criterion is convex, it can be checked the optimality of a particular design using the celebrated General Equivalence Theorem (GET) [24]. If the criterion function, Ψ, is differentiable the GET has a friendly version. Thus, a design Φ_D^* is Ψ_D-optimum if and only if $\forall \omega \in \chi$, the dispersion function

$$d(\omega, \Phi_D^*) = \nabla_\theta Z(\omega)^H M^{-1}(\Phi_D^*) \nabla_\theta Z(\omega) = \text{Tr}\left[M^{-1}(\Phi_D^*) \tilde{M}(\omega, \theta)\right] \tag{20}$$

achieves its maximum values at the support points. In particular, for the D-optimum criterion this condition proves the optimality of Φ_D^* if and only if

$$d(\omega, \Phi_D^*) \leq k, \quad \forall \omega \in \chi \tag{21}$$

being k the number of the parameters of the model.

The GET allows us to check the optimality of a design, but it does not tell us how to find it. However, this theorem is useful for building efficient algorithms that allow computing optimal designs.

Another fundamental tool commonly used by the algorithmic techniques is the efficiency of a design. This value is interpreted as the goodness of a design and is defined as

$Eff_\Psi(\Phi) = \Psi[M(\Phi)]/\Psi[M(\Phi^*)]$, being Φ^* the Ψ-optimal design. Thus the D-efficiency of a design Φ_D is computed as:

$$Eff_D(\Phi_D) = \left[\frac{\det M(\Phi_D)}{\det M(\Phi_D^*)}\right]^{-\frac{1}{k}} \qquad (22)$$

If the criteron function has a homogeneity property, as in this case, there is a practical statistical interpretation. Thus, if a design has 50 % efficiency, then half of the observations with the optimal design will produce the same results with respect to the criterion function. Although this quantity cannot be calculated when the optimal design is unknown, it is possible to obtain lower limits of efficiency to make a stopping rule. An important bound for the D-optimization criterion is the one proposed by Atwood [27]

$$Eff_D(\Phi_D) \geq \frac{k}{\max_{\omega \in \chi} d(\omega, \Phi_D)} \qquad (23)$$

Modified Algorithms

The search for analytical solutions for the problem of construction of optimal designs turns out to be a difficult task and, in most of the real problems, it is not possible to calculate analytically the designs under a certain criterion. There is a rich literature on numerical computational algorithms proposed to obtain optimal designs under different scenarios. In exact design problems, we do not have a convex optimization problem in general and, so, finding optimal design is not an easy task because it is a discrete optimization problem and there is no general analytical tool for confirming whether an exact design is optimal or not. There are several numerical algorithms for finding optimal exact designs based on exchange methods. In this paper, we proposed the Atkinson and Donev KL exchange algorithm [28] to calculate exact D-optimal designs. The procedure starts with a non-singular random design. Then, two sets of points are constructed from the dispersion function. One with K "least promising" support points of the current design, for which exchanges are attempted. The other one with L "most promising" candidate design points. Finally, it adds and deletes observation points that lead to the greatest increase in the determinant of the FIM, under the standard constraint of the required number of points and the maximum execution time of the algorithm. Each exchange of improvement is executed immediately. Because this is only a heuristic, it cannot be guaranteed to reach the global optimum, so it is convenient to run the algorithm several times. The end result is the best design found in all runs.

For optimal approximate design problems, there are many analytic methods to construct them. Due to the performance and the flexibility to be applied in a broad range of problem structures and sizes, the randomized exchange algorithm (REX) [29] has been considered in this work. The REX method, which is a simple batch-randomized exchange algorithm, can be viewed as an efficient extension or combination of both the vertex exchange method for D-optimality of Böhning [30] and the KL exchange algorithm. The procedure begins with a random design of non-singular points and their respective proportions. Then, a batch consisting of a pair of points is repeatedly selected: a random support point of the current design, ω_k, and a random design point, ω_l, where optimal ratio exchanges between these pairs are made. The batch selection depends on the dispersion function. The key to making the optimal random exchanges of proportions between the selected batch is the optimal step length value $\alpha_{k,l}^*(\Phi_D)$ (see Appendix A in [29]), which gives the value to be added or subtracted from the proportions of each observation point. Finally, it adds and deletes observation points that lead to the largest increase in the efficiency bound. This algorithm has a standard threshold constraint on the minimum design efficiency to stop the computation. The limit used as the stopping rule is the Atwood limit (23).

These algorithms were adapted to involve complex variables. The matrix of Equation (13) is given as input for both algorithms. We develop a complex type null matrix and then it is completed by creating a loop, where each row of the complex null matrix is replaced by the components of (13). Each row corresponds to a value of ω within χ previously defined. Next, we adapt the definition of the single frequency FIM (see Equation (15)) and the dispersion function (20). Modified codes to adapt the algorithms to this case study can be found in Appendix C.

The general procedure followed by these algorithms can be summarized as:

1. An initial design is chosen. In principle, it can be any arbitrary design, $\Phi_D^{(0)}$, such that the criterion function for this design verifies $[\det M(\Phi_D^{(0)})]^{-\frac{1}{k}} \neq 0$.
2. A succession of designs $\Phi_D^{(1)}, \Phi_D^{(2)}, \ldots$ is obtained computationally in an iterative way, where $\Phi_D^{(q+1)}$ is calculated by slightly disturbing the previous design $\Phi_D^{(q)}$ and requiring that $[\det M(\Phi_D^{(q+1)})]^{-\frac{1}{k}} \neq 0$.
3. The process of generating the previous designs will end in the qth step after verifying that the design $\Phi_D^{(q)}$ obtained is close enough to the optimum according to a stopping rule.

4. Real Applications

As mentioned earlier, biological tissues, cells, and ETIs can be characterized from their electrical behaviour. Figure 2 shows a portion of tissue (group of similar cells) with an implanted electrode. In general, the passive electrical behaviour of the tissue and the ETI involve electrical capacitance (capacity to store charges) and resistance (ability to oppose dc-current flow). Figure 2 also shows several basic EECs [1–4]. Intra- (pink colour) and extracellular (blue colour) media are resistive parts (electrolyte solutions), and thus are modelled by the resistances R_I (Figure 2A) and R_E (Figure 2B), respectively. The passive electrical behaviour of a cell membrane (green colour) is described by a parallel combination of a cell membrane capacitance C_M and the membrane resistance R_M (see Figure 2C). A basic model of ETI is shown in the EEC of Figure 2D, that is, a double layer capacitance C_{DL} in parallel with the polarization resistance R_P [1,3]. The EEC shown in Figure 1A involves those of Figure 2C,D with an additional resistance R_1. Moreover, the impedance of the EEC of Figure 1A is equivalent to that proposed by Cole when the biological tissue involves an ideal capacitance [2,4].

It should be mentioned that the optimal design of experiments is of great interest for two main reasons: to obtain an optimal characterization of the process and to minimize the measurement acquisition time.

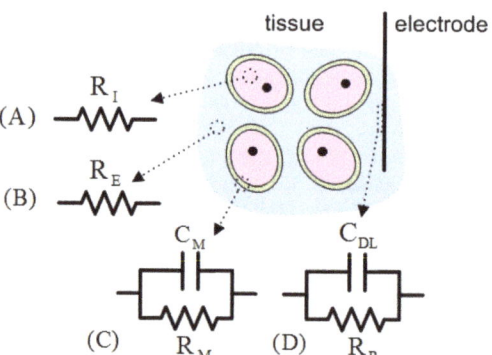

Figure 2. Biological tissue and basic EECs for intra- (**A**), extracellular media (**B**), cell membrane (**C**), and electrode-tissue interface (**D**).

4.1. Methods

The modified algorithms were applied to the circuit shown in Figure 1A. Let $R_1 = 100\ \Omega$, $R_2 = 10^6\ \Omega$ and $C = 10^{-6}$ F the nominal values of the parameters and $\chi = [2\pi 10^{-1}, 2\pi 10]$ rad/s. For numerical study, we consider the frequency design space to be a set of grid points spread equidistantly by 0.01.

We have used the RStudio 1.3.1093 program to obtain the optimal designs. The Autolab PGSTAT204 potentiostat/galvanostat (Figure 3A), equipped with the FRA32M module, was used to perform the impedance measurements. The equipment, controlled by a computer and NOVA electrochemistry software, is connected to a dummy cell containing the circuit described above to perform the test (Figure 3B). We used sinusoidal current signals of 10^{-6} A peak amplitude.

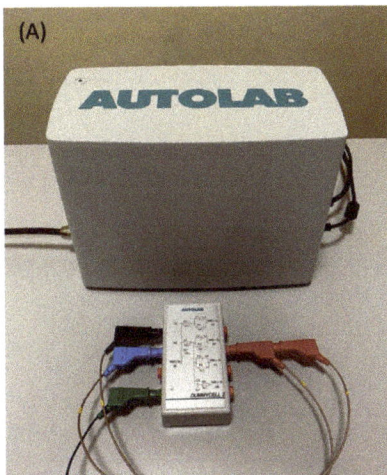
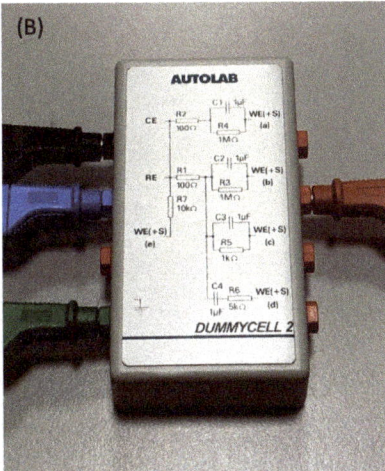

Figure 3. Autolab PGSTAT potentiostat/galvanostat equipment (**A**) connected to the dummy cell (**B**) containing the EEC.

The objective of this experimental test was to compare the efficiency of the classical design commonly used by experimenters with the D-optimal designs obtained in the adapted KL and REX algorithms. The classic design is based on measuring impedance at certain frequencies equally spaced on a logarithmic scale. In particular

$$\Phi^{classic} = \{2\pi 10^{-1}, 2\pi 10^{-0.8}, 2\pi 10^{-0.6}, \ldots, 2\pi 10^{0.8}, 2\pi 10\} \quad (24)$$

where $N = 11$. For comparison purposes, the adapted KL algorithm was executed considering the same number of support points as the classic design ($N = 11$). In the case of the REX algorithm, from a theoretical point of view, it is not necessary to set N. The algorithm provides points and the proportions to be measured at those points. In order to be able to compare the design obtained, the proportion was rounded to the nearest integer, that is, if the design puts weight p_i on ω_i, $i = 1, \ldots, M$ and the total number of observations we want is $N = 11$, then approximately $N \cdot p_i$ observations will be taken at ω_i, $i = 1, \ldots, M$.

4.2. Results and Discussion

Figure 4 shows the Nyquist plot for the EEC of Figure 3B. Experimental impedance data obtained for the frequencies of (24) draw a semicircle like that of Figure 1B. Subsequently, experimental data have been fitted to the EEC of Figure 1A and the values of its parameters are given in Table 1.

In this experimental test, there was a prior knowledge of the EEC parameters with a certain tolerance. In this case, the following initial values were considered to execute the algorithms:

$$b_1 = 10, \quad b_0 = 50500, \quad a_0 = 50 \quad (25)$$

where $R_1 = 10\ \Omega$, $R_2 = 1000\ \Omega$ and $C = 20 \times 10^{-6}$ F. To avoid dependence on the value of these parameters, a sequential approach was applied with the estimates obtained in the previous step. The stabilization of the process was fast (Table 1). Finally, the optimal design obtained with the two algorithms was the following:

$$\Phi_D^* = \left\{ \begin{array}{cc} 2\pi 0.1 & 2\pi 10 \\ 7 & 4 \end{array} \right\} \qquad (26)$$

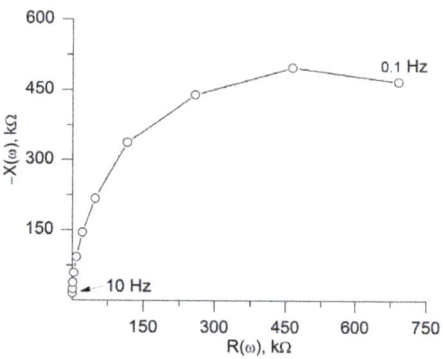

Figure 4. Nyquist plot obtained from the classic design.

Table 1. EEC parameters values estimated using the different optimal designs.

Design	Iteration	N	R_1, Ω	R_2, Ω	C, F
Classic	-	11	90.86	1.0103×10^6	1.0750×10^{-6}
KL	1	11	263.9	1.0056×10^6	1.0679×10^{-6}
KL	2	11	100.7	1.0061×10^6	1.0745×10^{-6}
REX	1	11	99.62	1.0079×10^6	1.0695×10^{-6}

The dispersion function (20), shown in Figure 5, reaches the maximums at the support points (that is, the extremes of the interval) and remains less than 3 (the number of parameters) throughout the design space, so the design obtained is D-optimal.

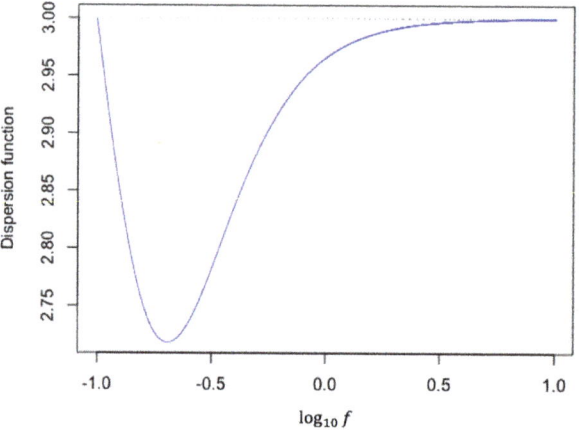

Figure 5. Dispersion function for the D-optimal design for the EEC shown in Figure 1A. The abscissa axis represents the logarithm of the frequency f ($f = \omega/2\pi$).

Figure 6 illustrates the support points of the D-optimal designs obtained with $N = 11$ after executing the algorithms and the classic design. Table 2 shows the values of the D-optimal criterion (19) for the designs obtained from REX, KL and classical. It is observed that the values obtained with the algorithms are greater than the value obtained with the classical design, therefore, the value of the D-optimal criterion has been maximized. Optimal designs are an interesting tool to measure the value of an experimental design, through efficiency. This efficiency is the percentage of observations that the optimal design would need to achieve the precision of the experimental design being compared. The efficiency (22) of the classic design is also presented in Table 2. This shows how the same information can be obtained by reducing the number of experimental conditions by using optimal inputs.

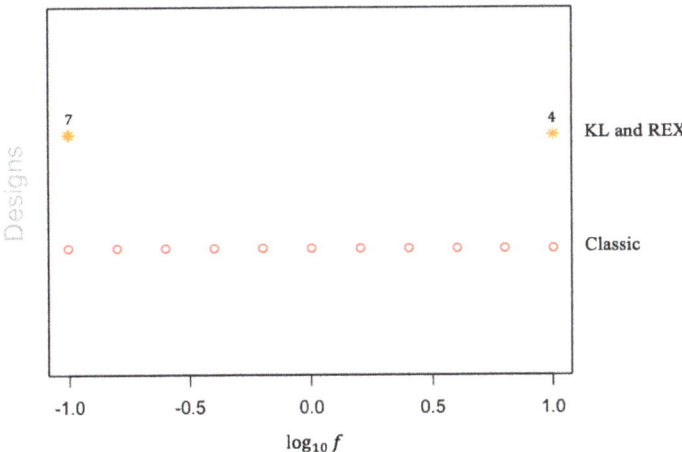

Figure 6. Support points of the D-optimal designs obtained by the adapted algorithms and the classic design. The values on the points obtained with the algorithms (7 and 4) are the number of replicas of each point.

Table 2. Criterion values.

Design	$\Psi_D[M(\Phi_D^*)]$	$Eff_D(\Phi_D)$
KL	2488.52	
REX	2488.52	
Classic	1632.01	0.65

Finally, a sensitivity study has been performed by analysing the fluctuations of the efficiency values against the initial variations of the parameters. In particular, each initial parameter was modified by $\pm 20\%$ of the real values. The efficiencies of the designs obtained have been calculated in relation to the $3^3 = 27$ possible designs. For all cases, as can be seen from Figure 7, the efficiency for both REX and the KL was never lower than 99.21% and higher than 99.99% for most variations.

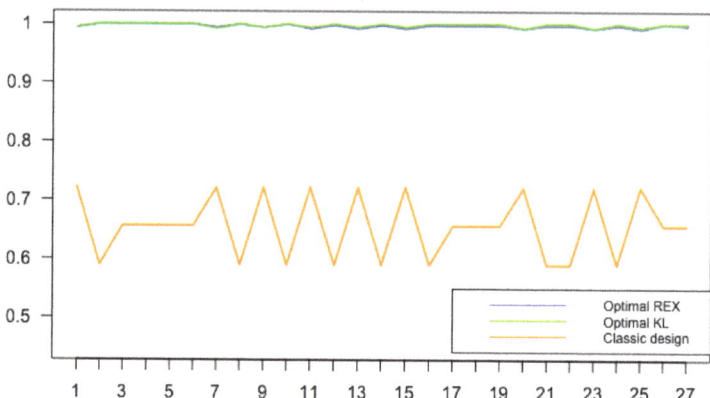

Figure 7. Efficiencies of the 27 possible designs.

5. Conclusions

This paper expands the existing tools to create optimal designs regarding SISO LTI systems in the context of electrical impedance measurements, based on the frequency domain description of an input signal. We have considered the most used optimization criterion, D-optimality. Two algorithms (KL and REX) were modified to calculate D-optimal designs and estimate the parameters of the EEC describing the electrical behaviour of bioelectrodes, cell membranes, or biological tissues. We have checked that the efficiency remains high for different initial values of the parameters. The estimation of the parameters has also been discussed. The application of a sequential approximation with the estimates obtained by means of least squares stabilize the process quickly. We have calculated the D-optimal designs with the same number of points as those of the classical design to obtain an efficiency comparison. It has been seen that optimal designs computed may save 35% of the observations to get the same results as the classic design.

The generation of new results for the design of optimal input signals in impedance models is very useful both in the characterization of biological tissues and the electrode–tissue interface. Specifically, the KL exchange and random exchange REX algorithms that we have adapted are a good option to be used by experimenters to obtain a good estimate of the parameters with lower time-consuming.

Author Contributions: Conceptualization, R.M.M. and J.-L.P.S.; methodology, À.S.B., R.M.M. and J.-L.P.S.; software, À.S.B. and R.M.M.; writing—original draft preparation, À.S.B. and R.M.M.; writing—review and editing, À.S.B., J.-L.P.S. and R.M.M. All authors have read and agreed to the published version of the manuscript.

Funding: This research was funded by the Ministerio de Economía, Industria y Competitividad-Agencia Estatal de Investigación (Project MTM2016-80539-C2-1-R), the Consejería de Educación, Cultura y Deportes of Junta de Comunidades de Castilla-La Mancha (Project SBPLY/17/180501/000380), and the European Regional Development Fund (FONDOS FEDER).

Institutional Review Board Statement: Not applicable.

Informed Consent Statement: Not applicable.

Data Availability Statement: Not applicable.

Conflicts of Interest: The authors declare no conflict of interest. The funders had no role in the design of the study; in the collection, analyses, or interpretation of data; in the writing of the manuscript, or in the decision to publish the results.

Appendix A. Obtaining the Differential Equation

Kirchhoff's current law provides

$$i(t) = i_C(t) + i_{R_2}(t) \tag{A1}$$

Applying Kirchhoff's voltage law, we obtain

$$v_C(t) = v(t) - v_{R_1}(t) \tag{A2}$$

As shown in Figure 1A, C and R_2 are in parallel, and therefore have the same voltage $v_C(t)$. Using the characteristic equations of the elements

$$v_C(t) = R_2 i_{R_2}(t) \tag{A3}$$

$$v_{R_1}(t) = R_1 i(t) \tag{A4}$$

$$i_C(t) = C\frac{dv_C(t)}{dt} \tag{A5}$$

Using the Equations (A3) and (A5) in Equation (A1), we obtain

$$i(t) = C\frac{dv_C(t)}{dt} + \frac{v_C(t)}{R_2} \tag{A6}$$

And, using Equations (A2) and (A4) in Equation (A6), we obtain

$$i(t) = C\frac{dv(t)}{dt} - CR_1\frac{di(t)}{dt} + \frac{v(t)}{R_2} - \frac{R_1}{R_2}i(t) \tag{A7}$$

Finally, dividing both members by C and rearranging we arrive at the ODE:

$$\frac{dv(t)}{dt} + \frac{1}{R_2 C}v(t) = R_1\frac{di(t)}{dt} + \frac{R_1 + R_2}{R_2 C}i(t), \quad t \in [0, T] \tag{A8}$$

Appendix B. Fisher Information Matrix of a LTI System

Appendix B.1. Time Domain

The impulse response fully characterizes LTI systems and allows the output of an LTI system to be calculated against any input. As indicated above, an LTI circuit, with input $i(t)$ and output $v(t)$, can be described by an ODE with constant coefficients (see Equation (1)). The output $v(t)$ of the continuous LTI system is given by a convolution integral:

$$v(t) = z(t) * i(t) = \int_{-\infty}^{+\infty} z(t-\tau)i(\tau)d\tau \tag{A9}$$

where $z(t)$ is the voltage response to a unit-impulse current at the input. Therefore, taking into account that the FIM for a non-linear model has the form

$$M(i(t), \theta) = \int_{-\infty}^{\infty}\int_{-\infty}^{\infty}\int_{-\infty}^{\infty} \nabla_\theta z(t-\tau, \theta)\nabla_\theta^T z(t-v, \theta)i(\tau)i(v)d\tau\, dv\, dt$$
$$= \int_{-\infty}^{\infty}\int_{-\infty}^{\infty}\int_{-\infty}^{\infty} \nabla_\theta z(\tau, \theta)\nabla_\theta^T z(v, \theta)\underbrace{i(t-\tau)i(t-v)}_{(\star)}\, d\tau\, dv\, dt \tag{A10}$$

The function $(\star)$ will be needed for the next subsection.

Appendix B.2. Frequency Domain

Assuming that $i(t)$ is a time stationary process (the value of the covariance between two periods depends only on the distance between these two periods of time) and applying the limit to the function $(\star)$, we obtain the next

$$\lim_{T \to \infty} \frac{1}{2T} \int_{-T}^{T} i(t-\tau)i(t-\nu)dt = \lim_{T \to \infty} \frac{1}{2T} \int_{-T}^{T} i(t)i(t+\tau-\nu) = R_i(\tau-\nu) \quad \text{(A11)}$$

where the time period is $t - \nu - (t - \tau) = \tau - \nu$ and R_i is the autocorrelation function of the signal $i(t)$.

The normalized FIM is defined as

$$\begin{aligned}
M(R_i(\tau)) &= \lim_{T \to \infty} \frac{1}{2T} M(i(t), \theta) \\
&= \lim_{T \to \infty} \frac{1}{2T} \int_{-T}^{T} \int_{-T}^{T} \int_{-T}^{T} \nabla_\theta z(\tau,\theta) \nabla_\theta^T z(\nu,\theta) i(t-\tau) i(t-\nu) d\tau \, d\nu \, dt \\
&= \int_{-\infty}^{\infty} \int_{-\infty}^{\infty} \nabla_\theta z(\tau,\theta) \nabla_\theta^T z(\nu,\theta) \lim_{T \to \infty} \frac{1}{2T} \left[\int_{-T}^{T} i(t-\tau) i(t-\nu) dt \right] d\tau d\nu \\
&= \int_{-\infty}^{\infty} \int_{-\infty}^{\infty} \nabla_\theta z(\tau,\theta) \nabla_\theta^T z(\nu,\theta) R_i(\tau-\nu) \, d\tau \, d\nu
\end{aligned} \quad \text{(A12)}$$

The Wiener–Khinchin theorem establishes a relationship between the autocorrelation function of a signal and its power spectral density function, that is, the Fourier transform of the autocorrelation function $R_i(\tau)$ of a time stationary process is the function spectral density $\Phi(\omega)$ ($\mathcal{F}[R_i](\omega) = \Phi(\omega)$). Therefore, by Parseval's Theorem, we find that the FIM in the frequency domain is given by

$$\begin{aligned}
M(\mathcal{F}[R_i]) \underset{\text{Notation}}{\equiv} M(\Phi) &= \frac{1}{2\pi} \int_{-\infty}^{\infty} \mathcal{F}[\nabla_\theta z(\tau,\theta)] \mathcal{F}[\nabla_\theta z(\nu,\theta)] \mathcal{F}(R_i(\tau-\nu)) d\omega \\
&= \frac{1}{2\pi} \int_{-\infty}^{\infty} \Re \left\{ \nabla_\theta \mathcal{F}[z(\tau,\theta)] \nabla_\theta \mathcal{F}[z(\nu,\theta)] \right\} \Phi(\omega) d\omega \\
&= \frac{1}{2\pi} \int_{-\infty}^{\infty} \Re \left\{ \nabla_\theta Z(\omega) \nabla_\theta Z(\omega)^H \right\} \Phi(\omega) d\omega
\end{aligned} \quad \text{(A13)}$$

where $\Re\{z\}$ is the real part of the number $z \in \mathbb{C}$, $\nabla_\theta = \frac{\partial}{\partial \theta}$ and the superscript H denotes the conjugate transpose operator. Indeed, the Fourier integral of $z(\tau,\theta)z(\nu,\theta)$ is the function $Z(\omega)Z(\omega)^H$.

Appendix C. Modified Algorithm Codes

```
space <-seq(0.62,62.83,by=0.01)
n <-length(space)
m <-3
MATRIX_F <- matrix(0 ^ 1i, n, m)

b1 <-100
b0 <-1000100
a0 <-1

j <-1
for(i in space)
{
f <-function(x)
c(complex(real=0,imaginary=x)/complex(real=a0,imaginary=x),
1/complex(real=a0,imaginary=x),
complex(real=b0,imaginary=b1*x)/
(complex(real=x,imaginary=-a0))^2)
```

```
          M_row <- f(i)
          MATRIX_F[j,] <- M_row
          j <- j+1
          }
```

Appendix C.1. REX

Modification of the FIM:

```
M <- (t(sqrt(w.supp)*Conj(Fx.supp)) %*% (sqrt(w.supp)*Fx.supp))
M <- Re(M)
```

Modification of the dispersion function:

```
Mp <- matrix(NA, n, 1)
for(i in 1:n) {
Mpp <- Fx[i,] %*% t(Conj(Fx[i,]))
Mpp <- Re(Mpp)
Z <- solve(M+E) %*% Mpp
traza <- sum(diag(Z))
Mp[i,] <- traza
}
```

Appendix C.2. KL

Modification of the FIM:

```
M1 <- t((w %*% one) * F) %*% Conj(F)
M2 <- Re(M1)
```

Modification of the dispersion function:

```
H <- Conj(F) %*% solve(M2 + E)
H2 <- H * F
d.fun <- apply(Re(H2), 1, sum)
```

References

1. Barsoukov, E.; Macdonald, J.R. *Impedance Spectroscopy: Theory, Experiment, and Applications*, 3rd ed.; John Wiley and Sons: Hoboken, NJ, USA, 2018.
2. Hernández-Balaguera, E.; López-Dolado, E.; Polo, J.L. Obtaining electrical equivalent circuits of biological tissues using the current interruption method, circuit theory and fractional calculus. *RSC Adv.* **2016**, *6*, 22312–22319. [CrossRef]
3. Hernández-Balaguera, E.; Polo, J.L. On the potential-step hold time when the transient-current response exhibits a Mittag-Leffler decay. *J. Electroanal. Chem.* **2020**, *856*, 113631.
4. Grimnes, S.; Martinsen, Ø.G. *Bioimpedance and Bioelectricity Basics*, 3rd ed.; Academic Press: London, UK, 2015.
5. Oppenheim, A.V.; Willsky, A.S.; Nawab, H. *Signals and Systems*, 2nd ed.; Prentice Hall: Upper Saddle Rider, NJ, USA, 1997.
6. Ferris, C.D. A General Definition for Impedance. *IEEE Trans. Educ.* **1964**, *E-7*, 6–8. [CrossRef]
7. Ziemer, R.E.; Tranter, W.H. *Principles of Communications Systems: Modulation, and Noise*, 7th ed.; John Wiley and Sons: Hoboken, NJ, USA, 2015.
8. Kalaba, R.; Spingarn, K. *Control, Identification, and Input Optimization*, 1st ed.; Plenum Press: New York, NY, USA, 1982.
9. Mehra, R.K. Optimal input signals for parameter estimation in dynamic systems-survey and new results. *IEEE Trans. Autom. Control* **1974**, *19*, 753–768. [CrossRef]
10. Mehra, R.K. Optimal inputs for linear system identification. *IEEE Trans. Autom. Control* **1974**, *19*, 192–200. [CrossRef]
11. Goodwin, G.C.; Payne, R.L. *Dynamic System Identification: Experiment Design and Data Analysis*, 1st ed.; Academic Press: New York, NY, USA, 1977.
12. Titterington, D.M. Aspects of Optimal Design in Dynamic Systems. *Technometrics* **1980**, *22*, 287–299. [CrossRef]
13. Rafajlowicz, E. Optimal experiment design for identification of linear distributed-parameter systems: Frequency domain approach. *IEEE Trans. Autom. Control* **1983**, *28*, 806–808. [CrossRef]
14. Walter, E.; Pronzato, L. *Identification of Parametric Models from Experimental Data*; Springer: Berlin/Heidelberg, Germany; New York, NY, USA, 1997.
15. Zarrop, M.B. *Optimal Experiment Design for Dynamic System Identification*; Springer: Berlin/Heidelberg, Germany; New York, NY, USA, 1979.

16. Gevers, M. Identification for control. From the early achievements to the revival of experimental design. *Eur. J. Control* **2005**, *11*, 335–352. [CrossRef]
17. Hjalmarsson, H. From experiment design to closed-loop control. *Automatica* **2005**, *41*, 393–438. [CrossRef]
18. Ljung, L. *System Identification, Theory for the User*, 2nd ed.; Prentice Hall: Upper Saddle Rider, NJ, USA, 1999.
19. Sanchez, B.; Vandersteen, G.; Bragos, R.; Schoukens, J. Optimal multisine excitation design for broadband electrical impedance spectroscopy. *Meas. Sci. Technol.* **2011**, *22*, 1156011. [CrossRef]
20. Sanchez, B.; Rojas, C.R.; Vandersteen, G.; Bragos, R.; Schoukens, J. On the calculation of the D-optimal multisine excitation power spectrum for broadband impedance spectroscopy measurements. *Meas. Sci. Technol.* **2012**, *23*, 085702. [CrossRef]
21. Kwon, H.; Rojas, C.R.; Butkove, S.B.; Sanchez, B. Three-harmonic optimal multisine input power spectrum for bioimpedance identification. *Physiol. Meas.* **2019**, *40*, 05NT02. [CrossRef] [PubMed]
22. Imhof, L.; Lopez-Fidalgo, J.; Wong, W.K. Efficiencies of optimal approximate designs for small samples. *Stat. Neerl.* **2001**, *55*, 301–318. [CrossRef]
23. Kay, S.M. *Fundamentals of Statistical Signal Processing: Estimation Theory*; Prentice Hall: Upper Saddle River, NJ, USA, 1993.
24. Kiefer, J.; Wolfowitz, J. Optimum Designs in Regression Problems. *Ann. Math. Stat.* **1959**, *30*, 271–294. [CrossRef]
25. Karlin, S.; Studden, W.J. Optimal Experimental Designs. *Ann. Math. Stat.* **1966**, *37*, 783–815. [CrossRef]
26. Fedorov, V.V. *Theory of Optimal Experiments*; Academic Press: New York, NY, USA, 1972.
27. Atwood, C.L. Optimal and Efficient Designs of Experiments. *Ann. Math. Stat.* **1969**, *40*, 1570–1602. [CrossRef]
28. Atkinson, A.C.; Donev, A.N.; Tobias, R.D. *Optimum Experimental Designs, with SAS*; Oxford University Press: New York, NY, USA, 2007.
29. Harman, R.; Filová, L.; Richtárik, P. A Randomized Exchange Algorithm for Computing Optimal Approximate Designs of Experiments. *J. Am. Stat. Assoc.* **2020**, *115*, 348–361. [CrossRef]
30. Böhning, D. A Vertex-Exchange-Method in D-optimal Design Theory. *Metrika* **1986**, *33*, 337–347. [CrossRef]

Discriminative Convolutional Sparse Coding of ECG Signals for Automated Recognition of Cardiac Arrhythmias

Bing Zhang and Jizhong Liu *

Nanchang Key Laboratory of Medical and Technology Research, School of Advanced Manufacturing, Nanchang University, Nanchang 330031, China
* Correspondence: liujizhong@ncu.edu.cn

Abstract: Electrocardiogram (ECG) is a common and powerful tool for studying heart function and diagnosing several abnormal arrhythmias. In this paper, we present a novel classification model that combines the discriminative convolutional sparse coding (DCSC) framework with the linear support vector machine (LSVM) classification strategy. In the training phase, most existing convolutional sparse coding frameworks are unsupervised in the sense that label information is ignored in the convolutional filter training stage. In this work, we explicitly incorporate a label consistency constraint called "discriminative sparse-code error" into the objective function to learn discriminative dictionary filters for sparse coding. The learned dictionary filters encourage signals from the same class to have similar sparse codes, and signals from different classes to have dissimilar sparse codes. To reduce the computational complexity, we propose to perform a max-pooling operation on the sparse coefficients. Using LSVM as a classifier, we examine the performance of the proposed classification system on the MIT-BIH arrhythmia database in accordance with the AAMI EC57 standard. The experimental results show that the proposed DCSC + LSVM algorithm can obtain 99.32% classification accuracy for cardiac arrhythmia recognition.

Keywords: electrocardiogram signal; discriminative convolutional sparse coding; dictionary filter learning; linear SVM

MSC: 68U01

1. Introduction

Electrocardiogram (ECG) is used to record cardiac activity and detect different abnormalities in cardiac function and is a commonly used non-invasive tool for non-invasive diagnosis of cardiac arrhythmias. However, visual analysis is extremely limited and imprecise due to the large amount of information contained in the ECG, which may lead to misdiagnosis or inaccurate detection of arrhythmias. Therefore, computer-aided analysis helps doctors to detect cardiac arrhythmias quickly and efficiently.

The automatic arrhythmia detection system mainly includes feature extraction, feature selection, and classifier construction. ECG signal feature extraction techniques can be divided into time-based methods [1–3], frequency methods [4–6], and time-frequency techniques [7,8]. The time domain features mainly include heartbeat interval, duration parameters, and amplitude parameters. Due to the subtle changes in ECG amplitude and duration, time-based methods do not provide good discrimination [9,10]. Therefore, frequency methods using such as Fourier transform and power spectral density (PSD) and time-frequency methods using wavelet transform are proposed. However, the frequency method does not provide time information from the ECG signal. Time-frequency technology based on wavelet transform is widely used in time-frequency feature extraction of ECG signals. Before the time-frequency feature vectors extracted by wavelet transform are applied to the classifier, it is important to choose the best dimensionality reduction method. Dimensionality reduction methods for linear and non-linear transforms based on wavelet transforms have been proposed [7,11–13]. Martis et al. [7] transformed the ECG heartbeat using DWT and then applied independent component analysis (ICA) methods to extract features. The experimental results show that the features extracted using the ICA method combined with a probabilistic neural network (PNN) have better classification results. In the classification step, the most commonly used techniques in ECG signal classification are support vector machines (SVM) [1,14] and artificial neural networks [15].

In this paper, unlike most existing methods, we propose a novel classification model that combines the discriminative convolutional sparse coding framework with the linear support vector machines (LSVM) classification strategy.

The convolutional sparse coding (CSC) model assumes that the signal can be represented as a superposition of a few local filters, convolved with sparse feature maps. The CSC model handles the signal globally, and yet pursuit and dictionary learning are feasible due to the specific structure of the dictionary involved. CSC has been utilized for a variety of computer vision and pattern recognition tasks, such as inpainting [16], image separation [17], image fusion [18], object recognition [19], pedestrian detection [20], and tissue classification [21].

Although the CSC model has achieved state-of-the-art performance in many fields, most of the existing CSC frameworks are unsupervised and ignore label information in the convolutional filter training stage. Chen et al. [22] proposed a novel convolutional sparse coding classification (CSCC) approach, which introduces label information during the training process. The results show that dictionaries trained by convolution with label information can obtain more representative image information and achieve better classification performance. However, in the CSCC model, a set of dictionary filters are trained for each class of data, and then the dictionary filters from all classes build the final discriminative filter bank. This is not an efficient approach. At the same time, the intra-class and inter-class information are not considered, so the coding coefficients have small within-class scatter but large between-class scatter.

How to improve the classification performance of convolutional sparse coding has become a research direction in this field. One of the solutions is to obtain a discriminative dictionary filter bank through training so that the samples of different classes encoded by the dictionary filter bank are discriminative. Methods for learning a discriminative dictionary for sparse coding from training data have been recently proposed. Zhang and Li [23] proposed a discriminative KSVD dictionary learning algorithm. The algorithm incorporated the "classification error" term into the objective function, obtained the dictionary through the KSVD algorithm, and finally realized the classification task through a linear classifier. Yang et al. [24] learned a structured dictionary with class labels by adding Fisher's discriminant criterion during encoding. The method considers the intra-class and inter-class information in the coding process so that the coding coefficients have small within-class scatter but large between-class scatter. Following the work in [23], Jiang et al. [25] proposed to incorporate a "discriminative sparse code error" term into the objective function to enhance the discriminative power. It forces the signals from the same class to have very similar sparse representations, which results in good classification performance even using a simple linear classifier.

Obtaining a discriminative dictionary for classification by sparse coding has been successfully applied and achieved excellent performance. However, the discriminative dictionary obtained by sparse coding also has shortcomings, that is, it cannot capture the shifted local features in the sample, and at the same time, for high-dimensional signals, there is a curse of dimensionality. The dictionary filter bank obtained by convolutional sparse coding has shift invariance, local features at the sample translation position are extracted by convolution, and there is no curse of dimensionality.

However, how to learn discriminative convolutional dictionary filters with convolutional sparse representation and classification functions by supervised training is still an issue worth investigating. In this work, we propose a discriminative convolutional sparse coding (DCSC) model to learn discriminative dictionary filters for sparse coding of ECG signals. Different from the CSCC algorithm, we explicitly incorporate a label consistency constraint called "discriminative sparse-code error" into the objective function, transform the DCSC model to the Fourier domain to reduce the computational cost [26], and optimize the DCSC model using the alternating direction method of the multiplier framework [27] (ADMM) algorithm. By adding label information to the training phase of the convolutional dictionary filters, the learned dictionary filters encourage signals from the same class to have similar sparse codes, and signals from different classes to have dissimilar sparse codes. To reduce the computational complexity, we use the max-pooling operation on the sparse coefficients. These pooled coefficients are then used as features and fed to an LSVM classifier for the ECG classification task.

Our contributions are as follows:

- We propose a discriminative convolutional sparse coding (DCSC) model in which the "discriminative sparse-code error" is inserted into the objective function.
- In the process of solving the objective function, the DCSC model is first transformed into the Fourier domain, the convolution operation is converted into a multiplication operation, and then the function solution is obtained using the alternating direction method of the multiplier framework.
- The discriminative sparse coefficients are obtained via convolutional sparse coding, then dimensionally reduced by the max-pooling method, and finally fed into the LSVM classifier to complete the ECG classification task.

The rest of the paper is organized as follows: Section 2 presents the background of CSC, CDL, and LC-KSVD. Section 3 describes the proposed DCSC model. Section 4 describes the experimental results. The conclusion is given in Section 5.

2. Literature Survey

2.1. Convolutional Sparse Coding

The convolutional sparse coding (CSC) model assumes that a signal $\mathbf{s} \in \Re^N$ can be represented by the sum of M convolutions. These are built by feature maps $\{\mathbf{x}_m\}$, each of length N, convolved with M small support filters $\{\mathbf{d}_m\}$ of length $n \ll N$, $*$ denotes convolution, and the CSC model can be formulated as:

$$\underset{\{\mathbf{x}_m\}}{\operatorname{argmin}} \frac{1}{2} \left\| \sum_m \mathbf{d}_m * \mathbf{x}_m - \mathbf{s} \right\|_2^2 + \lambda \sum_m \|\mathbf{x}_m\|_1 \qquad (1)$$

where $\lambda > 0$ is a regularization parameter. Given the filters, the above problem becomes the CSC pursuit task of finding the representations $\{\mathbf{x}_m\}$.

2.2. Convolutional Dictionary Learning

A common approach for convolutional dictionary learning (CDL) [26] entails using a batch of K training data to optimize the filters and sparse coefficient maps. This problem can be formulated as follows:

$$\underset{\{\mathbf{d}_m\},\{\mathbf{x}_{m,k}\}}{\operatorname{argmin}} \frac{1}{2} \sum_k \left\| \sum_m \mathbf{d}_m * \mathbf{x}_{m,k} - \mathbf{s}_k \right\|_2^2 + \lambda \sum_k \sum_m \|\mathbf{x}_{m,k}\|_1 \text{ such that } \|\mathbf{d}_m\|_2 = 1 \; \forall m \qquad (2)$$

where the constraint on the norms of dictionary filters $\{\mathbf{d}_m\}$ is required to avoid the scaling ambiguity between filters and coefficients. We denote the number of filters and the amount of training data by M and K, respectively.

The CDL problem is usually addressed by alternating optimization with respect to $\{\mathbf{x}_{m,k}\}$ and $\{\mathbf{d}_m\}$. Several works have shown that solving (2) with respect to $\{\mathbf{d}_m\}$ can also be done effectively and efficiently using ADMM in the frequency domain [26,28].

2.3. Label Consistent KSVD

Jiang et al. [25] proposed a label consistent KSVD (LC-KSVD1) algorithm to learn a discriminative dictionary. The objective function is defined as follows:

$$< \mathbf{D}, \mathbf{A}, \mathbf{X} > = \arg\min_{\mathbf{D},\mathbf{A},\mathbf{X}} ||\mathbf{S} - \mathbf{D}\mathbf{X}||_2^2 + \alpha ||\mathbf{Q} - \mathbf{A}\mathbf{X}||_2^2 \quad \text{s.t.} \ ||\mathbf{x}_i||_0 < T \qquad (3)$$

where $||\mathbf{S} - \mathbf{D}\mathbf{X}||_2^2$ denotes the reconstruction error and $\mathbf{D}$ is the learned dictionary. $||\mathbf{Q} - \mathbf{A}\mathbf{X}||_2^2$ represents the discriminative sparse-code error, $\mathbf{Q}$ are the "discriminative" sparse codes of input signals $\mathbf{S}$ used for classification, and $\mathbf{A}$ is a linear transformation matrix. α is the scalar that controls the relative contribution of the corresponding term. $\mathbf{X}$ are the sparse codes of input signals $\mathbf{S}$ and $\mathbf{x}_i$ is the column vector of $\mathbf{X}$. T is a sparsity constraint factor (each signal has fewer than T non-zero items in its decomposition). By adding a discriminative sparse-code error constraint, the LC-KSVD1 model has good classification performance even with a simple linear classifier.

3. The Proposed ECG Signal Classification System

The proposed DCSC-based automatic arrhythmia identification system framework is shown in Figure 1. The proposed method consists of four stages, namely (1) in the discriminative convolutional sparse dictionary filters learning stage, we trained the DCSC model to obtain a discriminative dictionary filter. (2) In the sparse coding stage, we used the CSC model to obtain the discriminative sparse coefficients of the training and the test signals. (3) Pooling was performed on those sparse coefficients to reduce the large amount of data to an appropriate level. More importantly, it is used to obtain a compact representation of features that are invariant to local transformations. (4) In the ECG heartbeat testing stage, we used the pooled coefficients as features and fed them to an LSVM classifier for ECG classification.

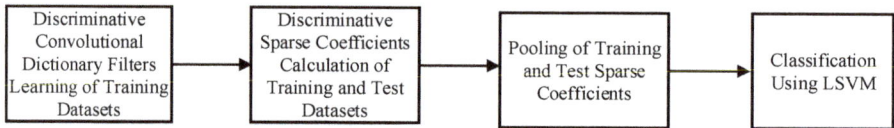

Figure 1. Block diagram of the proposed ECG classification system.

3.1. Discriminative Convolutional Sparse Dictionary Learning Model

To improve the discriminative properties of the convolutional sparse coefficients, we incorporate the discriminative terms into the objective function during training. It can be formulated as the following optimization problem:

$$\arg\min_{\{\mathbf{d}_m\},\{\mathbf{a}_m\},\{\mathbf{x}_{k,m}\}} \frac{1}{2} \sum_k \left\| \sum_m \mathbf{d}_m * \mathbf{x}_{m,k} - \mathbf{s}_k \right\|_2^2 + \frac{1}{2}\alpha \sum_k \left\| \sum_m \mathbf{a}_m * \mathbf{x}_{m,k} - \mathbf{q}_k \right\|_2^2 + \lambda \sum_k \sum_m ||\mathbf{x}_{m,k}||_1 \qquad (4)$$

such that $||\mathbf{d}_m||_2 = 1, ||\mathbf{a}_m||_2 = 1 \forall m$

where $\mathbf{s}_k$ is the kth training data set, $\mathbf{s}_k \in \Re^N$. $\lambda > 0$ is a regularization parameter and α is the scalar that controls the relative contribution of the corresponding terms. $\{\mathbf{d}_m\}$ and $\{\mathbf{a}_m\}$ are a set of M dictionary filters, and $\{\mathbf{x}_{m,k}\}$ is a set of coefficient maps corresponding to the mth dictionary filter and the kth training data, each having the same size as $\mathbf{s}_k$. $\mathbf{q}_k = [0, \ldots, 1, 1, \ldots, 0]^t \in \Re^N$ is a "discriminative" sparse code corresponding to an input signal $\mathbf{s}_k$, and $\mathbf{q}_k$ is the column vector of $\mathbf{Q}$, whose size is the same as $\mathbf{s}_k$. For example, assuming that $S = [s_0, s_1, s_2, s_3]$, where s_0, s_1 are from class 1, s_2, s_3 are from class 2, and the length of the training data set $N = 6$, then Q can be defined as:

$$Q = \begin{bmatrix} 1 & 1 & 0 & 0 \\ 1 & 1 & 0 & 0 \\ 1 & 1 & 0 & 0 \\ 0 & 0 & 1 & 1 \\ 0 & 0 & 1 & 1 \\ 0 & 0 & 1 & 1 \end{bmatrix} \quad (5)$$

The codes $\{x_{m,k}\}$ and the dictionary filters $\{d_m\}$ and $\{a_m\}$ can then be efficiently updated in an alternating manner, as follows.

A. Convolutional sparse coding (CSC) step

Given the dictionary filters $\{d_m\}$ and $\{a_m\}$, the codes can be updated by using ADMM in the frequency domain.

$$\underset{\{x_{m,k}\}}{\operatorname{argmin}} \frac{1}{2} \sum_k \left\| \sum_m d_m * x_{m,k} - s_k \right\|_2^2 + \frac{1}{2}\alpha \sum_k \left\| \sum_m a_m * x_{m,k} - q_k \right\|_2^2 + \lambda \sum_k \sum_m \left\| x_{m,k} \right\|_1 \quad (6)$$

If we define the linear operators D_m and A_m such that $D_m x_{m,k} = d_m * x_{m,k}$, $A_m x_{m,k} = a_m * x_{m,k}$, and denote

$$D = (D_0 \quad D_1 \quad \ldots), \; A = (A_0 \quad A_1 \quad \ldots), \; S = (s_0 \quad s_1 \quad \ldots), \; Q = (q_0 \quad q_1 \quad \ldots), \; X = \begin{pmatrix} x_{0,0} & x_{0,0} & \cdots \\ x_{1,0} & x_{0,0} & \cdots \\ \vdots & \vdots & \ddots \end{pmatrix} \quad (7)$$

then we can rewrite Equation (6) as

$$\underset{X}{\operatorname{argmin}} \frac{1}{2} \|DX - S\|_2^2 + \frac{1}{2}\alpha \|AX - Q\|_2^2 + \lambda \|X\|_1 \quad (8)$$

The ADMM algorithm and shrinkage/soft thresholding algorithm can be employed to solve Equation (8), as described in Appendix A.

B. Convolutional dictionary update (CDU) step

In developing the dictionary filter update, it is convenient to switch the index of the coefficient map from $\{x_{m,k}\}$ to $\{x_{k,m}\}$. With the codes fixed, the dictionary filters $\{d_m\}$ and $\{a_m\}$ can be updated by solving the following optimization problems,

$$\underset{\{d_m\},\{a_m\},\{x_{k,m}\}}{\operatorname{argmin}} \frac{1}{2} \sum_k \left\| \sum_m x_{k,m} * d_m - s_k \right\|_2^2 + \frac{1}{2}\alpha \sum_k \left\| \sum_m x_{k,m} * a_m - q_k \right\|_2^2 \quad (9)$$

$$\text{such that } \|d_m\|_2 = 1, \|a_m\|_2 = 1 \forall m$$

Updating $\{d_m\}$

With the $\{x_{k,m}\}$ and $\{a_m\}$ fixed, the dictionary filters $\{d_m\}$ can be updated by solving the following optimization problem,

$$\underset{\{d_m\}}{\operatorname{argmin}} \frac{1}{2} \sum_k \left\| \sum_m x_{k,m} * d_m - s_k \right\|_2^2 \text{ such that } \|d_m\|_2 = 1 \; \forall m \quad (10)$$

Addressing the CDL optimization problem (10) over $\{d_m\}$ is equivalent to solving the following optimization problem

$$\underset{\{d_m\}}{\operatorname{argmin}} \frac{1}{2} \sum_k \left\| \sum_m x_{k,m} * d_m - s_k \right\|_2^2 + \sum_m \iota_{CPN}(d_m) \quad (11)$$

where $\iota c_{PN}(\mathbf{d}_m)$ is an indicator function [26]. Problem (11) can be solved efficiently using the consensus ADMM method, please refer to Appendix B.

Updating $\{\mathbf{a}_m\}$

With the $\{\mathbf{x}_{k,m}\}$ and $\{\mathbf{d}_m\}$ fixed, the dictionary filters $\{\mathbf{a}_m\}$ can be updated by solving the following optimization problem,

$$\underset{\{\mathbf{a}_m\}}{\operatorname{argmin}} + \frac{1}{2}\sum_k \left\| \sum_m \mathbf{x}_{k,m} * \mathbf{a}_m - \mathbf{q}_k \right\|_2^2 \text{ such that } \|\mathbf{a}_m\|_2 = 1 \ \forall m \qquad (12)$$

Addressing the CDL optimization problem (12) over $\{\mathbf{a}_m\}$ is similar to problem (10), please refer to Appendix B.

Algorithm 1: The DCSC Algorithm.

Input: sample $\{\mathbf{s}_k\}$, parameters λ, α
Output: $\{\mathbf{d}_m\}$
Precompute: $\mathbf{s}_k \to \hat{\mathbf{s}}_k$, $\mathbf{q}_k \to \hat{\mathbf{q}}_k$,
Initialize: $\{\mathbf{Y}\} = \{\mathbf{U}\} = \{\mathbf{g}_m\} = \{\mathbf{h}_m\} = 0$,
while $j = 0$ to convergence **do**

    (CSC step)
    Compute FFTs of $\{\mathbf{Y}\} \to \{\hat{\mathbf{Y}}\}$, $\{\mathbf{U}\} \to \{\hat{\mathbf{U}}\}$, $\{\mathbf{d}_m\} \to \{\hat{\mathbf{D}}\}$, $\{\mathbf{a}_m\} \to \{\hat{\mathbf{A}}\}$
    Compute $\hat{\mathbf{X}}$ with the algorithm in Appendix A.
    Compute inverse FFTs of $\hat{\mathbf{X}} \to \mathbf{X}$
    $\mathbf{Y}^{(j+1)} = S_{\lambda/\rho}(\mathbf{X}^{(j+1)} + \mathbf{U}^{(j)})$
    $\mathbf{U}^{(j+1)} = \mathbf{U}^{(j)} + \mathbf{X}^{(j+1)} - \mathbf{Y}^{(j+1)}$
    (CDU step)
    Compute FFTs of $\{\mathbf{x}_{k,m}\} \to \{\hat{\mathbf{X}}_k\}$, $\{\mathbf{g}_m\} \to \{\hat{\mathbf{g}}_m\}$, $\{\mathbf{h}_m\} \to \{\hat{\mathbf{h}}_m\}$
    Compute $\hat{\mathbf{d}}$ with the algorithm in Appendix B.
    Compute inverse FFTs of $\hat{\mathbf{d}} \to \{\mathbf{d}_m\}$
    Compute $\{\mathbf{g}_m\}$ with the algorithm in Appendix B.
    $\mathbf{h}_m^{(j+1)} = \mathbf{h}_m^{(j)} + \mathbf{d}_m^{(j+1)} - \mathbf{g}_m^{(j+1)}$
    Compute $\{\mathbf{a}_m\}$

end

We trained the DCSC algorithm with the training data and obtained the dictionary filters. The dictionary filters $\{\mathbf{d}_m\}$ were then used to obtain the sparse coefficients of both the training and test signals for each class in the sparse coding stage.

3.2. Sparse Coding of Training and Test Signals

We obtained $\{\mathbf{d}_m\}$ by employing the DCSC algorithm (Algorithm 1). Sparse coefficient vectors $\{\mathbf{x}_{m,k}\}$ for each signal were obtained by using the CSC algorithm as follows:

$$\underset{\{\mathbf{x}_{m,k}\}}{\operatorname{argmin}} \frac{1}{2} \sum_k \left\| \sum_m \mathbf{d}_m * \mathbf{x}_{m,k} - \mathbf{s}_k \right\|_2^2 + \lambda \sum_k \sum_m \|\mathbf{x}_{m,k}\|_1 \qquad (13)$$

The sparse coefficient vectors of each signal thus obtained were then combined column-wise to form a vector of larger dimensions. This process is depicted in Figure 2. The sparse coefficients of these training data were used to train the LSVM model for ECG classification.

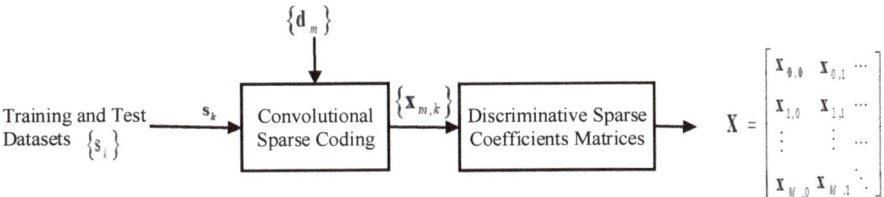

Figure 2. Extraction of sparse coefficients using convolutional sparse coding.

3.3. Pooling of Coefficient Matrix

Inspired by the feature extraction methods [29,30], we apply max-pooling methods to each column of the sparse coefficient matrix X.

The max-pooling function

$$\mathbf{f}_k = \max(\mathbf{x}_k^{n \times 1} u(n,1)) \qquad (14)$$

applies a window function $u(n,1)$ to each column of the sparse coefficient matrix X and computes the maximum value in the neighborhood.

These pooled features can then be ℓ_2 normalized by

$$\mathbf{f}_k = \mathbf{f}_k / \|\mathbf{f}_k\|_2 \qquad (15)$$

These pooled sparse coefficients from each sub-region are concatenated and normalized to the final feature representation for the classification.

3.4. Classification by LSVM

The schematic diagram of the proposed ECG classification system is shown in Figure 3. By learning discriminative dictionary filters, it forces signals from the same class to have very similar sparse representations, so we use the LSVM for our ECG classification task. In the classification stage, each class in the training dataset contains 300 training samples, and the test dataset contains 51,722 ECG segments.

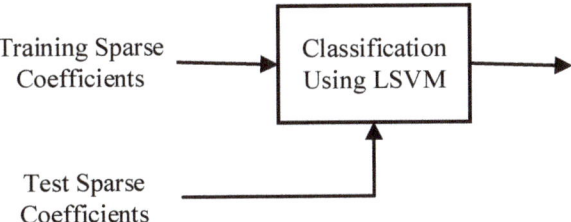

Figure 3. ECG classification using LSVM.

4. Experiments and Discussion

In this section, we test on the PhysioNet MIT-BIH arrhythmia database and compare the performance of the DCSC + LSVM method with other state-of-the-art classifiers.

4.1. Dataset

The proposed methodology is validated on the PhysioNet MIT-BIH Arrhythmia database [31] comprising 48 ECG records of about 30 min, sampled at 360 Hz with 11-bit resolution from 47 different patients. As recommended by the American Association of Medical Instrumentation (AAMI) [32], the MIT-BIH arrhythmia database is projected into five AAMI heartbeat classes, as described in Table 1. The ECG signal downloaded from the MIT-BIH database is processed with the help of wavelet techniques to remove baseline wander and high-frequency noise. The ECG signals sampled at 360 Hz were decomposed up to eight levels using the Bior2.6 wavelet to remove various kinds of noise [33]. The ECG would not contain much information after 45 Hz. The high-frequency noise is removed by excluding the first and second detail coefficients, which consist of bands of 90–180 Hz and 45–90 Hz. The baseline wander is removed by excluding the approximate coefficients at the fourth level. After the corresponding wavelet reconstruction, it is obvious that we can obtain a denoised ECG signal. Then, the R-peak is detected from the denoised ECG signal followed by a window across each R-peak to isolate the ECG segments for processing. After detection of the QRS complex, 99 samples preceded the QRS peak and 180 samples after the peak, and the QRS peak itself are considered as 280 samples segment as a single beat for subsequent analysis. The mapping of the MIT-BIH arrhythmia database into the AAMI recommendations along with the summary of the training and testing datasets for five classes is summarized in Table 2.

Table 1. Heartbeats of the MIT-BIH arrhythmia database classified based on the ANSI/AAMI EC57:1998 standard.

N	S	V	F	Q
• Normal • Left bundle branch block • Right bundle branch block • Nodal (junctional) escape beat • Atrial escape beat	• Atrial premature beat • Aberrated atrial premature beat • Nodal (Junctional) premature beat • Supraventricular premature beat	• Premature ventricular contraction • Ventricular escape beat	• Fusion of ventricular and normal beat	• Paced beat • Fusion of paced and normal beat • Unclassifiable beat

Table 2. A summary of the 5 classes of beat subtypes.

AAMI Classes	Training Data	Testing Data	Total Data
N	300	40,212	40,512
S	300	1388	1688
V	300	4610	4910
F	300	501	801
Q	300	5011	5311
Total	1500	51,722	53,222

4.2. Signal Preprocessing

Roshan et al. [7,11] pointed out that through wavelet transform decomposition, the power spectral density of each type of different heartbeat has discriminative information in these two sub-bands (level 4 approximation and detail), and independent component analysis (ICA) based on wavelet transform coefficients has strong robustness and high classification accuracy. Each beat consisting of 280 samples was decomposed into four levels using the FIR approximation of Mayer's wavelet ("dmey"). The ICA method was applied independently to the two DWT sub-bands, the fourth level approximation, and the details [7]. From each of the sub-bands fifteen ICA components were selected, so a total of thirty features from the two sub-bands were selected for subsequent pattern recognition.

4.3. Parameter Selection

In the first set of experiments reported in Figure 4, we compare the effects of λ and α values on classification accuracy. The λ and α values vary from 10^{-5} to 0. We can observe that good performance is achieved at $\lambda = 10^{-1}$ and $\alpha = 10^{-2}$.

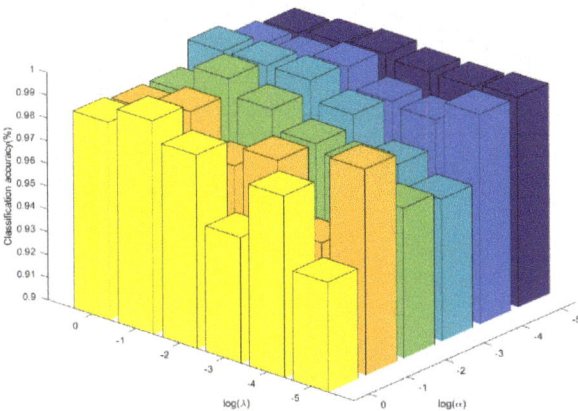

Figure 4. Effects of λ and α parameter selection on classification accuracy.

The effect of the number of iterations on the classification accuracy is shown in Figure 5. With the increase in the number of iterations, the accuracy also increases. When the number of iterations increases to 130, the accuracy rate changes very little and stabilizes to a certain value. In order to balance accuracy and complexity, the number of iterations was fixed at 130.

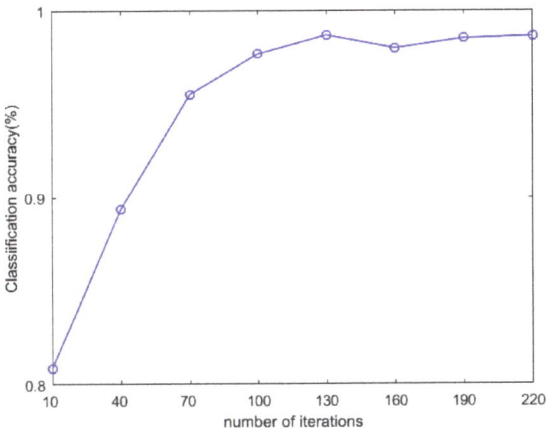

Figure 5. The effect of the number of iterations on the classification accuracy.

Figure 6 shows the classification accuracy when the variable dictionary filter dimension is changed from 6 to 20. In this experiment, we choose the dictionary size $M = 128$, and the number of training samples per class is 300. However, the overall trend is that the dictionary filter dimension has little effect on the classification performance.

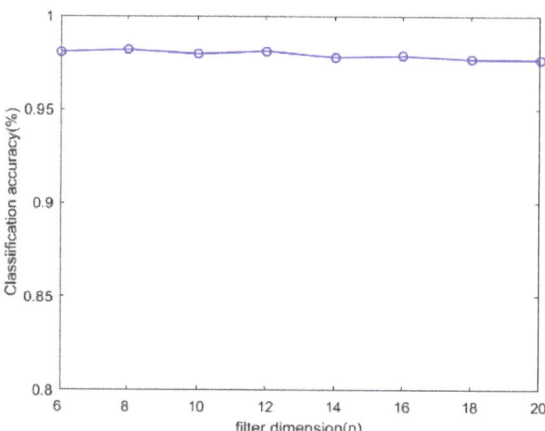

Figure 6. Classification accuracy based on variable dictionary filter dimension.

Figure 7 shows the classification results for the variable dictionary size M changing from 128 to 576. We can see that DCSC + LSVM shows an improvement of about 2.3% over LC-KSVD in all cases. In particular, even with the dictionary size $M = 128$, DCSC + LSVM can still have higher classification accuracy than LC-KSVD with $M = 576$. Moreover, from dictionary size $M = 576$ to $M = 128$, the recognition rate of DCSC + LSVM drops by 1.41%, while that of LC-KSVD drops by 6.25%. In the following classification experiments, we choose the dictionary filter dimension $M = 128$.

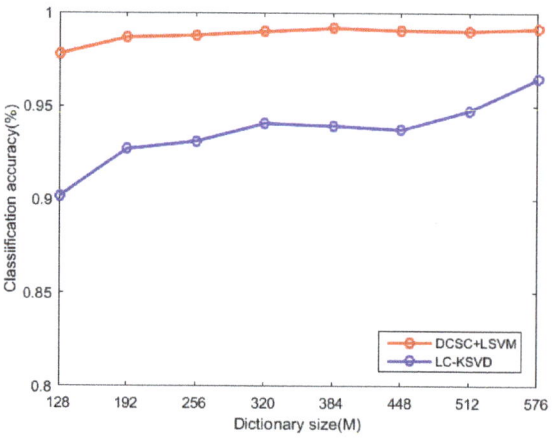

Figure 7. Classification accuracy based on variable dictionary size M.

Figure 8 shows the classification results with different numbers of training samples per class. We trained 100, 150, 200, 250, 300, 350, and 400 samples per class. We can see that the different number of training samples per class has little effect on the classification performance of the DCSC + LSVM algorithm, and in all cases, the classification results of the DCSC + LSVM algorithm outperform the LC-KSVD algorithm. The classification performance of the LC-KSVD algorithm is strongly influenced by the number of training samples per class. When the number of training samples per class is less than 250, the classification results of the LC-KSVD algorithm differ from those of the DCSC + LSVM algorithm by a maximum of 9%. In the following classification experiments, we set 300 training samples per class for training.

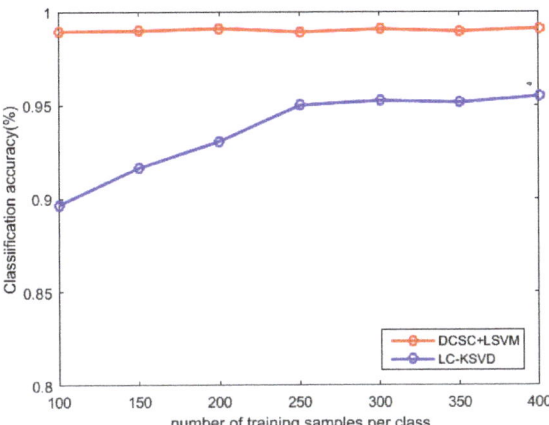

Figure 8. Classification accuracy based on different numbers of training samples per class.

Figure 9 shows the effect of pooling kernel size on classification accuracy. In this experiment, the pooling stride is 2, and the pooling kernel is increased from 3 to 8. It can be seen from Figure 9 that with the increase of the pooling kernel, the classification accuracy decreases. At the same time, comparing the effects of max pooling and average pooling on the classification accuracy, it can be seen that the classification effect of max pooling is better than that of average pooling. So, we choose the max-pooling method, and the pooling kernel is set to 3.

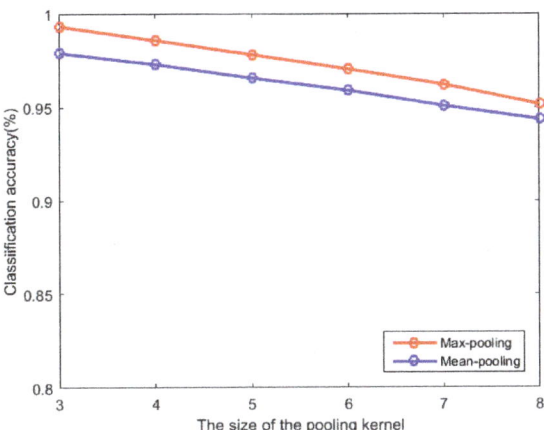

Figure 9. Effects of the Pooling Kernel Size on the Classification Accuracy.

4.4. Statistical Parameters

In order to analyze the performance of the classifiers, four evaluation metrics are used: sensitivity (SEN), positive predictive value (PPV), F_1, and accuracy (Acc). The SEN, PPV, F_1, and Acc can be written as

$$SEN = TP/(TP + FN) \times 100 \tag{16}$$

$$PPV = TP/(TP + FP) \times 100 \tag{17}$$

$$F_1 = 2TP/(2TP + FP + FN) \times 100 \tag{18}$$

$$Acc = (TP + TN)/(TP + FP + FN + TN) \times 100 \qquad (19)$$

where true positive (TP) corresponds to the number of times that the classifier correctly predicts a heartbeat without arrhythmia, i.e., normal. False positive (FP) gives the number of arrhythmic heartbeats classified as normal. True negative (TN) quantifies the number of heartbeats with arrhythmia that are predicted correctly. False negative (FN) indicates the total of normal beats misclassified as arrhythmic. F_1 being defined as the harmonic mean of precision and sensitivity.

4.5. Results

We evaluated our approach on the PhysioNet MIT-BIH arrhythmia database and compared our approach with LC-KSVD [25], Fisher discrimination dictionary learning (FDDL) [24], class-specific dictionary learning (CSDL) [34], Euler label consistent KSVD (ELC-KSVD) [35], convolutional sparse coding classification (CSCC) [22], label embedded dictionary learning (LEDL) [36]. The hardware platform is Intel Xeon Gold 5122 CPU 3.60 GHz, 128.0 GB RAM, and the experimental analysis is performed by the MATLAB 2015b software package installed on the Windows 10 21H2 Microsoft USA platform. During the experiment, we also adjust the parameters of other classifiers to obtain the best classification effect. For example, in the LC-KSVD algorithm, $\alpha = 2^{-2}$ and $\beta = 2^{-6}$. In the FDDL algorithm, $\lambda_1 = 0.005$, $\lambda_2 = 0.05$. In the CSDL algorithm, $\alpha = 2^{-8}$. In the ELC-KSVD algorithm, $\alpha = 10^{-1}$, $\beta = 10^{-4}$, $\gamma = 2^{-6}$. In the LEDL algorithm, $\lambda = 10^{-1}$, $\omega = 10^{-5}$, and $\varepsilon = 10^{-3}$. The number of atoms per class for the FDDL, CSDL, and CSCC algorithms is the same as the number of training samples per class, which is 300. The dictionary atomic number of LC-KSVD, ELC-KSVD, and LEDL algorithms is set to 1500. The experimental results are as follows.

Figure 10 illustrates the confusion matrix using the LSVM method. The test dataset contains 51,722 ECG signal segments, the accuracy of the LSVM method was 87.09%, and 45,044 ECG signals were correctly classified. Figure 11 demonstrates the confusion matrix using the LC-KSVD method. The accuracy of the LC-KSVD method was 96.97%, and 50,156 ECG signals were correctly classified. Figure 12 illustrates the confusion matrix using the FDDL method. The accuracy of the FDDL method was 98.80%, and 51,100 ECG signals were correctly classified. Figure 13 illustrates the confusion matrix using the CSDL method. The accuracy of the CSDL method was 94.15%, and 48,698 ECG signals were correctly classified. Figure 14 illustrates the confusion matrix using the ELC-KSVD method. The accuracy of the ELC-KSVD method was 99.02%, and 51,213 ECG signals were correctly classified. Figure 15 illustrates the confusion matrix using the CSCC method. The accuracy of the CSCC method was 94.70%, and 48,983 ECG signals were correctly classified. Figure 16 illustrates the confusion matrix using the LEDL method. The accuracy of the LEDL method was 95.17%, and 49,222 ECG signals were correctly classified. Figure 17 illustrates the confusion matrix using the DCSC + LSVM method. The accuracy of the DCSC + LSVM method was 99.32%, and 51,371 ECG signals were correctly classified.

	N	S	V	F	Q
N	36,463	451	32	1588	1678
S	98	1168	0	71	51
V	958	38	2251	701	662
F	8	0	0	491	2
Q	142	33	47	118	4671

Figure 10. Confusion matrix using the LSVM model.

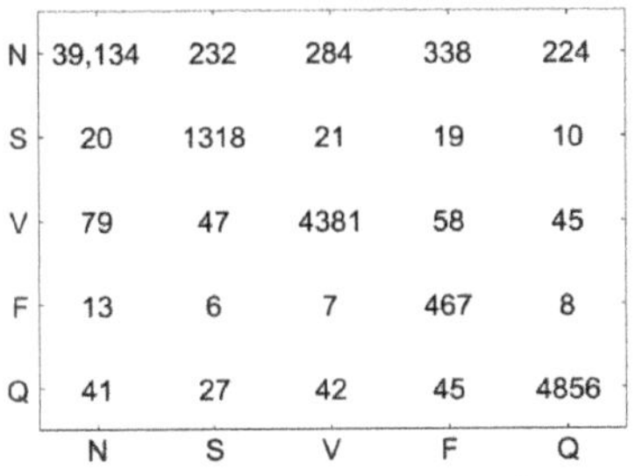

	N	S	V	F	Q
N	39,134	232	284	338	224
S	20	1318	21	19	10
V	79	47	4381	58	45
F	13	6	7	467	8
Q	41	27	42	45	4856

Figure 11. Confusion matrix using the LC-KSVD model.

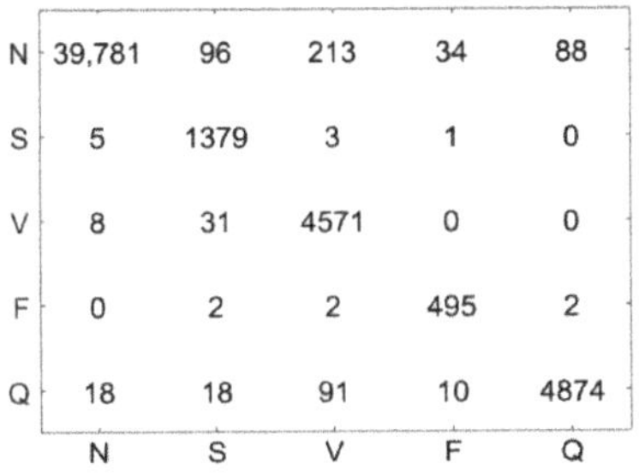

	N	S	V	F	Q
N	39,781	96	213	34	88
S	5	1379	3	1	0
V	8	31	4571	0	0
F	0	2	2	495	2
Q	18	18	91	10	4874

Figure 12. Confusion matrix using the FDDL model.

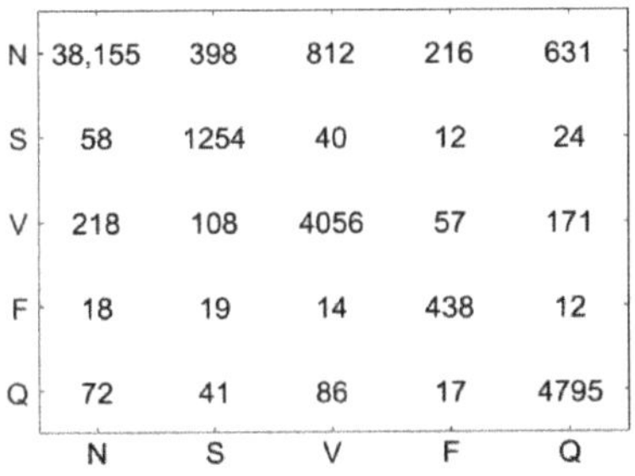

	N	S	V	F	Q
N	38,155	398	812	216	631
S	58	1254	40	12	24
V	218	108	4056	57	171
F	18	19	14	438	12
Q	72	41	86	17	4795

Figure 13. Confusion matrix using the CSDL model.

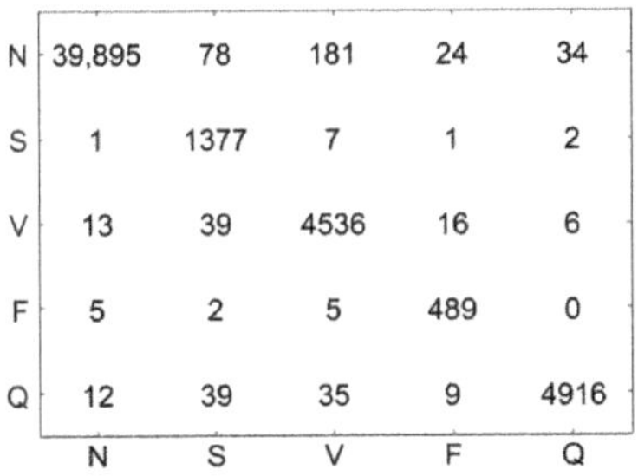

	N	S	V	F	Q
N	39,895	78	181	24	34
S	1	1377	7	1	2
V	13	39	4536	16	6
F	5	2	5	489	0
Q	12	39	35	9	4916

Figure 14. Confusion matrix using the ELC-KSVD model.

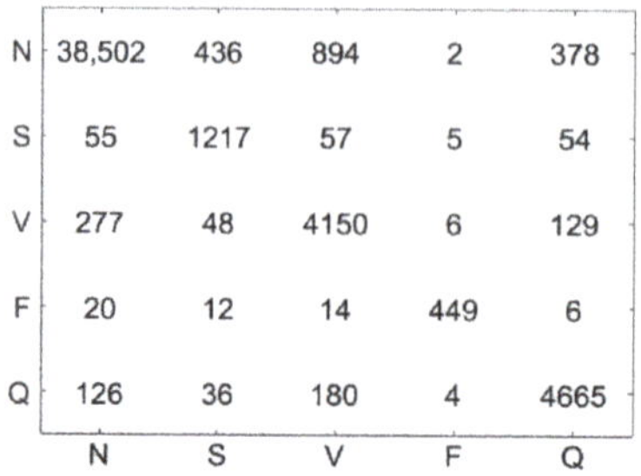

	N	S	V	F	Q
N	38,502	436	894	2	378
S	55	1217	57	5	54
V	277	48	4150	6	129
F	20	12	14	449	6
Q	126	36	180	4	4665

Figure 15. Confusion matrix using the CSCC model.

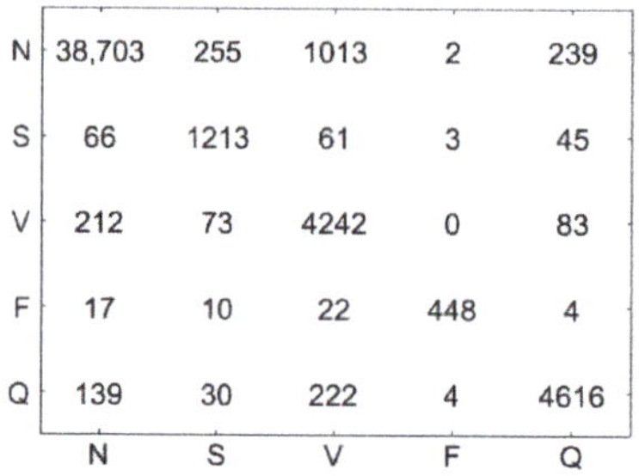

	N	S	V	F	Q
N	38,703	255	1013	2	239
S	66	1213	61	3	45
V	212	73	4242	0	83
F	17	10	22	448	4
Q	139	30	222	4	4616

Figure 16. Confusion matrix using the LEDL model.

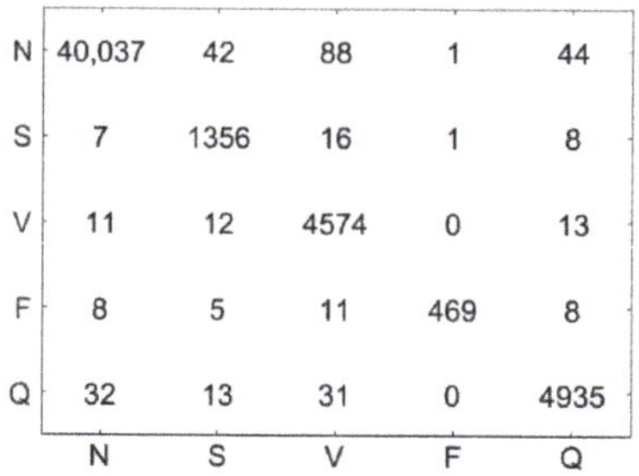

	N	S	V	F	Q
N	40,037	42	88	1	44
S	7	1356	16	1	8
V	11	12	4574	0	13
F	8	5	11	469	8
Q	32	13	31	0	4935

Figure 17. Confusion matrix using the DCSC + LSVM model.

Table 3 shows the classification performance (Acc, SEN, PPV, and F_1) obtained by different models on the test dataset. Compared with the LSVM algorithm, after DCSC coding, the classification accuracy is improved by 12.23%. Meanwhile, compared with LC-KSVD, FDDL, CSDL, ELC-KSVD, CSCC and LEDL, the accuracy of the proposed DCSC + LSVM is improved by 2.35%, 0.52%, 5.17%, 0.3%, 4.62%, and 4.15%, respectively. The disadvantage is that 32 S-class and 32 F-class ECG beats are misclassified. This explains why the SEN of class S and class F are lower, and this also affects the PPV value of class N and Q. Future efforts will look for discriminable features which get higher accuracy for classifying these beats.

In this system, to complete the classification of a segment of ECG signal, it needs to go through four stages, namely, the DWT feature extraction stage, the DCSC encoding stage, the pooling stage, and the classification stage. Since the test results of the same ECG signal were slightly different each time, we calculated the average of 10 test times as the final time. Table 4 lists the calculation time of each stage. The results show that the DCSC coding stage requires the longest computation time, the classification stage requires the shortest computation time due to the use of the linear SVM classifier, and a segment of ECG signal needs 0.336 s to complete the classification process.

Table 3. Performance metrics of different algorithms.

Method	Acc	N			S			V			F			Q		
	%	SEN	PPV	F_1	SEN	PPV	F_1	SEN	PPV	F_1	SEN	PPV	F_1	SEN	PPV	F_1
LSVM	87.09	90.68	96.80	93.64	84.15	69.11	75.89	48.83	96.61	64.87	98.00	16.54	28.30	93.21	66.12	77.37
LC-KSVD	96.97	97.32	99.61	98.45	94.96	80.86	87.34	95.03	92.52	93.76	93.21	50.38	65.41	96.91	94.42	95.65
FDDL	98.80	98.93	99.92	99.42	99.35	90.37	94.65	99.15	93.67	96.33	98.80	91.67	95.10	97.27	98.19	97.72
CSDL	94.15	94.88	99.05	96.92	90.35	68.90	78.18	87.98	80.99	84.34	87.43	59.19	70.59	95.69	85.12	90.10
ELC-KSVD	99.02	99.21	99.92	99.57	99.21	89.71	94.22	98.39	95.21	96.78	97.60	90.72	94.04	98.10	99.15	98.63
CSCC	94.70	95.75	98.77	97.24	87.68	69.58	77.59	90.02	78.38	83.80	89.62	96.35	92.86	93.10	89.16	91.09
LEDL	95.17	96.25	98.89	97.55	87.39	76.72	81.71	92.02	76.29	83.42	89.42	98.03	93.53	92.12	92.56	92.34
DCSC + LSVM	99.32	99.56	99.86	99.71	97.69	94.96	96.31	99.22	96.91	98.05	93.61	99.58	96.50	98.48	98.54	98.51

Table 4. Computation time for each stage for a test sample.

Methods	DWT + ICA	DCSC	Pooling	Classification
Time(s)	0.058	0.198	0.078	0.002

4.6. Discussion

In this work, we explicitly incorporated a label consistency constraint called "discriminative sparse-code error" into the objective function of learning discriminative dictionary filters for sparse coding. The learned dictionary filters encouraged signals from the same class to have similar sparse codes, and signals from different classes to have dissimilar sparse codes. These discriminative coding coefficients allowed us to obtain good classification results even with simple linear classifiers. Compared with the LSVM algorithm, after DCSC coding, the classification accuracy is improved by 12.23%, which means that by adding label information, after DCSC coding, the coding coefficients of different classes have more obvious differences. Compared with the CSCC algorithm, the algorithm trains filter banks for each class separately but does not use the intra-class and inter-class information of the training samples during the training process, so it does not achieve good classification results. The FDDL, LC-KSVD, CSDL, ELC-KSVD, and LEDL algorithms are all supervised training algorithms and incorporate label information. The reason why their classification effect is lower than the DCSC + LSVM algorithm is that the dictionary filter bank has shift-invariance. The local features at translated positions of the sample can be extracted through the convolution operation, so a better classification effect can be obtained. We also arranged comparative experiments between DCSC + LSVM algorithm and the LC-KSVD algorithm under different dictionary sizes and different training numbers. The experimental results show that the discriminative convolutional dictionary-based learning model can obtain better classification results than LC-KSVD at a smaller dictionary size. At the same time, it is less affected by the number of training datasets. This shows that the DCSC + LSVM algorithm can be applied to a database with a small number of samples.

A comprehensive summary of the automated classification of ECG beats using the MIT-BIH arrhythmia database is shown in Table 5. Mathews et al. [7] used ICA on DWT coefficients to extract features and reported an accuracy of 99.28% using the PNN classifier. Desai et al. [37] also used ICA on DWT coefficients to extract features and obtained 98.49% accuracy using SVM quadratic kernels. Elhaj et al. [38] used PCA on DWT and ICA on HOS cumulants as features and obtained 98.91% accuracy using the SVM-RBF classifier. Acharya et al. [39] classified with an accuracy of 94.03% using a 9-layer deep convolutional neural network. Kachuee et al. [40] used a deep residual CNN network to classify with an accuracy of 93.40%. Yildirim et al. [41] used CAE and LSTM networks to classify with an accuracy of 99.00%. Romdhane et al. [42] classified with an accuracy of 98.41% using a deep CNN model and a focal loss function. Li et al. [43] used a deep residual network to classify with an accuracy of 99.06%.

Table 5. Comparison of works on ECG heartbeat classification from MIT-BIH.

Literature	Features	Classifier	Classes	Acc
Mathews et al. [7]	DWT + ICA	PNN	5	99.28
Desai et al. [37]	DWT + ICA	SVM quadratic kernel	5	98.49
Elhaj et al. [38]	PCA + DWT + HOS + ICA	SVM-RBF	5	98.91
Acharya et al. [39]		9-layer deep convolutional neural network	5	94.03
M. Kachuee et al. [40]		deep residual CNN	5	93.40
Yıldırım et al. [41]		CAE and LSTM	5	99.00
Romdhane et al. [42]		Deep CNN	5	98.41
Li et al. [43]		Deep residual network	5	99.06
Proposed	DWT + ICA	DCSC + LSVM	5	99.32

The results show that the proposed model achieves higher classification accuracy compared to existing works presented in the literature and can be utilized for automated computer-aided diagnosis of several cardiovascular diseases.

5. Conclusions

In this paper, we present a novel classification model that combines the DCSC model with the LSVM classification strategy. In this work, we explicitly incorporate a label consistency constraint called "discriminative sparse-code error" into the objective function and transform the DCSC model into the Fourier domain to reduce the computational cost and optimize the DCSC model using the ADMM algorithm. By adding label information to the training phase of the convolutional dictionary filters, the learned dictionary filters encourage signals from the same class to have similar sparse codes, and signals from different classes to have dissimilar sparse codes. To reduce the computational complexity, we used a max-pooling operation for the sparse coefficients. These pooled coefficients were then used as features and fed to the LSVM classifier for the ECG classification task. The evaluation and experiments on the MIT-BIH arrhythmia database for the five classes as recommended by AAMI validate the effectiveness of the proposed DCSC + LSVM method and show that the proposed DCSC + LSVM model outperforms LSVM, LC-KSVD, FDDL, CSDL, ELC-KSVD, CSCC, LEDL and achieves state-of-the-art performance.

Author Contributions: Conceptualization, B.Z. and J.L.; methodology, B.Z. and J.L.; software, B.Z. and J.L.; validation, B.Z.; investigation, B.Z. and J.L.; writing—original draft preparation, B.Z.; writing—review and editing, B.Z. All authors have read and agreed to the published version of the manuscript.

Funding: This work was supported by the National Natural Science Foundation of China (Grant no. 61863027), the Key Research and Development Plan of Jiangxi Province (Grant no. 20202BBGL73057), the Natural Science Foundation of Jiangxi Province (Grant no. 20171BAB201013), and the Project of Nanchang Key Laboratory of Medical and Technology Research (Grant no. 2018-NCZDSY-002).

Institutional Review Board Statement: Not applicable.

Informed Consent Statement: Not applicable.

Conflicts of Interest: The authors declare that there are no conflicts of interest regarding the publication of this paper.

Appendix A. The Coding Algorithm

Using variable splitting, problem (8) in ADMM form can be reformulated as follows:

$$\underset{\mathbf{X}}{\operatorname{argmin}} \frac{1}{2} \|\mathbf{DX} - \mathbf{S}\|_2^2 + \frac{1}{2}\alpha \|\mathbf{AX} - \mathbf{Q}\|_2^2 + \lambda \|\mathbf{Y}\|_1 \quad \text{s.t.} \quad \mathbf{X} - \mathbf{Y} = 0 \qquad (A1)$$

for which we have the ADMM iterations with dual variables $\mathbf{U}$, which are

$$\mathbf{X}^{(j+1)} = \underset{\{\mathbf{x}_m\}}{\operatorname{argmin}} \frac{1}{2}\|\mathbf{DX} - \mathbf{S}\|_2^2 + \frac{1}{2}\alpha\|\mathbf{AX} - \mathbf{Q}\|_2^2 + \frac{\rho}{2}\sum_m \|\mathbf{X} - \mathbf{Y}^{(j)} + \mathbf{U}^{(j)}\|_2^2 \tag{A2}$$

$$\mathbf{Y}^{(j+1)} = \underset{\{\mathbf{y}_m\}}{\operatorname{argmin}} \lambda \sum_m \|\mathbf{Y}\|_1 + \frac{\rho}{2}\sum_m \|\mathbf{X}^{(j+1)} - \mathbf{Y} + \mathbf{U}^{(j)}\|_2^2 \tag{A3}$$

$$\mathbf{U}^{(j+1)} = \mathbf{U}^{(j)} + \mathbf{X}^{(j+1)} - \mathbf{Y}^{(j+1)} \tag{A4}$$

Sub-problem Equation (A3) is solved via shrinkage/soft thresholding as

$$\mathbf{Y}^{(j+1)} = S_{\lambda/\rho}(\mathbf{X}^{(j+1)} + \mathbf{U}^{(j)}) \tag{A5}$$

where

$$S_\gamma(\mathbf{u}) = sign(\mathbf{u}) \odot \max(0, |\mathbf{u}| - \gamma) \tag{A6}$$

with $sign(\cdot)$ and $|\cdot|$ of a vector being considered to be applied element-wise and $\odot$ denoting element-wise multiplication.

The most computationally expensive step is Equation (A2), which requires solving the linear system

$$(\mathbf{D}^T\mathbf{D} + \alpha\mathbf{A}^T\mathbf{A} + \rho\mathbf{I})\mathbf{X} = \mathbf{D}^T\mathbf{S} + \alpha\mathbf{A}^T\mathbf{Q} + \rho(\mathbf{Y} - \mathbf{U}) \tag{A7}$$

Since $\mathbf{D}^T\mathbf{D}$ is a very large matrix, it is impractical to solve this linear system using the approaches that are effective when $\mathbf{D}$ is not a convolutional dictionary. An obvious approach is to attempt to efficiently implement convolution via the DFT convolution theorem using the Fast Fourier Transform (FFT). The variables $\mathbf{D}$, $\mathbf{A}$, $\mathbf{X}$, $\mathbf{S}$, $\mathbf{Q}$, $\mathbf{Y}$, and $\mathbf{U}$ in the DFT domain are denoted by $\hat{\mathbf{D}}$, $\hat{\mathbf{A}}$, $\hat{\mathbf{X}}$, $\hat{\mathbf{S}}$, $\hat{\mathbf{Q}}$, $\hat{\mathbf{Y}}$, and $\hat{\mathbf{U}}$, respectively. It is easy to demonstrate via the DFT convolution theorem that Equation (A7) is equivalent to

$$(\hat{\mathbf{D}}^H\hat{\mathbf{D}} + \alpha\hat{\mathbf{A}}^H\hat{\mathbf{A}} + \rho\mathbf{I})\hat{\mathbf{X}} = \hat{\mathbf{D}}^H\hat{\mathbf{S}} + \alpha\hat{\mathbf{A}}^H\hat{\mathbf{Q}} + \rho(\hat{\mathbf{Y}} - \hat{\mathbf{U}}) \tag{A8}$$

Appendix B. Convolutional form of Method of Optimal Directions

The consensus ADMM formulation of problem (11) is given as

$$\underset{\{\mathbf{d}_m\},\{\mathbf{g}_m\}}{\operatorname{argmin}} \frac{1}{2}\sum_k \left\|\sum_m \mathbf{x}_{k,m} * \mathbf{d}_m - \mathbf{s}_k\right\|_2^2 + \sum_m \iota_{C_{PN}}(\mathbf{g}_m) \text{ s.t. } \mathbf{d}_m - \mathbf{g}_m = 0 \; \forall m \tag{A9}$$

with ADMM iterations

$$\{\mathbf{d}_m\}^{(j+1)} = \underset{\{\mathbf{d}_m\}}{\operatorname{argmin}} \frac{1}{2}\sum_k \left\|\sum_m \mathbf{x}_{k,m} * \mathbf{d}_m - \mathbf{s}_k\right\|_2^2 + \frac{\sigma}{2}\sum_m \|\mathbf{d}_m - \mathbf{g}_m^{(j)} + \mathbf{h}_m^{(j)}\|_2^2 \tag{A10}$$

$$\{\mathbf{g}_m\}^{(j+1)} = \underset{\{\mathbf{g}_m\}}{\operatorname{argmin}} \frac{1}{2}\sum_m \iota_{C_{PN}}(\mathbf{g}_m) + \frac{\sigma}{2}\sum_m \|\mathbf{d}_m^{(j+1)} - \mathbf{g}_m + \mathbf{h}_m^{(j)}\|_2^2 \tag{A11}$$

$$\mathbf{h}_m^{(j+1)} = \mathbf{h}_m^{(j)} + \mathbf{d}_m^{(j+1)} - \mathbf{g}_m^{(j+1)} \tag{A12}$$

The problem with the $\{\mathbf{d}_m\}$ update is of the form

$$\underset{\{\mathbf{d}_m\}}{\operatorname{argmin}} \frac{1}{2}\sum_k \left\|\sum_m \mathbf{x}_{k,m} * \mathbf{d}_m - \mathbf{s}_k\right\|_2^3 + \frac{\sigma}{2}\sum_m \|\mathbf{d}_m - \mathbf{p}_m\|_2^2 \tag{A13}$$

The variables $\mathbf{d}_m$, $\mathbf{x}_{k,m}$, $\mathbf{s}_k$ and $\mathbf{p}_m$ are denoted in the DFT domain by $\hat{\mathbf{d}}_m$, $\hat{\mathbf{x}}_{k,m}$, $\hat{\mathbf{s}}_k$, and $\hat{\mathbf{p}}_m$, respectively, where $\hat{\mathbf{X}}_{k,m} = diag(\hat{\mathbf{x}}_{k,m})$, which becomes

$$\underset{\{\mathbf{d}_m\}}{\operatorname{argmin}} \frac{1}{2} \sum_k \left\| \sum_m \hat{\mathbf{X}}_{k,m} \hat{\mathbf{d}}_m - \hat{\mathbf{s}}_k \right\|_2^2 + \frac{\sigma}{2} \sum_m \| \hat{\mathbf{d}}_m - \hat{\mathbf{p}}_m \|_2^2 \tag{A14}$$

Defining

$$\hat{\mathbf{X}}_k = (\hat{\mathbf{X}}_{k,0} \quad \hat{\mathbf{X}}_{k,1} \quad \ldots) \hat{\mathbf{d}} = \begin{pmatrix} \hat{\mathbf{d}}_0 \\ \hat{\mathbf{d}}_1 \\ \vdots \end{pmatrix} \hat{\mathbf{p}} = \begin{pmatrix} \hat{\mathbf{p}}_0 \\ \hat{\mathbf{p}}_1 \\ \vdots \end{pmatrix} \tag{A15}$$

this problem can be expressed as

$$\underset{\hat{\mathbf{d}}}{\operatorname{argmin}} \frac{1}{2} \sum_k \| \hat{\mathbf{X}}_k \hat{\mathbf{d}} - \hat{\mathbf{s}}_k \|_2^2 + \frac{\sigma}{2} \| \hat{\mathbf{d}} - \hat{\mathbf{p}} \|_2^2 \tag{A16}$$

with solution

$$\left(\sum_k \hat{\mathbf{X}}_k^H \hat{\mathbf{X}}_k + \sigma \mathbf{I} \right) \hat{\mathbf{d}} = \sum_k \hat{\mathbf{X}}_k^H \hat{\mathbf{s}}_k + \sigma \hat{\mathbf{p}} \tag{A17}$$

Equation (A11) is of the form

$$\underset{\mathbf{x}}{\operatorname{argmin}} \frac{1}{2} \| \mathbf{x} - \mathbf{y} \|_2^2 + \iota c_{PN}(\mathbf{x}) = prox_{\iota c_{PN}}(\mathbf{y}) \tag{A18}$$

It is clear from the geometry of the problem that

$$prox_{\iota c_{PN}}(\mathbf{y}) = \frac{PP^T \mathbf{y}}{\| PP^T \mathbf{y} \|_2} \tag{A19}$$

or, if the normalization $\|\mathbf{d}_m\|_2 \leq 1$ is desired instead

$$prox_{\iota c_{PN}}(\mathbf{y}) \begin{cases} PP^T \mathbf{y} & \text{if } \| PP^T \mathbf{y} \|_2 \leq 1 \\ \frac{PP^T \mathbf{y}}{\| PP^T \mathbf{y} \|_2} & \text{if } \| PP^T \mathbf{y} \|_2 \geq 1 \end{cases} \tag{A20}$$

References

1. Zhu, W.; Chen, X.; Wang, Y.; Wang, L. Arrhythmia recognition and classification using ECG morphology and segment feature analysis. *IEEE/ACM Trans. Comput. Biol. Bioinform.* **2019**, *16*, 131–138. [CrossRef]
2. Jekova, I.; Bortolan, G.; Christov, I. Assessment and comparison of different methods for heartbeat classification. *Med. Eng. Phys.* **2008**, *30*, 248–257. [CrossRef]
3. Alfaras, M.; Soriano, M.C.; Ortin, S. A fast machine learning model for ECG-Based heartbeat classification and arrhythmia detection. *Front. Phys.* **2019**, *7*, 103. [CrossRef]
4. Marinho, L.B.; Nascimento, N.D.M.M.; Souza, J.W.M.; Gurgel, M.V. A novel electrocardiogram feature extraction approach for cardiac arrhythmia classification. *Future Gener. Comput. Syst.* **2019**, *97*, 564–577. [CrossRef]
5. Plawiak, P. Novel methodology of cardiac health recognition based on ECG signals and evolutionary-neural system. *Expert Syst. Appl.* **2018**, *92*, 334–349. [CrossRef]
6. Aziz, S.; Ahmed, S.; Alouini, M. ECG-based machine learning algorithms for heartbeat classification. *Sci. Rep.* **2021**, *11*, 18738. [CrossRef]
7. Martis, R.J.; Acharya, U.R.; Min, L.C. ECG beat classification using PCA, LDA, ICA and discrete wavelet transform. *Biomed. Signal Proces.* **2013**, *85*, 437–448. [CrossRef]
8. Minhas, F.A.; Arif, M. Robust electrocardiogram (ECG) beat classification using discrete wavelet transform. *Physiol. Meas.* **2008**, *29*, 555–570. [CrossRef]
9. Martis, R.J.; Chakraborty, C.; Ray, A.K. An integrated ECG feature extraction scheme using PCA and wavelet transform. In Proceedings of the 2009 Annual IEEE India Conference, Ahmedabad, India, 18–20 December 2009; p. 422.
10. Lin, C. Frequency-domain features for ECG beat discrimination using grey relational analysis-based classifier. *Comput. Math. Appl.* **2008**, *55*, 680–690. [CrossRef]

11. Martis, R.J.; Acharya, U.R.; Mandana, K.M.; Ray, A.K. Application of principal component analysis to ECG signals for automated diagnosis of cardiac health. *Expert Syst. Appl.* **2012**, *39*, 11792–11800. [CrossRef]
12. Wan, M.; Lai, Z.; Yang, G.; Yang, Z. Local graph embedding based on maximum margin criterion via fuzzy set. *Fuzzy Set. Syst.* **2017**, *318*, 120–131. [CrossRef]
13. Wan, M.; Chen, X.; Zhan, T.; Xu, C. Sparse Fuzzy Two-Dimensional Discriminant Local Preserving Projection (SF2DDLPP) for Robust Image Feature Extraction. *Inform. Sci.* **2021**, *563*, 1–15. [CrossRef]
14. Hammad, M.; Maher, A.; Wang, K.; Jiang, F. Detection of abnormal heart conditions based on characteristics of ECG signals. *Measurement* **2018**, *125*, 634–644. [CrossRef]
15. Matta, S.C.; Sankari, Z.; Rihana, S. Heart rate variability analysis using neural network models for automatic detection of lifestyle activities. *Biomed. Signal Process* **2018**, *42*, 145–157. [CrossRef]
16. Heide, F.; Heidrich, W.; Wetzstein, G. Fast and flexible convolutional sparse coding. In Proceedings of the IEEE Conference on Computer Vision and Pattern Recognition (CVPR), Boston, MA, USA, 7–12 June 2015; pp. 5135–5143.
17. Papyan, V.; Romano, Y.; Sulam, J.; Elad, M. Convolutional dictionary learning via local processing. In Proceedings of the 16th IEEE International Conference on Computer Vision (ICCV), Venice, Italy, 22–29 October 2017; pp. 5306–5314.
18. Liu, Y.; Chen, X.; Ward, R.K.; Wang, Z.J. Image fusion with convolutional sparse representation. *IEEE Signal Proc. Let.* **2016**, *23*, 1882–1886. [CrossRef]
19. Zeiler, M.D.; Taylor, G.W.; Fergus, R. Adaptive deconvolutional networks for mid and high level feature learning. In Proceedings of the IEEE International Conference on Computer Vision (ICCV), Washington, DC, USA, 6–13 November 2011; pp. 2018–2025.
20. Sermanet, P.; Kavukcuoglu, K.; Chintala, S.; LeCun, Y. Pedestrian detection with unsupervised multistage feature learning. In Proceedings of the 26th IEEE Conference on Computer Vision and Pattern Recognition (CVPR), Portland, OR, USA, 23–28 June 2013; pp. 3626–3633.
21. Zhou, Y.; Chang, H.; Barner, K.; Spellman, P. Classification of histology sections via multispectral convolutional sparse coding. In Proceedings of the 27th IEEE Conference on Computer Vision and Pattern Recognition (CVPR), Columbus, OH, USA, 23–28 June 2014; pp. 3081–3088.
22. Chen, B.; Li, J.; Ma, B.; Wei, G. Convolutional sparse coding classification model for image classification. In Proceedings of the IEEE International Conference on Image Processing ICIP, Phoenix, AZ, USA, 25–28 September 2016; pp. 1918–1922.
23. Zhang, Q.; Li, B. Discriminative K-SVD for dictionary learning in face recognition. In Proceedings of the 23rd IEEE Conference on Computer Vision and Pattern Recognition (CVPR), Portland, OR, USA, 23–28 June 2010; pp. 2691–2698.
24. Yang, M.; Zhang, L.; Feng, X.; Zhang, D. Fisher discrimination dictionary learning for sparse representation. In Proceedings of the IEEE International Conference on Computer Vision (ICCV), Barcelona, Spain, 6–13 November 2011; pp. 543–550.
25. Jiang, Z.L.; Lin, Z.; Davis, L.S. Label consistent K-SVD: Learning a discriminative dictionary for recognition. *IEEE Trans. Pattern Anal.* **2013**, *35*, 2651–2664. [CrossRef] [PubMed]
26. Wohlberg, B. Efficient algorithms for convolutional sparse representations. *IEEE T Image Process.* **2016**, *25*, 301–315. [CrossRef]
27. Boyd, S.; Parikh, N.; Chu, E.; Peleato, B. Distributed optimization and statistical learning via the alternating direction method of multipliers. *Found. Trends Mach. Learn.* **2010**, *3*, 1–122. [CrossRef]
28. Garcia-Cardona, C.; Wohlberg, B. Convolutional dictionary learning: A comparative review and new algorithms. *IEEE Trans. Comput. Imag.* **2018**, *4*, 366–381. [CrossRef]
29. Zubair, S.; Yan, F.; Wang, W. Dictionary learning based sparse coefficients for audio classification with max and average pooling. *Digit. Signal Process.* **2013**, *23*, 960–970. [CrossRef]
30. Wang, J.; Yang, J.; Yu, K.; Lv, F. Locality-constrained linear coding for image classification. In Proceedings of the 23rd IEEE Conference on Computer Vision and Pattern Recognition (CVPR), San Francisco, CA, USA, 13–18 June 2010; pp. 3360–3367.
31. Moody, G.; Mark, R. The impact of the MIT-BIH arrhythmia database. *IEEE Eng. Med. Biol.* **2001**, *20*, 45–50. [CrossRef] [PubMed]
32. *ANSI/AAMI EC57:1998*; Testing and Reporting Performance Results of Cardiac Rhythm and ST Segment Measurement Algorithms. Association for the Advancement of Medical Instrumentation: American National Standards Institute, Inc. (ANSI): Washington, DC, USA, 1998.
33. Singh, B.N.; Tiwari, A.K. Optimal selection of wavelet basis function applied to ECG signal denoising. *Digit. Signal Process.* **2006**, *16*, 275–287. [CrossRef]
34. Liu, B.D.; Shen, B.; Gui, L. Face recognition using class Specific dictionary learning for sparse representation and collaborative representation. *Neurocomputing* **2016**, *204*, 198–210. [CrossRef]
35. Song, Y.; Liu, Y.; Gao, Q.; Gao, X. Euler label consistent k-svd for image classification and action recognition. *Neurocomputing* **2018**, *310*, 277–286. [CrossRef]
36. Shao, S.; Xu, R.; Liu, W.; Liu, B. Label embedded dictionary learning for image classification. *Neurocomputing* **2020**, *385*, 122–131. [CrossRef]
37. Desai, U.; Martis, R.J.; Nayak, C.G.; Sarika, K. Machine intelligent diagnosis of ECG for arrhythmia classification using DWT, ICA and SVM techniques. In Proceedings of the 12 IEEE International Conference on Elect Energy Env Communications Computer Control, New Delhi, India, 17–20 December 2015; p. 2015.
38. Elhaj, F.A.; Salim, N.; Harris, A.R.; Swee, T.T. Arrhythmia recognition and classification using combined linear and nonlinear features of ECG signals. *Comput. Method Prog. Biomed.* **2016**, *127*, 52–63. [CrossRef]

39. Acharya, U.R.; Oh, S.L.; Hagiwara, Y. A deep convolutional neural network model to classify heartbeats. *Comput. Biol. Med.* **2017**, *89*, 389–396. [CrossRef]
40. Mohammad, K.; Shayan, F.; Majid, S. ECG heartbeat classification: A deep transferable representation. In Proceedings of the International Conference Healthcare Informativa ICHI, New York, NY, USA, 4–7 June 2018; pp. 443–444.
41. Yildirim, O.; Baloglu, U.B.; Tan, R. A new approach for arrhythmia classification using deep coded features and LSTM networks. *Comput. Method Prog. Biomed.* **2019**, *176*, 121–133. [CrossRef]
42. Romdhane, T.F.; Alhichri, H.; Ouni, R.; Atri, M. Electrocardiogram heartbeat classification based on a deep convolutional neural network and focal loss. *Comput. Biol. Med.* **2020**, *123*, 103866. [CrossRef]
43. Li, Z.; Zhou, D.; Wan, L.; Li, J. Heartbeat classification using deep residual convolutional neural network from 2-lead electrocardiogram. *J. Electrocardiol.* **2020**, *58*, 105–112. [CrossRef]

Article

Teaching Probabilistic Graphical Models with OpenMarkov

Francisco Javier Díez [1],*, Manuel Arias [1], Jorge Pérez-Martín [1] and Manuel Luque [2]

[1] Department of Artificial Intelligence, Universidad Nacional de Educación a Distancia (UNED), 28040 Madrid, Spain
[2] Department of Statistics, Operations Research and Numerical Calculation, Universidad Nacional de Educación a Distancia (UNED), 28040 Madrid, Spain
* Correspondence: fjdiez@dia.uned.es

Abstract: OpenMarkov is an open-source software tool for probabilistic graphical models. It has been developed especially for medicine, but has also been used to build applications in other fields and for tuition, in more than 30 countries. In this paper we explain how to use it as a pedagogical tool to teach the main concepts of Bayesian networks and influence diagrams, such as conditional dependence and independence, d-separation, Markov blankets, explaining away, optimal policies, expected utilities, etc., and some inference algorithms: logic sampling, likelihood weighting, and arc reversal. The facilities for learning Bayesian networks interactively can be used to illustrate step by step the performance of the two basic algorithms: search-and-score and PC.

Keywords: OpenMarkov; Bayesian Networks; d-separation; inference; Learning Bayesian Networks

MSC: 68T37

1. Introduction

Bayesian networks (BNs) [1] and influence diagrams (IDs) [2,3] are two types of probabilistic graphical models (PGMs) [4–6] widely used in artificial intelligence. Unfortunately, the mathematical theory that supports them may be tough for beginners. Our computer science students, despite having a relatively strong mathematical background, find it hard to intuitively grasp some of the fundamental concepts, such as conditional independence and d-separation. Additionally, we have been teaching PGMs to health professionals, most of them physicians, for more than 25 years, and although we avoid the more complex aspects (for instance, we do not mention d-separation and only teach them the variable elimination algorithm), some of the basic notions important for them, such as conditional independence, are difficult to convey. In this paper we show how OpenMarkov, an open-source tool with an advanced graphical user interface (GUI), has allowed us to explain more intuitively some concepts that we found very difficult to explain before we had it.

This article is an extended version of the paper "Teaching Bayesian networks with OpenMarkov", presented at the 9th International Conference on Probabilistic Graphical Models, Prague, 2018 [7]. The rest of this paper is structured as follows: Section 2 introduces the background (notation, definitions, and an overview of OpenMarkov); Sections 3 and 4, the core of the paper, explain how to teach BNs and IDs respectively; Section 5 contains a brief discussion and the conclusion.

2. Background

2.1. Basic Definitions about Probability and Graphs

In the literature about PGMs it is usual to represent variables with capital letters (X) and their values with lower-case letters (x). A bold upper-case letter (**X**) denotes a set of variables and a bold lower-case letter (**x**) denotes a configuration of them, i.e., the assignment of a value to each variable in **X**. In this paper we assume that all the variables are discrete, i.e., each variable has a finite set of values, called *states*. When a variable X is Boolean, we denote by $+x$ the state "true", "present", or "positive", and by $\neg x$ the state "false", "absent", or "negative".

Definition 1 (Conditional independence). *Given a probability distribution P, two variables X and Y, and a set of variables **Z** containing neither X nor Y, we define $I_P(X, Y \mid \mathbf{Z})$ as follows:*

$$I_P(X, Y \mid \mathbf{Z}) \iff \forall x, \forall y, \forall \mathbf{z}, \; P(x, y \mid \mathbf{z}) = P(x \mid \mathbf{z}) \cdot P(y \mid \mathbf{z}). \tag{1}$$

When $I_P(X, Y \mid \mathbf{Z})$ holds, we say that X and Y are *conditionally independent* given **Z**. In this case, if $P(y) \neq 0$ for a particular value of Y, then

$$\forall x, \; P(x \mid \mathbf{z}, y) = P(x \mid \mathbf{z}), \tag{2}$$

i.e., if we already know $\mathbf{Z} = \mathbf{z}$, knowing later that $Y = y$ does not alter the probability of X.

In these expressions **Z** can be the empty set, which only has one configuration, usually denoted by ♦. We have $P(x \mid \blacklozenge) = P(x)$ and $P(x \mid \blacklozenge, y) = P(x \mid y)$. If $I_P(X, Y \mid \varnothing)$ holds, we say that X and Y are *a priori* independent.

The graphs considered in this paper can have at most one link between each pair of nodes. A graph is *directed* when all its links are directed. A *directed path* is a sequence of nodes $\{X_1, \ldots, X_n\}$ such that there is a link $X_i \to X_{i+1}$ between each pair of consecutive nodes. A *cycle* is a sequence of nodes $\{X_1, \ldots, X_n\}$ such that there is a link $X_i \to X_{i+1}$ between each pair of consecutive nodes and a link $X_n \to X_1$. Directed graphs containing no cycles are said to be *acyclic*.

When there is a link $X \to Y$, we say that X is a *parent* of Y and Y is a *child* of X. The set of parents of a node X is denoted by $\mathrm{Pa}(X)$. When there is a directed path from X to Y, we say that X is an *ancestor* of Y and Y is a *descendant* of X.

A pair of consecutive links in a path is called a *trail* [5]. A trail can be convergent ($X \to Z \leftarrow Y$), divergent ($Y \leftarrow X \to Z$), or consecutive ($X \to Y \to Z$); these three types are sometimes called head-to-head, tail-to-tail, and head-to-head, respectively [4].

The following two definitions for acyclic directed graphs are relevant to PGMs.

Definition 2 (d-separation). *A path consisting of one link is always active. Let X, Y, and Z be three nodes and **E** a set of nodes in an acyclic directed graph G, such that **E** contains neither X nor Y. A convergent trail $X \to Z \leftarrow Y$ is active if Z or at least one of its descendants is in **E**. A divergent trail $Y \leftarrow X \to Z$ is active if X is not in **E**. A sequential trail $X \to Y \to Z$ is active if Y is not in **E**. A path consisting of more than one link is active when all its trails are active.*

*Given two nodes, X and Y, and a set **E** containing neither X nor Y, if there is at least one active path connecting them, we say that they are* connected given **E**; *otherwise, we say that they are* separated given **E** *and denote it as $S_G(X, Y \mid \mathbf{E})$.*

Proposition 1. *Let X and Y be two nodes and **E** a set of nodes in an acyclic directed graph G, such that **E** contains neither X nor Y. A path (not necessarily a directed path) between X and Y is active if and only if it consists of a single link or every node W between X and Y in the path satisfies this property:*

1. *if the arrows that connect W with its two neighbors in the path converge in it (head-to-head trail), then W or at least one of its descendants is in **E**;*
2. *else (i.e., if W is the middle of a divergent or a sequential trail), then W is not in **E**.*

This proposition is a consequence of Definition 2, but it could alternatively be taken as the definition of d-separation.

2.2. Probabilistic Graphical Models

A PGM consists of a set of variables $\mathbf{V}$ [4,5], a probability distribution $P(\mathbf{v})$, and a graph G such that each node in the graph represents a variable in $\mathbf{V}$; for this reason, it is usual to speak indifferently of nodes and variables. The relation between G and P depends on the type of PGM. In this paper we focus on two types of PGMs whose graphs are directed and acyclic, namely, BN and IDs.

2.2.1. Bayesian Networks

In a BN every node has a conditional probability distribution for each configuration of its parents, $P(x \mid pa(X))$. Since we assume that all the variables are discrete, the set of distributions for a node can be encoded as a *conditional probability table* (CPT).

The relation between G and P is given by the following properties; we can take any one of them as the definition of a BN and then prove that the other two follow from it [4,5,8]:

1. **Factorization of the probability:** The joint probability is the product of the probability of each node conditioned on its parents, i.e.,

$$P(\mathbf{v}) = \prod_{X \in \mathbf{V}} P(x \mid pa(X)). \quad (3)$$

   (In this equation, the value x and the configuration $pa(X)$ in the right-hand side are given by the projection of $\mathbf{v}$ onto X and $Pa(X)$ respectively. The same holds for the equations in the next section.)

2. **Markov property.** Each node is independent of its non-descendants given its parents, i.e., if $\mathbf{Y}$ is a set of nodes such that none of them is a descendant of X, then

$$P(x \mid pa(X), \mathbf{y}) = P(x \mid pa(X)). \quad (4)$$

3. **d-separation.** If two nodes X and Y are d-separated in the graph given $\mathbf{E}$ (cf. Definition 2), then they are probabilistically independent given $\mathbf{E}$:

$$\forall X, \forall Y, \forall \mathbf{E}, \ S_G(X, Y \mid \mathbf{E}) \Longrightarrow I_P(X, Y \mid \mathbf{E}). \quad (5)$$

2.2.2. Influence Diagrams

IDs [2,3] have three different types of nodes: chance ($\mathbf{V}_C$), decision ($\mathbf{V}_D$), and utility ($\mathbf{V}_U$). In this paper we assume that utility nodes have no children; for a more general presentation, see [9]. Every chance node C has a CPT and each utility node U has a table, ψ, that represents the decision maker's values for each configuration of the parents of U, $\psi_U(pa(U))$.

The meaning of a link (sometimes called *arc*) depends on the type of nodes it connects. A link from a decision D_i to a decision D_j means that D_i is made before D_j. A link from a chance node C to a decision node D_j means that the value of variable C is known when making the decision D_j. Links into utility nodes represent functional dependency.

IDs require that there is a directed path connecting all the decisions; it induces a total ordering $\{D_0, \ldots, D_{n-1}\}$, the order in which they are made. It is usual to assume the *non-forgetting hypothesis*, which means that a variable C known for a decision D_j is also known for any subsequent decision D_k. The set of chance variables, $\mathbf{V}_C$, can be partitioned into $\{\mathbf{C}_0, \mathbf{C}_1, \ldots, \mathbf{C}_n\}$, where $\mathbf{C}_i$ is the subset of variables unknown for D_{i-1} and known for D_i. The set of variables known to the decision maker when deciding on D_i is called the *informational predecessors* of D_i and denoted by $InfPred(D_i)$ [10].

A *stochastic policy* for a decision D is a probability distribution $P_D(d \mid infPred(D))$. If P_D is degenerate (i.e., consisting of ones and zeros only) then the policy is *deterministic*. A *strategy* Δ for an ID is a set of policies, one for each decision, $\{P_D \mid D \in \mathbf{V}_D\}$. A strategy Δ *induces* a joint probability distribution over $\mathbf{V}_C \cup \mathbf{V}_D$ defined as follows:

$$P_\Delta(\mathbf{v}_C, \mathbf{v}_D) = \prod_{C \in \mathbf{V}_C} P(c \mid pa(C)) \prod_{D \in \mathbf{V}_D} P_D(d \mid \mathit{infPred}(D)) \,, \tag{6}$$

so that the *expected utility under the strategy* Δ is

$$EU(\Delta) = \sum_{\mathbf{v}_C} \sum_{\mathbf{v}_D} P_\Delta(\mathbf{v}_C \mid \mathbf{v}_D) \sum_{U \in \mathbf{V}_U} \psi_U(pa(U)) \,, \tag{7}$$

where $\mathit{infPred}(D)$ and $pa(U)$ are the projections of the configuration $(\mathbf{v}_C, \mathbf{v}_D)$ onto $\mathit{InfPred}(D)$ and $Pa(U)$ respectively. The *maximum expected utility* (*MEU*) is

$$MEU = \max_{\Delta \in \Delta^*} EU(\Delta) \,, \tag{8}$$

where Δ^* is the set of all the strategies. A strategy Δ_{opt} is *optimal* if it maximizes the expected utility, i.e., if $EU(\Delta_{opt}) = MEU$. Each policy in an optimal strategy is an *optimal policy*.

The evaluation of an ID consists in finding the *MEU* and an optimal strategy. It can be proved [11] that

$$MEU = \sum_{\mathbf{c}_0} \max_{d_0} \ldots \sum_{\mathbf{c}_{n-1}} \max_{d_{n-1}} \sum_{\mathbf{c}_n} P(\mathbf{v}_C \mid \mathbf{v}_D) \sum_{U \in \mathbf{V}_U} \psi_U(\mathbf{v}_C, \mathbf{v}_D) \,. \tag{9}$$

When the information available for D_i is $\mathit{infPred}(D_i)$, the best choice for this decision is

$$\delta_i = \arg\max_{d_i \in D_i} \sum_{\mathbf{c}_i} \max_{d_{i+1}} \ldots \sum_{\mathbf{c}_{n-1}} \max_{d_n} \sum_{\mathbf{c}_n} P_\Delta(\mathbf{v}_C \mid \mathbf{v}_D) \sum_{U \in \mathbf{V}_U} \psi_U(pa(U)) \,,$$

which implies that, in the optimal strategy, the policy for D_1 is

$$P_{D_i}^{opt}(d_i \mid \mathit{iPred}(D_i)) = \begin{cases} 1 & \text{if } d_i = \delta_i \\ 0 & \text{otherwise} \end{cases}. \tag{10}$$

2.2.3. Arc Reversal Algorithm

An arc (a link) $X \to Y$ in a BN can be inverted without modifying the joint probabilities or the expected utilities of the network, as long as there is no other path from X to Y [2]. It proceeds as follows. Let $\mathbf{A} = pa(X) \cap pa(Y)$, $\mathbf{B} = pa(X) \setminus \mathbf{A}$, and $\mathbf{C} = pa(Y) \setminus \mathbf{A}$, which are disjoint sets. The CPT for the two nodes in the original network are $P(x \mid \mathbf{a}, \mathbf{b})$ and $P(y \mid x, \mathbf{a}, \mathbf{c})$, respectively. In the new BN, this link is replaced with $Y \to X$ and the new CPTs are $P(y \mid \mathbf{a}, \mathbf{b}, \mathbf{c})$ and $P(x \mid y, \mathbf{a}, \mathbf{b}, \mathbf{c})$:

$$P(x, y \mid \mathbf{a}, \mathbf{b}, \mathbf{c}) = P(x \mid \mathbf{a}, \mathbf{b}) \cdot P(y \mid x, \mathbf{a}, \mathbf{c})$$
$$P(y \mid \mathbf{a}, \mathbf{b}, \mathbf{c}) = \sum_x P(x, y \mid \mathbf{a}, \mathbf{b}, \mathbf{c})$$
$$P(x \mid y, \mathbf{a}, \mathbf{b}, \mathbf{c}) = \frac{P(x, y \mid \mathbf{a}, \mathbf{b}, \mathbf{c})}{P(y \mid \mathbf{a}, \mathbf{b}, \mathbf{c})}$$

In order to maintain the consistency of the BN, it is then necessary to *share the parents* by drawing a link from each node in $\mathbf{C}$ to X and from each node in $\mathbf{B}$ to Y.

Arc reversal can be applied to compute the posterior probability $P(v \mid \mathbf{e})$ of a variable of interest, V, in a BN. A node is said to be *barren* when it is not V, is not in $\mathbf{E}$, and is not an ancestor of any evidence variable. Due to the Markov property, barren nodes can be removed from the network without altering the posterior probability of V. If necessary, some links can be inverted one by one to create new barren nodes until the evidence variables are the parents of X and all the other nodes have been removed; the probability of interest can be read from the CPT for X—we will see an example in Section 3.3.1.

Similarly, a link $X \to Y$ between two chance nodes in an ID can be inverted to remove all the chance and decision nodes one by one, and some utility nodes can be fused, until only one utility node remains [12,13]—there is an example in Section 4.1.2. A chance node X whose only descendants are utility nodes can be *absorbed* as follows. If the only child of X is U, the algorithm adds a link from each node in $\mathbf{V} = pa(X) \setminus pa(U)$ to U and removes X. The new utility potential is

$$U(\mathbf{v}') = \sum_x P(x \mid pa(X)) \cdot U(x, pa(U)) . \tag{11}$$

where $\mathbf{V}' = (pa(X) \cup pa(U)) \setminus \{X\}$. If X has more than one utility node, $\mathbf{U}_X = \{U_1, \ldots, U_n\}$, they must be fused into a new utility node U, with $Pa(U) = \cup_{U_i \in \mathbf{U}_X} Pa(U_i)$ and $\psi_U = \sum_{U_i \in \mathbf{U}_X} \psi_{U_i}$.

Similarly, a decision D whose only descendant is U can be absorbed, so that the new utility is

$$U(\mathbf{v}') = \max_d U(d, \mathbf{v}') , \tag{12}$$

where $\mathbf{V}' = pa(U) \setminus \{D\}$. If D has more than one utility node, they must be fused, as above.

2.3. OpenMarkov

There are many software tools for PGMs, either commercial (AgenaRisk, BayesFusion, BayesiaLab, Bayes Server, HUGIN, Netica...), free (SamIam), or open-source (OpenMarkov, UnBBayes, Weka...). OpenMarkov has been developed at the National University for Distance Education (UNED) in Madrid, Spain (http://www.openmarkov.org; accessed on 20 September 2022). It consists of around 115,000 lines of Java code (excluding comments and blank lines), structured in 44 Maven subprojects and stored in a Git repository at Bitbucket (https://maven.apache.org, https://git-scm.com, https://bitbucket.org; accessed on 20 September 2022). The first versions were distributed under the European Union Public License (EUPL), version 1.1 (https://eupl.eu; accessed on 20 September 2022); recent versions are distributed under the GNU public license, version 3 (GPLv3) (https://www.gnu.org/licenses/gpl-3.0.en.html; accessed on 20 September 2022).

OpenMarkov offers support for editing and evaluating several types of PGMs, such as BNs, IDs, Markov IDs [14], and decision analysis networks [15]. It can also edit limited-memory IDs (LIMIDs) [16] and several types of temporal models, such as dynamic Bayesian networks [17], which include Markov chains and hidden Markov models as a particular case, factored Markov decision processes (MDPs) [18], factored partially observable MDPS (POMDPs) [19], and DLIMIDs [20]. Its native format for encoding these models is Prob-ModelXML (http://www.ProbModelXML.org; accessed on 20 September 2022).

OpenMarkov has been designed primarily for medicine and for teaching. With this tool and its predecessor, Elvira [21], our research group has built complex models for several real-world health problems. (Some of those networks and other examples are available at http://www.probmodelxml.org/networks; accessed on 20 September 2022.) Other groups have used it to build PGMs in other fields, such as planning and robotics [22]. Both Elvira and OpenMarkov have paid special attention to the explanation of reasoning [23,24], a topic whose importance has been acknowledged in the area of expert systems since the 1980s [25], and is now an issue of utmost relevance in modern AI—see [24] and references therein.

To our knowledge, OpenMarkov has been used for research and tuition in more than 30 countries, from top universities, large companies, and centers of the Government of the United States to students in low-income countries who cannot afford paying for commercial software for PGMs.

3. Teaching Bayesian Networks

3.1. Evidence Propagation in BNs with OpenMarkov

In a diagnostic problem, the assignment of a value to a variable as a result of an observation is called a *finding*. The set of findings is called *evidence*. The *propagation* of evidence consists in computing the posterior probability of some variables given the evidence.

In OpenMarkov chance variables are drawn as rounded rectangles and colored in cream, as shown in Figure 1. When a finding is entered (usually by double-clicking on the value/state of the variable), OpenMarkov propagates it and shows the posterior probability by means of a horizontal bar. It is possible to have several sets of findings, each called an *evidence case*, and display several bars for each state. Figure 1 shows three evidence cases: in the first one, corresponding to the red bars, there is no finding ($\mathbf{E} = \varnothing$); in the second one, shown in blue, the presence of virus A is confirmed, so $\mathbf{E} = \{V_A\}$ and $\mathbf{e} = (+v_A)$; in the third one, shown in green, this virus is known to be absent, i.e., $\mathbf{E} = \{V_A\}$ and $\mathbf{e} = (\neg v_A)$. This allows the user to see how the probabilities of the variables change when new findings are entered.

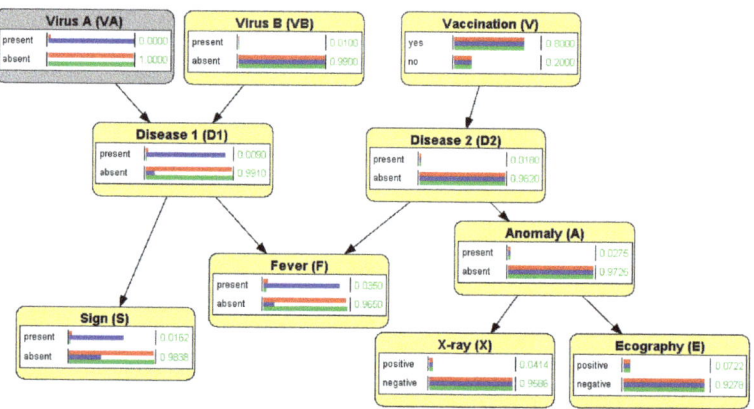

Figure 1. A Bayesian network for the differential diagnosis of two hypothetical diseases. The horizontal bars represent the probability of each state for each evidence case. We can check that V_A and V_B are a priori independent by introducing evidence about V_A and observing that the probability of V_B does not change. The same holds for the 5 variables at the right of F. In contrast, the 4 descendants of V_A do depend on the evidence for this variable.

3.2. Correlation and Independence

3.2.1. Conditional Independence

Even though the concepts of probabilistic dependence (correlation) and independence are mathematically very simple (cf. Equation (1)), many students have difficulties to understand them intuitively, especially in the case of conditional independence. In our teaching, we use the network in Figure 1, which has a clear causal interpretation: all the variables are Boolean, and for each link $X \to Y$, the finding $+x$ increases the probability of $+y$, except in the case of vaccination, $+v$, which decreases the probability of D_2 being present.

In order to illustrate a priori independence, we point out that in this model there is no link between the two viruses, V_A and V_B, and they have no common ancestors. Therefore, they are d-separated in the graph, and because of Property (5) (with $\mathbf{E} = \varnothing$), they are a priori independent. We can check it by introducing a finding for V_A and observing that the probability of V_B does not change, or vice versa; for example, $P(+v_B|+v_A) = P(+v_B|\neg v_A) = P(+v_B) = 0.01$, as shown in Figure 1, which confirms that Equation (2) holds. In contrast, we can see that the variables V_A and D_1 are *correlated* by introducing evidence about the one and observing that the probability of the other changes; for example, in Figure 1 we observe that $P(+d_1 | +v_A) = 0.9009 > P(+d_1) = 0.0268 > P(+d_1 | \neg v_A) = 0.009$.

We can also see that in this graph each node at the left of F is separated from each variable at its right when $\mathbf{E} = \varnothing$, which implies that they are pairwise a priori independent— see again Figure 1. We can verify it by introducing evidence for one variable in one side and observing that the probabilities on the other side do not change.

To illustrate conditional independence, we first show that S (a sign) and F (fever) are a priori correlated by introducing evidence on one of them and seeing that the probability of the other changes. However, if we first introduce evidence about D_1, which plays the role of **E**, and introduce a finding S (by generating a new evidence case in OpenMarkov), then the probability of F does not change, as we can observe in Figure 2. This shows that F and S, despite being correlated a priori, are conditionally independent given D_1 (it is an instance of Equation (1) with $\mathbf{E} = \{D_1\}$). Our students easily understand that the correlation between fever and the sign is due to a common cause, and when we know with certainty whether this cause is present or absent, the correlation disappears. OpenMarkov confirms that our intuitive understanding of causation leads to the numerical results we expected.

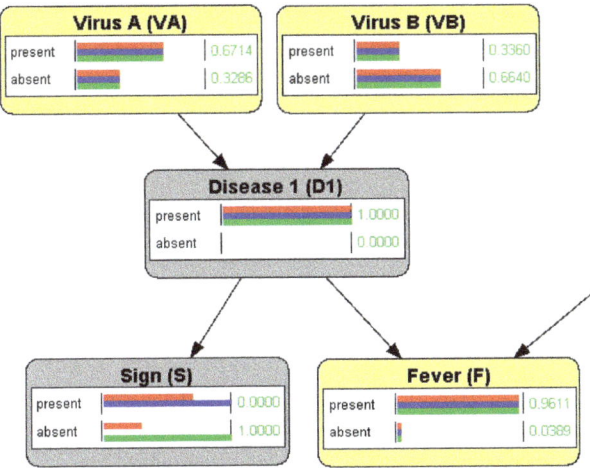

Figure 2. An example of conditional independence: once we know with certainty that disease 1 is present, no finding about sign S affects the probability of fever or the suspicion about the viruses.

3.2.2. d-Separation

Section 2.2.1 introduced the definition of d-separation. If we just left our students with it (or with its equivalent definition in Proposition 1), they would be absolutely unable to understand the rationale behind it—so would we! In particular, it is difficult to understand why some trails are active if and only if the intermediate node is in **E**, while for other trails the opposite is true—see Definition 2. Additionally, a convergent path $X \to Z \leftarrow Y$, which is a priori inactive, can be activated not only by Z but also by any of its descendants, while a divergent path $Y \leftarrow X \to Z$, which is a priori active, can be blocked by X but not by its ancestors. It sounds arbitrary, if not esoteric.

To make d-separation intuitive, we explain that this property is a consequence of the factorization of the probability (cf. Equation (3)) and that it agrees with our notions of causality, provided that **E** in Definition 2 is interpreted as the evidence, i.e., a set of findings for the observed variables. We first consider that a path containing just one link is always active, by definition, whatever the evidence. We can observe for the network in Figure 1 that introducing a finding for one variable affects the posterior probabilities of all its neighbors, even if there is evidence for other nodes. The correlation in this case is explained by a direct cause-effect relation.

We then consider a divergent trail, such as $S \leftarrow D_1 \to F$. Definition 2 says that this path is active a priori, i.e., when there is no evidence. We can verify it by introducing a finding for S or for F, as explained above. This correlation is intuitive because S and F are effects of a common cause. However, when the presence or the absence of this disease is confirmed or ruled out by direct observation, then $\mathbf{E} = \{D_1\}$, and $S_G(S, F \mid \{D_1\})$ implies $I_P(S, F \mid \{D_1\})$. We can check it by first entering evidence for D_1 and then, in a new evidence case, adding a finding for S, either $+s$ or $\neg s$; the probability of F does not change, as shown in Figure 2. This also agrees with our notion of causal influence.

The behavior of a sequential trail is similar; for example, the path $V_A \to D_1 \to S$ means that the causal influence of V_A on S is mediated by D_1. This path is active a priori because detecting virus A increases the probability of the disease and, consequently, that of the symptom (deductive reasoning). Similarly, the symptom makes us suspect the presence of the virus (abductive reasoning). However, the finding $+d_1$ blocks this path, because once we know that the disease is present (or absent), the information about the virus does not affect the probability of the symptom, and vice versa. We can check it with OpenMarkov. Again, d-separation agrees with our intuitive notion of causality.

Let us now consider the convergent trail $V_A \to D_1 \leftarrow V_B$. When $\mathbf{E} = \emptyset$, it is inactive and V_A and V_B are separated. (At this point, it may be worth warning our students that, contrary to intuition, "being connected" is not a transitive property: V_A is connected with D_1 and D_1 is connected with V_B, but V_A is not connected with V_B. The analysis of whether a path is active cannot be done link by link, because an individual link is always active; it is necessary to consider every pair of consecutive links, i.e., every trail, as in Definition 2 and Proposition 1. The lesson is that, even though intuition is very useful in mathematics, it must be properly trained and supported by formal reasoning.)

We can check that V_A and V_B are separated—and, because of Property (5), a priori independent—by introducing evidence for V_A and observing that the probability of V_B does not change, as shown in Figure 1. This is intuitive, because there is no common cause for these variables. In contrast, when there is evidence about D_1, the trail $V_A \to D_1 \leftarrow V_B$ becomes active and, consequently, V_A and V_B are no longer separated: $\neg S_G(V_A, V_B \mid \{D_1\})$. We can verify it by first introducing evidence about D_1—for example, $+d_1$—, generating a new evidence case, introducing evidence about V_A, and observing that now the probability of V_B changes: $P(+v_B \mid +d_1, +v_A) < P(+v_B \mid +d_1) < P(+v_B \mid +d_1, \neg v_A)$. This is consistent with the causal interpretation of the BN, because when a patient has the first disease, we suspect that the cause is virus A or virus B; if additional evidence (for example, the result of a test) leads us to ruling out virus A, we then suspect that the cause of the disease is virus B; conversely, if the presence of A is confirmed, our suspicion of B decreases. Put another way, the finding $+d_1$ creates a negative correlation between V_A and V_B, which were are a priori independent. This phenomenon, called *explaining away* [4], is the most typical case of intercausal reasoning; in particular, it is a property of the noisy-OR model [4,26]. (In this network there is another noisy OR at F.)

It also follows from the definition of d-separation that the convergent trail $V_A \to D_1 \leftarrow V_B$ is not only activated by D_1 itself, but also by any of its descendants. We can verify it with OpenMarkov by introducing the findings $+s$ or $+f$. This is another instance of explaining-away because any of these findings makes us suspect the presence of at least one of the viruses, with a negative correlation between V_A and V_B.

We may now ask ourselves: if the middle node in a divergent trail can block it, and the descendants of the middle node can activate a convergent trail, why cannot the ancestors of the middle node in a divergent trail block it? We can check with OpenMarkov that this is the case; for example, given the trail $S \leftarrow D_1 \to F$, if we first introduce the finding $+v_A$ and then add in a new evidence case the finding $+s$, we observe that the probability increases, which proves that S and F are not conditionally independent given V_A. The reason for this correlation is that the presence of a virus increases the probability of the disease, but— unlike the case in which the disease is confirmed by direct observation—the probability is not yet 100%, so it can be further increased by $+s$. We can also try other combinations of findings to check that no ancestor of D_1 blocks this trail.

3.2.3. Markov Property and Markov Blankets

As we saw in Section 2.2.1 (cf. Equation (4)), the Markov property means that every node is conditionally independent of its non-descendants given its parents. Again, this definition may be difficult to understand for students when stated in abstract, but it is intuitive when explained with examples. In particular, when a node has no parents, it is conditionally independent of its non-descendants. We can illustrate it with the two-diseases network (Figure 1) by showing, for example, that the probability of *Disease 1* does not change when introducing evidence for the nodes at the right of *Fever*, which are not descendants of that disease; and vice versa. Similarly, we can introduce evidence for the parents of a node—for example, *Fever*—and then see that adding evidence about other nodes that are not its descendants does not alter its probability.

We can illustrate in the same manner the concept of *Markov blanket*, which denotes a set of nodes that surround a node, making it conditionally independent of the other variables in the network [4]. One might think that the set of parents and children of a node D_1 constitute a Markov blanket for it. However, this is not the case: if we introduce evidence for the parents and children of D_1, i.e., for V_A, V_B, S, and F, we can see that D_1 is not yet separated from all the other nodes in the network; in fact, every node in $\{V, D_2, A, X, E\}$ is correlated with D_1 because F has activated the trail $D_1 \to F \leftarrow D_2$. Therefore, the Markov blanket of a node must include not only its parents and children, but also the parents of its children.

3.3. Inference Algorithms for Bayesian Networks

We have seen that OpenMarkov is able to propagate evidence, but so far we have not discussed inference algorithms. In this section, we explain how this tool can help illustrate some of the basic algorithms, namely, arc reversal, logic sampling, and likelihood weighting.

3.3.1. Arc Reversal for Bayesian Networks

Arc reversal was initially designed to transform IDs into decision trees [2], but in our opinion, students understand it better if it is first introduced for BNs.

Let us use again the two-diseases network (Figure 1) as an example. When processing the query $P(+d_1|+f, +s, \neg v)$, D_1 is the variable of interest and F, S, and V are the evidence variables. Then X and U can be removed in OpenMarkov's GUI because they are barren nodes. Then A becomes a barren node, which can also be removed. The user can invert link $B \to D_1$ by right-clicking on it; OpenMarkov replaces it with $D_1 \to B$, adds a new link $A \to B$ (because A was a parent of D_1), and computes the new probability table $P(b \mid a, d_1)$; the probability $P(a)$ does not change because A has received no new parent. Now B is barren and can be removed. The user can then invert $A \to D_1$ to remove A. After inverting $D_2 \to S$, which adds the links $D_1 \to D_2$ and $V \to S$, it is possible to remove D_2. In each step the user can inspect the new CPTs and check that they have been computed correctly. Finally, after inverting $D_1 \to S$ and $D_1 \to F$ the parents of D_1 (the variable of interest) are the three evidence nodes, and the user can retrieve the probability $P(+d_1|+f, +s, \neg v)$ by opening the CPT for D_1.

When there is a link $X \to Y$ and another directed path from X to Y, the option for inverting the link is disabled in its contextual menu (it appears in gray) because it would create a cycle. In the future, we might add a dialog that would suggest to the user the node deletions and arc reversals that will lead to calculating the probability of the variable of interest.

3.3.2. Stochastic Algorithms

OpenMarkov currently implements two stochastic algorithms: logic sampling [27] and likelihood weighting [28]. Both start by sampling a value for each node without parents, using its prior distribution, and then proceed in topological order (i.e., downwards), sampling each other node in accordance with the probability distribution for the configuration of its parents. This way, every iteration of the algorithm obtains a sample—a configuration of all the nodes. OpenMarkov is able to store these configurations in a spreadsheet and compute some statistics, including the posterior probability of each variable, as shown in Figure 3.

The left side of this figure displays the output of the logic sampling algorithm. The 10,000 configurations obtained are stored in the "Samples" sheet (not visible in the figure), with a sample per row and a variable per column; those compatible with the evidence are colored in green and those incompatible in red. The "General stats" tab shows that only 37 samples are compatible (see cell B6), a clear indication of the inefficiency of this algorithm.

	A	B	C		A	B	C
1	Bayesian network	two-diseases.pgmx		1	Bayesian network	two-diseases.pgmx	
2	Approximate algorithm	logic sampling		2	Approximate algorithm	likelihood weighting	
3	Total number of samples	10,000		3	Total number of samples	10,000	
4	Computing time (ms)	24.25		4	Computing time (ms)	26.46	
5	Computing time per sample (ms)	0.0024		5	Computing time per sample (ms)	0.0026	
6	Non-null samples	37		6	Non-null samples	10,000	
7	Accumulated weight	37.00		7	Accumulated weight	188.15	
8	Exact algorithm	clustering		8	Exact algorithm	clustering	
9				9			
10	Variable	States		10	Variable	States	
11				11			
12	Virus A (VA)	absent	present	12	Virus A (VA)	absent	present
13	number of ocurrences	9,773	227	13	number of ocurrences	9,807	193
14	approximate probability	0.2778	0.7222	14	approximate probability	0.3475	0.6525
15	exact probability	0.3482	0.6518	15	exact probability	0.3482	0.6518
16				16			
17	Virus B (VB)	absent	present	17	Virus B (VB)	absent	present
18	number of ocurrences	9,898	102	18	number of ocurrences	9,902	98
19	approximate probability	0.7222	0.2778	19	approximate probability	0.6778	0.3222
20	exact probability	0.6738	0.3262	20	exact probability	0.6738	0.3262
21				21			
22	Disease 1 (D1)	absent	present	22	Disease 1 (D1)	absent	present
23	number of ocurrences	9,714	286	23	number of ocurrences	9,729	271
24	approximate probability	0.0278	0.9722	24	approximate probability	0.0290	0.9710
25	exact probability	0.0293	0.9707	25	exact probability	0.0293	0.9707
26				26			
27	Vaccination (V)	no	yes	27	Disease 2 (D2)	absent	present
28	number of ocurrences	2,063	7,937	28	number of ocurrences	9,494	506
29	approximate probability	1.0000	0.0000	29	approximate probability	0.9018	0.0982
30	exact probability	1.0000	0.0000	30	exact probability	0.9254	0.0746
31				31			
32	Disease 2 (D2)	absent	present	32	Anomaly (A)	absent	present
33	number of ocurrences	9,815	185	33	number of ocurrences	9,408	592
34	approximate probability	0.9444	0.0556	34	approximate probability	0.8843	0.1157
35	exact probability	0.9254	0.0746	35	exact probability	0.9176	0.0824
36				36			
37	Fever (F)	absent	present	37	X-ray (X)	negative	positive
38	number of ocurrences	9,464	536	38	number of ocurrences	9,303	697
39	approximate probability	0.0000	1.0000	39	approximate probability	0.8849	0.1151
40	exact probability	0.0000	1.0000	40	exact probability	0.9157	0.0843
41				41			
42	Sign (S)	absent	present	42	Ecography (E)	negative	positive
43	number of ocurrences	9,728	272	43	number of ocurrences	9,019	981

Figure 3. Output of two stochastic algorithms: logic sampling (**left**) and likelihood weighting (**right**), for the evidence $\{+f, +s, \neg v\}$. The latter only samples the variables that are not part of the evidence.

For each variable, the spreadsheet displays the number of samples in which each state has appeared; for example, D_1 has taken the state "absent" in 9714 samples (cell B23) and "present" in 286 (cell C23). It also shows the posterior probability for each state, which is not proportional to the number of occurrences because the samples incompatible with the evidence do not count.

The right side of Figure 3 shows the output of likelihood weighting. One difference with the previous algorithm is that it only samples the variables that do not make part of the evidence; therefore, the evidence variables are not shown in the sheet. Another difference is that now the number of non-null samples (cell B6) equals the number of samples, because all of them are valid. However, each sample has a weight between 0 and 1 (in logic sampling it was either 0 or 1), as shown in the "Samples" sheet. As a consequence, the total weight for this simulation is 188.15 (cell B6), much higher than the value of 37 obtained for logic sampling, and this usually leads to more accurate estimates of the posterior probabilities, as we can see by comparing the approximate probabilities with their exact probabilities for both algorithms.

3.4. Learning Bayesian Networks

BNs can be built from human knowledge, data, or a combination of both. OpenMarkov implements the two basic algorithms for learning BNs from data: search-and-score [29] and PC [30]. Other tools offer many more algorithms, but the advantage of OpenMarkov is the possibility of interactive learning [31]: in every step, the GUI displays a list of the *edits* (operations) that it is ready to perform and a motivation for each edit, as shown in Figures 4 and 5. This way, the user can monitor how the algorithm proceeds, step by step, and either accept the next edit proposed by the algorithm, or select another one from the list, or do a different edit at the GUI.

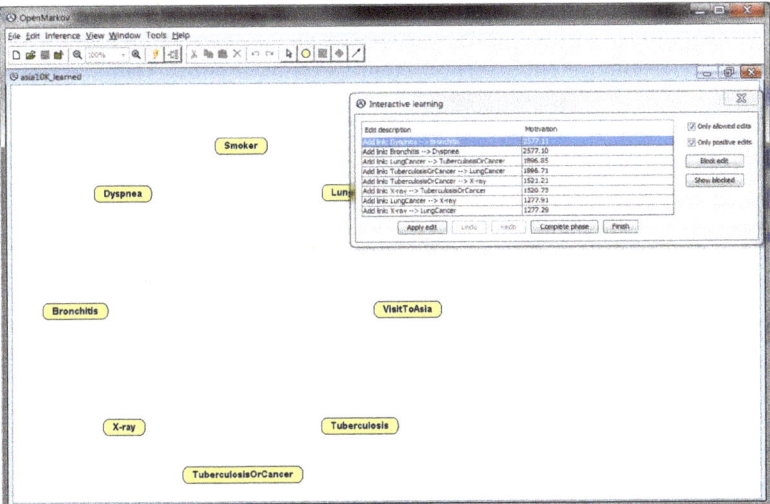

Figure 4. Initial state of the interactive search-and-score algorithm when applied to a dataset generated from the Bayesian network *Asia*. The "Motivation" column shows the score of each edit for the metric selected.

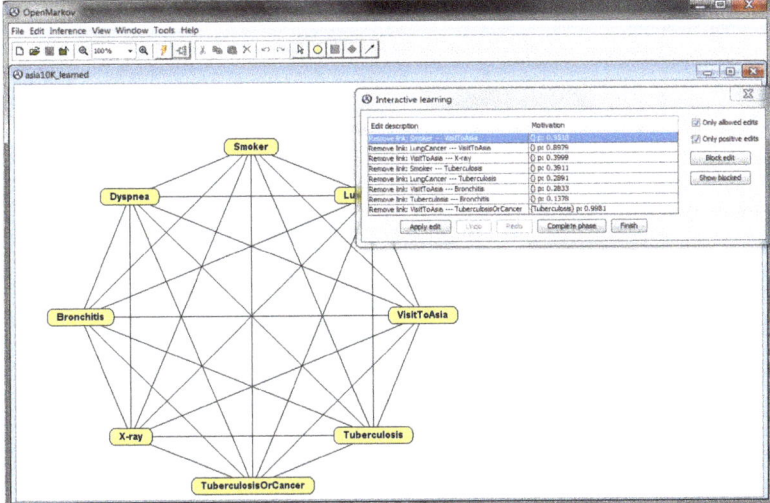

Figure 5. Initial state of the interactive PC algorithm when applied to the same dataset as in the previous figure. The "Motivation" column shows, for each edit, the *p*-value obtained for the test of independence conditioned on the variables in curly brackets.

The search-and-score algorithm, also called "hill climbing", departs from a network with a node for each variable in the data, and no link (cf. Figure 4). The possible edits are: adding a directed link (the most common edit), deleting one of the existing links, or inverting a link. This process is guided by a metric chosen by the user. Currently OpenMarkov offers six well-known metrics: BD, Bayesian, K2, entropy, AIC, and MDLM. When learning the network, it selects the edits compatible with the restrictions of the network (for example, a BN cannot have cycles) and ranks them according to their scores. This way, a student can see, for example, that when the network has no link yet, the K2 metric usually assigns different scores to the links $X \rightarrow Y$ and $Y \rightarrow X$, although the resulting networks represent exactly the same probability distribution, which is an unsatisfactory property of this metric. It is also possible to see that every edit (for example, adding a link) usually changes the scores of future edits.

In contrast, the PC algorithm departs from a fully connected undirected graph (Figure 5) and removes the links one by one depending on the conditional independencies found in the database. For each undirected link X–Y, OpenMarkov performs a statistical test that returns the p-value for the "null hypothesis" that X and Y are a priori independent; if p is below a certain threshold, α—called significance level, set by the user—, the null hypothesis is rejected and the link is kept; otherwise, it is removed. Links with higher p-values, which correspond to correlations that can be explained by chance, are proposed to be removed first. Then the PC algorithm tests, for each pair of variables, whether they are independent given a third variable, and then given a pair of other variables, and so on. In each step, the GUI shows the user a list of the links that might be removed, and for each link, the conditioning variables and the p-value. This way, the user can not only see the removals that the algorithm is considering, but also the certainty for each one. Finally, the algorithm assigns a direction to each link.

The tutorial of OpenMarkov, available at www.openmarkov.org/docs/tutorial; accessed on 20 September 2022, explains in detail the options it offers for learning BNs, either automatically or interactively.

4. Teaching Influence Diagrams

4.1. Evaluation of Influence Diagrams

4.1.1. Expected Utility and Optimal Policies

In Section 2.2.2 we mentioned that the evaluation of an ID consists in finding the maximum expected utility (MEU) and an optimal strategy. When OpenMarkov evaluates an ID in the GUI, it presents to the user the posterior probability of each chance and decision node and the expected utility of each utility node, as shown in Figure 6.

One way to evaluate an ID—the original method proposed by Howard and Matheson [2] when introducing this formalism—is to convert it into an equivalent decision tree (DT). For example, the ID in Figure 6 can be expanded into the DT in Figure 7, where each branch is labeled with its expected utility, obtained when evaluating the tree from the leaves to the root; for every decision node, one of its branches is marked with a small red rectangle to indicate the optimal choice in that scenario (in the case of a tie, more than one branch would have this mark). This evaluation method is very inefficient, because the size of the tree grows exponentially with the number of nodes in the ID. In fact, in our group we have built IDs for some medical problems [32,33], having fewer than 30 nodes, whose equivalent DTs contain tens of thousands of leaves. However, when teaching PGMs it is very useful to compare IDs with DTs for small problems because, in our opinion, an ID can only be understood as a compact representation of a DT, and all the algorithms for evaluating IDs take the DT as a reference. For these reasons, we implemented in OpenMarkov the automatic conversion of IDs into DTs.

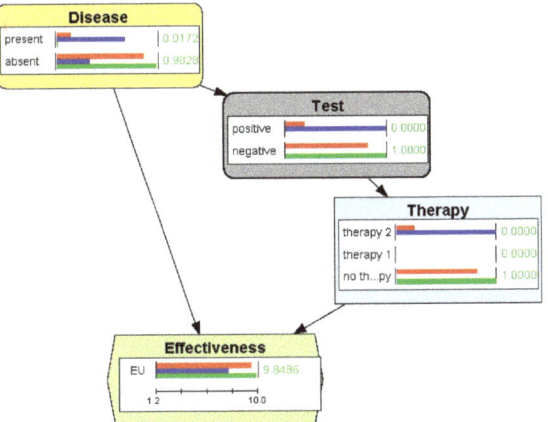

Figure 6. An influence diagram (ID) for deciding the optimal therapy based on the result of a test. The red bars represent the probabilities and the utility when no finding is introduced, i.e., the values for the general population. The blue and green bars correspond to a positive and a negative test result respectively.

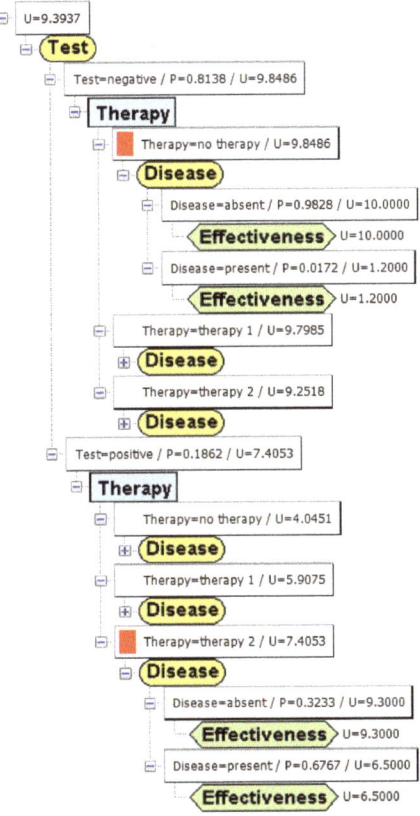

Figure 7. A decision tree equivalent to the ID in Figure 6. A red rectangle denotes the optimal choice for each decision. Some branches have been collapsed to make the figure more compact.

However, OpenMarkov can also evaluate IDs with more efficient algorithms; by default, the GUI uses variable elimination [9,34]. After the evaluation, in addition to showing the posterior probability of each chance variable, with a bar for each evidence case, as in the case of BNs, it also displays a bar for every state (option) of every decision and for the expected utility of every utility node. For example, Figure 6 displays the probabilities and the expected utility for three evidence cases: when the test is not yet done (red bars), when it is positive (blue bars), and when it is negative (green bars).

The optimal strategy calculated by OpenMarkov can be examined in different ways. One of them is to open for each decision D the probability table $P_D(d|iPred(D))$ for the optimal policy—cf. Section 2.2.2. Since the optimal policies are deterministic—except in the case of ties—these tables usually contain only 0's and 1's, as in Figure 8, where the only informational predecessor of the decision (the only variable known when making it) is the result of the test.

Test	negative	positive
therapy 2	0	1
therapy 1	0	0
no therapy	1	0

Figure 8. Optimal policy of *Therapy*: the best choice (with probability 1) is "therapy 2" when the test is positive and "no therapy" when it is negative.

More insight about this policy is presented in Figure 9, which shows the expected utilities obtained when calculating the optimal policy for *Therapy*—cf. Equation (10).

Test	negative	positive
therapy 2	9.251831	7.405263
therapy 1	9.798501	5.907519
no therapy	9.848611	4.045113

Figure 9. Expected utility for *Therapy*. When the test is positive, "therapy 2" is chosen because it has the highest expected utility. When the test is negative, the highest expected utility is obtained for "no therapy".

An alternative way to see the optimal strategy in OpenMarkov is to display the *strategy tree* [35], which summarizes all the policies in one figure. It is more compact than the DT—please compare Figures 7 and 10—because it prunes the suboptimal branches (which implies that only one branch goes out from each decision node, except in the case of a tie) as well as the branches with null probability (for example, when we decide not to do a test, its result is neither "positive" nor "negative"). The strategy tree is very useful for large IDs; for example, the optimal-policy table for the last decision in Mediastinet, an ID for lung cancer [32], contained more than 15,000 columns, but only 5 were relevant because the others corresponded to impossible or suboptimal scenarios. In contrast, the strategy for that ID only has 5 leaves, one for each relevant column [35].

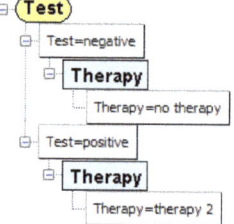

Figure 10. Optimal strategy for the ID of Figure 6. It is much more compact than the decision tree in Figure 7.

4.1.2. Arc Reversal for Influence Diagrams

As mentioned above, arc reversal was introduced by Howard and Matheson [2] to transform IDs and convert them into DTs. Later, Olmsted [12] designed an algorithm that iteratively removes the nodes from the graph, one by one, until only the utility node remains; this is much more efficient than expanding a DT—see also [13].

Again, we can illustrate this algorithm with OpenMarkov. For example, when evaluating the ID in Figure 6, we should remove first the node *Disease* because it is not an informational predecessor of any decision; but this node has a descendant that is not a utility node. We can then invert the link *Disease* $\rightarrow$ *Test* by right-clicking on it, as in BNs. Now *Effectiveness*, a utility node, is the only descendant of *Disease*, so the user can click "Absorb node" on the contextual menu of this node, which adds a link from *Test* to *Effectiveness* and computes the new utility table with Equation (11). If *Disease* were the parent of more than one utility node, OpenMarkov would fuse them into a single node, as explained in Section 2.2.3. Then the only descendant of *Therapy* is the utility node, and this decision can be absorbed by applying Equation (12); the optimal policy is obtained from Equation (10). Now the only descendant of *Test* is the utility node, so this chance node can be absorbed by applying again Equation (11). At the end, only one utility node remains in the ID; its potential contains a single numerical parameter, which is the MEU.

4.1.3. Expected Value of Perfect Information (EVPI)

A relevant concept in decision analysis is the EVPI [36], which measures the advantage we would obtain from a certain piece of information, such as knowing the exact value of a parameter or the value taken by a variable. For example, given the ID in Figure 6, we may ask ourselves: "What would be the value of knowing for sure whether the patient has the disease (or not) before deciding about the therapy?" In OpenMarkov this question can be easily solved by drawing an information link from *Disease* to *Therapy*. Students can observe that the expected utility (effectiveness) increases from 9.3937—see Figure 6—to 9.5100, which means that the EVPI is 0.1163. This example illustrates the advantages of IDs, because if the original problem had been modeled with a decision tree, computing the EVPI would require building a new decision tree almost from scratch.

4.2. Explanation of Reasoning

OpenMarkov offers several options for explaining the conclusions achieved by an ID, most of them developed for its predecessor, Elvira [24]. These options have been useful for our research group when building BNs and IDs for medicine [23] and also for teaching PGMs to our students.

4.2.1. Imposing Policies for What-If Reasoning

OpenMarkov allows the user to impose policies on some decision nodes, in which case the evaluation algorithm only calculates optimal policies for the other decisions, which may differ from those obtained without imposed policies. This functionality allows the user to analyze decision scenarios that can never occur if the decision maker applies the optimal strategy, thus performing *what-if reasoning* [24].

For example, the optimal strategy for the ID in Figure 6 is: "if the result of test is negative, then do not apply any therapy; otherwise, apply therapy 2". However, the user might wish to investigate other policies, such as applying therapy 1 instead of therapy 2 when the test is positive, or applying therapy 1 in all cases, and calculate the expected utility for different results of the test, as shown in Figure 11.

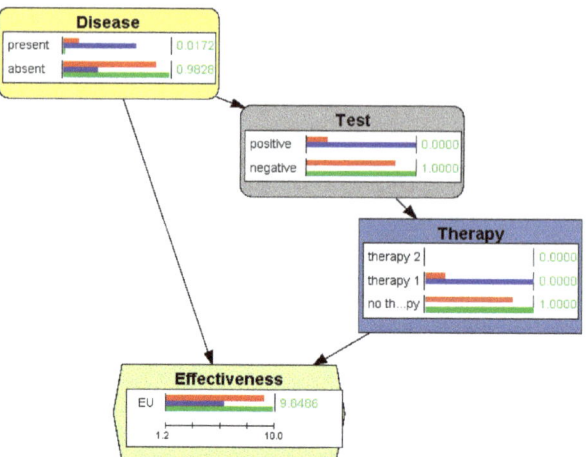

Figure 11. What-if reasoning: OpenMarkov allows the user to analyze what would happen if the decision maker applied a non-optimal policy. The node *Therapy* is colored in dark blue to indicate that a policy was imposed, instead of allowing the evaluation algorithm find the optimal strategy. The colors of the bars have the same meaning as in Figure 6.

4.2.2. Introducing Evidence

Lacave et al. [24] distinguished two types of evidence in the context of IDs: *pre-resolution* and *post-resolution*. Post-resolution evidence is introduced when every decision has been assigned a policy, either by the user or by the evaluation algorithm. The goal is to see how some findings affect the posterior probabilities—as in BNs—and the expected utilities. We have already seen two examples in Figures 6 and 11: OpenMarkov displays the utility expected before doing the test (which is the same as the utility for the general population, because some people test positive and others test negative), but we can also compute the expected utility and the posterior probability of the disease for those people having a positive test result and for those having a negative result.

In contrast, pre-resolution evidence corresponds to the classical definition of evidence in IDs [37]. In this case the question is: "What would the optimal strategy and the expected utilities be if we had that information when making the decisions?"

4.2.3. Example: Justifying a Policy

The usefulness of these two explanation facilities can be illustrated with the following example, adapted from a situation we encountered during the construction of an ID for lung cancer [32], when the pneumologist did not understand why the model built so far advised against doing a test that, in his opinion, would be useful.

The ID in Figure 12 presents a similar situation, in which it is better not doing the test, which might be counterintuitive. The reason seems to be that the result of the test does not modify the optimal policy. To confirm it, we first perform the sensitivity analysis shown in Figure 13, which shows that when the probability of disease is below 3.45% no therapy should be applied. Then we try to find out the posterior probability of disease after a positive test, but when we try to introduce the finding "Result of test = positive". OpenMarkov throws an error message saying that this finding is incompatible with the optimal policy, which precludes doing the test. A workaround consists in imposing the policy "Do test? = yes", which allows us introducing that finding and observing that the posterior probability increases of disease increases only to 2.51% (see Figure 14), still below the 3.45% threshold.

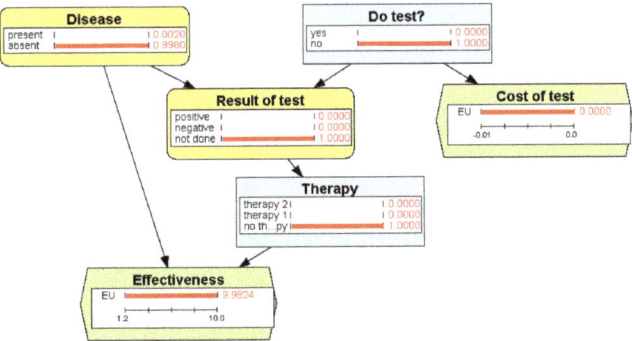

Figure 12. What-if reasoning: OpenMarkov allows the user to analyze what would happen if the decision maker applied a non-optimal policy. The node *Therapy* is colored in dark blue to indicate that a policy was imposed, instead of allowing the evaluation algorithm find the optimal strategy.

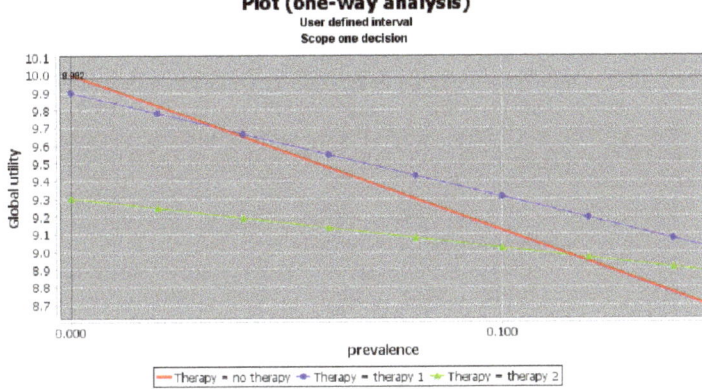

Figure 13. Sensitivity analysis for the ID in Figure 12, showing that when the probability of disease is below 0.0345, the best option is no therapy.

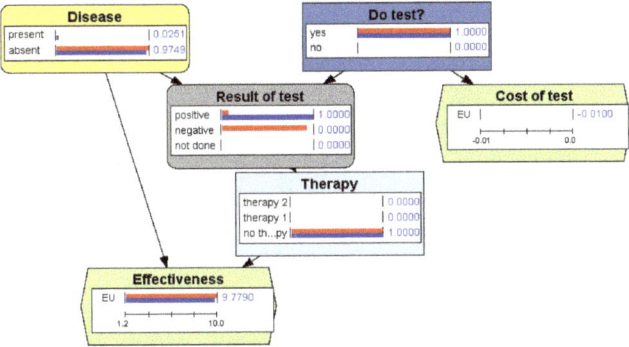

Figure 14. OpenMarkov allows the user to impose the suboptimal policy "Do test? = yes" and observe that a positive test result is unable to raise the posterior probability of disease above the 0.0345 threshold. This explains why it is not worth doing the test. The colors of the bars have the same meaning as in Figures 6 and 11.

5. Discussion and Conclusions

OpenMarkov is an open-source tool for building and evaluating several types of PGMs. It has been especially designed for medical applications and for teaching. It has been used for research and tuition in more than 30 countries.

In this paper we have illustrated with several examples how to teach several aspects of PGMs with OpenMarkov. Some of them—for example, the properties of d-separation, which are far from intuitive for beginners—might be illustrated with any other tool having a graphical user interface (GUI) able to show on a screen the graph of the model and a probability bar for each node, such as those mentioned in Section 2.3, but the explanation is much clearer if there is a probability bar for each evidence case, a feature that is only available in OpenMarkov. This tool also allows building networks in which some conditional probability tables (CPTs) are encoded as canonical models based on the independence of causal interactions, such as the noisy and leaky of the OR, AND, MAX, MIN, etc. [4,26], and implements efficient algorithms for evaluating them [38]. Students can learn how to apply these models and how they behave when propagating evidence.

Additionally OpenMarkov is useful to illustrate the execution of several iterative algorithms for inference and learning. In particular, it is able to display on a spreadsheet the samples generated by stochastic algorithms, as well the number of valid samples, the accumulated weights, and the posterior probabilities. It also allows the user to apply arc reversal iteratively for both BNs and IDs, showing how the probabilities and the utility tables are updated in each step. Similarly, it can learn BNs from a database using several variations of the two basic algorithms, search-and-score (hill climbing) and PC; in this case, the GUI offers several edits (such as adding, removing, or inverting a link), along with a qualitative score for each one, so that the user can understand what the algorithm intends to do and why. Students can compare the performance of different algorithms by observing not only the differences in the networks learned from the same database, but also how the algorithms differ step by step.

Our tool offers several possibilities for evaluating IDs. One of them is the conversion into decision trees, which can only be done for very small problems, but is very useful to intuitively understand the relation between the two formalisms. OpenMarkov can also apply efficient algorithms, such as variable elimination and arc reversal, and show the optimal policy (a table) for each decision, as well as the expected utility and the posterior probability of each chance and decision node, with the possibility of entering pre- and post-resolution evidence to observe how those utilities and probabilities vary. It can also show the optimal strategy in the form of a tree (cf. Figure 10), which is much more compact than the decision tree and the policy tables. Most of these features are not available in any other tool, whether commercial, free, or open-source.

Finally, OpenMarkov has novel types of PGMs, such as Markov influence diagrams [14] and decision analysis networks [15], developed by our research group, as well as new algorithms for cost-effectiveness analysis with these models [14,39,40]. They can be very useful for teaching health technology assessment (HTA), but that topic is out of the scope of this paper.

A limitation of OpenMarkov is that, although it implements several algorithms for exact inference, it only offers the most basic algorithms for stochastic inference and for learning. We implemented them just for pedagogical purposes, because these topics fall outside the priorities of our research group.

However, being open-source is an important advantage of OpenMarkov because it allows students with some knowledge of Java to inspect the implementation of the algorithms. For example, in the abstract class StochasticPropagation.java the students can find the data structures and methods common to the two algorithms discussed in this paper, while the classes that extend it, namely, LogicSampling.java and LikelihoodWeighting.java, implement the aspects in which the algorithms differ. Furthermore, advanced students can add new features—see [41] as an example. In fact, a significant part of OpenMarkov's code has been written by undergraduate, master, and Ph.D. students. In the future, other researchers and students, not necessarily from our university, might contribute new algorithms for inference and learning. This tool can be especially useful as a workbench for new learning algorithms because it has been carefully designed to allow implementing other algorithms, integrating them in the GUI, and executing them interactively.

Given that nowadays PGMs make part of the computer science curriculum in all universities around the world, we hope that many teachers and students may consider using OpenMarkov as a pedagogical tool, and some of them will later use it for building real-world applications.

Author Contributions: M.A. implemented Carmen, the first prototype of this software tool. All authors have contributed to the design and implementation of OpenMarkov, and to writing, reviewing, and editing the manuscript. All authors have read and agreed to the published version of the manuscript.

Funding: This work has been supported by grant PID2019-110686RB-I00 from the Spanish Government. The development of OpenMarkov has also received support from other grants of the Spanish Government and from the Regional Government of Madrid, most of them co-financed by the European Regional Development Fund.

Data Availability Statement: Some of the networks shown in this paper, together with several PMGs for real-world medical problems, are available at http://www.probmodelxml.org/networks; accessed on 20 September 2022.)

Acknowledgments: We thank the reviewers of this journal and those of the PGM-2018 conference for their comments and corrections. We thank all the students who have collaborated in the development of OpenMarkov, in particular, José Enrique Mendoza and Antonio Sáez for their work on the GUI, and Iago París for implementing arc reversal and the stochastic algorithms.

Conflicts of Interest: The authors declare no conflict of interest.

Abbreviations

The following abbreviations are used in this manuscript:

BN	Bayesian network
CPT	Conditional probability table
DT	Decision tree
GUI	Graphical user interface
ID	Influence diagram
MEU	Maximum expected utility
PGM	Probabilistic graphical model

References

1. Pearl, J. Fusion, propagation and structuring in belief networks. *Artif. Intell.* **1986**, *29*, 241–288. [CrossRef]
2. Howard, R.A.; Matheson, J.E. Influence diagrams. In *Readings on the Principles and Applications of Decision Analysis*; Howard, R.A., Matheson, J.E., Eds.; Strategic Decisions Group: Menlo Park, CA, USA, 1984; pp. 719–762.
3. Howard, R.A.; Matheson, J.E. Influence diagrams. *Decis. Anal.* **2005**, *2*, 127–143. [CrossRef]
4. Pearl, J. *Probabilistic Reasoning in Intelligent Systems: Networks of Plausible Inference*; Morgan Kaufmann: San Mateo, CA, USA, 1988.
5. Koller, D.; Friedman, N. *Probabilistic Graphical Models: Principles and Techniques*; The MIT Press: Cambridge, MA, USA, 2009.
6. Sucar, L.E. *Probabilistic Graphical Models. Principles and Applications*; Springer: London, UK, 2015.
7. Díez, F.J.; París, I.; Pérez-Martín, J.; Arias, M. Teaching Bayesian networks with OpenMarkov. In Proceedings of the Ninth European Workshop on Probabilistic Graphical Models (PGM'18), Prague, Czech Republic, 11–14 September 2018.
8. Neapolitan, R.E. *Probabilistic Reasoning in Expert Systems: Theory and Algorithms*; Wiley-Interscience: New York, NY, USA, 1990.
9. Luque, M.; Díez, F.J. Variable elimination for influence diagrams with super-value nodes. *Int. J. Approx. Reason.* **2010**, *51*, 615–631. [CrossRef]
10. Nielsen, T.D.; Jensen, F.V. Welldefined decision scenarios. In Proceedings of the Fifteenth Conference on Uncertainty in Artificial Intelligence (UAI'99), Stockholm, Sweden, 30 July–1 August 1999; Laskey, K., Prade, H., Eds.; Morgan Kaufmann: San Francisco, CA, USA, 1999; pp. 502–511.
11. Cowell, R.G.; Dawid, A.P.; Lauritzen, S.L.; Spiegelhalter, D.J. *Probabilistic Networks and Expert Systems*; Springer: New York, NY, USA, 1999.

12. Olmsted, S.M. On Representing and Solving Decision Problems. Ph.D. Thesis, Dept. Engineering-Economic Systems, Stanford University, Stanford CA, USA, 1983.
13. Shachter, R.D. Evaluating influence diagrams. *Oper. Res.* **1986**, *34*, 871–882. [CrossRef]
14. Díez, F.J.; Yebra, M.; Bermejo, I.; Palacios-Alonso, M.A.; Arias, M.; Luque, M.; Pérez-Martín, J. Markov influence diagrams: A graphical tool for cost-effectiveness analysis. *Med. Decis. Mak.* **2017**, *37*, 183–195. [CrossRef] [PubMed]
15. Díez, F.J.; Luque, M.; Bermejo, I. Decision analysis networks. *Int. J. Approx. Reason.* **2018**, *96*, 1–17. [CrossRef]
16. Lauritzen, S.L.; Nilsson, D. Representing and solving decision problems with limited information. *Manag. Sci.* **2001**, *47*, 1235–1251. [CrossRef]
17. Dean, T.; Kanazawa, K. A model for reasoning about persistence and causation. *Comput. Intell.* **1989**, *5*, 142–150. [CrossRef]
18. Boutilier, C.; Dearden, R.; Goldszmidt, M. Stochastic dynamic programming with factored representations. *Artif. Intell.* **2000**, *121*, 49–107. [CrossRef]
19. Boutilier, C.; Poole, D. Computing optimal policies for partially observable decision processes using compact representations. In Proceedings of the Thirteenth National Conference on Artificial Intelligence (AAAI'96), Portland, OR, USA, 4–8 August 1996; Clancey, W.J., Weld, D.S., Eds.; AAAI Press/MIT Press: Portland, OR, USA, 1996; pp. 1168–1175.
20. Díez, F.J.; van Gerven, M.A.J. Dynamic LIMIDs. In *Decision Theory Models for Applications in Artificial Intelligence: Concepts and Solutions*; Sucar, L.E., Hoey, J., Morales, E., Eds.; IGI Global: Hershey, PA, USA, 2011; pp. 164–189.
21. Elvira Consortium. Elvira: An environment for creating and using probabilistic graphical models. In Proceedings of the First European Workshop on Probabilistic Graphical Models (PGM'02), Cuenca, Spain, 6–8 November 2002; pp. 1–11.
22. Oliehoek, F.A.; Spaan, M.T.J.; Terwijn, B.; Robbel, P.; Messias, J.V. The MADP Toolbox: An open source library for planning and learning in (multi-)agent systems. *J. Mach. Learn. Res.* **2017**, *18*, 1–5.
23. Lacave, C.; Oniśko, A.; Díez, F.J. Use of Elvira's explanation facilities for debugging probabilistic expert systems. *Knowl.-Based Syst.* **2006**, *19*, 730–738. [CrossRef]
24. Lacave, C.; Luque, M.; Díez, F.J. Explanation of Bayesian networks and influence diagrams in Elvira. *IEEE Trans. Syst. Man Cybern.—Part B Cybern.* **2007**, *37*, 952–965. [CrossRef] [PubMed]
25. Teach, R.L.; Shortliffe, E.H., An analysis of physician's attitudes. In *Rule-Based Expert Systems: The MYCIN Experiments of the Stanford Heuristic Programming Project*; Addison-Wesley: Reading, MA, USA, 1984; pp. 635–652.
26. Díez, F.J.; Druzdzel, M.J. *Canonical Probabilistic Models for Knowledge Engineering*; Technical Report CISIAD-06-01; UNED: Madrid, Spain, 2006.
27. Henrion, M. Propagation of uncertainty by logic sampling in Bayes' networks. In Proceedings of the Uncertainty in Artificial Intelligence 4 (UAI'88), Minneapolis, MN, USA, 10–12 July 1988; Shachter, R.D., Levitt, T., Kanal, L.N., Lemmer, J.F., Eds.; Elsevier Science Publishers: Amsterdam, The Netherlands, 1988; pp. 149–164.
28. Fung, R.; Chang, K.C. Weighing and integrating evidence for stochastic simulation in Bayesian networks. In Proceedings of the Uncertainty in Artificial Intelligence 6 (UAI'90), Cambridge, MA, USA, 27–29 July 1990; Bonissone, P., Henrion, M., Kanal, L.N., Lemmer, J.F., Eds.; Elsevier Science Publishers: Amsterdam, The Netherlands, 1990; pp. 209–219.
29. Cooper, G.F.; Herskovits, E. A Bayesian method for the induction of probabilistic networks from data. *Mach. Learn.* **1992**, *9*, 309–347. [CrossRef]
30. Spirtes, P.; Glymour, C. An algorithm for fast recovery of sparse causal graphs. *Soc. Sci. Comput. Rev.* **1991**, *9*, 62–72. [CrossRef]
31. Bermejo, I.; Oliva, J.; Díez, F.J.; Arias, M. Interactive learning of Bayesian networks with OpenMarkov. In Proceedings of the Sixth European Workshop on Probabilistic Graphical Models (PGM'12), Granada, Spain, 19–21 September 2012; pp. 27–34.
32. Luque, M.; Díez, F.J.; Disdier, C. Optimal sequence of tests for the mediastinal staging of non-small cell lung cancer. *BMC Med. Inform. Decis. Mak.* **2016**, *16*, 9. [CrossRef] [PubMed]
33. León, D. A Probabilistic Graphical Model for Total Knee Arthroplasty. Master's Thesis, Department Artificial Intelligence, UNED, Madrid, Spain, 2011.
34. Jensen, F.V.; Nielsen, T.D. *Bayesian Networks and Decision Graphs*, 2nd ed.; Springer: New York, NY, USA, 2007.
35. Luque, M.; Arias, M.; Díez, F.J. Synthesis of strategies in influence diagrams. In Proceedings of the Thirty-third Conference on Uncertainty in Artificial Intelligence (UAI'17), Sydney, Australia, 11–15 August 2017; AUAI Press: Corvallis, OR, USA, 2017; pp. 1–9.
36. Felli, J.C.; Hazen, G.B. Sensitivity Analysis and the Expected Value of Perfect Information. *Med. Decis. Mak.* **1998**, *18*, 95–109. [CrossRef] [PubMed]
37. Ezawa, K.J. Value of evidence on influence diagrams. In Proceedings of the Tenth Conference on Uncertainty in Artificial Intelligence (UAI'94), Seattle, WA, USA, 29–31 July 1994; de Mántaras, R.L., Poole, D., Eds.; Morgan Kaufmann: San Francisco, CA, USA, 1994; pp. 212–220.
38. Díez, F.J.; Galán, S.F. Efficient computation for the noisy MAX. *Int. J. Intell. Syst.* **2003**, *18*, 165–177. [CrossRef]
39. Arias, M.; Díez, F.J. Cost-effectiveness analysis with influence diagrams. *Methods Inf. Med.* **2015**, *54*, 353–358. [CrossRef] [PubMed]
40. Díez, F.J.; Luque, M.; Arias, M.; Pérez-Martín, J. Cost-effectiveness analysis with unordered decisions. *Artif. Intell. Med.* **2021**, *117*, 102064. [CrossRef] [PubMed]
41. Li, L.; Ramadan, O.; Schmidt, P. Improving visual cues for the interactive learning of Bayesian networks. UC Berkeley. Available online: http://vis.berkeley.edu/courses/cs294-10-fa14/wiki/images/0/0a/Li_Ramadan_Schmidt_Paper.pdf (accessed on 20 September 2022).

Article

A Framework to Assist in Didactic Planning at Undergraduate Level

Daniel Alfredo Hernández-Carrasco [1,†], César Enrique Rose-Gómez [1,†], Samuel González-López [2,†], Aurelio López-López [3,†], Jesús Miguel García-Gorrostieta [4,*,†] and Gilberto Borrego [5,†]

1. Tecnologico Nacional de Mexico, Instituto Tecnológico de Hermosillo, Hermosillo 83170, Mexico; danielalfredohdez@gmail.com (D.A.H.-C.); crose@ith.mx (C.E.R.-G.)
2. Tecnologico Nacional de Mexico, Instituto Tecnológico de Nogales, Nogales 84065, Mexico; samuel.gl@nogales.tecnm.mx
3. Instituto Nacional de Astrofísica, Óptica y Electrónica, Sta María Tonantzintla, Puebla 72840, Mexico; allopez@inaoep.mx
4. Department of Computer Science, Universidad de la Sierra, Moctezuma 84560, Mexico
5. Departamento de Computación y Diseño, Instituto Tecnológico de Sonora, Ciudad Obregón 85000, Mexico; gilberto.borrego@itson.edu.mx
* Correspondence: jgarcia@unisierra.edu.mx
† These authors contributed equally to this work.

Abstract: In the teaching-learning process under the competency-based educational model, the instructor is a facilitator and seeks to generate a flexible and adaptable environment for student learning. One of the first tasks of the facilitator is the structuring of didactic planning. Didactic planning includes strategies for teaching and learning, evidence gathering, and choice of evaluation instruments. In this paper, we propose a framework based on natural language processing techniques with the support of an ontology grounded in the experience of instructors and university level course plans in the information systems area. We employ Bloom's taxonomy in the ontology design, producing an ascending structure for didactic planning, which allows the student to learn gradually. The developed framework can analyze the key elements that a didactic plan must contain and identify inter-related areas. Evaluation results with Cohen's kappa coefficient between expert judgement and our framework show that is possible to assist instructors in structuring their didactic planning. Out of the nine processes analyzed with the framework, an almost perfect kappa level was achieved in five processes, a substantial level in three processes, and a moderate level for one process.

Keywords: competency-based model; didactic planning; ontology; natural language processing; Bloom's taxonomy

MSC: 68T50

1. Introduction

In the teaching-learning process under the competency-based educational model, the instructor plays the role of a facilitator in the classroom. Following this paradigm, a flexible and adaptable environment is generated to support student learning. The learner becomes the center in the teaching process, seeking to acquire competencies. From the operational perspective, competencies require skills and behaviors that go from the simple to the complex. According to Westera, the individual's cognitive structure contains theory and practical knowledge [1].

Knowledge can be used in everyday activities, although some tasks require strategic thinking. In more complex situations, the competencies combine the acquired skills with specific attitudes. Under this approach, the student must grasp the theoretical knowledge (knowing), practical experience (knowing how to do it), and strategic thinking.

Preparation of didactic planning is one of the initial tasks to carry out in the competency-based approach. Didactic planning is a documented process that provides the instructor and the student with a guide to the teaching process in the classroom [2]. For the preparation of didactic planning, some instructors reflect on their experience to choose the didactic material supporting the course syllabus, or they try to replicate previous approaches. We propose a framework based on natural language processing techniques with the support of an ontology grounded in the experience of instructors and university level course plans in the information systems area. We employ the original Bloom taxonomy [3] in the ontology design, producing an ascending structure for didactic planning, which allows the student to learn gradually.

An experiment with students and teachers for the development of a product in six stages (planning, concept development, system-level, design, detailed design, implementation and testing, and production) for the engineering discipline was undertaken. This showed how the levels of Bloom's taxonomy appear gradually and allow students to reflect as they solve the problem [4]. In the early stages of development, the knowledge level of the taxonomy reaches the highest peak, while in the final stages of product development, the level of analysis and evaluation reach a high value. Furthermore, the experiment provided evidence of the link between engineering design and Bloom's taxonomy. In this study, the inclusion of verbs in Bloom's taxonomy led to a positive perception of the students. This research provided the motivation to consider Bloom's taxonomy as a guide for instructors to develop didactic planning.

Below, we present the elements of didactic planning:

- Learning strategies: activities carried out by students to participate in the training process to reinforce the instructor's knowledge or acquire new knowledge in an autodidactic way.
- Teaching strategies: activities, techniques, methods, or procedures that the facilitator uses to conduct the teaching process in the classroom.
- Evidence of learning: products of individual or group activities that demonstrate the student's learning process.
- Evaluation instruments: tools used by the instructor to assess student performance evidence in the teaching process.

In this study, the developed framework has two main components, the first is intended to manage the created ontology, and the second performs several text analyses. These two components are detailed in corresponding sections later on. The framework can analyze the didactic planning section-by-section from this combined interaction of the two components, as shown in Table 1.

There is little reported use of methods based on natural language processing for textual analysis in the formulation and writing of teaching and learning activities. To fill this gap, we developed the present framework. Our work is particularly helpful for novice instructors who are starting to write learning activities as they can receive an automatic analysis of their writing based on prior knowledge of the ontology and NLP methods. The framework can automatically validate if a given learning activity has the structure of verb + activity + topic—if any component is missing, the instructor is immediately given feedback. With this, a more complete and structured set of learning and teaching activities is obtained, since several rules, relations and inferences are verified or enforced. For example, in the case of the teaching activity "Explain examples about the use of vectors in programming", for this sentence the framework detects the absence of the topic which must be related to data structures according to the competence "Identify the different data structures, their classification, and how to manipulate them to find the most efficient way to solve problems through their classification and memory management".

Our framework's evaluation was carried out with 715 elements to produce an analysis report applying our approach and then this was compared it against the results of expert analysis. For the assessment, a Cohen's kappa agreement analysis was performed. The framework comprises nine analysis processes: competence, learning activities, teaching activities, learning evidence, evaluation instruments, competence-learning relationship, learning-evidence relationship, evidence-learning relationship, and evidence-instruments relationship.

Table 1. Didactic planning, unit I of computer engineering program.

Competence: Identify the fundamentals of user-computer interaction, based on knowledge of the human cognitive process and the principles of object-oriented design.		
Course outline	Learning activities	Teaching activities
- Human cognitive process - Human learning process - Cognitive ergonomics - Basic concepts - Design fundamentals - Principles of object-oriented design	- Create a concept map of basic terms of user-computer interaction - Analysis of case studies of user interfaces - Exercises of application of design principles to the design of virtual objects - Development of documents with a definition of the user interface project	- Introduction to the concepts and design principles through the development of a PowerPoint presentation and the use of examples - Presentation of case studies - Question formulation
Learning evidence		Evaluation instruments
- Data collection instrument - Data analysis report and results - Requirements document		- Checklist - Rubric - Rubric

Contributions:
- A framework that applies the knowledge managed in an ontology, combined with natural language processing (NLP) techniques to identify deficiencies in didactic planning, either in learning strategies, teaching strategies, evidence of learning, or evaluation instruments.
- Our study seeks to potentiate the ontology by implementing methods based on NLP as a complement. Previous related studies explored are mainly based on the use of ontologies.
- A framework designed to analyze text in Spanish, which can be equally adapted to other languages.

The article is structured as follows: Section 2 describes recent studies related to ontologies for designing and evaluating didactic planning. Section 3 provides an overview of the developed framework. Section 4 details the created ontology, including a binary relation scheme taking Bloom's taxonomy as a reference. The text analysis component is detailed in Section 5, including the four modules: text segmenter, match process, evidence-learning, and instrument-evidence. The statistical results are shown in Section 6. Section 7 focuses on the results of analysis on the test set. Finally, Section 8 addresses conclusions and discusses future research.

2. Related Work

In the educational environment, the design of learning objectives, teaching methods, techniques, and pedagogical approaches are part of the process called learning design (LD) [5]. The concept of learning design refers to the "process of designing effective learning experiences with the use of technological innovations and resources" [5]. In our work, didactic plan refers to a document that fits within the LD process, specifically in the competency model, to help the instructor organize the course plan. The use of educational data mining and learning analytic approaches to help improve LD has evolved with different computational techniques. Educational data mining (EDM) refers to creating methods to explore data that has an origin in educational environments. Learning analytics (LA) is defined as measuring, collecting, and analyzing data from students to understand and improve learning environments. Among the main areas closely related to EDM/LA are: computer science, computer-based education, education, educational statistics, data mining/machine learning, and statistics [6].

In [7], we reviewed recent trends in educational technology in the Computers & Education Journal, from 1976 to 2018. The authors performed a topic-based bibliometric analysis of 3963 articles. We observe that our research is aligned with topics such as assessment, teacher training, technology acceptance models, E-learning, and policy, which correspond to increasing trends identified by [7]. Another study that supports the importance of artificial intelligence in education is [8] which highlights the relevance of using data-driven learning to personalize and deliver immediate feedback in real-time. Our framework using AI techniques offers immediate feedback to the instructor.

Educational Data Mining and Learning Analytics

The design of strategies to improve student learning in online courses is approached using different algorithms [9], for example, longitudinal k-means cluster analysis. For this purpose, student groups were characterized using measurable features, such as the percentage of reading, instructional videos watched, the number of times task guides were viewed, the number of times task instructions were viewed, and the order of completed assignments. On this basis, the authors defined several groups: novice careful, confident traditional, knowledgeable confident, and no main group. Then a pattern was created for each kind of student. These groups represent the strategies developed by the students. For example, 21% of students were grouped under the novice careful strategy, so these students would have to read more text and watch many more videos. Analysis of this data helps instructional designers to focus their efforts.

Student performance prediction through clustering was analyzed in [10]. The authors grouped students with the objective that students with the same performance were placed together; thus, three groups were defined according to lecture materials, activity description, source, and the IP address of the student who accessed the e-course. To obtain a prediction, the authors built three decision trees, one for each group; in this way, they produced a general profile for each group. The smallest group contained the best-performing students. The result was that teachers could identify student behavior and design better techniques to encourage them to improve their reading time before tests.

The authors of [11] proposed monitoring of students to identify variables affecting student productivity. The authors focused on learning analytics, and using statistical tools, such as non-parametric tests and multivariate regression. They found five variables were related to student learning behaviors: total time spent, off-task behavior, the closeness of the first attempt to the due date, number of attempts, and the spacing of the study sessions. These variables provided instructors with valuable information to design and implement activities that could improve student learning.

PLATON is a system focused on stimulating self-reflection and providing support to teachers for understanding planned activities, asking questions such as, "How much time is scheduled for action—is that realistic?" [12]. In contrast, our framework seeks to computationally analyze the text and provide suggestions to instructors to improve teaching planning. Research-related work addresses aspects of ontologies and competency-based models.

Studies have also been undertaken using ontologies as a resource to organize expert knowledge. In some cases, this architecture is combined with other methods. For instance, in [13], we identified an ontology for designing competency-based learning applications that combines the concepts of knowledge, skill, attitudes, and performance. The ontology provides ways to semantically annotate resources to define individual actors' competencies, prerequisites, and goals for activities and resource content, evaluation criteria, and personalization capabilities for e-learning and knowledge management applications. The author also presents a competency management framework with an evaluation grid tool used by facilitators to assess learners' actual competencies. The author suggests that it can be used to adapt the learning environments to the learners' characteristics. In the same way, our framework utilizes an ontology to manage the information of the competencies. However, our ontology is based on Bloom's taxonomy and incorporates natural language processing (NLP) techniques for the analysis of new unprocessed texts.

The design of activities and assessment instruments are relevant for the student to understand his/her progress. In [14], the authors propose creating five ontologies to conceptualize the e-assessment domain to support the semi-automatic generation of assessment. They present an ontologies course domain specification, an educational resource specification, a learning object, assessment, and assessment instruments. The ontologies are connected through membership relationships. First, the course's domain incorporates the education resource, which, in turn, integrates the assessment ontology. This provides a means of ensuring that the suggested assessment instrument is appropriate for the course domain.

In [15], the authors introduce a pedagogic model within an ontology, placing the levels around the student, including learning style, learning objective learning domain, tag, and emotion, which are intended to provide better feedback to the student. In our work, all relationships revolve around the competence of didactic planning. However, we only have one ontology organized hierarchically according to Bloom's taxonomy. In the ontology of assessment, a deep hierarchy is observed, including three types of evaluation: formative, diagnostic, and summative.The ontology for evaluation includes a battery of assessment instruments, for example, essays and conceptual maps.

Under the competencies model, we found an ontology to support the teacher in designing a didactic sequence [16]. The ontology includes five elements: competence, resources (communication tools and digital resources), integrative tasks (learning scenarios), learning activities, and evaluation criteria (evaluation instruments and evidence). The authors employed the methontology [17] approach for the design of the ontology. We follow the same approach. One feature of their approach is the systematic creation of learning activities. However, the authors did not consider any text analysis as has been proposed and applied in our work.

In [18], the authors proposed an evaluation instrument for competencies using a rubric applied to a didactic sequence. The rubric considers the aspects of planning, intervention, and reflection. Experts who reviewed the consistency of the instrument analyzed the rubric. The authors performed a pilot test to validate its applicability. However, the aspects considered in the rubric require the interpretation of an expert for the rubric's application. Therefore, it is advantageous to have an approach, such as our framework, which employs a method to automatically evaluate the didactic planning document based on the ontology and language processing techniques.

One key difference between our work and the previously mentioned study is that most of the analyses focus on the English language, while our didactic planning framework was developed for the Spanish language. A closely related work [19] used ontology and NLP techniques but was oriented to the evaluation of essays. We found that the authors employed the same processes, including tokenization and identification of grammatical class as a verb. These authors used only cosine similarity, while we employed two metrics, cosine similarity and Levenshtein distance. The inclusion of NLP techniques to link the text, according to the ontology rules for didactic planning assessment, is also one of our main contributions.

3. Framework Overview

A framework based on natural language processing techniques to analyze college-level subjects' didactic planning is presented below. In addition, we create an ontology considering the information from didactic plans that an evaluation committee had previously approved. The basic assumptions of the competency learning model are:

- The instructor must be a facilitator of the learning process, motivating the learner to develop skills and aptitudes in a self-taught way. The teacher must prepare the learning environment with teaching strategies that consider the context.
- According to the desired graduate profile, the teaching process must focus on developing competencies, emphasizing actual problems and context applications.
- Depending on the established competencies, the formative assessment takes into account the student's achievements and development of their abilities during the course.

The goal was to develop a framework capable of detecting the key elements that each of the planning sections should contain and identifying the inter-related sections. Below, we describe the framework architecture.

In Figure 1, we can observe two components: the first focuses on ontology, while the second shows the methods employed for the extraction and analysis of text in free format. Both components maintain inter-communication for the retrieval and extraction of information. One of the first steps in this model is to segment competence into three elements, the verb, object, and purpose, where the main verb of the competence is analyzed under Bloom's taxonomy. It is essential to note that when the didactic planning is designed, there is a gradual increase in the student's activities and expected results. For instance, it is commonly observed that, in the first unit of planning, the concepts of the main topics are established and activities are defined for the student to appropriate that knowledge. Later, in subsequent units, the subject is deepened, and the learning evidence requires further elaboration by the student.

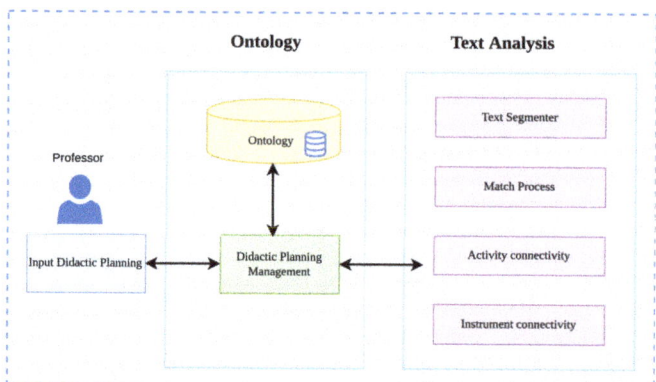

Figure 1. Framework architecture.

Bloom's taxonomy, proposed by Benjamin Bloom, is a six-part cognitive model focused on a person's thinking skills. This model increases in complexity as one progresses from higher-order to lower-order thinking skills [3]. Bloom sought to order the cognitive processes of the students hierarchically. For example, the ability to evaluate is based on the assumption that the student must have the necessary information, understand that information, apply it, analyze it, synthesize it and, finally, evaluate it. The six levels are knowledge, comprehension, application, analysis, synthesis, and evaluation. In Anderson's work [20], a review of Bloom's taxonomy is presented, redefining some of the levels. At the highest level of the original taxonomy is assessment, while in the revised taxonomy this is before the creation level. The six levels established in the revised taxonomy are: memorize, understand, apply, analyze, evaluate, and create. In addition, the definitions of the levels was changed from using nouns to verbs. Our work employs the original taxonomy as a reference, since we found it to be more suitable for the engineering discipline of our research.

This taxonomy leads the instructor to use appropriate verbs in each thematic unit of planning in our work. In this way, when the instructor carries out the planning, this gradually influences the student's learning level upwards.

The framework's input data to perform the analysis are: competence, syllabus, learning activities, teaching activities, the learning evidence, and assessment instruments. These elements are part of the didactic planning. Figure 2 shows a flow diagram of the processes that are carried out to evaluate didactic planning.

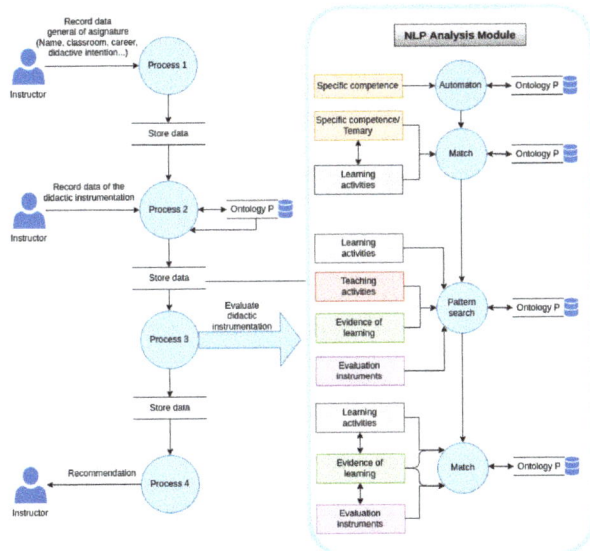

Figure 2. Flow diagram of the processes to evaluate didactic planning.

- Process 1: As a first step, the instructor submits the general course data for the didactic planning, such as the name, the course code, degree level, and the didactic intention, among other data contained in the official document of the course.
- Process 2: In this process, the instructor writes (in his/her own words) the data that will be analyzed by the algorithm presented in this article, as shown in Table 1. Starting from a specific competence and the course syllabus, the instructor will plan which learning and teaching activities to apply during the course, considering the student's evidence to deliver, and the instruments to evaluate the course results.
- Process 3: Subsequently, an evaluation of the sections that make up the didactic instrumentation registered by the teacher is carried out. The evaluation sequence involves four stages:
  – Automaton: the specific competence segmentation is carried out to identify if it complies with the three elements that it must contain and determine the verb level in Bloom's taxonomy. The correct wording of this sentence is essential to improve the probability of a match in the following process.
  – Match: In the first match process, the aim is to identify a relationship between the learning activities and the specific competence of the unit, considering that the activities must be planned to comply with the competence.
  – Search for patterns: an activity or evidence has a pattern, i.e., a verb followed by an activity and a topic associated with the current unit.
  – Evidence of activities: As a result of a learning activity, there must be at least one piece of evidence expected from the student. Three different evaluations were employed to find the connection: a match between the learning activity and the evidence activity, a fuzzy match to find a paraphrase in its counterpart, and

finally, an unsupervised clustering technique. Based on the three evaluations, an estimate is obtained to determine whether there is evidence for each proposed activity.
- Evidence evaluation: Finally, whether the instructor's evaluation instrument is adequate for the learner's evidence is judged.

In each of the steps just described, the algorithm relies on the relationships inferred by the knowledge model to increase the probability of finding patterns between the analyzed sections.

- Process 4: Finally, the results obtained by the NLP method and the knowledge model are sent to a recommendation module that, based on the metrics, indicates to the instructor whether its didactic planning complies with the grammatical structures and relationships necessary to move on to the final phase: the human review. In this work, we focus on the didactic planning analysis method. However, in an advanced version of this project, the system sends thirteen types of recommendations because two kinds of advice are given for each of the elements: verb, infinitive verb, the relationship between competence and learning activities, the relationship between learning activities and learning evidence, and the connection between learning evidence and assessment instruments. The first time an error is found, a list of recommended learning objects is displayed for each specific case. For example, if the competence does not have a verb and it is the first attempt, the recommendation will be displayed: "Remember that competence requires a verb that indicates what the student will do to demonstrate its performance. It is recommended that you review the following learning objects and try again".

4. Ontology Component

The ontology design was based on the methontology methodology [17], which integrates five tasks: specification, conceptualization, formalization, implementation, and maintenance. The domain of the proposed ontology is limited to the elements of didactic planning of academic program subjects at the undergraduate level in information systems in the Spanish language.

The acquisition of knowledge was carried out with experts in the area to create a glossary. The ontology was fed from the knowledge of two instructors of the computing area. Both instructors had completed graduate studies, with around 20 years experience of teaching, lecturing, and doing didactic planning. One of the instructors had also completed speciality studies in education. In addition, we followed recommendations of teachers in the design of didactic sequences based on high school education competencies [16]. Table 2 shows a partial view of the results for the concepts of teaching activities and generic competencies. There were 83 classes (21 main classes and 69 subclasses) and 486 previously defined individuals, representing the most used didactic material in the domain and corresponding to those described in Bloom's taxonomy. The organization of tacit (empirical) knowledge is complemented with explicit (theoretical) knowledge regarding the methodology to elaborate correct didactic plans. The main elements are related to a specific competence that determines what goal should be met at each thematic unit's end.

Table 2. Short view of glossary of two concepts.

Concepts	Activities
Teaching activities	Practical lesson Lead commented reading Lead a workshop Watch a video Case studies Make teams Organize dialogue
Development of generic competences	Capacity for analysis and synthesis Ability to organize and plan Oral and written communication Knowledge of a second language Basic knowledge of the career Basic general knowledge

Based on the experts' information, a relationship was identified between the unit's specific competences and Bloom's taxonomy, indicating the level of cognitive ability to be achieved in the thematic unit. A competency can belong to more than one level of the six that make up the taxonomy. The learning and teaching activities must consider the maximum level of competence and include activities for the previous levels until reaching it. For example, if the application level (level 3) is chosen, then activities at the knowledge, comprehension, and application levels must be considered to comply with the methodology.

Consequently, the ontology makes sense of the different classifications needed and the relationships established between the individuals that belong to more than one cognitive level. Therefore, it is not necessary to establish all the relationships in the model. Employing the inference engine, it is possible to deduce some correlations that generate knowledge.

Figure 3 shows a partial diagram of the class hierarchy. This hierarchy is defined based on Bloom's taxonomy. Within each concept, there are six levels of verbs of the taxonomy.

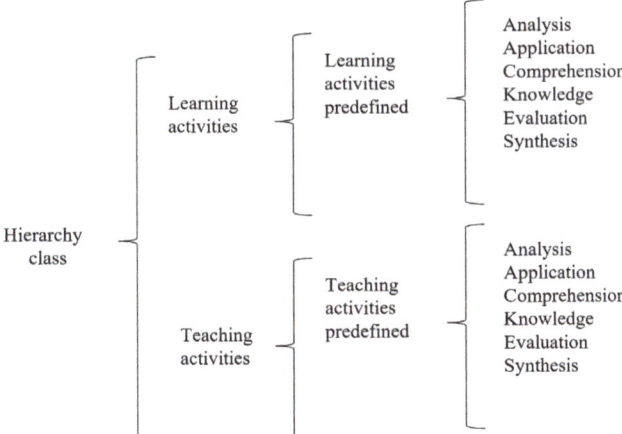

Figure 3. Hierarchical view of concepts "learning and teaching activities".

Figure 4 shows the general diagram of the existing binary relationships between the main classes of the ontology, where the categories that are classified based on Bloom's taxonomy are "Learning evidence", "Evaluation instruments", "Learning activities", and "Teaching activities". The competence class is directly related to the learning activities, the teaching activities, and the evaluation method. Teaching and learning activities should consider a domain verb, while the evidence may omit it. Ontology super classes are those whose levels have subclasses, and are shown in a dark color tone.

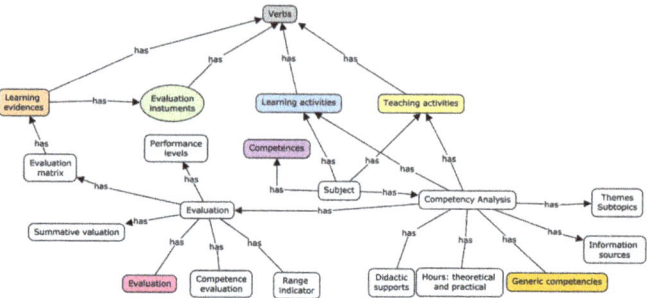

Figure 4. Binary relation scheme.

To implement the ontological model, the open-source ontology editor Protege was employed. The ontology is involved in several processes; one of them is when component two extracts the main verb. The first step is to identify the verb in the ontology, the related verbs, and their activities with respect to Bloom's taxonomy. If the verb is applicable, then the levels of knowledge and comprehension are considered, alongside the inference engine's activities. The ontology is also in charge of finding similar concepts. For instance, from the sentence "make a PowerPoint presentation with slides on NLP", three activities are detected: "presentation", "PowerPoint", and "slides". A query is submitted to the ontology to find similar concepts—if any activity corresponds to a verb, this is removed. Subsequently, which activity is accompanied by a verb is sought (in this case, PowerPoint). Therefore, the "slides" activity is discarded.

An example of learning activities and evidence is given below:

- Activities: make a comparative table of programming languages.
- Evidence: deliver a synoptic table on C.

In this case, the algorithm does not identify that C# is a programming language but identifies that the synoptic table is a diagram. Using the synonyms, it is possible to identify that a synoptic table can be a comparative table. This knowledge is inferred, since both elements are related to the word diagram's knowledge model (ontology). Therefore, the relationship is valid. Finally, each piece of evidence has associated instruments, and then it is identified which activity is the evidence. After that, a query is submitted to the ontology with that activity, and the possible evaluation instruments are retrieved. The ontology's function is to facilitate the classification based on Bloom's taxonomy of activities and verbs and to infer the relationships to obtain synonyms and relationships between words.

5. Text Analysis Component

The second component of our framework focuses on the application of natural language processing techniques. The search for existing patterns in the sections that make up the didactic planning involves evaluating the text in free format. Figure 5 shows the general design, starting from the segmentation of the unit's specific competence to finding the competence's linguistic structure and its main components. Afterwards, a lexical-syntactic comparison is performed between the filtered elements to determine their similarity (match process). The evidence and activities process identifies whether the learning activities are connected for at least one evidence example. Finally, the last process matches the evidence with the instruments to determine whether the selected instrument is adequate, based on the evidence. Each process can be carried out separately and gives an evaluation result, but they need to maintain the sequence since each depends on the previous one.

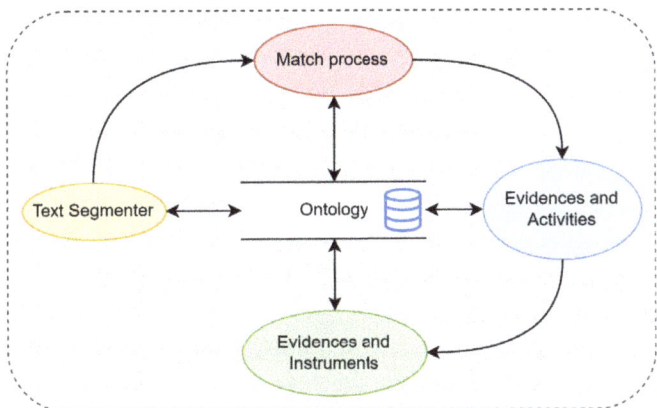

Figure 5. Text analysis component.

5.1. Text Segmenter

In this process, the component considers that a specific competence must contain a verb that identifies the domain to which it pertains, based on Bloom's taxonomy. Competence is composed of three sections:

Competence = verb + object + purpose or performance condition

We designed a method to carry out the segmentation, using morpho-syntactic analysis to find the words' root (lemma) and identify each grammatical role of the terms (tokens) in the sentence. We used the Freeling Library [21], that returns the base form of words and POS tagging (part of speech category tagging). Figure 6 illustrates how the segmentation process works. The verb that accompanies the learning object allows retrieval of the information stored in the ontology, establishing a filter dependent on the cognitive level for the written competence. Identifying the third element is also essential because it must maintain a relationship with the unit's learning activities.

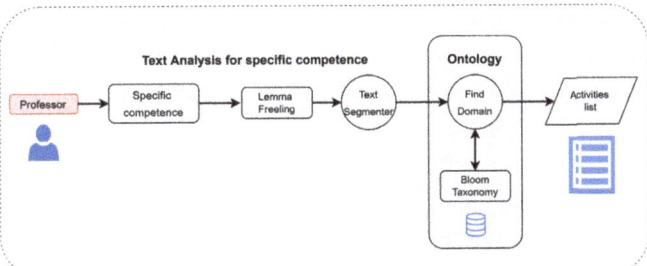

Figure 6. Segmentation process scheme.

The morphological analysis by Freeling allows generation of the label of the grammatical category of a sentence's words, providing a nomenclature depending on its classification, such as category, type, or gender, among others. The segmenter uses the words whose label indicates that it is a verb (V), conjunction (C), a noun (N), a pronoun (P), a preposition (S), or punctuation mark (F). For example, when the competence "Comprehends and applies linear data structures for problem-solving" is analyzed, the result of the competence segmentation process is the following:

- Verb: Comprehend and apply.
- Object: Data structures.
- Purpose: For problem-solving.

5.2. Match Process

The matching process consists of two parts. First, the unit's specific competence and learning activities are compared, so the different activities (learning, teaching, evidence, and instruments) have to be recovered and formulated by the instructor. Similar to a competence, an activity has a structure, as shown below:

Activity = verb + activity + topic

Figure 7 indicates the flow of information from the written activity to the result. The first step performs a pre-processing of the text, eliminating functional words (such as connectors and prepositions), and normalizing (eliminating capital letters, punctuation marks, word stemming), leaving only the words that provide relevant information for the analysis. Subsequently, the main activity is identified to detect later if there is a verb that accompanies it. Note that the activity and verb must belong to the catalogue available in the ontology. Later, it was identified if the activity is related to any subtopic of the current unit, to finally perform a joint evaluation of the three elements, resulting in a Boolean value that indicates whether the structure of the activity has been met.

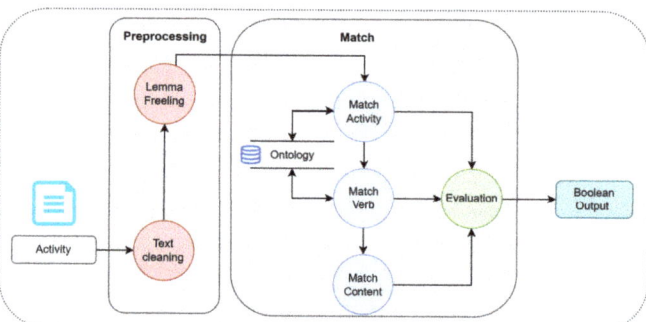

Figure 7. Match process scheme.

The instrumentation elements analyzed in this process are teaching activities, learning activities, learning evidence, and assessment instruments. Within the match process, it is defined that the evidence may lack a verb, and, even if it does, its wording is considered adequate. The instruments lack a verb and subject, so the activity is only searched in the match process.

5.3. Evidence-Learning Activity Connection

This process seeks to identify the existence of evidence for each learning activity. Figure 8 includes the diagram corresponding to this process, where three different methods can be identified that together produce a single correspondence value.

Match: The activity found in the previous process must appear in both texts. In addition, the synonyms stored in the ontology are considered, increasing the probability of a match. From this analysis, a Boolean value is obtained that indicates the existence or not of the relation.

Fuzzy match: This comparison is based on the Levenshtein distance that reflects the editing distance to determine the difference between two sentences. The writing of the evidence is considered a paraphrase of the proposed activity. When doing a partial analysis of the texts, their similarity should be high concerning the rest of the group, determining their similarity level by considering an acceptance threshold, which results in a numerical value.

Unsupervised clustering [22]: Clustering organizes elements that share particularities, finding patterns using feature extraction techniques and the cosine similarity metric. TF-IDF (frequency of term-inverse document frequency) allows evaluation of the relevance of a word within a text by converting the strings into a vector representation of n components, where the angle between the vectors is measured through the cosine function, resulting in their degree of similarity. Finally, we obtain a vector with similar elements grouped. This was performed employing the library sklearn.cluster.KMeans.

The results obtained from the three methods give higher relevance to the match method since it was clear that the activity must appear in both texts. The other two processes allow for confirmation of the relationship and establish the degree dependent on its values. When combining the methods, a correlation threshold was obtained, classifying the relationship as acceptable, under review, or non-existent. For instance, suppose that the didactic planning contains the learning activity: "Develop a conceptual map to explain artificial intelligence", and it also contains the evidence: "Develop a presentation that allows you to explain artificial intelligence". If we employ the Levenshtein distance and clustering functions with the above learning activity and evidence as inputs, then the output will be a high similarity score. However, the relationship between the concept map and presentation is non-existent, so that it would be considered as "under review".

The existence of the activity is not enough. For example, if the didactic planning has "Create a conceptual map to explain artificial intelligence", and, as evidence, "Create a conceptual map on mobile devices", the predicates do not correspond to each other, leading to low similarity, that, according to the threshold, would not be enough to be considered suitable (even when the learning object is available). For this, the fuzzy match and clustering process are pertinent to identify if the sentence predicates match.

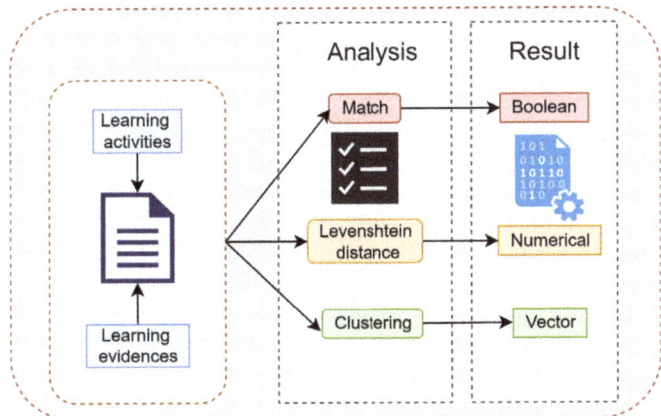

Figure 8. Scheme for the analysis of evidence and learning activities.

5.4. Instrument-Evidence Connection and a Short Example

The last process is intended to evaluate whether the instructor's instrument is appropriate, based on the evidence that the learner has requested. The didactic planning document contains a table, called the evaluation matrix, that indicates a direct relationship between both elements, unlike the previous process, where the correlation does not follow an order. Within the ontology, the match process's activity for the current evidence is validated and is identified if the instrument is adequate for its evaluation. The learning activities are the nucleus of the process as they have to be related to the specific competence, the teaching activities, and the learning evidence. Therefore, the result of the relationships is dependent on the correct writing of this element.

In Table 3, we provide a short output example of evaluation for the didactic planning by our framework. In the first step, we identify the following elements of the competence using the method in the text segmenter scheme: "Verb": Identify, "Competence Object": different data structures, their classification, and how to manipulate them, "Purpose": to find the most efficient way to solve problems, "Condition": through their classification and memory management.

Next, we show the output of three processes of the didactic planning analysis. Table 4 shows the result of evaluating the teaching activities looking for a match between the activities retrieved from the ontology and those written by the instructor. In this process, we consider whether the domain verb has been used and the topic to be addressed. The method is described in Section 5.2 Match process.

We can observe in Table 4 the phrase under review, which means that the absence of a topic (course outline) allows identification of the vectors as data structures. In this case, the instructor has to review the activity. This match process is repeated with the learning activities, learning evidence, and assessment instruments.

In Table 5, an evaluation of the evidence and learning activities is carried out. In this analysis, the match, Levenshtein distance, and clustering methods are employed, that were detailed in a previous section. There is no associated element in the example below for the first learning activity (under review). Therefore, the instructor must review the learning evidence.

Table 3. Evaluation didactic planning data structure.

Competence: Identify the different data structures, their classification, and how to manipulate them to find the most efficient way to solve problems through their classification and memory management.		
Course outline	Learning activities	Teaching activities
Data structures introduction. 1.1 Classification of data structures. 1.2 Abstract data types. 1.3 Examples of abstract data types. 1.4 Memory management 1.4.1 Static memory. 1.4.2 Dynamic memory. 1.5 Algorithm efficiency.	- Formulate a synoptic table of the different data structures and their classification. - Formulate a summary on abstract data types and implementation in object-oriented programming. - Formulate a comparative table of static and dynamic memory management.	- Use of technologies to search for information about data structures. - Organize a discussion among the students about the types of memory. - Explain examples about the use of vectors in programming.
Learning evidences		Evaluation instruments
Summary of abstract data types. Static memory and dynamic memory practices. Design exercises for virtual objects.		- Evidence folder. - Evidence folder. - Check list.

Table 4. Match of teaching activities.

Teaching Activities	Our Framework
Use of technologies to search for information about data structures	Result: Acceptable Activity: Search for information Topic: Data structures introduction
Organize a discussion among the students about the types of memory	Result: Acceptable Activity: Organize discussion Topic: Memory management
Explain examples about the use of vectors in programming	Result: Under review Activity: Explain examples Topic: Not found

Table 5. Evidence associated with learning activities.

Learning Activities	Learning Evidences	Our Framework Result
Formulate a synoptic table of the different data structures and their classification	Not found	Under Review
Formulate a summary on abstract data types and implementation in object-oriented programming	Summary of abstract data types	Acceptable
Formulate a comparative table of static and dynamic memory management	Static memory and dynamic memory practices	Acceptable

Finally, in the third evidence of Table 6, the identified activity "exercise" is not related to the evaluation instrument. It is incorrect to evaluate "exercises" with a checklist, so the framework generates a recommendation to the instructor, to review such activity.

Table 6. Instruments associated with learning evidences.

Learning Evidences	Evaluation Instruments	Our Framework
Summary of abstract data types	Evidence folder	Acceptable Activity: Summary
Static memory and dynamic memory practices	Evidence folder	Acceptable Activity: Practices
Design exercises for virtual objects	Check list	Under review Activity: Exercises

5.5. Framework as a Feedback System

Our framework is responsible for evaluating the didactic planning of college-level subjects using PLN techniques and a knowledge model. The framework belongs to a system dedicated to instructor training and education. Figure 9 shows the main components of the recommender system.

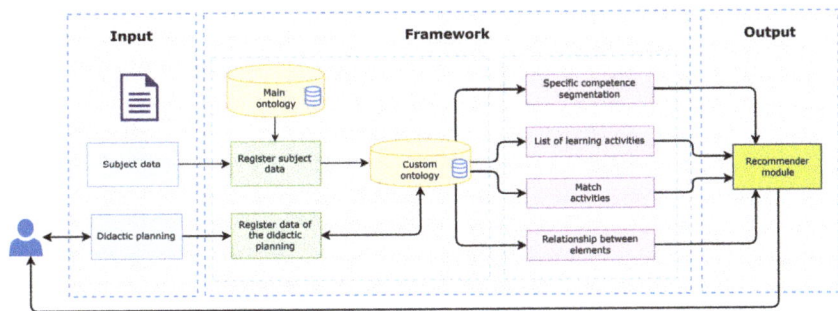

Figure 9. Framework as a feedback system.

- Input: In this section, the instructor can specify (write) his/her didactic planning, and is able to consult the available material related to the course and the suggestions made by the recommendation module.
- Framework: The function of the framework is to examine the didactic planning data using the components described in Section 3. As a result of the analysis, metadata is obtained and sent to the recommendation module.

- Output: Finally, this module receives the data from the analysis module to provide feedback. In the event of detecting deficiencies in the didactic planning, the system sends the instructor the pertinent recommendations. For example, suppose the competence does not correspond to the type of learning activities, and it is the first attempt. In that case, the recommendation will be displayed: "Remember that the learning activity must reflect the action indicated in the verb and the object on which that action is executed on". In addition, a list of learning objects linked to the competence is displayed. If the instructor requires a second attempt, a list of learning activities is displayed.

The analysis time for didactic planning lasted 30 to 40 s. Each planning contained four to five planning units. This time covered the following:

- If the competition was well written using the automaton
- Comparison between competence and learning activities
- Analyze if each activity is well-written
- Analyze the relationship between learning activities and evidence of learning (Using ontology, fuzzy logic, and clustering)
- Analyze the relationship between learning activities and evaluation instruments.

6. Statistical Results

For the analysis of the results of the nine processes, we found the following: Out of the 715 elements, 658 elements had a match between the human expert and our framework. The rest were non-matches (57). These descriptive results indicate that the percentage of agreement between the expert and our framework was 92%.

Below, in Figure 10, we detail the percentages in each of the nine processes. We can observe that the "Competence-learning relationship" process obtained the least correct answers, i.e., 75%. Competence-learning is a match of the competence with the activities to verify if the activities that the teacher is planning will help fulfill the unit's specific competence. Reviewing the didactic plan, we observe that the teacher paraphrased the competence in an activity or placed complementary activities that were not directly related to the competence. Our algorithm does not detect this paraphrasing phenomenon and this is an improvement to include in a further version. However, reaching human performance at this point will be difficult, as it requires a process of understanding, possibly with additional costly processing (such as parsing) or resources (e.g., sentence embeddings). In the work of [23], an analysis of classification tasks between humans and methods that used NLP was carried out; one of the conclusions was that humans will calibrate the learning results, and the algorithms will focus on refining the structure of the text. In contrast, the relationship between evidence instruments, evaluation instruments, and competence relationships reached 100% of correct answers. The complexity was lower since, at this stage, the instruments were already established, and the instructor only performed the selection. In this way, the match was facilitated for the computational algorithm.

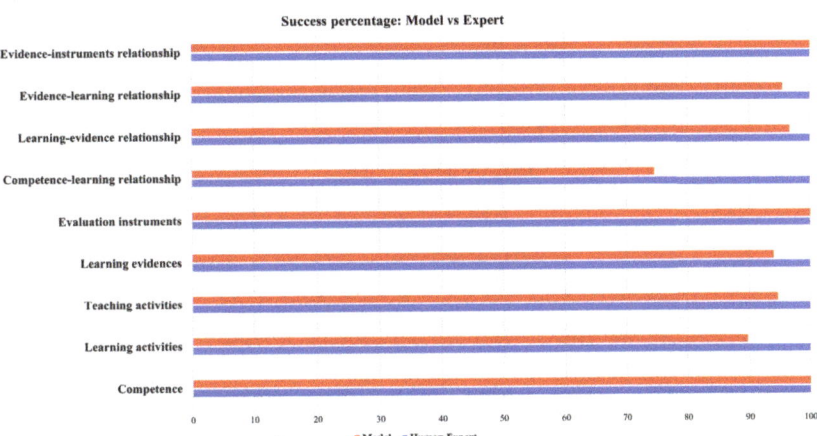

Figure 10. Success percentage: Framework vs. Human expert.

We calculated Cohen's kappa to obtain a result that would minimize randomness in the measurement. This coefficient reflects the level of agreement reached between our framework and the expert (instructor). Kappa is a statistical measure that adjusts for the effect of chance on the relationships involved [24].

$$K = \frac{Pr(a) - Pr(e)}{1 - Pr(e)} \quad (1)$$

Pr(a) are those elements in which both experts have had a relative agreement, while *Pr(e)* is the hypothetical probability of agreement by chance. Considering the results of this calculation, Table 7 shows the 715 elements evaluated and the levels achieved.

Table 7. Cohen's Kappa test results.

Didactic Planning Sections	Elements	Cohen's Kappa Statistics	Strength of Agreement
Competence	19	1	Almost Perfect
Learning activities	116	0.75	Substantial
Teaching activities	91	0.88	Almost Perfect
Learning evidences	65	0.75	Substantial
Evaluation instruments	65	1	Almost Perfect
Competence-learning relationship	114	0.48	Moderate
Learning-evidence relationship	115	0.91	Almost Perfect
Evidence-learning relationship	65	0.7	Substantial
Evidence-instruments relationship	65	1	Almost Perfect

The Cohen's kappa scale for a value under 0 indicates that there is no agreement and in the interval from 0.01 to 0.20 is null or very slight. A regular agreement, is considered between 0.21 and 0.40, while 0.41 to 0.60 is a moderate agreement. At a higher acceptance level, a value of 0.61 to 0.80 is a substantial agreement, and, finally, between 0.81 and 1.00 is an almost perfect agreement. The lowest value of agreement obtained was 0.48 in the comparison between specific competence and learning activities. This was because in the set of elements analysed (114 items) there were cases where the learning activity did not appear in the competence. However, the expert was able to identify it based on his experience. The match between evaluation instruments reached the almost perfect level because the instructor only selected the instrument from an established list. The agreement analysis of learning evidences and learning activities obtained a value of 0.91; we believe that in this section the use of natural language processing with synonyms, in addition to clustering and Levenshtein distance, helped to obtain an almost perfect level. Regarding the first evaluation that was analysed, it managed to obtain an almost perfect level of agreement for the task of identifying the competence.

7. Analysis on Test Set

The number of elements where the expert and the framework obtained an "Acceptable" prediction was also counted, i.e., the content of the didactic planning document elaborated by the instructor fitted correctly with the knowledge of the ontology and the text analysis component. The number of elements was counted where the expert and our framework sent "Under review" (this indicates that a phrase revision was necessary). In the figure below, the nine processes are represented on the X-axis and the test set on the Y-axis.

Figure 11 depicts in blue the frequency where the expert and the framework achieved an "Acceptable" prediction, while in red, it depicts those contents that were sent for review. That is, both points (in blue and red) represent coincidences. We can infer that instructors have a lower frequency of errors or failures when writing the didactic plan. It was observed that most of the framework's errors were due to the lack of a verb that accompanies the learning activity. The objective of this graph is to show that the failures of the designed method will be less than the successes. In the previous section, the kappa level was computed for each component. However, we sought to identify if this behavior could be supported statistically. Although there are no definitive results through a pilot test, this result indicates that the method is feasible to implement and put into practice. We performed a non-parametric correlation test to generalize the behaviour between the predictions "Acceptable" and "Under review". After running the Spearman test, we obtained r (s) = 0.033, p (2-tailed) = 0.93, which indicates that it is very likely that this behaviour is present in most of the didactic planning that instructors develop. We might think that most learning and teaching activities will be appropriate for students to perform better. Finally, our framework's precision depends on the handling of requirements indicated by the rubrics that the experts use to determine if planning complies with the competency-based model's indications. However, it may be feasible for the framework to be used as a tool that assists the instructor in writing the didactic plan document. We do not intend to replace the instructor, and we intend to provide support to improve their planning, and therefore impact students at undergraduate level. However, an interesting issue is that our framework takes from an ontology the expert's previous knowledge without training some learning model, for example, a neural network. Our approach helps a great deal in implementation processing because we require fewer resources. Our framework could, however, be complemented with a learning model, such as the BERT (bidirectional encoder representations from transformers) [25], which would allow identifying relationships between conceptually connected words. BERT has multilingual-trained models that would serve our purposes. For instance, in Table 3, the word "Android" was not linked to the word "mobile", but using the BERT models, we will probably find a relationship between both words.

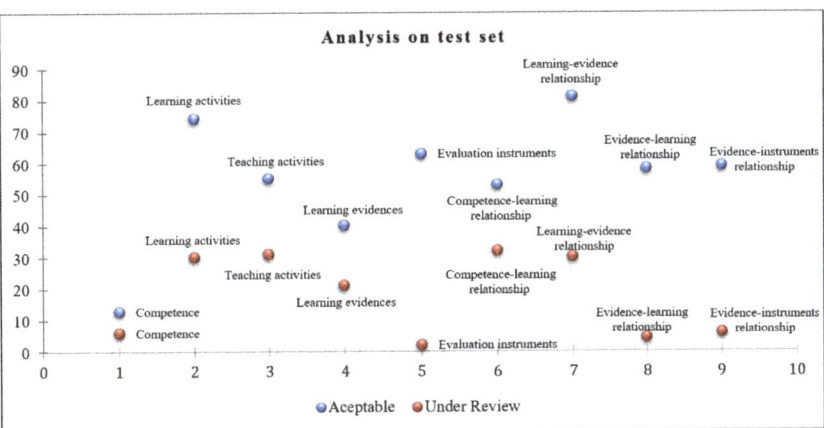

Figure 11. Analysis on test set.

8. Conclusions

The evaluations performed in the didactic planning of instructors of high technological education identified deficiencies in the writing of the learning objects, which for the most part corresponded to the omission of a verb that identifies the maximum cognitive domain that was expected to be achieved when carrying out the activity, considering the levels of Bloom's taxonomy. In a detailed results analysis, we observed that those elements where the algorithm and the expert did not coincide in the evaluation were due to the empirical knowledge resulting from years of experience in the evaluation of didactic plans, which allows human evaluators to infer relationships between elements, even when they are written implicitly. Therefore, modeling this knowledge and incorporating an infinity of possible options would imply having new rules and relationships that could harm the knowledge inference of the current framework, although they benefit it on some occasions.

Our framework's results show that it is feasible to use NLP techniques and knowledge models for the analysis of didactic plans of higher education instructors. It is also vital to understand that the framework is not intended to impersonate certified evaluators but to be a support for them and for the instructor, who will benefit from obtaining immediate feedback. We observe that our method's time to evaluate didactic planning was approximately 25 s against the more than 30 min that a human evaluator would invest in performing the same task. In light of this, we consider that the use of the proposed framework can reduce the workload of instructors.

The designed knowledge model, based on experts' knowledge from the department, is another contribution of this research since it contains properties that allow inferring knowledge, given the predetermined relationships. However, it is not possible to consider all the possible situations presented in didactic planning, so its viability depends on the experts' evaluation perspectives who were the source of the modeled knowledge.

We expect to integrate the framework into a platform dedicated to instructor training and education based on the competency-based model in future work. We plan to carry out a pilot test with new didactic plans that follow the methodology to obtain a new evaluation comparison that helps determine if the instructor has improved in the writing of his/her activities and the relationship between the sections, starting from the specific competence up to the evaluation instruments.

The knowledge model designed is limited to the technological domain, so evaluating other knowledge areas is beyond its scope. That is the reason we plan to increase the number of predetermined elements of the framework to provide higher coverage.

Author Contributions: Conceptualization, D.A.H.-C., C.E.R.-G., S.G.-L. and A.L.-L.; data curation, D.A.H.-C.; formal analysis, D.A.H.-C., C.E.R.-G., S.G.-L. and J.M.G.-G.; investigation, D.A.H.-C., C.E.R.-G., S.G.-L., A.L.-L. and J.M.G.-G.; methodology, S.G.-L.; project administration, C.E.R.-G., A.L.-L., J.M.G.-G. and G.B.; supervision, G.B.; validation, J.M.G.-G. and G.B.; visualization, S.G.-L.; writing—original draft, D.A.H.-C., C.E.R.-G., S.G.-L. and A.L.-L.; writing—review and editing, J.M.G.-G. and G.B. All authors have read and agreed to the published version of the manuscript.

Funding: This research received no external funding.

Institutional Review Board Statement: Not applicable.

Informed Consent Statement: Not applicable.

Data Availability Statement: The data presented in this study are available upon reasonable request from the corresponding author.

Acknowledgments: We want to thank the annotators of the collection. All authors were partially supported by SNI-Conacyt.

Conflicts of Interest: The authors declare no conflict of interest.

References

1. Westera, W. Competences in education: A confusion of tongues. *J. Curric. Stud.* **2001**, *33*, 75–88. [CrossRef]
2. Arnold, K.H. Didactics, Didactic Models and Learning. In *Encyclopedia of the Sciences of Learning*; Seel, N.M., Ed.; Springer: Boston, MA, USA, 2012; pp. 986–990. [CrossRef]
3. Bloom, B.S.; Engelhart, M.D.; Furst, E.; Hill, W.H.; Krathwohl, D.R. *Handbook I: Cognitive Domain*; David McKay: New York, NY, USA, 1956.
4. Sharunova, A.; Wang, Y.; Kowalski, M.; Qureshi, A.J. Applying Bloom's taxonomy in transdisciplinary engineering design education. *Int. J. Technol. Des. Educ.* **2020**, *32*, 987–999. [CrossRef]
5. Blumenstein, M. Synergies of Learning Analytics and Learning Design: A Systematic Review of Student Outcomes. *J. Learn. Anal.* **2020**, *7*, 13–32. [CrossRef]
6. Romero, C.; Ventura, S. Educational data mining and learning analytics: An updated survey. *Wiley Interdiscip. Rev. Data Min. Knowl. Discov.* **2020**, *10*, 1942–4787. [CrossRef]
7. Chen, X.; Zou, D.; Cheng, G.; Xie, H. Detecting latent topics and trends in educational technologies over four decades using structural topic modeling: A retrospective of all volumes of Computers & Education. *Comput. Educ.* **2020**, *151*, 103855. [CrossRef]
8. Srinivasan, V. AI & learning: A preferred future. *Comput. Educ. Artif. Intell.* **2022**, *3*, 100062. [CrossRef]
9. Davies, R.; Allen, G.; Albrecht, C.; Bakir, N.; Ball, N. Using Educational Data Mining to Identify and Analyze Student Learning Strategies in an Online Flipped Classroom. *Educ. Sci.* **2021**, *11*, 668. [CrossRef]
10. Križanić, S. Educational data mining using cluster analysis and decision tree technique: A case study. *Int. J. Eng. Bus. Manag.* **2020**, *12*, 1–9. [CrossRef]
11. Harindranathan, P.; Folkestad, J. Learning Analytics to Inform the Learning Design: Supporting Instructors' Inquiry into Student Learning in Unsupervised Technology-Enhanced Platforms. *Online Learn.* **2019**, *23*, 34–55. [CrossRef]
12. Strickroth, S. PLATON: Developing a graphical lesson planning system for prospective teachers. *Educ. Sci.* **2019**, *9*, 254. [CrossRef]
13. Paquette, G. An ontology and a software framework for competency modeling and management. *J. Educ. Technol. Soc.* **2007**, *10*, 1–21.
14. Romero, L.; North, M.; Gutiérrez, M.; Caliusco, M.L. *Pedagogically-Driven Ontology Network for Conceptualizing the E-Learning Assessment Domain*; JSTOR: New York, NY, USA, 2015; Volume 18, pp. 312–330.
15. Halimi, K.; Seridi-Bouchelaghem, H. A Web 3.0-based intelligent learning system supporting education in the 21st century. *J. Univ. Comput. Sci.* **2019**, *25*, 1373–1393.
16. Garnica, C.C.; Archundia-Sierra, E.; Martínez, B.B.; Márquez, A.P.C.; Cruz, J.L.G. Elaboración de una ontología para apoyar el diseño de secuencias didácticas basadas en competencias en la práctica del docente de educación media superior. *Res. Comput. Sci.* **2015**, *99*, 115–126. [CrossRef]
17. Corcho, O.; Fernández-López, M.; Gómez-Pérez, A.; López-Cima, A. Building legal ontologies with METHONTOLOGY and WebODE. In *Law and the Semantic Web*; Springer: Berlin/Heidelberg, Germany, 2005; pp. 142–157.
18. Ávila-Camacho, M.G.; Juárez-Hernández, L.G.; Arreola-González, A.L.; Palmares-Villarreal, O.G. Construcción y validación de un instrumento de valoración del desempeño docente en la ejecución de una secuencia didáctica. *Rev. Investig. Educ.* **2019**, *17*, 122–142.
19. Contreras, J.O.; Hilles, S.; Abubakar, Z.B. Automated essay scoring with ontology based on text mining and nltk tools. In Proceedings of the IEEE 2018 International Conference on Smart Computing and Electronic Enterprise (ICSCEE), Kuala Lumpur, Malaysia, 11–12 July 2018; pp. 1–6.
20. Anderson, L.W.; Krathwohl, D.R. *A Taxonomy for Learning, Teaching, and Assessing: A Revision of Bloom's Taxonomy of Educational Objectives*; Addison Wesley Longman: New York, NY, USA, 2001.

21. Padró, L.; Stanilovsky, E. Freeling 3.0: Towards wider multilinguality. In Proceedings of the Eighth International Conference on Language Resources and Evaluation (LREC2012), Istanbul, Turkey, May 2012; European Language Resources Association (ELRA): Istanbul, Turkey, 2012; pp. 2473–2479.
22. Gupta, M.K.; Chandra, P. A comprehensive survey of data mining. *Int. J. Inf. Technol.* **2020**, *12*, 1243–1257. [CrossRef]
23. McMahon, M.; Garrett, M. Mind vs. Machine: A comparison between human analysis and autonomous natural language processing in the classification of learning outcomes. In *EdMedia+ Innovate Learning*; Association for the Advancement of Computing in Education (AACE): Vancouver, BC, Canada, 2016; pp. 641–649
24. Landis, J.R.; Koch, G.G. The measurement of observer agreement for categorical data. *Biometrics* **1977**, *33*, 159–174. [CrossRef] [PubMed]
25. Devlin, J.; Chang, M.W.; Lee, K.; Toutanova, K. BERT: Pre-training of Deep Bidirectional Transformers for Language Understanding. In Proceedings of the 2019 Conference of the North American Chapter of the Association for Computational Linguistics: Human Language Technologies, Volume 1 (Long and Short Papers), Minneapolis, MN, USA, June 2019; Association for Computational Linguistics: Minneapolis, MN, USA, 2019; pp. 4171–4186. [CrossRef]

Article

Discovery Model Based on Analogies for Teaching Computer Programming

Javier Alejandro Jiménez Toledo [1,*], César A. Collazos [2] and Manuel Ortega [3]

1. Faculty of Engineering, Systems Engineering, CESMAG University, Pasto 520001, Colombia
2. System Department, Faculty of Electronic Engineering and Telecommunications, University of Cauca, Popayán 190001, Colombia; ccollazo@unicauca.edu.co
3. Department of Technologies and Information Systems, Higher School of Informatics, Castilla-La Mancha University, 13001 Ciudad Real, Spain; manuel.ortega@uclm.es
* Correspondence: jajimenez@unicesmag.edu.co; Tel.: +57-310-495-4875

Citation: Jiménez Toledo, J.A.; Collazos, C.A.; Ortega, M. Discovery Model Based on Analogies for Teaching Computer Programming. *Mathematics* **2021**, *9*, 1354. https://doi.org/10.3390/math9121354

Academic Editor: Radi Romansky

Received: 28 March 2021
Accepted: 9 June 2021
Published: 11 June 2021

Publisher's Note: MDPI stays neutral with regard to jurisdictional claims in published maps and institutional affiliations.

Copyright: © 2021 by the authors. Licensee MDPI, Basel, Switzerland. This article is an open access article distributed under the terms and conditions of the Creative Commons Attribution (CC BY) license (https://creativecommons.org/licenses/by/4.0/).

Abstract: Teaching the fundamentals of computer programming in a first course (CS1) is a complex activity for the professor and is also a challenge for them. Nowadays, there are several teaching strategies for dealing with a CS1 at the university, one of which is the use of analogies to support the abstraction process that a student needs to carry for the appropriation of fundamental concepts. This article presents the results of applying a discovery model that allowed for the extraction of patterns, linguistic analysis, textual analytics, and linked data when using analogies for teaching the fundamental concepts of programming by professors in a CS1 in university programs that train software developers. For that reason, a discovery model based on machine learning and text mining was proposed using natural language processing techniques for semantic vector space modeling, distributional semantics, and the generation of synthetic data. The discovery process was carried out using nine supervised learning methods, three unsupervised learning methods, and one semi-supervised learning method involving linguistic analysis techniques, text analytics, and linked data. The main findings showed that professors include keywords, which are part of the technical computer terminology, in the form of verbs in the statement of the analogy and combine them in quantitative contexts with neutral or positive phrases, where numerical examples, cooking recipes, and games were the most used categories. Finally, a structure is proposed for the construction of analogies to teach programming concepts and this was validated by the professors and students.

Keywords: machine learning; modeling; programming; text analysis

1. Introduction

Learning to program computers is a difficult process for novice students and also for professors [1] as it not only means acquiring new knowledge, but also fundamentally applying this knowledge to solve problems [2]. Therefore, it becomes a complex task because it requires students to master higher-order cognitive skills [3].

On the other hand, analogies are didactic tools used very frequently in the educational sector, and from observed experience, it can be determined that some professors include them in their curricula in a planned way and others adopt them only as part of their explanations in the classroom.

The scientific literature reports few experiences in the use of analogies for teaching-learning in a CS1, one of which is Collece 2.0, a programming learning environment that has been extended with mixed reality techniques and uses the analogy of roads and traffic signs for the study of recursion concepts [4–6]. In turn, Sukamto and Megasari [7] developed a model that converts source code into analogy images using state machines for teaching programming.

Likewise, there are models based on analogies for teaching processes in fields other than a CS1, which is how Strunz and Louie [8] proposed a model of analogy between energy storage and data processing in a computer for teaching electrical engineering concepts. For his part, Plappally [9] designed a model of analogies using concept maps for the first year of mechanical engineering courses. Additionally, Stockdill et al. [10] implemented a correspondence-based analogy model to choose representations of mathematical problems, among others.

Taking into consideration the ease of incorporating analogies in a teaching–learning process and the difficulties reported in the scientific literature in a CS1, this study proposed a model of knowledge discovery based on machine learning and text mining, which took as input the didactic teaching strategy with analogies and obtained a set of patterns for possible scenarios that can be used with a greater degree of assertiveness when presenting an analogy on a CS1.

In the collection of information, a semi-structured questionnaire was used to characterize the formal and non-formal analogical processes developed in a CS1 class with university professors. This questionnaire collected information from the professor, university, course, and the analogies used in teaching for four fundamental concepts: entries, exits, conditionals, and cycles. The application of this survey reported a total of 570 examples of analogies in 15 universities of five countries (Mexico, Ecuador, Argentina, Spain, and Colombia) with a total of 33 expert professors in CS1 in university computer programs that train professionals in software development.

The proposed knowledge model has three stages: initial processing, discovery, and results. In the initial processing stage, three activities were developed: data collection, extraction, and pre-processing. Two major activities were carried out in the discovery stage: transformation and mining. Finally, in the results stage, the findings found in the mining process were complemented, for this, techniques of the Natural Language Toolkit (NLTK) were implemented through three tasks: linguistic analysis, textual analytics, and experimental analysis.

The rest of this paper is organized as follows. In Section 2, the conceptual foundation of this study is presented. Section 3 describes the proposed discovery model. Section 4 shows the results obtained when applying the discovery model. In Section 5, the results are discussed and a structural model is presented to build analogies to teach programming concepts, which was validated through an experiment with professors and students. Finally, Section 6 presents the conclusions and future work.

2. Literature Review

The teaching–learning processes of computer programming are a complex task, and the results of teaching programming show that professors do not generate a reflection process in problem solving [11], despite the fact that many students do not have previous training experience in this field [12]. This is even more so when facing a CS1 as it requires cognitive abstraction skills, logical-mathematical skills, and the ability to solve problems algorithmically [13].

On the other hand, the learning of programming through analogous representations is a process where work has been underway for some years and whose purpose is to reduce the level of abstraction that programming requires to facilitate its understanding [4,14].

This is how an analogy is a connection of two situations with common relationship patterns between them and they are bidirectional [15]. Analogy can be explanatory when it poses new concepts and principles in familiar terms and creative when it stimulates the solution and the identification of a new problem and the generalization of knowledge [16].

The word analogy was initially a mathematical concept that meant proportion [17] and it was later considered as not corresponding to an identity of two relationships but rather ensures a similarity of correlations [18]. That is to say, it does not imply symmetric equality, but a relationship used with the purpose of clarifying, structuring, and evaluating the unknown from what is known [19].

Through analogies, one can develop the creativity, imagination, skills, and attitudes necessary for the critical use of scientific models and to shape one's own reality [20,21].

Furthermore, analogies can stimulate the professor-researcher to take into consideration the students' prior knowledge [22].

Analogies are a relevant research topic in the field of teaching [23]. Currently, there is an analog didactic model (ADM), which helps students find concepts that already exist in their cognitive structures on which a new learning is built [24].

Alternatively, artificial intelligence (AI) is a simulation of the human intelligence process in machines [25,26], where one of its most important fields is machine learning, which together with natural language processing (NLP) are contributing significantly to the development of science through research [27].

In addition, Knowledge Discovery in Databases (KDD) is a process that facilitates findings and analysis with the purpose of extracting unusual patterns in the form of rules or functions [28–30] through techniques that include data mining (DM) and text mining (TM) [31] as fundamental elements of machine learning.

Despite the beginning of machine learning dating back several decades, it is currently considered as an emerging field for developing research processes [32], demonstrating unexpected results in complex situations that resemble processes developed by human experts or superior to them [33].

Machine learning generates learning with low computational complexity [34] by which it is possible to extract behavior patterns from a dataset and build predictive models [35] using two phases in data processing: training and testing [33]. Furthermore, the training data requires standardization processes to ensure its efficiency [36]. An important feature of machine learning is the continuous upgrade, which can lead to changes in training data [37].

Additionally, machine learning takes into consideration three types of learning: supervised, unsupervised, and semi-supervised [38,39]. In supervised learning, classification, regression, and prognosis tasks are identified with techniques such as trees and decision rules, neural networks, support vector machines, and Bayesian classifiers, among others. Unsupervised learning features grouping tasks, association, and reduction with techniques such as clustering and dimensionality reduction techniques, while techniques such as transductive support vector machines and hope maximization are found in semi-supervised learning [40–42].

Another important area of machine learning is deep learning [43,44], natural language processing (NLP) [25], and text mining, which are computer and statistical techniques developed in the early nineties [45] used to discover new non-explicit information in source documents [46,47] and was aimed at discovering patterns through the right combination of artificial intelligence, machine learning, statistics, and data mining [48]. Text mining is currently used for various operations such as in image analysis [49], in biomedical fields (hospitals and clinics) [50,51], in the analysis of profiles of university students [52], in geosciences (geology, geophysics, geochemistry and remote sensing) [53], and in the automotive sector [54], among others.

There are several moments in the methodological processes formulated in text mining. Verma, Ranjan, and Mishra proposed two stages: classification and extraction [55]. In contrast, Sukanya and Biruntha established five different steps: purpose of study, information retrieval, processing, extraction, and results [56]. Similarly, Miner et al. proposed four tasks: collecting, organizing, analyzing, and assimilating [57]. Uysal and Gunal introduced four stages: pre-processing, extraction, selection, and classification [58]. In addition, text mining incorporates data mining tasks that are also used in machine learning within its learning types. These tasks are association, classification, and segmentation [27,28,41,59].

3. Materials and Methods

In this study, a knowledge discovery model based on machine learning and text mining is proposed. It takes the didactic teaching strategy as an input together with analogies for processes of abstraction of the fundamental concepts in a CS1 developed by professors in their classes. This model (see Figure 1) consists of three stages: (1) Initial processing; (2) discovery, and (3) results.

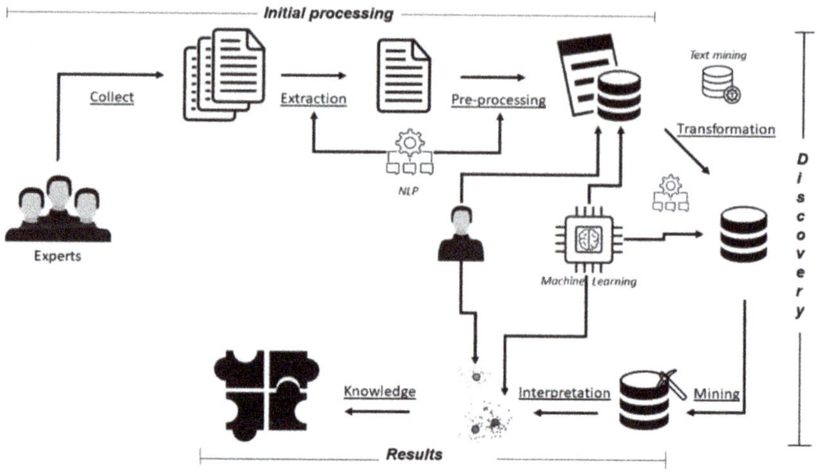

Figure 1. Knowledge discovery model.

3.1. Initial Processing Stage

The initial processing stage consists of three activities: Data collection, extraction, and pre-processing. For the collection, the survey was used as a technique and a semi-structured questionnaire was constructed in which the objective was to characterize the formal and non-formal analog processes developed in class for a CS1 with university professors. This survey was divided into two parts. The first part was related to the general characterization data of the professor, the university, and the course. In the second part, the experience of incorporating analogies in four fundamental concepts was investigated: inputs, outputs, conditionals, and cycles.

The extraction activity allowed us to carry out a characterization of professors and courses, in addition, it classified the examples of analogies in each of the following thematic units: analogies for inputs, outputs, simple conditionals, compound conditionals, nested conditionals, selective structures, cycle for, cycle while, and cycle do while. In this activity, there were a total of 570 examples of analogies used by professors in a CS1.

In the pre-processing activity, a dataframe was built under a data matrix structure and a cleaning process was carried out using NLTK [60] that consisted of: eliminating white spaces at the beginning, at the end, and between words, eliminating special characters, converting all words to lowercase, removing spelling accents, identifying words with plural and singular, and correct misspelled words.

3.2. Discovery Stage

Two major activities were carried out in the discovery stage: transformation and mining.

3.2.1. Transformation Activity

During the transformation activity, the text mining technique called the semantic vector space model [61] was used through the distributional semantics approach Gensim [62] that analyzes the words individually using: keyword extraction, summary extraction, tokens, and tagging part of speech (PoS).

With the previous activities, the following grammatical elements were created: main verbs and noun. Moreover, with the participation of three experts, a classification technique was applied under the intent detection model [63], which allowed us to extract the following semantic fields: action, context, and category.

Finally, during the transformation, it was necessary to resort to the synthetic data generation method [64] to balance the dataset using Python's NLTK to generate synonyms for each contemplated variable, which allowed for balancing the number of tuples of the input and output concepts versus conditionals and cycles.

3.2.2. Mining Activity

Before starting the mining activity, it was necessary to split the dataset into two: training (to build the model) and testing (to evaluate its behavior). Therefore, stratified sampling was used and the variable "Concept" (input, output, conditional, and cycle) was taken as a parameter. With these considerations, a setting of 80% for the training dataset and 20% for testing was done using cross validation to obtain better results [65].

In turn, the purpose of the mining activity was to identify patterns that allow the professor to use appropriate analogies to teach fundamental concepts of computer programming in CS1. In that way, and to obtain better results in the detection of patterns, three types of learning were applied: supervised, unsupervised, and semi-supervised learning with their corresponding tasks [66].

In the mining activity, the balanced dataset was used and began with the supervised type of learning through the classification task [67]; as it is one of the most widely used, it has great importance in this study due to its purpose of classifying data into categories that allow for the discovery of patterns in a CS1.

In contrast, the type of unsupervised learning was initiated through the association task [68] with the purpose of discovering frequent actions that were present in the bank of analogies used by professors in CS1. There were two methods used for this task: Apriori (to search for groups of frequent items) and Predictive Apriori (to extract the best rules with support and trust parameters).

Finishing with the mining activity and in order to obtain more information from the set of examples collected as analogies used in a CS1, the type of semi-supervised learning was applied using the expectation maximization technique (EM) [69] that obtains groups using a probabilistic approach.

3.3. Results Stage

Once the mining activity was completed and to strengthen the pattern detection process, the findings were complemented with three additional techniques: linguistic analysis [70], textual analysis [71], and experimental analysis [72] for each of the four main concepts established in this study.

For linguistic analysis, the techniques of flexive lemmatization and morphosyntactic labelling [73] were used. For the textual analysis, extraction techniques were used which involved keywords, multi-word, entities, and sentiment analyzer [74]. Finally, in the experimental analysis, the technique of extracting data linked by triplets was used [75].

Consequently, for the interpretation of results, the findings of the three techniques described above and the results of the mining stage were used, supported under the semantic vector space model with Tf-idf [61] with the Python OpenCv library. In addition, scripts were used to generate frequency graphs, point diagrams, word clouds, hierarchical grouping with elimination of dispersed terms and visualization of dendrograms by levels.

Likewise, with WEKA, the different cluster display models, trees, and margin curves were implemented. With these tools, it was possible to complement the process of the extraction of patterns from the bank of analogies used in teaching a CS1 by the 33 professors involved in this study.

Finally, an experiment was conducted in two moments, first by professors of a CS1, and then with their students.

4. Results

This section presents the results obtained in each stage of the knowledge model proposed in this study.

4.1. Initial Processing Stage

There were 15 state and private universities in five countries (Mexico, Ecuador, Argentina, Spain, and Colombia) that participated in this process, with a total of 33 professors who are experts in CS1 in university computer programs that train professionals in software development.

After the completion of the data collection, the extraction activities began. They, revealed that out of the 33 experts, 20 were from state universities and 13 from private ones. In addition, 21% of them had a doctoral degree, 70% had master's degree and 9% were specialists. Furthermore, in the characterization of courses, it was seen that the courses with the highest enrolment were Introduction to Programming, Algorithms and Programming, Programming I, and Fundamentals of Programming, which corresponded to 82% of the name of the courses. Additionally, the names of the professional programs that offer these courses corresponded to Systems Engineering, Computing, and Computer Engineering, which represent 95%. Finally, all the courses consulted were taught in the first semester of each academic program.

The pre-processing activity ends with the construction of the dataframe that had the following variables: Name of the university, country where the university is located, type of university, last study done by the professor, name of the course, semester in which it is taught, program or faculty, description of the analogy, concept that was intended to be taught, and if it was used directly in classes. Table 1 shows some analogies described by the professors at this stage.

Table 1. Some analogies used in a CS1.

Analogy	Concept
To Add an ingredient to prepare food	Input
To Enter password in ATM	
To Print sales invoice	Output
To Calculate total to pay	
To Choose menu of the day	Conditional
To Evaluate based on age, whether you are younger or older	
To Generate the first ten numbers	Cycle
To Add products in a cash register	

4.2. Discovery Stage

4.2.1. Transformation

With the results of the pre-processing and transformation activities, a relational database model was built (implemented in MySQL) with the following entities: Countries, Universities, Types Universities, Departments, Courses, Professors, Analogies, Concepts, and Descriptors.

The transformation activity incorporated the creation of datasets through dynamic views that allowed for the inclusion of the fields required for the construction of training algorithms necessary for the mining phase.

Before carrying out the mining activity, a pre-analysis was made using NLTK with the first data contained in the initial dataset, where the following information was obtained: Number of records for each concept: input (57), output (43), simple conditional (76), compound conditional (72), nested conditional (64), multiple selective (64), cycle for (66), cycle while (69), and cycle do while (59).

Additionally, this dataset contained the following peculiarities: out of the 570 cases of analogies used by professors, 523 were used in class with students and 47 were proposed because the professor had not used them for a certain concept and they suggested that they could be used. It was also observed that the same analogy was used to explain more than one concept.

Likewise, the most widely used contexts in the analogies for "Inputs" were Food, Shopping and Recipes. For "Outputs", the contexts used were Product, Invoices, and Purchases while for "Simple Conditional", the contexts used included Climate, Purchase, and Clothing. For "Compound Conditional", Transportation, Age, and Supermarket were used. Purchases, Salary, and Dress were the contexts used for "Nested Conditional". For "Selective Structure", Calculator, Food, and Cashier were used whereas Multiples, Students, and Clock were the contexts used for "Cycle For". For "Cycle While", Students, Play, and Multiples were the contexts used while Game, Students, and Shopping were used for "Cycle Do While".

A total of 116 different verbs were also found and the most frequent was "Evaluate". There were 309 nouns where the most widely used was "Age". Additionally, there were 402 actions and the most frequent was "Evaluate age". There were 272 contexts and the one with the highest concurrence was "Game", and finally, there were 11 categories where the most repeated was "Activity".

These findings applied to a CS1 are related to the teaching–learning processes of programming in studies carried out in children as presented by Pérez et al. [76,77], Sukamto and Megasari [7], or through metaphors by Chibaya [78].

4.2.2. Mining

Supervised Learning

The mining activity started with the type of supervised learning through the classification task and with the purpose of obtaining an appropriate model to the training dataset. In this task, the "general concept" attribute was chosen as the class variable that categorizes the analogies for inputs, outputs, conditionals, and cycles. In addition, there were five techniques used: decision trees, classification rules, vector support machines, envelope classifiers, and meta classifiers. The implementation of these methods was done with Weka.

There were two methods used for the decision tree classification task: J48 (which in turn contains the decision tree algorithm C4.5) and logistic model trees (LMT).

Due to the size of the dataset, the trees generated were complex to analyze due to the number of leaves and the size of the tree, therefore, it was necessary to use three pre-pruning techniques, taking into consideration to not affect the threshold of the percentage of instances classified correctly. The first pruning technique consisted of manipulating the confidence factor in each node (CF); the second by means of the minimum number of instances per leaf (IH); and the third by the elimination of attributes (EA).

Thus, a set of training models was planned by applying values from 10% to 40% to the CF; for IH, there were values from 2 to 40 records and EA up to three negations of the main attribute, for a total of 48 analyzed trees. In addition, a post-pruning process was also necessary. This consisted of discarding the generated rules that were under the established threshold of trust and support of the data.

As a result of the pre-pruning process, one of the generated decision trees that considered attributes of action, verb, noun, and context, correctly classified 93.3% of the instances with a minimum confidence of 83.9%. This tree took the verb attribute as the root node and the general rules with the highest value are shown in Table 2.

Table 2. Pre-pruning with J48.

Rule	Concept	% Confidence	Records by Rule
Verb = 'to enter'	Input	83.9	31
Verb = 'to get'	Output	88.6	21
Verb = 'to evaluate'	Conditional	97.5	193
Verb = 'to do'	Cycle	91.2	131

The J48 and LMT methods in the pre-pruning process classified the following verbs: to enter, to register, to obtain, to calculate, to evaluate, to do, and to play and the arithmetic and shopping contexts with the highest scores. In the post-pruning process, important variables related to noun, action, and context are evidenced, some results were: Noun (ingredient, row, plate, area, higher, assistance, products, budget, etc.), action (insert, ingredient, get, receive money, assess age, evaluate number, make multiples, play numbers, etc.), and context (recipe, bus, product, factory, students, purchases, game, students, etc.)

For the classification task using rules, four methods were employed. They were the Ripper algorithm (Jrip), machine learning sequential coverage algorithms (Modlem), One Rules based on ID3 (OneR), and Part Decision List based on C4. 5 (Part). In total, 678 rules were obtained.

In turn, the classification by means of vector support machines was performed with the SMO method, which is a sequential algorithm of minimum optimization through which a total of 1756 rules were obtained.

In the classification using envelopes, the input mapped classifier method was used taking into consideration the training and test dataset. This algorithm classified 21 rules.

Additionally, using the IterativeClassifierOptimizer Meta classifier, 10 iterations were performed with cross validation, obtaining 40 rules.

Finally, the results for supervised learning in the classification task were obtained considering the precision indicators, area under the curve, classification, and the positive rate for each of the methods used. The indicators in the classification task for the inputs, outputs, conditionals, and cycles concepts are presented in Table 3.

Table 3. Correctly Classified Instances.

Method	Input %	Output %	Cond. %	Cycle %
J48	98.4	98.4	98.4	98.4
LMT	94.4	94.4	94.4	94.4
Jrip	81.1	81.1	81.1	81.1
Modlem	99.1	98.9	99.1	99.1
OneR	98.6	98.6	98.6	98.6
Part	80.5	86.1	80.5	86.1
SMO	86.9	86.9	86.9	86.9
InputMappedClassifier	97.7	97.7	97.7	97.7
IterativeClassifierOptimizer	85.8	85.8	85.8	85.8

The most important findings of supervised learning for each of the concepts established in this study are presented below.

In the bank of analogies proposed for the input concept, the most important classification rules obtained in the nine methods were:

If [(verb in {enter} & noun in {ingredient, food} context in {recipe})] or [(verb in {enter, place} & context in {recipe, salary, arithmetic, student, price})] or [(verb in {register, type, read} & context in {salary, arithmetic, student, price})] then Input.

In the analogies proposed for the output concept, the most important classification rules obtained in the nine methods were:

If [(verb in {get} & noun in {ingredient, food} context in {recipe})] or [(verb in {get, calculate} & noun in {total, area, value} & actions in {get result})] or [(verb in {print, compute} & context in {arithmetic})] then Output.

Likewise, the most important classification rules for the concept of conditional were:

If [(verb in {choose} & noun in {food, time} & context in {food, restaurant})] or [(verb in {evaluate} & context in {mathematical, student} & noun in {age, number, grade, price})] or [(verb in {choose, determine, evaluate} & context in {arithmetic})] or [(action in {evaluate # noun})] then Conditional.

Furthermore, the most important classification rules for the concept of Cycle were:

If [(verb in {do, count, repeat} & noun in {age, multiple})] or [(verb in {add, average} & actions in {add ages, add wages, average age})] or [(verb in {add, count} & context in {arithmetic, student})] or [(noun in {row, money, bill, energy, shift} & context in {shopping, cashier, playing, television})] then Cycle.

Unsupervised Learning

This was started by the association task through two methods: Apriori and Predictive Apriori.

During the generation of rules with Apriori, a minimum support of 1% was used with a confidence of at least 70% and in total, 328 rules were obtained of which the main ones are shown in Table 4.

Table 4. Association with Apriori.

Concept	Rule
Input	(verb in {enter} & (noun in {ingredient}))
Output	(verb in {get, generate, print})
Conditional	(verb in {choose, evaluate, determine} & (noun in {operation, number, note, options, food} or (context in {purchase, food, student})))
Cycle	(verb in {make, play, count, assemble, add} & (noun in {multiples, vehicle} or (context in {arithmetic}))

In the search for rules with Predictive Apriori, the same parameters of support and confidence were configured as Apriori. Thus, we obtained 361 association rules.

This was then complemented with the grouping or segmentation task, which allows intra-group differences to be minimized and extra-group differences to be maximized.

Before applying this technique, a scaling, weighing, and selection process was performed with the data in order to obtain a more reliable segmentation level. For the grouping task, the K-means technique was used to search for characteristics iteratively.

This technique was configured with a value of 120 as seed in the generation of random numbers and four for the number of groups. For K-means, the grouping for inputs, outputs, conditionals and cycles according to the data classified in the dataset had a success of 89%, 91%, 99%, and 85%, respectively.

The most important findings of unsupervised learning are presented below.

The results for unsupervised learning in the association task for the input concept obtained the following rules:

If (verb in {enter} & noun in {ingredient, key}) then Input.

If [(verb in {enter} & context in {purchase})] or [(verb in {read, enter, type, insert} & noun in {price, side, key, money, card, code})] or [(verb in {digit, insert} & noun in {arithmetic})] or [(verb in {read, enter} & noun in {student})] or [(verb in {enter, enter} & context in {food})] then Input.

Similarly, the association task for the output concept generated the following rules:

If [(verb in {get, generate, print})] or [(verb in {get, generate, receive, finish} & (noun in {plate, product, information} or context in {invoice, information}))] or [(verb in {print} & context in {invoice, document, arithmetic, calculation})] then Output.

Likewise, the most important conditional rules for the association task were:

If [(verb in {choose, evaluate, determine} & noun in {operation, number, note, purchase, options, food, weather, age} or context in {purchase, food, calculator, student})] or [(verb in {evaluate, choose, determine, validate} & noun in {number, note, purchase, food, color, age, climate, price} or context in {age, climate, note, purchase, salary})] or [(verb in {choose} & noun in {menu, food} & context in {restaurant})] then Conditional.

The most important cycle rules for the association task were:

If [(verb in {make, play, count, assemble, add} & noun in {multiples, vehicle} or (context in {arithmetic}))] or [((verb in {play, count, do, add, run}) or (noun in {multiples, student, product}) or (context in {arithmetic, student, budget})] or [(verb in {play} & noun in {numerical care, professions, parquet, ballot, Tingo_Tango, hideout, war fest, cards, Cucunova, Hanoi, guess_number})] then Cycle.

Finally, for unsupervised learning in the grouping or segmentation task and in order to determine similar characteristics of the input concept, a new dataset was generated with only the corresponding tuples and to which the input class attribute was discarded, therefore, the K-means technique was configured to partition them into three groups. Correspondingly, three more datasets were made with the same criteria for the concepts of output, conditional, and cycle. The most important results can be observed in Table 5.

Table 5. Grouping by the K-means concept.

Concept	Variable	Cluster 0	Cluster 1	Cluster 2
Input	Verb	To enter	To read	To register
	Context	Recipe	Arithmetic	Purchases
Output	Verb	To get	To calculate	To get
	Context	Arithmetic	Purchases	Recipe
Conditional	Verb	To choose	To evaluate	To decide
	Context	Various	Various	Various
Cycle	Verb	To do	To tell	To do
	Context	Calculations	Various	Activities

Semi Supervised Learning

EM was configured with the same seed value as K-means and although the cluster number was not configured in EM, it generated four of these. The most important results for the semi-supervised learning in the grouping or segmentation task with the EM technique and with the same methodology carried out with K-means with four. The dataset is shown in Table 6.

Table 6. Grouping by the EM concept.

Concept	Variable	Cluster 0	Cluster 1	Cluster 2
Input	Verb	Various	To enter	To enter
	Context	Activity	Recipe	Purchases
Output	Verb	To get	To generate	Various
	Context	Arithmetic	Action	Vehicle
Conditional	Verb	To evaluate	To evaluate	To evaluate
	Context	Numeric	Activity	Calculator
Cycle	Verb	To do	To play	To tell
	Context	Numeric	Games	Numeric

4.3. Results Stage

Once the mining activity was concluded and using NLTK, three tasks were applied: linguistic analysis, textual analytics, and experimental analysis for each of the four main concepts established in this study.

4.3.1. Linguistic Analysis

This activity was developed with NLTK and its purpose was to extract information from the corpus of the analogies analyzed here to complement the patterns obtained in the discovery phase.

As a result of the linguistic analysis in the analogies described by the professors to face the abstraction of the input concept, there was a lexical variety of 81% where the use of verbs was 12.2% and nouns 43.5%. The main results for this analysis were:

Verbs: To enter, to register, to read, to place, to fill, to insert, to type, and to start. Additionally, the most frequent nouns were: ingredient, side, row, food, object, key, data, money, article, card, code and day. At the same time, the most recurring actions were: adding an ingredient, entering a password, reading text, entering a bus, turning on a circuit, filling a locker, queuing, filling fuel, and entering data. Regarding the context, the most used were: recipe, bus, arithmetic, student, data, restaurant, recipe, telephone, salary, and price. Figure 2 shows the morphosyntactic labelling process for the "key in cash machine" analogy.

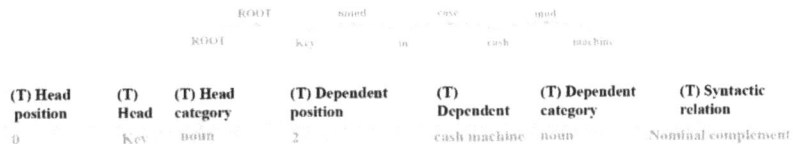

Figure 2. Input morphosyntactic labelling.

Similarly, linguistic analysis in analogies to teach the concept of output had a lexical variety of 71.2% where the use of verbs was 9.4% and nouns 25.9%. The main results for this analysis were:

The most used verbs were: to obtain, to calculate, to generate, to print and to invoice. The list of most common nouns was: total, area, shake, plate, information, power, shakes, clothing, result, bill, wages, sound, and value. On the other hand, the most mentioned actions were: obtaining a prescription, receiving money, getting off the bus, obtaining a solution, printing an invoice, obtaining an arithmetic result, and obtaining a prepared plate. The most frequent contexts reported were: product, factory, document, oven, arithmetic, printing and invoice.

In the results of the linguistic analysis in the analogies used for the study of conditionals, there was a lexical variety of 61.6% where the use of verbs was 7.8% and 16.9% nouns. The main results for this analysis were:

The most used verbs were: to evaluate, to choose, to determine, to validate, to take, to compare, and to calculate. The nouns were: major, minor, assistance, route, operation, transport, road, qualification, garment, purchase, options, health, color, signal, alternatives and subject, whereas the actions were: evaluate age, evaluate number, evaluate grade, evaluate purchase, choose transportation, choose route, determine age, determine gender, calculate higher, calculate lower, choose case, and evaluate number. The most common contexts included: student, shopping, arithmetic, and transportation.

Likewise, the linguistic results for the study of cycles had a lexical variety of 46.2% where the use of verbs was 6.4% and nouns 12.1%. The main results for this analysis were:

Verbs: to make, to play, to assemble, to count, to add, to perform, to loop, to execute, to count, to average, to determine, to repeat, to rinse, to collect, to put and to convert. The nouns included: product, users, arithmetic, budget, count, activity, game, card, age, multiple, routine, and Fibonacci. The actions were: making multiples, playing numbers, assembling vehicles, counting students, doing routines, doing operations, adding ages, adding wages and playing, whereas the contexts were: game, student, arithmetic, budget, tasks, payroll, cooking, health, reading, sports, counting, and assembling.

4.3.2. Textual Analytics

The main results for the textual analysis for the input concept showed that the most prominent keywords were: ingredient, keyboarding, dispenser and enter. The most frequent multi-words were: cooking recipe, food preparation, geometry figures, side height, beverage dispenser, bank affairs, quantity of items, and cashier code. Regarding the analysis of entities with the greatest presence in the analogies, there were: ingredient and geometry. The sentiment analyzer indicated that 17.9% of the examples presented were negative phrases, 57.1% were neutral phrases, and 25.0% were positive ones.

Likewise, in the textual analytics for the output concept, the main results of keywords were: plate, arithmetic, operation, and get. The most frequent multi-words were: prepared recipes, geometric figures, receipt, arithmetic operation, calculating salary, informational message, and cashier's money. In the analysis of entities with the highest presence in the analogies were area and concluded. The sentiment analyzer indicated that out of the examples presented, 15.9% were negative phrases, 54.5% were neutral phrases, and 29.6% were positive phrases.

Additionally, the main results of textual analytics for conditionals in terms of keywords were: if, menu, traffic light, cases, validation, and evaluation. The most frequent multi-words were: choice of garment, evaluating option, ideal weight, daily life, choosing destination, type of transport, restaurant menu, and evaluating proposal. In the analysis of entities with highest presence in the analogies were: menu, clothing, and cities. The sentiment analyzer indicated that 17.2% of the examples presented were negative phrases, 32.2% were neutral phrases, and 50.6% were positive phrases.

Moreover, the main results of the textual analysis in the analogies used for cycles provided keywords like: do, summation, factorial, Hanoi towers, iterate, count, play, and while. The most frequent multi-words were: race number, running game, building floor, and multiples. In the analysis of entities with the highest presence in the analogies were: numbers, Fibonacci, iterate, and summations. The sentiment analyzer indicated that 17.5% of the examples presented were negative phrases, 41.8.6% were neutral phrases, and 40.7% were positive phrases.

4.3.3. Linked Data

In the results of data extraction linked by triplets for the input concept, the most important relationships between subject and object were: they will be used for, represent, require, and enter, as shown in Table 7.

Table 7. Triplets.

Subject	Relationship	Object
Ingredients	They will be used to	A meal
Number	It represents	Value on a calculator
The flour	It requires	A baker to make bread
Beverage dispenser	It enters	Money

Similarly, in the extraction of triplets in the output concept, the most important relationships between subject and object were: get a, produce one, and exit.

Likewise, in the conditional triplets, the relations between subject and object with the highest frequency were: if it's there, if it complies, be, and travel in.

Finally, in the extraction of linked data for cycles, the most relevant relationships were: that they are repeated according to, do, add, until, and while.

5. Discussion

It can be seen in the vast majority of the analogies collected in this study that professors wrote them including key verbs that are commonly used in computational terminology and combined them with contexts and actions that are part of people's daily activities. Therefore, the most used categories were: cooking recipes, arithmetic calculations, purchases, sales, school situations, housework, and games, among others.

In addition, the professors used a greater proportion of analogies that could be computationally modeled instead of those that were general and could not be converted into computer programs.

The discussion for each of the three types of learning contemplated in this study is presented in greater detail below.

In supervised learning, professors incorporate verbs such as to enter, to read, to write and to register, to represent an input action, in addition, the examples are presented repetitively in the context of cooking recipes, payroll basic exercises, calculation of arithmetic operations, processing student's grades, transactions and purchases, and actions in electronic devices, among others.

In these rules, it can also be stated that professors include keywords in the use of verbs such as to obtain, to calculate, to generate, to invoice, and to print, which are commonly used in computational terminology to denote an output. In addition, some of the examples found were: obtaining a kitchen recipe, the calculation or printing a payroll, arithmetic, geometric operations, invoices, etc. There were also outputs that represent actions such as obtaining an adequate combination of garments, cars, and clothing, stimuli and the results of processes of electronic devices.

When analyzing the rules found for the analogies used to study the concept of conditional, it is also observed that professors included characteristic verbs of the specific terminology such as to choose, to evaluate, to determine, and to compare. The contexts analyzed were presented when choosing a meal from a menu, evaluating mathematical concepts, student's evaluation aspects, and activities such as doing housework, crossing the street, visiting, traveling, eating, dancing, choice of clothing, etc.

Finally, the rules generated in the analogies used to teach the concept of cycle also included verbs that are closely related to the specific terminology at the time of presenting a computational example for this concept, some of them were do, count, repeat, add, and average. Action such as sums, averages, age counts, wages, multiples, passengers, steps, students, among others, were also recorded.

In unsupervised learning, for the input concept, the association rules obtained were directly related to those extracted with the supervised learning techniques, in which the use of verbs plays an important role in the proposed sentence and with a greater emphasis on nouns in similar contexts.

The association rules for the output concept were more specific than the ones obtained in the classification task and they mainly used the same verbs and contexts. In addition, there were rules that involve actions in general contexts and not purely computational.

The association rules for the conditional concept were more detailed than those generated by classification techniques with a greater participation of nouns and contexts, but sharing the same verbs.

The association rules found in the analogies used for the teaching of cycles contained both the same verbs, nouns, and contexts as the classification rules, but these included more descriptors for verbs and nouns, which allowed us to contemplate a greater number of possibilities when analyzing analogical contexts to approach this concept with new examples.

In semi-supervised learning, the results of the grouping task in Tables 7 and 8 reaffirm the main rules obtained in both the classification and association task previously analyzed. Despite carrying out internal groupings in each concept, subgroups that used the same verbs and contexts were already found.

Table 8. Average grades for the control and experimental groups.

Group	Topic	Pre-Test	Pos-Test
G_1	Input/Output	2.30	4.32
	Conditional	1.70	3.56
	Cycle	2.12	3.87
G_2	Input/Output	2.43	4.03
	Conditional	1.81	3.12
	Cycle	2.40	3.26
G_3	Input/Output	2.60	4.67
	Conditional	2.40	4.26
	Cycle	2.91	4.39
G_4	Input/Output	2.57	4.28
	Conditional	2.13	3.75
	Cycle	2.12	4.00

According to the results found in supervised, unsupervised, semi-supervised learning, linguistic analysis, textual analytics, and linked data, it can be presented as a model (Figure 3) that integrates situated learning and the analogous didactic model to have a better approach to the fundamental concepts of programming to be taught by the professor.

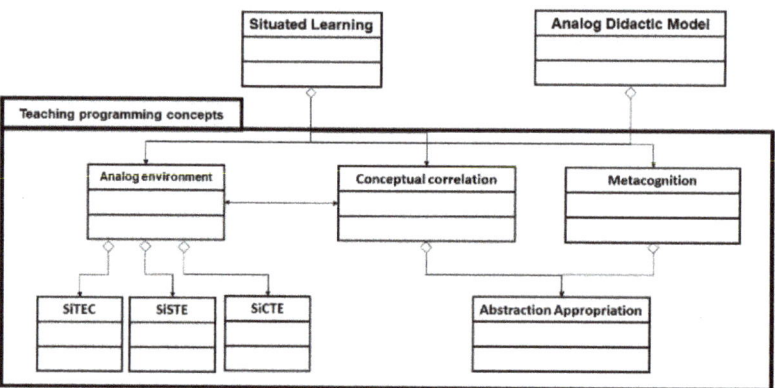

Figure 3. Model for teaching programming concepts.

Arias [79] states that the theory of situated learning establishes a relationship between the learner and the context, which is structured on a practical basis, therefore, to make the learning effective, the learner must be actively involved in actual instruction, that is, be part and product of the activity, the context, and the culture in which the instruction is developed and used [80].

On the other hand, the analogous didactic model constitutes a teaching strategy that implies the active construction, coming from the students, of the elements that constitute the base domain of the analogy [22].

The analogous environment refers to the real situation experienced by the students in their context; in this study, three environments were proposed:

1. Situated teaching environment in the classroom (SiTEC): When the situation is presented with physical elements in the classroom.

2. Situated and symbolic teaching environment (SiSTE): When it is observed indirectly (e.g., in simulated environments, immersive or digital environments, videos, among others).
3. Situated and Covert Teaching Environment (SiCTE): This occurs when the student who learns does so by imagining the situation.

In the conceptual correlation, the technical vocabulary is introduced, which is correlated with the options of the analogous environment to find meaning and understanding by comparing the concepts through the experiential analogy presented.

Finally, metacognition is the route of study of the professor's teaching process, which guides the planning, execution, and control of mental actions and operations of students, which have been oriented together with the aforementioned stages and there is an action to regulate the teaching of computer programming.

A key element of the model in Figure 3 is the analogy that the professor will use to teach a fundamental concept of programming. For the construction of an analogy, one must start from the concept to be taught, taking into consideration the three proposed analog environments (SiTEC, SiSTE, and SiCTE) and using experiential situations of the context where the learning takes place, so that the student can easily identify an analogy.

A proposal to build analogies and teach the concepts of programming fundamentals is to combine morphosyntactic elements with the most important findings of this study such as the inclusion of keywords from the terminology of computational examples, quantitative contexts, infinitive verbs, common nouns, and the sentiment analysis of sentences.

Therefore, Figure 4 presents the elements that an analogy may contain to teach these concepts through the use of sentences with elliptical or tacit subject that do not have the explicit subject in the grammatical structure, that is, they have the form of instructions and are categorized in the affirmative imperative grammatical mood.

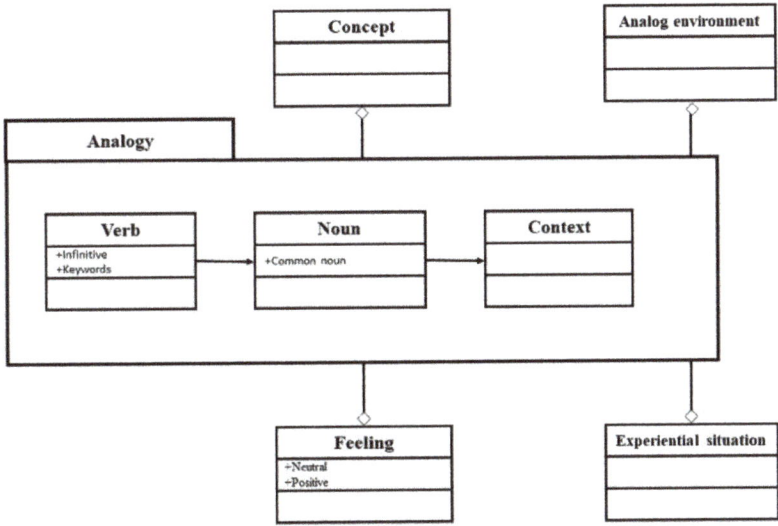

Figure 4. Elements of an analogy for programming concepts.

The findings presented in this study of supervised, unsupervised, semi-supervised learning, linguistic analysis, textual analytics, and linked data will allow us to select the most appropriate verbs, nouns and contexts for the concepts of input, output, conditional, and cycle, to later use computational thinking as a didactic strategy [81] in a CS1.

For example, according to the elements suggested in Figure 4, the following analogies can be used to teach the following concepts of programming fundamentals: enter a password in an ATM (input), obtain an invoice for the purchase of products (output), choose a dish from the restaurant menu (conditional), and add the values of each product of a purchase (cycle).

Validation

The evaluation process of this study was carried out in two moments, first with professors of a CS1 and then with their students. For the first moment of evaluation, the positivist paradigm was used, with a quantitative approach, using the analytical empirical method, with a descriptive type of research and through a pre-experiment with pre-test and post-test.

In this experimental process, two professors participated from two universities in Colombia, CESMAG University (private) and University of Nariño (public), who belong to the Systems Engineering program in the subject called Introduction to Programming and Fundamentals of Programming, respectively, which is in the first academic semester of each curriculum.

Consequently, the experimental design proposed was G O_1 X O_2, where G is the experimental group formed by the two professors who guide the CS1 in each university. Likewise, O_1 was formed by the bank of examples of analogies that these professors were asked to write to explain the concepts of input, output, conditional and cycles, presenting a total of 14 examples for the course Introduction to Programming and 17 examples for Programming Fundamentals.

Then, the professors were given the experimental treatment X, which consisted of the model of the creation of analogies proposed in this research. Finally, they were asked to re-build the analogies for each concept, according to the recommendations of the experimental treatment and whose result was O_2, obtaining the same number of initial examples raised by each professor.

When analyzing the analogies raised in O_1 with those obtained in O_2, it can be seen that the teachers considered elements such as the syntactic structure, the context, and the analogous environment. In addition, the first professor replaced six of the 14 examples initially proposed and the second professor changed five of the 17 examples. It was also observed that 100% of the initial analogies were restructured according to the syntactic recommendation to use a verb, a noun, and a context, incorporating the use of keywords as the main verb in each topic taught.

Similarly, all analogies in O_2 were shorter in length than those in O_1. For example, the analogy for teaching compound conditionals presented in O_1, whose wording was "when asking about the age of a student, you must establish if is of legal age or not", and in O_2, which was worded as follows: "Evaluate the age of a student and determine if is of legal age or not" being 37.2% smaller in extent, maintaining the context and adapting the syntactic structure.

In a second moment, the implementation of the analogies was evaluated according to the bank of examples obtained in O_2 with students of a CS1 and compared with the previous courses oriented by the same professors in which they used the analogies of O_1. In this case, the experiment had the same paradigm, approach, method, and type of research already mentioned with the professors, where the only difference was the research design, which was experimental with control groups and experimental with pre- and post-test.

In the experimental process, 154 students participated from the two universities already mentioned in San Juan de Pasto (Col) distributed in four groups and whose experimental design for CESMAG University was: G_1 O_3 X O_4 and G_2 O_5–O_6 and for The University of Nariño: G_3 O_7 X O_8 and G_4 O_9–O_{10}.

The groups G_1 and G_3 corresponded to the experimental groups of each university, while G_2 and G_4 were their control groups, respectively. In addition, X was the experimental treatment that consisted of using analogies with the model proposed in this research as a didactic strategy for teaching the fundamental concepts of programming in a CS1. In turn, O_3, O_5, O_7, and O_9 were the pre-tests implemented to evaluate the students' previous knowledge before facing the CS1. In addition, O_4, O_6, O_8, and O_{10} were the post-tests performed at the end of the experimental treatment for both the experimental and control groups.

The G_1 group was formed by 45 students (89% men and 11% women, aged between 16 and 20 years, and two students who retook the course) in the course Introduction to Programming of the first semester of Systems Engineering at CESMAG University, carried out between February and May of 2021, to whom O_3 was implemented by means of a questionnaire to verify their previous knowledge in the concepts of input, output, conditional, and cycle. Then, during the course, the topics were explained through the experimental treatment X, and finally, the notes obtained in the academic evaluation process were considered as O_4 posttests.

Likewise, the G_2 control group was made up of 31 students (87% men and 13% women, aged between 17 and 22 years and a student who retook the course) who received the same course with the same professor during the months of August and November 2020 at the same university. This group was given the same initial questionnaire as the G_1 group as a pre-test (O_5), but no experimental treatment was applied (X), that is, the professor used the analogies proposed in O_1 and the notes obtained were considered as O_6.

On the other hand, G_3 was formed by 40 students (83% men and 17% women, aged between 16 and 25 years, and no retaking of the course) of the course Fundamentals of Programming of the first semester of the Systems Engineering program at the University of Nariño, to whom O_7 was also applied as a result of the previous knowledge, then, during the course, the topics were explained through the experimental treatment X, and finally, the notes obtained in the academic evaluation process were O_8.

In the same way, G_4 was the control group with 42 students (89% men and 11% women, aged between 16 and 23 years, and no retaking of the course) who received the same course with the same professor during May and September 2020 at the same university. This group was also given the same initial questionnaire as the G_3 group as a pre-test (O_9), but no experimental treatment (x) was applied and the grades obtained were O_{10}.

The evaluation design for the two experimental groups and the two control groups was done through two academic follow-up activities: A group workshop (45%) and an individual quiz (55%) for each of the topics proposed in this study. The averages of the grades obtained in the pre- and post-test for the four groups are shown in Table 8.

The marks obtained in the pre-tests of both the experimental and control groups were never higher than those obtained in the different posttests, concluding that students from both the public and private universities learn the fundamental concepts of programming in a CS1, therefore, it highlights the importance of this study. In addition, it is evident the difficulty presented in the concept of conditionals, obtaining positives results in the management of cycles and achieving an optimal appropriation in the handling of data input and output.

Finally, a statistical analysis was performed to determine by means of the student's probability T distribution [80], the difference that exists between the grades obtained by the experimental group and the control group in each university. Thus, in both G_1 and G_3, the statistical values t (3.46 and 2.06) were greater than both the critical value of t of a queue (1.67 in both cases) and the critical value for two queues (1.99 in both cases). In addition, the record for one and two P tails was less than 5% in each case, which concludes that the grades obtained by G_1 and G_3, compared to those of G_2 and G_4, in each theme were statistically different.

Therefore, the aforementioned statistical analysis demonstrates the impact that the analogies built under the model proposed here can decrease the complexity of the topics for a student in a CS1.

6. Conclusions and Further Work

Professors included keywords that are typical of the terminology for computational examples in the writing of the analogies used in a CS1. Additionally, most of the contexts used in the analogies were of the quantitative type, where the numerical field has special importance.

In the sentence structure described by the professors when writing the analogy, the most significant grammatical element of value established by the NLP techniques was the verb, which at the same time was also the main attribute in the tasks of classification, association, and segmentation.

In turn, numerical examples, cooking recipes, and games were the most widely used categories as a reference for the construction of analogies that allow the student to abstract a fundamental concept of computer programming.

In addition, the results obtained in unsupervised and semi-supervised learning confirmed and complemented those obtained in supervised learning, the first being more specific and the second being more general.

It was also observed that the association rules generated in this study presented a higher level of confidence than those found in the classification rules. In addition, they allowed us to obtain patterns of greater specificity for each of the evaluated concepts.

Similarly, the results found by grouping ratified the rules obtained by association and classification in the four concepts.

On the other hand, the linguistic analysis showed us that despite having a wide lexical variety in the four concepts, due to the wide geographical area from which the data were taken, the professors used analogies in common contexts.

There was a high level of agreement among the results of the linguistic analysis, textual analysis, and data linked by each concept compared to the results obtained with the supervised and unsupervised analysis techniques.

For its part, the sentiment analysis showed that the analogies described by the professors had, on average, a neutral wording (46.6%) in the vast majority, followed by positive feelings (36.5%), and to a lesser degree negative (17.1%).

The design of an effective analogy to teach fundamental concepts in a CS1 must combine morphosyntactic elements with keywords in the form of verbs, and those must be typical of the terminology of computational examples. In addition, they must be in quantitative contexts and accompanied by common nouns and with neutral or positive phrases.

For future work, we will design a recommendation system that will guide the professor in the approach of an analogy to address a fundamental concept of a CS1 and develop a visualization tool that supports the process of abstraction in computing environments.

Author Contributions: Conceptualization, J.A.J.T., C.A.C., and M.O.; Methodology, J.A.J.T., C.A.C., and M.O.; Validation, J.A.J.T., C.A.C., and M.O.; Formal analysis, J.A.J.T., C.A.C., and M.O.; Investigation, J.A.J.T., C.A.C., and M.O.; Resources, J.A.J.T., C.A.C., and M.O.; Data curation, J.A.J.T., C.A.C., and M.O.; Writing—original draft preparation, J.A.J.T., C.A.C., and M.O.; Writing—review and editing, J.A.J.T., C.A.C., and M.O. All authors have read and agreed to the published version of the manuscript.

Funding: This research received no external funding.

Institutional Review Board Statement: Not applicable.

Informed Consent Statement: Not applicable.

Data Availability Statement: The data presented in this study are available on request from the corresponding author.

Conflicts of Interest: The authors declare no conflict of interest.

References

1. López Reguera, J.; Hernández Rivas, C.; Farran Leiva, Y. An Automatic Evaluation Platform with an Effective Methodology for Teaching/Learning in Computer Programming. *Ingeniare Rev. Chil. Ing.* **2011**, *19*, 265–277. [CrossRef]
2. Depetris, B.; Mallea, D.A.; Pendenti, H.; Tejero, G.; Prisching, G. Teaching and Learning Programming and Concurrent Programming with DaVinci. In Proceedings of the X Congress of Technology in Education and Education in Technology, Corrientes, Argentina, 11–12 June 2015; pp. 194–202.

3. Silva, G.; Arjona, P.; Castillo, F. More Time or Better Tools? A Large-Scale Retrospective Comparison of Pedagogical Approaches to Teach Programming. *IEEE Trans. Educ.* **2016**, *59*, 274–281. [CrossRef]
4. Sánchez, S.; García, M.Á.; Lacave, C.; Molina, A.I.; González, C.; Vallejo, D.; Redondo, M.Á.; Sanchez, E.S.; Gmarin, M.; Lacave, C.; et al. Applying Mixed Reality Techniques for the Visualization of Programs and Algorithms in a Programming Learning Environment. In Proceedings of the eLmL 2018: The Tenth International Conference on Mobile, Hybrid, and On-line Learning Applying, Rome, Italy, 25–29 March 2018; pp. 84–89.
5. Lacave, C.; Garcia, M.A.; Molina, A.I.; Sanchez, S.; Redondo, M.A.; Ortega, M. COLLECE-2.0: A Real-Time Collaborative Programming System on Eclipse. In Proceedings of the 2019 International Symposium on Computers in Education (SIIE), Tomar, Portugal, 21–23 November 2019; pp. 1–6. [CrossRef]
6. Redondo, M.Á.; Ortega, M. Colecce 2.0. Available online: http://blog.uclm.es/grupochico/proyecto-iapro/collece-2-0/ (accessed on 27 March 2021).
7. Sukamto, R.; Megasari, R. Analogy Mapping for Different Learning Style of Learners in Programming. In Proceedings of the 2017 3rd International Conference on Science in Information Technology (ICSITech), Bandung, Indonesia, 25–26 October 2017; pp. 626–631. [CrossRef]
8. Strunz, K.; Louie, H. Cache Energy Control for Storage: Power System Integration and Education Based on Analogies Derived From Computer Engineering. *IEEE Trans. Power Syst.* **2009**, *24*, 12–19. [CrossRef]
9. Plappally, A. The effect of joint role of creative analogy and concept-in-context map on the learning interest and performance of first year mechanical engineering undergraduates. In Proceedings of the 2016 IEEE 8th International Conference on Engineering Education (ICEED), Kuala Lumpur, Malaysia, 7–8 December 2016; pp. 126–130. [CrossRef]
10. Stockdill, A.; Raggi, D.; Jamnik, M.; Garcia, G.; Sutherland, H.; Cheng, P.; Sarkar, A. Correspondence-Based Analogies for Choosing Problem Representations. In Proceedings of the 2020 IEEE Symposium on Visual Languages and Human-Centric Computing (VL/HCC), Dunedin, New Zealand, 10–14 August 2020; pp. 1–5. [CrossRef]
11. Chaves, C.; Rosero, M.M. Teaching Model and Its Relationship with Metacognitive Processes in Systems Programming. *Rev. Educ. Ing.* **2014**, *9*, 1–12. [CrossRef]
12. Jiménez, J.; Collazos, C.; Hurtado, J.; Pantoja, W. Collaborative Strategy in Three-Dimensional Environments as a Didactic Strategy for Learning Iterative Structures in Computational Programming. *Investig. IRE Cienci. Soc. Hum.* **2015**, *6*, 80–92. [CrossRef]
13. Jiménez-Toledo, J.A.; Collazos, C.; Revelo-Sánchez, O. Considerations in the Teaching-Learning Processes for a First Course in Computer Programming: A Systematic Review of the Literature. *TecnoLógicas* **2019**, *22*, 83–117. [CrossRef]
14. Hundhausen, C.D.; Douglas, S.A.; Stasko, J.T. A Metastudy of Algorithm Visualization Effectiveness. *J. Vis. Lang. Comput.* **2002**, *13*, 259–290. [CrossRef]
15. Ruiz, F.J.; Luciano, C. Relating Relationships as a Functional Analytical Model of Analogy and Metaphor. *Acta Comport.* **2012**, *20*, 3–29.
16. Glynn, S.; Brillan, B.; Semrud Clikman, M.; Muth, K. Analogical Reasoning and Problem Solving in Science Textbooks. In *Handbook of Creativity*; PlenumPress: NewYork, NY, USA, 1989; pp. 383–398.
17. Haaparanta, L. The Analogy Theory of Thinking. *Dialectica* **1992**, *46*, 169–183. [CrossRef]
18. Perelman, C. *Analogie et Metaphore En Science, Poesie et Philosophie*; Presses Universitaires de Bruxelles: Bruxelles, Belgium, 1970.
19. Oliva, J.M. Actividades Para La Enseñanza/Learning chemistry through analogies. *Eureka Mag. Sci. Teach. Dissem.* **2006**, *3*, 104–114. [CrossRef]
20. Gilbert, J.K. *Multiple Representations in Chemical Education*; Gilbert, J.K., Treagust, D., Eds.; Models and Modeling in Science Education; Springer: Dordrecht, The Netherlands, 2009; Volume 4. [CrossRef]
21. Harrison, A.G.; Treagust, D.F. A Typology of School Science Models. *Int. J. Sci. Educ.* **2000**, *22*, 1011–1026. [CrossRef]
22. Galagovsky, L.; Adúriz-Bravo, A. Models and Analogies in the Teaching of Natural Sciences. The Concept of Analogical Didactic Model. *Enseñ. Cienc.* **2001**, *19*, 231–242.
23. Fernández González, J.; González González, B.M.; Moreno Jiménez, T. Considerations about Research in Analogies. *Estud. Front.* **2004**, *5*, 79–105. [CrossRef]
24. Malachías, M.E.I.; Borges dos Santos, D. Critical Meaningful Learning through the Explanatory Proposition of Analogies Through the Analog Didactic Model (MDA). *Electron. J. Res. Sci. Educ.* **2013**, *8*, 21–33.
25. Wang, D.; Su, J.; Yu, H. Feature Extraction and Analysis of Natural Language Processing for Deep Learning English Language. *IEEE Access* **2020**, *8*, 46335–46345. [CrossRef]
26. Ahmet, C. *Artificial Intelligence: How Advance Machine Learning Will Shape the Future of Our Word*; Independently published, 2018. Available online: https://www.amazon.com/Artificial-Intelligence-Advanced-Machine-Learning/dp/1790129753 (accessed on 27 March 2021).
27. Sharda, R.; Delen, D.; Turban, E. *Pearson Etext Analytics, Data Science, & Artificial Intelligence*, 11th ed.; Pearson Education: London, UK, 2019.
28. Timarán, S.; Hernández, I.; Caicedo, S.; Hidalgo, A.; Alvarado, J. *Discovery of Academic Performance Patterns with Decision Trees in Generic Professional Training Competencies*, 1st ed.; Universidad Cooperativa de Colombia: Bogotá, Colombia, 2016. [CrossRef]
29. Gomes, R.P.; Ribeiro, V.G.; Corrêa, Y.; Zabadal, J.R.S. Aplicação de Revisão Sistemática Com Suporte de Mineração de Dados e de Textos: O Caso Do Periódico Design Studies. *Em. Quest.* **2019**, *25*, 156–183. [CrossRef]

30. Arce, D.; Lima, F.; Orellana Cordero, M.P.; Ortega, J.; Sellers, C.; Ortega, P. Discovering Behavioral Patterns among Air Pollutants: A Data Mining Approach. *Enfoque UTE* **2018**, *9*, 168–179. [CrossRef]
31. Tan, P.-N.; Steinbach, M.; Karpatne, A.; Kumar, V. *Introduction to Data Mining*; Pearson: Edinburgo, UK, 2019.
32. Jordan, M.I.; Mitchell, T.M. Machine Learning: Trends, Perspectives, and Prospects. *Science* **2015**, *349*, 255–260. [CrossRef]
33. Xue, M.; Yuan, C.; Wu, H.; Zhang, Y.; Liu, W. Machine Learning Security: Threats, Countermeasures, and Evaluations. *IEEE Access* **2020**, *8*, 74720–74742. [CrossRef]
34. Qian, G.; Li, Z.; He, C.; Li, X.; Ding, X. Power Allocation Schemes Based on Deep Learning for Distributed Antenna Systems. *IEEE Access* **2020**, *8*, 31245–31253. [CrossRef]
35. Ledesma, S.; Ibarra-Manzano, M.; Cabal-Yepez, E.; Almanza-Ojeda, D.; Avina-Cervantes, J. Analysis of Data Sets with Learning Conflicts for Machine Learning. *IEEE Access* **2018**, *6*, 45062–45070. [CrossRef]
36. Bo, L.; Wang, L.; Jiao, L. Feature Scaling for Kernel Fisher Discriminant Analysis Using Leave-One-Out Cross Validation. *Neural Comput.* **2006**, *18*, 961–978. [CrossRef] [PubMed]
37. Jin, B.; Jing, Z.; Zhao, H. Incremental and Decremental Extreme Learning Machine Based on Generalized Inverse. *IEEE Access* **2017**, *5*, 20852–20865. [CrossRef]
38. Russell, S.; Norvig, P. *Artificial Intelligence: A Modern Approach*, 3rd ed.; Norvig, P., Ed.; Pearson: London, UK, 2016.
39. Marsland, S. *Machine Learning: An Algorithmic Perspective*, 2nd ed.; CRC Press: Boca Raton, FL, USA, 2015.
40. Godoy Viera, Á.F. Machine Learning Techniques Used for Text Mining. *Investig. Bibl. Arch. Bibl. Inf.* **2017**, *31*, 103. [CrossRef]
41. Verhaar, P. *Text and Data Mining: The Theory and Practice of Using TDM for Scholarship in the Humanities*; Facet Publishing: London, UK, 2020.
42. Alvarez Fernández, N.; Comin, X.J.; Merino Arranz, D. *Técnicas de Machine Learning y Desarrollo de Modelos Predictivos Aplicados a la Antropología Forense*; Universidad Oberta de Catalunya: Barcelona, Spain, 2018.
43. LeCun, Y.; Bengio, Y.; Hinton, G. Deep Learning. *Nature* **2015**, *521*, 436–444. [CrossRef] [PubMed]
44. Zhong, G.; Zhang, K.; Wei, H.; Zheng, Y.; Dong, J. Marginal Deep Architecture: Stacking Feature Learning Modules to Build Deep Learning Models. *IEEE Access* **2019**, *7*, 30220–30233. [CrossRef]
45. Arce García, S.; Menéndez Menéndez, M.I. Applications of Statistics to Framing and Text Mining in Communication Studies. *Inf. Cult. Soc.* **2018**, 61–70. [CrossRef]
46. Lin, F.; Hao, D.; Liao, D. Automatic Content Analysis of Media Framing by Text Mining Techniques. In Proceedings of the 2016 49th Hawaii International Conference on System Sciences (HICSS), Koloa, HI, USA, 5–8 January 2016; pp. 2770–2779. [CrossRef]
47. Kwartler, T. *Text Mining in Practice with R*, 1st ed.; Jhon Wiley & Sons Ltd.: Oxford, UK, 2017.
48. Ortíz, Z. Trends and Challenges for Information Science in Today's World. *Cienci. Inf.* **2019**, *9*, 196–208. [CrossRef]
49. Mandujano, S. Analysis and Trends of Photo-Trapping in Mexico: Text Mining in R. *Therya* **2019**, *10*, 25–32. [CrossRef]
50. Rashid, J.; Adnan Shah, S.M.; Irtaza, A.; Mahmood, T.; Nisar, M.W.; Shafiq, M.; Gardezi, A. Topic Modeling Technique for Text Mining Over Biomedical Text Corpora Through Hybrid Inverse Documents Frequency and Fuzzy K-Means Clustering. *IEEE Access* **2019**, *7*, 146070–146080. [CrossRef]
51. Kim, D.; Lee, J.; So, C.H.; Jeon, H.; Jeong, M.; Choi, Y.; Yoon, W.; Sung, M.; Kang, J. A Neural Named Entity Recognition and Multi-Type Normalization Tool for Biomedical Text Mining. *IEEE Access* **2019**, *7*, 73729–73740. [CrossRef]
52. Zhang, L.; Zhu, G.; Zhang, S.; Zhan, X.; Wang, J.; Meng, W.; Fang, X.; Wang, P. Assessment of Career Adaptability: Combining Text Mining and Item Response Theory Method. *IEEE Access* **2019**, *7*, 125893–125908. [CrossRef]
53. Shi, L.; Jianping, C.; Jie, X. Prospecting Information Extraction by Text Mining Based on Convolutional Neural Networks—A Case Study of the Lala Copper Deposit, China. *IEEE Access* **2018**, *6*, 52286–52297. [CrossRef]
54. Jia, S.; Wu, B. Incorporating LDA Based Text Mining Method to Explore New Energy Vehicles in China. *IEEE Access* **2018**, *6*, 64596–64602. [CrossRef]
55. Verma, V.K.; Ranjan, M.; Mishra, P. Text Mining and Information Professionals: Role, Issues and Challenges. In Proceedings of the 2015 4th International Symposium on Emerging Trends and Technologies in Libraries and Information Services, Noida, India, 6–8 January 2015; pp. 133–137. [CrossRef]
56. Sukanya, M.; Biruntha, S. Techniques on Text Mining. In Proceedings of the 2012 IEEE International Conference on Advanced Communication Control and Computing Technologies (ICACCCT), Ramanathapuram, India, 23–25 August 2012; pp. 269–271. [CrossRef]
57. Miner, G.; Nisbet, B.; Elder, J.; Fast, A.; Delen, D.; Hill, T. *Practical Text Mining and Statistical Analysis for Non-Structured Text Data Applications*; Academic Press Elsevier: Oxford, UK, 2012.
58. Uysal, A.; Gunal, S. The Impact of Preprocessing on Text Classification. *Inf. Process. Manag.* **2014**, *50*, 104–112. [CrossRef]
59. Raschka, S.; Mirjalili, V. *Python Machine Learning*, 2nd ed.; Packt Publishing: Birmingham, UK, 2017.
60. Lobur, M.; Romanyuk, A.; Romanyshyn, M. Using NLTK for Educational and Scientific Purposes. *IEEE Xplore* **2011**, *1*, 43.
61. Xu, L.; Sun, S.; Wang, Q. Text Similarity Algorithm Based on Semantic Vector Space Model. In Proceedings of the 2016 IEEE/ACIS 15th International Conference on Computer and Information Science (ICIS), Okayama, Japan, 26–29 June 2016; pp. 1–4. [CrossRef]
62. Torres, C.; Arco, L. Textual Representation in Semantic Vector Space. *Rev. Cuba. Cienci. Inf.* **2016**, *10*, 148–180.
63. Kim, J.-K.; Tur, G.; Celikyilmaz, A.; Cao, B.; Wang, Y.-Y. Intent Detection Using Semantically Enriched Word Embeddings. In Proceedings of the 2016 IEEE Spoken Language Technology Workshop (SLT), San Diego, CA, USA, 13–16 December 2016; pp. 414–419. [CrossRef]

64. Sano, N. Synthetic Data by Principal Component Analysis. In Proceedings of the 2020 International Conference on Data Mining Workshops (ICDMW), Sorrento, Italy, 17–20 November 2020; pp. 101–105. [CrossRef]
65. Yadav, S.; Shukla, S. Analysis of K-Fold Cross-Validation over Hold-Out Validation on Colossal Datasets for Quality Classification. In Proceedings of the 2016 IEEE 6th International Conference on Advanced Computing (IACC), Bhimavaram, India, 27–28 February 2016; pp. 78–83. [CrossRef]
66. Sedaghat, N.; Fathy, M.; Modarressi, M.H.; Shojaie, A. Combining Supervised and Unsupervised Learning for Improved MiRNA Target Prediction. *IEEE/ACM Trans. Comput. Biol. Bioinform.* **2018**. [CrossRef] [PubMed]
67. Cedeno, D.; Vargas, M. Application of Machine Learning with Supervised Classification Algorithms: In the Context of Health. In Proceedings of the 2019 7th International Engineering, Sciences and Technology Conference (IESTEC), Panama, 9–11 October 2019; pp. 613–618. [CrossRef]
68. Nijhawan, R.; Srivastava, I.; Shukla, P. Land Cover Classification Using Super-Vised and Unsupervised Learning Techniques. In Proceedings of the 2017 International Conference on Computational Intelligence in Data Science (ICCIDS), Chennai, India, 2–3 June 2017; pp. 1–6. [CrossRef]
69. Karacali, B. Improved Quasi-Supervised Learning by Expectation-Maximization. In Proceedings of the 2013 21st Signal Processing and Communications Applications Conference (SIU), Haspolat, Turkey, 24–26 April 2013; pp. 1–4. [CrossRef]
70. Lytvyn, V.; Vysotska, V.; Veres, O.; Rishnyak, I.; Rishnyak, H. Content Linguistic Analysis Methods for Textual Documents Classification. In Proceedings of the 2016 XIth International Scientific and Technical Conference Computer Sciences and Information Technologies (CSIT), Lviv, Ukraine, 6–10 September 2016; pp. 190–192. [CrossRef]
71. Weir, G.; Owoeye, K.; Oberacker, A.; Alshahrani, H. Cloud-Based Textual Analysis as a Basis for Document Classification. In Proceedings of the 2018 International Conference on High Performance Computing & Simulation (HPCS), Orleans, France, 16–20 July 2018; pp. 672–676. [CrossRef]
72. Yun, D.; Liu, W.; Wu, C.Q.; Rao, N.S.V.; Kettimuthu, R. Performance Prediction of Big Data Transfer Through Experimental Analysis and Machine Learning. In Proceedings of the 2020 IFIP Networking Conference (Networking), Paris, France, 22–26 June 2020; pp. 181–189.
73. Gamallo, P.; García, M. *Methods on Natural Language Processing for Information Retrieval*; Universidade de Santiago de Compostela: Santiago, Chile, 2012.
74. Pérez-Guadarramas, Y.; Rodríguez-Blanco, A.; Simón-Cuevas, A.; Hojas-Mazo, W.; Olivas, J.Á. Combining Lexical—Syntactic Patterns and Topic Analysis for Automatic Keyphrase Extraction from Texts. *Proces. Leng. Nat.* **2017**, *59*, 39–46.
75. Rodriguez-Blanco, A.; Simon-Cuevas, A.; Hojas-Mazo, W.; Perea-Ortega, J. Extraction of Linked Data from Unstructured Information Applying NLP Techniques and Ontologies. *CEUR Workshop Proc.* **2016**, *1797*, 80–91.
76. Perez-Marin, D.; Hijon-Neira, R.; Martin-Lope, M. A Methodology Proposal Based on Metaphors to Teach Programming to Children. *IEEE Rev. Iberoam. Tecnol. Aprendiz.* **2018**, *13*, 46–53. [CrossRef]
77. Pérez-Marín, D.; Hijón-Neira, R.; Bacelo, A.; Pizarro, C. Can Computational Thinking Be Improved by Using a Methodology Based on Metaphors and Scratch to Teach Computer Programming to Children? *Comput. Hum. Behav.* **2020**, *105*, 105849. [CrossRef]
78. Chibaya, C. A Metaphor-Based Approach for Introducing Programming Concepts. In Proceedings of the 2019 International Multidisciplinary Information Technology and Engineering Conference (IMITEC), Vanderbijlpark, Kimberley, South Africa, 21–22 November 2019; pp. 1–8. [CrossRef]
79. Arias, L. Situated Learning and Cognitive Development. Available online: https://docplayer.es/27825700-El-aprendizaje-situado-y-el-desarrollo-cognitivo-comparacion-entre-las-teorias-aprendizaje-situado-y-desarrollo-cognitivo-de-brunner.html (accessed on 27 March 2021).
80. Sanchez, R. T-Student, uses and abuses. *Rev. Mex. Cardiol.* **2015**, *26*, 59–61.
81. Ramos, X.; Jiménez, J. *Methodological Proposal for the Development of Computational Thinking*, 1st ed.; CESMAG University: Pasto, Colombia, 2020; Available online: http://repositorio.unicesmag.edu.co:8080/xmlui/handle/123456789/126 (accessed on 27 March 2021).

Article

Predicting High-Risk Students Using Learning Behavior

Tieyuan Liu [1,2], Chang Wang [1], Liang Chang [1,*] and Tianlong Gu [1,3]

1 Guangxi Key Laboratory of Trusted Software, Guilin University of Electronic Technology, Guilin 541000, China; lty205@guet.edu.cn (T.L.); 19032201031@mails.guet.edu.cn (C.W.); cctlgu@guet.edu.cn (T.G.)
2 School of Information and Communication, Guilin University of Electronic Technology, Guilin 514000, China
3 College of Information Science and Technology/College of Cyber Security, Jinan University, Guangzhou 510000, China
* Correspondence: changl@guet.edu.cn

Abstract: Over the past few years, the growing popularity of online education has enabled there to be a large amount of students' learning behavior data stored, which brings great opportunities and challenges to the field of educational data mining. Students' learning performance can be predicted, based on students' learning behavior data, so as to identify at-risk students who need timely help to complete their studies and improve students' learning performance and online teaching quality. In order to make full use of these learning behavior data, a new prediction method was designed based on existing research. This method constructs a hybrid deep learning model, which can simultaneously obtain the temporal behavior information and the overall behavior information from the learning behavior data, so that it can more accurately predict the high-risk students. When compared with existing deep learning methods, the experimental results show that the proposed method offers better predicting performance.

Keywords: learning behavior; student performance prediction; deep neural network (DNN); recurrent neural network (RNN); educational data mining (EDM)

MSC: 68T01

1. Introduction

In the past few decades, Educational Data Mining (EDM) has been a very active research field, applying machine learning, data mining, and statistical learning methods to mine the hidden information in educational data [1]. As one of the important research directions of EDM, student performance prediction is essential for evaluating and improving teaching quality and guiding students' personalized development [2].

The development of information technology has promoted the reform of educational methods. Online learning platforms represented by virtual learning environments (VLEs) and large-scale open online courses (MOOCS) have become a new way of learning. The emergence of these online education platforms has broken the restrictions of time and space and met the diverse learning needs of different learners. However, online learning faces great challenges. According to the 2019 Harvard MOOC Research Report [3], many learners cannot pass the course examination. The number of students in online learning is much higher than that in traditional classrooms. It is difficult for teachers to track the learning situation of each student and provide timely teaching guidance to students with learning risks, which makes the quality of online education difficult to be effectively guaranteed. Through student performance prediction, students needing time and help to complete their studies can be identified, which can help these students improve their academic performance [4]. Therefore, for teachers, accurate student performance prediction can effectively help them improve the quality of online teaching and realize all the potential advantages of online learning platforms.

Early student performance prediction mainly attempts to predict student performance by considering factors such as the student's grade point average, demographic information, and usual test scores [5]. The development of online learning platforms has enabled a large amount of student learning behavior to be collected, such as learning resource access time, number of visits, etc. [6]. The online behavior reflects the learning situation of students and can be used to predict student performance [7].

In recent years, more and more researchers regard PSP as a time series classification problem. Among the existing temporal algorithms, recurrent neural networks, such as long short-term memory (LSTM), have outstanding performance in analyzing students' learning behavior sequences, and the extracted temporal behavior features precisely reflect the learning process of students [8]. Recurrent neural networks can provide a persistence mechanism by implementing feedback loops [9]. These feedback loops will pass the information from the current time step to the next time step, in order for the networks to retain the hidden information extracted from the previous time step. When predicting student performance, after the training of student learning behavior sequences at different periods, the recurrent neural network can finally extract the temporal behavior information from the learning behavior sequence.

The method based on the recurrent neural network can predict the performance of students very well, however, it does so at the expense of paying too much attention to the temporal behavior information while ignoring the overall behavior information. In actual learning, as shown in Table 1, some students will study conscientiously within a specific period of time to pass the course, when compared to other students, their overall learning behavior is similar, but their learning behavior during different periods is different. Therefore, some information on the overall learning behavior will help improve the accuracy of student performance prediction.

Table 1. Comparison of the distribution of students' main learning behaviors.

ID	Flag	Week	Forumng	Oucontent	Quzie	Subpage
FFF2014B544271	Pass	16	260	970	715	297
FFF2013J595386	Pass	22	275	1486	656	329
FFF2014B617965	Pass	31	299	1515	809	339

This research aims to use students' learning behavior to predict student performance. The learning behavior of students is commonly found in the logs of various online learning systems, recording students' visits to online platforms, and hiding the students' learning process. Unfortunately, the existing PSP method does not fully utilize the information on the student's learning behavior, which affects the accuracy of student performance prediction. In order to make full use of the information hidden in the student's learning behavior, a new method is proposed based on existing research, which extracts the temporal behavior information and the overall behavior information from student's learning behavior data by using deep neural networks and recurrent neural networks, respectively. Finally, a variety of modeling techniques are compared with the proposed method. Experiments show that this method has the best prediction performance. Compared to related work, the contributions are mainly as follows:

(1) This article proposes a new prediction method, which can simultaneously obtain the temporal behavior features and the overall behavior features of student's learning behavior from student's learning behavior data.
(2) To better integrate the temporal behavior features and the overall behavior features of student's learning behavior, using an attention mechanism to evaluate the importance of the temporal behavior features and the overall behavior features.
(3) Extensive experiments have been conducted on a real dataset, and the results show that the proposed method has a more accurate prediction performance than some other prediction methods.

The remainder of this paper is organized as follows. Section 2 will introduce the related works. In Section 3 we introduce the dataset and the data preprocessing we have done. Section 4 will outline the model we propose. In Section 5 we show an analysis and the experimental results of the model. Lastly, Section 6 briefly summarizes the conclusions and future work.

2. Related Work

The application of distance education and large-scale open online learning systems have provided a large amount of data for educational data mining, which has ushered in a new turning point in educational data mining which has begun to receive more and more attention [10]. Among the many research fields of data mining, student performance prediction is widely studied to solve problems such as poor academic performance, rising university dropout rates, and delayed graduation [11]. The learning process of students is complicated, and how to model them more comprehensively and accurately has always been the focus of research in the field of student performance prediction.

The early studies of student performance prediction are mainly based on traditional machine learning methods, such as regression analysis [12,13], decision trees [14,15], Naive Bayes [16], etc. These traditional machine learning algorithms have good interpretability and simple implementation and have achieved good results in the field of student performance prediction. Compared with these algorithms, most deep learning models are data-driven black box models. Although they lack interpretability, they have been applied to the field of student performance prediction because of their superior prediction performance and have become a research hotspot in the field of performance prediction. Deep neural networks have perfect fitting capabilities and can approximate any complex function. They contain many hidden layers, whilst having a very powerful and expressive ability. They can also learn the complex nonlinear relationships between features. The performance prediction of students based on deep neural networks is better than traditional machine learning [17–19].

In recent years, recurrent neural networks have been successfully applied in various fields, such as handwriting recognition [20] and speech synthesis [21]. Due to the fact that learning behavior data generated by students during the learning process has an obvious time series in the existing work, the ways to predict student performance based on recurrent neural networks has become a research phenomenon in student performance prediction. Corrigan et al. [22] extracted student interaction data from the virtual learning environment and simply counted the number of times students visit Moodle each week as the input of the student performance prediction model. When considering the good performance of the recurrent neural network on time series data, the most popular variant, long and short-term memory (LSTM), wass used to predict the learning performance of students. When compared with the current most effective method, random forest, the experimental results show that the performance of the recurrent neural network is better. Kőrösi et al. [23] used the original row-level user log data in the learning platform to generate statistics based on the different learning behaviors of students in each week as the input of the student performance prediction model. Using the GRU recurrent neural network to predict the performance of students at the end of the course and comparing it with a standard classifier that uses manual synthesis of features, it was found that the recurrent neural network has a better predictive effect. Wu et al. [24] believe that students' online behavior is related to students' learning performance. They classified different websites by type and counted the number of visits to different types of websites as the input to the student's performance prediction model. They then mplemented the commonly used student performance prediction methods which included Logistic Regression (LR), Naive Bayes (NB), Support Vector Machine (SVM), Multilayer Perceptron (MLP), and LSTM methods to predict student performance. The experimental results showed that the prediction accuracy of LSTM was the highest.

3. Dataset

3.1. Dataset Introduction

In order to effectively analyze the relationship between learning behavior and student performance, the data set needs to contain a large number of students, diverse types of learning behavior, and frequent learning behavior. Therefore, we use the data related to the FFF course in the Open University Learning Analysis Data Set (OULAD) [25]. It is worth noting that, in order to establish a model to achieve early prediction of student performance, only the data of the previous 32 weeks is used.

The FFF course data set contains two years of student learning data. For two years, FFF courses were offered every semester. The information on the students participating in the course and the students' learning behavior on the platform are stored in different tables. These tables include the student information table (StudentInfo), the student learning behavior table (StudentVle) and the learning behavior table (Vle). The StudentInfo table stores the results of students' course learning, whilst the StudentVle stores the learning behaviors of students. Related information on various learning behavior is stored in Vle.

There are two characteristics of student learning behavior:

(1) There is a large amount of data. In the FFF course, a total of 7762 students studied the course. During the students' learning process, a total of 4,014,499 learning records were generated.
(2) There is a wide variety of learning behaviors. Different learning behavior numbers represent different learning behaviors. There are 1967 different learning behavior numbers in the FFF course, which means that there are 1967 different learning behaviors in total.

3.2. Dataset Preprocessing

Due to the large amount of data, diversified learning behavior types, and missing data in the data set, further processing of the data set is required, which is described in detail as follows:

(1) Record Extraction: The original log involved the course study of 7762 students, of which only 7046 students studied only on the course FFF and only studied once. The learning behavior of some students was not recorded, so we deleted them. In the end, we had 6455 students and their learning records.
(2) Learning behavior category: The extracted data set involved 1967 different learning behaviors. Categorizing these learning behaviors can help us better understand students' learning behavior. From the original data set, 20 categories of learning behavior can be summarized. The learning behavior categories absent from the FFF course were deleted, and 18 categories of learning behavior were obtained; the details of the learning behavior categories are shown in Table 2.
(3) Performance Classification: In the FFF course, students' final course learning results are divided into four categories: excellent, passed, failed, and dropped out. As shown in Figure 1, in the original data, the distribution of students' different performance results is unbalanced. Therefore, we classify distinction and pass as pass whilst we classify fail and withdrawn as fail.

Table 2. Introduction to learning behavior categories.

Index	Learning Behavior Category	Description
1	Dataplus	Total clicks on the additional information such as videos, audio, sites, etc.
2	Dualpane	Total clicks on the information on site and activity related to that information
3	Folder	Total clicks on the files relevant to the course
4	Forumng	Total clicks on the discussion forum
5	Homepage	Total clicks on the course homepage
6	Oucollaborate	Total clicks on the online video discussions
7	Oucontent	Total clicks on the contents of the assignment
8	Ouwiki	Total clicks on the Wikipedia content
9	Page	Total clicks on the information related to the course
10	Questionnaire	Total clicks on the questionnaires related to the course
11	Quiz	Total on the course quiz
12	RepeatActivity	Total clicks on the course contents from previous weeks
13	Resource	Total clicks on the pdf resources such as books
14	Subpage	Total clicks on the other sites enabled in the course
15	Url	Total clicks on the links to audio/video
16	Ouelluminate	Total clicks on the online tutorial sessions
17	Glossary	Total clicks on the basic glossary related to the contents of the courseF45 BC
18	Htmlactivity	Total clicks on the interactive html page

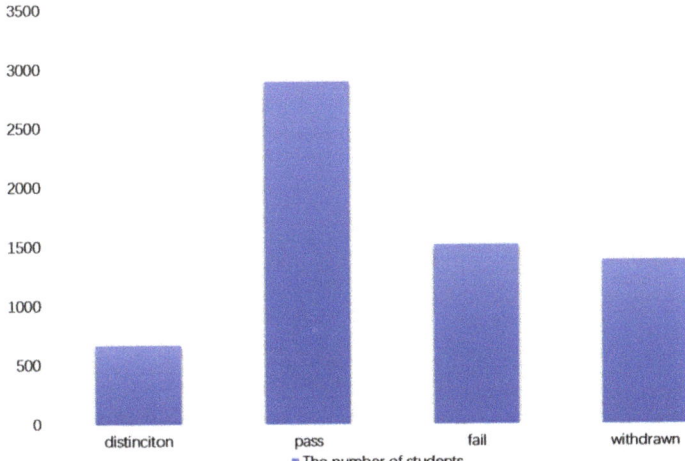

Figure 1. The distribution of students with different performances.

3.3. Dataset Analysis

In order to effectively prove the relationship between student learning behavior and student learning performance, we conducted a detailed analysis of the data set.

Firstly, we accumulated the learning behavior of students with different performance types in different weeks and used the average value to visualize the learning behavior of students with different performance types in different weeks. As shown in Figure 2, during the learning process, the students who passed always had more learning behavior than those who failed the course, this shows that the more learning behaviors students use during the learning process, the more likely they are to pass the course.

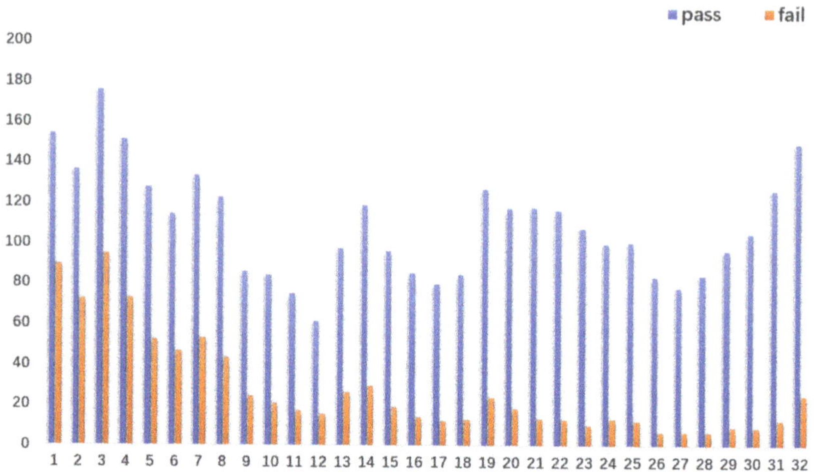

Figure 2. Average weekly learning behavior of students.

Secondly, we accumulated the different learning behavior types of students with different performance types and used the average value to visualize the learning behavior of students with different performance types on different learning behaviors. However, due to the large difference in the magnitude of learning behavior types, we will show them separately. As shown in Figure 3, during the learning process, the students who passed were more active than those who failed in all types of learning behaviors. It shows that the number of students in different learning behavior types hides some information that may help distinguish students with different performances. It also indicates that integrating the overall behavioral information will help improve the accuracy of student performance prediction.

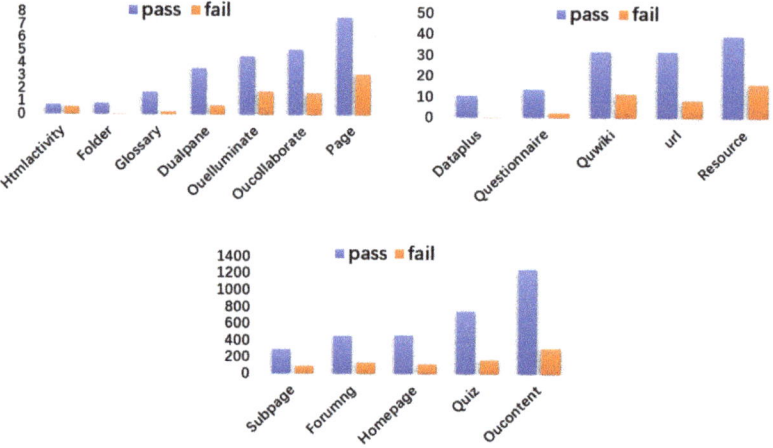

Figure 3. Comparison of students with different performances in different learning behaviors.

4. Methodology

4.1. Task Definition

In course learning, when a student is given and only the student's learning behavior is provided, the model we then build can make accurate early predictions of their learning performance. We accumulate the learning behavior of students in two different time spans to obtain the process-learning behavior and the overall-learning behavior of students and use these two types of learning behavior as the input of the model.

The process-learning behavior. Use P to define the student's process-learning behavior. The process-learning behavior of student s can be defined as: $P(s) = P_{1:T} = [p_1, \ldots, p_T]$, where T is the number of weeks of learning. Each element $p_i (1 \leq i \leq T)$ is defined as a one-dimensional matrix $[a_{i,1}, \ldots, a_{i,N}]$, where N is the number of learning behavior types, and $a_{i,j} (1 \leq j \leq N)$ is defined as the number of clicks by student s on the j-th type of learning behavior in the i-th study week (for example, the number of clicks on the homepage during the 12th study week). The data structure of this behavior is shown in Figure 4.

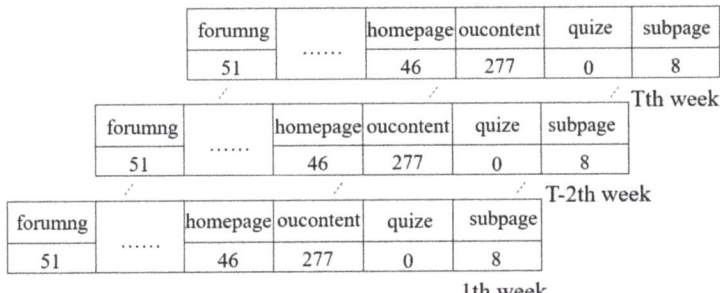

Figure 4. The process-learning behavior data structure.

The overall-learning behavior. Use Q to define the student's overall-learning behavior. The overall-learning behavior of student s can be defined as: $Q(s) = Q_{1:N} = [q_1, \ldots, q_N]$, where N is the number of learning behavior types, and $q_i (1 \leq i \leq N)$ is defined as the number of clicks on the i-th learning behavior type of s during the entire learning process (for example, the number of clicks on the forum during the entire learning process). As shown in Figure 5.

forumng	......	homepage	oucontent	quize	subpage
698		754	2883	678	472

all weeks

Figure 5. The overall-learning behavior data structure.

Task description. We represent the student performance prediction task as a two-category prediction problem. Given a student's process-learning behavior $P(s)$ and the overall-learning behavior $Q(s)$ during a course, we can predict the student's learning performance y, where $y \in \{0,1\}$, 0 means that the student cannot pass the course, and 1 means that the student can pass the course.

4.2. GDPN Framework

The method proposed in this paper, based on deep learning technology, aims to obtain potential behavioral features that can predict students' learning performance from students' learning behavior. It is different from existing student performance prediction methods, and we can learn separately from student learning data accumulated in different time spans to obtain more comprehensive potential behavior features. Specifically, we propose a new student performance prediction method (GRU&DNN Performance Prediction), GDPN. The method includes three important components which include the temporal behavior feature generator based on a gated unit neural network, the overall behavior feature generator based on a deep neural network, and the feature connect mechanism with an attention mechanism. The main purpose of our method is to use different generators to learn from student learning behavior data and extract the hidden information in this behavior data. In addition to that, through the feature connect mechanism, this hidden information is fully integrated, so as to better classify the students' learning performance. The workflow of our method is shown in Figure 6:

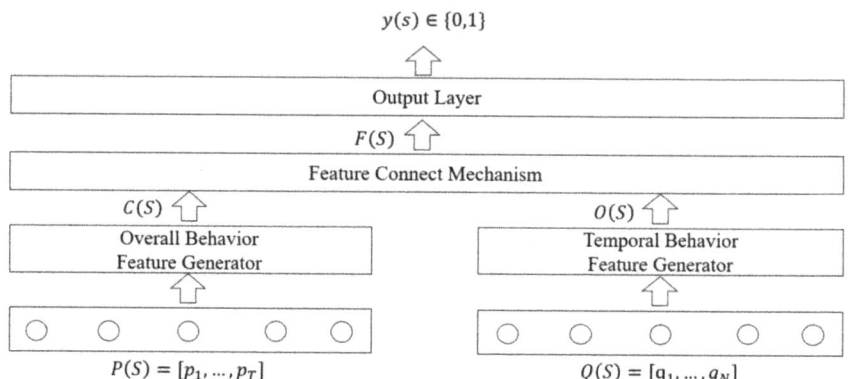

Figure 6. The GDPN framework.

Firstly, we take the process-learning behavior $P(s) = [p_1, \ldots, p_T]$ of student s as the input of the temporal behavior feature generator (GRU) and extract the hidden information $C(s) = [c_1, \ldots, c_K]$, where K is the number of GRU network units. As a special recurrent neural network, GRU can realize the memory function through its own feedback mechanism and effectively mine the time information and semantic information in the learning behavior sequence. GRU can control the flow of information by the reset gate and the update gate to capture the short-term and long-term relationships in the time series. Using the input of learning behavior in different time periods, GRU will compare the input and historical hidden information to obtain the output hidden information. This hidden information contains not only the information on the current learning behavior, but also the previous learning behavior information on the student, therefore it can describe the specific learning process of the student. Since this hidden information is extracted from the student's process-learning behavior, we refer to this type of hidden information as the temporal behavior features.

Secondly, we take the student's overall-learning behavior $Q(s) = [q_1, \ldots, q_N]$ as the input of the overall behavior feature generator (DNN) and dig out the hidden information $O(s) = [o_1, \ldots, o_D]$, where D is the number of neurons in the output layer of the DNN. It is a given that DNN possesses good non-linear mapping and generalization abilities and can fully learn the relationship between different features. When using DNN to process the overall-learning behavior, through the full connection between the different neural network layers and the nonlinear processing of neurons, it can simulate the complex nonlinear relationship between different learning behaviors to obtain the hidden information. This hidden information reflects well the overall-learning behavior pattern of students and describes the overall learning characteristics of students. Since this hidden information is extracted from the overall-learning behavior, we refer to this type of hidden information as the overall behavior feature.

Finally, we incorporate the previously obtained two types of hidden information C and O input feature connect mechanism. In the feature connect mechanism, a simplified neural attention mechanism is used to assign appropriate weights to this hidden information, and the hidden information is multiplied by the corresponding weights to output student behavior features for prediction $F(s) = [f_1, \ldots, f_L]$, where L is the sum of the dimensions of different hidden information. In this way, we have realized the joint training of different feature generators, which can better learn the influence weights of different types of hidden information on student performance and optimize all parameters.

4.2.1. Temporal Behavioral Feature Generator

Using the temporal behavior feature generator, our purpose is to extract temporal behavior features through GRU. Cho et al. [26] proposed GRU inspired by LSTM, which is relatively simple to calculate and implement. As opposed to a traditional recurrent neural network, GRU can retain important features through various goalkeepers to ensure that it will not be lost in the long-term propagation process. Therefore, we use GRU to extract the temporal behavior features hidden in the process-learning behavior.

The structure of the temporal behavior feature generator is shown in Figure 7. When the model is trained to the last time step, we input the learning behavior $p(s)_T = [a_{T,1}, \ldots, a_{T,N}]$ of student s in the last week into the GRU, and the GRU can output temporal behavior features describing the specific learning process of the student. The gating mechanism in GRU can effectively control the flow of information and better capture the association relationship with longer time steps in the time series. There are reset and update gates in GRU. The reset gate is used to help capture the short-term relationships in the learning behavior sequence, and the update gate is used to help capture the long-term relationships in the learning behavior sequence. When we assume that the number of hidden units in the GRU is K and the historical hidden information is $h_{T-1} \in \mathbb{R}^{1 \times K}$, the calculation process of the reset gate and update gate at time step T is as follows:

$$r_T = \sigma\big(p(s)_T w_{pr} + h_{T-1} w_{Kr} + b_r\big) \tag{1}$$

$$z_T = \sigma\big(p(s)_T w_{pz} + h_{T-1} w_{Kz} + b_z\big) \tag{2}$$

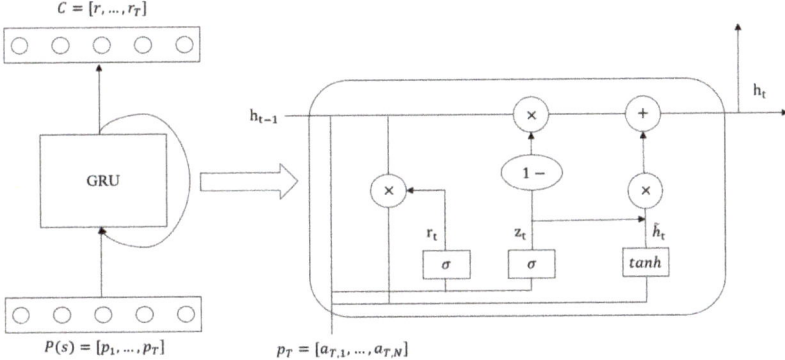

Figure 7. The temporal behavioral feature generator.

The inputs of the reset gate r_T and the update gate z_T are the input at the current time step and the historical hidden information $p(s)_T$, which are calculated through a fully connected layer with an activation function of *sigmoid*.

GRU will calculate candidate hidden information for time step T based on the output r_T of the reset gate, historical hidden information h_{T-1}, and learning behavior $p(s)_T$ in the current week. The calculation process is as follows:

$$\tilde{h}_T = tanh\big(p(s)_T w_{pk} + (r_T \odot h_{T-1}) w_{KK} + b_K\big) \tag{3}$$

In Formula (3), r_T and h_{T-1} perform element-wise multiplication (its symbol is $\odot$). It then connects the result of the element-wise multiplication operation with $p(s)_T$, and calculates the candidate hidden state $\tilde{h}_T \in \mathbb{R}^{1 \times K}$ through a fully connected layer with an activation function of $tanh$. In this calculation process, the reset gate controls how the hidden information on the history flows into the candidate's hidden information of the current time step and discards the historical information that has nothing to do with student performance.

Finally, the hidden information h_T trained at the time step T, that is, the time series feature $C(s)$, will be calculated according to the output z_T of the update gate, the historical hidden information h_{T-1}, and the current candidate hidden information $\tilde{h}_T$:

$$h_T = z_T \odot h_{T-1} + (1 - z_T) \odot \tilde{h}_T \tag{4}$$

In Formula (4), the update gate controls how the historical hidden information is updated by the candidate hidden information containing the learning behavior information of the current week. After the last week of learning behavior training, the $C(s)$ obtained not only hides the information in the current week's learning behavior, but also hides the information on the other week's learning behavior. Therefore, the extracted time-series features can describe the specific learning process of students.

4.2.2. Overall Behavioral Feature Generator

Different from the temporal feature generator, using the overall behavior feature generator, our purpose is to extract the overall behavior feature through DNN [27]. Since the time-series features extracted by GRU from the process-learning behavior mainly describes the specific learning process of the student, some key information hidden in the overall-learning behavior of the student will be ignored. DNN can learn hidden information related to student performance from the overall-learning behavior, which can increase the importance of this information.

Among the students who pass the course, the students' specific learning process will be different, but the students' investment in learning is similar. For example, some students who have passed the course will start to study diligently at a certain stage at the beginning of the course. Compared with students who pass the course normally, these students have different learning behavior sequences in the learning process, but their overall-learning behavior is similar. They will have a similar number of forum visits, homepage visits, etc. throughout the learning process. Therefore, when predicting student performance, we need to pay attention to the important information hidden in the overall-learning behavior of students to ensure that such students can be correctly classified.

When extracting hidden important information from the overall-learning behavior of students, compared with traditional machine learning, DNN can fit more complex nonlinear features, and extract deeper hidden information by learning high-level feature interactions. Therefore, we use DNN to extract the overall behavior features hidden in the overall-learning behavior. The structure of the overall behavior feature generator is shown in Figure 8. The overall-learning behavior $Q(s) = Q_{1:N} = [q_1, \ldots, q_N]$ of student s is sent to the hidden layer of DNN. After the training of the hidden layer in the neural network, the hidden information in the overall-learning behavior is output, that is, the overall behavior feature. The calculation process of each hidden layer is as follows:

$$A^{(l+1)} = \sigma\left(\sum W^{(l)} A^{(l)} + B^{(l)}\right) \tag{5}$$

where $A^{(l+1)}$ is the input of the l-th hidden layer and the output of the l-th hidden layer, $W^{(l)}$ and $B^{(l)}$ are the weight and bias of the l-th hidden layer, respectively, and $\sigma(\cdot)$ is the activation function of the neuron.

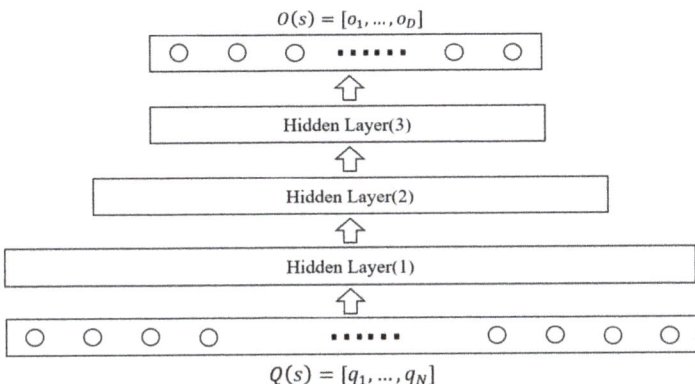

Figure 8. The overall behavioral feature generator.

DNN learns the complex relationship between different behaviors through the full connection between different layers and the nonlinear calculation of the activation function. The complex relationship between these different behaviors reflects the overall learning characteristics of students so that the overall behavioral feature $O(s)$ related to student performance prediction can be extracted.

4.2.3. Feature Connect Mechanism

In the feature connect mechanism, we use the attention mechanism to evaluate the importance of temporal behavior features and overall behavior features. Then, after processing the two different types of features according to the evaluation results, the feature vector $F(s)$ for prediction is obtained. Finally, we input $F(s)$ into a fully connected layer whose activation function is *sigmoid* for joint training to achieve early prediction of students' learning performance.

The structure of the feature connect mechanism is shown in Figure 9. When evaluating the importance of different types of behavior features, we used the feed-forward neural network attention mechanism proposed by Cho et al. [28]. When studying machine translation, the author uses this model to calculate the correlation of each source word, helping the decoder to focus more on the correct source word vector when decoding. Therefore, when we use both temporal and overall behavior features to predict student performance, the feed-forward neural network attention mechanism can help the model to focus more on the features related to student performance when predicting.

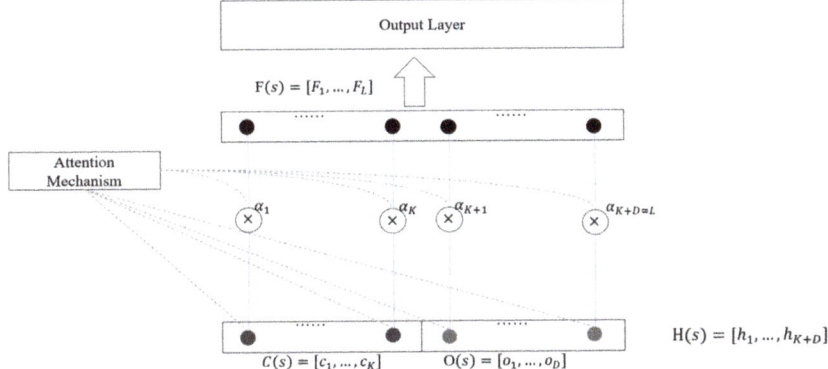

Figure 9. The feature connect mechanism framework.

We input the temporal and overall behavior features of student s into the attention mechanism to learn the importance of different types of features. The calculation process is as follows:

$$e_t = a(h_t) \tag{6}$$

$$\alpha_t = \frac{\exp(e_t)}{\sum_{t=1}^{T} \exp(e_t)} \tag{7}$$

The attention mechanism uses the learning function a to learn the influence factor e_t of each feature vector h_t on the result and standardizes e_t to obtain the weight α_t corresponding to the feature vector. Finally, we multiply the feature vector by its corresponding weight to reach the final feature vector $F(s)$ for prediction. The feed-forward neural network attention mechanism is essentially a hidden layer with a $softmax$ activation function.

Its input is a feature vector, and the output is a weight assigned to each feature vector. In the feature connect mechanism of this paper, we will use the attention mechanism based on different activation functions to obtain the most suitable personalized attention mechanism for the GDPN model.

5. Experiment

5.1. Compared Methods & Evaluation Metrics

We used a series of deep learning-based algorithms and models: Deep Neural Network (DNN), Simple Recurrent Network (SRN), Long Short-Term Memory Neural Network (LSTM), Gate Recurrent Unit Neural Network (GRU), and Convolutional Neural Network (CNN).

The following are the models proposed in this paper:

GDPN: The model proposed in this article;

For comparative evaluation, we used several evaluation metrics commonly used to evaluate classification algorithms: Accuracy, Precision, Recall, F1-score, and AUC.

5.2. Experimental Results and Discussion

In order to compare the predictive effect of student performance between our proposed model and the baseline model, we conducted the following experiments. Each experiment was run 10 times and the average of the results was taken.

5.2.1. Impact of the Attention Mechanism with Different Neuron Functions

The effect of the attention mechanism will be different if the activation function of the hidden neuron is set differently. In the attention mechanism, $softmax$ is often used as the activation function, whose purpose is to ensure that the sum of the weights assigned to each feature is 1. The features used for student performance prediction in this article are extracted from two different models and the weight sum of each feature may not be 1, so it is necessary to consider the impact of different activation functions on the prediction performance of the model. The commonly used activation functions are $relu$, $tanh$, $softmax$, and $sigmoid$. This article compares the effects of the attention mechanism using these four activation functions on the prediction performance of the model. The experimental results are shown in Table 3:

Table 3. Comparison of attention mechanism of different activation functions.

Activation Functions	Accuracy	Precision	Recall	F1-Score	AUC
softmax	0.892	0.877	0.936	0.906	0.886
tanh	0.917	0.892	0.965	0.927	0.912
relu	0.918	0.901	0.956	0.928	0.913
sigmoid	**0.925**	**0.906**	**0.965**	**0.935**	**0.92**

From the experimental results, it can be found that when the $softmax$ function is used as the activation function in the attention mechanism, the effect of predicting student performance is poor. When using the *sigmoid* function, the best performance is obtained on various evaluation metrics, so in subsequent experiments, we will use the sigmoid function as the activation function of the attention mechanism.

5.2.2. Impact of Different Components of the Model on Prediction

The GDPN model mainly includes the overall behavior feature generator and the temporal behavior feature generator. In order to study the impact of different components of the model on the predictive ability, we split the model structure and conducted separate experiments to explore the influence of different parts. The experimental results are shown in Table 4:

Table 4. Comparison of different components of the model.

	Accuracy	Precision	Recall	F1-Score	AUC
DNN	0.891	0.87	0.941	0.904	0.886
GRU	0.917	0.892	0.967	0.928	0.912
GDPN	0.925	0.906	0.965	0.935	0.92

When only the DNN model is used to predict student performance, its accuracy rate is 89.1%. The results show that using overall behavior features can predict student performance well. When only the GRU model is used to predict student performance, its various evaluation metrics standards are better than that of the DNN model, which shows that students' temporal behavior features play a more important role in predicting student performance. When the GDPN model is used to predict student performance, the model can simultaneously extract the temporal features and the overall features of students' learning behavior. When modeling the students' learning process, not only the specific learning process of the students, but also the overall learning characteristics of the students are considered. The model uses a feed-forward neural network attention mechanism, which can assign appropriate weights to different types of features, thereby achieving better prediction of student performance. It can be seen from Table 5 that using the GDPN model to predict student performance achieved good results in various evaluation indicators.

Table 5. Comparison of different deep learning methods.

Method	Accuracy	Precision	Recall	F1-Score	AUC
CNN	0.903	0.898	0.927	0.912	0.898
RNN	0.911	0.891	0.956	0.922	0.906
LSTM	0.915	0.897	0.957	0.926	0.91
GDPN	0.925	0.906	0.965	0.935	0.92

5.2.3. Comparison of Different Deep Learning Prediction Methods

In the last experiment, it was shown that the GDPN prediction model is superior to DNN and GRU, so in this experiment, we compared GDPN with other deep learning prediction methods of student performance prediction. The comparison results are shown in Table 5.

It can be seen from Table 5 that LSTM is better than SRN; this is because compared with SRN, LSTM is more complex in that the mechanism that inputs information at different times affects each other and solves the long-term dependency problem of SRN. The GDPN model proposed in this study achieved good prediction results on each evaluation index set. Compared with other methods, the method proposed in this study can consider both time-series information and overall information on click behavior, therefore, it achieves better prediction results. The GDPN model proposed in this study achieved good prediction results with each evaluation metric. Compared with other methods, the method proposed in this study can consider both temporal information and overall information on click behavior, therefore, it achieves better prediction results.

6. Conclusions and Future Work

The low pass rate of courses is an important phenomenon affecting the development of online education. As one of the current research hotspots, research on student performance prediction has been proven to be the most effective way to solve students' learning risk identification and improve the pass rate of online courses. In the online learning environment, the existing performance prediction research methods, based on recurrent neural networks, often focus on extracting the temporal information on students' learning behavior, ignoring the important impact of the overall information on learning behavior on students' performance, therefore, a new student performance prediction model, GDPN, is proposed. The model can achieve more accurate performance prediction by extracting the timing information and overall information on students' learning behavior at the same time. Experimental results on public online education data sets show that our model is superior to other performance prediction models based on deep learning.

In future work, we will use visual aids to more accurately analyze the relationship between students' learning behavior and their performance. Furthermore, we will explore how to design learning behaviors to build a higher-quality online learning platform based on existing research.

Author Contributions: Investigation, L.C.; Supervision, T.L. and T.G.; Writing—original draft, C.W.; Writing—review & editing, T.L. and L.C. All authors have read and agreed to the published version of the manuscript.

Funding: This research received no external funding.

Institutional Review Board Statement: Not applicable for studies not involving humans or animals.

Data Availability Statement: https://analyse.kmi.open.ac.uk/open_dataset (accessed on 3 September 2021).

Acknowledgments: This work was supported by the Natural Science Foundation of China (Nos. U1811264, 62066010), the Natural Science Foundation of Guangxi Province (No. 2020GXNSFAA159055), Innovation Project of Guang Xi Graduate Education (No. YCBZ2021072), Guangxi Key Laboratory of Trusted Software (No. KX202058).

Conflicts of Interest: The authors declare no conflict of interest.

References

1. Romero, C.; Ventura, S.; Pechenizkiy, M.; Baker, R.S. (Eds.) *Handbook of Educational Data Mining*; Taylor & Francis Group, LLC.: Boca Raton, FL, USA, 2010.
2. Al Breiki, B.; Zaki, N.; Mohamed, E.A. Using Educational Data Mining Techniques to Predict Student Performance. In Proceedings of the 2019 International Conference on Electrical and Computing Technologies and Applications (ICECTA), Ras Al Khaimah, United Arab Emirates, 19–21 November 2019. [CrossRef]
3. Bogdanova, D.; Snoeck, M. Using MOOC technology and formative assessment in a conceptual modelling course: An experience report. In Proceedings of the 21st ACM/IEEE International Conference on Model Driven Engineering Languages and Systems: Companion Proceedings, Copenhagen, Denmark, 14–19 October 2018; ACM: New York, NY, USA, 2018; pp. 67–73.
4. Zhou, Q.; Quan, W.; Zhong, Y.; Xiao, W.; Mou, C.; Wang, Y. Predicting high-risk students using Internet access logs. *Knowl. Inf. Syst.* **2018**, *55*, 393–413. [CrossRef]
5. Shahiri, A.M.; Husain, W.; Rashid, N.A. A Review on Predicting Student's Performance Using Data Mining Techniques. *Procedia Comput. Sci.* **2015**, *72*, 414–422. [CrossRef]
6. Hernandez-Blanco, A.; Herrera-Flores, B.; Tomas, D.; Navarro-Colorado, B. A Systematic Review of Deep Learning Approaches to Educational Data Mining. *Complexity* **2019**, *2019*, 1306039. [CrossRef]
7. Meier, Y.; Xu, J.; Atan, O.; van der Schaar, M. Personalized grade prediction: A data mining approach. In Proceedings of the IEEE International Conference on Data Mining, ICDM, Atlantic City, NJ, USA, 14–17 November 2015; Volume 2016, pp. 907–912. [CrossRef]
8. Qu, S.; Li, K.; Wu, B.; Zhang, S.; Wang, Y. Predicting Student Achievement Based on Temporal Learning Behavior in MOOCs. *Appl. Sci.* **2019**, *9*, 5539. [CrossRef]
9. Hopfield, J.J. Neural networks and physical systems with emergent collective computational abilities. In *Feynman and Computation*; CRC Press: Boca Raton, FL, USA, 2018; pp. 7–19. [CrossRef]

10. Jin, C. Dropout prediction model in MOOC based on clickstream data and student sample weight. *Soft Comput.* **2021**, *25*, 8971–8988. [CrossRef]
11. Bonafini, F.C.; Chae, C.; Park, E.; Jablokow, K.W. How Much Does Student Engagement with Videos and Forums in a MOOC Affect Their Achievement? *OLJ* **2017**, *21*. [CrossRef]
12. Saqr, M.; Fors, U.; Tedre, M. How learning analytics can early predict under-achieving students in a blended medical education course. *Med. Teach.* **2017**, *39*, 757–767. [CrossRef] [PubMed]
13. Zhang, W.; Huang, X.; Wang, S.; Shu, J.; Liu, H.; Chen, H. Student Performance Prediction via Online Learning Behavior Analytics. In Proceedings of the 2017 International Symposium on Educational Technology (ISET), Hong Kong, China, 27–29 June 2017; pp. 153–157. [CrossRef]
14. Wang, G.-H.; Zhang, J.; Fu, G.-S. Predicting Student Behaviors and Performance in Online Learning Using Decision Tree. In Proceedings of the 2018 Seventh International Conference of Educational Innovation through Technology (EITT), Auckland, New Zealand, 12–14 December 2018; pp. 214–219. [CrossRef]
15. Figueroa-Canas, J.; Sancho-Vinuesa, T. Early Prediction of Dropout and Final Exam Performance in an Online Statistics Course. *IEEE Rev. Iberoam. Tecnol. Aprendiz.* **2020**, *15*, 86–94. [CrossRef]
16. Zhou, Q.; Zheng, Y.; Mou, C. Predicting students' performance of an offline course from their online behaviors. In Proceedings of the 2015 Fifth International Conference on Digital Information and Communication Technology and Its Applications (DICTAP), Beirut, Lebanon, 29 April–1 May 2015; pp. 70–73. [CrossRef]
17. Widyahastuti, F.; Tjhin, V.U. Predicting students performance in final examination using linear regression and multilayer perceptron. In Proceedings of the 2017 10th International Conference on Human System Interactions, HSI 2017, Ulsan, Korea, 17–19 July 2017; pp. 188–192. [CrossRef]
18. Raga, R.C.; Raga, J.D. Early Prediction of Student Performance in Blended Learning Courses Using Deep Neural Networks. In Proceedings of the 2019 International Symposium on Educational Technology (ISET), Hradec Kralove, Czech Republic, 2–4 July 2019; pp. 39–43. [CrossRef]
19. Altaf, S.; Soomro, W.; Rawi, M.I.M. Student Performance Prediction using Multi-Layers Artificial Neural Networks: A case study on educational data mining. In Proceedings of the 3rd International Conference on Information System and Data Mining, Houston, TX, USA, 6–8 April 2019; pp. 59–64. [CrossRef]
20. Wu, Y.-C.; Yin, F.; Chen, Z.; Liu, C.-L. Handwritten Chinese Text Recognition Using Separable Multi-Dimensional Recurrent Neural Network. In Proceedings of the International Conference on Document Analysis and Recognition, ICDAR, Kyoto, Japan, 9–15 November 2017; Volume 1, pp. 79–84. [CrossRef]
21. Zen, H.; Agiomyrgiannakis, Y.; Egberts, N.; Henderson, F.; Szczepaniak, P. Fast, compact, and high quality LSTM-RNN based statistical parametric speech synthesizers for mobile devices. In Proceedings of the Annual Conference of the International Speech Communication Association, INTERSPEECH, San Francisco, CA, USA, 8–12 September 2016; pp. 2273–2277. [CrossRef]
22. Corrigan, O.; Smeaton, A.F. A course agnostic approach to predicting student success from vle log data using recurrent neural networks. In *Lecture Notes in Computer Science*; Springer: Cham, Switzerland, 2017; Volume 10474, pp. 545–548. [CrossRef]
23. Krosi, G.; Farkas, R. MOOC Performance Prediction by Deep Learning from Raw Clickstream Data. In *Communications in Computer and Information Science*; Springer: Singapore, 2020; Volume 1244, pp. 474–485. [CrossRef]
24. Wu, B.; Qu, S.; Ni, Y.; Zhou, Y.; Wang, P.; Li, Q. Predicting student performance using weblogs. In Proceedings of the 14th International Conference on Computer Science and Education, ICCSE 2019, Toronto, ON, Canada, 19–21 August 2019; pp. 616–621. [CrossRef]
25. Kuzilek, J.; Hlosta, M.; Zdrahal, Z. Open University Learning Analytics dataset. *Sci. Data* **2017**, *4*, 170171. [CrossRef] [PubMed]
26. Cho, K.; Van Merriënboer, B.; Gulcehre, C.; Bahdanau, D.; Bougares, F.; Schwenk, H.; Bengio, Y. Learning phrase representations using RNN encoder-decoder for statistical machine translation. In Proceedings of the 2014 Conference on Empirical Methods in Natural Language Processing (EMNLP), Doha, Qatar, 25 October 2014; pp. 1724–1734. [CrossRef]
27. Covington, P.; Adams, J.; Sargin, E. Deep neural networks for youtube recommendations. In Proceedings of the 10th ACM Conference on Recommender Systems, Boston, MA, USA, 15–19 September 2016; pp. 191–198. [CrossRef]
28. Cho, K. Introduction to Neural Machine Translation with GPUs (Part 3). 2015. Available online: https://devblogs.nvidia.com/parallelforall/introduction-neural-machine-translation-with-gpus (accessed on 12 September 2021).

Article

An Empirical Analysis of the Impact of Continuous Assessment on the Final Exam Mark

María Morales [1,*], Antonio Salmerón [1], Ana D. Maldonado [1], Andrés R. Masegosa [2] and Rafael Rumí [1]

[1] Department of Mathematics, University of Almería, 04120 Almería, Spain
[2] Department of Computer Science, Aalborg University, 2450 Copenhagen SV, Denmark
* Correspondence: maria.morales@ual.es

Abstract: Since the Bologna Process was adopted, continuous assessment has been a cornerstone in the curriculum of most of the courses in the different degrees offered by the Spanish Universities. Continuous assessment plays an important role in both students' and lecturers' academic lives. In this study, we analyze the effect of the continuous assessment on the performance of the students in their final exams in courses of Statistics at the University of Almería. Specifically, we study if the performance of a student in the continuous assessment determines the score obtained in the final exam of the course in such a way that this score can be predicted in advance using the continuous assessment performance as an explanatory variable. After using and comparing some powerful statistical procedures, such as linear, quantile and logistic regression, artificial neural networks and Bayesian networks, we conclude that, while the fact that a student passes or fails the final exam can be properly predicted, a more detailed forecast about the grade obtained is not possible.

Keywords: continuous assessment; Bayesian networks; artificial neural networks; classification

MSC: 62P25

1. Introduction

The interest in the Assessment for Learning (AFL) [1,2] which started in the last decades of the 20th century has grown during the 21st century, especially in European Higher Education due to the Bologna Process. The adaptation of the universities to the European Higher Education Area as well as the increasing interest of the different governmental agencies in learning outcomes [3,4] causes the effective assessment of the students to become particularly important for academic institutions. In this framework, Continuous Assessment (CA) is considered to be a useful tool to assess what students know and the competencies that they have achieved.

The main principle of the AFL is that any assessment should help students to learn and to succeed [2] and some research papers have highlighted this formative function of the continuous assessment. Nair and Pillay [5] assert that continuous assessment "makes teaching, learning and assessment part of the same process", highlighting the capacity to collect more evidence of the students learning in different ways and paces. Day et al. [6] point out two main benefits of continuous assessment: the first one is the enhancement of the retention of knowledge when it is repeatedly tested; the second benefit is that this retention is enlarged when the study period is spread by the CA. Some research in the bibliography concludes that CA helps the students to improve their understanding of the course content by removing the stress involved in the final exams [7–9] and helping them to manage their workload [5,8] or engaging them with the course materials [10,11]. Other researchers claim that CA improves students' motivation for learning [12] and increases the students' engagement throughout the course and the class attendance [11,13].

The advantage most emphasized in the literature is the feedback that CA offers to students and teachers [11,12,14,15]. Lopez-Tocón [16] found that Moodle quizzes let the teachers know failures in the students' understanding as well as information about students' learning processes while students are provided with self-assessment from the quizzes. Carles et al. [17] state that learning skills are developed thanks to the feedback provided by iterative assignments. Deeley et al. [18] and Scott [19] affirm that feedback brings the students' performance close to the one required by the assessment criteria. Timing is the main factor to make the feedback valuable [18] because if it is given too late, the students are not able to identify their weaknesses and change what is needed to improve the quality of their work. Timely feedback is challenging for the instructors [20], especially when teaching in large groups.

The positive perception of the students about CA has been indexed in the literature [21]. In Holmes' research [11], students affirmed that the improvement in their learning and understanding were a consequence of the continuous assessment while students surveyed by Scott [19] and Deeley et al. [18] reported that feedback given by their continuous assessment enhanced their understanding of the assessment processes, boosted their confidence and enabled them to improve the quality of their work.

Almost all the authors agree on the significant effect of continuous assessment on student behavior. Gibbs [22] and Bloxham and Boyd [10] found that CA has more impact on the learning process than teaching.

However, this effect is not always positive. Bloxham and Boyd [10] warn of strategic students who avoid making an effort in activities that do not contribute to their marks. Moreover, it has been reported [14,23] that students reduce their work once they obtain a satisfactory mark in their CA part and this attitude has consequences on the final exam. Finally, Dejene [20] found that some students perceive the CA as "continuous testing" that makes them busy and tired.

Another drawback of the CA lies in an increase in the workload for teachers, as well as the time required to plan and mark the CA [10,12,24], especially in large groups where individualized attention is highly time-consuming for teachers [14,18,20]. Deeley et al. [18] describe how staff could feel demotivated when their feedback is not taken into consideration by their students whereas the students feel disengaged when feedback does not provide clear and personalized information.

In the literature, we can find studies where CA enhances student performance in the final exams [15,24]. Nair and Pillay [5] assert that CA increases the percentage of students completing their studies in the minimum stipulated time while reducing the drop-out volume. Lopez-Tocón [16] finds that online tests help students to pass the exam in the ordinary call and the study of González et al. [25] reveals a positive effect of CA on students' success as well as a positive statistically significant correlation between the grades got in the CA and the final exam marks.

However, opposing conclusions about whether CA enhances student performance in the final exams can also be found in the literature [6,14,23]. The analysis carried out by Day et al. [6] concludes that students' results do not depend on whether CA has been used or the type of assessment followed in the course; even the positive correlation found by Gonzalez et al. [25] are low (below 0.4 in eight of the nine subjects studied) and the researchers did not find a significant relation between the continuous assessment grades and the final exam marks in the tail ends of the distribution.

Facing the number of studies yielding opposing conclusions, the goal of this study is to find statistical evidence of a significant effect of the CA on the performance of the students in the final exam of a course. In particular, we try to determine to what extent the final mark of a student can be predicted by their performance in the CA activities. We have collected the outcomes of 2397 students enrolled in courses of Statistics taught at the University of Almería. In an attempt to obtain as many heterogeneous students as possible we have selected courses of Statistics in seven degree programs belonging to different branches (Science, Technology, Economy and Social Sciences), taught in different semesters, shifts and with different methodologies (in-person, online or blended teaching). All these variables have been included in the models as explanatory variables. Moreover, as Reina et al. [24] found that the weight of the CA in the final grade has a significant influence on the final exam, we have also added this variable to the models. Our initial attempt was to predict the final mark by using linear and quantile regression to predict the highest and lowest scores. The poor quality of the predictions led us to use artificial neural networks for regression, also getting unreliable results. As a solution, we transformed the regression problem into a classification problem where, given the explanatory variables, we try to determine the range of grades in which the student will score in the final exam by using artificial neural networks and Bayesian networks. Finally, we simplify the problem by trying to predict whether a student will pass or fail the final exam.

2. Methods

We have recorded the performance of 2397 students enrolled in courses of Statistics in seven degree programs of the University of Almería:

- Economy: 1104 students;
- I.T. Engineering: 453 students;
- Industrial Engineering: 109 students;
- Mathematics: 288 students;
- Public Management: 188 students;
- Labor Relations: 166 students;
- Physical Activity and Sport Science: 89 students.

For each student, the following variables are studied:

- Degree program;
- Shift: Morning or Afternoon;
- Teaching: type of teaching(in-person, e-learning or blended);
- Weight of the CA in the final grade of the course;
- Continuous: performance of the student in the CA, measured as the percentage out of the maximum mark possible (values between 0 and 100);
- Exam: mark of the student in the final exam of the course, measured as the percentage out of the maximum mark possible (values between 0 and 100). When a student, following the CA, does not sit the final exam, we have entered a zero in this variable to take into account the failure in finishing the course.

We consider the shift of the course of interest because when the same course is taught in different shifts, students choose their shift in an order determined by their marks, so students with higher marks are expected to choose morning shifts whereas students usually choose the afternoon shifts only when the morning course is full or if they combine study with work. Therefore, the performance of students in morning shifts is typically better than in afternoon shifts.

Table 1 displays the number of students in each category.

Table 1. Frequency distribution of some explanatory variables in the data set.

Shift		Type of Teaching		Weight	
Morning	1236	In-person	1239	20%	47
		E-learning	781	30%	800
Afternoon	1161	Blended	377	40%	166
				50%	1192
				60%	192

To assess the performance of the model, we have randomized the data set and divided it into a training set and a test set with 70% and 30% of the data, respectively.

We have carried out two analyses: Firstly, we try to predict the score in the final exam of a generic student, that is, without using the variable *Degree* as an explanatory variable. In the second part of the study, we use the same statistical procedures applied in the first analysis but include the degree of the student in order to assess if more precise results are obtained.

The task of predicting the numeric value of the mark obtained in an exam was approached by using linear regression. We also used quantile regression, since it does not make any previous assumption (such as homoscedasticity in the linear model) and to predict the marks in the tails. In order to handle potential nonlinearities, we used artificial neural networks. The task of predicting the qualitative value of the mark obtained in an exam was approached using two state-of-the-art classification methods, namely artificial neural networks and Bayesian networks [26], taking as a benchmark for comparison a standard logistic regression model.

2.1. Regression Analysis

2.1.1. Linear Regression and Quantile Regression

Our first aim is to predict the target variable *Exam* as a function of the explanatory variables *Shift*, *Teaching*, *Weight* and *Continuous*.

The first method used has been a linear regression model. However, a first analysis of the data set reveals problems in terms of heteroscedasticity (Breusch–Pagan's *p*-value lower than 0.001) and normality (Shapiro–Wilk's *p*-value lower than 0.001). We have checked several transformations of the response variable (Box–Cox transformations, $log(y + \lambda_2)$ where λ_2 = smallest non-zero value/2 or $\lambda_2 = \frac{Q_1^2}{Q_3}$ or the arc-sin-square root transformation) but they got a higher dependency between the variance and the mean except for the arc-sin-square root transformation that got similar results than the raw data (Figure 1), so we decided to keep the original response variable for the sake of simplicity, taking into account the limitations of the regression model given the non-constant variance.

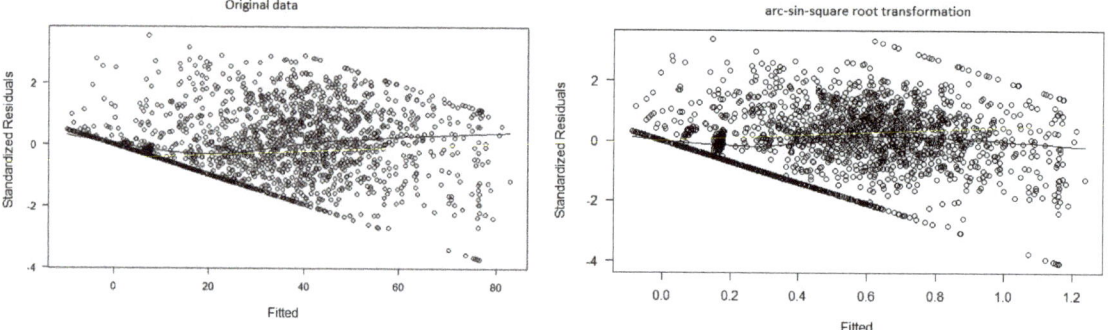

Figure 1. Standardized residuals versus fitted values with the original data and after transforming by arc−sin−square root.

On the other hand, the QQ plot of the standardized residuals (see Figure 2) shows non-normal errors with the apparently long-tailed distribution. To address this problem, we have used robust regression models [27,28]. To choose the most suitable robust method for the estimation of the coefficients, we have compared the RMSE (root mean squared error) of the models fitted by using Huber's M-estimator [29], the least trimmed squares (LTS) robust (high breakdown point) regression [30], least-absolute-deviations (LAD) regression [31] and the S-estimators proposed by Koller and Stahel [32]. We have used the MASS [33] and robustbase [34] R packages to fit the models.

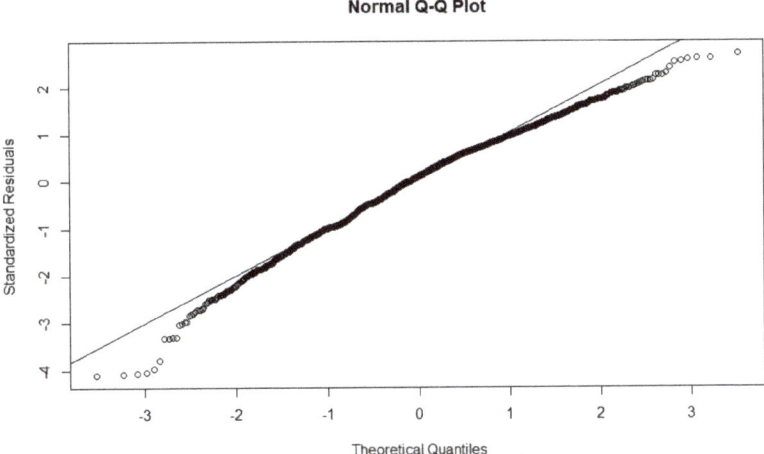

Figure 2. QQ—plot of the standardized residuals.

Due to the problems with the requirements of the linear regression, we propose the use of quantile regression [35–37] which makes no assumption on the errors. Quantile regression estimates the conditional median (or any other quantile) of the response variable instead of the conditional mean estimated by linear regression. However, not only can the median be predicted but also any quantile from the response variable's distribution, so we will try to predict the lowest (lower quartile) and highest marks (upper quartile, 80th and 90th percentile) in the final exam. As goodness of fit measurement, we have computed the coefficient proposed by Koenker and Machado [38], defined as one minus the ratio between the sum of absolute deviations in the fully parameterized model and the sum of absolute deviations in the null (non-conditional) quantile model.

2.1.2. Artificial Neural Networks

Our last attempt for the prediction of the mark obtained in the final exam was the use of Artificial Neural Networks (ANN). ANNs [39,40] are computational models which consist of nodes connected by links. The nodes, called neurons, are distributed in layers that can be divided into three classes: the first layer, called input layer, contains the nodes that represent the explanatory variables for the model; the last layer called output layer produces the result of the model; between the input and output layers the nodes are distributed in layers called hidden layers where the processing of the information is carried out. The nodes in each hidden layer are connected with all the neurons in the previous and next layers but there is no link between the nodes in the same layer. The number of hidden layers and the number of nodes in each one are hyperparameters that can be fixed by the research before training the ANN. Figure 3 shows the structure of an ANN with one hidden layer and three nodes in it.

The processing of the information in the hidden layers is performed inside each neuron as follows: each link connecting two neurons i and j has associated a numerical parameter called *weight* and denoted w_{ij}, which determines how strongly the neuron i affects the neuron j. So, the information that a neuron j receives is the value taken by the neurons in the previous layer multiplied by the weights of the links plus a bias to adjust the information along with the weighted sum of the inputs to the neuron. Figure 4 illustrates the information received by the first neuron in the hidden layer of the ANN in Figure 3. The weights are estimated in the training of the ANN in such a way that the error of the output of the ANN is minimized.

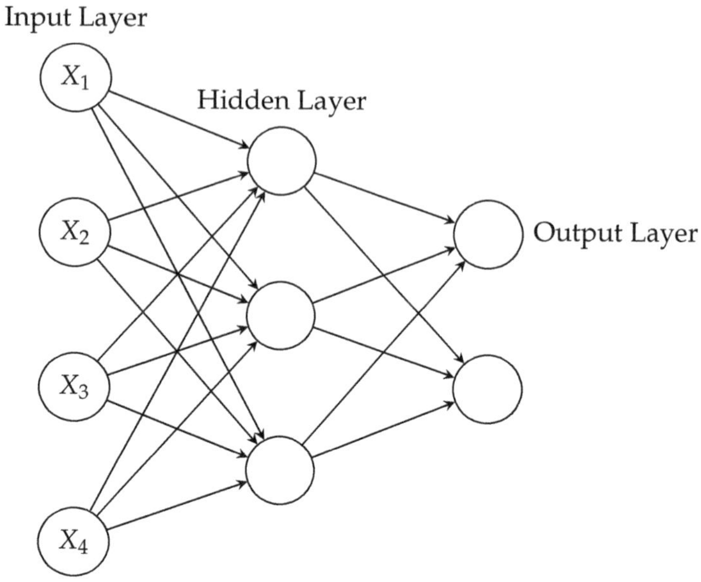

Figure 3. An example of an ANN with one hidden layer.

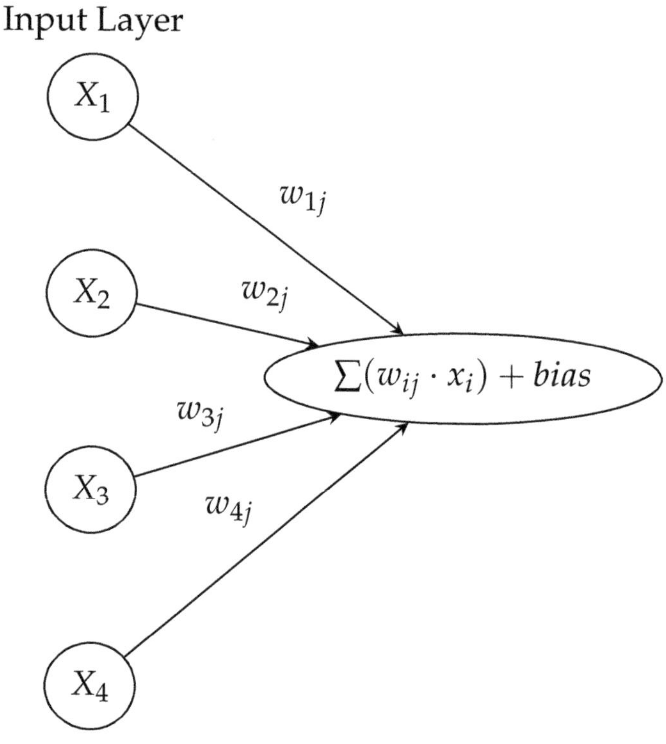

Figure 4. An example of the information received by a neuron in the hidden layer.

A function is applied to the weighted sum of the inputs with the bias to produce the output of the neuron. This function is called the activation function and it decides whether the information in the neuron is important enough to be incorporated into the process. The activation function must be chosen by the researcher among a wide range of functions such as the identity, the logistic or sigmoid, the hyperbolic tangent, Rectified Linearity Units (ReLu) or Softmax functions, introducing the non-linearity in our model.

In this work, we used the most common type of ANN, the multilayer perceptron (MLP) [39]. We have trained nine different MLPs with one hidden layer and a total of 527 MLPs with two hidden layers varying the number of neurons in the layers. To learn each MLP, we used three activation functions: identity, ReLU and Softplus. The explanatory variable *SHIFT* was transformed into a 0–1 variable, whereas *TEACHING* was converted into three binary variables and the numeric variables were re-scaled to the interval $[-1,1]$. The assessment measure to choose the best model is the RMSE.

2.2. Multiclass Classification

As it is shown in Section 3, we were not able to accurately predict the mark in the final exam due to the high errors obtained in both regression models and ANNs so we decided to approach the problem as a classification task where the target variable *EXAM* is categorized into four classes: *Fail*, *PassingGrade*, *GradeB* and *GradeA*. As we did when training the ANNs for regression, the variable *SHIFT* is transformed into a 0-1 variable, *TEACHING* into three binary variables and *WEIGHT* and *CONTINUOUS* have been re-scaled to the interval $[-1,1]$.

The first method used to classify the exam score of a student was an MLP with a logistic activation function. We trained different MLPs with one and two hidden layers varying the number of nodes in them. To assess the accuracy of the ANNs we computed the following performance metrics, where TP denotes the number of true positives, TN the number of true negatives, FP the false positives and FN the number of false negatives:

- Classification ACCURACY: ratio between the number of correct predictions and the total number of predictions

$$Accuracy = \frac{TP+TN}{TP+TN+FP+FN}; \quad (1)$$

- GEOMETRIC MEAN (GM): tries to measure the equilibrium between the performance on classifying both the majority and the minority classes

$$GM = \sqrt{\frac{TP}{TP+FN} \cdot \frac{TN}{TN+FP}}; \quad (2)$$

- MATTHEW'S CORRELATION COEFFICIENT (MCC): takes on values in the range $[-1,1]$. A value of $MCC = -1$ indicates that the model predicts all negatives as positives and vice versa (perfect negative correlation), $MCC = 0$ indicates that the model predicts randomly (no correlation), and $MCC = +1$ indicates perfect agreement. It is computed as

$$MCC = \frac{TN \cdot TP - FP \cdot FN}{\sqrt{(TN+FN)(FP+TP)(TN+FP)(FN+TP)}}; \quad (3)$$

- YOUDEN'S INDEX (J): aggregates the values of specificity and sensitivity. It ranges between 0 and 1. $J = 0$ indicates that the classifier is useless whereas $J = 1$ indicates perfect agreement.

$$J = \frac{TP}{TP+FN} + \frac{TN}{TN+FP} - 1; \quad (4)$$

- COEH'S KAPPA SCORE (K): measures how much better the classifier is performing with respect to random classification according to the frequency of each class. It takes on values under or equal to 1, considering that the classifier is useless when $J \leq 0$ and as acceptance criterium, we can consider a good performance when $J > 0.6$ [41]. Its formula is

$$K = \frac{P_o - P_e}{1 - P_e}, \quad (5)$$

where P_o is the ratio of observed agreements and P_e the expected agreements.

GM, *MCC* and *J* are computed for each class of the response variable and the measure given is the weighted mean, using as weights the relative frequency of each class in the test data set.

Unlike *Accuracy*, the metrics *GM*, *MCC*, *J* and *K* take into account the difference in the size of the classes of the response variable in the test data set. As Table 2 shows, the *Fail* class contains over eight times more items than *GradeB* class and over 33 times more items than *GradeA*. Therefore, *Accuracy* can be misleading, for instance, if the model only classifies properly the *Fail* class.

Table 2. Frequency distribution of the categorized variable *EXAM* in the test data set.

Class	n_i
Fail	504
PassingGrade	106
GradeB	62
GradeA	15

Besides ANNs, we have also addressed the classification problem using Bayesian networks.

Bayesian Networks

In what follows, we will use uppercase letters to denote random variables and lowercase letters to denote a value of a random variable. Boldfaced characters will be used to denote sets of variables. The set of all possible combinations of values of a set of random variables $\mathbf{X}$ is denoted as $\Omega_\mathbf{X}$. A Bayesian Network (BN) [42] with variables $\mathbf{X} = \{X_1, \ldots, X_n\}$ is formally defined as a directed acyclic graph with n nodes where each one corresponds to a variable in $\mathbf{X}$. Attached to each node $X_i \in \mathbf{X}$, there is a conditional distribution of X_i given its parents in the network, $Pa(X_i)$, so that the joint distribution of the random vector $\mathbf{X}$ factorizes as

$$p(x_1, \ldots, x_n) = \prod_{i=1}^{n} p(x_i | pa(x_i)), \quad (6)$$

where $pa(x_i)$ denotes a configuration of the values of the parents of X_i.

An example of a BN representing the joint distribution of the variables $\mathbf{X} = \{X_1, \ldots, X_5\}$ is shown in Figure 5. It encodes the factorization

$$p(x_1, x_2, x_3, x_4, x_5) = p(x_1) p(x_2 | x_1) p(x_3 | x_1) p(x_5 | x_3) p(x_4 | x_2, x_3).$$

A remarkable feature of BNs is their modularity, in the sense that the factorization simplifies the specification of large multivariate distributions that are replaced by a set of smaller ones (with a lower number of parameters to specify). For example, the factorization encoded by the network in Figure 5 replaces the specification of a joint distribution over 5 variables with the specification of 5 smaller distributions, each one of them with at most 3 variables. Another advantage is that the network structure describes the interaction between the variables in the model, in a way that can be easily interpretable, according to the *d*-separation criterion [42]. As an example, the structure in Figure 5 determines that variables X_1 and X_5 are independent if the value of X_3 is known, and likewise, X_2 and X_3 are independent if X_1 is known.

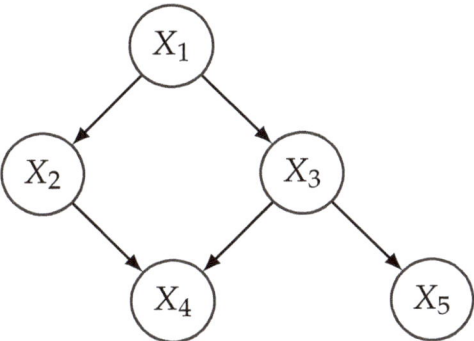

Figure 5. An example of a BN structure with 5 variables.

Building a BN from data involves two tasks: (i) learning the network structure and (ii) estimating the conditional distributions corresponding to the selected structure. Assuming that all the variables in the network are discrete or qualitative, maximum likelihood estimations of the conditional distributions can be obtained from the relative frequencies in the data of each combination of possible values of the variables involved. Structure learning [43] can be cast as an optimization problem, where the space of possible network structures is traversed trying to maximize some score function that measures how accurately a given structure fits the data. In this work, we have used the BIC score, which is a typical choice in the literature [44], defined as

$$BIC(M|D) = \sum_{l=1}^{N} \ln p(\mathbf{x}_l|\hat{\boldsymbol{\theta}}) - \frac{1}{2} d \ln N, \qquad (7)$$

where $D = \{\mathbf{x}_1, \ldots, \mathbf{x}_N\}$ is the dataset, M is the network under evaluation, and $p(\mathbf{x}_l|\hat{\boldsymbol{\theta}})$ is the joint distribution corresponding to network M, with parameters $\hat{\boldsymbol{\theta}}$ estimated by maximum likelihood. The idea of using the BIC score is to obtain networks that fit the data accurately while prioritizing simple networks. That is why the number of parameters, d, necessary to specify the probability distributions in the network, is used as a penalty factor. Other popular choices are the AIC and BDE scores [44]. In this paper, we have used the Hill Climbing (HC) optimization procedure with BIC score as a metric to optimize, using the implementation in the bnlearn [45] R package.

It is also possible to fix a given network structure beforehand, and only estimate the conditional distributions from data. This choice is typically adopted in practice when the network is going to be used for prediction purposes, where one could be more interested in the value of a target variable than in the interactions between the other variables. An example of such a fixed structure is the so-called Naive Bayes (NB) [46], where the variable whose value we want to predict is the root of the network and the only existing links go from that variable to the rest of the variables in the network (see Figure 6 for an example of such a structure).

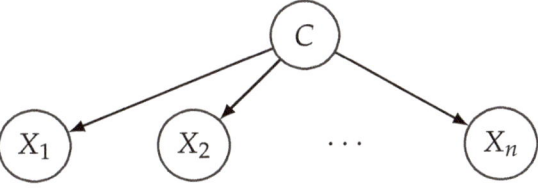

Figure 6. A Naive Bayes structure with n predictive variables and class C.

NB structures impose a strong independence assumption (all the variables are conditionally independent given the root variable C), but in practice, it is compensated by the low number of parameters that need to be estimated from data. Notice that, in this case, the factorization encoded by the network results in

$$p(c, x_1, \ldots, x_n) = p(c) \prod_{i=1}^{n} p(x_i|c), \tag{8}$$

meaning that n one-dimensional conditional distributions must be specified, instead of one n-dimensional conditional distribution.

A BN can be used for classification by computing the posterior distribution of the class variable given an observed value $\{x_1, \ldots, x_n\}$ of the predictive variables so that the result would be the value $c^* \in \Omega_C$ such that

$$c^* = \arg\max_{c \in \Omega_C} p(c|x_1, \ldots, x_n).$$

Since $p(c|x_1, \ldots, x_n) \propto p(c, x_1, \ldots, x_n)$, in the case of an NB structure, and taking into account Equation (8), it amounts to computing

$$c^* = \arg\max_{c \in \Omega_C} p(c) \prod_{i=1}^{n} p(x_i|c).$$

Unlike the learning of MLPs, to train the BNs, the variable *TEACHING* is a unique variable with three categories: the rest of the variables (*SHIFT*, *WEIGHT*, *CONTINUOUS* and *EXAM*) are the same as the variables used with the MLPs.

2.3. Binary Classification

In an attempt to improve the reliability of the predictions, we have compared the performance of MLPs and BNs with a logistic regression model where the mark in the final exam is categorized into two classes: *Fail* and *Pass*. As in the previous section, the input variables for training the MLPs are: *SHIFT* (a 0–1 variable), *TEACHING* (split into three binary variables), *WEIGHT* and *CONTINUOUS*, both re-scaled to the interval $[-1,1]$. Twelve MLPs with one hidden layer have been learned varying the number of nodes in the intermediate layer from 3 to 14. The activation function used was the logistic.

To get the models based on BNs, we have trained a Naive Bayes model, as well as a BN with structure, learned using the HC optimization procedure with BIC score as a metric.

Finally, we compared the performance of the aforementioned classifiers with the results obtained by the logistic regression where the input variables are the same as those used with the MLP.

2.4. Prediction Using Degree as Explanatory Variable

In the last part of this study, we repeated the steps followed in the previous sections but introduced the degree program as an explanatory variable in an attempt to improve the quality of the predictions.

For the regression analysis, we fitted a linear model for each degree program in the study. We kept the rest of the explanatory variables with the following exceptions:

- In the linear model fitted for students enrolled in *Industrial Engineering*, *Labor Relations* and *Physical Activity and Sport Science* we have removed the variable *WEIGHT* from the model because it takes the same value in all the courses analyzed (30% in Industrial Engineering and 50% in both, Labor Relations and Physical Activity and Sport Science).
- In the linear model fitted in *Industrial Engineering* and *Physical Activity and Sport Science* the variable *TEACHING* is not used because the courses in these degrees were taught with the same methodology (in-person and eLearning, respectively).

The analysis of the standardized errors show lack of normality (Shapiro–Wilk's *p*-value lower than 0.001) in all the degrees with exception of *Mathematics*, *Public Management* and *Physical Activity and Sport Science* (Shapiro–Wilks' *p*-value = 0.1888, 0.1824 and 0.0575, respectively). Neither is the homoscedasticity requirement accomplished in all the degrees (Breusch–Pagan's *p*-value under 0.001) except for *I.T. Engineering* (Breusch–Pagan's *p*-value = 0.6045). Therefore, the coefficient of each model has been computed both by Least Squared Error and robust estimators and the RSME compared.

To learn the MLP the degree is entered as 7 binary variables while for the BNs the degree is one variable with 7 categories.

3. Results

3.1. Regression Results

Regarding the use of robust estimators to fit the linear model to our data, the resulting values of RMSE yield by the models estimated by Huber's M-estimator, Least Trimmed Squares (LTS) robust regression, Least-Absolute-Deviations (LAD) regression and the S-estimator proposed by Koller and Stahel are displayed in Table 3. All the models except the one fitted by the LTS method are similar, getting the minimum RMSE with the estimations proposed by Koller and Stahel, so we will use this linear model to study the relationship between the explanatory variables and the mark obtained in the final exam. The results of this estimation are shown in Table 4.

Table 3. Comparison of the RMSE obtained by the different methods of estimation: Huber = Huber's M-estimator, LTS = least trimmed squares robust regression, LAD = least-absolute-deviations regression and KS = S-estimator proposed by Koller and Stahel.

Method of Estimation	RMSE
Huber	20.44772
LTS	40.45228
LAD	20.49332
KS	20.43824

Table 4. Estimations of the regression coefficients using the KS estimator.

Parameter	Value	Std.Error	*t* Value	*p*-Value
Intercept	−45.76676	3.61698	−12.653	$<2 \times 10^{-16}$
SHIFTMorning	10.16746	1.09684	9.270	$<2 \times 10^{-16}$
TEACHINGe-learning	0.64087	1.58107	0.405	0.685
TEACHINGIn-person	18.69717	1.66811	11.209	$<2 \times 10^{-16}$
WEIGHT	0.70788	0.06454	10.968	$<2 \times 10^{-16}$
CONTINUOUS	0.69939	0.01883	37.143	$<2 \times 10^{-16}$

Since the reference level for *TEACHING* is *blended* learning, the fitted regression within this group is

$$EXAM = -45.76676 + 10.16746 \cdot SHIFT + 0.70788 \cdot WEIGHT + 0.69939 \cdot CONTINUOUS, \qquad (9)$$

where *SHIFT* takes on the value 0 for the afternoon shift and 1 for courses in the morning shift.

When the course is taught online, there is no significant change in the model (*p*-value = 0.685) and the regression model when the course is taught face to face is

$$EXAM = -27.06959 + 10.16746 \cdot SHIFT + 0.70788 \cdot WEIGHT + 0.69939 \cdot CONTINUOUS. \qquad (10)$$

From these regression models, we can deduce that when the teaching is not in-person, students score lower in the final exam and, as was expected, students on the morning shift score higher than students on the afternoon shift.

The variable with the highest weight in the explanation of the mark obtained in the final exam (Table 5) is the score in the continuous evaluation followed by whether the type of teaching is "In-Person" and the shift. The percentage of the continuous evaluation in the assessment of the subject (WEIGHT) is the predictor with the lowest impact on the result of the final exam.

Table 5. Standardized coefficient estimated by the S-estimator proposed by Koller and Stahel.

Intercept	SHIFT	TEACHING e-Learning	TEACHING In-Person	WEIGHT	CONTINUOUS
−0.5254	0.3435	0.0217	0.6318	0.2550	0.6682

The robust residual standard error of the models in Equations (9) and (10) is 20.13 that, together with the RMSE obtained when validating the model in the test data set (20.44), indicates that the regression model fails at predicting accurately the mark in the final exam (which takes on values between 0 and 100). Thus, we tried quantile regression in an attempt to obtain better predictions of the mark in the final exam by predicting its median instead its mean as well as predictions for the lower and higher estimated marks.

The values of the goodness of fit measurement proposed by Koenker and Machado are shown in Table 6, suggesting that neither quantile regression model explains appropriately the scores in the final exam, especially for quantiles under the median.

Table 6. Goodness of fit of quantile regression for determined percentiles.

P_{10}	P_{20}	P_{25}	P_{50}	P_{75}	P_{80}	P_{90}
0.0002697	0.1134626	0.1761121	0.3841547	0.3940505	0.3801269	0.3402591

The values of the coefficients, their standard error and p-values of the fitted models for the lower and upper quantiles (P_{25} and P_{75}), the median (P_{50}) and the 80th and 90th percentiles are displayed in Table 7.

Table 7. Coefficients of the quantile regression for P_{25}, P_{50}, P_{75}, P_{80} and P_{90}.

		Intercept	SHIFT	TEACHING e-Learning	TEACHING In-Person	WEIGHT	CONTINUOUS
P_{25}	Value	−28.15909	8.45455	−0.81818	9.18182	0.34136	0.45455
	Std.Error	3.52704	0.78454	0.85138	1.44456	0.06642	0.02121
	p-value	<0.001	<0.001	0.33669	<0.001	<0.001	<0.001
P_{50}	Value	−37.01504	8.31228	−1.81706	13.00710	0.57015	0.72903
	Std.Error	4.30834	0.98214	1.29218	1.64289	0.07828	0.02158
	p-value	<0.001	<0.001	0.15985	<0.001	<0.001	<0.001
P_{75}	Value	−40.59302	4.07737	1.84492	18.05048	0.75142	0.90754
	Std.Error	2.98465	0.86038	1.59524	1.27903	0.05460	0.01913
	p-value	<0.001	<0.001	0.24763	<0.001	<0.001	<0.001
P_{80}	Value	−38.15904	4.24812	1.42903	16.12104	0.73460	0.95913
	Std.Error	5.38077	1.58888	2.17907	2.08862	0.10189	0.02961
	p-value	<0.001	0.00757	0.51204	<0.001	<0.001	<0.001
P_{90}	Value	−39.51856	7.91199	14.70176	28.41365	0.79037	0.92436
	Std.Error	7.51783	1.97941	2.27543	2.81211	0.14375	0.03541
	p-value	<0.001	<0.001	<0.001	<0.001	<0.001	<0.001

The linear models to estimate the different percentiles for the mark in the exam of courses taught in-person are:

$$P_{25} = -18.97727 + 8.45455 \cdot SHIFT + 0.34136 \cdot WEIGHT + 0.45455 \cdot CONTINUOUS \tag{11}$$
$$P_{50} = -24.00794 + 8.31228 \cdot SHIFT + 0.57015 \cdot WEIGHT + 0.72903 \cdot CONTINUOUS \tag{12}$$
$$P_{75} = -22.54254 + 4.07737 \cdot SHIFT + 0.75142 \cdot WEIGHT + 0.90754 \cdot CONTINUOUS \tag{13}$$

The linear models to estimate the different percentiles for the mark in the exam of blended courses taught (there are no significant differences between the models of online courses and blended courses except for the 90th percentile) are:

$$P_{25} = -28.15909 + 8.45455 \cdot SHIFT + 0.34136 \cdot WEIGHT + 0.45455 \cdot CONTINUOUS \tag{14}$$
$$P_{50} = -37.01504 + 8.31228 \cdot SHIFT + 0.57015 \cdot WEIGHT + 0.72903 \cdot CONTINUOUS \tag{15}$$
$$P_{75} = -40.59302 + 4.07737 \cdot SHIFT + 0.75142 \cdot WEIGHT + 0.90754 \cdot CONTINUOUS \tag{16}$$

where SHIFT takes on the value 0 for the afternoon shift and 1 for courses in the morning shift.

Notice that the magnitude of the coefficients of variables WEIGHT and CONTINUOUS increases along with the percentile, whereas the higher the percentile is the lower the coefficient of SHIFT.

However, the RMSE for these models (Table 8) remains very large considering that the fitted models offer accurate predictions, particularly if we are interested in predicting low or high percentiles. This result is in line with the analysis made by Gonzalez et al. [25] in which no significant relation between the scores in CA and the final exam was found in the tails of the distribution. Neither does the estimate of the median by the quantile regression improve the accuracy of the estimation of the mean by the robust regression used in Equations (9) and (10).

Table 8. Root mean square error (RMSE) of quantile regression models for P_{25}, P_{50}, P_{75}, P_{80} and P_{90}.

P_{25}	P_{50}	P_{75}	P_{80}	P_{90}
26.09989	20.49223	24.42311	26.12923	34.35438

Finally, we used MLPs for regression. More precisely, we trained nine MLPs with one hidden layer varying the number of nodes in the layer from 1 up to 21 and 527 MLPs with two hidden layers; the activation function used in all of them was the identity. The RMSE barely changes among all the MLPs achieving the minimum value (0.4082447) for the MLP with two neurons in the first hidden layer and 10 neurons in the second one. As the target variable EXAM was scaled to the interval $[-1, 1]$, the RMSE obtained is the worst among the three methods of regression used in this study. When we used ReLU or Softplus as an activation function, the procedure did not converge.

Thus, the results indicate that it is not possible to predict in an accurate way the mark in the final exam from the explanatory variables selected in this study.

Our next attempt is to transform the regression problem into a classification problem.

3.2. Classification Results

In the fist attempt, we address a multiclass classification problem where the target variable is categorized into four classes (*Fail*, *PassingGrade*, *GradeB* and *GradeA*).

Table 9 displays the values of the performance measures obtained with the one hidden layer MLPs trained. MLPs with two hidden layers do not usually converge when six or more neurons are used in one of the layers while for structures with a low number of neurons the MLP is not able to classify classes either *GradeB* or *GradeA*. The low values of MCC, J and K indicate very poor performance of the classifier. The measure Accuracy reaches an acceptable value, but it is misleading because, as it is shown in the confusion matrix in Table 10, the MLP only predicts correctly the class Fail.

Table 9. Performance [1] of MLP with one hidden layer.

Neurons	Accuracy	GM	MCC	J	K
4	0.7423581	0.3767619	0.1912527	0.1126921	0.2307464
5	0.7379913	0.4528189	0.2253644	0.16143641	0.2574133
6	0.7336245	0.3500356	0.1491623	0.08828901	0.2047303
7	0.7423581	0.3556055	0.1814024	0.10156554	0.2145427
8	0.7365357	0.3506387	0.1600189	0.09149303	0.2081272
9	**0.7481805**	**0.4758372**	**0.2611203**	**0.18915434**	**0.2929113**
10	0.7190684	0.4247192	0.1597665	0.12140248	0.2293730
15	0.7350801	0.4675948	0.2243916	0.1694903	0.275774

[1] GM = Geometric, MCC = Matthew's correlation coefficient, J = Youden's Index and K = Coeh's Kappa Score.

Table 10. Confusion matrix obtained from the one-hidden layer MLP with 9 neurons.

		Predicted			
		Fail	PassingGrade	GradeB	GradeA
Observed	Fail	472	27	3	2
	PassingGrade	75	25	4	2
	GradeB	37	13	6	6
	GradeA	6	6	1	2

To compare the performance of the MLP with the BNs at classifying the exam mark, we trained a Naive Bayes structure and a BN with a structure determined using the HC algorithm. Tables 11 and 12 display the performance values and the confusion matrix, respectively, for the Naive Bayes model. The BN trained with the HC method was not able to predict any category but *Fail*.

Table 11. Performance [1] of the Naive Bayes classifier.

Accuracy	GM	MCC	J	K
0.7263464	0.3564184	0.1386113	0.08551829	0.1859933

[1] GM = Geometric, MCC = Matthew's correlation coefficient, J = Youden's Index and K = Coeh's Kappa Score.

Table 12. Confusion matrix obtained from the Naive Bayes classifier.

		Predicted			
		Fail	PassingGrade	GradeB	GradeA
Observed	Fail	477	19	1	7
	PassingGrade	83	18	2	3
	GradeB	38	14	3	7
	GradeA	11	3	0	1

The performance of the Naive Bayes classifier is even worse than the MLP when predicting *PassingGrade*, *GradeB* and *GradeA* categories.

In the last attempt to improve the prediction of the students' performance in the final exam, we ask if, at least, the fact of failing or passing the exam can be predicted from the continuous evaluation and the other variables considered. We have trained MLPs with one hidden layer and the logistic activation function, modifying the number of neurons in the hidden layer from 3 up to 14. Additionally, we trained a Naive Bayes classifier as well as a BN learned by the HC algorithm. Finally, we also tried logistic regression. Tables 13 and 14 show the measures of performance and the confusion matrix of the three classifiers: the MLP with six neurons in the hidden layer (best performance achieved among the MLPs trained), the NB model and the results from the logistic regression. The BN learned by the HC algorithm was not able to predict the *Pass* category. In this case, the MLP accomplishes almost acceptable results and shows more superior behavior than the NB and the logistic regression. Logistic regression classifies better the *Fail* category but does not succeed in predicting the *Pass* category. NB has a similar performance to the MLP when predicting the fails but, as the logistic regression does, is unsuccessful with the students passing the exam.

Table 13. Assessment [1] of the classifiers MLP, NB and logistic regression.

	Accuracy	GM	MCC	J	K
MLP	0.8195051	0.7660164	0.5414379	0.5451470	0.5413786
NB	0.7787482	0.6759694	0.4128719	0.3956219	0.4113708
Log.Reg.	0.7947598	0.6390402	0.4252452	0.365242	0.4102143

[1] GM = Geometric, MCC = Matthew's correlation coefficient, J = Youden's Index and K = Coeh's Kappa Score.

Table 14. Confusion matrices obtained from the classifiers MLP, NB and logistic regression.

		MLP				NB				Log.Reg.	
		Predicted				Predicted				Predicted	
		Fail	Pass			Fail	Pass			Fail	Pass
Observed	Fail	437	67	Observed	Fail	439	65	Observed	Fail	465	39
	Pass	70	113		Pass	87	96		Pass	102	81

To finish the study, we have added the degree to which the student is enrolled as an explanatory variable.

3.3. Improvement in the Accuracy When the Degree is Added to the Previous Models

When the degree is introduced as a predictor in the linear models, the variable *WEIGHT* cannot be included for *Industrial Engineering* (whose value is 30% in all the cases), *Labor Relations* (50%) and *Physical Activity and Sport Science* (50%) as well as variable *TEACHING* neither can be included for *Industrial Engineering* (only in-person) nor *Physical Activity and Sport Science* (only e-learning). Only *Economy* and *Mathematics* have the three types of teaching, the rest (*I.T, Labor Relations* and *Public Management*) have been only taught by e-learning and in-person, taking as reference the e-learning group.

Table 15 shows the RSME of the different linear models depending on the estimator used to compute the coefficients of the linear model. Now, the robust estimators of the coefficients that minimize the RMSE depend on the degree program considered. If we compare the RMSE of the best choice with the results in Table 3 we can notice that the change in RMSE depends strongly on the degree: whereas in Economy the RMSE decreases about 20%, in others as I.T. or Mathematics it barely changes. In any case, the RMSEs remain high enough to consider the predictions reliable.

Table 15. Comparison of the RMSE obtained by the different methods of estimation in each degree: Huber = Huber's M-estimator, LTS = least trimmed squares robust regression, LAD = least-absolute-deviations regression and KS = S-estimator proposed by Koller and Stahel.

Degree	Method of Estimation			
	Huber	LTS	KS	LAD
Economy	16.25501	31.41839	16.23750	16.54850
I.T.	22.30481	31.54442	22.30931	23.04748
INDUS	14.81322	20.37739	14.76142	14.50819
Mathematics	19.65349	42.74780	19.70359	20.22910
Public Management	18.23688	28.85815	17.99737	31.80174
Labour Relations	12.72984		33.55746	12.47861
Sports	19.07092	18.70723	19.07724	21.53974

In Table 16, we can observe how the mark obtained in the CA contributes in a positive and significant way, no matter the degree. However, the weight of the CA in the assessment of the course has a negative effect on the degrees of Economy and Mathematics, being positive in the rest of the degrees. Moreover, it is remarkable that Mathematics is the only degree for which in-person teaching has a negative effect on the performance of the students in the final exam. This could be due to the sharpest peak in performance during the COVID pandemic in comparison with the rest of the degrees.

Table 16. Coefficients of the regression model fitted for each degree. Inside the parenthesis not significant coefficients.

Degree	Intercept	Teaching e-Learning	Teaching In-Person	Weight	Continuous
Economy	13.70546	−3.89268	(1.36264)	−0.40290	0.64196
I.T.	−33.2755	-	19.2129	0.7942	0.5798
INDUS	(0)	-	-	-	0.40710
Mathematics	272.1077	15.9608	−49.8121	−5.7813	1.0668
Public Management	−70.39375	-	20.32998	1.04353	0.88170
Labour Relations	−8.99644	-	5.04751	1.04353	0.89074
Sports	(−1.9231)	-	-	-	1.1134

Regarding the multiclass classification task, Table 17 displays the performance measures of the MLP with eight neurons in the hidden layer (structure with the best performance among the twelve one-hidden-layer MLPs trained) and the NB classifier (BN learned with the HC method keeps on being unable to classify classes different from *Fail*. There is a noticeable improvement in the performance of both classifiers, especially in the MLP, although the assessment measures are still low.

Table 17. Assessment [1] of the multiclass classifiers MLP and NB when degree is entered in the model.

	Accuracy	GM	MCC	J	K
MLP	0.7583697	0.6247160	0.3795430	0.3470143	0.4080537
NB	0.7292576	0.3983517	0.1689443	0.1145226	0.23902

[1] GM = Geometric, MCC = Matthew's correlation coefficient, J = Youden's Index and K = Coeh's Kappa Score.

If we reduce the problem to determine whether a student will pass or fail the final exam, Table 18 shows the performance of the three classifiers and the logistic regression. In this case, the BN learned with the HC algorithm is able to predict the passing students although its performance is poor. The results show how the MLP and the logistic regression improve their accuracy while the NB loses precision as a classifier.

Table 18. Assessment [1] of the classifiers MLP, NB and logistic regression when degree is entered in the model.

	Accuracy	GM	MCC	J	K
MLP	0.8529840	0.7737900	0.6077984	0.5733802	0.6038537
NB	0.7947598	0.6223217	0.4193111	0.3478402	0.39845
HC	0.7554585	0.3443093	0.2337671	0.1063297	0.14525
Log.Reg.	0.8107715	0.7120422	0.4926073	0.4636352	0.4891726

[1] GM = Geometric, MCC = Matthew's correlation coefficient, J = Youden's Index and K = Coeh's Kappa Score.

4. Discussion

From the results detailed in Section 3, the prediction of the student performance in the final exam of a course is a difficult task. The variables used to explain the score in the final exam: shift, type of teaching, the weight of the continuous evaluation in the assessment of the subject and the performance of the students in the continuous evaluation, turn out to be insufficient to explain the score obtained in the final exam. The first issue that we face when trying to fit a linear model to the data is the difference in variability. This problem remains even when one regression model is fitted for each degree. The measures of error (Robust Residual Standard Error and RMSE) indicate that the regression model has no acceptable predictability, so there must be important variables in explaining the efficiency of the students when taking the final exam, that this study has not taken into account. These results are in agreement with the conclusions obtained in the studies of Bjælde et al. [23] and Day et al. [6]. However, the regression model shows that the student achievements in the continuous assessment play an important role in the final exam mark. Actually, it is the explanatory variable with the highest weight in the prediction of the final exam score followed by the fact of teaching the course face to face. This result agrees with findings in [25], Gidado [47], Onihunwa et al. [48] or Santos et al. [49]. Actually, every course at the University of Almeía has a mandatory CA in its assessment procedure which implies that the positive effect of the CA remains even when the rest of the courses taken by students have CA, as opposed to what Perez-Martínez et al. [50] infer from their studies.

From the regression models, we can also deduce that when the teaching is not in-person, students score lower in the final exam. This conclusion is opposed to the findings in the literature about the better performance of students during the COVID-19 outbreak [51–53]. A possible explanation for this different behavior could be that during the COVID-19 lockdown, the University of Almería fixed a mandatory 50% of CA in all the courses; the marks in the CA part are significantly higher in e-learning teaching (50.51% for e-learning against 36.5% got in in-person taught courses) lowering the motivation for exam preparation in some students as have been reported in [10,14,23]. This rise in online CA was also reported by De Santos Berbel et al. [54] but the authors also found a growth in the dropout rate, which could have a negative effect on the variable *Exam* because the student's withdrawal is recorded in this variable with zero. Another possible explanation could be that there is more room for cheating in online CA: instructors could have made a bigger effort to avoid cheating in the online final exam by, for example, increasing the bank of questions or setting a tight completion time whereas in blended teaching the final exam is face to face. This could cause a larger gap between the marks obtained in the continuous assessment and in the final exam.

Neither quantile regression offers an accurate forecast of the final exam outcomes. The low values of the Koenker and Machado R index, especially in low percentiles, denote that the quantile model also fails in explaining the variability in the response variable. The RMSE of the forecast of the percentiles are high, particularly when fitting high percentiles in line with what was stated by Gonzalez et al. [25].

The use of ANNs to predict the mark in the final exam yields the worst result in comparison with the linear model and the quantile regression, almost doubling the RMSE of the estimations.

Splitting the grades in the final exam into four intervals to use classification procedures in an attempt to make predictions about the results of the exam neither improves the outcomes. The MLP with one hidden layer outperforms the NB increasing by more than 50% the assessment measures MCC and K and doubling the Youden's index. Accuracy measure is similar in both methods because NB is able to properly predict the *Fail* category (more than 94.6% of agreements) but fails for higher categories, likely due to the limited number of cases in the dataset.

If the problem is reduced to just predicting whether a student will pass or fail the final exam, we obtain more accurate results, particularly by using the MLP, which outperforms both, NB and logistic regression, being able to rightly predict 61.7% of the students passing the exam (against the 52.5% of the NB and the 44.3% of the logistic regression). The three methods are accurate when predicting the failures: MLP predicts this class 86.7% of the time, NB 87.1% of the time and logistic regression 92.3%.

The inclusion of the degree read by the student barely improves the accuracy of the methods studied, which is in line with Pérez Martínez et al. [50] who suggest the improvement in the student's performance does not depend on the degree.

5. Conclusions

Continuous evaluation has been adopted by most of the courses taught in Spanish universities due to, either academic decisions or because colleges or accreditation agencies make a percentage of CA in the assessment of the courses mandatory. There is no doubt about the benefits of including a CA in a course playing both roles: as summative and formative assessment, mainly when the continuous evaluation offers feedback to the students and they take advantage of that feedback. However, what is less clear is the magnitude of this positive effect on the learning of the students as well as on their results in the final exam of the course in that case. Furthermore, there is no evidence about whether the benefits of the CA outweigh the increase in the workload of students and teachers.

There is a number of papers in the literature studying the relationship between the continuous assessment and the final exam mark [21,23–25,47–49], but the statistical procedures used are traditional: descriptive Statistics, T tests, Pearson's correlation test, ANOVA or linear regression. In this study, we have tried to find statistical evidence about whether the effect of the CA is a determinant in students' performance on the final exam by using and comparing state-of-the-art methods as it is suggested by [55]. Although it has been shown that CA has actually an effect on the final exam score, this effect is not decisive to predict how a student will perform in the final exam.

The results obtained seem to encourage the instructors to move CA activities closer to the final exam requirements. Given that the weight of the CA in the assessment of the course has a positive effect on the fitted regression model, the increase in this percentage could enhance students' performance in the final exam. Moreover, the type of CA used in the course could be a variable to take into account when it comes to improving the students' learning, despite there is no agreement in the literature about this point: Day et al. [6] found no differences in the students' scores on courses with different assessment types while Deeley et al. [18] assert that diverse assessment with a more flexible approach and assessment method that let the students be actively involved in making choices about their assessment would increase students' motivation. The large differences in the regression models fitted for each degree suggest that the design of the assessment must be customized to match the student's characteristics.

Supplementary Materials: The following supporting information can be downloaded at: https://www.mdpi.com/article/10.3390/math10213994/s1.

Author Contributions: Conceptualization, A.D.M., A.R.M., M.M., R.R. and A.S.; methodology, A.D.M., M.M. and A.S.; software, M.M. and A.S.; validation, M.M. and A.S.; formal analysis, M.M. and A.S.; investigation, M.M. and A.S.; resources, A.D.M., M.M. and A.S.; data curation, A.D.M., M.M. and A.S.; writing—original draft preparation, M.M. and A.S.; writing—review and editing, A.D.M., M.M. and A.S.; visualization, A.D.M., M.M. and A.S.; supervision, M.M. and A.S.; project administration, M.M., R.R. and A.S.; funding acquisition, R.R. and A.S. All authors have read and agreed to the published version of the manuscript.

Funding: This research is part of Project PID2019-106758GB-C32 funded by MCIN/AEI/10.13039/501100011033, FEDER "Una manera de hacer Europa" funds. This research is also partially funded by Junta de Andalucía grant P20-00091 and University of Almería grant UAL2020-FQM-B196.

Data Availability Statement: Training and test data sets used in this research are available as Supplementary Materials.

Acknowledgments: We would like to acknowledge the support given by the Vice-chancellorship for Academic planning of the University of Almería.

Conflicts of Interest: The authors declare no conflict of interest.

Abbreviations

The following abbreviations are used in this manuscript:

AFL	Assessment for Learning
ANN	Artificial Neural Network
BN	Bayesian Network
CA	Continuous Assessment
DAG	Directed acyclic graph
GM	Geometric Mean
HC	Hill-climbing
J	Youden's index
K	Coeh's kappa score
KS	Koller and Stahel robust estimator
LAD	least-absolute-deviations regression
LTS	Least trimmed squares robust regression
MCC	Matthew's correlation coefficient
MLP	Multilayer perceptron
NB	Naive Bayes
RMSE	Root mean square error
TAN	Tree augmented network

References

1. McDowell, L.; Wakelin, D.; Montgomery, C.; King, S. Does assessment for learning make a difference? The development of a questionnaire to explore the student response. *Assess. Eval. High. Educ.* **2011**, *36*, 749–765. [CrossRef]
2. Sambell, K.; McDowell, L.; Montgomery, C. *Assessment for Learning in Higher Education*; Routledge: Oxfordshire, UK, 2012.
3. Zlatkin-Troitschanskaia, O.; Shavelson, R.J.; Pant, H.A. Assessment of learning outcomes in higher education: International comparisons and perspectives. In *Handbook on Measurement, Assessment, and Evaluation in Higher Education*; Routledge: Oxfordshire, UK, 2017; pp. 686–698.
4. Zahl, S.; Jimenez, S.; Huffman, M. Assessment at the highest degree(s): Trends in graduate and professional education. In *Trends in Assessment: Ideas, Opportunities, and Issues for Higher Education*; Stylus: Sterling, TX, USA, 2019.
5. Nair, P.; Pillay, J. Exploring the validity of the continuous assessment strategy in higher education institutions: Research in higher education. *South Afr. J. High. Educ.* **2004**, *18*, 302–312.
6. Day, I.N.; van Blankenstein, F.M.; Westenberg, P.M.; Admiraal, W.F. Explaining individual student success using continuous assessment types and student characteristics. *High. Educ. Res. Dev.* **2018**, *37*, 937–951. [CrossRef]
7. Poza-Lujan, J.L.; Calafate, C.T.; Posadas-Yagüe, J.L.; Cano, J.C. Assessing the impact of continuous evaluation strategies: Tradeoff between student performance and instructor effort. *IEEE Trans. Educ.* **2015**, *59*, 17–23. [CrossRef]
8. Combrinck, M.; Hatch, M. Students' experiences of a continuous assessment approach at a Higher Education Institution. *J. Soc. Sci.* **2012**, *33*, 81–89. [CrossRef]
9. Shields, S. 'My work is bleeding': Exploring students' emotional responses to first-year assignment feedback. *Teach. High. Educ.* **2015**, *20*, 614–624. [CrossRef]
10. Bloxham, S.; Boyd, P. *Developing Effective Assessment in Higher Education: A Practical Guide*; McGraw-Hill Education: New York, NY, USA, 2007.
11. Holmes, N. Student perceptions of their learning and engagement in response to the use of a continuous e-assessment in an undergraduate module. *Assess. Eval. High. Educ.* **2015**, *40*, 1–14. [CrossRef]
12. Hernández, R. Does continuous assessment in higher education support student learning? *High. Educ.* **2012**, *64*, 489–502. [CrossRef]
13. Holmes, N. Engaging with assessment: Increasing student engagement through continuous assessment. *Act. Learn. High. Educ.* **2018**, *19*, 23–34. [CrossRef]
14. Martín-Carrasco, F.; Granados, A.; Santillan, D.; Mediero, L. Continuous Assessment in Civil Engineering Education-Yes, but with Some Conditions. *CSEDU* **2014**, *2*, 103–109.
15. Rubio-Escudero, C.; Asencio-Cortés, G.; Martínez-Álvarez, F.; Troncoso, A.; Riquelme, J.C. Impact of auto-evaluation tests as part of the continuous evaluation in programming courses. In Proceedings of the 13th International Conference on Soft Computing Models in Industrial and Environmental Applications, San Sebastian, Spain, 6–8 June 2018; pp. 553–561.
16. López-Tocón, I. Moodle Quizzes as a Continuous Assessment in Higher Education: An Exploratory Approach in Physical Chemistry. *Educ. Sci.* **2021**, *11*, 500. [CrossRef]
17. Carless, D.; Salter, D.; Yang, M.; Lam, J. Developing sustainable feedback practices. *Stud. High. Educ.* **2011**, *36*, 395–407. [CrossRef]
18. Deeley, S.J.; Fischbacher-Smith, M.; Karadzhov, D.; Koristashevskaya, E. Exploring the 'wicked' problem of student dissatisfaction with assessment and feedback in higher education. *High. Educ. Pedagog.* **2019**, *4*, 385–405. [CrossRef]

19. Scott, G.W. Active engagement with assessment and feedback can improve group-work outcomes and boost student confidence. *High. Educ. Pedagog.* **2017**, *2*, 1–13. [CrossRef]
20. Dejene, W. The practice of modularized curriculum in higher education institution: Active learning and continuous assessment in focus. *Cogent Educ.* **2019**, *6*, 1611052. [CrossRef]
21. Sanz-Pérez, E. Students' performance and perceptions on continuous assessment. Redefining a chemical engineering subject in the European higher education area. *Educ. Chem. Eng.* **2019**, *28*, 13–24. [CrossRef]
22. Gibbs, G. How assessment frames student learning. In *Innovative Assessment in Higher Education*; Routledge: Oxfordshire, UK, 2006; pp. 43–56.
23. Bjælde, O.E.; Jørgensen, T.H.; Lindberg, A.B. Continuous assessment in higher education in Denmark. *Dan. Univ. Tidsskr.* **2017**, *12*, 1–19. [CrossRef]
24. Reina-Paz, M.D.; Rodriguez-Oromendia, A.; Sevilla-Sevilla, C. Effect of Continuous Assessment Tests on Overall Student Performance in the Case of the Spanish National Distance Education University (UNED). *J. Int. Educ. Res. (JIER)* **2014**, *10*, 61–68. [CrossRef]
25. Gonzalez, M.d.l.O.; Jareño, F.; López, R. Impact of students' behavior on continuous assessment in Higher Education. *Innov. Eur. J. Soc. Sci. Res.* **2015**, *28*, 498–507. [CrossRef]
26. Gil-Begue, S.; Bielza, C.; Larrañaga, P. Multi-dimensional Bayesian network classifiers: A survey. *Artif. Intell. Rev.* **2021**, *54*, 519–559. [CrossRef]
27. Li, G. Robust regression. *Explor. Data Tables Trends Shapes* **1985**, *281*, U340.
28. Faraway, J.J. *Linear Models with R*; CRC: Boca Raton, FL, USA, 2004.
29. Huber, P.J. Robust Estimation of a Location Parameter. *Ann. Math. Stat.* **1964**, *35*, 73–101. [CrossRef]
30. Giloni, A.; Padberg, M. Least trimmed squares regression, least median squares regression, and mathematical programming. *Math. Comput. Model.* **2002**, *35*, 1043–1060. [CrossRef]
31. Thanoon, F.H. Robust regression by least absolute deviations method. *Int. J. Stat. Appl.* **2015**, *5*, 109–112.
32. Koller, M.; Stahel, W.A. Nonsingular subsampling for regression S estimators with categorical predictors. *Comput. Stat.* **2017**, *32*, 631–646. [CrossRef]
33. Ripley, B.; Venables, B.; Bates, D.M.; Hornik, K.; Gebhardt, A.; Firth, D.; Ripley, M.B. Package 'mass'. *Cran R* **2013**, *538*, 113–120.
34. Maechler, M.; Rousseeuw, P.; Croux, C.; Todorov, V.; Ruckstuhl, A.; Salibian-Barrera, M.; Verbeke, T.; Koller, M.; Conceicao, E.L.; di Palma, M.A. Package 'Robustbase'. 2022. Available online: https://cran.r-project.org/web/packages/robustbase/index.html (accessed on 10 October 2021).
35. Koenker, R.; Hallock, K.F. Quantile regression. *J. Econ. Perspect.* **2001**, *15*, 143–156. [CrossRef]
36. Hao, L.; Naiman, D.Q. *Quantile Regression*; Number 149; Sage: Thousand Oaks, CA, USA, 2007.
37. Yu, K.; Lu, Z.; Stander, J. Quantile regression: Applications and current research areas. *J. R. Stat. Soc. Ser.* **2003**, *52*, 331–350. [CrossRef]
38. Koenker, R.; Machado, J.A. Goodness of fit and related inference processes for quantile regression. *J. Am. Stat. Assoc.* **1999**, *94*, 1296–1310. [CrossRef]
39. Haykin, S. *Neural Networks: A Comprehensive Foundation*; Prentice Hall: Hoboken, NJ, USA, 1998.
40. Goodfellow, I.; Bengio, Y.; Courville, A. *Deep Learning*; MIT Press: Cambridge, MA, USA, 2016.
41. Landis, J.R.; Koch, G.G. The measurement of observer agreement for categorical data. *Biometrics* **1977**, *1*, 159–174. [CrossRef]
42. Pearl, J. *Probabilistic Reasoning in Intelligent Systems*; Morgan-Kaufmann: San Mateo, CA, USA, 1988.
43. Scanagatta, M.; Salmerón, A.; Stella, F. A survey on Bayesian network structure learning from data. *Prog. Artif. Intell.* **2019**, *8*, 425–439. [CrossRef]
44. Neapolitan, R.E. *Learning Bayesian Networks*; Prentice Hall: Hoboken, NJ, USA, 2003.
45. Scutari, M. Learning Bayesian Networks with the bnlearn R Package. *J. Stat. Softw.* **2010**, *35*, 1–22. [CrossRef]
46. Friedman, N.; Geiger, D.; Goldszmidt, M. Bayesian Network Classifiers. *Mach. Learn.* **1997**, *29*, 131–163. [CrossRef]
47. Gidado, B.K. The corelation between continuous assessment and examination scores of public administration students of the University of Abuja. *Sokoto Educ. Rev.* **2021**, *20*, 12–20.
48. Onihunwa, J.; Adigun, O.; Irunokhai, E.; Sada, Y.; Jeje, A.; Adeyemi, O.; Adesina, O. Roles of Continuous Assessment Scores in Determining the Academic Performance of Computer Science Students in Federal College of Wildlife Management. *Am. J. Eng. Res.* **2018**, *7*, 7–20.
49. Santos, J.M.; Ortiz, E.; Marín, S. Variation indexes of marks due to continuous assessment. Empirical approach at university/Índices de variación de la nota debidos a la evaluación continua. Contrastación empírica en la enseñanza universitaria. *Cult. Educ.* **2018**, *30*, 491–527. [CrossRef]
50. Pérez-Martínez, J.E.; García-García, M.J.; Perdomo, W.H.; Villamide-Díaz, M.J. Analysis of the results of the continuous assessment in the adaptation of the Universidad Politécnica de Madrid to the European Higher Education Area. In Proceedings of the Research in Engineering Education Symposium, Palm Cove, QLD, Australia, 20–23 July 2009; Volume 90.
51. Gonzalez, T.; De La Rubia, M.A.; Hincz, K.P.; Comas-Lopez, M.; Subirats, L.; Fort, S.; Sacha, G.M. Influence of COVID-19 confinement on students' performance in higher education. *PLoS ONE* **2020**, *15*, e0239490. [CrossRef]

52. Iglesias-Pradas, S.; Hernández-García, Á.; Chaparro-Peláez, J.; Prieto, J.L. Emergency remote teaching and students' academic performance in higher education during the COVID-19 pandemic: A case study. *Comput. Hum. Behav.* **2021**, *119*, 106713. [CrossRef]
53. Moravec, L.; Ječmínek, J.; Kukalová, G. Evaluation of final examination performance at Czech University of Life Sciences during the COVID-19 outbreak. *J. Effic. Responsib. Educ. Sci.* **2022**, *15*, 47–52. [CrossRef]
54. De Santos-Berbel, C.; Hernando García, J.I.; De Santos Berbel, L. Undergraduate Student Performance in a Structural Analysis Course: Continuous Assessment before and after the COVID-19 Outbreak. *Educ. Sci.* **2022**, *12*, 561. [CrossRef]
55. Yang, X.; Ge, J. Predicting Student Learning Effectiveness in Higher Education Based on Big Data Analysis. *Mob. Inf. Syst.* **2022**, *2022*, 8409780. [CrossRef]

Article

A Method to Automate the Prediction of Student Academic Performance from Early Stages of the Course

Alicia Nieto-Reyes [1,*], Rafael Duque [1] and Giacomo Francisci [2]

[1] Department of Mathematics, Statistics and Computer Science, University of Cantabria, 39005 Santander, Spain; rafael.duque@unican.es
[2] Department of Mathematics, University of Trento, 38122 Trento, Italy; giacomo.francisci@unitn.it
* Correspondence: alicia.nieto@unican.es

Abstract: The objective of this work is to present a methodology that automates the prediction of students' academic performance at the end of the course using data recorded in the first tasks of the academic year. Analyzing early student records is helpful in predicting their later results; which is useful, for instance, for an early intervention. With this aim, we propose a methodology based on the random Tukey depth and a non-parametric kernel. This methodology allows teachers and evaluators to define the variables that they consider most appropriate to measure those aspects related to the academic performance of students. The methodology is applied to a real case study obtaining a success rate in the predictions of over the 80%. The case study was carried out in the field of Human-computer Interaction.The results indicate that the methodology could be of special interest to develop software systems that process the data generated by computer-supported learning systems and to warn the teacher of the need to adopt intervention mechanisms when low academic performance is predicted.

Keywords: computer-supported cooperative learning; non-parametric statistics; predictive methods; statistical data depth; supervised classification; random methods

Citation: Nieto-Reyes, A.; Duque, R.; Francisci, G. A Method to Automate the Prediction of Student Academic Performance from Early Stages of the Course. *Mathematics* **2021**, *9*, 2677. https://doi.org/10.3390/math9212677

Academic Editors: Ana Isabel Molina and Carmen Lacave

Received: 16 September 2021
Accepted: 15 October 2021
Published: 22 October 2021

Publisher's Note: MDPI stays neutral with regard to jurisdictional claims in published maps and institutional affiliations.

Copyright: © 2021 by the authors. Licensee MDPI, Basel, Switzerland. This article is an open access article distributed under the terms and conditions of the Creative Commons Attribution (CC BY) license (https://creativecommons.org/licenses/by/4.0/).

1. Introduction

Recent technological innovations are currently reflected in the proliferation of groupware systems aimed at facilitating communication and coordination between users, as well as providing shared workspaces where users build artifacts that solve tasks. Collaboration supported by groupware is characterized by a large number of interactions that each user performs to cooperate with other members of a common group. An analysis of these interactions can be used to improve these collective processes. Duque et al. [1] propose a methodology for carrying out this analysis based on the following three phases:

(i) to capture descriptive information of the interactions,
(ii) to categorize and characterize the information collected and
(iii) to intervene in the improvement of the collaborative activity.

Among these improvements, it is worth highlighting those that refer to providing better mechanisms to be aware of the interactions performed by other users [2], optimizing business processes to achieve strategic goals of organizations [3], and adapting academic processes supported by collaborative learning environments [4].

Computer-Supported Collaborative Learning (CSCL) is the research field that studies how groupware can be exploited in academic environments. Thus, groupware systems support processes that enable students to build new knowledge. These processes are usually oriented towards solving academic problems using social interaction with classmates. Students discuss and interchange ideas about solutions that solve a problem proposed by the teacher. Therefore, students acquire new knowledge due to the arguments and reasonings that arise in these discussions. One of the main research challenges in the CSCL field is building groupware that generate interventions in the collective process to optimize the student academic performance. Bravo et al. [5] define intervention mechanisms in CSCL systems with three components:

(i) information to be processed by the students (analysis indicators to be displayed, advice to be shown, new exercise to be solved, etc.),
(ii) a trigger moment or situation that puts the intervention in action,
(iii) learners who receive each intervention.

1.1. Related Work

Intervention mechanisms have been deeply studied in the CSCL field to improve students learning. Thus, Anderson et al. [6] establish a set of theoretical principles to integrate software agents that simulate the role of a teacher who helps the student by issuing advice. Selker [7] follows this theoretical proposal with a generic architecture that allows modeling the behavior of the student and offering advice based on how users interact with the system. Meanwhile, Paolucci et al. [8] focus interventions in guiding students to solve academic problems. According to the criteria used by [9], it is possible to intervene in the work of students not only to optimize solutions but also to ensure optimal collaboration between classmates.

Some alternatives have already been explored to include artificial intelligence (in some of its variants) to the field of teaching, such as incorporating virtual assistants adapted to specific classes and different levels of students [10] or in online courses to mitigate the impact of the volume of students [11]. The aim of these intelligent systems is to provide continuous support to students, overcoming some of the disadvantages of online teaching, such as long response times by teachers or the correction of common errors. This support can be particularly interesting in courses based on significant problems in which the student learns by doing [12]. These methodologies can be applied in such a way that students are structured into groups that must carry out small tasks throughout the course. These tasks are related to each other in such a way that the solutions produced in one task are essential for the completion of the next tasks since they are taken as inputs [13]. Thus, students are increasingly producing larger solutions to more complex problems, generating at the end of the course a product close to the quality standards required in professional environments. Artificial Intelligence [14] can be used to analyze academic performance, being able to train different machine learning models [15,16] so that the different types of students are detected and classified. After extracting the characteristics of the students and classifying them, it can be given a series of warnings or personalized hints and feedback [17]. Therefore, Artificial Intelligence techniques are a useful tool to characterize learning activities and provide interventions. Intervention mechanisms have been generally focused on guiding specific activities. However, these research proposals do not provide information that enables teachers to guide a course or subject.

1.2. Our Research Contribution

This work is dedicated to propose a methodology that enables teachers to identify the factors with most impact in the academic performance of the students in a course, using an interaction and collaboration analysis of the earliest activities of the subject. The idea is to obtain a flexible methodology that can be adapted to any subject and software system that supports the learning process, individually or collaboratively. Thus, the intention is that the methodology does not adhere to predefined indicators or competencies, but rather that the teacher establishes, in a flexible manner, how to measure those aspects of the learning process that he/she considers of interest. Additionally, the methodology is based on a statistical technique that can be carried out in an automated manner by software tools. Therefore, the amount of information generated by CSCL systems is not an obstacle for the execution of the prediction process, as is automated by software support. Thus, a generic and flexible solution is obtained, providing a state of the art proposal that automates the process of predicting academic performance while providing the teacher with the freedom of configuration, not sticking to specific competencies or indicators. This methodology is useful to intervene, not only in specific problem-solving activities but also in adapting the course development to the students. It is based on statistical data depth [18] and non-parametric kernel classification [19] and is here applied to the Human-computer Interaction subject of the Computer Science degree at the University of Cantabria.

This paper has four additional sections. Section 2 describes the methodology for predicting the academic performance of the students from the interactions collected in early stages. Section 3 shows the results of a case study in which the methodology is applied to predict academic performance in a university course. Section 4 discusses the results of this work. The computations have been carried out using the R software.

2. Materials and Methods

Our main research problem is about knowing whether it is possible to predict successfully the performance of students in an academic course from the earliest activities supported by groupware, by making use of the performance of the students who took the course in previous years. Denoting by $N = 6$ the amount of tasks performed by the students, the research problem is divided into the following research subproblems:

1. Is it possible to predict successfully the average grade over the N tasks based on the *two* first tasks performed by the students?
2. Is it possible to predict successfully the average grade over the N tasks based on the *three* first tasks performed by the students?
3. Is it possible to predict successfully the average grade over the N tasks based on the *four* first tasks performed by the students?
4. Is it possible to predict successfully the average grade over the N tasks based on the *five* first tasks performed by the students?

To design a methodology that allows for this, the following three types of data, commonly used to characterize groupware [20], are taken as input:

- Communication between classmates: These data measure the fluency in exchanging ideas on how to solve the activities (e.g.: contributions from each student, perception of the quality of the proposals of others, etc.).
- Coordination to distribute tasks: These data allow us to quantify how the efforts are distributed between the members of the group (e.g.: hours of work of each member of the group, perception of the effort of the classmates, etc.).
- Collaboration for building quality solutions: These data quantify whether the collective process allowed the student to improve solutions (e.g.: grades in collaborative activities, perception of how solutions are improved by the classmates, etc.).

The measurement of the students' academic performance was carried out through the analysis indicators proposed by [5]. This proposal includes a set of indicators that measure three dimensions of the students' academic work:

1. The individual work of the students. Examples of these indicators are the number of proposal of each learner and the amount of individual interaction with the solution.
2. The degree of collaboration. Examples of these indicators are the number of proposals commented by other learners and the degree in which the task distribution was equitable.
3. The solutions generated. Examples are the degree to which the solution is well-formed according to the syntax rules of the programming language and the assessment of whether the solution solves the task goals.

Finally, the technological framework proposed by [21] was used to automate the calculation of a single variable that measures student performance as an average of the value of these indicators. Each indicator has the same weight in the calculation of the final variable. These data are multivariate and are processed by means of data depth to reduce their dimensionality, resulting in univariate data, which allows to easily predict the students performance. This prediction is done in terms of non-parametric supervised classification. We employ the *random Tukey depth* [22] as statistical data depth. As this is a more novel technique, we explore it in what follows. After that, we propose the methodology employed in practice and introduce the studied dataset.

2.1. Statistical Data Depth

According to the recent paper [23], statistical depth is a current hot research topic in statistical analysis [24–28] in some papers on the topic. Given a probability distribution P on $\mathbb{R}^p$, a statistical depth function orders the points in $\mathbb{R}^p$ from the "center of P" to the "outer of P". Obviously, this problem includes data sets if we take P to be the empirical distribution associated to the dataset at hand. Note that in the one-dimensional case this order is trivial; being reasonable to order the points using the order induced by the function

$$x \rightarrow D_1(x, P) := \min\{P(-\infty, x], P[x, \infty)\}. \tag{1}$$

This implies that the data is ordered using the decreasing order of the difference between 50 and their percentiles, in absolute values, and the deepest points are the medians of P. Ordering multivariate data is, however, neither trivial nor pursued in a unique manner. Therefore, several multidimensional depths have been proposed [29–32]. Here we are mainly interested in the random Tukey depth function, which is a random approximation of the Tukey (or halfspace) depth [33]. The problematic of the Tukey depth is the required high computational time [34]. This issue is addressed by its random approximation. According to Zuo and Serfling [18], the Tukey depth behaves very well in comparison with the existing competitors. The random Tukey depth inherits the good theoretical properties of the Tukey depth and, in particular, that it characterizes discrete distributions [35], which comes in handy. for the study performed in this paper.

For $x \in \mathbb{R}^p$, the random Tukey depth of x with respect to P, $D_R(x, P)$, is the minimal probability which can be attained over a set of randomly closed halfspaces containing x; i.e., $D_R(x, P)$ is the minimum of the one-dimensional depths (see (1)) of a finite number of randomly chosen one-dimensional projections of x, where those depths are calculated with respect to the corresponding marginal of P. In this paper we make use of 50 random projections. Let us, then, concentrate further on explaining what the idea of deepness inside the definition of random Tukey depth is. Given n points, let us denote one of them by x. Then, we want to compute the random Tukey depth of x with respect to the set of n points. For that, we compute the number of points in the set that are contained in each of the randomly chosen closed halfspaces that has x in its border. Then, we record any of those halfspaces that contain the fewest points from the set and the depth of x is this number of points divided by n. In the left-hand side plot of Figure 1, in $\mathbb{R}^2$, n is equal to ten and the random Tukey depth of x is given, among others, by the randomly obtained closed halfspace painted in pastel blue. As there are four points inside this halfspace, the random Tukey depth of x is 0.4. Note that x is the deepest point in the set. From the right-hand side plot of Figure 1 we can observe that, taking sufficient randomly chosen halfspaces, the random Tukey depth of point y is 0.3 because among all the closed halfspaces that have y on their border, the ones that contain fewer points from the set do contain three points. Alternatively, taking into account that (1) coincides with the definition of random Tukey depth in $\mathbb{R}$, to compute the random Tukey depth of a point $x \in \mathbb{R}^p$ with respect to a set $A \subset \mathbb{R}^p$ of size n we can do the following. For each randomly selected vector v in the unit sphere of $\mathbb{R}^p$, we compute the one-dimensional depth, (1), of the projection of x on v with respect to the projection of A on v. Then, the minimum of the one-dimensional depths over the drawn $v's$ is the random Tukey depth of x. Note that when A is finite it suffices to take an amount of vectors, v, equal to the number of combinations of $(p-1)$ elements taking $(n-1)$ at a time without repetition.

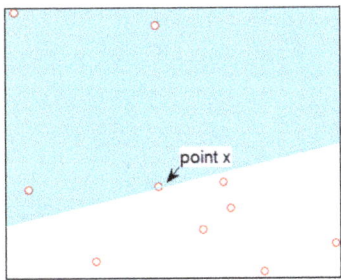 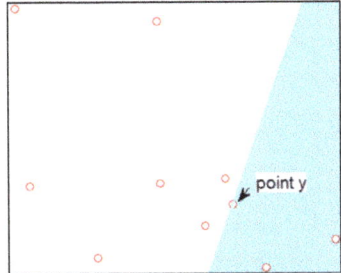

Figure 1. n is equal to ten and the random Tukey depth of x (left-hand side) and y (right-hand side) are, respectively, given, among others, by the randomly obtained closed halfspaces painted in pastel blue.

2.2. Methodology in Practice

To evaluate the performance of the students, we make use of their grades. There are a variety of grade systems. For instance:

- A letter in the set $\{A*, A, B, C, D, E, U\}$ with $A*$ the highest possible grade and U the lowest. This is a common grading system in the United Kingdom.
- A number in the set $\{1, 1.3, 1.7, 2, 2.3, 2.7, 3, 3.3, 3.7, 4, 5\}$, with 1 the highest possible grade and 5 the lowest. This is the system used in Germany.
- A number in the interval $[0, 10]$ with 0 the lowest possible grade and 10 the highest. This system is the one established in Spain.

The methodology we present here is valid for any grading system. The reason is that any system can be translated into a success percentage. That is, any grade can be transformed into a number $g \in [0, 100]$ with $g\%$ the percentage of right answers, for instance. Thus, to particularize it, we focus on the Spanish grading system.

Let $t := \{t_1, \ldots, t_s\}$ be the dataset under study where $t_i \in \mathbb{R}^p$ for any $i \in \{1, \ldots, s\}$ with $s, p \in \mathbb{N}$, both larger than two. t_i represents the grades of student i. Thus, if $p = 6$, we have theoretically recorded 6 grades for each student. Missing grades will be assigned the lowest possible grade. The dataset is split into training sample, $r := \{r_1, \ldots, r_m\}$, and test sample $e := \{e_1, \ldots, e_n\}$. Thus, $r \cup e = t$, $r \cap e = \emptyset$ and $m + n = s$. $r_i, e_j \in \mathbb{R}^p$ for any $i \in \{1, \ldots, m\}$ and $j \in \{1, \ldots, n\}$. Then, each $r_i = (r_{i,1}, \ldots, r_{i,p})$ and, analogously, each $e_j = (e_{j,1}, \ldots, e_{j,p})$. Let $d \in \mathbb{N} \cap [2, p]$. The objective in this manuscript is to predict the average grade $E_j := 1/p \sum_{k=1}^{p} e_{j,k}$, for each $j \in \{1, \ldots, n\}$, making use of:

$$r_i^{(d)} := (r_{i,1}, \ldots, r_{i,d}) \text{ for } i \in \{1, \ldots, m\}, \tag{2}$$

$$R_i := \frac{1}{p} \sum_{k=1}^{p} r_{i,k} \text{ for } i \in \{1, \ldots, m\} \text{ and} \tag{3}$$

$$e_j^{(d)} := (e_{j,1}, \ldots, e_{j,d}) \text{ for } j \in \{1, \ldots, n\}. \tag{4}$$

As a large range of grades are possible in the Spanish system, $R_i \in [0, 10]$, we summarize it by substituting R_i by IR_i, that provides the membership of R_i to one of the intervals in the following set:

$$G := \{[0, 4), [4, 5), [5, 6), [6, 7), [7, 8), [8, 9), [9, 10), \{10\}\}. \tag{5}$$

These intervals have been set by taking into account that a student passes with a grade larger or equal than 5. Thus, we use the interval $[0,4)$ for those grades where the student clearly fails. The largest possible grade posses also an interval, $\{10\}$, since it is a distinction.

Then, noting that G in (5) denotes the set of all labels, it is easy to see that we are given a series of data with label:

- the training sample consists of the pairs $(r_i^{(d)}, IR_i) \in \mathbb{R}^d \times G$ for $i \in \{1, \ldots, m\}$,
- the test sample is given by the pairs $(e_j^{(d)}, IE_j) \in \mathbb{R}^d \times H$ for $j \in \{1, \ldots, n\}$,

where, for each $j \in \{1, \ldots, n\}$, IE_j provides the membership to the intervals in

$$H := \{[0,4], [3,5], [4,6], [5,7], [6,8], [7,9], [8,10], [9,10]\}. \tag{6}$$

of $E_j := \frac{1}{p} \sum_{k=1}^{p} e_{j,k}$. Note that these intervals are of larger length, to emulate confidence bands.

The idea is to first construct a model making use of the training sample. To construct it, we simply employ a supervised classification procedure where first the random Tukey depth is used to reduce the dimensionality, and then a normal kernel classifier is applied to perform the classification. In what follows we explain in what consists this classifier; for which we refer to Ferraty and Vieu [36] and Ferraty and Vieu [37], Chapter 8 for more technical details, consistency, and rate of convergence of posterior probabilities. For that, we suppose that $(r_i^{(d)}, IR_i)$ and $(e_j^{(d)}, IE_j)$, $i \in \{1, \ldots, m\}$ and $j \in \{1, \ldots, n\}$, are independent and identically distributed (i.i.d.) as (X, Y); where X takes values in $\mathbb{R}^d$ and Y takes values in G. The classifier is based on a general Bayes classification rule. For a general pair (x, g), where $g \in G$ and $x \in \mathbb{R}^d$, it is defined the posterior probability

$$p_g(x) := P(Y = g | X = x). \tag{7}$$

Note that P denotes the underlying probability. Then, $x \in \mathbb{R}^d$ is classified to the class $g \in G$ yielding maximum posterior probability. In particular, for classifying points in the training sample we take $(x, g) = (r_i^{(d)}, IR_i)$ for some $i \in \{1, \ldots, m\}$, while for classifying points in the test sample $(x, g) = (e_j^{(d)}, IE_j)$ for some $j \in \{1, \ldots, n\}$. For this purpose, we need to estimate $p_g(x)$. As the training sample $(r_i^{(d)}, IR_i)$, $i \in \{1, \ldots, m\}$, consists of i.i.d. copies of (X, Y), we use it to estimate the underlying probability distribution. Specifically, we replace $p_g(x)$ by its Nadaraya–Watson estimator [38,39], which is given by

$$\hat{p}_g(x) := \frac{\sum_{i=1, IR_i=g}^{m} K(h^{-1} \|x - r_i^{(d)}\|)}{\sum_{i=1}^{m} K(h^{-1} \|x - r_i^{(d)}\|)}, \tag{8}$$

where $h > 0$, $\|\cdot\|$ is the Euclidean norm on $\mathbb{R}^d$, and K is a probability kernel satisfying $K(0) > 0$, $K(u) = 0$ for $u < 0$, and it is non-increasing in u, for u is positive. Notice that the sum at the numerator is only over those i such that $IR_i = g$ yielding

$$\sum_{g \in G} \hat{p}_g(x) = 1. \tag{9}$$

Additionally, the closer the point x is to r_i, the closer the quantity $h^{-1} \|x - r_i^{(d)}\|$ is to 0, the maximal point of the kernel K; thus, yielding a higher probability. Specifically, we choose K to be 2 times the standard normal density if u is non-negative and 0 otherwise. The parameter h is chosen so that the classification error in the training sample is minimized. Then, we introduce into the model the $e_j^{(d)}$ for $j \in \{1, \ldots, n\}$ and obtain the predictions $\hat{IE}_1, \ldots, \hat{IE}_n$ of the $IE_1, \ldots, IE_n$.

2.3. The Dataset

The proposed method was applied in the *Human-computer Interaction* (HCI) subject taken by students in the third year of the Computer Science degree at the University of Cantabria, in Spain. The HCI discipline deals with studying how people interact with computers. Some of the main objectives pursued by this discipline are the definitions of methodologies to develop more efficient and intuitive user interfaces, the creation of methods that allow evaluating and comparing the characteristics of user interfaces and the design of models that allow the interaction between people and computers to be represented. HCI studies the relationship of people with computers and this makes it necessary to apply knowledge from fields as varied as Psychology, Computer Science, Telecommunications and Sociology. Therefore, HCI has a multidisciplinary nature that bases it on many classical fields of knowledge.

This subject follows a Project-Based Learning (PBL) approach through tasks in which students work collaboratively to design and build different types of user interfaces (for mobile phones, web applications, or desktop tools). The methodology is applied to predict academic performance using data from a few early activities. The main goal of this experimentation is to identify elements of the learning process (tasks, group composition, etc.) that should be intervened to have a real impact in the academic performance of the students in a course.

Data collected quantify the activity of 205 students:

- 43 of them took the subject during the academic period 2017/18,
- 41 during 2018/19,
- 63 during 2019/20 and
- 61 during 2020/21.

As part of their academic course, these students performed 6 tasks that required designing user interfaces. These tasks are the following:

1. Prototype a mockup of a user interface for smartphones.
2. Build user interfaces using the Android platform.
3. Design and build user interfaces for desktop computers using a WIMP (windows icons menus and pointers) style.
4. Design and build user interfaces for desktop computers using a WYSIWYG (What You See Is What You Get) style.
5. Design and build the user interfaces of a website.
6. Perform a usability test process.

Software support used by the students was a videoconferencing tool with a shared whiteboard and chat, a shared folder and Axure, a UX tool to prototype interfaces. These user interfaces were later built using Android technologies and Java and HTML languages. Students collaborated in groups, resulting in a total of 79 groups:

- 14 of them for the academic period 2017/18,
- 15 for 2018/19,
- 21 for 2019/20 and
- 29 for 2020/21.

The dataset was used to experiment with the proposed methodology as shown in Figure 2. The students collaborated in groups to solve the proposed tasks. This collaboration was made with the support of software tools that recorded their communications, how the workload was distributed, and the solutions to the tasks. The teacher used all this information to grade each assignment. Finally, the methodology was applied to verify if a small number of tasks allowed to predict the final grade of the student.

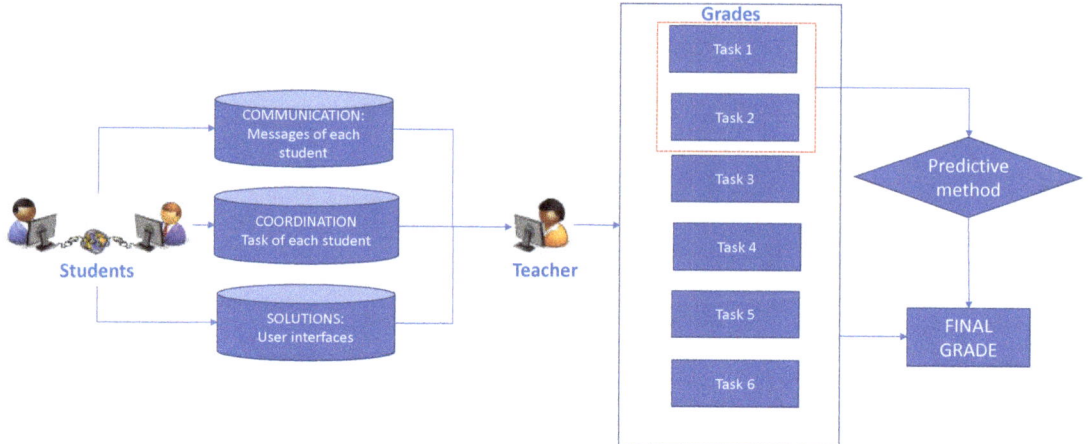

Figure 2. Outline of the process followed to experiment with the methodology.

To illustrate the dataset, we have plotted in Figure 3 the grades of the groups over the six tasks of the different academic periods. These grades are in the range 0–10, 0 being the lower possible grade and 10 the highest one. These grades are the result of quantifying the following three aspects:

(i) the quality of the user interfaces,
(ii) the extent to which group members distribute the workload equitably, and
(iii) the contributions and proposals that arise to establish a real collaboration.

The left plot corresponds to the grades in Task 1 against those in Task 2, the central plot to those in Task 3 against those in Task 4 and the right plot to those in Task 5 against those in Task 6. The grades of the academic period 2017/18 are represented in black, those of 2018/19 in red, those of 2019/20 in green, and those of 2020/21 in blue. In each of these academic periods we have labeled each group by a number. Thus, we can observe, for instance, that:

- Group 3 of the academic period 2017/18 had grades in the interval [6,8) in Tasks 1 and 2 that improved to the range [8,10] for Tasks 3, 4 and 5 and decreased to the range [4,6) for Task 6.
- Group 5 of the academic period 2018/19 had grades in the range [8,10] in Task 1 that worsened to the range [2,4) for Tasks 2 and 3 and slighted improved to the interval [4,6) for Tasks 4 an 5 and again improved to the interval [6,8) for Task 6.
- Group 19 of the academic period 2019/20 had grades in the range [6,8) in Tasks 1 and 2 that improved to the range [8,10] for Tasks 3, decreased to the range [4,6) for Tasks 4 and 5 and then highly increased to a 10 for Task 6.

This leads us to realize that the patterns among the different groups is different, which makes the analysis more difficult.

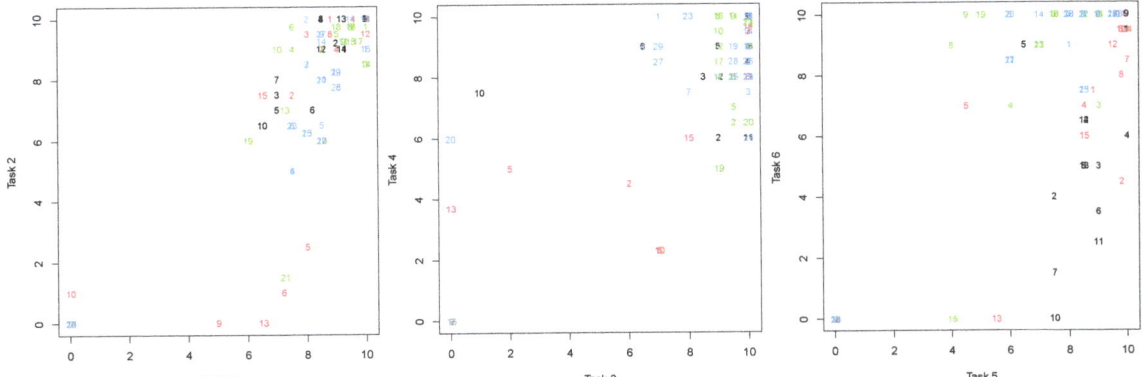

Figure 3. Illustration of the grades of the different groups in the academic periods 2017/18 (black), 2018/19 (red), 2019/20 (green) and 2020/21 (blue). Grades of Tasks 1 and 2 in the left plot, of Tasks 3 and 4 in the central plot and of Tasks 5 and 6 in the right plot. Each group in an academic period is labeled by a corresponding number.

3. Results

The objective of this section is to provide the results for the research problem proposed in Section 2, which consist in predicting the average grade of the students taking an academic course based on their early performance in the course and the performance of the students who took the course in previous academic years. In particular, we use the grades of the courses 2017/18, 2018/19, 2019/20 as training sample; obtaining a training sample of size $m = 50$. We use as test sample the early grades recorded during the course 2020/21 to predict the average grade over the six tasks (in groups); having a test sample of size $n = 29$. The research problem has four subproblems where the first one regards as early grades the first two, the second research problem the first three grades, the third the first four grades, and the fourth problem the first five grades. Making use of the methodology expressed in Section 2, we perform here a supervised classification to predict the average grade over the six tasks of the groups in the test sample. To do this, we take d, the amount of tasks done by the student, in the range from 2 to 5.

At the top of Table 1 we observe the results of applying the model to the test data with $d = 2$ (research problem 1). That is, we have constructed the model making use of the training data $(r_{i,1}, r_{i,2})$, which are the grades for the first two Tasks, and the label IR_i, which is the average grade of the six Tasks, for $i \in \{1, \ldots, 50\}$. Then, we have reported in the top panel of Table 1 the summary of the range values $\hat{IE}_1, \ldots, \hat{IE}_{29}$, that is, the estimated values of $IE_1, \ldots, IE_{29}$. We report the values by providing a wider ranger, of a $\pm$ grade, than the one used to summarize the given values. Thus, we obtain that the three test groups of students whose average grade is in the interval [0,4) are correctly classified in the interval [0,4]. Analogously, the four groups of students with average grade in the interval [7,8) are appropriately classified in the interval [6,8].

There are 13 groups of students in the average grade range [8,9), 3 of them are classified in the [6,8] interval and the other 10 in the [7,9]. Although both classifications should be considered correct, to be on the safe side, we have only considered successful for a later analysis (Figure 4) those classified in [7,9]. Similarly, there are seven groups of students with average grade in [9,10) which are correctly classified in [8,10] and another one which is not so clear as it is classified in [7,9]. Thus, for the later analysis we only consider as correct the seven classified in [8,10]. Furthermore, there is one case in the analysis that is clearly wrongly classified. That is the one of the group of students with average grade in [9,10) whose estimation is in [6,8].

Table 1. Four confusion matrices between the real average grade intervals (columns) and the estimated average grade intervals (rows) for the $n = 29$ test data (academic course 2020/21) on the model constructed using the $m = 50$ training data (academic courses 2017/18, 2018/19, 2019/20). 3 test data belong to the interval [0,4), 4 to [7,8), 13 to [8,9), and 9 to [9,10) (intervals reported in (6)). The analysis is based on: Tasks 1 and 2 (top matrix), Tasks 1, 2 and 3 (second matrix from the top), Tasks 1, 2, 3, and 4 (third matrix from the top) and Tasks 1, 2, 3, 4, and 5 (bottom matrix). The average grades make use of the six Tasks. The groups of students whose average grade is clearly correctly classified are in blue. The omitted values correspond to zeros.

		TEST SAMPLE				
		Tasks 1–2 (research problem 1)				
				estimated		
		[0,4]	[5,7]	[6,8]	[7,9]	[8,10]
real	[0,4)	3				
	[7,8)			4		
	[8,9)			3	10	
	[9,10)			1	1	7
		Tasks 1–3 (research problem 2)				
				estimated		
		[0,4]	[5,7]	[6,8]	[7,9]	[8,10]
real	[0,4)	2		1		
	[7,8)		1	3		
	[8,9)				13	
	[9,10)				2	7
		Tasks 1–4 (research problem 3)				
				estimated		
		[0,4]	[5,7]	[6,8]	[7,9]	[8,10]
real	[0,4)	1		2		
	[7,8)			4		
	[8,9)				13	
	[9,10)					9
		Tasks 1–5 (research problem 4)				
				estimated		
		[0,4]	[5,7]	[6,8]	[7,9]	[8,10]
real	[0,4)	1		2		
	[7,8)			4		
	[8,9)				13	
	[9,10)					9

When making use of the grades of Tasks 1, 2, and 3 (research problem 2) to predict the average grade over the six tasks, the obtained results when classifying test sample are, as expected, slightly better than those obtained by just using Tasks 1 and 2 (research problem 1) and worse than when also using Task 4 (research problem 3). They are reported in the second block of Table 1. In particular, we can observe only one clear misclassification, which is that of a group with an average grade in the interval [0,4) whose estimated average grade belongs to the interval [6,8]. The results obtained when making use of just Tasks 1, 2, 3, and 4 (research problem 3) are the same than those obtained when also adding Task 5 (research problem 4). In particular, the absolute number of misclassifications increases to two in both cases. As reported in Table 1, they correspond to groups with average grade in the interval [0,4) that is estimated as in the interval [6,8].

We have reported above the absolute misclassifications when predicting the test data making use of a model that is based on just Tasks 1 and 2 (research problem 1) to a model based on Tasks 1, 2, 3, 4, and 5 (research problem 4). All these misclassifications are summarized in Table 2 where we report the relative success rate of the procedure under the different studied scenarios. There, we can observe that, when applying to the test data the model that only makes use of Tasks 1 and 2 (research problem 1), we are able to predict the interval to which the average grade over the six Tasks belongs with a success rate of the 82.76%. This rate increases to the 86.21% when also making use of Task 3 (research problem 2) and stabilizes to the 93.10% success rate when making use of Tasks 1, 2, 3, and 4 (research problem 3). A display of these success rates is in Figure 4 where a rapid increase and stabilization of the success rates is observed. It is worth saying that we have been conservative in computing these success rates, considering as successful the entries in blue in Table 1 although, as explained above, there are other entries that could also be considered successful.

Table 2. Success rates for the supervised classification of average grade intervals over 6 tasks for the test data on the model constructed using the training data. Test data refer to the $n = 29$ groups in the academic course 2020/21 and training data to the $m = 50$ groups along the academic courses 2017/18, 2018/19, and 2019/20. The analysis is based on: Tasks 1 and 2 (left column), Tasks 1, 2, and 3 (second left column), Tasks 1, 2, 3, and 4 (third left column) and Tasks 1, 2, 3, 4, and 5 (right column). For the success rate, it is used as correctly classified only the groups of students whose average grade is displayed in blue in Table 1.

	Tasks 1–2 (Research Problem 1)	Tasks 1–3 (Research Problem 2)	Tasks 1–4 (Research Problem 3)	Tasks 1–5 (Research Problem 4)
Test	82.76%	86.21%	93.10%	93.10%

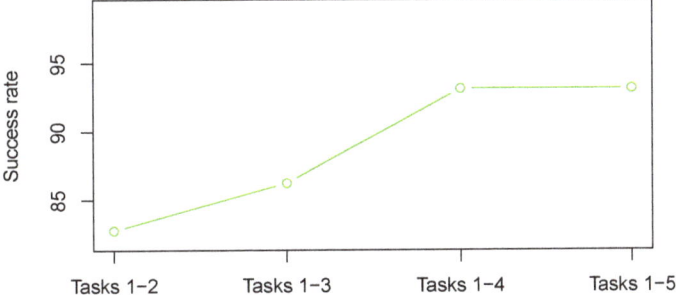

Figure 4. Display of the success rates in Table 2. The OX-axis shows the tasks used in the model to predict the interval of the average grade; it goes from Tasks 1 and 2 (research problem 1) in the left corner of the axis to Tasks 1, 2, 3, 4, and 5 (research problem 4) in the right corner.

The obtained results are extremely good as after the student has completed just the two first tasks, we can predict their average final grade over the six tasks with a success rate of over the 80%; when completing the first three tasks with a success rate over the 85% and when completing the first four tasks with a success rate of over the 90%.

4. Discussion

The algorithm used is powerful in that it makes use of the random Tukey depth. This is due to two main reasons:

1. The random Tukey depth is computationally effective in reducing the dimension to one even if the original data dimension is high, as it happens with high dimensional or functional data [40].
2. The random Tukey depth behaves adequately [35] as it generally inherits the good properties of the Tukey depth, which is the most well-known in the literature but for it expensive computational time.

Furthermore, the kernel classifier performed on the resulting one-dimensional data is a well-known one but could be substituted by any other one-dimensional classifier. The only requirement being that the process can be automated as it occurs in this case.

Other works have carried out data-driven analysis of student academic activity with different objectives. Thus, ref [41] stores information on how students solve collaborative activities using CSCL systems and analyzed them to propose 17 strategies to optimize student performance. In other cases, the studies have focused on predicting the optimal number of students who should collaborate on the tasks [42]. Our study has a broader temporal scope. It is not about analyzing specific activities but rather predicting performance in an academic year.

The obtained results show a high success rate in predicting the average grade by just using the first two tasks performed by the students.

Thus, something that can be considered is the possibility of reducing the amount of tasks required of the students. Additionally, this would also allow an early intervention to improve the performance of the groups whose predicted grade is lower.

We can deduce that academic collaborative tasks imply greater richness and complexity due to the social interactions that take place, this work opens the door to consider the first tasks that students solve as predictive of academic performance in the rest of the course. The case study of this work illustrates how the method proposed can achieve this goal. This approach complements other works in the CSCL field that analyzes collaboration and interaction without predicting future academic performance [1,13,14]. However, our work has not delved into mechanisms that detail the causes (lack of communication, problems with the groupware system, etc.) that lead to an academic performance problem or in proposing automatic intervention strategies (adapting the groupware system, changing the composition of working groups, etc.).

5. Conclusions

This work has presented a proposal to automatically predict the academic performance of students using only the data recorded in the first tasks of the academic year. The interactions that students carry out with software tools to solve academic activities allow us to have datasets with which to try to carry out this prediction. In many active learning methodologies these activities are carried out collaboratively. For this reason, the work focused on experimenting with a real case in which the students collaborate in solving the tasks.

The proposal is based on a statistical depth based supervised classification technique, which first performs the random Tukey depth to lower to one the data dimension and then applies a kernel classifier. This means that the prediction can be carried out in an automated way, using support software that processes a significant amount of data. The experimentation carried out during four academic years in a university subject shows promising results, as just making use of the first two tasks that the students perform we obtain over an 80% success rate in predicting their final grade. This success rate increases to over the 90% success rate if the first four tasks, out of six, are known in predicting the final grade.

We propose that the results of the predictive mechanisms serve not only to inform what the academic performance of students would be at the end of the academic year but also to intervene in the automated development of activities. Our future work will address the analysis of the causes of task failures and to design intervention mechanisms in CSCL systems.

Author Contributions: Conceptualization, R.D.; methodology, A.N.-R.; validation, A.N.-R.; resources, R.D.; writing, A.N.-R., R.D. and G.F. All authors have read and agreed to the published version of the manuscript.

Funding: For A.N.-R., this research was funded by grant number MTM2017-86061-C2-2-P of the Spanish Ministry of Economy, Industry and Competitiveness. For R.D. this work was funded by the

University of Cantabria through the teaching innovation project "Implantación de la técnica focus group para diseñar interfaces de usuario en la asignatura Interacción Persona-Computador" and "Utilización de las TIC para monitorizar y gestionar actividades colaborativas orientadas a resolver tareas de programación de algoritmos en el Grado en Ingeniería Informática."

Institutional Review Board Statement: Not applicable.

Informed Consent Statement: This study does not involve personal information. Grades have been treated confidentially according to the regulations of the University of Cantabria.

Conflicts of Interest: The authors declare no conflict of interest.

Abbreviations

The following abbreviations are used in this manuscript:

CSCL	Computer-Supported Cooperative Learning
HCI	Human-computer interaction
HTML	HyperText Markup Language
i.i.d.	independent and identically distributed
PBL	Project-Based Learning
WIMP	Windows Icon Menu Pointer

References

1. Duque, R.; Bollen, L.; Anjewierden, A.; Bravo, C. Automating the Analysis of Problem-solving Activities in Learning Environments: The Co-Lab Case Study. *J. Univ. Comput. Sci.* **2012**, *18*, 1279–1307.
2. Kutlu, B.; Aggul, Y.G.; Atasu, I.; Kaymaz, Z. A Meta-Analysis of Studies on Groupware for Collaborative Work Environments. *Proceedings* **2021**, *74*, 9. [CrossRef]
3. Dennis, A.R.; Carte, T.A.; Kelly, G.G. Breaking the rules: Success and failure in groupware-supported business process reengineering. *Decis. Support Syst.* **2003**, *36*, 31–47. [CrossRef]
4. Duque, R.; Gómez-Pérez, D.; Nieto-Reyes, A.; Bravo, C. Analyzing collaboration and interaction in learning environments to form learner groups. *Comput. Hum. Behav.* **2015**, *47*, 42–49. [CrossRef]
5. Bravo, C.; Redondo, M.A.; Verdejo, M.F.; Ortega, M. A framework for process–solution analysis in collaborative learning environments. *Int. J. Hum. Comput. Stud.* **2008**, *66*, 812–832. [CrossRef]
6. Anderson, J.R.; Boyle, C.; Corbett, A.T.; Lewis, M.W. Cognitive modeling and intelligent tutoring. *Artif. Intell.* **1990**, *42*, 7–49. [CrossRef]
7. Selker, T. COACH: A Teaching Agent That Learns. *Commun. ACM* **1994**, *37*, 92–99. [CrossRef]
8. Paolucci, M.; Suthers, D.; Weiner, A. Automated advice-giving strategies for scientific inquiry. In *Intelligent Tutoring Systems*; Frasson, C., Gauthier, G., Lesgold, A., Eds.; Springer: Berlin/Heidelberg, Germany, 1996; pp. 372–381.
9. Mørch, A.; Jondahl, S.; Dolonen, J. Supporting Conceptual Awareness with Pedagogical Agents. *Inf. Syst. Front.* **2005**, *7*, 39–53. [CrossRef]
10. du Boulay, B. Artificial Intelligence as an Effective Classroom Assistant. *IEEE Intell. Syst.* **2016**, *31*, 76–81. [CrossRef]
11. Goel, A.K.; Polepeddi, L. Jill Watson: A Virtual Teaching Assistant for Online Education. In *Learning Engineering for Online Education: Theoretical Contexts and Design-Based Examples*; Routledge: New York, NY, USA, 2018.
12. Uskola Ibarluzea, A.; Madariaga Orbea, J.M.; Arribillaga Iriarte, A.; Maguregi González, G.; Fernández Alonso, L. Categorisation of the Interventions of Faciliting Tutors on PBL and Their Relationship with Students' Response. *Profesorado: Revista de curriculum y formación del profesorado* **2018**, *22*, 153–170. [CrossRef]
13. Splichal, J.M.; Oshima, J.; Oshima, R. Regulation of collaboration in project-based learning mediated by CSCL scripting reflection. *Comput. Educ.* **2018**, *125*, 132–145. [CrossRef]
14. Chen, L.; Chen, P.; Lin, Z. Artificial Intelligence in Education: A Review. *IEEE Access* **2020**, *8*, 75264–75278. [CrossRef]
15. Li, Z.; Hoiem, D. Learning without Forgetting. *IEEE Trans. Pattern Anal. Mach. Intell.* **2018**, *40*, 2935–2947. [CrossRef]
16. Aljundi, R.; Chakravarty, P.; Tuytelaars, T. Expert Gate: Lifelong Learning with a Network of Experts. In Proceedings of the 2017 IEEE Conference on Computer Vision and Pattern Recognition (CVPR), Honolulu, HI, USA, 21–26 July 2017; pp. 7120–7129. [CrossRef]
17. Phielix, C.; Prins, F.J.; Kirschner, P.A. The Design of Peer Feedback and Reflection Tools in a CSCL Environment. In Proceedings of the 9th International Conference on Computer Supported Collaborative Learning, Rhodes, Greece, 8–13 June 2009; Volume 1, pp. 626–635.
18. Zuo, Y.; Serfling, R. General notions of statistical depth function. *Ann. Statist.* **2000**, *28*, 461–482. [CrossRef]
19. Härdle, W. *Applied Nonparametric Regression*; Econometric Society Monographs, Cambridge University Press: Cambridge, UK, 1990. [CrossRef]

20. Gerosa, M.A.; Pimentel, M.; Fuks, H.; de Lucena, C.J.P. Development of Groupware Based on the 3C Collaboration Model and Component Technology. In *Groupware: Design, Implementation, and Use*; Dimitriadis, Y.A., Zigurs, I., Gómez-Sánchez, E., Eds.; Springer: Berlin/Heidelberg, Germany, 2006; pp. 302–309.
21. Duque, R.; Bravo, C.; Ortega, M. A model-based framework to automate the analysis of users' activity in collaborative systems. *J. Netw. Comput. Appl.* **2011**, *34*, 1200–1209. [CrossRef]
22. Cuesta-Albertos, J.A.; Nieto-Reyes, A. The random Tukey depth. *Comput. Statist. Data Anal.* **2008**, *52*, 4979–4988. [CrossRef]
23. Zuo, Y. On General Notions of Depth for Regression. *Stat. Sci.* **2021**, *36*, 142–157. [CrossRef]
24. Nieto-Reyes, A.; Battey, H. A Topologically Valid Definition of Depth for Functional Data. *Stat. Sci.* **2016**, *31*, 61–79. [CrossRef]
25. Nieto-Reyes, A.; Battey, H. A topologically valid construction of depth for functional data. *J. Multivar. Anal.* **2021**, *184*, 104738. [CrossRef]
26. Nieto-Reyes, A.; Battey, H.; Francisci, G. Functional Symmetry and Statistical Depth for the Analysis of Movement Patterns in Alzheimer's Patients. *Mathematics* **2021**, *9*, 820. [CrossRef]
27. Saraceno, G.; Agostinelli, C. Robust multivariate estimation based on statistical depth filters. *TEST* **2021**, 1–25. [CrossRef]
28. Pandolfo, G.; Iorio, C.; Staiano, M.; Aria, M.; Siciliano, R. Multivariate process control charts based on the Lp depth. *Appl. Stoch. Model. Bus. Ind.* **2007**, *37*, 229–250. [CrossRef]
29. Liu, R.Y. On a notion of data depth based on random simplices. *Ann. Statist.* **1990**, *18*, 405–414. [CrossRef]
30. Serfling, R. A depth function and a scale curve based on spatial quantiles. In *Statistical Data Analysis Based on the L_1-norm and Related Methods (Neuchâtel, 2002)*; Stat. Ind. Technol.: Basel, Switzerland, 2002; pp. 25–38.
31. Liu, R.Y.; Serfling, R.; Souvaine, D.L. (Eds.) *Data Depth: Robust Multivariate Analysis, Computational Geometry and Applications*; DIMACS Series in Discrete Mathematics and Theoretical Computer Science, 72; American Mathematical Society: Providence, RI, USA, 2006; p. xiv+246.
32. Liu, Z.; Modarres, R. Lens data depth and median. *J. Nonparametric Stat.* **2011**, *23*, 1063–1074. [CrossRef]
33. Tukey, J.W. Mathematics and the picturing of data. In Proceedings of the International Congress of Mathematicians (Vancouver, B. C., 1974), Vancouver, Canada, 21–29 August 1974; Canadian Mathematical Congress, 1975; Volume 2, pp. 523–531. Available online: https://www.mathunion.org/fileadmin/ICM/Proceedings/ICM1974.2/ICM1974.2.ocr.pdf (accessed on 20 October 2021).
34. Dyckerhoff, R.; Mozharovskyi, P. Exact computation of the halfspace depth. *Comput. Stat. Data Anal.* **2016**, *98*, 19–30. [CrossRef]
35. Cuesta-Albertos, J.; Nieto-Reyes, A. The Tukey and the random Tukey depths characterize discrete distributions. *J. Multivar. Anal.* **2008**, *99*, 2304–2311. [CrossRef]
36. Ferraty, F.; Vieu, P. *Nonparametric Functional Data Analysis: Theory and Practice (Springer Series in Statistics)*; Springer: Berlin/Heidelberg, Germany, 2006.
37. Ferraty, F.; Vieu, P. Curves discrimination: A nonparametric functional approach. *Comput. Stat. Data Anal.* **2003**, *44*, 161–173. [CrossRef]
38. Nadaraya, E.A. On estimating regression. *Theory Probab. Appl.* **1964**, *9*, 141–142. [CrossRef]
39. Watson, G.S. Smooth regression analysis. *Sankhyā Ser.* **1964**, *26*, 359–372.
40. Cuesta-Albertos, J.A.; Nieto-Reyes, A. Functional Classification and the Random Tukey Depth. Practical Issues. In *Combining Soft Computing and Statistical Methods in Data Analysis*; Borgelt, C., González-Rodríguez, G., Trutschnig, W., Lubiano, M.A., Gil, M.Á., Grzegorzewski, P., Hryniewicz, O., Eds.; Springer: Berlin/Heidelberg, Germany, 2010; pp. 123–130.
41. Zheng, L. Optimize CSCL Activities Based on a Data-Driven Approach. In *Data-Driven Design for Computer-Supported Collaborative Learning: Design Matters*; Springer: Singapore, 2021; pp. 147–162. [CrossRef]
42. Omae, Y.; Furuya, T.; Mizukoshi, K.; Oshima, T.; Sakakibara, N.; Mizuochi, Y.; Yatsushiro, K.; Takahashi, H. Machine learning-based collaborative learning optimizer toward intelligent CSCL system. In Proceedings of the 2017 IEEE/SICE International Symposium on System Integration (SII), Taipei, Taiwan, 11–14 December 2017; pp. 577–582. [CrossRef]

Article

Automatic Group Organization for Collaborative Learning Applying Genetic Algorithm Techniques and the Big Five Model

Oscar Revelo Sánchez [1,*], César A. Collazos [2] and Miguel A. Redondo [3]

1 Galeras.NET Research Group, Universidad de Nariño, San Juan de Pasto 52001, Colombia
2 IDIS Research Group, Universidad del Cauca, Popayán 190001, Colombia; ccollazo@unicauca.edu.co
3 CHICO Research Group, Universidad de Castilla-La Mancha, 13071 Ciudad Real, Spain; Miguel.Redondo@uclm.es
* Correspondence: orevelo@udenar.edu.co

Citation: Revelo Sánchez, O.; Collazos, C.A.; Redondo, M.A. Automatic Group Organization for Collaborative Learning Applying Genetic Algorithm Techniques and the Big Five Model. *Mathematics* **2021**, *9*, 1578. https://doi.org/10.3390/math9131578

Academic Editors: Basil Papadopoulos and Amir Mosavi

Received: 29 March 2021
Accepted: 1 July 2021
Published: 5 July 2021

Publisher's Note: MDPI stays neutral with regard to jurisdictional claims in published maps and institutional affiliations.

Copyright: © 2021 by the authors. Licensee MDPI, Basel, Switzerland. This article is an open access article distributed under the terms and conditions of the Creative Commons Attribution (CC BY) license (https://creativecommons.org/licenses/by/4.0/).

Abstract: In this paper, an approach based on genetic algorithms is proposed to form groups in collaborative learning scenarios, considering the students' personality traits as a criterion for grouping. This formation is carried out in two stages: In the first, the information of the students is collected from a psychometric instrument based on the Big Five personality model; whereas, in the second, this information feeds a genetic algorithm that is in charge of performing the grouping iteratively, seeking for an optimal formation. The results presented here correspond to the functional and empirical validation of the approach. It is found that the described methodology is useful to obtain groups with the desired characteristics. The specific objective is to provide a strategy that makes it possible to subsequently assess in the context what type of approach (homogeneous, heterogeneous, or mixed) is the most appropriate to organize the groups.

Keywords: collaborative learning; collaborative work; genetic algorithms; group formation; personality traits

1. Introduction

Due to the current needs of society, education requires changes in the teaching–learning processes through the implementation of innovative and motivating pedagogical actions. Among those that have shown effective results are collaborative teaching strategies. These have become a more common practice today thanks to their high educational potential [1]. One of the key processes when implementing this type of strategy is the formation of working groups.

Outside the academic scope, groups are formed with various objectives, for example, people group together in social situations, at work, or when they seek common interests. Groups are considered as a basic social structure. Although in the academic scope groups are also formed with ease and for various purposes, the establishment of groups in the classroom can be a complicated and stilted process, always depending on the objective being pursued [2]. However, for collaborative learning to succeed, it is important to form effective groups, since the result of the group depends largely on the fulfilment of the responsibilities of each of its members, good academic and empathy relationships are fundamental among them [3].

The grouping problem is critical in collaborative learning, due to the complexity and difficulty of achieving an adequate grouping, based on different criteria and numerous students [4]. Group formation in collaborative environments is not a trivial task when it comes to achieving homogeneity or heterogeneity within the groups. Applying a good strategy in their forming, which considers not only one, but several characteristics of the students depends largely on the general academic benefit [5]. Therefore, it is very useful to have a solution that automates this process, to do it as efficiently as possible and increase the chances of success of the groups.

There are various criteria for the automatic formation of learning groups. These criteria have been used in a wide variety of studies that can be found in the literature. These studies usually consider factors such as the students' learning style [6,7], their thinking style [8], their knowledge and behaviour [9,10], or characteristics such as their gender, skills, and personality [11–16], among others.

Considering the above, one of the aspects to be evaluated in the group formation may be the students' personality. However, in the literature review developed by Borges et al. [17], it is observed that personality is one of the grouping criteria that is least used in studies, showing great potential for research on this topic.

The proposed approach in this paper seeks to find homogeneous, heterogeneous, or mixed groups, considering each student's personality traits. Personality traits are measured under the "Big Five" model, using the self-assessment instrument based on this model named Big Five Questionnaire—BQF. The traits of each person within a global group are evaluated, to later find the group mean in each dimension contemplated by the Big Five model, and groups are formed seeking to optimize a certain intra-heterogeneity and inter-homogeneity measure. Since group formation is a combinatorial problem that involves multiple characteristics, the heuristic search offered by evolutionary algorithms was used as an optimization technique.

The characteristics from which groups are formed and the operators implemented in the genetic algorithm are the main contributions of this work. Most of the existing studies in group formation that use genetic algorithms focus the grouping according to the students' knowledge level and use crossover and mutation basic operators. The proposed strategy exploits the traits derived from the five dimensions of the Big Five personality model (Extraversion, Agreeableness, Conscientiousness, Neuroticism, and Openness), to improve collaboration and learning outcomes at group and individual level. Likewise, a modification of the crossover operator named C1 is used, which is suggested for problems where genes should not be repeated, as is the case under study; and, for mutation, a variation of the swap mutation operator is used. These modified genetic operators allow a more complete search in the solution space, providing new genetic information to the population, preventing the algorithm from being trapped in a local minimum.

The proposed approach was empirically validated through a controlled experiment with 82 students from four programming courses, belonging to Systems Engineering and Electronic Engineering programs of the University of Nariño of the City of San Juan de Pasto-Colombia during the academic semester B-2020. The experiment consisted of developing collaborative activities by the students, obtaining the required groups through the proposed strategy and by students' preference, to evaluate the academic performance achieved by the participants finally. To somehow guarantee the initial equivalence of the groups, a pre-test was applied to both the experimental and control groups. Section 4.3 describes the empirical study in detail.

The rest of this paper is organized as follows: Section 2 addresses the relevant theoretical foundation of the Big Five model, work and collaborative learning, and genetic algorithms; Section 3 shows some related work about group formation; subsequently, Section 4 describes the proposed approach divided into two parts, the first describes the psychometric instrument used, while the second poses the use of genetic algorithms; and finally, Sections 5 and 6 present the results obtained, the conclusions and the future work.

2. Theoretical Foundations

This section presents the theoretical foundations that support the research carried out. Topics about personality, work, and collaborative learning, group formation and genetic algorithms as optimization technique used are addressed.

2.1. The "Big Five" Model

Currently, a wide variety of models and personality theories that offer different perspectives on how to approach a person's personality are available. Some of these theories are: Carl Jung's Psychological Types [18], Keirsey's Personality Types Theory [19], The "Big Five" Factors Personality Model [20], and Myers–Briggs Type Indicator (MBTI) [21], among others.

In this work, we decided to use the "Big Five" or "Five-Factor Model (FFM)" personality model because it has obtained the greatest consensus in the area of psychology and because it is one of the most widely used in the literature [22,23]. The "Big Five" is a personality trait hierarchical model composed of five big factors, where each represents personality characteristics at a more general abstraction level. These factors or dimensions are traditionally referred to as Extraversion (E), Agreeableness (A), Conscientiousness (C), Neuroticism (N), and Openness (O). Each value combination in the different dimensions generates a personality type with a different tendency to behave, interact, react, and reason.

Since the Big Five model is a purely descriptive personality model, psychologists have developed various tests and questionnaires that evaluate each of the five factors or dimensions in individuals; for example, NEO Personality Inventory-Revised (NEO-PI-R), Sixteen Personality Factor Fifth Edition (16PF-5), Big Five Questionnaire (BFQ), Big Five Questionnaire-Children (BFQ-C), 100 Trait-Descriptive Adjectives (TDA-100), Big Five Inventory (BFI), Hogan Personality Inventory (HPI), and Five-Factor Personality Inventory(FFPI), among others [24,25].

2.2. Work and Collaborative Learning

In the educational context, collaborative work is an interactive learning model, in which students build together, uniting efforts, talents and competencies, through activities that in consensus lead to reaching the established goals. More than a technique, collaborative work is considered an interaction philosophy and a personal way of working, that involves managing aspects such as respecting the individual contributions of group members [26].

From the above, the Collaborative Learning construct arises. Chaljub Hasbún [27] affirms that collaborative learning is a result of collaborative work. For Johnson et al. [28], collaborative learning is a carefully designed interaction system that organizes and induces reciprocal influence between team members. It is developed through a gradual process in which each member and everyone feels mutually committed to each other's learning, generating a positive interdependence that does not imply competition.

Collaborative learning is achieved through group work methods characterized by the interaction and contribution of all in the acquisition of knowledge, sharing authority, accepting responsibility and the point of view of the other, and building consensus with others [29].

2.3. Genetic Algorithms

Genetic algorithms were described by Holland [30] and are considered as a computational model family inspired by evolutionary biology [31]. To date, their use has spread beyond the original conception, as a more general type of evolutionary algorithm that attempts to simulate Darwinian evolution and natural selection through the recombination and mutation of individuals [32]. These algorithms use a data structure to encode the potential solutions to the problem in question, generally a vector, as a chromosome and apply recombination operators seeking to preserve the critical information that guides towards a satisfactory solution [33].

In general, a genetic algorithm is structured in a three-step iterative process [31]: (i) an initial population of solutions (individuals) is created, represented by a chromosome that encodes the solution to the problem; (ii) a group of individuals is selected through a specific strategy, based on the fitness function, and the next population is generated by applying genetic operators (crossover and mutation) to the selected individuals; (iii) step (ii) is repeated until the remaining individuals in the generation are good enough according to the fitness function and the stop criteria. This process is outlined in Figure 1.

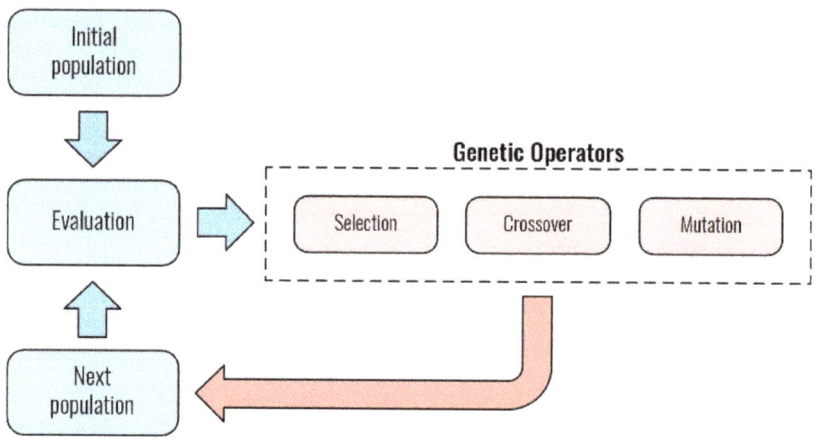

Figure 1. GA general scheme.

Regarding their application, genetic algorithms have been used, particularly during the last two decades, in a wide range of combinatorial optimization problems, including TSP (Travel Salesman Problem), KP (Knapsack Problem), sequencing and scheduling of tasks (Scheduling), vehicle routing, among others [34–39], which makes this technique a good candidate to solve the grouping problem outlined in this paper.

3. Related Works

In collaborative work, it is essential to have very well formed work teams, in which the members are comfortable with their peers and where the academic level of each allows a favourable interdependence. However, in practice, self-selection and random assignment of members are the most popular approaches used in group formation, although they do not always produce good results [40]. Currently, it is difficult to find group formation techniques, as research is based on the correct functioning of collaborative learning, but formation as such is neglected or undervalued. In the literature, however, there are several works where certain elements that must exist within the group are discussed and roles that must be fulfilled in each work team [41]. Below are some of the most important related works of recent years, including a brief description of their application.

Battur et al. [16] propose in their study that teams be formed based on the student's complementary skills and ensuring that each team has an expert member in each identified skill. Wichmann et al. [9] investigated how group formation based on student behaviour affects productivity on a small group task. Amara et al. [42] carried out research to form homogeneous groups in a mobile collaborative learning environment, with a grouping attributes personalized selection; the technique used was the K-Means algorithm. Sadeghi and Kardan [13] and Amarasinghe et al. [12] propose binary integer linear programming based on task assignment, gender, and language preferences as a group formation optimization technique. Manske and Hoppe [10] used a semantic algorithm, which maximized the knowledge diversity in the groups. Odo et al. [43] analysed how the student's affective state can affect their performance in collaborative study groups. Lykourentzou et al. [14]

and Reis [15] highlight in their work the importance of personality traits as critical elements that affect collaboration and students' interaction, affirming that this factor can influence performance and student satisfaction, and induce various actions and behaviours in group work.

On the other hand, the literature review carried out by Cruz and Isotani [44] regarding group formation demonstrates the great researcher's interest in using the genetic algorithm technique as a solution to the problem, given its relevance when dealing with a large variable number and its ability to quickly generate optimal solutions, that is, useful groups.

4. Proposed Approach

As previously mentioned, the approach proposed in this paper seeks to find three types of groups, homogeneous, heterogeneous, and mixed, attending to the student's personality traits, contrasting the five dimensions of the Big Five model. The measurement of these dimensions can be obtained employing the "Big Five Inventory" (BFI), to then find the group mean in each of the dimensions, and finally form groups seeking to optimize a certain measure of heterogeneity, homogeneity, or mixture.

The approach is explained below in three sections—the first one describes the proposed psychometric test to measure personality traits, followed by the formation of workgroups as such, through the application of genetic algorithms, and finally, the empirical design is described as used for validation.

4.1. Big Five Inventory (BFI)

As described in Section 2.1, the Big Five model, on which this work is theoretically and psychologically based, is a purely descriptive personality model, which has led psychologists to develop various tests and questionnaires that evaluate each of the five factors or dimensions in individuals. In the specific case, an adaptation to Spanish of the Big Five Inventory-BFI by John et al. [45] is used as an instrument to measure the students' personality traits.

The use of this instrument is considered a scientifically accepted resource to quantify personality traits, which, as described below, are the input required by the grouping algorithm. It is not intended to issue a concept or psychological diagnosis of the participants, as this is outside the scope of the study.

Table 1 shows the Spanish and English versions of the instrument, the latter as a reference for non-Spanish-speaking readers, which were reconstructed from the original paper "Los Cinco Grandes Across Cultures and Ethnic Groups: Multitrait Multimethod Analysis of the Big Five in Spanish and English" [46]. It consists of 44 multiple-response items (Likert type) that measure the dimensions proposed for the Big Five model.

4.2. Algorithm for Group Formation

The proposed method for group formation is described in detail in this section. It is based on the previous work of Moreno et al. [47], who propose a method to group elements in a homogeneous way. The mathematical and algorithmic formulation of the model is generally described, from the representation of the elements to be grouped (students), the solutions (feasible groupings) and their fitness measures, to the operators employed in applying the genetic algorithm.

Table 1. Spanish and English Big Five Inventory.

Spanish Big Five Inventory

Las siguientes expresiones le describen a usted con más o menos precisión. Por ejemplo, ¿está de acuerdo en que usted es alguien "chistoso, a quien le gusta bromear"? Por favor escoja un número para cada una de las siguientes expresiones, indicando así hasta qué punto está de acuerdo o en desacuerdo en cómo le describe a usted.

Muy en desacuerdo 1	Ligeramente en desacuerdo 2	Ni de acuerdo ni en desacuerdo 3	Ligeramente de acuerdo 4	Muy de acuerdo 5

Me veo a mi mismo-a como alguien que ...

___ 1. es bien hablador
___ 2. tiende a ser criticón
___ 3. es minucioso en el trabajo
___ 4. es depresivo, melancólico
___ 5. es original, se le ocurren ideas nuevas
___ 6. es reservado
___ 7. es generoso y ayuda a los demás
___ 8. puede a veces ser algo descuidado
___ 9. es calmado, controla bien el estrés
___ 10. tiene intereses muy diversos
___ 11. está lleno de energía
___ 12. prefiere trabajos que son rutinarios
___ 13. inicia disputas con los demás
___ 14. es un trabajador cumplidor, digno de confianza
___ 15. con frecuencia se pone tenso
___ 16. tiende a ser callado
___ 17. valora lo artístico, lo estético
___ 18. tiende a ser desorganizado
___ 19. es emocionalmente estable, difícil de alterar
___ 20. tiene una imaginación activa
___ 21. persevera hasta terminar el trabajo
___ 22. es a veces mal educado con los demás
___ 23. es inventivo
___ 24. es generalmente confiado
___ 25. tiende a ser flojo, vago
___ 26. se preocupa mucho por las cosas
___ 27. es a veces tímido, inhibido
___ 28. es indulgente, no le cuesta perdonar
___ 29. hace las cosas de manera eficiente
___ 30. es temperamental, de humor cambiante
___ 31. es ingenioso, analítico
___ 32. irradia entusiasmo
___ 33. es a veces frío y distante
___ 34. hace planes y los sigue cuidadosamente
___ 35. mantiene la calma en situaciones difíciles
___ 36. le gusta reflexionar, jugar con las ideas
___ 37. es considerado y amable con casi todo el mundo
___ 38. se pone nervioso con facilidad
___ 39. es educado en arte, música, o literatura
___ 40. es asertivo, no teme expresar lo que quiere
___ 41. le gusta cooperar con los demás
___ 42. se distrae con facilidad
___ 43. es extrovertido, sociable
___ 44. tiene pocos intereses artísticos

Por favor, compruebe que ha escrito un número delante de cada frase.

English Big Five Inventory

Here are a number of characteristics that may or may not apply to you. For example, do you agree that you are someone who likes to spend time with others? Please choose a number for each statement to indicate the extent to which you agree or disagree with that statement.

Disagree strongly 1	Disagree a little 2	Neither agree nor disagree 3	Agree a little 4	Agree strongly 5

I see myself as someone who ...

___ 1. is talkative.
___ 2. tends to find fault with others.
___ 3. does a thorough job.
___ 4. is depressed, blue.
___ 5. is original, comes up with new ideas.
___ 6. is reserved.
___ 7. is helpful and unselfish with others.
___ 8. can be somewhat careless.
___ 9. is relaxed, handles stress well.
___ 10. is curious about many different things.
___ 11. is full of energy.
___ 12. starts quarrels with others.
___ 13. is a reliable worker.
___ 14. can be tense.
___ 15. is ingenious, a deep thinker.
___ 16. generates a lot of enthusiasm.
___ 17. has a forgiving nature.
___ 18. tends to be disorganized.
___ 19. worries a lot.
___ 20. has an active imagination.
___ 21. tends to be quiet.
___ 22. is generally trusting.
___ 23. tends to be lazy.
___ 24. is emotionally stable, not easily upset.
___ 25. is inventive.
___ 26. has an assertive personality.
___ 27. can be cold and aloof.
___ 28. perseveres until the task is finished.
___ 29. can be moody.
___ 30. values artistic, aesthetic experiences.
___ 31. is sometimes shy, inhibited.
___ 32. is considerate and kind to almost everyone.
___ 33. does things efficiently.
___ 34. remains calm in tense situations.
___ 35. prefers work that is routine.
___ 36. is outgoing, sociable.
___ 37. is sometimes rude to others.
___ 38. makes plans and follows through with them.
___ 39. gets nervous easily.
___ 40. likes to reflect, play with ideas.
___ 41. has few artistic interests.
___ 42. likes to cooperate with others.
___ 43. is easily distracted.
___ 44. is sophisticated in art, music, or literature.

Please check: Did you write a number in front of each statement?

4.2.1. Student Representation

Each student n can be represented through a vector, where M is the number of characteristics, which could have a different nature, for example, demographic (age, gender), psychological (personality traits, abilities, capacities), academic (grades, pre-tests, self-assessment), and cognitive (learning styles, intelligence types), among others.

$$E_n = \{C_1, C_2, \ldots, C_M\} \quad (1)$$

Each characteristic m ($1 \leq m \leq M$) must be a value in a predefined numerical range. If categorical attributes are considered, a prior numerical discretization process would be required. For example, if a characteristic takes "high", "medium", and "low" values, these could be changed to 1, 2, and 3, respectively.

A set of students can be represented by an $N \times M$ matrix, where N is the number of students and M is the number of characteristics, as shown in Table 2.

Table 2. Representation of a set of students.

Id	C_1	C_2	$\ldots$	C_M
1	70	0.50	$\ldots$	25
2	20	0.83	$\ldots$	-10
$\vdots$	$\vdots$	$\vdots$		$\vdots$
N	45	1.22	$\ldots$	13

The data must be scaled to a common range so that there are no alterations in calculating the objective function. One way to do this is by applying the min–max normalization [48], which allows all the data to remain, for example, in the range 0–1, using the following expression, where $V_{\max}$ and $V_{\min}$ are the maximum and minimum values of the corresponding characteristic.

$$V' = \frac{V - V_{\min}}{V_{\max} - V_{\min}} \quad (2)$$

4.2.2. Individual Representation

In the group formation problem, an individual corresponds to a given set of G groups, each with up to N/G students, where N is the total number of students. For the representation of individuals, it is proposed to use a matrix, where the number of rows corresponds to the number of groups G and the number of columns corresponds to the maximum size of each group N/G. In this way, each gene that makes up the chromosome contains the identifier of an element, and its position within the matrix defines the group to which it belongs. This representation facilitates the coding of the chromosome and the use of the genetic operators described below.

As in other combinatorial problems, in group formation, a chromosome cannot have repeated genes, which means that an individual (feasible solution) is one in which each element (student) is in a single position on the chromosome. For example, if you have a set of 20 students and you want to form 4 groups, each group would contain 5 students. A possible individual, if the students are numbered consecutively, is presented in Table 3.

Table 3. Representation of an individual.

	S_1	S_2	S_3	S_4	S_5
G_1	1	2	3	4	5
G_2	6	7	8	9	10
G_3	11	12	13	14	15
G_4	16	17	18	19	20

4.2.3. Fitness Measure

As mentioned above, the objective of the proposed approach is to form homogeneous, heterogeneous, or mixed groups concerning all the students, considering their personality traits. The way to measure this classification criterion would be given by the fitness measure. One possible way to calculate it is described below:

The average of each characteristic of all students (*TM*) is calculated:

$$TM = \{\overline{C_1}, \overline{C_2}, \ldots, \overline{C_M}\} \quad (3)$$

For each group g ($1 \leq g \leq G$) of each individual i the average of each characteristic is calculated. Considering that individual i is represented as a vector of X^i, these averages (*IM*) are represented as follows:

$$IM_g^i = \{\overline{X_{g,1}^i}, \overline{X_{g,2}^i}, \ldots, \overline{X_{g,M}^i}\} \quad (4)$$

The sum of the squared differences between the *M* characteristics of each group g of individual i and the average of each characteristic in all the students is calculated, like this:

$$D^i = \sum_{g=1}^{G} \left[\left(\overline{C_1} - \overline{X_{g,1}^i}\right)^2 + \left(\overline{C_2} - \overline{X_{g,2}^i}\right)^2 + \ldots + \left(\overline{C_M} - \overline{X_{g,M}^i}\right)^2 \right] \quad (5)$$

The lower this value (with a minimum of 0), the more similar each group will be on average concerning all the students (*TM*), in the case of homogeneous group formation; and the higher this value, the less similar each group will be on average concerning all the students, in the case of heterogeneous group formation. The objective function is expressed as follows:

$$\min|\max Z = \sum_{g=1}^{G} \left[\left(\overline{C_1} - \overline{X_{g,1}^i}\right)^2 + \left(\overline{C_2} - \overline{X_{g,2}^i}\right)^2 + \ldots + \left(\overline{C_M} - \overline{X_{g,M}^i}\right)^2 \right] \quad (6)$$

For mixed group formation, that is, heterogeneous for certain characteristics and homogeneous for others, the problem becomes one of multi-objective optimization: it is required to maximize the differences for the heterogeneous characteristics and at the same time minimize the differences for the homogeneous characteristics. Considering the above, a possible way to deal with this situation is described below.

Let *HT* and *HM* be the vectors of characteristic for which heterogeneity and homogeneity are considered, respectively, represented as follows:

$$HT = \{C_1, C_2, \ldots, C_J\} \subset E_n \quad (7)$$

$$HM = \{C_{J+1}, C_{J+2}, \ldots, C_M\} \subset E_n \quad (8)$$

For the fitness measure, the sum of the squared differences between the *J* characteristics of heterogeneity for each group g of individual i and the average of each characteristic in all the students is calculated, and the value obtained from the sum is subtracted from the differences squared between the *M* characteristics of homogeneity for each group g of individual i and the average of each characteristic in all the students, like this:

$$D^i = \sum_{g=1}^{G} \left[\left(\overline{C_1} - \overline{X_{g,1}^i}\right)^2 + \left(\overline{C_2} - \overline{X_{g,2}^i}\right)^2 + \ldots + \left(\overline{C_J} - \overline{X_{g,J}^i}\right)^2 \right] - \sum_{g=1}^{G} \left[\left(\overline{C_{J+1}} - \overline{X_{g,J+1}^i}\right)^2 + \left(\overline{C_{J+2}} - \overline{X_{g,J+2}^i}\right)^2 + \ldots + \left(\overline{C_K} - \overline{X_{g,M}^i}\right)^2 \right] \quad (9)$$

The greater the difference in objectives, the better heterogeneity the groups would have in the *HT* characteristics and the better homogeneity in the *HM* characteristics, simultaneously. The objective function can be expressed as follows:

$$\max Z = \sum_{g=1}^{G}\left[\left(\overline{C_1}-\overline{X_{g,1}^i}\right)^2+\left(\overline{C_2}-\overline{X_{g,2}^i}\right)^2+\ldots+\left(\overline{C_J}-\overline{X_{g,J}^i}\right)^2\right]- \\ \sum_{g=1}^{G}\left[\left(\overline{C_{J+1}}-\overline{X_{g,J+1}^i}\right)^2+\left(\overline{C_{J+2}}-\overline{X_{g,J+2}^i}\right)^2+\ldots+\left(\overline{C_K}-\overline{X_{g,M}^i}\right)^2\right] \quad (10)$$

To clarify the entire process described, the data in Table 4, corresponding to a list of 6 students and 3 assessed characteristics, are considered as an example.

Table 4. Example students.

Id	C_1	C_2	C_3
1	0.12	1.00	0.90
2	0.97	0.00	0.30
3	0.00	0.64	0.98
4	1.00	0.45	1.00
5	0.35	0.07	0.93
6	0.59	0.84	0.00

Now we want to form two groups, each with three students. Two possible individuals are shown in Table 5.

Table 5. Two possible example individuals.

Individual 1			Individual 2		
1	2	3	1	3	5
4	5	6	2	4	6

By applying (3), the following is obtained:

$$TM = \{0.505, 0.500, 0.685\} \quad (11)$$

Table 6 shows the $\overline{X_{g,C}^i}$ calculation from Tables 4 and 5, necessary to obtain IM_g^i according to (4).

$$IM_g^1 = \left\{\begin{array}{ccc} 0.363 & 0.547 & 0.727 \\ 0.647 & 0.453 & 0.643 \end{array}\right\} \quad (12)$$

$$IM_g^2 = \left\{\begin{array}{ccc} 0.157 & 0.570 & 0.937 \\ 0.853 & 0.430 & 0.433 \end{array}\right\} \quad (13)$$

Finally, calculating the fitness measures applying (5), $D^1 = 0.048$ and $D^2 = 0.380$ are obtained.

$$D^1 = \left[\begin{array}{c}(0.505-0.363)^2+(0.500-0.547)^2+(0.685-0.727)^2+\\(0.505-0.647)^2+(0.500-0.453)^2+(0.685-0.643)^2\end{array}\right] = 0.048 \quad (14)$$

$$D^2 = \left[\begin{array}{c}(0.505-0.157)^2+(0.500-0.570)^2+(0.685-0.937)^2+\\(0.505-0.853)^2+(0.500-0.430)^2+(0.685-0.433)^2\end{array}\right] = 0.379 \quad (15)$$

Table 6. $\overline{X^i_{g,C}}$ calculation.

Individual	Group	Id	C_1	C_2	C_3
1	1	1	0.120	1.000	0.900
		2	0.970	0.000	0.300
		3	0.000	0.640	0.980
		$\overline{X^1_{1,C}}$	0.363	0.547	0.727
	2	4	1.000	0.450	1.000
		5	0.350	0.070	0.930
		6	0.590	0.840	0.000
		$\overline{X^1_{2,C}}$	0.647	0.453	0.643
2	1	1	0.120	1.000	0.900
		3	0.000	0.640	0.980
		5	0.350	0.070	0.930
		$\overline{X^2_{1,C}}$	0.157	0.570	0.937
	2	2	0.970	0.000	0.300
		4	1.000	0.450	1.000
		6	0.590	0.840	0.000
		$\overline{X^2_{2,C}}$	0.853	0.430	0.433

The grouping represented by Individual 1 is more inter-homogeneous than Individual 2; with this distribution, all the groups of Individual 1 reflect all the students (*TM*) with greater precision when all the characteristics are considered as a whole. On the contrary, the grouping represented by Individual 2 is more inter-heterogeneous than Individual 1; with this distribution, all the groups of Individual 2 present greater variability concerning all the students (*TM*) when all the characteristics are considered in whole.

Now a mixed formation is desired, which is homogeneous for C_2 and at the same time heterogeneous for C_1 and C_3. According to (7) and (8), we obtain:

$$HT = \{C_1, C_3\} \tag{16}$$

$$HM = \{C_2\} \tag{17}$$

Calculating the fitness measures applying (9), the following is obtained:

$$D^1_{HT} = \begin{bmatrix} (0.505 - 0.363)^2 + (0.684 - 0.727)^2 + \\ (0.505 - 0.647)^2 + (0.684 - 0.643)^2 \end{bmatrix} = 0.044 \tag{18}$$

$$D^1_{HM} = \left[(0.500 - 0.547)^2 + (0.500 - 0.453)^2 \right] = 0.004 \tag{19}$$

$$D^1 = 0.044 - 0.004 = 0.040 \tag{20}$$

$$D^2_{HT} = \begin{bmatrix} (0.505 - 0.157)^2 + (0.684 - 0.937)^2 + \\ (0.505 - 0.853)^2 + (0.684 - 0.433)^2 \end{bmatrix} = 0.369 \tag{21}$$

$$D^2_{HM} = \left[(0.500 - 0.570)^2 + (0.500 - 0.430)^2 \right] = 0.010 \tag{22}$$

$$D^2 = 0.369 - 0.010 = 0.359 \tag{23}$$

The grouping represented by Individual 2 is more inter-homogeneous for C_2 and inter-heterogeneous for C_1 and C_3 than Individual 1; with this distribution, all groups of Individual 2 more accurately reflect similarity and variability with the whole set of students (TM), when simultaneously seeking homogeneity for C_2 and heterogeneity for C_1 and C_3.

4.2.4. Initial Population and Evolution

The example in Table 5 shows a trivial group formation: each student is assigned in an orderly manner to a group based on their identifier. The first N/G students (in this case 3) belong to Group 1, the next N/G to Group 2 and so on. Although this formation is valid, the idea of the initial population is to randomly generate k individuals, using the matrix representation described above and satisfying the restriction that each student must be in one and only one of the array positions.

Once the initial population is obtained, the process of evolution is carried out, passing from one generation to another using genetic operators, until a desired fitness measure is obtained or until a certain number of generations is reached.

The main objective of the proposed algorithm is to improve the quality of group formation and its effectiveness in collaborative processes. To do this, a set of configurations are tested, and some modifications are made to the classical genetic operators. The flow of the genetic algorithm used for the student group formations based on personality traits is:

Step 1—Measure students' personality traits: The first step is to measure the characteristics of the students based on which the groups are formed, in this case, their personality traits. This measurement is crucial for structuring good groups that promote efficient and effective collaboration and achieve better learning outcomes.

Step 2—Define genetic parameters: Before executing the genetic algorithm, the genetic parameters concerning group size, population size, number of generations, and crossover and mutation probabilities must be established. This process is described in Section 4.2.5.

Step 3—Encode chromosome: In this step, the chromosome is represented into a predefined data structure to allow genetic operators to apply. In this study, a matrix structure is used, as described in Section 4.2.2.

Step 4—Initialize population: The genetic algorithm is started by creating an initial population that consists of a set of feasible encoded solutions (chromosomes). This population is generated randomly to ensure its diversity.

Step 5—Evaluate fitness: A fitness function based on the students' personality traits is used to evaluate the chromosomes of the population, as described in Section 4.2.3.

Step 6—Generate a new population: This step is the core of the genetic algorithm, where new and better solutions are generated. The genetic operators applied are: (a) selection, where two parents are selected for crossing, (b) crossover, where, based on a probability, a recombination of the parents' genes is carried out, and (c) mutation, where, based on a probability, parts of the chromosome of the new population are mutated.

Step 7—End search: After several generations, the algorithm ends and converges to the fittest chromosome, which represents a feasible solution.

Step 8—Form optimal groups: Student groups are formed based on the genetic algorithm results, and students are notified to begin working in their groups on the development of the proposed collaborative activity.

Figure 2 illustrates the main flow of the student group formation process, using the proposed genetic algorithm, grouping the different steps into four stages: input (1), GA settings preparation (2, 3), GA procedure (4, 5, 6, 7), and output (8).

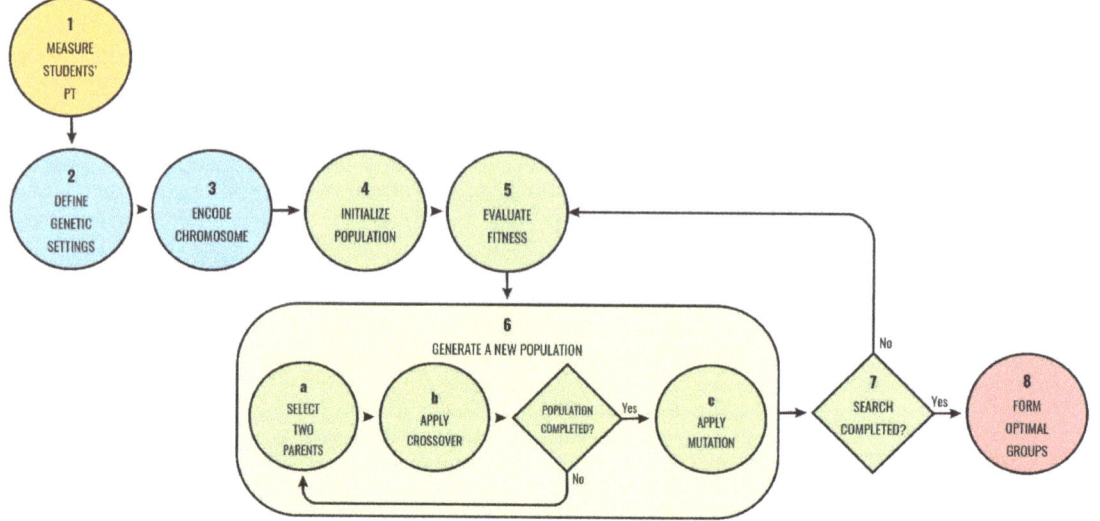

Figure 2. The main flow of the student group formation process using GA.

4.2.5. Search Complexity and Algorithm Performance

The estimation of the exhaustive search complexity of the proposed algorithm is associated with the combinatorial explosion generated by the group formation process, it goes hand in hand with the total number of students to group and the number of groups that want to be formed, which, in turn, is directly related to the size of the groups. In general, the number of G different groups of N/G students that can be obtained from a whole set of N students, considering the ordering of the groups relevant, can be calculated through multinomial coefficients [49] with the following expression:

$$\frac{N!}{\left(\left(\frac{N}{G}\right)!\right)^G} \qquad (24)$$

Thus, for example, if you want to organize 50 students into 10 groups of 5, this value would amount to 4.91×10^{43} possible combinations (applying (24)), which makes finding the best solution from an exhaustive search not very feasible in many cases. Hence the usefulness of the proposed method.

On the other hand, before presenting the results of the implemented genetic algorithm, the process of defining its general parameters is described: crossover probability, mutation probability, population size and generation number (termination criterion). The values obtained for these parameters were generalized for the different cases of model validation.

To define good values for both the crossover probability (p_c) and the mutation probability (p_m), values of each of the parameters were simulated in the ranges suggested by the literature [50,51], and others slightly outside of them, selecting the set with the best results. A high crossover probability allows greater exploration of the solution space, reducing the possibility of establishing a false optimum; but if the probability is very high, it causes a great investment in computation time in the exploration of unpromising regions of the solution space. As for the mutation probability, if it is very low, some genes that could have been produced are never tested; if it is too high, there will be much random disturbance, the children would begin to lose their parental likeness.

The simulation was performed on a base case: the example described in Section 4.2.3; the formation of two groups of three students is considered; formation of the three types: homogeneous, heterogeneous, and mixed; with three-valued characteristics; establishing a population size of 100 individuals; 100 generations of execution of the genetic algorithm; and, with 100 simulation runs. Since this is a case with low complexity in the calculations, its verification was possible through the example implementation in an electronic sheet. The simulation results are shown in Table 7.

Table 7. Simulation results of crossover and mutation probabilities.

	Homogeneous Optimal Value: 0.04259					Heterogeneous Optimal Value: 0.37947					Mixed (Het 1,3; Hom 2) Optimal Value: 0.35975				
$p_c \backslash p_m$	0.001	0.005	0.01	0.05	0.1	0.001	0.005	0.01	0.05	0.1	0.001	0.005	0.01	0.05	0.1
0.2	100	100	100	64	62	100	100	100	56	59	100	100	100	65	64
0.3	100	100	100	70	63	100	100	100	59	59	100	100	100	59	61
0.4	99	100	100	59	51	99	100	100	64	63	100	100	100	63	58
0.6	74	94	89	65	56	87	93	91	60	61	89	98	91	72	56
0.8	61	67	49	50	52	61	59	53	58	43	66	59	52	51	49

The results show that statistically similar values are obtained for the three types of formation. In the three cases, with crossover probability from 0.2 to 0.4 and with mutation probability from 0.001 to 0.01, practically 100 times out of the 100 simulation runs, the corresponding optimal values were obtained. Therefore, for the case under study, it was decided to take the mean values in each interval as appropriate values, that is, $p_c = 0.4$ and $p_m = 0.01$.

Likewise, to define good values, both for the population size and the generations number (termination criterion of the genetic algorithm), each of the parameters was simulated by selecting the set of those with the best results. Small populations run the risk of not adequately covering the search space, while large populations can generate a high computational cost. On the other hand, as the number of generations increases, the average fitness is more likely to approach that of the best individual, but the computational cost increases.

The simulation was performed with randomly generated data for 50 students; heterogeneous group formation of four members; with five valued characteristics (corresponding to the five dimensions of the Big Five model); establishing a crossover of 0.4 and mutation of 0.01 probabilities; and with 100 simulation runs. The simulation results are shown in Table 8.

Table 8. Results of population size and generation number simulation (time (T) in milliseconds, fitness value (F)).

G\PS	100		250		500		1000	
	T	F	T	F	T	F	T	F
50	670	2.86807	2793	2.95261	6039	2.57977	6440	2.41648
100	1294	3.19189	5196	3.11056	9153	2.68289	12,071	2.43724
250	3413	3.38202	13,152	3.27827	16,379	2.80822	29,856	2.45063
500	6311	3.65009	15,166	3.12584	30,225	2.77663	57,944	2.52308
1000	11,553	4.08895	30,642	3.24229	57,730	2.89469	115,698	2.56421

The results show that, for the case under analysis, a good population size (PS) is 100 individuals; with higher values, it is observed that fitness (F) decreases. Regarding the generations number (G), the above is ratified: the greater the number, the greater the computational cost (time (T) in milliseconds); and, in addition, as can be seen in Figure 3, after 1000 generations the fitness value stabilizes, which would indicate that the algorithm has found a value close to the optimal; so, it was decided to handle a value around 1000 generations.

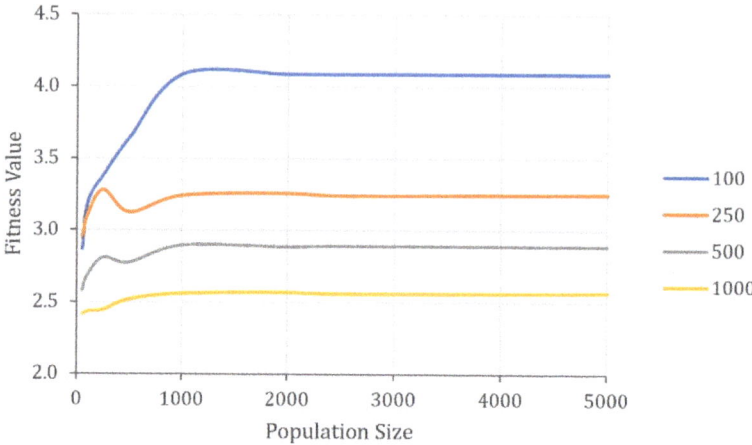

Figure 3. GA performance.

The implemented genetic algorithm was validated from randomly simulated data with a structure like that presented in Table 4, considering five valued characteristics (corresponding to the five dimensions of the Big Five model). Three tests were carried out with lists of 20, 50, and 100 students; formation of the three types; groups of 4 and 5 members; a population size of 100 individuals; a generation number of 1000; and a run simulation number of 100.

For the first genetic operator, selection, a survivor's number equal to population size was chosen by the tournament selection method. The choice of individuals (with replacement) was made randomly, although proportional to the fitness functions, that is, that the fittest individuals have a greater possibility of cloning to the next generation.

The crossover operator was applied to the resulting population, choosing two parents randomly according to the crossover probability of 0.4. Every two parents produce two children using the C1 operator, which chooses a crossing point between the parents' chromosomes, combines the first segment of the first parent with the second segment, but in the order in which they appear in the second parent and vice versa [52].

Given the nature of the problem, a variation of the swap mutation operator was used [53]. It is proposed in two steps: in the first step, the individuals to be mutated are randomly selected; and, in the second step, two genes to be mutated are randomly selected. The gene mutation will consist of the swap of values of a specific allele in each gene, also selected randomly. Considering the matrix representation used, it is necessary to clarify that the swap's allele cannot be in the same row since the change would not affect it (the order within a group has no relevance). The mutation operator was applied to the entire population of each generation with a probability of 0.01.

Under all these parameters, the execution of the algorithm programmed in Java™, on a laptop with an Intel Core I7 processor of 1.8 GHz and 8 Gb of RAM, generated the results presented in Tables 9 and 10.

Table 9. Results of the 4-student group formation (time (T) in milliseconds, fitness value (F)).

Students	Homogeneous		Heterogeneous		Mix (Ht123, Hm45)	
	T	F	T	F	T	F
20	2384	0.02564	2837	1.45408	3425	0.79947
50	12,244	0.15691	12,120	4.09133	12,406	2.58507
100	42,644	0.40598	40,700	6.79100	40,434	4.15891

Table 10. Results of the 5-student group formation (time (T) in milliseconds, fitness value (F)).

Students	Homogeneous		Heterogeneous		Mix (Ht123, Hm45)	
	T	F	T	F	T	F
20	2711	0.01084	3038	1.04431	2908	0.60869
50	11,065	0.06563	12,240	2.97906	12,235	1.93656
100	41,801	0.20536	51,146	4.92599	41,940	3.26345

These results show that the algorithm implemented does not differentiate between the types of groups to be formed, practically the computational performance (time in milliseconds) is the same for the three in each of the lists, for groups of 4 or 5 members. On the other hand, the time used, and the fitness value are increasing for each of the lists, since as the total number of students increases, the complexity of the search increases, that is, there are more combinations to consider in determining the optimal value. It is important to consider the above: the tests were performed using a generations number of 1000 as the termination criterion of the genetic algorithm; if this parameter is increased, the adaptation value improves, but the processing time is also increased.

These results demonstrate the effectiveness of the proposed algorithm, which, being a heuristic search method, does not guarantee to reach the global optimum, but a very close value, despite the simplicity of its formulation and its low demand for computational resources (time and memory), even when the number of possible combinations is very high.

4.3. Empirical Design

The experiment consisted in conducting a collaborative learning activity, specifically an activity named "Peer Code Evaluation" [54], with 82 students from 4 programming courses, belonging to the programs of Systems Engineering and Electronic Engineering of the University of Nariño of the City of San Juan de Pasto-Colombia, in the academic semester B-2020. It is worth mentioning that for this period, given the COVID-19 situation, the courses were developed in virtual mode. Table 11 shows the characterization of each of the courses.

Table 11. Characterization of the working groups.

Program-Course	N	Group Type	Number of Groups	Grouping Type
Electronic Engineering-	22	Experimental	6/3–1/4	Heterogeneous
Computer Programming	17	Control	3/3–2/4	Students' preference
Systems Engineering-	24	Experimental	8/3	Homogeneous
Graphic Programming	19	Control	5/3–1/4	Students' preference

The research process was developed with an empirical design based on a quasi-experiment as shown in Table 12, seeking to verify one of the following hypotheses: H_0: the means of the grades obtained by the students in the topic of the collaborative activity are equal (null hypothesis); H_1: the means of the grades obtained by the students in the topic of the collaborative activity are different (research hypothesis). It is a quasi-experiment since the study groups (described below) were already formed before the experimentation, they were intact groups (the reason why they arose and the way they were formed have nothing to do with the experiment, it is a task that corresponds to the registration and academic control University office for each new academic period) [55]. This is a common situation in educational contexts, as teachers must evaluate the efficacy of their teaching methods, but pure experiments in these contexts are seldom politically, administratively, or ethically feasible [56].

Table 12. Experimental design.

Group Type	Group	Pre-Test	Experimental Stimulus	Post-Test
Experimental	G_1	O_1	X	O_5
	G_2	O_2	X	O_6
Control	G_3	O_3	-	O_7
	G_4	O_4	-	O_8

G_1 and G_2 groups were the experimental groups and G_3 and G_4 were the control groups in each course. In addition, X was the experimental treatment that consisted of forming the required groups using the proposed approach, carrying out a collaborative learning activity during work sessions scheduled. In the control groups, to which the experimental treatment was not applied, the groups required for the collaborative activity, which was the same as for the experimental ones, were formed by students' preference.

O_1, O_2, O_3, and O_4, were the pre-tests applied at the beginning of the experiment, both for the experimental and control groups, seeking to guarantee in some way the initial equivalence of the groups, which in turn guarantees the internal validity of the experiment. The pre-tests consisted of the individual response to the same questionnaire (for each of the courses), related to the topics of the collaborative activity.

In turn, O_5, O_6, O_7, and O_8 were the post-tests applied at the end of the experiment for both experimental and control groups, seeking to determine the implication of the experimental treatment. The post-tests consisted of individual responses to the same pre-test questionnaire (for each of the courses), related to the topics of collaborative activity.

The first experimental group G_1 consisted of 22 students from the Computer Programming course—Group 1 of the second semester of Electronic Engineering, who were applied the experimental treatment X and the post-test O_5. The control group G_3 consisted of 17 students from the Computer Programming course—Group 2, from the same semester and academic period, and who were not experimentally treated, but the O_7 post-test was applied. The second experimental group G_2 consisted of 24 students from the Graphic Programming course—Group 1 of the tenth semester of Systems Engineering, for whom the experimental treatment X and the post-test O_6 were applied. The control group G_4 consisted of 19 students from the Graphic Programming course—Group 2, from the same semester and academic period, and who were not experimentally treated, but the O_8 post-test was applied. As mentioned above, all groups were given pre-tests O_1, O_2, O_3, and O_4, seeking to guarantee the initial equivalence of the groups in each of the courses.

All participant students in the study were informed about the research's purpose and scope and were assured of their anonymity.

5. Results

The proposal presented in this paper contemplates applying an instrument for measuring personality traits and an approach using genetic algorithms for group formation. The results described here correspond to the validation of the model and its application in a controlled experiment with students in a collaborative learning scenario. It is verified that the methodology described in Section 4 is useful to obtain groups with the desired characteristics, and it is empirically verified that the academic results obtained through the collaborative work of these groups are favourable.

As mentioned in Section 4.3, at the beginning of the experiment the pre-tests were applied to the study groups, the objective of which was to guarantee in some way the initial equivalence of the groups, since they are intact groups. These pre-tests consisted of questionnaires for individual response, about the specific topics of the collaborative activity developed in each course.

Figure 4 shows the apparent initial equivalence of the study groups. The results show that, on average, the grades obtained in the pre-tests by the experimental groups are like those obtained by the control groups in each of the courses.

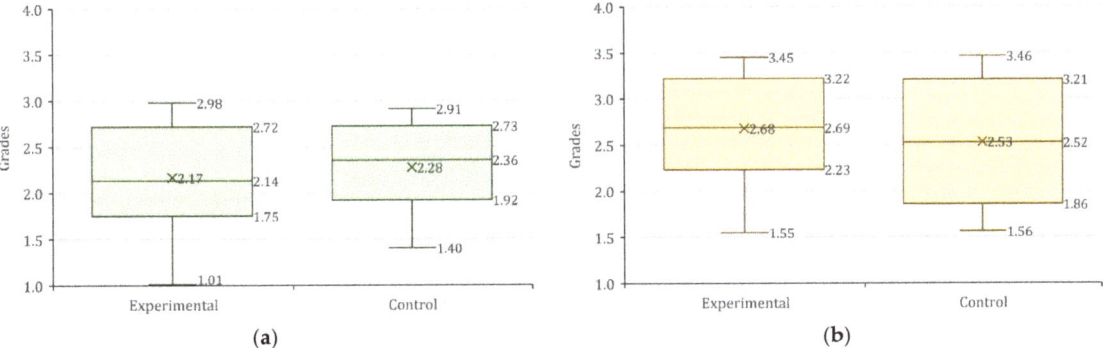

Figure 4. Pre-test results. (**a**) Computer Programming; (**b**) Graphic Programming.

To provide a solid conclusion regarding the initial equivalence of the groups, a statistical analysis was carried out using the Mann–Whitney U test, a non-parametric test used to compare two independent samples, seeking to statistically confirm the apparent similarity between the grades obtained by the experimental groups and those obtained by the control groups in the pre-tests, that is to say, that the students, in general, handle the same pre-concepts in each of their courses, before carrying out the experimentation. This test was used considering that the students' pre-test grades do not follow a normal distribution.

The results of the application of the Mann–Whitney U test are shown in Table 13, which were obtained using SPSS™, with a confidence level of 95% and considering the following hypotheses: H_0: the means of the grades obtained by the students in the pre-test are similar; H_1: the means of the grades obtained by the students in the pre-test are different.

Table 13. Mann–Whitney U test for pre-tests.

Course	Group	N	Tests	p
Computer Programming	Experimental (G_1)	22	O_1–O_3	0.589
	Control (G_3)	17		
Graphic Programming	Experimental (G_2)	24	O_2–O_4	0.607
	Control (G_4)	19		

When comparing the experimental group G_1 with the control group G_3 of the Computer Programming course, a p-value of 0.589 was obtained. As this value is greater than 0.05, the alternative hypothesis (H_1) is rejected in favour of the null hypothesis (H_0), with a confidence level of 95%, that is, that the means of the grades obtained by the students in the pre-test are similar.

When comparing the experimental group G_2 with the control group G_4 of the Graphic Programming course, a p-value of 0.607 was obtained. As this value is greater than 0.05, the alternative hypothesis (H_1) is rejected in favour of the null hypothesis (H_0), with a confidence level of 95%, that is, that the means of the grades obtained by the students in the pre-test are similar.

The results of these tests show that there is no statistically significant difference between the means of the grades obtained in the pre-tests by the experimental groups and those obtained by the control groups in each of the courses, that is, that the pre-concepts that students handle about the topics required for the development of collaborative activity in each of the courses are similar. This adds validity to the experiment.

On the other hand, as mentioned in Section 4.3, at the end of the experiment, post-tests were applied to the study groups, the objective of which was to determine the implication of the experimental treatment. These post-tests consisted of questionnaires for individual response, about the specific topics of the collaborative activity developed in each course. This process made it possible to contrast the grades of the experimental groups versus those of the control groups, seeking to verify in a basic way if there is an improvement in the learning process by applying the proposed group formation technique based on personality traits, concerning the formation technique by students' preference, traditionally used by teachers, when developing a collaborative activity.

Figure 5 shows the apparent positive incidence of the proposed experimental treatment. The results show that, on average, the grades obtained in the post-test by the experimental groups are higher than those obtained by the control groups.

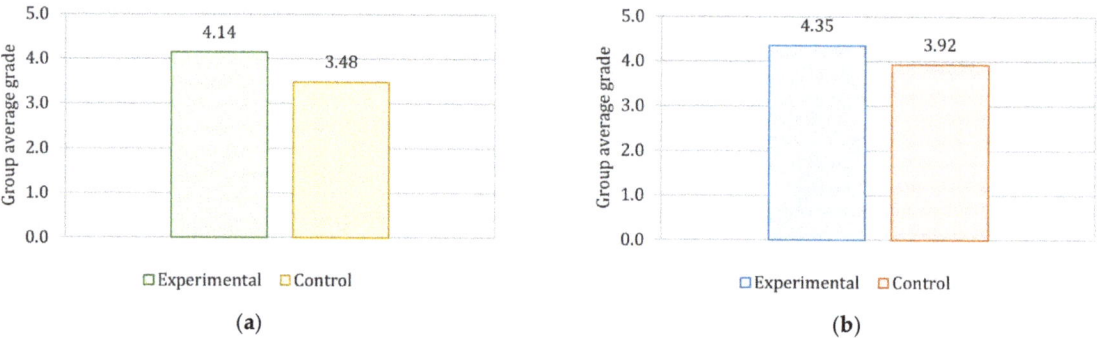

Figure 5. Post-test results. (a) Computer Programming; (b) Graphic Programming.

To provide a solid conclusion regarding the goodness of the proposed group formation technique, a statistical analysis was performed using the Mann–Whitney U test, seeking to statistically confirm the difference between the grades obtained by the experimental groups compared to those obtained by the control groups, that is, a basic difference in the level of learning achieved by the students in the specific subject. This test was used considering that the students' post-test grades do not follow a normal distribution. In addition, the effect size of the experimental treatment was calculated through Hedges' g [57], a metric that allows to quantify the magnitude of the difference between two independent samples analysed through non-parametric tests, giving it greater reliability to test results.

The results of the application of the Mann–Whitney U test, which were obtained using SPSS™, are shown in Table 14 with a confidence level of 95% and considering the following hypotheses: H_0: the means of the grades obtained by the students in the post-test are similar; H_1: the means of the grades obtained by the students in the post-test are different.

Table 14. Mann–Whitney U Test for post-tests.

Course	Group	N	Tests	p	g
Computer Programming	Experimental (G_1)	22	O_5–O_7	0.029	0.729
	Control (G_3)	17			
Graphic Programming	Experimental (G_2)	24	O_6–O_8	0.039	0.579
	Control (G_4)	19			

When comparing the experimental group G_1 with the control group G_3 of the Computer Programming course, a p-value of 0.029 was obtained. As this value is less than 0.05, the null hypothesis (H_0) is rejected in favour of the alternative hypothesis (H_1), with a confidence level of 95%, that is, that the means of the grades obtained by the students in the post-test are different, with a difference of 0.6545 in favour of G_1. According to the classification made by Cohen [58], the effect size of the experimental treatment (g) with a value of 0.729 is considered as medium, approaching large, which implies that there is a significant difference between the results of the experimental group versus the control group not due to chance.

When comparing the experimental group G_2 with the control group G_4 of the Graphic Programming course, a p-value of 0.039 was obtained. As this value is less than 0.05, the null hypothesis (H_0) is rejected in favour of the alternative hypothesis (H_1), with a confidence level of 95%, that is, that the means of the grades obtained by the students in the post-test are different, with a difference of 0.4311 in favour of G_2. According to the classification made by Cohen [58], the effect size of the experimental treatment (g) with a value of 0.579 is considered as medium, which implies that there is a moderate difference between the results of the experimental group versus the control group that is not due to chance.

Finally, Table 15 shows the results of the application of the Mann–Whitney U test to the contrast between post-tests and pre-tests, which were obtained using SPSS™, with a confidence level of 95% and considering the following hypotheses: H_0: the means of the grades obtained by the students in the post-test and the pre-test are similar; H_1: the means of the marks obtained by the students in the post-test and the pre-test are different.

Table 15. Mann–Whitney U Test for post-tests vs. pre-tests.

Course	Group	N	Tests	p	g
Computer Programming	Experimental (G_1)	22	O_1–O_5	0.000	2.860
	Control (G_3)	17	O_3–O_7	0.002	1.433
Graphic Programming	Experimental (G_2)	24	O_2–O_6	0.000	2.713
	Control (G_4)	19	O_4–O_8	0.000	1.735

When comparing the post-tests with the pre-tests in both courses, it can be observed that in all cases the p-value is less than 0.05. Therefore, the null hypothesis (H_0) is rejected in favour of the alternative hypothesis (H_1), with a confidence level of 95%, that is, the means of the grades obtained by the students in the post-test and the pre-test are different. According to the classification made by Cohen [58], the effect size of the experimental treatment (g) with values (in all cases) greater than 0.8 is considered large, which implies that there is a very significant difference between the results of the post-tests and pre-tests that are not due to chance. In addition, these results indicate that there is an improvement on the part of the students in the domain of the specific topics in each course, independent of the group formation strategy that is used, which is more evident in the experimental groups than in the control ones.

The previous statistical analysis shows the positive impact of the experimental treatment applied in this research to the experimental groups compared to the control groups, allowing us to confirm that forming groups for collaborative learning scenarios considering the students' personality traits benefits their academic performance.

6. Conclusions and Further Work

Considering that the problem of obtaining homogeneous, heterogeneous, or mixed groups from a set of students, where several of their characteristics are taken into account (for example, the personality dimensions of the Big Five model), is difficult to solve by analytical or exhaustive search methods, given the combinatorial explosion that occurs depending on the number of students and groups, a heuristic search method, such as genetic algorithms, turned out to be a good alternative for solving it.

The model presented in this paper aims to be a contribution to collaborative learning scenarios since it addresses one of its fundamental requirements: group formation. Therefore, it is very useful to have a solution that automates this process, to do it as efficiently as possible and increase the chances of success of the groups. The proposal aims to make the groups obtained as homogeneous as possible (as similar as possible to the general characteristics of the whole group), as heterogeneous as possible among themselves (to differ as far as possible from the general characteristics of the whole group), or showing a mixture among themselves (that are similar in some characteristics and that differ in others at the same time, concerning the general characteristics of the whole group). To achieve this, the model is made up of two parts. First, it considers the five dimensions proposed by the Big Five model to assess personality: extraversion, agreeableness, conscientiousness, neuroticism, and openness, proposing a specific instrument to measure them. Secondly, it uses genetic algorithms defining an objective function for each individual (a possible grouping), considering grouping as a multi-objective optimization problem.

The innovations of the proposed strategy lay in the grouping criterion considered and in the genetic operators used. Most studies in student group formation that use genetic algorithm approaches focus on grouping based on the students' knowledge level and use crossover and mutation basic operators. The proposed approach took advantage of the personal characteristics arising from the five dimensions of the Big Five model, to improve collaboration and learning outcomes, both at the group and individual level. Additionally, a modification of the named C1 operator was used, a crossover operator for problems where there should not be repeated genes, as is the case under study; and, for mutation, a variation of the swap mutation operator was used. These modified genetic operators allow a more thorough search in the solution space, inserting new genetic information into the population, preventing the algorithm from being trapped in a local minimum.

The validation of the proposed model was carried out concerning the goodness of the genetic algorithms so that the group formation achieves the desired objectives; the results were satisfactory to the extent that the grouping obtained for each of the types (one of the possible ones) ensures that each group reflects more precisely similarity and/or variability with the whole set of students when considering the five dimensions of the Big Five Model as a grouping criterion.

As future work from the pedagogical perspective, it is desirable to improve the evaluation process by measuring not only the academic results of the students but also their performance at a collaborative level in these types of scenarios, which can facilitate knowledge, control, and improvement group work, leading to a progressive acquisition of this competence by students.

After this, it is proposed to assess in each context, also through controlled experiments, what type of approach is most suitable for organizing groups (homogeneous, heterogeneous, or mixed), bearing in mind that a technique and tool are available that facilitate this work and automate it.

In addition, it is suggested to explore which specific dimensions of the personality, evaluated through the Big Five Model, can most directly influence the learning process, particularly programming and software engineering in general. Based on this, eventually a recommendation system could be proposed that suggests what should be the ideal formation of workgroups, considering the specific characteristics of the students and the proposed collaborative activities.

Considering the above, from the computational point of view, the proposed group formation strategy works for any knowledge area—from the pedagogical point of view, an eventual generalization of the proposal would initially require characterization of the personality dimensions that favour collaborative performance in a specific area of knowledge, especially for mixed groups.

It is also proposed as future work to evaluate the additional effort that applying the proposed approach would imply on teachers and students, trying to determine if this "amount of additional effort" is worth making and under what circumstances.

Author Contributions: Conceptualization, O.R.S., C.A.C. and M.A.R.; methodology, O.R.S., C.A.C. and M.A.R.; software, O.R.S.; validation, O.R.S.; formal analysis, O.R.S.; investigation, O.R.S.; writing—original draft preparation, O.R.S.; writing—review and editing, O.R.S., C.A.C. and M.A.R.; supervision, C.A.C. and M.A.R.; funding acquisition, M.A.R. All authors have read and agreed to the published version of the manuscript.

Funding: This research received no external funding.

Institutional Review Board Statement: Ethical review and approval were waived for this study because all participant students were informed about the research's purpose and scope and were ensured their anonymity.

Informed Consent Statement: Informed consent was obtained from all students involved in the study.

Data Availability Statement: The data presented in this study are available on request from the corresponding author.

Acknowledgments: The authors express their thanks to the respective research groups for allowing and supporting the development of this work: Galeras.NET Group, Universidad de Nariño; IDIS Group, Universidad del Cauca; and CHICO Group, Universidad de Castilla-La Mancha. In addition, special recognition to CHICO Research Group of the Universidad de Castilla-La Mancha for having funded the publication of this paper.

Conflicts of Interest: The authors declare no conflict of interest.

References

1. Moreno-Guerrero, A.-J.; Rondón García, M.; Martínez Heredia, N.; Rodríguez-García, A.-M. Collaborative Learning Based on Harry Potter for Learning Geometric Figures in the Subject of Mathematics. *Mathematics* **2020**, *8*, 369. [CrossRef]
2. Cárdenas, M.L.B.; Malagón, L. The Formation of Study Groups: Experiences in the Outset of a Permanent English Teacher Development Program. *Signum Estud. da Ling.* **2007**, *10*, 73–93. [CrossRef]
3. Barkley, E.F.; Major, C.H.; Cross, K.P. *Collaborative Learning Techniques: A Handbook for College Faculty*, 2nd ed.; Jossey-Bass: San Francisco, CA, USA, 2014; ISBN 9781118761557.
4. Lin, Y.-S.; Chang, Y.-C.; Chu, C.-P. Novel Approach to Facilitating Tradeoff Multi-Objective Grouping Optimization. *IEEE Trans. Learn. Technol.* **2016**, *9*, 107–119. [CrossRef]
5. Bekele, R. *Computer-Assisted Learner Group Formation Based on Personality Traits*; University of Hamburg: Hamburg, Germany, 2005.
6. Costaguta, R.; Menini, M.D.L.Á. An Assistant Agent for Group Formation in CSCL Based on Student Learning Styles. In *Proceedings of the 7th Euro American Conference on Telematics and Information Systems—EATIS '14*; ACM Press: Valparaiso, Chile, 2014; pp. 1–4.
7. Lescano, G.; Costaguta, R.; Amandi, A. Genetic Algorithm for Automatic Group Formation Considering Student's Learning Styles. In *Proceedings of the 8th Euro American Conference on Telematics and Information Systems (EATIS)*; IEEE: Cartagena, Colombia, 2016; pp. 1–8.
8. Wang, D.-Y.; Lin, S.S.J.; Sun, C.-T. DIANA: A Computer-Supported Heterogeneous Grouping System for Teachers to Conduct Successful Small Learning Groups. *Comput. Human Behav.* **2007**, *23*, 1997–2010. [CrossRef]
9. Wichmann, A.; Hecking, T.; Elson, M.; Christmann, N.; Herrmann, T.; Hoppe, H.U. Group Formation for Small-Group Learning. In *Proceedings of the 12th International Symposium on Open Collaboration*; ACM: Berlin, Germany, 2016; pp. 1–4.
10. Manske, S.; Hoppe, H.U. Managing Knowledge Diversity: Towards Automatic Semantic Group Formation. In Proceedings of the 17th International Conference on Advanced Learning Technologies (ICALT), Timisoara, Romania, 3–7 July 2017; IEEE: Timisoara, Romania, 2017; pp. 330–332.
11. Zheng, Z.; Pinkwart, N. A Discrete Particle Swarm Optimization Approach to Compose Heterogeneous Learning Groups. In Proceedings of the 14th International Conference on Advanced Learning Technologies, Athens, Greece, 7–10 July 2014; IEEE: Athens, Greece, 2014; pp. 49–51.
12. Amarasinghe, I.; Hernandez-Leo, D.; Jonsson, A. Intelligent Group Formation in Computer Supported Collaborative Learning Scripts. In Proceedings of the 17th International Conference on Advanced Learning Technologies (ICALT), Timisoara, Romania, 3–7 July 2017; IEEE: Timisoara, Romania, 2017; pp. 201–203.
13. Sadeghi, H.; Kardan, A.A. Toward Effective Group Formation in Computer-Supported Collaborative Learning. *Interact. Learn. Environ.* **2016**, *24*, 382–395. [CrossRef]
14. Lykourentzou, I.; Antoniou, A.; Naudet, Y.; Dow, S.P. Personality Matters. In *Proceedings of the 19th ACM Conference on Computer-Supported Cooperative Work & Social Computing*; ACM: San Francisco, CA, USA, 2016; pp. 260–273.
15. Duque Reis, R.C. *Formação de Grupos Em Ambientes Cscl Utilizando Traços de Personalidade Associados Às Teorias de Aprendizagem Colaborativa*; Universidade de São Paulo: São Carlos, Brazil, 2019.

16. Battur, S.; Patil, M.S.; Desai, P.; Vijayalakshmi, M.; Raikar, M.M.; Hegde, P.; Joshi, G.H. Enhancing the Students Project with Team Based Learning Approach: A Case Study. In Proceedings of the 4th International Conference on MOOCs, Innovation and Technology in Education (MITE); IEEE: Madurai, India, 2016; pp. 275–280.
17. Borges, S.; Mizoguchi, R.; Bittencourt, I.I.; Isotani, S. Group Formation in CSCL: A Review of the State of the Art. In *Higher Education for All. From Challenges to Novel Technology-Enhanced Solutions. HEFA 2017. Communications in Computer and Information Science*; Cristea, A.I., Bittencourt, I.I., Lima, F., Eds.; Springer: Cham, Switzerland, 2018; Volume 832, pp. 71–88, ISBN 9783319979335.
18. Jung, C. *Psychological Types*; Taylor & Francis Ltd.: London, UK, 2017; ISBN 9781138687424.
19. Keirsey, D. *Please Understand Me II: Temperament, Character, Intelligence*; Prometheus Nemesis Book Company: Carlsbad, CA, USA, 2006; ISBN 9781885705020.
20. McCrae, R.R.; Allik, J. *The Five-Factor Model of Personality Across Cultures*; Springer: Boston, MA, USA, 2002; ISBN 9780306473555.
21. Torrin, K. *A Guide to Myers-Briggs Type Indicator (MBTI), Including Its Background, Concepts, Applications, and More*; Webster's Digital Services: New York, NY, USA, 2012; ISBN 9781276177030.
22. Aguilar, R.A.; De Antonio, A.; Imbert, R. Searching Pancho's Soul: An Intelligent Virtual Agent for Human Teams. In Proceedings of the Electronics, Robotics and Automotive Mechanics Conference (CERMA 2007), Morelos, Mexico, 25–28 September 2007; IEEE: Morelos, Mexico, 25 September 2007; pp. 568–571.
23. Soto, C.J.; Kronauer, A.; Liang, J.K. Five-Factor Model of Personality. In *The Encyclopedia of Adulthood and Aging*; Krauss Whitbourne, S., Ed.; John Wiley & Sons, Inc.: Hoboken, NJ, USA, 2015; pp. 1–5. ISBN 9781118528921.
24. John, O.P.; Naumann, L.P.; Soto, C.J. Paradigm shift to the integrative Big Five trait taxonomy: History, measurement, and conceptual issues. In *Handbook of Personality: Theory and Research*; John, O.P., Robins, R.W., Pervin, L.A., Eds.; The Guilford Press: New York, NY, USA, 2008; pp. 114–158. ISBN 9781606237380.
25. Sleep, C.E.; Lynam, D.R.; Miller, J.D. A Comparison of the Validity of Very Brief Measures of the Big Five/Five-Factor Model of Personality. *Assessment* **2020**, *28*, 739–758. [CrossRef] [PubMed]
26. Maldonado Pérez, M. El Trabajo Colaborativo En El Aula Universitaria. *Laurus Rev. Educ.* **2007**, *13*, 263–278.
27. Chaljub Hasbún, J.M. Trabajo Colaborativo Como Estrategia de Enseñanza En La Universidad/Collaborative Work as a Teaching Strategy in the University. *Cuad. Pedagog. Univ.* **2015**, *11*, 64–71. [CrossRef]
28. Johnson, D.W.; Johnson, R.T.; Johnson Holubec, E. *The New Circles of Learning: Cooperation in the Classroom and School*; ASCD: Alexandria, VI, USA, 1994; ISBN 9780871202277.
29. Revelo-Sánchez, O.; Collazos-Ordóñez, C.A.; Jiménez-Toledo, J.A. El Trabajo Colaborativo Como Estrategia Didáctica Para La Enseñanza/Aprendizaje de La Programación: Una Revisión Sistemática de Literatura. *TecnoLógicas* **2018**, *21*, 115–134. [CrossRef]
30. Holland, J.H. *Adaptation in Natural and Artificial Systems: An Introductory Analysis with Applications to Biology, Control, and Artificial Intelligence*; MIT University Press: Cambridge, MA, USA, 1992; ISBN 9780262275552.
31. Wang, R.; Sato, Y.; Liu, S. Mutated Specification-Based Test Data Generation with a Genetic Algorithm. *Mathematics* **2021**, *9*, 331. [CrossRef]
32. Díaz, D.; Valledor, P.; Ena, B.; Iglesias, M.; Menéndez, C. Improved Method for Parallelization of Evolutionary Metaheuristics. *Mathematics* **2020**, *8*, 1476. [CrossRef]
33. Goldberg, D.E. *Genetic Algorithms*; Pearson Education: New York, NY, USA, 2006; ISBN 9788177588293.
34. Alba, E.; Dorronsoro, B. Solving the Vehicle Routing Problem by Using Cellular Genetic Algorithms. In *Evolutionary Computation in Combinatorial Optimization. EvoCOP 2004. Lecture Notes in Computer Science*; Gottlieb, J., Raidl, G.R., Eds.; Springer: Berlin, Germany, 2004; Volume 3004, pp. 11–20. ISBN 9783540213673.
35. Asadzadeh, L. A Local Search Genetic Algorithm for the Job Shop Scheduling Problem with Intelligent Agents. *Comput. Ind. Eng.* **2015**, *85*, 376–383. [CrossRef]
36. Pongcharoen, P.; Hicks, C.; Braiden, P.M.; Stewardson, D.J. Determining Optimum Genetic Algorithm Parameters for Scheduling the Manufacturing and Assembly of Complex Products. *Int. J. Prod. Econ.* **2002**, *78*, 311–322. [CrossRef]
37. Rezoug, A.; Bader-El-Den, M.; Boughaci, D. Guided Genetic Algorithm for the Multidimensional Knapsack Problem. *Memetic Comput.* **2018**, *10*, 29–42. [CrossRef]
38. Vaishnav, P.; Choudhary, N.; Jain, K. Traveling Salesman Problem Using Genetic Algorithm: A Survey. *Int. J. Sci. Res. Comput. Sci. Eng. Inf. Technol.* **2017**, *2*, 105–108.
39. Zhang, W.; Lu, J.; Zhang, H.; Wang, C.; Gen, M. Fast Multi-Objective Hybrid Evolutionary Algorithm for Flow Shop Scheduling Problem. In *Proceedings of the Tenth International Conference on Management Science and Engineering Management. Advances in Intelligent Systems and Computing*; Xu, J., Hajiyev, A., Nickel, S., Gen, M., Eds.; Springer: Baku, Azerbaijan, 2016; pp. 383–392.
40. Ani, Z.C.; Yasin, A.; Husin, M.Z.; Hamid, Z.A. A Method for Group Formation Using Genetic Algorithm. *Int. J. Comput. Sci. Eng.* **2010**, *2*, 3060–3064.
41. Deleón, A.F.; Gómez, S.; Moreno, J. Uso de Tests de Aptitud y Algoritmos Genéticos Para La Conformación de Grupos En Ambientes Colaborativos de Aprendizaje. *Av. Sist. Inf.* **2009**, *6*, 165–172.
42. Amara, S.; Macedo, J.; Bendella, F.; Santos, A. Group Formation in Mobile Computer Supported Collaborative Learning Contexts: A Systematic Literature Review. *Educ. Technol. Soc.* **2016**, *19*, 258–273.
43. Odo, C.; Masthoff, J.; Beacham, N.; Alhathli, M. Affective State for Learning Activities Selection. In Proceedings of the Intelligent Mentoring Systems Workshop Associated with the 19th International Conference on Artificial Intelligence in Education, AIED 2018, London, UK, 27 June 2018; pp. 1–10.

44. Cruz, W.M.; Isotani, S. Group Formation Algorithms in Collaborative Learning Contexts: A Systematic Mapping of the Literature. In *Collaboration and Technology. CRIWG 2014. Lecture Notes in Computer Science*; Baloian, N., Burstein, F., Ogata, H., Santoro, F., Zurita, G., Eds.; Springer: Cham, Switzerland, 2014; Volume 8658, pp. 199–214. ISBN 9783319101651.
45. John, O.P.; Robins, R.W.; Pervin, L.A. *Handbook of Personality*, 3rd ed.; The Guilford Press: New York, NY, USA, 2008; ISBN 9781593858360.
46. Benet-Martínez, V.; John, O.P. Los Cinco Grandes across Cultures and Ethnic Groups: Multitrait-Multimethod Analyses of the Big Five in Spanish and English. *J. Pers. Soc. Psychol.* **1998**, *75*, 729–750. [CrossRef]
47. Moreno, J.; Rivera, J.C.; Ceballos, Y.F. Agrupamiento Homogéneo de Elementos Con Múltiples Atributos Mediante Algoritmos Genéticos. *DYNA* **2011**, *78*, 246–254.
48. Han, J.; Kamber, M. *Data Mining: Concepts and Techniques*, 2nd ed.; Elsevier Inc.: San Francisco, CA, USA, 2006; ISBN 9780080475585.
49. Conradie, W.; Goranko, V. *Logic and Discrete Mathematics: A Concise Introduction*; John Wiley & Sons, Ltd.: Hoboken, NJ, USA, 2015; ISBN 9781118751275.
50. Kramer, O. Evolutionary Self-Adaptation: A Survey of Operators and Strategy Parameters. *Evol. Intell.* **2010**, *3*, 51–65. [CrossRef]
51. Mirjalili, S. Genetic Algorithm. In *Evolutionary Algorithms and Neural Networks. Studies in Computational Intelligence*; Springer: Cham, Switzerland, 2018; pp. 43–55. ISBN 9783319930251.
52. Reza Hejazi, S.; Saghafian, S. Flowshop-Scheduling Problems with Makespan Criterion: A Review. *Int. J. Prod. Res.* **2005**, *43*, 2895–2929. [CrossRef]
53. Araujo, L.; Cervigón, C. *Algoritmos Evolutivos: Un Enfoque Práctico*; Alfaomega Grupo Editor: Ciudad de México, México, 2009; ISBN 9786077686293.
54. Revelo-Sánchez, O.; Collazos, C.A.; Solano, A.F.; Fardoun, H. Diseño Colaborativo Basado En ThinkLets Como Apoyo a La Enseñanza de La Programación. *Rev. Colomb. Comput.* **2020**, *21*, 22–33. [CrossRef]
55. Kirk, R.E. *Experimental Design—Procedures for the Behavioral Sciences*, 4th ed.; SAGE Publications, Inc.: Los Angeles, CA, USA, 2013; ISBN 9781412974455.
56. Duzhin, F.; Gustafsson, A. Machine Learning-Based App for Self-Evaluation of Teacher-Specific Instructional Style and Tools. *Educ. Sci.* **2018**, *8*, 7. [CrossRef]
57. Ledesma, R.; Macbeth, G.; Cortada De Kohan, N. Tamaño Del Efecto: Revisión Teórica y Aplicaciones Con El Sistema Estadístico ViSta. *Rev. Latinoam. Psicol.* **2008**, *40*, 425–439.
58. Cohen, J. *Statistical Power Analysis for the Behavioral Sciences*, 2nd ed.; Lawrence Erlbaum Associates: New York, NY, USA, 1988; ISBN 9780805802832.

Article

Machine Learning Prediction of University Student Dropout: Does Preference Play a Key Role?

Marina Segura [1,*], **Jorge Mello** [2] **and Adolfo Hernández** [1]

[1] Department of Financial and Actuarial Economics & Statistics, Universidad Complutense de Madrid, 28223 Madrid, Spain
[2] Faculty of Exact and Technological Sciences, Universidad Nacional de Concepción, Concepción 010123, Paraguay
* Correspondence: marina.segura@ucm.es

Abstract: University dropout rates are a problem that presents many negative consequences. It is an academic issue and carries an unfavorable economic impact. In recent years, significant efforts have been devoted to the early detection of students likely to drop out. This paper uses data corresponding to dropout candidates after their first year in the third largest face-to-face university in Europe, with the goal of predicting likely dropout either at the beginning of the course of study or at the end of the first semester. In this prediction, we considered the five major program areas. Different techniques have been used: first, a Feature Selection Process in order to identify the variables more correlated with dropout; then, some Machine Learning Models (Support Vector Machines, Decision Trees and Artificial Neural Networks) as well as a Logistic Regression. The results show that dropout detection does not work only with enrollment variables, but it improves after the first semester results. Academic performance is always a relevant variable, but there are others, such as the level of preference that the student had over the course that he or she was finally able to study. The success of the techniques depends on the program areas. Machine Learning obtains the best results, but a simple Logistic Regression model can be used as a reasonable baseline.

Keywords: student dropout; machine learning; Feature Selection; Artificial Neural Networks; Support Vector Machines; decision trees; logistic regression

MSC: 62-07; 62H12; 62P25

Citation: Segura, M.; Mello, J.; Hernández, A. Machine Learning Prediction of University Student Dropout: Does Preference Play a Key Role? *Mathematics* **2022**, *10*, 3359. https://doi.org/10.3390/math10183359

Academic Editor: Vassilis C. Gerogiannis

Received: 7 August 2022
Accepted: 13 September 2022
Published: 16 September 2022

Publisher's Note: MDPI stays neutral with regard to jurisdictional claims in published maps and institutional affiliations.

Copyright: © 2022 by the authors. Licensee MDPI, Basel, Switzerland. This article is an open access article distributed under the terms and conditions of the Creative Commons Attribution (CC BY) license (https://creativecommons.org/licenses/by/4.0/).

1. Introduction

Dropping out at the university level is a problem for education systems around the world, as well as for academic and financial managers from different institutions, teachers, and students themselves. University dropouts have an economic and social impact, in addition to the students' negative self-perception due to the feeling of failure and frustration that is generated. In 2017, the average percentage of university dropouts in public institutions the Bachelor's level remained at around 30% in OECD member countries [1]. For the European community, student dropout is a major challenge since one of its objectives is to improve the knowledge and skills to meet the needs of the labor market and to implement a more productive and socially equitable environment [2].

Previous studies carried out in Spain indicate that the phenomenon is linked to the students' type of degree program. The program areas with the highest dropout rate are the Arts and Humanities (45.9%), while science degrees have the lowest percentage (16.6%), and it takes place mainly from the first year onwards [3–5]. These studies have also emphasized the time students spend per week studying in different program areas, and it has been observed that the longer the study time, the lower the dropout rate [6].

A problem that has been widely addressed is the design of predictive systems to anticipate the risk of students dropping out of higher education and identify students with a high probability of dropping out to implement retention policies [7]. To this end, several educational data mining techniques have been implemented, such as the use of Decision Trees, K-Nearest Neighbors (KNN), Support Vector Machines (SVM), Bayesian Classification, Artificial Neural Networks (ANN), Logistic Regression, a combination of classifiers and others (Agrusti et al., 2020). Machine learning techniques have also been used to predict students' academic performance [8,9].

According to Behr et al. [6], the development of an accurate prediction model for student dropout should be the focus of further empirical research, identifying groups of students with similar dropout motives, detecting the reason for dropping out may reveal details within the dropout process and the development of early warning systems and individual or group support mechanisms for at-risk students in order to prevent dropout at an early stage. The objective of this work is the development of statistical methods that allow the early detection of student dropout. The statistical models to be implemented are those typified in the literature as Learning Analytics or Educational Data Mining. These data analysis techniques, although novel, are already a reference in recent international scientific publications in the area of statistics and Big Data and remain a subject of research for their scope and usefulness with complex data from institutional educational platforms. This research will allow significant advances in the prevention of university dropout, as well as help address the economic and social impacts of this phenomenon.

Referential Framework

University dropout is a polysemic concept, and for its use, it needs a clear definition in order to avoid ambiguity. Larsen et al. [10] analyzed the different aspects and use of the term and defined it in a negative sense as the "non-completion" of a given university program of study. It is necessary to differentiate the level at which dropout occurs, in that students may change degrees but remain in the field of study, move to another university for different reasons, or drop out of the university system [6].

In the report by Fernández-Mellizo [11] on the dropout of undergraduate students in on-site universities in Spain, it was defined as the dropout of any undergraduate university study, excluding the change of degree. It was calculated with respect to a cohort of new entrants and was limited to students enrolled for the first time in a degree program and who did not re-enroll for two consecutive years. In particular, dropping out after the first year refers to the number of new students who, having enrolled in the first year, have not enrolled in the following two years. The dropout rate is obtained by dividing this number by the total number of new students. According to this report, the first year is the most delicate moment from the point of view of dropouts, and after this moment, the probability of dropping out decreases.

In order to reduce the dropout rate, it is necessary to identify the factors and the profile of students who dropped out of university studies. In a previous study [12], the main predictors were identified as the student's time commitment, whether part-time or full-time, the access score, and the area of knowledge. In this study, multilevel logistic regression and decision tree techniques were applied with a mainly descriptive purpose.

One of the purposes of this work is to predict and identify students at risk of dropping out as accurately and quickly as possible. A feature of data mining techniques that allow combining determinants from several areas, e.g., personal, academic and non-academic characteristics, to a single rule to predict dropout, program change, or continuation of studies [13]. For a review of data mining in education, see [14] for an example.

According to Frawley et al. [15], data mining is the non-trivial extraction of implicit, previously unknown, and potentially useful information from data through machine learning algorithms with the purpose of identifying patterns or relationships in a data set, being one of its main tasks in predictive modeling. In this study, a set of data mining techniques, including Decision Tree, KNN, SVM, ANN and Logistic Regression, are implemented with the purpose of contrasting the results obtained, drawing conclusions from coinciding results, and assessing the relevant information provided by some of these techniques in a specific way.

The rest of the paper is organized as follows: Section 2 presents the dataset and introduces the different Machine Learning methods applied. Section 3 includes the main results. Finally, the discussion and conclusions are presented in Section 4.

2. Materials and Methods

2.1. The Dataset

The proposed analysis of student dropouts and the determination of the most relevant variables was carried out using data obtained from the Integrated Institutional Data System (Sistema Integrado de Datos Institucionales—SIDI) of the Universidad Complutense de Madrid (UCM), a well-known Spanish public university and the third largest on-site university in Europe.

The data identify enrolled first-year students in the 17–18 academic year of 10 degrees taught at the university in five different areas: Social Sciences and Law, Sciences, Health Sciences, Engineering and Arts and Humanities (Figure 1).

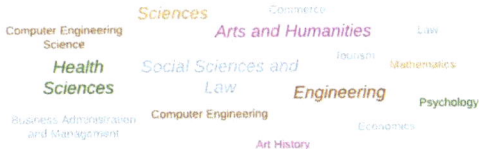

Figure 1. Areas and university degrees under study.

The students have been characterized according to a set of variables that can be grouped into three categories: socio-economic variables, enrollment variables, and academic performance variables during the first semester of university. The first category includes variables, such as gender, age, parents' or guardians' level of education, municipality of residence, and nationality, among others. The second group has variables such as type of school (public or private), university entrance mark, number of degree preferences for the student, and entrance study (school, professional training, and entrance specialization). Finally, among the variables of the first semester of the university are the amount of the enrollment fee, the number of European Credit Transfer System (ECTS) (enrolled and passed), the average mark for the first semester, and whether the student holds a scholarship. The list and description of all the variables used are detailed in Appendix A. The number of students enrolled for the first time in the different degrees in each of the academic years is shown in Table 1.

Table 1. Number of enrolled students and dropouts per degree and its percentage.

Degree	Enrollees	Dropouts	Percentage
Business Administration and Management	564	86	15.25%
Economics	275	78	28.36%
Commerce	223	30	13.45%
Tourism	217	32	14.75%
Law	869	119	13.69%
Mathematics	154	19	12.34%
Psychology	705	75	10.64%
Computer Engineering	70	27	38.57%
Computer Science Engineering	116	16	13.79%
Art History	235	59	25.11%
Total	3428	541	15.78%

2.2. Data Processing

Once the database of students has been obtained, the processing of those who dropped out after the first year begins. According to the definition of dropout considered in this study, a student drops out when they do not enroll for any ECTS in the following two years. Table 1 shows the number of students who have dropped out of the degree in which they enrolled, the dropout has been verified both by the number of ECTS enrolled and by the payment of the enrollment fee.

The steps we followed to obtain University Dropouts Predictions are illustrated in Figure 2. First, search for the most relevant variables to predict dropout. Second, clean the data taking care of missing data and errors. Third, code the database to perform statistical analysis and machine learning techniques. Fourth, perform the statistical analysis of the preliminary variables and the application of the machine learning models. Finally, analyze the predictions of dropouts and the techniques used.

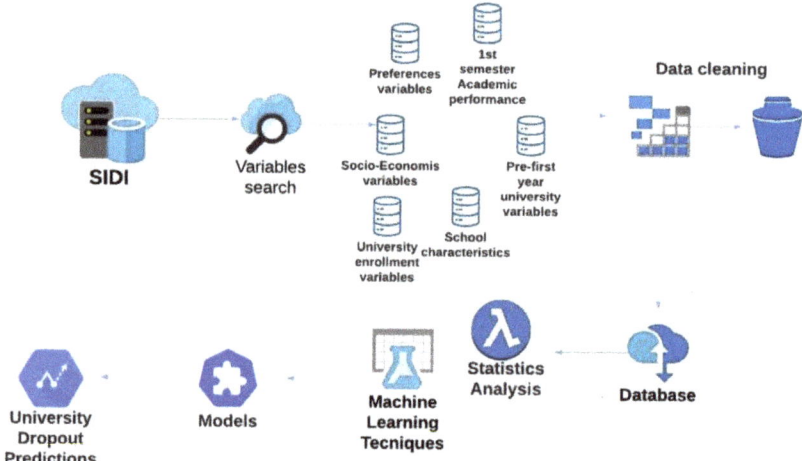

Figure 2. Set of processes followed to obtain University Dropout Predictions.

2.3. Machine Learning Methods

Machine Learning is generally divided into three categories: supervised, unsupervised and semi-supervised. Supervised learning is the task of mapping inputs to the corresponding output, where there is a prior set of input–output pairs given as examples [16,17]. Supervised learning methods whose target variable is discrete are called supervised classification.

In this study, Feature Selection (FS) is implemented in the first stage, and then five predictive machine learning methods are applied: ANN, SVM, KNN, Decision Tree and Logistic Regression. These techniques were chosen considering the effectiveness demonstrated in related works consulted in the literature [18,19].

For model training, the dataset was divided into two parts: training (70%) and test (30%). The performance of each technique was measured through the confusion matrices and the accuracy in predicting dropout and non-dropout [7].

2.3.1. Feature Selection

Feature selection (FS) aims to select a smaller and appropriate subset of features (predictor variables) to improve classification efficiency so the redundant and unimportant features can be removed. FS favors minimizing overfitting, reducing data dimensionality, improving accuracy, eliminating irrelevant data, and speeding up training, among many other advantages. FS does not transform the original set of variables, thus preserving the interpretation and validating them in line with the objective of the analysis. FS methods are generally classified into filters, wrappers, embedded and hybrids [20].

The filter methods prove to be fast, scalable, computationally simple and classifier-independent. Multivariate filter methods consider feature dependencies and interaction with the classification algorithm [21]. One of the most commonly used filter methods is the so-called Correlation-based Feature Selection. This method uses the correlation coefficient to determine the features that are strongly correlated with the target variable and, at the same time, have a low inter-correlation with the other features [22].

For the ranking of the variables, one variable at a time and its relationship to the target variable is considered. The importance value of each variable is calculated as 1-p, where p is the p-value of the test statistic between the candidate variable and the target variable.

2.3.2. Artificial Neural Networks

ANN are considered one of the most efficient machine learning techniques. As their name suggests, they are computational networks that attempt to simulate the decision process in networks of neurons of a biological central nervous system. ANNs have been used in different scientific fields for prediction, classification and modeling tasks. Several studies have used this technique to predict student performance and to determine the factors that influence the educational process [23].

The ANN model is based on three main layers: an input layer, which links the input signal (X_j) to the neuron through a set of weights (W_{kj}). The next step involves a hidden layer, which compiles the bias values b_k and also the input signals. This layer is weighted by the corresponding weights of the neuron. Lastly, the output layer is applied to limit the amplitude of the output of the neuron utilizing the activation transfer function. To increase or decrease the net output of the neuron, a bias must be added [24,25].

ANN is represented as the following mathematical structure of a neuron k:

$$U_k = \sum_{j=1}^{n} \left(W_{kj} X_j \right)$$
$$Y_k = f(U_k + b_k)$$
(1)

where U_k represents the linear combiner, X_j are the input signals, W_{kj} are the weights for neuron k, b_k is the bias value, $f(\cdot)$ is the activation transfer function, and Y_k is the output signal of the neuron; a detailed explanation can be found in [26]. Multilayer perceptron (MLP) and radial basis function (RBF) networks are widely used as supervised training methods.

According to [27], MLP is applied to classification problems by using the error back-propagation algorithm. The main objective of this algorithm is to minimize the estimation error by calculating all the weights of the network, and systematically updating these weights to achieve the best neural network configuration.

The ability of ANNs to learn from provided examples makes it a powerful and flexible technique, but its effectiveness is related to the amount of data and the proper selection of the neural network architecture.

2.3.3. Support Vector Machines

SVM has been used to predict student performance, risk of failure, and overall, as a predictive technique in educational data mining [19] and is a widely used supervised learning approach for classification analysis. It transforms the training data into a high-dimensional feature space and determines an optimal linear solution by means of a separating hyperplane [17].

Consider the non-linear transformation $\Phi : R^m \to H$ in order to represent the input vectors in a new feature space $\Phi(x) \in H$. The kernel function indicates similarity, which is obtained by scalar product between two given vectors in the transformed space $\Phi(u) \cdot \Phi(v) = K(u,v)$ [24,28]. The most used kernel function is:

$$\text{Gaussian } K(u,v) = exp\left(-\sigma \|u-v\|^2\right) \quad (2)$$

Given the problem of binary classification consisting of N examples of training. Each example is indicated by a tuple (X_i, y_i) where X corresponds to the set of attributes, for example i, and the class denomination is indicated by $y_i \in \{1, -1\}$. The learning task with SVM can be formalized as the following constrained optimization problem [29]:

$$\begin{array}{l} \text{Max } L = \sum_i^N \lambda_i + \frac{1}{2} \sum_{i,j} \lambda_i \lambda_j y_i y_j K(X_i, X_j) \\ \text{such that } \sum_i^N \lambda_i y_i = 0 \text{ and } \lambda_i \geq 0 \text{ for all } i. \end{array} \quad (3)$$

A test case Z can be classified using the equation $f(z) = sign(\sum_i^n \lambda_i y_i K(X_i, Z) + b)$, where λ_i is a Lagrange multiplier, b is a parameter, and K is a kernel function.

SVM is a technique known to adapt well to high-dimensional data; as a limitation, it can be noted that its performance depends on the proper selection of its parameters and the kernel function.

2.3.4. K-Nearest Neighborhood

The KNN algorithm is a simple nonparametric classification method. It has achieved excellent results in previous studies on university dropouts [30]. The classification of an object is based on the assumption that data points similar to each other belong to the same class [31].

According to [32], the k-Nearest Neighborhood classifies an object O by taking into account the class of the object which is most similar to O. To begin, we need to find an objective way to measure the similarity. It is possible to achieve this by representing objects in the training set as numerical vectors $x \in R^n$ being n is the number of features of each object. In order to give an objective measure that states how similar two objects are, it is possible to use any distance function defined in the n-dimensional space, for instance, the Euclidean distance function. The Euclidean distance function for two objects x and y is shown in Equation (4):

$$d(x,y) = \sqrt{\sum_{i=1}^n (x_i - y_i)^2} \quad (4)$$

The object C in the training set with the smallest distance to O will be the nearest to O assigning C to this class. Different approach assigns the set S of the first k objects nearest to O and selects the class in which most of the objects in S belong. Ties are arbitrarily broken.

The strengths of KNN include its interpretability and easy implementation; however, it can take longer to run for larger datasets.

2.3.5. Decision Tree

The Decision Tree has been shown to effectively predict students' academic performance, dropout and retention behaviors [33,34]. Decision Trees use a recursive partitioning mechanism for their construction. At each node, the data is divided into two distinct groups according to a given criteria; these groups are further divided into smaller subsets with the same procedure, and so on, until their completion.

Consider $U = \{A_1, \ldots, A_n\}$ representing a set of attributes of a set Ω of objects. In the Decision Tree approach, each node i is related to an attribute A_i and a subset of objects in Ω. The tree structure includes a root node, internal nodes and leaf nodes. The root node contains all the objects in Ω. Internal node i comes from the root node, and S_i is the subset of Ω associated to i. A leaf node contains all objects of the same class. The procedure to classify an object starts from the root node and inspects each node i until a leaf node is reached [32].

The CHAID (CHi-squared Automatic Interaction Detector) is one of the oldest decision tree algorithms [35]. It uses the Chi-square independence test to decide on the splitting rule for each node. The Pearson chi-square statistic is calculated as follows:

$$X^2 = \sum_{j=1}^{J} \sum_{i=1}^{I} \frac{(n_{ij} - \hat{m}_{ij})^2}{\hat{m}_{ij}} \tag{5}$$

where $n_{ij} = \sum_n f_n I(x_n = i, y_n = j)$ is the observed cell frequency and $\hat{m}_{ij}$ is the expected cell frequency for cell $(x_n = i, y_n = j)$ from the independence model. The corresponding p-value is calculated as $p = P(\chi^2 > X^2)$, where χ^2 follows a chi-square distribution with $d = (J-1)(I-1)$ degrees of freedom.

Decision Tree has a simple and easily understandable schematic representation. Its main limitation is that it can overfit the data.

2.3.6. Logistic Regression

Logistic Regression is a very popular classification model used in different program areas and problems, including educational data mining and dropout prediction [36]. It is analogous to linear regression but uses a categorical target field instead of a numerical one, instead of a numeric one.

The LR considers n data records $x_{i1}, \ldots, x_{ip}$, which represent p input variables. Each record contains an observation y_i. The observations $y_1, \ldots, y_n$ are binary (values 0 or 1). The LR methodology is based on estimating the probability that the observation is 1.

The problem presented by linear probabilistic models as LR, in terms of the existence of out-of-range predictions (negative or greater than one), is due to the fact that they use a probability function that depends linearly on the explanatory variables, which would be solved by narrowing the probability distribution. To solve this problem, the regression function is transformed with a function F:

$$F(t) = \frac{exp(t)}{1 + exp(t)} \tag{6}$$

where $t = h(x_{i1}, \ldots, x_{ip}) = \beta_0 + \beta_1 x_{i1} \ldots + \beta_p x_{ip}$. This model is called the Logit model, due to the transformation function F, and it is the most common regression model for binary target variables.

Logistic Regression is a traditional classification technique, easy to implement and interpret. Due to the initial assumptions, the technique has limitations with non-linear and correlated data. More details on the Logistic Regression algorithm can be found at [31].

2.4. Predictor Importance

Predictor importance uses sensitivity analysis to determine the reduction in variance in the target variable attributable to each predictor. Let Y represent the target variable and X_j the predictors, where $j = 1, \ldots, k$. Predictor importance is then computed as the normalized sensitivity:

$$VI_i = \frac{S_i}{\sum_{j=1}^{k} S_j} \tag{7}$$

where $S_i = \frac{V(E(Y/X_i))}{V(Y)}$ and $V(Y)$ is the unconditional output variance.

In this work, the method of calculating the importance of the predictor indicated above was used in the ANN, SVM, Logistic Regression and Decision Tree machine learning methods [31]. The determination of predictors with the highest importance for the KNN method is based on the envelope approach of Cunningham and Delany [37]. The predictors of greatest importance sequentially consider the variable that causes the greatest decrease in error rate or sum of squares error.

3. Results

3.1. Preliminary Analysis

First, we categorized the groups of students into those who dropped out in the first year and those who did not. Then, we analyzed the statistical patterns of the different variables in both groups in order to find significant differences. To this end, it is possible to opt for inference techniques such as Chi-square or *t*-test, depending on the nature of the variables (Tables 2 and 3). Some relevant outcomes of the study are highlighted below, i.e., the significant differences at 99%, 95% and 90%. See Appendix B for details.

Table 2. Preliminary results of significant qualitative variables.

Variables	Not Dropout	Dropout
Degree	Business Administration and Management (84.8%) Economics (71.6%) Commerce (86.5%) Tourism (85.3%) Law (86.3%) Mathematics (87.7%) Psychology (89.4%) Computer Engineering (61.4%) Computer Science Engineering (86.2%) Art History (74.9%)	Business Administration and Management (15.2%) Economics (28.4%) Commerce (13.5%) Tourism (14.7%) Law (13.7%) Mathematics (12.3%) Psychology (10.6%) Computer Engineering (38.6%) Computer Science Engineering (13.8%) Art History (25.1%)
Area	Social Science and Law (83.9%) Sciences (87.7%) Health Sciences (89.4%) Engineering (76.9%) Arts and Humanities (74.9%)	Social Science and Law (16.1%) Sciences (12.3%) Health Sciences (10.6%) Engineering (23.1%) Arts and Humanities (25.1%)
Gender	Men (81.6%), Women (87.2%)	Men (18.4%), Women (12.8%)
Access Specialty	Social Science and Humanities (82.8%) Technical Sciences (87.1%) Health Sciences (73.3%) Arts (61.1%)	Social Science and Humanities (17.2%) Technical Sciences (12.9%) Health Sciences (26.7%) Arts (38.9%)
Mother's or guardian's level of studies	Illiterate (100.0%) No education (85.0%) Primary education (81.9%) Secondary education (83.3%) Higher education (86.6%)	Illiterate (0.0%) No education (15.0%) Primary education (18.1%) Secondary education (16.7%) Higher education (13.4%)
Father's or guardian's level of studies	Illiterate (96.6%) No education (81.8%) Primary education (83.7%) Secondary education (82.7%) Higher education (86.3%)	Illiterate (3.4%) No education (18.2%) Primary education (16.3%) Secondary education (17.3%) Higher education (13.7%)
Scholarship holder	Yes (85.8%), No (82.9%)	Yes (14.2%), No (17.1%)
Type of scholarship	Education Ministry (85.4%) University (94.8%)	Education Ministry (14.6%) University (5.2%)
PAU Call	Ordinary (85.3%), Extraordinary (77.5%)	Ordinary (14.7%), Extraordinary (22.5%)
Admission Reason	General (84.5%) Disabled (81.3%) Elite athletes (61.5%)	General (15.5%) Disabled (18.8%) Elite athletes (38.5%)

Significant differences have been found linked to the degree and the area to which they belong with regard to the percentage of students who dropped out of the degree program in the first year. The degree with the highest dropout rate is Computer Engineering (38.6%), followed by Economics (28.4%) and Art History (25.1%). In the rest of the degrees, the dropout rate is between 10 and 15%, where Psychology has the lowest rate (10.6%) and

Business Administration and Management the highest (15.2%). The areas with the highest dropout rates are Humanities and Engineering, with 25.1% and 23.1%, respectively.

Table 3. Preliminary results of significant quantitative variables.

Variables	Not Dropout	Dropout
Academic Amount	$\overline{A.A.} = 1516.74$ €	$\overline{A.A.} = 1612.36$ €
Admission Option	$\overline{A.O.} = 1.28$	$\overline{A.O.} = 1.37$
PAU grade	$\overline{PAU\ g.} = 6.75$	$\overline{PAU\ g.} = 6.48$
Access grade	$\overline{Access\ g.} = 8.50$	$\overline{Access\ g.} = 8.00$
Age	$\overline{Age} = 19.22$ years	$\overline{Age} = 19.68$ years
First-semester grade	$\overline{Grade\ 1st\ sem.} = 5.69$	$\overline{Grade\ 1st\ sem.} = 3.57$
No. of ECTS Passed 1st semester	$\overline{No\ ECTS\ P.\ 1st} = 19.76\ ECTS$	$\overline{No\ ECTS\ P.\ 1st} = 8.46\ ECTS$
No. of ECTS Enrolled 1st semester	$\overline{No\ ECTS\ E.\ 1st.} = 30.14\ ECTS$	$\overline{No\ ECTS\ E.\ 1st.} = 29.79\ ECTS$
Ratio of subject passes 1st semester	$\overline{R.\ p.\ 1st} = 0.66$	$\overline{R.\ p.\ 1st} = 0.29$

Values are the mean of each variable for each group.

The gender differences are significant; men are dropping out more than women, 18.4% compared to 12.8%. The university entrance specialties in which most students drop out in the first year of their studies are Arts (38.9%) and Health Sciences (26.7%), and the lowest are Technical Sciences (12.9%) and Humanities and Social Sciences (17.2%).

The dropout rate is lower when the students' parents have attended higher education, around 13%, and rises when they have only primary, secondary, or no education (15–18%). In the case of illiterate parents, the dropout rate is very low (less than 5%), but this is a very small group.

Scholarship holders drop out in a lower proportion than students who do not have a scholarship (14.2% compared to 17.1%). In relation to the type of grant, there is a significant difference between those with a state grant, who dropped out to a greater extent (14.6%) compared to those with a grant from the university itself, where only 5.2% dropped out.

The dropout rate is 7% higher when students enter with entering after a retake exam, even though it is a very small group, 38.5% of elite sportsmen and women drop out in the first year.

If the same analysis is carried out for qualitative variables differentiating by areas to which the university degrees under study belong, the following significant results can be found. In the area of Social Sciences and Law, students entering from Arts and Health Sciences drop out in a very high percentage, 50% and 35.3% respectively, although these are small groups. In Humanities, greater differences are observed between dropouts and non-dropouts when the mother has attended higher education (15.3%), and when she did not (25%). A higher percentage of dropouts is observed in students who attended the retake exam (34.9%) and when the gender is male (34.3%). On the contrary, in Science, no gender differences are observed and it is worth noting there are no students who entered with an extraordinary entrance exam. In Health Sciences, there are differences in the number of dropouts between students who studied science in high school (7.2%) and those who did not (19%). Finally, in Engineering, it is worth highlighting that a large number of students dropped out when they entered the program from a vocational learning route and that, although the percentage of women is very small, the percentage of men who dropped out is still higher (25%) compared to the 7.7%.

In the quantitative variables, significant differences can also be observed between students who dropped out and those who did not drop out in the first year. The admission option is significant at 90%, with the mean being lower in the group of non-dropouts. The PAU exam grade and access grade follow the same line and are higher in those who did not dropout, 6.75 and 8.50 compared to 6.47 and 8.00. On the other hand, the age is lower for those who did not drop out—19.22 years compared to 19.68 years on average for those who dropped out.

As for the differences between the areas, in the area of Social Sciences and Law and Arts and Humanities, no differences were found between the admission option and age, but in the latter, no differences were found in the access grade, either. In Sciences, there were greater differences in the admission option and, in Health Sciences, in the access grade. Engineering shows the biggest differences between the admission option, 1.27 on average, for those who dropped out compared to 1.1 for those who did not drop out, and also significant differences in the access grade of 9.33 compared to 8.7.

Finally, the continuous variables of the first semester mark, ECTS passed, and pass rate in the first semester are clearly significant for the analysis in general and for all areas, with significant differences between students who dropped out in the first year and those who did not.

3.2. Machine Learning Methods

Table 4 shows the chosen variables after the application of Correlation-based FS at two different moments of time: enrollment and the end of the first semester. The cut-off point for the value of 1-p (see Section 2.3.1) has been taken as the typical 0.95.

Table 4. Chosen Variables in Feature Selection.

Variable	Type	Feature Importance Enrollment	Feature Importance after 1st Semester
Degree	Nominal	1.000	1.000
Access grade	Continuous	1.000	1.000
Area	Nominal	1.000	1.000
PAU grade	Continuous	1.000	1.000
Access Specialty	Nominal	1.000	1.000
Gender	Nominal	1.000	1.000
PAU Call	Nominal	1.000	1.000
Mother's or guardian's level of studies	Nominal	0.998	0.998
Age	Continuous	0.994	0.994
School holder	Nominal	0.978	0.978
Father's or guardian's level of studies	Nominal	0.965	0.965
Admission Option	Continuous	0.962	0.962
Academic Amount	Continuous	0.955	0.955
Ratio of subject passes 1st semester	Continuous	NA [1]	1.000
First-semester grade	Continuous	NA [1]	1.000

[1] Not applicable.

Variables that have not been selected are the number of ECTS enrolled, Time Commitment, Country of Birth, Family Township, Follow the Path, Type of Scholarship, Type of School, School Holder, Location of the School and Admission Reason.

The variable, Admission Option, which measures the level of preference of the students with regard to the studies they want to take, appears both at enrollment and at the end of the first semester.

Table 5 shows the predictive accuracy of the different Machine Learning methods, at both periods of time, globally or considering each area of knowledge apart. We have distinguished the success rates in the groups of dropouts and not dropouts. As a general remark, none of the methods seem to work well considering only the variables prior to university entrance, and the dropout success rates are very low apart from Engineering and Arts and Humanities. On the other hand, the results improve greatly when we introduce the variables describing academic performance over the first semester. Finally, Logistic Regression always takes values closest to the best results.

Table 5. Predictive accuracy of Machine Learning methods.

Technique	Groups	Enrollment Variables			After 1st Semester		
		Global [1]	Not Dropouts	Dropouts	Global [1]	Not Dropouts	Dropouts
SVM	Total	82.90%	95.58%	9.38%	85.57%	94.72%	**32.50%** [2]
	Social Sciences and Law	81.40%	96.92%	10.00%	83.18%	95.11%	28.33%
	Arts and Humanities	62.67%	77.59%	11.76%	76.00%	89.66%	29.41%
	Sciences	87.76%	100.00%	0.00% [3]	87.76%	97.67%	16.67% [3]
	Health Sciences	86.67%	93.78%	5.88%	88.57%	93.78%	29.41% [5]
	Engineering	75.41%	89.36%	**28.57%** [2]	70.49%	85.11%	21.43%
ANN	Total	85.11%	99.78%	0.00% [3]	87.13%	96.88%	30.63%
	Social Sciences and Law	81.99%	99.46%	1.67%	84.97%	97.10%	29.17%
	Arts and Humanities	74.67%	96.55%	0.00% [3]	70.67%	81.03%	**35.29%** [2]
	Sciences	86.00%	93.33%	20.00% [2,4]	85.00%	100.00%	14.29% [3]
	Health Sciences	90.95%	97.93%	11.76%	90.95%	96.37%	29.41% [5]
	Engineering	77.05%	97.87%	7.14%	78.69%	95.74%	21.43%
Decision Tree	Total	82.05%	98.58%	0.58% [3]	85.32%	95.05%	33.33% [5]
	Social Sciences and Law	81.33%	98.68%	1.72%	86.71%	96.15%	35.24%
	Arts and Humanities	71.43%	82.14%	**28.57%** [2]	79.73%	89.83%	**40.00%** [2]
	Sciences	80.77%	89.13%	16.67%	83.64%	97.83%	11.11%
	Health Sciences	86.22%	98.82%	3.85%	85.45%	95.90%	4.00% [3]
	Engineering	78.79%	97.92%	27.78% [4]	71.19%	83.72%	37.50% [5]
KNN	Total	85.59%	98.95%	16.36% [2,4]	88.72%	99.01%	29.30%
	Social Sciences and Law	86.47%	99.46%	14.85% [4]	88.48%	97.55%	39.05% [5]
	Arts and Humanities	74.07%	98.31%	9.09%	88.89%	96.83%	**61.11%** [2,5]
	Sciences	91.23%	100.00%	0.00% [3]	87.27%	100.00%	22.22%
	Health Sciences	87.83%	98.02%	14.29% [4]	87.83%	98.02%	14.29%
	Engineering	89.06%	100.00%	12.50%	82.26%	100.00%	31.25%
Logistic Regression	Total	83.37%	99.77%	0.00% [3]	87.22%	97.02%	30.57%
	Social Sciences and Law	83.74%	98.74%	0.99%	87.59%	97.38%	34.29%
	Arts and Humanities	76.47%	86.96%	**31.25%** [2,4]	75.31%	85.71%	**38.89%** [2]
	Sciences	91.23%	100.00%	0.00% [3]	85.45%	95.65%	33.33% [5]
	Health Sciences	88.98%	99.52%	13.79%	90.45%	98.46%	28.00% [3]
	Engineering	75.00%	84.75%	11.11%	72.58%	84.78%	37.50% [5]

[1] Global is the predictive accuracy for the overall model, not-dropouts and dropouts. [2] Highest predictive accuracy for dropouts with only enrollment variables and after 1st semester variables for each technique. [3] Lowest predictive accuracy for dropouts with only enrollment variables and after 1st semester variables for each technique. [4] Highest predictive accuracy for dropouts with only enrollment variables for each group. [5] Highest predictive accuracy for dropouts with after 1st semester variables for each group.

The information contained in Table 5 has been used to construct Figures 3 and 4, which show the minimum, average and maximum predictive accuracy for all students (global) and those who did not drop out, and those who dropped out, respectively. In both figures, the methods that attained the minimum and maximum are highlighted.

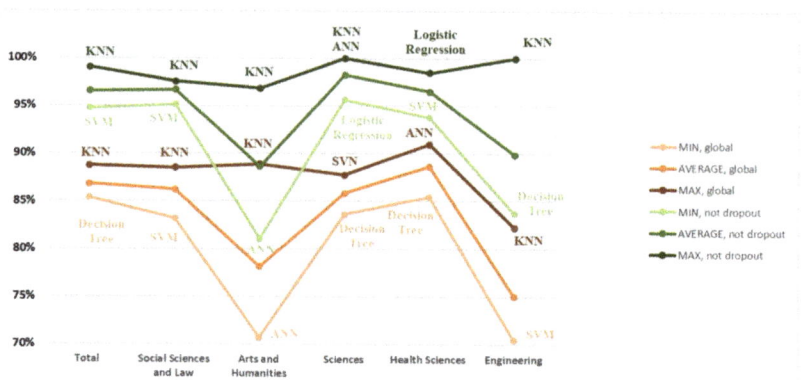

Figure 3. Predictive accuracy: minimum, average and maximum for global and who did not drop out.

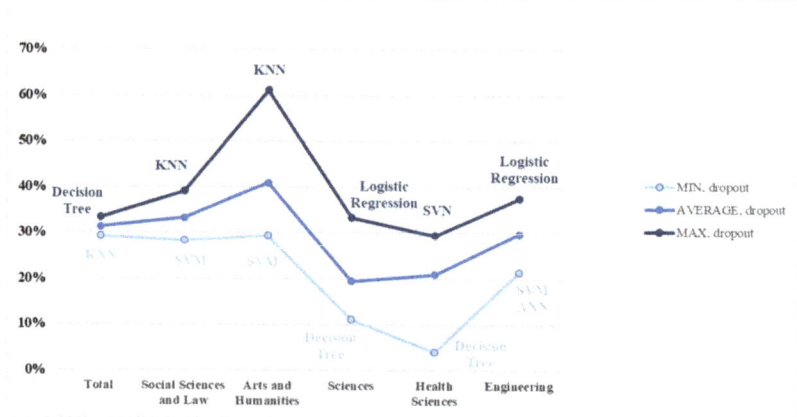

Figure 4. Predictive accuracy: minimum, average and maximum only for those that dropped out.

As can be seen in Figure 3, on average, the worst results are obtained in Arts and Humanities and in Engineering, in both the global and non-dropout results. KNN has the best results. except for Health Sciences and Sciences in the global results.

Figure 4 illustrates how dropouts obtain the worst results in Sciences and Health Sciences. Similar prediction results were obtained in all areas, although with different techniques. KNN stands out for Arts and Humanities (61.1%).

With regard to the predictor importance in the different Machine Learning Models, as expected, the ratio of subject passes the first semester and first-semester grades are always the most important variables. The admission option, which expresses the preference of the student for the course they finally study, is always a relevant variable and, in Sciences, has the third highest value.

There are other rather important variables, but they depend on the area of knowledge. For instance, the mother or guardian's level of studies has high importance, but mainly in Sciences and Arts and Humanities, while the PAU grade and Access Grade appear in Arts and Humanities, Social Sciences and Law. Table 6 shows the heat map of all variables for

Logistic Regression; the heat maps of all variables in all other techniques are detailed in Appendix C.

Table 6. Predictors Importance after 1st semester (Logistic Regression).

Variables	Total	Sciences	Engineering	Arts and Humanities	Health Sciences	Social Sciences and Law
Area	0.043					
Scholarship holder	0.045	0.087	0.046		0.068	0.036
PAU Call		0.049		0.045	0.057	
Age	0.043	0.062		0.034	0.039	0.043
Access Specialty	0.044	0.049	0.061	0.056	0.082	0.048
Degree	0.100		0.074			
Academic Amount		0.158		0.084	0.039	
Mother's or guardian's level of studies		0.175	0.069	0.126		0.040
Father's or guardian's level of studies			0.052	0.099		
First-semester grade	0.212	0.058	0.175		0.124	0.254
Access grade	0.043	0.074	0.044		0.041	0.045
PAU grade		0.049	0.043	0.038	0.061	
Admission Option	0.045	0.051		0.050	0.058	0.042
Ratio of subject passes 1st semester	0.285		0.186	0.260	0.263	0.244
Gender	0.042		0.044	0.085		0.048

Color increases in intensity as the importance of the predictor increases.

4. Discussion and Conclusions

In this work, we addressed the problem of early detection of university dropouts. We have focused on the dropouts that occur at the end of the first year of studies because it is the one that takes the highest values and has the greatest negative impact. For example, at an economic level for universities, the expected income for the remaining study period (at least two more years) is lost.

We used data from the students of one of the largest face-to-face universities in Europe. One of the strengths of our study is that we considered the students who are studying in different program areas. To the best of our knowledge, this is the first time this has been done in the university dropout literature (see, for example, [38]). More specifically, we considered ten university degrees corresponding to the five major program areas. This allowed us to compare the different performance of the models in the different areas, and also to discuss which variables are more relevant in the prediction models depending on these fields of knowledge.

Another aspect to highlight is the very good quality of our data. Fortunately, we have been able to count on the collaboration of the academic authorities, and we have complete information. Specifically, we have been able to obtain information on a total of 28 variables. Some of them are academic, but others correspond to the socio-economic situation of the students or their environment.

With regard to the obtained results, the element of note is that an early detection model with good performance cannot be obtained only with the enrollment data. We are aware that this result goes against the results obtained in previous studies (see, for example, Fernández-García et al. [7]), but these studies worked with data corresponding only to engineering students, which is a very homogeneous group with a high entry grade, and led to a low dropout rate. As mentioned previously, our study covers the degrees corresponding to very different program areas, with dropout rates ranging between 15% and 40%.

When we introduce academic performance variables corresponding to the first semester of the studies, the predictions of the models improve remarkably. We believe that this is very timely because the academic authorities can implement retention policies for students who have been detected as being at risk of dropping out. We believe that the dropout rate could be drastically reduced with these policies, which would result in an improvement of the university system and would have positive repercussions on the social and economic situation of the country.

In general, all Machine Learning methods obtain similar predictions, as previously mentioned in the literature. However, there are some notable exceptions: for example, the well-behaved KNN methods in the area of Arts and Humanities. There are areas, such as Sciences and Health Sciences, where all the methods consistently give worse results in predicting early leaving.

In all cases, a Logistic Regression model has also been used. We understand that this model is much easier to use for non-specialized audiences. The results are that although this method is never the best compared to the other more sophisticated techniques, it is always among the top three or four. Our advice to university managers is not to stop using dropout prediction techniques due to the complexity of the algorithms. The recommendation is that in those universities where sufficient resources cannot be invested in the development of powerful Machine Learning techniques, Logistic Regression should at least be used as a good approximation to the dropout phenomenon.

Last but not least, our study has also considered the importance of the different variables when building the model that best predicts dropout. Specifically, we wanted to consider the relevance of the variable Admission Option. In the Spanish university system, as in many others at the international level, students must place their degree options in preference order. Based on their grades, a system assigns them the studies they can take. It can happen that students ends up studying their first choice (this happens when the student has a very good grade), but it can also happen that the student ends up taking studies that he or she had placed as a lower option. It is logical to consider whether this variable, which measures the student's preference for the studies that he/she ends up taking, is relevant in the models. It is to be expected that the lower the preference for studies, the higher the probability of dropping out. First, we have used correlation-based Feature Selection methods for variable extraction. As expected, the variable Admission Option always appears as relevant both in the overall number of students and in each of the program areas. Next, we measured the importance of the variables in the different methods used. Again, the variable Admission Option is relevant, but it does not have the same importance in the different program areas. For example, the high importance of this variable in the area of Science should be highlighted. We know that university autonomy is subject to higher-ranking laws, but from the academic field, we dare to suggest, based on the results obtained, that the methods of assigning students to studies should take this variable into account and, perhaps students should not enroll in programs that were not among their first choices, especially when it comes to Science. As this is both difficult to apply and subject to political debate (it could violate the right of students to pursue university studies, even if they were not their first choices), we could at least recommend that special attention should be paid to this type of student.

This research presents some limitations. We only consider first-year dropouts, we used data corresponding to ten different degrees, and the Machine Learning techniques used are limited to those that the literature review has shown to be useful for predicting university dropouts. Thus, it would be interesting for future research to study university dropouts after the first year, assess more degrees in the different program areas, and compare the data obtained from other machine learning techniques, such as Random Forest or Gradient Boosting. In addition, although the results did not find that gender was a significant predictor of dropping out of university in the specific context of this study, it is likely necessary to deepen the analysis of the characteristics of the phenomenon from the perspective of gender.

Author Contributions: M.S., J.M. and A.H. conceptualization, literature review, methodology, writing and interpretation of the data and results. M.S. and A.H. carried out the data curation, and J.M. did the formal analysis. All authors have read and agreed to the published version of the manuscript.

Funding: This research was funded by Ministerio de Ciencia e Innovación de España [grant number ABANRED2020, PID2020-116293RB-I00)] and Santander—Universidad Complutense de Madrid 2020 [grant number PR108/20-10]. The APC was funded by Department of Financial and Actuarial Economics & Statistics, Universidad Complutense de Madrid.

Data Availability Statement: The data sets were obtained from the Integrated Institutional Data System (Sistema Integrado de Datos Institucionales-SIDI), which belongs to the Institutional Intelligence Center of the Complutense University of Madrid (http://www.ucm.es/cii (accessed on 1 April 2022)).

Acknowledgments: The data sets were obtained thanks to the Institutional Intelligence Center of the Complutense University of Madrid (http://www.ucm.es/cii (accessed on 1 April 2022)). We also thank the reviewers for their suggestions on improving the paper.

Conflicts of Interest: The authors declare no conflict of interest.

Appendix A

Table A1. Variables and explanations.

Variable	Explanation
Student ID	ID that identifies the student.
Academic Amount	Cost of the student's enrollment.
Degree	The subject area the student is studying (Business Administration and Management, Economics, Commerce, Tourism, Law, Mathematics, Psychology, Computer Engineering, Computer Science Engineering, Art History).
Area	Area to which the student's degree belongs (Social Sciences and Law, Sciences, Health Sciences, Engineering, Arts and Humanities).
Dropout	A dichotomous variable that identifies whether the student dropped out of the degree after the first year or not.
Family Township	A dichotomous variable that identifies whether the student has a family in the region of Madrid or not.
Admission Option	The Spanish public university access system is competitive on the basis of student performance. A student can choose up to 12 options between degree and university to access university studies.
Gender	Dichotomous variable identifying the sex of the student.
Country of Birth	A dichotomous variable that identifies whether the student is Spanish or foreign.
Admission Study	A dichotomous variable that identifies whether the student has entered university from high school or from a professional training degree.
Access Specialty	In the last years of school, the student must choose between subjects from different areas that will determine the specialty with which they mainly enter university (Social Sciences and Humanities, Arts, Technical Sciences, Health Sciences). However, this requirement is not compulsory; a science student can enter social science degrees and vice-versa.
Follow the path	A dichotomous variable that identifies whether the student who has taken subjects in a field in the last years of school has chosen a related university degree or not.
Time commitment	A dichotomous variable that identifies whether the student has enrolled in the first year of the full course or not.
PAU grade	University entrance exam grade (over 10).

Table A1. Cont.

Variable	Explanation
Access grade	University entrance grade, an average between the mark of the last two years of high school and the entrance exam (over 14).
Mother's or guardian's level of studies	Mother or guardian's level of studies (illiterate, no education, primary education, secondary education, higher education).
Father's or guardian's level of studies	Father or guardian's level of studies (illiterate, no education, primary education, secondary education, higher education).
Scholarship holder	A dichotomous variable that identifies whether the student receives a scholarship or not.
Type of scholarship	A dichotomous variable that identifies whether the scholarship is from the Education Ministry or from the university.
Type of school	A variable that identifies whether the school is a comprehensive school, only an upper secondary school, or only a professional degree school.
School holder	A variable that identifies whether the school is public, private, or private with public subsidy.
Location of the school	A dichotomous variable that identifies whether the student has attended school in the region of Madrid or not.
PAU Call	The university entrance examination has two calls, ordinary and extraordinary.
Admission Reason	A student can be accepted under different quotas (general, disabled, elite athletes).
Age	Age of student in the first year of university.
First-semester grade	Average first-semester grade at university.
No. of ECTS Passed 1st semester	The number of ECTS passed in the first semester at university.
No. of ECTS enrolled 1st semester	The number of ECTS enrolled in the first semester at university.
Ratio of subject passes 1st semester	The ratio between ECTS passed and enrolled in the first semester.

Appendix B

Table A2. Significance level.

Variables	Total	Social Sciences and Law	Arts and Humanities	Sciences	Health Sciences	Engineering
Academic Amount	0.081 +	0.052 +	0.317	0.225	0.550	0.585
Degree	<0.001 ***	0.098 +	a	a	a	<0.001 ***
Area	<0.001 ***	a	a	a	a	a
Family Township	0.462	0.842	0.626	0.848	0.746	0.255
Admission Option	0.061 +	0.098 +	0.352	0.107	0.240	0.03 *
Gender	<0.001 ***	0.013 *	0.038 *	0.805	0.260	0.051 +
Country of Birth	0.195	0.362	0.513	0.606	0.800	0.095 +
Admission Study	0.636	0.676	0.530	a	0.101	0.002 **
Access Specialty	<0.001 ***	0.003 **	0.468	a	0.009 **	0.072 +
Follow the path	0.562	0.408	0.751	a	0.087 +	0.517
Time commitment	0.104	0.710	0.724	0.111	0.073 +	0.212
No. of ECTS credits enrolled	0.002 **	0.052+	0.349	0.113	0.070+	0.781
PAU grade	<0.001 ***	<0.001 ***	0.022 *	0.346	0.397	0.096 +
Access grade	<0.001 ***	<0.001 ***	0.170	0.080 +	0.016 *	0.015 *

Table A2. Cont.

Variables	Total	Social Sciences and Law	Arts and Humanities	Sciences	Health Sciences	Engineering
Mother's or guardian's level of studies	0.012 *	0.05 *	0.016 *	<0.001 ***	0.978	0.295
Father's or guardian's level of studies	0.054 +	0.150	0.665	0.399	0.712	0.268
Scholarship holder	0.022 *	0.188	0.386	0.126	0.948	0.988
Type of scholarship	0.044 *	0.100+	0.257	0.652	0.651	0.264
Type of school	0.211	0.241	0.467	0.736	0.446	0.909
School holder	0.243	0.621	0.121	0.238	0.405	0.470
Location of the school	0.843	0.938	0.496	0.992	0.893	0.195
PAU Call	<0.001 ***	0.091 +	0.007 **	a	0.145	a
Admission Reason	0.070 +	0.590	0.414	0.277	<0.001 ***	a
Age	0.023 *	0.381	0.661	0.289	0.159	0.295
First-semester grade	<0.001 ***	<0.001 ***	<0.001 ***	<0.001 ***	<0.001 ***	<0.001 ***
First-year grade	<0.001 ***	<0.001 ***	<0.001 ***	0.009 **	<0.001 ***	<0.001 ***
No. of ECTS Passed 1st semester	<0.001 ***	<0.001 ***	<0.001 ***	<0.001 ***	<0.001 ***	<0.001 ***
No. of ECTS Enrolled 1st semester	0.046 *	0.032 *	0.563	0.318	0.543	0.459
Ratio of subject passes 1st semester	<0.001 ***	<0.001 ***	<0.001 ***	<0.001 ***	<0.001 ***	<0.001 ***

Significance levels: + 10%, * 5%, ** 1%, *** 0.1%, a means that is a constant.

Appendix C

Table A3. Predictors Importance after 1st semester (SVN).

Variables	Total	Sciences	Engineering	Arts and Humanities	Health Sciences	Social Sciences and Law
Area	0.059					
Scholarship holder	0.084	0.062	0.070		0.114	
PAU Call	0.094	0.058	0.077	0.049		0.039
Age	0.047	0.058	0.074	0.043	0.045	
Access Specialty		0.059	0.069	0.104	0.071	0.093
Degree	0.104			0.055	0.042	0.075
Academic Amount	0.052		0.077	0.058	0.041	
Mother's or guardian's level of studies	0.051	0.109	0.089	0.065	0.044	0.048
Father's or guardian's level of studies		0.092				0.087
First-semester grade	0.193	0.081	0.109	0.086	0.139	0.175
Access grade		0.061				0.038
PAU grade						0.040
Admission Option	0.046	0.058	0.076	0.062	0.047	
Ratio of subject passes 1st semester	0.163	0.086		0.302	0.305	0.171
Gender			0.065			0.072

Color increases in intensity as the importance of the predictor increases.

Table A4. Predictors Importance after 1st semester (ANN).

Variables	Total	Sciences	Engineering	Arts and Humanities	Health Sciences	Social Sciences and Law
Area						
Scholarship holder		0.018				
PAU Call						
Age	0.084	0.013	0.133	0.036	0.134	0.130
Access Specialty		0.036	0.063	0.055	0.054	
Degree	0.075		0.054			0.088
Academic Amount	0.078	0.315	0.073	0.135	0.111	0.070
Mother's or guardian's level of studies	0.043		0.065	0.104	0.045	0.036
Father's or guardian's level of studies	0.039	0.017	0.137	0.058	0.042	0.037
First-semester grade	0.180	0.369	0.112	0.086	0.254	0.172
Access grade	0.049	0.017	0.072		0.106	0.090
PAU grade	0.046	0.034		0.061	0.072	0.074
Admission Option	0.088	0.145	0.071	0.073	0.040	0.073
Ratio of subject passes 1st semester	0.177	0.026	0.149	0.229	0.073	0.134
Gender				0.086		

Color increases in intensity as the importance of the predictor increases.

Table A5. Predictors Importance after 1st semester (KNN).

Variables	Total	Sciences	Engineering	Arts and Humanities	Health Sciences	Social Sciences and Law
Area	0.067					
Scholarship holder		0.071	0.074	0.073	0.072	
PAU Call	0.068	0.073	0.069	0.071	0.072	0.072
Age	0.066	0.073	0.069		0.071	0.072
Access Specialty	0.067		0.073	0.073	0.072	0.071
Degree	0.068	0.073	0.080	0.070	0.071	0.071
Academic Amount	0.067	0.073		0.071		0.072
Mother's or guardian's level of studies		0.071	0.072	0.071	0.072	0.071
Father's or guardian's level of studies		0.073	0.070	0.070	0.072	0.071
First-semester grade	0.068			0.071	0.073	0.074
Access grade	0.067	0.073	0.076	0.073	0.072	
PAU grade	0.066	0.073		0.080		
Admission Option		0.073	0.069			0.071
Ratio of subject passes 1st semester	0.068				0.071	0.074
Gender			0.077			

Color increases in intensity as the importance of the predictor increases.

Table A6. Predictors Importance after 1st semester (Decision Tree).

Variables	Total	Sciences	Engineering	Arts and Humanities	Health Sciences	Social Sciences and Law
Area						
Scholarship holder	0.090					
PAU Call	0.055					
Age				0.120		
Access Specialty					0.144	
Degree	0.054					
Academic Amount	0.051	0.643				
Mother's or guardian's level of studies	0.054			0.243		
Father's or guardian's level of studies						
First-semester grade	0.197				0.066	0.124
Access grade				0.019		
PAU grade	0.058				0.294	
Admission Option					0.235	
Ratio of subject passes 1st semester	0.442	0.357	1.000	0.618	0.260	0.876
Gender						

Color increases in intensity as the importance of the predictor increases.

References

1. Organisation for Economic Co-operation and Development (OECD). *Education at a Glance 2019: OECD Indicators*; OECD Publishing: Paris, France, 2019.
2. Ortiz-Lozano, J.M.; Rua-Vieites, A.; Bilbao-Calabuig, P.; Casadesús-Fa, M. University student retention: Best time and data to identify undergraduate students at risk of dropout. *Innov. Educ. Teach. Int.* **2018**, *57*, 74–85. [CrossRef]
3. Ortiz, E.A.; Dehon, C. Roads to Success in the Belgian French Community's Higher Education System: Predictors of Dropout and Degree Completion at the Universite Libre de Bruxelles. *Res. High. Educ.* **2013**, *54*, 693–723. [CrossRef]
4. Cabrera, L.; Bethencourt, J.T.; Alvarez Pérez, P.; González Afonso, M. El problema del abandono de los estudios universitarios. *Rev. Electrónica Investig. Evaluación Educ.* **2006**, *12*, 171–203. [CrossRef]
5. Lassibille, G.; Navarro Gómez, M.L. Why do higher education students drop out? Evidence from Spain. *Educ. Econ.* **2008**, *1*, 89–106. [CrossRef]
6. Behr, A.; Giese, M.; Teguim Kamdjou, H.D.; Theune, K. Dropping out of university: A literature review. *Rev. Educ.* **2020**, *8*, 614–652. [CrossRef]
7. Fernandez-Garcia, A.J.; Preciado, J.C.; Melchor, F.; Rodriguez-Echeverria, R.; Conejero, J.M.; Sanchez-Figueroa, F. A Real-Life Machine Learning Experience for Predicting University Dropout at Different Stages Using Academic Data. *IEEE Access* **2021**, *9*, 133076–133090. [CrossRef]
8. Nieto-Reyes, A.; Duque, R.; Francisci, G. A Method to Automate the Prediction of Student Academic Performance from Early Stages of the Course. *Mathematics* **2021**, *9*, 2677. [CrossRef]
9. Liu, T.; Wang, C.; Chang, L.; Gu, T. Predicting High-Risk Students Using Learning Behavior. *Mathematics* **2022**, *10*, 2483. [CrossRef]
10. Larsen, M.S.; Kornbeck, K.P.; Kristensen, R.; Larsen, M.R.; Sommersel, H.B. Dropout Phenomena at Universities: What Is DROPOUT? Why Does Dropout Occur? What Can Be Done by the Universities to Prevent or Reduce It? Danish Clearinghouse for Educational Research: Aarhus, Denmark, 2013.
11. Fernández-Melizo, M. *Análisis del Abandono de Los Estudiantes de Grado en Las Universidades Presenciales en España*; Ministerio de Universidades: Madrid, Spain, 2022.
12. Constante-Amores, A.; Fernández-Melizo, M.; Florenciano Martínez, E.; Navarro Asencio, E. Factores asociados al abandono universitario. *Educ. XX1* **2021**, *24*, 17–44.
13. Rodriguez-Muniz, L.J.; Bernardo, A.B.; Esteban, M.; Diaz, I. Dropout and transfer paths: What are the risky profiles when analyzing university persistence with machine learning techniques? *PLoS ONE* **2019**, *14*, e0218796. [CrossRef]
14. Romero, C.; Ventura, S. Educational Data Mining: A Review of the State of the Art. *IEEE Trans. Syst. Man Cybern. Part C-Appl. Rev.* **2010**, *40*, 601–618. [CrossRef]
15. Frawley, W.J.; Piatetskyshapiro, G.; Matheus, C.J. Knowledge discovery in databases—An overview. *Ai Mag.* **1992**, *13*, 57–70.

16. Grillo, S.A.; Roman, J.C.M.; Mello-Roman, J.D.; Noguera, J.L.V.; Garcia-Torres, M.; Divina, F.; Sotomayor, P.E.G. Adjacent Inputs With Different Labels and Hardness in Supervised Learning. *IEEE Access* **2021**, *9*, 162487–162498. [CrossRef]
17. Lee, Y.W.; Choi, J.W.; Shin, E.H. Machine learning model for predicting malaria using clinical information. *Comput. Biol. Med.* **2021**, *129*, 104151. [CrossRef] [PubMed]
18. Viloria, A.; Padilla, J.G.; Vargas-Mercado, C.; Hernandez-Palma, H.; Llinas, N.O.; David, M.A. Integration of Data Technology for Analyzing University Dropout. *Procedia Comput. Sci.* **2019**, *155*, 569–574. [CrossRef]
19. Shahiri, A.M.; Husain, W.; Rashid, N.A. A Review on Predicting Student's Performance using Data Mining Techniques. *Procedia Comput. Sci.* **2015**, *72*, 414–422. [CrossRef]
20. Jovic, A.; Brkic, K.; Bogunovic, N. A review of feature selection methods with applications. In Proceedings of the 2015 38th International Convention on Information and Communication Technology, Electronics and Microelectronics (Mipro), Opatija, Croatia, 25–29 May 2015; IEEE: New York, NY, USA, 2015; pp. 1200–1205.
21. Saeys, Y.; Inza, I.; Larranaga, P. A review of feature selection techniques in bioinformatics. *Bioinformatics* **2007**, *23*, 2507–2517. [CrossRef]
22. Wah, Y.B.; Ibrahim, N.; Hamid, H.A.; Abdul-Rahman, S.; Fong, S. Feature Selection Methods: Case of Filter and Wrapper Approaches for Maximising Classification Accuracy. *Pertanika J. Sci. Technol.* **2018**, *26*, 329–339.
23. Sandoval-Palis, I.; Naranjo, D.; Vidal, J.; Gilar-Corbi, R. Early Dropout Prediction Model: A Case Study of University Leveling Course Students. *Sustainability* **2020**, *12*, 9314. [CrossRef]
24. Mello-Roman, J.D.; Mello-Roman, J.C.; Gomez-Guerrero, S.; Garcia-Torres, M. Predictive Models for the Medical Diagnosis of Dengue: A Case Study in Paraguay. *Comput. Math. Methods Med.* **2019**, *2019*, 7307803. [CrossRef]
25. Ghorbani, M.A.; Zadeh, H.A.; Isazadeh, M.; Terzi, O. A comparative study of artificial neural network (MLP, RBF) and support vector machine models for river flow prediction. *Environ. Earth Sci.* **2016**, *75*, 1–14. [CrossRef]
26. Haykin, S. *Neural Networks: A Comprehensive Foundation*; Prentice Hall PTR: Hoboken, NJ, USA, 1994; p. 842.
27. Kayri, M. An Intelligent Approach to Educational Data: Performance Comparison of the Multilayer Perceptron and the Radial Basis Function Artificial Neural Networks. *Educ. Sci.-Theory Pract.* **2015**, *15*, 1247–1255.
28. Shawe-Taylor, J.; Cristianini, N. *Kernel Methods for Pattern Analysis*; Cambridge University Press: Cambridge, UK, 2004; p. 460.
29. Tan, P.N.; Steinbach, M.; Kumar, V. *Introduction to Data Mining*; Pearson Education India: Noida, India, 2016; p. 169.
30. Yukselturk, E.; Ozekes, S.; Turel, Y.K. Predicting dropout student: An application of data mining methods in an online education program. *Eur. J. Open Distance E-Learn.* **2014**, *17*, 118–133. [CrossRef]
31. Wendler, T.; Gröttrup, S. *Data Mining with SPSS Modeler: Theory, Exercises and Solutions*; Springer: Cham, Switzerland, 2016; p. 1059.
32. Agrusti, F.; Mezzini, M.; Bonavolonta, G. Deep learning approach for predicting university dropout: A case study at Roma Tre University. *J. E-Learn. Knowl. Soc.* **2020**, *16*, 44–54. [CrossRef]
33. Mello-Román, J.D.; Hernández, A. Un estudio sobre el rendimiento académico en Matemáticas. *Rev. Electrónica Investig. Educ.* **2019**, *21*, e29. [CrossRef]
34. Tan, M.J.; Shao, P.J. Prediction of Student Dropout in E-Learning Program Through the Use of Machine Learning Method. *Int. J. Emerg. Technol. Learn.* **2015**, *10*, 11–17. [CrossRef]
35. Kass, G.V. An exploratory technique for investigating large quantities of categorical data. *Appl. Stat.* **1980**, *29*, 119–127. [CrossRef]
36. Ahuja, R.; Kankane, Y. Predicting the Probability of Student's Degree Completion by Using Different Data Mining Techniques. In Proceedings of the 2017 Fourth International Conference on Image Information Processing (ICIIP), Near Shimla, India, 21–23 December 2017; IEEE: New York, NY, USA, 2017; pp. 474–477.
37. Cunningham, P.; Delany, S.J. k-Nearest Neighbour Classifiers—A Tutorial. *Acm Comput. Surv.* **2021**, *54*, 1–25. [CrossRef]
38. Opazo, D.; Moreno, S.; Alvarez-Miranda, E.; Pereira, J. Analysis of First-Year University Student Dropout through Machine Learning Models: A Comparison between Universities. *Mathematics* **2021**, *9*, 2599. [CrossRef]

Article

Quantile Regression Analysis between the After-School Exercise and the Academic Performance of Korean Middle School Students

Kyulee Shin [1] and Sukkyung You [2,*]

1. Department of Sports Science, Seoul National University of Science & Technology, Seoul 01811, Korea; kyuleeshin@seoultech.ac.kr
2. College of Education, Hankuk University of Foreign Studies, Seoul 130-791, Korea
* Correspondence: skyou@hufs.ac.kr

Abstract: This study deepens our understanding of the prediction and structural relationship between a student's academic performance and his/her regular after-school exercise by estimating models based upon the quantile regression and the instrumental variable quantile regression methods, respectively. Using data on Korean middle school students, we found that negative relationships were dominant for the prediction models, whereas the relationships were reversed for the structural models, affirming the theoretical and experimental hypotheses observed in prior literature. Furthermore, we also found that the low-performing students, in terms of the academic performance, had stronger associations between the two variables than the high-performing students, overall.

Keywords: after-school exercise; academic performance; structural relationship; quantile regression; instrumental variable quantile regression

1. Introduction

Investigating the relationship between mental health and physical activity has been a popular research topic in literature. For example, Correa-Burrows et al. [1] and Tomporowski et al. [2] reviewed theoretical works on the relationship, indicating a positive structural association between a student's regular physical exercise and his/her academic achievement. Furthermore, Shin, Yoo, and Kim [3] empirically examined students' academic performance and after-school exercise using Korean middle school student data, affirming the theoretical and experimental hypotheses.

Nevertheless, we note that every student does not behave according to the same theoretical hypothesis, and the extent of the relationship between the academic performance and regular exercise is different from student to student, although the theoretical hypothesis may still be valid overall.

This aspect motivates the current study. The goal of this study is to empirically identify the relationship between students' academic performance and their after-school exercise by separately estimating structural models for the students belonging to different groups, thereby deepening the prior empirical results on the two variables. For this purpose, we classified the students according to the quantile levels of their academic performance score and examined whether the students belonging to each quantile level behaved according to the hypothesized theory or not. In addition to this, we also further examined which quantile level of students were more strongly supported by the hypothesized theory on the two variables.

For the purpose of this study, we investigated the empirical data collected by the National Youth Policy Institute (NYPI) in Korea from middle school students in 2011, using both quantile regression (QR) and instrumental variable quantile regression (IVQR) methods. The QR method, developed by Koenker and Bassett [4], estimates the quantile prediction model by using observations belonging to the different quantile levels of the

dependent variable, and it does not necessarily estimate the structural relationship between the variables of interest. On the other hand, the IVQR method, developed by Chernozhukov and Hansen [5], in parallel to the two-stage least squares (TSLS) estimation, estimates the structural model by using the observations belonging to the different quantile levels of the dependent variable, similarly to the QR method. To the best of our knowledge, the IVQR method has not been applied to the quantile structural equation between a student's academic performance and his/her physical activity. This study contributes to the literature by providing empirical evidence on the positive structural relationship between Korean middle school students' physical activity and their academic performance by applying the IVQR method.

The paper is organized as follows. In Section 2, we discuss the motivation for the use of the IVQR method in comparison with the QR method, in parallel to the comparison between the ordinary least squares (OLS) and the TSLS methods. In addition, we provide the models estimated by QR and IVQR and the variables used for the empirical analysis, describing our strategy to estimate the quantile structural relationship between the two variables, along with the instrumental variables that are employed for the application of the IVQR method. The prior literature relevant to the current study goal is also provided. In Section 3, the estimation results are provided, and we compare the results with the hypotheses given in the existing literature and discuss them. Concluding remarks are provided in Section 4.

2. Model Estimation Strategy and Literature
2.1. Benchmark Model

Our study concept is based upon the following model:

$$\log(acps_i) = \alpha_* + \beta_* excd_i + \gamma_* prvl_i + \delta_* \log(yinc_i) + u_i, \tag{1}$$

where *acps* stands for the student's average exam scores of Korean, English, mathematics, science, and social science, which measures students' academic performance; and *excd* and *prvl* denote the dummy variables for weekly after-school exercise and weekly after-school private lessons for Korean, English, mathematics, science, or social science, respectively. For example, *excd* is equal to 1 if the student attends after-school private lessons for exercise and is 0, otherwise. This model was specified to capture the effect of the after-school exercise on the student's academic performance. Therefore, the exam score of physical education was not included in *acps*. In addition, *yinc* stands for the parent's yearly income measured in 10,000 Korean won. The logarithm was taken to *acps* and *yinc*, so that we could interpret the coefficient δ_* as the income elasticity of the academic performance. Finally, the subscript i denotes the student index.

This empirical model was motivated by the hypothesis that regular exercise positively affects students' academic performance. For example, Alkadhi [6], de Greeff, Bosker, Oosterlaan, Visscher, and Hartman [7], Tomporowski, McCullick, Pendleton, and Pesce [8], and Xiang et al. [9], among others, provided theoretical bases for a positive association between physical and cognitive or mental activities. Furthermore, Belcher et al. [10] reported experimental results indicating that regular exercises modified the structure and function of brain, positively affecting brain activities. These theoretical and experimental works imply that students' regular after-school exercises are helpful in raising their academic performances, and Model (1) was specified to capture this effect empirically. Here, a student's regular exercise is denoted as any form of after-school exercise lessons, but excludes casual exercises, such as irregular or regular gym classes held at the school. They are excluded because such classes are common for all students in Korea, and therefore it is difficult to capture the different activities among different students and their affection to the academic performance.

Models similar to (1) have been empirically investigated in prior literature. For example, using Korean middle school student data, Shin, Yoo, and Kim [3] showed that the academic performance was positively and structurally associated with after-school exercise hours, although their relationship was negative in terms of the prediction model. In obtaining this result, Shin, Yoo, and Kim [3] employed the OLS and TSLS estimation methods. The OLS method estimates the prediction model, and a negative relationship is captured between the two variables. Meanwhile, the TSLS method estimates the structural relationship between the two variables, estimating a positive relationship, affirming the structural hypothesis on the two variables in the literature.

The current study deepens the empirical results in prior literature. Note that students' responses to the after-school exercise would not be the same for every student, and this can lead to various results in terms of raising their academic performance. For example, a student with high academic performance is expected to respond to the after-school exercise differently from a student with low academic performance. Specifically, if the academic performance is positively associated with the student's cognitive power and his/her regular exercise is helpful in raising the student's cognitive power, attending the after-school exercise class is expected to raise the cognitive power of the low-performing student more effectively than the high-performing student. It is mainly because the latter is likely to have already reached the level that cannot be easily raised by attending the physical exercise class. We estimated these different responses by specifying the QR model. Specifically, the responses were assumed to be different among the students belonging to the different quantile levels in terms of their academic performance, and we estimated the different coefficients by modifying Model (1) to have different parameters at different quantile levels. That is, if we let τ denote the quantile level of the student's academic performance, the parameters in Model (1) are modified to depend on τ, as follows: for each $\tau \in (0, 1)$,

$$\log(acps_i) = \alpha_{(\tau)*} + \beta_{(\tau)*} excd_i + \gamma_{(\tau)*} prvl_i + \delta_{(\tau)*} \log(yinc_i) + u_{(\tau)i}. \qquad (2)$$

The parameters on the right side now depend on the quantile level τ, so that the top 10-% students can now be differently associated with the right-side variables from the bottom 10-% students.

We estimated Model (2) by the QR method. Koenker and Bassett [4] provided the estimation method for the model specified by the same motivation as that of this study, under a general model assumption, and showed that their estimator was consistent for the desired parameters and was asymptotically normal around the unknown parameter values. In addition, Koenker [11] demonstrated how to test hypotheses on the unknown parameters using the asymptotic normal distribution provided by Koenker and Bassett [4]. In particular, Koenker [11] employed the robust standard error to define the t-test and showed that its null limit distribution was a standard normal. Below, we exploit the technical advances in Koenker [11] to estimate Model (2).

Nevertheless, the QR method does not estimate the structural relationship between the academic performance and the after-school exercise. Note that when Model (2) is estimated by QR for different quantiles, their weighted average with respect to τ turns out to be identical to that estimated by OLS. This implies that the QR method cannot be associated with the structural relationship between the variables.

We therefore estimated the structural form of Model (2) by IVQR. Chernozhukov and Hansen [5] provided a method to estimate the structural parameters in Model (2) under the condition that proper instrumental variables are available. They showed that their estimator could consistently estimate the unknown structural parameters and, also, that its limit distribution was normal under some mild regularity conditions, that enables us to construct the t-test for the QR method. The model estimated by IVQR was different from that estimated by QR. For each quantile level, we emphasize that it consistently estimated the structural quantile equation instead of the quantile equation, viz., the quantile prediction model. The relationship between the QR and IVQR estimations is parallel to that between the OLS and TSLS estimations in terms of their structures. Exploiting the advances in Chernozhukov and Hansen [5], we estimated the structural quantile model and drew the model implications that were different from those of the QR method. (The following URL provides the stata code to estimate the model by the IVQR method: http://sites.google.com/site/dwkwak/dataset-and-code (accessed on 23 November 2021)).

The instrumental variables play a critical role in estimating the structural quantile model. For the goal of the current study, we employed the logarithms of the students' height, weight, and sleeping hours on the weekend. There were two motivations for these instrumental variables. First, a student's height and weight are closely associated with outside activities [12], so they are highly correlated. Second, a student attending the regular after-school exercise class tends to sleep more than other students on the weekend in order to recover from physical fatigue because they cannot oversleep during weekdays; hence, students' sleeping hours on weekends tend to be correlated with regular after-school exercise. Nihayah et al. [13] and Zeek et al. [14] also provided case studies on the relationship between students' sleeping hours and their academic performance. Based upon these two facts, the logarithms of students' height, weight, and sleeping hours on weekends were employed as our instrumental variables to apply to the IVQR method. The same instrumental variables were also selected by Shin, Yoo, and Kim [3] when estimating their structural model by TSLS.

In addition to the after-school exercise, the other explanatory variables on the right side of Model (2) were included in order to explain the variation of the academic performance score. The after-school private lessons for school subjects are certainly helpful in raising the academic performance score, which allows the after-school exercise (*excd*) to maintain its explanatory power. In addition, the parent's income level was also included on the right side, by noting that parent's high-income level provides the student with more opportunities to take high-quality private lessons, raising the student's academic performance. If these variables were to be omitted from the right side, the explanatory power of the after-school exercise may be overwhelmed by the variation of the error term. We called Model (2) our benchmark model and estimate it by both QR and IVQR.

2.2. Model Extensions

We next extended the model scope by including other explanatory variables on the right side and tested the robust model estimation property. For this goal, we applied the strategy taken by Shin, Yoo, and Kim [3] to our QR and IVQR models. As our first extension, we specified the following model:

$$\begin{aligned}\log(acps_i) &= \alpha_{(\tau)*} + \beta_{(\tau)*}excd_i + \gamma_{(\tau)*}prvl_i + \delta_{(\tau)*}\log(yinc_i) \\ &+ \pi_{(\tau)*}gndr_i + \xi_{(\tau)*}expl_i + \rho_{(\tau)*}nsib_i \\ &+ \eta_{(\tau)*}moed_{m_i} + \theta_{(\tau)*}moed_{h_i} + \kappa_{(\tau)*}moed_{p_i} \\ &+ \lambda_{(\tau)*}moed_{u_i} + \mu_{(\tau)*}moed_{g_i} + u_{(\tau)i},\end{aligned} \quad (3)$$

where *gndr* denotes students' gender, such that it is 1 and 0 for male and female students, respectively; *expl* denotes the monthly expenditure on the after-school private lessons measured in 10,000 KRW; *nsib* denotes the number of siblings; and *moed_x* denotes the mother's education level. The attachment *x* indicates the education level. That is, *m*, *h*, *p*, *u*, and *g* denote middle school, high school, polytechnic school, university, and graduate school, respectively. For example, if *moed_u* is 1, it implies that the student's mother was educated up to the university education.

These additional explanatory variables were included in order to examine how they are associated with the academic performance score. First, according to Alkadhi [6], and de Greeff, Bosker, Oosterlaan, Visscher, and Hartman [7], among others, male and female students have relative advantages in different disciplines, so a student's academic performance score for different disciplines can be gender-dependent. Therefore, we expected the coefficient of *gndr* in Model (3) to be significantly different from zero, and to further diverge depending on the quantile levels. Second, we included the monthly expenditure on private lessons (*expl*) and the number of siblings (*nsib*) in order to explain the partial effect of the parent's income on the academic performance. If the parents' income is spent on the student's private lessons in order to raise the academic performance, the income effect can be better explained by including the expenditure on the private lessons in addition to parent's income. Similarly, the income effect of parents with multiple children can reduce if the total parents' income is divided for each child's private lessons. We therefore included the number of siblings on the right side and capture the split-income effect. Finally, we included the mother's education level on the right side and detected the parental-involvement effect. Bogenschneider [15], Boonk, Gijselaers, Ritzen, and Brand-Gruwel [16], and Glick and Hohmann-Marriott [17], among others, pointed out that a student's academic performance was closely related to parental involvement and, further, that parental involvement can exist in various forms, suggesting that the parent's education level can be a proper form for parental involvement, although it is generally difficult to measure it objectively. By following the suggestions in prior studies, we included the mothers' education level to measure parental involvement and examined how it affected the student's academic performance at the different quantile levels [15,17–19].

By estimating Model (3) by both QR and IVQR, we can examine the hypothesis for the newly included explanatory variables on the right side. The given hypothesis may be relevant to some quantile levels but not to all of the quantile levels, or it may be relevant at all quantile levels. There can be many different results depending on the quantile levels. Below, we empirically examine whether the given hypothesis is valid or not at each quantile level, and from this we draw detailed empirical inference on the Korean middle school students.

As our final model extension, we further included more explanatory variables in Model (3). As mentioned above, parental involvement is a critical variable that explains a student's academic performance but including only the mother's education level on the right side may be insufficient to capture the effect of parental involvement on a student's academic performance. We, therefore, compensated the mother's education level by complementing it with the father's education level, as follows:

$$
\begin{aligned}
\log(acps_i) &= \alpha_{(\tau)*} + \beta_{(\tau)*} excd_i + \gamma_{(\tau)*} prvl_i + \delta_{(\tau)*} \log(yinc_i) \\
&+ \pi_{(\tau)*} gndr_i + \xi_{(\tau)*} expl_i + \rho_{(\tau)*} nsib_i \\
&+ \eta_{(\tau)*} moed_{m_i} + \theta_{(\tau)*} moed_{h_i} + \kappa_{(\tau)*} moed_{p_i} + \lambda_{(\tau)*} moed_{u_i} \\
&+ \mu_{(\tau)*} moed_{g_i} + \sigma_{(\tau)*} faed_{m_i} + \tau_{(\tau)*} faed_{h_i} + \phi_{(\tau)*} faed_{p_i} \\
&+ \psi_{(\tau)*} faed_{u_i} + \omega_{(\tau)*} faed_{g_i} + u_{(\tau)i},
\end{aligned} \quad (4)
$$

where $faed\_x$ is a dummy variable indicating the father's education level, and the attachment x denotes the same education level as for the mother's education level.

We estimated the extended models in Models (3) and (4) in order to affirm the estimation results made by both QR and IVQR. If the quantile prediction and structural quantile equations in Model (2) are consistently estimated by both QR and IVQR, respectively, they should be similar to those obtained by Models (3) and (4). By estimating these multiple models, we attempted to ensure that our model estimates were robust to model variation.

3. Estimation and Inference

3.1. Data

The data set for our study was collected by the NYPI in South Korea. The NYPI panel survey is collected to understand the comprehensive conditions and environmental changes in youth and childrens' education in South Korea. For our study goal, we used the second wave that provides the observations for the variables in 2011. Shin, You, and Kim [3] also estimated the prediction and structural models by OLS and TSLS, respectively, using the same data. There were 2280 students in the data set, but some students did not provide information. We estimated the models by excluding the missing observations, and the number of missing observations was different from model to model.

3.2. Estimation and Inference Results

3.2.1. Estimation and Inference Results Using Model 2

Tables 1 and 2 report the estimation results of Model (2) obtained by QR and IVQR, respectively. The selected quantile levels were 0.1, 0.2, ... , 0.8, and 0.9, and the total number of observations was 2099 after removing the missing observations. The estimated coefficients are provided in Tables 1 and 2, and figures in parentheses denote the p-values of the t-tests, testing whether the estimated coefficient was zero or not. We also provide the OLS and TSLS estimation results at the final columns of Tables 1 and 2, respectively, and affirm that the averages of the coefficients estimated by QR and IVQR approximate the corresponding coefficients obtained by OLS and TSLS, respectively.

Table 1. Estimation results obtained by quantile regression.

Variables\Quantiles	0.1	0.2	0.3	0.4	0.5	0.6	0.7	0.8	0.9	OLS
const	2.223	1.946	2.310	2.706	3.073	3.373	3.648	3.890	4.182	2.907
	(0.000)	(0.000)	(0.000)	(0.000)	(0.000)	(0.000)	(0.000)	(0.000)	(0.000)	(0.000)
excd	0.011	−0.084	−0.105	−0.118	−0.070	−0.051	−0.059	−0.054	−0.026	−0.067
	(0.828)	(0.245)	(0.038)	(0.281)	(0.089)	(0.028)	(0.003)	(0.006)	(0.185)	(0.047)
prvl	0.249	0.277	0.264	0.234	0.177	0.145	0.094	0.057	0.026	0.157
	(0.000)	(0.000)	(0.000)	(0.000)	(0.000)	(0.000)	(0.000)	(0.000)	(0.013)	(0.000)
log(yinc)	0.158	0.219	0.193	0.161	0.133	0.108	0.086	0.065	0.038	0.143
	(0.000)	(0.000)	(0.000)	(0.000)	(0.000)	(0.000)	(0.000)	(0.000)	(0.000)	(0.126)
Sample size	2099	2099	2099	2099	2099	2099	2099	2099	2099	2099

Figures in parentheses are the p-values of the t-test statistics computed by robust standard error. The dependent variable is log(acps). R^2 of the OLS model is 0.1262.

Table 2. Estimation results obtained by instrumental variable quantile regression.

Variables\Quantiles	0.1	0.2	0.3	0.4	0.5	0.6	0.7	0.8	0.9	TSLS
const	2.256	1.862	2.384	2.619	3.046	3.419	3.618	3.877	4.173	2.910
	(0.000)	(0.000)	(0.000)	(0.000)	(0.000)	(0.000)	(0.000)	(0.000)	(0.000)	(0.000)
excd	0.662	2.102	2.073	2.038	1.037	0.839	0.439	0.300	0.169	1.055
	(0.464)	(0.002)	(0.000)	(0.000)	(0.003)	(0.000)	(0.018)	(0.026)	(0.158)	(0.006)
Prvl	0.239	0.228	0.231	0.194	0.169	0.123	0.081	0.049	0.026	0.138
	(0.000)	(0.000)	(0.000)	(0.000)	(0.000)	(0.000)	(0.000)	(0.000)	(0.000)	(0.000)
log(yinc)	0.152	0.224	0.178	0.165	0.132	0.100	0.089	0.066	0.039	0.140
	(0.000)	(0.000)	(0.000)	(0.000)	(0.000)	(0.000)	(0.000)	(0.000)	(0.000)	(0.000)
Sample size	2099	2099	2099	2099	2099	2099	2099	2099	2099	2099

Figures in parentheses are the p-values of the t-test statistics testing whether the estimated parameter was zero or not. The dependent variable is log(acps).

We summarize the estimation results as follows. First, in terms of the quantile prediction model, the effect of the after-school exercise on the academic performance is statistically significant or insignificant, depending on the quantile level, implying that the after-school exercise is not always significantly associated with the academic performance. This quantile effect was obtained by integrating both the direct and indirect effects of the after-school exercise on the academic performance. For the 1% level of significance, the after-school exercise is negatively significant on the academic performance only for $\tau = 0.7$ and 0.8. If the level of significance is raised to 5%, it becomes also significant for $\tau = 0.3$ and 0.6, but it is insignificant for the other quantile levels. This implies that the after-school exercise is most negatively associated with the academic performance for the students with $\tau = 0.7$ and 0.8. In other words, the loss of the academic performance score is more severe for the students with $\tau = 0.7$ and 0.8. In other words, the opportunity cost of attending the after-school exercise class is most expensively perceived for the students with $\tau = 0.7$ and 0.8. On the other hand, for the extremely high-performing students (i.e., $\tau = 0.9$), attending the after-school exercise class is not perceived as an opportunity cost.

Second, the after-school exercise is positively associated with the academic performance score for most of the quantile levels in terms of the quantile structural model. The estimated coefficients of the after-school exercise in Table 2 are positive and statistically significant for $\tau = 0.2$ to 0.8 at a 1% level of significance, implying that most students directly raise their academic performance by attending the after-school exercise class. These overall positive effects have to be sharply distinguished from the negative effects in Table 1 that are obtained by integrating the direct and indirect effects of the after-school exercise, and they also empirically ensure the hypothetical and experimental positive relationship between the two variables, posited by de Greeff, Bosker, Oosterlaan, Visscher, and Hartman [7], and Tomporowski, McCullick, Pendleton, and Pesce [8], among others. In addition to this, the effect of the after-school exercise diminishes as the quantile level increases. That is, the students with low τ receive more direct benefit from the after-school exercise than the students with high τ. That is, as τ increases from $\tau = 0.2$ to $\tau = 0.9$, the estimated coefficient of *excd* persistently decreases. This aspect implies that the after-school exercise does not raise the academic performance score of the high-performing students as much as for the low-performing students, excluding the extreme quantile levels. From this aspect, we affirm that the hypothetical and experimental positive relationship is more effective for the students with low academic performance.

Third, the overall average effects of the parent's income and the after-school private lessons for the other subjects are positively associated with the student's academic performance. These positive associations are more or less similar between the QR and IVQR estimations. The obtained quantile coefficients of the parent's income and the private lessons decrease as τ increases, excluding the low-performing students, i.e., $\tau = 0.2$. This implies that the overall average effect of these two variables is more effective for the students with low academic performance. For the students with high academic performance, the overall average effect is still positive, but not as strong as for the low-performing students. From this aspect, we conclude that the marginal effect of taking the private lessons is greater for the low-performing students, and this also holds for the parent's income effect.

3.2.2. Estimation and Inference Results Using Model 3

We next discuss the estimation results of Model (3) reported in Tables 3 and 4. As for Model (2), Tables 3 and 4 are estimated by QR and IVQR, respectively. After removing the missing observations, we used a total of 2083 observations.

We summarize the estimation results as follows. First, the estimation results of Model (2) are valid even for Model (3). All estimated coefficients are more or less similar to those in Tables 1 and 2, and their statistical significance is also similarly obtained.

Second, we observed different gender effects between the quantile prediction and structural equations. Voyer and Voyer [20] and Gneezy, Niederle, and Rustichini [21], among others, assert that students' academic performance exhibits a gender effect, but this effect cannot be observed from the prediction models reported in Table 3. None of the estimated gender coefficients are statistically significant. In contrast, the gender effect becomes more evident for low quantile levels if the IVQR method is applied. For $\tau = 0.1, 0.2$, and 0.3, Table 4 reports that the estimated coefficients are negatively valued and statistically significant, implying that the gender effect asserted in the prior literature is more easily verifiable for the students. The estimated coefficient increases as τ increases, from -0.16 to close to 0 as τ increases from 0.1 to 0.4, and it stays around 0 for τ greater than 0.4.

Third, we examined the effects of the after-school lesson expenditure for private lessons and the number of siblings. As expected in Section 2.2, for both prediction and structural models, the overall sign of *expl* is positive, whereas it is weakly reversed for *nsib*. Although the coefficients of the number of siblings are statistically insignificant for the quantile prediction model, some of them in the quantile structural model are statistically significant. On the other hand, for most of the quantile levels, the coefficients of *expl* are statistically significant for both the quantile prediction and the structural models. This result implies that the parent's income effect can be better captured by including the expenditure effect rather than the number of siblings. In addition, the expenditure effect is stronger for the low-performing students than the students with high academic performance. The estimated coefficient of *expl* overall decreases as τ increases, implying that the academic performance of the low-performing students can be more easily raised by taking the private lessons than the high-performing students.

Table 3. Estimation results obtained by quantile regression.

Variables\Quantiles	0.1	0.2	0.3	0.4	0.5	0.6	0.7	0.8	0.9	OLS
const	3.086	2.907	2.934	3.252	3.513	3.665	3.926	4.122	4.283	3.355
	(0.000)	(0.000)	(0.000)	(0.000)	(0.000)	(0.000)	(0.000)	(0.000)	(0.000)	(0.000)
excd	−0.019	−0.089	−0.101	−0.093	−0.077	−0.049	−0.050	−0.043	−0.025	−0.064
	(0.868)	(0.060)	(0.148)	(0.129)	(0.087)	(0.067)	(0.033)	(0.027)	(0.210)	(0.058)
prvl	0.097	0.203	0.220	0.171	0.148	0.122	0.073	0.037	0.014	0.111
	(0.060)	(0.000)	(0.000)	(0.000)	(0.000)	(0.000)	(0.000)	(0.007)	(0.182)	(0.000)
$\log(yinc)$	0.057	0.089	0.101	0.087	0.068	0.057	0.048	0.033	0.024	0.082
	(0.076)	(0.001)	(0.000)	(0.000)	(0.000)	(0.000)	(0.000)	(0.000)	(0.002)	(0.000)
gndr	−0.064	−0.039	−0.011	0.014	0.010	0.009	0.004	0.002	−0.004	−0.012
	(0.148)	(0.166)	(0.617)	(0.418)	(0.441)	(0.400)	(0.621)	(0.794)	(0.559)	(0.360)
expl	0.004	0.003	0.002	0.001	0.001	0.001	0.000	0.000	0.000	0.002
	(0.030)	(0.001)	(0.004)	(0.001)	(0.005)	(0.000)	(0.016)	(0.038)	(0.006)	(0.000)
nsib	−0.008	−0.024	−0.017	−0.029	−0.018	−0.006	−0.012	−0.008	−0.008	−0.016
	(0.743)	(0.300)	(0.499)	(0.156)	(0.134)	(0.499)	(0.125)	(0.155)	(0.114)	(0.143)
moed_m	−0.113	−0.074	−0.109	−0.144	−0.078	−0.010	−0.065	−0.039	0.006	−0.059
	(0.183)	(0.243)	(0.430)	(0.188)	(0.524)	(0.890)	(0.200)	(0.409)	(0.876)	(0.294)
moed_h	−0.017	0.074	0.088	0.061	0.082	0.107	0.037	0.043	0.021	0.041
	(0.706)	(0.148)	(0.254)	(0.404)	(0.046)	(0.013)	(0.212)	(0.051)	(0.312)	(0.206)
moed_p	0.057	0.226	0.239	0.176	0.153	0.144	0.066	0.062	0.027	0.114
	(0.714)	(0.000)	(0.004)	(0.020)	(0.000)	(0.001)	(0.032)	(0.009)	(0.210)	(0.002)
moed_u	0.186	0.261	0.267	0.209	0.179	0.167	0.085	0.082	0.047	0.146
	(0.030)	(0.000)	(0.001)	(0.004)	(0.000)	(0.000)	(0.005)	(0.000)	(0.023)	(0.000)
moed_g	0.166	0.294	0.319	0.250	0.210	0.197	0.101	0.094	0.046	0.139
	(0.294)	(0.098)	(0.000)	(0.001)	(0.000)	(0.000)	(0.002)	(0.000)	(0.049)	(0.011)
Sample size	2083	2083	2083	2083	2083	2083	2083	2083	2083	2083

Figures in parentheses are the *p*-values of the *t*-test statistics computed by robust standard error. The dependent variable is $\log(acps)$. R^2 of the OLS model is 0.1660.

Fourth, we examined the effect of the parental involvement on the academic performance measured by the mother's education level. Overall, for each quantile level, the effect of the mother's education level is positive and becomes statistically more significant as the mother's education level increases for the quantile prediction model. On the other hand, for the quantile structural model, the effect of the mother's education level is maximized when the mother receives education up to university level. If the mother is educated only up to the middle school or high school level, it does not affect the student's academic performance significantly for neither the prediction nor the structural model. Furthermore, the effect of the mother's education level is most influential for $\tau = 0.2$ or 0.3 for both models.

3.2.3. Estimation and Inference Results Using Model 4

We finally discuss the estimation of Model (4) reported in Tables 5 and 6. As for Models (1) and (2), Tables 5 and 6 are estimated by QR and IVQR, respectively. After removing the missing observations, a total of 2083 observations remained.

Table 4. Estimation results by obtained instrumental variable quantile regression.

Variables\Quantiles	0.1	0.2	0.3	0.4	0.5	0.6	0.7	0.8	0.9	TSLS
const	2.882	2.903	2.924	3.274	3.484	3.681	3.955	4.072	4.288	3.353
	(0.000)	(0.000)	(0.000)	(0.000)	(0.000)	(0.000)	(0.000)	(0.000)	(0.000)	(0.000)
excd	2.480	2.292	2.641	1.818	1.151	0.692	0.624	0.439	0.214	1.655
	(0.028)	(0.017)	(0.000)	(0.001)	(0.008)	(0.061)	(0.004)	(0.056)	(0.131)	(0.007)
prvl	0.070	0.158	0.157	0.139	0.116	0.112	0.055	0.029	0.009	0.078
	(0.184)	(0.000)	(0.000)	(0.000)	(0.000)	(0.000)	(0.000)	(0.009)	(0.207)	(0.007)
$\log(yinc)$	0.078	0.085	0.098	0.075	0.066	0.054	0.042	0.037	0.022	0.077
	(0.044)	(0.009)	(0.000)	(0.000)	(0.000)	(0.000)	(0.000)	(0.000)	(0.000)	(0.000)
gndr	−0.160	−0.127	−0.086	−0.036	−0.023	−0.013	−0.016	−0.015	−0.010	−0.065
	(0.001)	(0.002)	(0.004)	(0.142)	(0.237)	(0.441)	(0.087)	(0.141)	(0.102)	(0.018)
expl	0.004	0.002	0.001	0.001	0.001	0.001	0.001	0.000	0.000	0.002
	(0.003)	(0.006)	(0.020)	(0.050)	(0.009)	(0.004)	(0.003)	(0.144)	(0.000)	(0.002)
nsib	−0.013	−0.020	−0.034	−0.033	−0.021	−0.007	−0.015	−0.009	−0.007	−0.022
	(0.615)	(0.420)	(0.051)	(0.020)	(0.078)	(0.488)	(0.011)	(0.148)	(0.111)	(0.186)
moed_m	−0.030	−0.059	−0.097	−0.100	−0.058	−0.016	−0.047	−0.022	0.010	−0.026
	(0.806)	(0.579)	(0.204)	(0.127)	(0.269)	(0.724)	(0.070)	(0.432)	(0.590)	(0.728)
moed_h	0.027	0.124	0.149	0.127	0.122	0.107	0.058	0.057	0.021	0.088
	(0.744)	(0.068)	(0.003)	(0.003)	(0.000)	(0.000)	(0.001)	(0.001)	(0.065)	(0.066)
moed_p	0.027	0.185	0.182	0.164	0.150	0.115	0.067	0.051	0.022	0.094
	(0.773)	(0.017)	(0.001)	(0.001)	(0.000)	(0.000)	(0.000)	(0.013)	(0.110)	(0.084)
moed_u	0.219	0.319	0.335	0.280	0.217	0.168	0.110	0.093	0.047	0.197
	(0.013)	(0.000)	(0.000)	(0.000)	(0.000)	(0.000)	(0.000)	(0.000)	(0.000)	(0.000)
moed_g	0.100	0.274	0.263	0.253	0.203	0.168	0.101	0.086	0.040	0.124
	(0.483)	(0.023)	(0.003)	(0.001)	(0.001)	(0.001)	(0.001)	(0.008)	(0.064)	(0.147)
Sample size	2083	2083	2083	2083	2083	2083	2083	2083	2083	2083

Figures in parentheses are the p-values of the t-test statistics testing whether the estimated parameter was zero or not. The dependent variable is $\log(acps)$.

Table 5. Estimation results obtained by quantile regression.

Variables\Quantiles	0.1	0.2	0.3	0.4	0.5	0.6	0.7	0.8	0.9	OLS
const	3.037	2.872	3.004	3.332	3.535	3.661	3.982	4.128	4.281	3.431
	(0.000)	(0.000)	(0.000)	(0.000)	(0.000)	(0.000)	(0.000)	(0.000)	(0.000)	(0.000)
excd	−0.031	−0.054	−0.093	−0.069	−0.064	−0.055	−0.040	−0.049	−0.026	−0.062
	(0.815)	(0.385)	(0.098)	(0.259)	(0.166)	(0.042)	(0.065)	(0.008)	(0.236)	(0.069)
prvl	0.103	0.187	0.205	0.170	0.135	0.121	0.076	0.039	0.017	0.112
	(0.036)	(0.000)	(0.000)	(0.000)	(0.000)	(0.000)	(0.000)	(0.004)	(0.109)	(0.000)
$\log(yinc)$	0.061	0.094	0.078	0.063	0.058	0.057	0.040	0.034	0.024	0.069
	(0.086)	(0.001)	(0.002)	(0.009)	(0.003)	(0.000)	(0.001)	(0.001)	(0.004)	(0.000)
gndr	−0.085	−0.046	−0.014	0.007	0.014	0.009	0.003	0.001	−0.005	−0.013
	(0.034)	(0.137)	(0.499)	(0.674)	(0.294)	(0.378)	(0.711)	(0.942)	(0.474)	(0.350)
expl	0.003	0.003	0.001	0.001	0.001	0.001	0.000	0.000	0.000	0.002
	(0.026)	(0.006)	(0.022)	(0.003)	(0.000)	(0.000)	(0.010)	(0.148)	(0.012)	(0.000)
nsib	−0.015	−0.021	−0.015	−0.038	−0.020	−0.009	−0.013	−0.010	−0.007	−0.018
	(0.511)	(0.428)	(0.388)	(0.045)	(0.144)	(0.290)	(0.096)	(0.106)	(0.179)	(0.098)
moed_m	−0.038	−0.047	0.031	−0.062	−0.060	−0.004	−0.036	−0.048	−0.015	−0.040
	(0.690)	(0.508)	(0.764)	(0.610)	(0.713)	(0.948)	(0.556)	(0.427)	(0.777)	(0.505)
moed_h	−0.009	0.039	0.130	0.086	0.070	0.082	0.038	0.031	0.027	0.040
	(0.824)	(0.462)	(0.026)	(0.248)	(0.176)	(0.022)	(0.211)	(0.232)	(0.208)	(0.220)
moed_p	0.065	0.164	0.239	0.174	0.145	0.128	0.067	0.047	0.036	0.104
	(0.603)	(0.021)	(0.000)	(0.024)	(0.007)	(0.000)	(0.040)	(0.092)	(0.128)	(0.007)
moed_u	0.116	0.165	0.255	0.182	0.153	0.133	0.073	0.061	0.049	0.121
	(0.211)	(0.016)	(0.000)	(0.014)	(0.004)	(0.000)	(0.020)	(0.025)	(0.026)	(0.001)

Table 5. Cont.

Variables\Quantiles	0.1	0.2	0.3	0.4	0.5	0.6	0.7	0.8	0.9	OLS
moed_g	−0.001	0.184	0.285	0.219	0.188	0.169	0.099	0.080	0.041	0.109
	(0.993)	(0.179)	(0.001)	(0.005)	(0.001)	(0.000)	(0.004)	(0.008)	(0.102)	(0.052)
faed_m	−0.041	−0.065	−0.098	0.062	0.040	−0.009	−0.042	0.000	0.017	−0.005
	(0.630)	(0.342)	(0.259)	(0.676)	(0.742)	(0.890)	(0.457)	(1.000)	(0.681)	(0.927)
faed_h	0.037	0.043	0.081	0.091	0.062	0.037	−0.001	−0.001	−0.010	0.031
	(0.453)	(0.438)	(0.119)	(0.266)	(0.397)	(0.496)	(0.966)	(0.980)	(0.563)	(0.361)
faed_p	−0.015	0.074	0.143	0.118	0.066	0.009	−0.005	−0.009	−0.018	0.037
	(0.883)	(0.376)	(0.020)	(0.171)	(0.383)	(0.871)	(0.884)	(0.737)	(0.351)	(0.356)
faed_u	0.127	0.123	0.164	0.165	0.097	0.045	0.019	0.012	−0.007	0.069
	(0.087)	(0.031)	(0.003)	(0.046)	(0.201)	(0.408)	(0.512)	(0.585)	(0.693)	(0.054)
faed_g	0.245	0.163	0.208	0.180	0.093	0.034	0.000	0.007	0.003	0.084
	(0.049)	(0.067)	(0.003)	(0.043)	(0.235)	(0.535)	(0.998)	(0.779)	(0.890)	(0.072)
Samplesize	2083	2083	2083	2083	2083	2083	2083	2083	2083	2083

Figures in parentheses are the p-values of the t-test statistics computed by robust standard error. The dependent variable is $\log(acps)$. R^2 of the OLS model is 0.1687.

Table 6. Estimation results obtained by instrumental variable quantile regression.

Variables\Quantiles	0.1	0.2	0.3	0.4	0.5	0.6	0.7	0.8	0.9	OLS
const	3.133	3.088	3.052	3.417	3.576	3.767	4.000	4.125	4.298	3.504
	(0.000)	(0.000)	(0.000)	(0.000)	(0.000)	(0.000)	(0.000)	(0.000)	(0.000)	(0.000)
excd	2.662	2.111	2.428	2.093	1.129	0.816	0.636	0.504	0.214	1.686
	(0.005)	(0.050)	(0.000)	(0.000)	(0.011)	(0.023)	(0.011)	(0.019)	(0.161)	(0.008)
prvl	0.071	0.158	0.146	0.130	0.115	0.108	0.059	0.029	0.010	0.078
	(0.109)	(0.001)	(0.000)	(0.000)	(0.000)	(0.000)	(0.000)	(0.005)	(0.174)	(0.008)
log(yinc)	0.027	0.044	0.058	0.036	0.041	0.035	0.032	0.027	0.020	0.045
	(0.464)	(0.300)	(0.035)	(0.106)	(0.021)	(0.013)	(0.001)	(0.002)	(0.001)	(0.073)
gndr	−0.163	−0.111	−0.080	−0.050	−0.019	−0.017	−0.015	−0.019	−0.010	−0.066
	(0.000)	(0.015)	(0.007)	(0.040)	(0.330)	(0.275)	(0.160)	(0.040)	(0.121)	(0.018)
expl	0.003	0.002	0.001	0.001	0.001	0.001	0.001	0.000	0.000	0.002
	(0.003)	(0.039)	(0.017)	(0.018)	(0.005)	(0.003)	(0.010)	(0.065)	(0.001)	(0.002)
nsib	−0.025	−0.035	−0.034	−0.041	−0.023	−0.013	−0.016	−0.013	−0.008	−0.027
	(0.275)	(0.202)	(0.053)	(0.004)	(0.049)	(0.197)	(0.019)	(0.033)	(0.089)	(0.106)
moed_m	0.077	−0.002	0.042	−0.035	−0.049	0.022	0.005	−0.002	−0.007	0.005
	(0.489)	(0.986)	(0.612)	(0.609)	(0.387)	(0.637)	(0.862)	(0.929)	(0.735)	(0.949)
moed_h	0.035	0.127	0.147	0.112	0.094	0.103	0.064	0.057	0.031	0.078
	(0.585)	(0.084)	(0.003)	(0.005)	(0.005)	(0.000)	(0.001)	(0.000)	(0.009)	(0.100)
moed_p	0.047	0.148	0.156	0.127	0.120	0.115	0.074	0.053	0.032	0.079
	(0.551)	(0.095)	(0.008)	(0.009)	(0.003)	(0.000)	(0.001)	(0.007)	(0.029)	(0.167)
moed_u	0.208	0.273	0.291	0.235	0.174	0.162	0.108	0.091	0.057	0.173
	(0.006)	(0.001)	(0.000)	(0.000)	(0.000)	(0.000)	(0.000)	(0.000)	(0.000)	(0.002)
moed_g	−0.015	0.226	0.201	0.171	0.159	0.171	0.095	0.085	0.042	0.087
	(0.894)	(0.103)	(0.030)	(0.023)	(0.011)	(0.001)	(0.008)	(0.004)	(0.087)	(0.331)
faed_m	0.038	0.023	0.004	0.131	0.078	0.022	−0.032	0.009	0.022	0.045
	(0.715)	(0.843)	(0.958)	(0.044)	(0.150)	(0.609)	(0.295)	(0.731)	(0.241)	(0.560)
faed_h	0.185	0.166	0.211	0.212	0.148	0.086	0.026	0.034	0.001	0.126
	(0.020)	(0.066)	(0.000)	(0.000)	(0.000)	(0.008)	(0.261)	(0.086)	(0.922)	(0.026)
faed_p	0.103	0.237	0.243	0.216	0.145	0.054	0.017	0.026	−0.006	0.126
	(0.255)	(0.021)	(0.000)	(0.000)	(0.001)	(0.144)	(0.512)	(0.260)	(0.741)	(0.052)
faed_u	0.238	0.243	0.269	0.251	0.172	0.086	0.035	0.040	0.002	0.147
	(0.004)	(0.008)	(0.000)	(0.000)	(0.000)	(0.008)	(0.125)	(0.044)	(0.895)	(0.009)
faed_g	0.382	0.342	0.342	0.310	0.188	0.082	0.037	0.038	0.014	0.191
	(0.001)	(0.006)	(0.000)	(0.000)	(0.001)	(0.075)	(0.250)	(0.179)	(0.509)	(0.018)
Sample size	2083	2083	2083	2083	2083	2083	2083	2083	2083	2083

Figures in parentheses are the p-values of the t-test statistics testing whether the estimated parameter was zero or not. The dependent variable is $\log(acps)$.

We summarize the estimation results as follows. First, the estimation results using Model (3) are still valid for Model (4). The estimated coefficients are more or less similar to those in Tables 3 and 4, and their statistical significance is also similarly obtained, ensuring that the model estimations are robust.

Second, we examined the effect of the father's education level on the student's academic performance as another form of parental involvement. In terms of the quantile prediction model, most of the father's education levels are not statistically significant. Nevertheless, for the students with $\tau = 0.4$, if his/her father receives education up to university level or more, it becomes statistically significant, implying that the highly educated fathers affect the academic performance of the student with $\tau = 0.4$.

Finally, we examined the effect of the father's education level on the student's academic performance in terms of the quantile structural model. Contrary to the quantile prediction model, the father's education level becomes significant, although the estimated coefficients are not significant, when the father receives education up to the middle school level. On the other hand, for each τ less than 0.7, the estimated coefficient overall increases as the father's education level increases, that is different from the effect of the mother's education level. For the structural model, the effect of the mother's education level is maximized when the mother receives education up to university level. In addition, the estimated coefficients are maximized for $\tau = 0.2, 0.3$, and 0.4.

4. Concluding Remarks

This study deepens our understanding of the prediction and structural relationship between a student's academic performance and his/her after-school exercise by employing the QR and IVQR methods, respectively. Using Korean middle school student data, our empirical investigation shows that the QR method detects negative relationships for all of the quantile levels of consideration, whereas a positive structural relationship is dominant between the two variables. This affirms the theoretical and experimental hypotheses on the two variables in prior literature. Furthermore, the low-performing students, in terms of academic performance, have stronger associations between the two variables than the high-performing students, overall.

Author Contributions: Conceptualization, formal analysis, writing—original draft preparation, K.S.; Methodology, supervision, review and editing, S.Y. All authors have read and agreed to the published version of the manuscript.

Funding: This work was supported by Hankuk University of Foreign Studies Research Fund 2021.

Institutional Review Board Statement: Not applicable.

Informed Consent Statement: Not applicable.

Data Availability Statement: Data on first-grade middle school students collected by NYPI in South Korea are used for our empirical analysis. The URL address is as follows (accessed on 1 November 2021): https://www.nypi.re.kr/archive/mps/program/examinDataCode/view?menuId=MENU00226&pageNum=1&titleId=15&schType=0&schText=&firstCategory=1&secondCategory=2. To access this webpage, users need to first provide brief information on the use of data at the URL given as follows (accessed on 1 November 2021): https://www.nypi.re.kr/archive/mps/program/examinDataCode/dataDwloadAgreeView?menuId=MENU00226.

Acknowledgments: Two anonymous referees provided helpful comments for which the authors are most grateful. The authors are also grateful to Jin Seo Cho for his helpful discussions and suggestions for this research.

Conflicts of Interest: The authors declare no conflict of interest.

References

1. Correa-Burrows, P.; Burrows, R.; Orellana, Y.; Ivanovic, D. Achievement in mathematics and language is linked to regular physical activity: A population study in Chilean youth. *J. Sports Sci.* **2014**, *32*, 1631–1638. [CrossRef] [PubMed]
2. Tomporowski, P.D.; Davis, C.L.; Miller, P.H.; Naglieri, J.A. Exercise and children's intelligence, cognition, and academic achievement. *Educ. Psychol. Rev.* **2008**, *20*, 111–131. [CrossRef] [PubMed]
3. Shin, K.; Yoo, S.; Kim, M. A comparison of Two-Stage Least Squares (TSLS) and Ordinary Least Squares (OLS) in estimating the structural relationship between after-school exercise and academic performance. *Mathematics* **2021**, *9*, 3105. [CrossRef]
4. Koenker, R.; Bassett, G. Regression quantiles. *Econometrica* **1978**, *46*, 33–50. [CrossRef]
5. Chernozhukov, V.; Hansen, C. An IV model of quantile treatment effects. *Econometrica* **2005**, *73*, 245–262. [CrossRef]
6. Alkadhi, K.A. Exercise as a positive modulator of brain function. *Mol. Neurobiol.* **2018**, *55*, 3112–3130. [CrossRef] [PubMed]
7. De Greeff, J.W.; Bosker, R.J.; Oosterlaan, J.; Visscher, C.; Hartman, E. Effects of physical activity on executive functions, attention and academic performance in preadolescent children: A meta-analysis. *J. Sci. Med. Sport* **2018**, *21*, 501–507. [CrossRef] [PubMed]
8. Tomporowski, P.D.; Mccullick, B.; Pendleton, D.M.; Pesce, C. Exercise and children's cognition: The role of exercise characteristics and a place for metacognition. *J. Sport Health Sci.* **2015**, *4*, 47–55. [CrossRef]
9. Xiang, M.; Gu, X.; Jackson, A.; Zhang, T.; Wang, X.; Guo, Q. Understanding adolescents' mental health and academic achievement: Does physical fitness matter? *Sch. Psychol. Int.* **2017**, *38*, 647–663. [CrossRef]
10. Belcher, B.R.; Zink, J.; Azad, A.; Campbell, C.E.; Chakravartti, S.P.; Herting, M.M. The roles of physical activity, exercise, and fitness in promoting resilience during adolescence: Effects on mental well-being and brain development. *Biol. Psychiatry Cogn. Neurosci. Neuroimaging* **2021**, *6*, 225–237. [CrossRef]
11. Koenker, R. *Quantile Regression*; Cambridge University Process: Cambridge, NY, USA, 2005.
12. Beets, M.W.; Beighle, A.; Erwin, H.; Huberty, J. After-school program impact on physical activity and fitness: A meta-analysis. *Am. J. Prev. Med.* **2009**, *36*, 527–537. [CrossRef] [PubMed]
13. Nihayah, M.; Ismarulyusda, I.; Syarif, H.L.; NurZakiah, M.S.; Baharudin, O.; Fadzil, M.H. Sleeping hours and academic achievements: A study among biomedical science students. *Procedia Soc. Behav. Sci.* **2011**, *18*, 617–621. [CrossRef]
14. Zeek, M.L.; Savoie, M.J.; Song, M.; Kennemur, L.M.; Qian, J.; Jungnickel, P.W.; Westrick, S.C. Sleep duration and academic performance among student pharmacists. *Am. J. Pharm. Educ.* **2015**, *79*, 63. [CrossRef] [PubMed]
15. Bogenschneider, K. Parental involvement in adolescent schooling: A proximal process with transcontextual validity. *J. Marriage Fam.* **1997**, *59*, 718–733. [CrossRef]
16. Boonk, L.; Gijselaers, H.J.; Ritzen, H.; Brand-Gruwel, S. A review of the relationship between parental involvement indicators and academic achievement. *Educ. Res. Rev.* **2018**, *24*, 10–30. [CrossRef]
17. Glick, J.; Hohmann-Marriott, B. Academic performance of young children in immigrant families: The significance of race, ethnicity, and national origins. *Int. Migr. Rev.* **2007**, *41*, 371–401. [CrossRef]
18. Daily, S.M.; Mann, M.J.; Kristjansson, A.L.; Smith, M.L.; Zullig, K.J. School climate and academic achievement in middle and high school students. *J. Sch. Health* **2019**, *89*, 173–180. [CrossRef] [PubMed]
19. Mann, M.J.; Kristjansson, A.L.; Sigfusdottir, I.D.; Smith, M.L. The role of community, family, peer, and school factors in group bullying: Implications for school-based intervention. *J. Sch. Health* **2015**, *85*, 477–486. [CrossRef] [PubMed]
20. Voyer, D.; Voyer, S.D. Gender differences in scholastic achievement: A meta-analysis. *Psychol. Bull.* **2014**, *140*, 1174. [CrossRef] [PubMed]
21. Gneezy, U.; Niederle, M.; Rustichini, A. Performance in competitive environments: Gender differences. *Q. J. Econ.* **2003**, *118*, 1049–1074. [CrossRef]

MDPI
St. Alban-Anlage 66
4052 Basel
Switzerland
Tel. +41 61 683 77 34
Fax +41 61 302 89 18
www.mdpi.com

Mathematics Editorial Office
E-mail: mathematics@mdpi.com
www.mdpi.com/journal/mathematics

www.ingramcontent.com/pod-product-compliance
Lightning Source LLC
LaVergne TN
LVHW070250100526
838202LV00015B/2199